ORTHODOX CHRISTIANITY

Volume II:
Doctrine and Teaching of the Orthodox Church

METROPOLITAN HILARION ALFEYEV

ORTHODOX CHRISTIANITY

Volume II:
Doctrine and
Teaching of the
Orthodox Church

WITH A FOREWORD BY
His Holiness Alexei II
Patriarch of Moscow and All Russia

Translated from the Russian by Andrew Smith

ST VLADIMIR'S SEMINARY PRESS
YONKERS, NEW YORK 10707
2012

Library of Congress Control Number 2011002385

Originally published by Sretensky Monastery, 2008, as

Pravoslavie
Tom 1: Istoriia, kanonicheskoe ustroistvo i verouchenie
Pravoslavnoi Tserkvi

ST VLADIMIR'S SEMINARY PRESS
575 Scarsdale Rd., Yonkers, NY 10707
1-800-204-2665
www.svspress.com

ISBN 978-0-88141-461-5

Table of Contents

Foreword

Beloved Brothers and Sisters in the Lord,

In writing these introductory words to this book by Bishop Hilarion of Vienna and Austria, I would like to note the timeliness of its appearance. Such an all-encompassing study of the history, teaching, and liturgical services of the Orthodox Church is long overdue. I am convinced that the publication of this first volume will inspire lively interest among readers both in Russia and abroad.

Orthodoxy is one of the few religious confessions whose membership is growing rather than declining. After many decades of persecution, a major revival of spiritual life is underway in Russia and other countries of the former Soviet Union, and it brings us joy that the number of parishes, monasteries, and theological schools is significantly increasing.

The Orthodox Church in Russia now occupies a fitting place in the life of the people and exerts a powerful and positive influence on many areas of society. Millions of people have found a spiritual home in the Church. The Church helps people to find a moral bearing; for centuries it has defended those values on which the stability and spiritual health of the nation, the family, and the individual are based.

Today, churches are accessible to all, religious literature is published in abundance, icons and reproductions of them are sold everywhere, services are broadcast on television, sermons of clergymen and bishops can be heard on the radio, and church music is available on compact discs.

Nevertheless, Orthodoxy remains a mystery for many people—both in our homeland and abroad. What does the Orthodox Church teach? What is its history, and how does it relate to the modern world? What are the foundations of Orthodox theology? What rules regulate the celebration of the liturgical services in Orthodox churches? What is the meaning of icons? What principles lie at the foundation of church art?

This book seeks to provide answers to these and many other questions. It examines not only the history and contemporary life of the Orthodox

Church, but also Orthodoxy as such: as a theological and ethical system, as a way of life and thinking.

The author of this book is not acquainted with the wealth of the theological and liturgical tradition of the Orthodox Church by hearsay. After receiving a broad education, Bishop Hilarion has authored numerous works on theology and church history, translated works from ancient languages, and composed liturgical music. His many years of service to the mother church, his rich creative activity, and his broad perspective enable him to present the tradition of the Orthodox Church in all its diversity.

I would like to express my hope for the success of this book not only in Russian but also in other languages. I would also like to wish its author God's help in his further archpastoral and theological work for the good of the Orthodox Church and the people of God. Finally, I pray that the reader will have a profound and meaningful encounter with the Orthodox Church, which is the "Church of the living God, the pillar and bulwark of the truth" (1 Tim 3.15).

+Alexei
Patriarch of Moscow and All Russia
August 7, 2007

Preface

THIS IS THE SECOND VOLUME of a detailed and systematic exposition of the history, canonical structure, doctrine, moral and social teaching, liturgical services, and spiritual life of the Orthodox Church.

The basic idea of this work is to present Orthodox Christianity as an integrated theological and liturgical system–a world view. In this system all elements are interconnected: theology is based on liturgical experience, and the basic characteristics of church art–including icons, singing, and architecture–are shaped by theology and the liturgy. Theology and the services, in their turn, influence the ascetic practice and the personal piety of each Christian. They shape the moral and social teaching of the Church as well as its relation to other Christian confessions, non-Christian religions, and the secular world.

Orthodoxy is traditional and even conservative (we use this term in a positive sense, to emphasize Orthodoxy's reverence to church tradition). The contemporary life of the Orthodox Church is based on its historical experience. Orthodoxy is historic in its very essence: it is deeply rooted in history, which is why it is impossible to understand the uniqueness of the Orthodox Church–its dogmatic teaching and canonical structure, its liturgical system and social doctrine–outside of a historical context. Thus, the reference to history, to the sources, is one of the organizing principles of this book.

This series covers a wide range of themes relating to the history and contemporary life of the Orthodox Church. It contains many quotations from works of the church fathers, liturgical and historical sources, and works of contemporary theologians. Nevertheless, we do not claim to give an exhaustive account of the subjects discussed: this work is neither an encyclopedia, a dictionary, nor a reference work. It is rather an attempt to understand Orthodoxy in all its diversity, in its historical and contemporary existence–an understanding through the prism of the author's personal perception.

A special feature of these books is that they strive to provide a sufficiently detailed wealth of material. It is addressed to readers who are already acquainted with the basics of Orthodoxy and who desire to deepen their knowledge and, above all, to systematize it.

The first volume in the series presented an account of the historical path of the Orthodox Church through almost twenty centuries. After examining the common heritage of the Christian church in east and west in the first millennium after Christ's nativity, it talks about the second millennium, with a focus on the history of the Russian Church and culture, in part as a "case study," as it were, of how Orthodoxy can infuse the literature, art, and philosophy of an entire culture. And finally, that volume examines the canonical structure of the Orthodox Church, treating of the emergence and development of diocesan structures, metropolias, and patriarchates in the Christian east. It concludes by discussing the contemporary structure of world Orthodoxy as well as the principle of "canonical territory," which forms the basis of inter-Orthodox relations.

This volume covers the doctrine of the Orthodox Church, beginning with an examination of the sources of Orthodox teaching, including the Old and New Testaments, the decrees of the ecumenical and local councils, the writings of the fathers and teachers of the Church, and works of liturgical poetry. It goes on to expound the Orthodox teaching on God, creation, and man. Further chapters are devoted to Orthodox christology, ecclesiology, and eschatology.

In future volumes, we will examine the services, sacraments, and rituals of the Orthodox Church, its ascetic and mystical teaching, as well as church art, including architecture, iconography, and liturgical singing. The moral and social teaching of the Orthodox Church as well as its relations with other Christian confessions, other religions, and the secular world, will also be discussed.

PART ONE

THE SOURCES OF ORTHODOX DOGMA

I

Scripture and Tradition

C HRISTIANITY APPEARS as a religion of divine revelation. In the Orthodox understanding, divine revelation is comprised of Holy Scripture and Holy Tradition. The Scripture is the whole of the Bible, that is to say, all the books of the Old and New Testaments. The term Tradition, however, demands a special explanation, since it is used with various meanings. Quite often one understands Tradition as the sum total of written and oral sources, by which aid Christian faith is transmitted from generation to generation. The Apostle Paul says "stand firm and hold fast to the traditions that you were taught by us, either by word of mouth or by our letter" (2 Thess 2.15).[1] By "word of mouth" one understands here oral Tradition, while by "letter" one understands the written Tradition. Sometimes though, one may understand Tradition chiefly as the oral transmission of the true faith, in contradistinction to the written sources of a dogmatic character. St Basil the Great says of oral Tradition:

> Concerning the teachings of the Church, whether publicly proclaimed (*kerygma*) or reserved to members of the household of faith (*dogmata*), we have received some from written sources, while others have been given to us secretly, through apostolic tradition. . . . If we attacked unwritten customs, claiming them to be of little importance, we would fatally mutilate the Gospel, no matter what our intentions. . . . For instance (to take the first and most common example), where is the written teaching that we should sign with the sign of the cross those who, trusting in the name of Our Lord Jesus Christ, are to be enrolled as catechumens? Which book teaches us to pray facing the East? Have any saints left for us in writing

---

[1]In general, translations of texts from the New Testament are based on the King James Version, while translations of Old Testament texts are based on the version of the Septuagint by Sir Lancelot Brenton. In some few instances, the translation was done ad hoc from the Russian. Chapter and verse numbering generally follows the conventions of the KJV.

the words to be used in the invocation over the eucharistic bread and the cup of blessing? As everyone knows, we are not content in the liturgy simply to recite the words recorded by St Paul or the Gospels, but we add other words both before and after, words of great importance for this mystery. We have received these words from unwritten teaching. We bless baptismal water and the oil for chrismation as well as the candidate approaching the font. By what written authority do we do this, if not from secret and mystical tradition? Even beyond blessing the oil, what written command do we have to anoint with it? What about baptizing a man with three immersions, or other baptismal rites, such as the renunciation of Satan and his angels?[2]

In the preceding words Basil the Great speaks chiefly of traditions of a liturgical or ceremonial character, passed down by word of mouth and thereby entering into church practice. In the time of Basil the Great (fourth century) much of what was enumerated remained unrecorded. Subsequently, though, all of these customs were recorded in written sources—in the works of the church fathers, in the decrees of the ecumenical and local councils, and in liturgical texts (particularly in the rubrics of the Divine Liturgy and the sacrament of baptism). The significant part in this is that it was all originally by oral Tradition, in "quiet and in secret," that it became written Tradition, which then continued to exist with oral Tradition.

If Tradition is understood in the sense of the sum total of oral and written sources, then how does it correspond with Scripture? Is it that Scripture is somehow on the outside with respect to Tradition, or does it present itself as a component of Tradition?

Before this question can be answered, it is necessary to note the problems of interrelation between Scripture and Tradition, although these problems are not reflected by many Orthodox authors, so they do not appear to be Orthodox in their provenance. The question of which is more important, Scripture or Tradition, was put at the forefront of the polemic between the Reformation and Counter-reformation during the sixteenth and seventeenth centuries. The leaders of the Reformation (Luther, Calvin) proposed the principle of the "sufficiency of Scripture," according to which only Scripture enjoyed absolute authority in the Church. So that which dealt with the latest dogmatic docu-

---

[2]Basil the Great *On the Holy Spirit* 27. (For publication data for this and other works cited in this book, please see the bibliography.)

ments, whether they be decrees of councils or the works of the church fathers, had authority to the extent that they agreed with the teachings of Scripture (the most radical reforms generally rejected the authority of the church fathers). Such dogmatic definitions, liturgical and ceremonial traditions, which were not founded on the authority of the Scripture, could not, in the opinion of the leaders of the Reformation, be accepted as legitimate and therefore were subject to abolition. The Reformation began the process of revising church Tradition, which continues in the heart of Protestantism even now.

To counterbalance the Protestant principle of *sola scriptura* the theologians of the Counter-reformation highlighted the importance of Tradition, without which, in their opinion, Scripture would not have authority. Luther's opponent at the Leipzig dispute in 1519 proved that "Scripture is not authentic without the authority of Tradition."[3] Those against the Reformation cited the words of the Blessed Augustine: "I would not have believed in the Gospel, had not the authority of the Catholic Church compelled me (*ego vero evangelio non crederem, nisi me catholicae ecclesiae commoverat auctoritas*)."[4] They pointed out, in particular, that the canon of Holy Scripture was formed precisely by church Tradition, which determined which books should be enrolled into it, and which should not be. At the Council of Trent in 1546 the theory of two sources was formulated, which agreed that Scripture could not be considered as the sole source of divine revelation: Tradition is not a less important source, but rather comprises a vital and important addition to Scripture.

Orthodox theologians in the nineteenth century, speaking about Scripture and Tradition, noted the nuance in a slightly different way. They insisted on the primacy of Tradition in relation to Scripture and traced the beginning of Christian Tradition not just to the Church of the New Testament, but back to the time of the Old Testament. St Philaret of Moscow emphasized that the Holy Scripture of the Old Testament began with Moses, but until Moses the true faith was preserved and spread by means of Tradition. With regard to the Holy Scripture of the New Testament then, it begins with the Evangelist Matthew, but previously the "foundation of dogmas, teachings on life, theological decrees, and laws concerning church governance" were all found in Tradition.[5]

---

[3]A. MacGraham, *The Theological Meaning of the Reformation* (Odessa: 1994), 178–179.
[4]Blessed Augustine *Contra epist. Manichaei*, cap. 5, 6, PL. 42: 176.
[5]Philaret of Moscow, *Words and Sayings*, T. III. C. 98.

Apostle and Evangelist John the Theologian with disciple—Book in miniature, 11th c.

For A.S. Khomiakov, the correlation of Tradition and Scripture can be considered in the context of the teachings of the actions of the Holy Spirit in the Church. Khomiakov considered that Tradition preceded Scripture, but that Tradition, or "action," by which he understood a religion of divine revelation, began with Adam, Noah, Abraham, and the other "forefathers and representatives of the Old Testament Church." The Church of Christ is a continuation of the Old Testament Church, and the Divine Spirit lived and continues to live in both the one and the other. This Spirit acts in the Church in many forms—in Scripture, in Tradition, and in other affairs. The unity of Scripture and Tradition is grasped by one who lives in the Church—outside the Church, it is impossible to grasp Scripture, Tradition, even other actions. A Christian understands Scripture to the extent that s/he guards Tradition and to the extent that s/he accomplishes "pleasing actions of wisdom." This wisdom, however, is not a personal one which belongs to the Christian alone, but it is given to the whole Church "in the fullness of the truth and unadulterated by lies." Khomiakov employs the understanding of the Holy Scriptures broadly, considering all of Scripture that the Church counts as its own, in particular the confession of faith of the Universal Church, to be holy. "The Holy Scripture existed before our own time," concludes Khomiakov, "and if it pleases God, there will always be Holy Scripture. But there has not been, and will never be, any kind of contradiction in the Church: not in Scripture, not in Tradition, not in any action, for the one and true Christ is in all three."[6]

In the twentieth century V.N. Lossky developed Khomiakov's thoughts on Tradition. He described Tradition as "the life of the Holy Spirit in the Church, a life which communicates to each member of the Body of Christ the ability to hear, understand, and recognize the Truth inherent in it in the world, but not that which is inherent in the natural world of human reason."[7] Highlighting the link between Tradition and the Church, Lossky wrote:

---

[6] A.S. Khomiakov, *The One Church* (Moscow: 2005), 14.
[7] *Tradition and Traditions* (Moscow: 2000), 525.

The notion of Tradition is richer than we habitually think. Tradition does not merely consist of an oral transmission of facts capable of supplementing the Scriptural narrative. It is the *complement* of the Bible and, above all, it is the *fulfillment* of the Old Testament in the New, as the Church becomes aware of it. It is Tradition which confers comprehension of the meaning of revealed truth (Lk 24). Tradition tells us not only *what* we must hear but, still more importantly, *how* we must keep what we hear. In this general sense, Tradition implies an incessant operation of the Holy Spirit, who could have his full outpouring and bear his fruits only in the Church, after the Day of Pentecost. It is only in the Church that we find ourselves capable of tracing the inner connections between the sacred texts which make the Old Testament and the New Testament into a single living body of truth, wherein Christ is present in each word. It is only in the Church that the seed sown by the word is not barren, but brings forth fruit; and this fruition of Truth, as well as the power to make it bear fruit, is called Tradition.[8]

Lossky sees the key to understanding the question concerning the correlation between Scripture and Tradition in the words of the holy martyr Ignatius the God-Bearer: "He who truly possesses the word of Christ can hear him even in silence."[9] In the revelation of the divine certain zones of silence are maintained, inaccessible to those who are "outsiders," explains Lossky. Silence accompanies the word of Holy Scripture and transmits to the Church, together with the words of the revelation, as a condition of their perception. For the perception of the fullness of revelation demands "an appeal to the vertical plan," so that one may not only grasp the *width and length* of the revelation, but that one may also grasp its *depth and height* (Eph 3.18). In this context "Scripture and Tradition may not be set against one another, nor set up as two opposing realities." Tradition is "not a word, but a living breath, given for the hearing of words and at the same time for the hearing of the silence from which the word has come."[10]

Thus there exists a verbal expression of Tradition, whether it be put down in writing or in an oral mode, but nevertheless it is there as a spiritual reality,

---

[8]Vladimir Lossky, *In the Image and Likeness of God* (Crestwood, NY: St Vladimir's Seminary Press, 1974), 198.

[9]Ignatius the God-Bearer *Epistle to the Ephesians* 15.2.

[10]*Tradition and Traditions*, 524–525 (ad hoc translation–Ed.).

which does not give way to verbal expression and which is kept in the silent experience of the Church, handed down from generation to generation. This reality is not something which is other, like the knowledge of God, divine contact, and vision of the divine, which were inherent in Adam until the expulsion of Paradise, in the biblical forefathers Abraham, Isaac, and Jacob, in the God-seer Moses and the prophets, and then in the eye-witnesses and servants of *the* Word (Cf. Lk 1.2): the apostles and disciples of Christ. The unity and continuity of these experiences, preserved in the Church right up until present times, is the essence of church Tradition. Access to such experiences is possible only for those who find themselves inside Tradition, inside the Church. The person who finds him or herself outside the Church, even if s/he studied all of the sources of church dogma, will not "hear the silence" of Jesus, because being outside the veil of the Tradition s/he will be unable to see within its heart. We have long understood that the Church is not only the Christian Church, but also the Church of the Old Testament, which was the custodian of divine revelation before the coming of Christ the Savior.

Answering the question put forth earlier concerning whether or not Scripture is somehow beyond any association with Tradition or is rather an integral part of the latter, we can decisively say that in the Orthodox understanding the Scriptures are a part of Tradition and that it is inconceivable to think otherwise. For this reason Scripture is by no means self-sufficient and cannot be in-and-of itself isolated from church tradition to serve as a criterion of the truth. The books of Holy Scripture were written in various times by various authors, and each one of these books reflect an experience of a concrete person, or a group of people, each one reflects a specific historical stage in the life of the Church (once again the Church is used in a broad sense, including the Old Testament "Church"). The experience was primary, while its expression in the books of Scripture was secondary. It is precisely the Church that offers these books (the Old Testament along with the New) in unity, which they are not lacking, unless they are considered from a purely historical or text-critical point of view:

> The books of the Old Testament, composed over a period of several centuries, written by different authors who have often brought together and fused different religious traditions, have only an accidental, mechanical unity for the eyes of the historian of religions. Their unity with writings of the New Testament will appear to him factitious and artificial. But a

son of the Church will be able to recognize the unity of inspiration and the unique object of the faith in these heteroclitic writings, woven by the same Spirit who, after having spoken by the prophets, preceded the Word in rendering the Virgin Mary apt to serve as means for the incarnation of God. It is only in the Church that one is able to recognize in full consciousness the unity of inspiration of the sacred books, because the Church alone possesses Tradition—the knowledge in the Holy Spirit of the Incarnate Word.[11]

Thus the Church considers Scripture to be inspired by God (2 Tim 3.16) not because the books which make up its contents were written by God, not because the Divine Spirit inspired its authors, opened the truth up to them, and ratified them as uncoordinated compositions set up in one whole. The understanding of "divine inspiration" in the Orthodox tradition shows that the authors of this or that book of the Holy Scriptures composed their texts with the assistance of the grace of the Holy Spirit, under his direct influence. But the action of the Holy Spirit is not some kind of violent force upon the reason, heart, and will of mankind. On the contrary, the Holy Spirit helped mobilize man's particular, inner resources with the intelligence of the hidden truths of Christian revelation. The creative process, resulting in the establishment of this or that book of the Holy Scriptures, can be thought of as a synergy which, combined with action, works between God and man. Man describes any sort of event or expounds various aspects of learning, and God helps him to become wiser and to adequately convey these things. The books of Holy Scripture were written by people who found themselves not in a trance-like state, but in a sober state of mind, and within each book lies a piece of the author's individual creativity.

It is exactly the work of the Holy Spirit which helped the Church to recognize the inner unity of the Old and New Testament books (composed by different authors in different ages) in all the varied, ancient literary texts placed in the canon of Scripture, books that are joined together by this unity, which has sorted the divinely inspired works from those not divinely inspired. This separation was not based on some sort of formal principle or criterion. It was rather based on the many centuries of experiencing the interior intuition and infallibility of the Church, which regulated this process.

[11]Ibid. 155.

Speaking on the correlation between Tradition and Scripture in the Church, Archimandrite Sophrony (Sakharov) writes:

> Sacred Tradition, as the eternal and immutable dwelling of the Holy Spirit in the Church, lies at the very root of her being, and so encompasses her life that even the Scriptures themselves come to be but one of its forms. Thus, were the Church to be deprived of Tradition she would cease to be what she is, for the ministry of the New Testament is the ministry of the Spirit "written not with ink, but with the Spirit of the living God; not in tables of stone, but in fleshy tables of the heart." Suppose that for some reason the Church were to be bereft of all her liturgical books, of the Old and New Testaments, the works of the holy Fathers—what would happen? Sacred Tradition would restore the Scriptures, not word for word, perhaps—the verbal form might be different—but in essence the new Scriptures would be the expression of that same 'faith which was once delivered unto the saints.' They would be the expression of the one and only Holy Spirit continuously active in the Church, her foundation and her very substance.[12]

---

[12] *Elder Silouan the Athonite* (Paris: 1952), 39.

2

The Holy Scripture in the Orthodox Church

I N THE ORTHODOX TRADITION the Old Testament, the Gospels, and the corpus of Apostolic Epistles come together as three parts of an undivided whole. As such, the Gospels are received as absolute predilections as to a source, bestowing on Christians the living voice of Jesus, while the Old Testament is comprised of foreshadowings of Christian truth, and the Apostolic Epistles are authoritative interpretations of the Gospels, offered by the closest disciples of Christ. By holding these concepts in tandem we understand when the holy martyr Ignatius the God-Bearer says, "[We] flee to the Gospel as to the flesh of Jesus and to the apostles as to the presbyters of the Church. And we should also love the prophets, because their proclamation anticipated the gospel and they hoped on him and awaited him."[1]

Origen gives us an understanding of the development of the teachings of the Gospel as the "flesh of Jesus," of his incarnation in word. He sees in all the Scriptures a "kenosis" (emptying) of God the Word, having become incarnate in the imperfect forms of human words: "Everything acknowledged by a divine word is a revelation of the incarnate Word of God, who *was in the beginning with God* (Jn 1.2) and emptied himself. This is why it is not for nothing that we men recognize the Word of God become man as the Word in the Scriptures which has become flesh and dwelt among us (Jn 1.14)."[2]

In Orthodox services the Gospel appears not just as a book for reading, but as an object of liturgical worship: the closed Gospel lies on the altar, and is brought out to be kissed. At the ordination of an archpriest an opened Gospel is laid on the head of the ordinand, and during the fulfillment of the mystery of Holy Unction an opened Gospel is placed on the head of the sick person. In its capacity as an object of liturgical worship, the Gospel acts as a symbol of the very Christ himself.

[1] *Epistle to the Philadelphians* 5.
[2] *Philokalia* 15.19, 26–31.

How do we then deal with the Old Testament, as seen in the Christian tradition as a foreshadowing of the New Testament reality and examined through the prism of the New Testament? In science, this kind of interpretation is referred to as "typological." The origin of this interpretation is presented by Christ himself, when he said of the Old Testament: "You search the scriptures because you think that in them you have eternal life; and it is they that testify on my behalf" (Jn 5.39). In accordance with this decree of Christ in the Gospels many events from his life are interpreted as a fulfillment of an Old Testament prophecy. Typological interpretations of the Old Testament are found in the Epistles of the Apostle Paul, especially in Hebrews, where all of the Old Testament story is interpreted as foreshadowing, from a typological point of view. Such traditions continue on in the texts of the divine services of the Orthodox Church, full of allusions to events from the Old Testament which are treated conformably to Christ and to events from his life, and thus to events from the life of the New Testament Church.

According to the teaching of Gregory the Theologian, all dogmatic truths of the Christian Church are included in the Holy Scriptures; one need only know how to recognize them. Gregory invites a certain method of reading the Scriptures which one may call "retrospective." He concludes that in order to examine all the scriptural texts, issuing forth from the succession of Church Tradition, one identifies in them those dogmas that are more fully formed in the latest epoch. Such an approach to Scripture appears to be based in the patristic period. In particular, in Gregory's opinion, it is not only New Testament, but also Old Testament texts that comprise the teachings on the Holy Trinity:

> Glorify Him with the Cherubim, who unite the Three Holies into one Lord (Isa 6.3), and so far indicate the Primal Substance as their wings open to the diligent. With David be enlightened, who said to the Light, "In your Light shall we see Light," that is, in the Spirit we shall see the Son;[3] and what can be of further reaching ray? With John thunder, sounding forth nothing that is low or earthly concerning God, but what is high and heavenly, who is in the beginning, and is with God, and is God the Word (Jn 1.1), and true God of the true Father. . . . And when you read, "I and the Father are One," keep before your eyes the Unity of Substance; but

[3] Basil the Great *On the Holy Spirit* 18.47; 26.24.

The appearance of the three Men to Abraham. Church of San Vitale, Ravenna, 6th c.

when you see, "We will come to him, and make Our abode with him," (Jn 14.23) remember the distinction of Persons; and when you see the names, Father, Son, and Holy Spirit, think of the Three Personalities. With Luke be inspired as you study the Acts of the Apostles. Why do you count yourself with Ananias and Sapphira . . . stealing the Godhead itself, and lying, not to men but to God, as you have heard?[4]

In other words, the Bible ought to be read in light of the dogmatic Tradition of the Church. In the fourth century both the Orthodox and Arians referenced scriptural texts to support their respective theological positions. The dependence of these positions on one or another text added various criteria which were then interpreted in different ways. For Gregory the Theologian, just as for other church fathers, especially Irenaeus of Lyons, there existed only one criterion for the correct approach to Scripture: loyalty to Church Tradition. Gregory considered any given interpretation of biblical texts to be legitimate, provided it was based on the Tradition of the Church—all other interpretations are false, as they "rob" the Divinity. Outside the context of

[4] *Oration* 34.13–14

Tradition, biblical texts lose their own dogmatic meaning. However, within Tradition even those texts that do not directly show dogmatic truth can receive a new interpretation. Christians see in the texts of Scripture that which non-Christians do not see; Orthodoxy reveals that which remains concealed from heretics. The mystery of the Trinity remains under a veil for those who find themselves outside of the Church, a veil that may only be removed by Christ, and only for those who are within the Church.

If the Old Testament is a foreshadowing of the New Testament, then the New Testament, in the mind of some interpreters, is the shadow of the Divine Kingdom which is to come: "The Law is the shadow of the Gospel, and the Gospel is the image of the future blessings,"[5] says Maximus the Confessor. St Maximus borrowed this idea from Origen, just like the allegorical method of scriptural interpretation, which he widely used. The allegorical method gave Origen and other representatives of the Alexandrian school the possibility to examine subjects from the Old and New Testaments as foreshadowings of the spiritual experience of the separate identity of mankind. One of the classical examples of the mystical interpretation in a similar vein is Origen's interpretation of Song of Songs, where the reader goes far beyond the literal meaning of the text and is transported into a new reality, by which the very text is perceived only as an image, a symbol of this reality.

After Origen, such a type of interpretation experienced wide dissemination in the Orthodox tradition: we find it specifically in Gregory of Nyssa, Macarius of Egypt and Maximus the Confessor. The latter, like Clement of Alexandria, spoke of two ways in which the Scripture makes itself manifest to people: the first—"simply and accessibly, which the many can see"—and the second—"more hidden and accessible only to the few, that is to those who like Peter, James, and John were already holy apostles, before whom the Lord was transfigured in glory, overcoming the senses."[6] Following in the footsteps of Origen, Maximus the Confessor divided Scripture into body and soul:

> The Old Testament is the body and the New is the soul, the meaning it contains, the spirit. From another viewpoint we can say that the entire sacred Scripture, Old and New Testament, has two aspects: the historical context that corresponds to the body, and the deep meaning, the goal at

---

[5] *Chapters on Theology and on Oikonomia* 1.90.
[6] Ibid. 1.97.

which the mind should aim, which corresponds to the soul. If we think of human beings, we see they are mortal in their visible properties but immortal in their invisible qualities. So too with Scripture. It contains the letter, the visible text, which is transitory. But it also contains the spirit hidden beneath the letter, and this is never extinguished and ought to be the object of our contemplation.[7]

Maximus the Confessor spoke about the interpretation of the Holy Scriptures as an ascent from letters to breath.[8] The anagogical method of scriptural interpretation (from the Greek *anagogē,–ἀναγογή–* ascent), just like an allegorical method, comes from the inexhaustible mystery of the biblical text: only the broader outline of the Scripture is restricted to the framework of the narrative, but "contemplation" (*theōria,* θεωρία), or the secret inner meaning, appears to be infinite. Everything in the Scriptures is connected with the inner spiritual life of man, and the letter of the Scripture derives from this spiritual meaning: "When the Word of God becomes for us bright and clear, his face shines like the sun and his raiment becomes white, and then the words of the Holy Evangelical Writings become clear, transparent and without any sort of veil. And with the Lord come (to us) Moses and Elijah, that is, the spiritual *logoi* of the Law and the Prophets."[9]

The typological, allegorical, and anagogical interpretation of Scripture is characteristic of divine worship in the Orthodox Church. The main target of the reading of Scripture is worship, to aid the faithful in becoming participants of the events described in it, to join in the experience of biblical personages and make it one's own personal experience. The Great Canon of St. Andrew of Crete read during Great Lent contains a whole range of biblical characters from the Old and New Testaments; in each occurrence an example of a biblical hero is accompanied by a commentary with links to a spiritual experience of the worshipper or a call to repentance. In such an interpretation each biblical persona becomes a foreshadowing of the faithful:

Adam was justly banished from Eden because he disobeyed one commandment of Thine, O Saviour. What then shall I suffer, for I am always rejecting Thy words of life?[10]

[7] *Mystagogia* 6.
[8] *Chapters on Theology and Oikonomia* 2.18.
[9] Ibid. 2.14.
[10] *The Lenten Triodion*, The Great Canon of St Andrew of Crete, Ode 1.

Like the woman of Canaan, I cry to Thee, "Have mercy on me, Son of David." Like the woman with an issue of blood, I touch the hem of Thy garment. I weep as Martha and Mary wept for Lazarus.[11]

The Priest saw me first, but passed by on the other side; the Levite looked on me in my distress, but despised my nakedness. O Jesus, sprung from Mary, do Thou come to me and take pity on me.[12]

In the liturgical texts of Holy Week we encounter a multitude of examples of scriptural interpretation with connections to the inner spiritual life of the Christian. Following Christ day by day, the believer himself becomes a participant in the events described in the Gospels. For example, the episode with the withered fig tree (Mt 21.19) is commented on thus: "O brethren, let us fear the punishment of the fig tree, withered because it was unfruitful; and let us bring worthy fruits of repentance unto Christ. . . ."[13] The narrative of Judas' betrayal rouses the author of the liturgical texts together with the listener to enter into direct dialogue with Judas: "What reason led thee, Judas, to betray the Saviour? Did he expel thee from the company of the apostles? Did he deprive thee of the gift of healing? When thou wast at supper with the others, did he drive thee from the table? When he washed the others' feet, did He pass thee by? How many are the blessings that thou hast forgotten! Thou art condemned for thine ingratitude. . . ."[14] In the canticles of the holy crucifixion, the author speaks from the point of view of the Virgin Mary, and in the canticles of the holy burial of Christ, from the point of view of Joseph of Arimathea. In the night after Holy Friday the order of divine services prescribes the fulfillment of the rite of burial for the Savior—services in which all those present take part with burning candles in hand. At these services the following words are sung: "O life, how hast Thou died? How art Thou placed in a tomb? . . . O my sweet Jesus and saving light, how art Thou covered in a dark tomb? . . . O blessed Joseph, thou didst bury the body of Christ the Giver of Life."[15] The believer is so deeply drawn in by the drama of Holy Week that he enters into dialogue with all the other participants, and with Christ himself. The Orthodox

[11]Ibid. Ode 8.
[12]Ibid. Ode 1.
[13]Great and Holy Monday, Matins, Stikheron at the Apostikha, Tone 8.
[14]Great and Holy Friday, Service of the 12 Gospels, Sedalen.
[15]Great and Holy Saturday, Matins, Praises.

Christian sympathizes with Christ's passion, and it becomes a part of his own personal experience of prayer.

If speaking on the Orthodox monastic tradition of the interpretation of the Holy Scripture, then before all else one must note that monastics had a special relationship with Holy Scripture, as to a source of religious inspiration: they not only read and interpreted Scripture, but even memorized it by heart.[16] Monastic tradition fully knows the special way in which to utilize Scripture—what is called *meletē*, μελέτη ("meditation," "diligent study"), contemplating a continual repetition, aloud or mumbled, of individual verses and passages from the Bible.[17]

Monks in the Eastern Church, as a rule, were not interested in the "scientific" exegesis of Scripture: they regarded Scripture as a set of directions to a practical activity and strove to understand it by means of the fulfillment of what was written in it. In their own compositions the holy ascetic fathers insist on the fact that everything said in Scripture is necessarily applicable to one's own life: the hidden meanings in Scripture become clear. Such an approach to Scripture is especially characteristic of *The Sayings of the Desert Fathers*. "Fulfill that which is written,"[18] writes Abba Gerontius, and in this simple formula is generalized all of the experience of scriptural interpretation and understanding in early monasticism. Significant also is the pronouncement of Anthony the Great: "Wherever you may go, always have the Lord before your eyes; whatever you may do, have the Holy Scriptures as a witness."[19] In this way, Scripture should be present in the life of the monk as truly as Christ Himself: it serves to check every individual deed against an evangelical witness. The monastic approach to Scripture, which one may define as exegesis through experience, is summarized in the following words of St Mark the Ascetic (fourth century):

> Being wise and diligent in spiritual matters, reading the Divine Scripture, all will be ascribed to itself, and not to others.[20] In reading the Divine Scripture, strive to comprehend that which is hidden within it, for

---

[16]In Egyptian monastic communities of the fourth century the memorization of scriptural texts was a requisite exercise for every monk.

[17]The Eastern Christian practice of *meletē* bears a large resemblance to what the western ascetic tradition calls *lectio divina* (lit. "divine reading").

[18]*Sayings of the Desert Fathers* Gerontius 1 PG 65, 152AB.

[19]Ibid. Anthony 3 PG 65, 76C.

[20]Mark the Ascetic *On Spiritual Law* 4 PG 65, 905B.

"whatsoever things were written beforehand were written for our learning (Rom. 15.4).[21]

Read the words of Divine Scripture as actions, not as verbiage vainly bestowing one simple (literal) meaning.[22]

Present in the ascetic tradition of the Eastern Church is the idea that the reading of the Holy Scripture is only a secondary means on the ascetic's path to spiritual life. St John Chrysostom says, "It were indeed meet for us not at all to require the aid of the written Word, but to exhibit a life so pure, that the grace of the Spirit should be instead as books to our souls, and that as these are inscribed with ink, even so should our hearts be with the Spirit. But, since we have utterly put away from us this grace, come, let us at any rate embrace the second best course."[23] This is similar to the thoughts found in Isaac the Syrian: "So long as man does not take in the Comforter, the Divine Scriptures are necessary for him . . . but when the strength of the Spirit deigns to become active in man's spiritual strength, then instead of the law of the Scriptures taking root in the heart of the commandment of the Spirit, he learns the Spirit's mystery and no longer has cares for sensual things."[24] According to the thoughts of Symeon the New Theologian, the necessity of Scripture falls away when man encounters God face to face:

He who consciously found himself with God, who gives knowledge to people, such a man read all of the Holy Scripture and collected all the fruit of profit from the reading: he will no longer require the readings found in books. Why is this so? It is so because in conversing with him who inspired the authors of the Divine Writings, having sanctified them in the hidden and unspoken mysteries, the same will become for others a divinely inspired book holding secrets both old and new, written with the quill of God.[25]

The above words of the Fathers of the Eastern Church by no means deny the necessity of the reading of the Holy Scriptures, nor do they lessen the significance of them. Rather, the quoted authors express here the traditional

[21]Ibid. 24.
[22]Ibid. 87.
[23]*Interpretation on Matthew* 1.1.
[24]*Oration* 58.
[25]*Chapters* 3.100.

Eastern Christian understanding that the experience of communion with Christ in the Holy Spirit is higher than verbal expression of this experience, whether it be Holy Scripture or any other authoritative written source. Christianity is a religion about contact with God, and not about a literary knowledge of God, and Christians are by no means "people of the Book."[26] Jesus Christ did not write even one book, and Archbishop Hilarion (Troitsky) does not consider this to be a coincidence. The essence of Christianity is not in moral commandments, nor is it in theological teachings, but it is rather in the salvation of man by the grace of the Holy Spirit through the founding of the Church by Christ:

> Did the incarnation of the Only-Begotten Son of God really need to be written and handed down to mankind through some kind of book? Is it absolutely necessary to be the Only-Begotten Son of God for a book to be written? And if the Church were to insist precisely on the Divine worthiness of its Creator, She would clearly not regard writing as the essence of His actions. The incarnation of the Son of God was necessary for the salvation of mankind, not for the writing of a book. There is no book that ever could, or can, save man. Christ is not the *Teacher*, but is rather the *Savior* of mankind. . . . Christ formed the Church. The Church existed when there was not even one book of the Holy New Testament Scripture. The books of the New Testament were written by the apostles already fifty years after the founding of the historical existence of the Church. In their written books the apostles left memorials of their own oral proclamation. They wrote for an already existing Church and handed their books down to the Church for its eternal edification. Clearly, the books of Holy Scripture do not make up the essence of Christianity because Christianity itself is not a teaching, but is precisely a *new life*, having originated in mankind through the Holy Spirit on the basis of the incarnation of the Son of God. For that reason it is not audacious to say that man is not saved through the Scripture as books, but through the Holy Spirit as it is alive in the Church.[27]

Insisting on the priority of the ecclesial experience, Orthodox Christianity rejects those interpretations of Holy Scripture that are not based on the

[26]In Islam, Jews and Christians are called "people of the Book," or "people of Scripture."
[27]Hilarion (Troitsky), *Holy Scripture and the Church* (Moscow: 2004), 150–153.

experience of the Church and which run counter to this experience or appear to be fruit of the action of man's autonomous intellect. This is the fundamental difference between Orthodox Christianity and Protestantism. Having proclaimed the principle of *sola Scriptura* and having rejected Church Tradition, Protestants have opened a wide space for arbitrary interpretation of Holy Scripture. Orthodox Christianity maintains that proper understanding of Scripture outside the Church and outside Tradition is impossible.

3

The Contents of the Bible. Biblical Criticism

T HE BIBLE IN THE ORTHODOX tradition differs
from that in the Roman Catholic tradition and
differs even more from that used by the Protestant
tradition. The differences revolve around a few
books in the Old Testament, as well as the order of
the arrangement of books in the New Testament.

In contemporary editions of the Bible the books
of the Old Testament are subdivided into those that
are canonical and those not canonical. Those books
that fall under the canonical category are understood to be those of the Hebrew canon. This canon

The codex sinaiticus
Bible, 4th c.

(i.e. the list of books recognized as holy in the Jewish tradition) was formed
over centuries and was finally solidified in the year 90 CE by the Sanhedrin
in the Galilean city of Jamnia.[1] The canonical texts differ from the non-
canonical in their antiquity; the former were written in the period between
the fifteenth and fifth centuries BCE, while the latter were written between
the fourth and first centuries BCE. As for the number of non-canonical
books concerned there are the books of Tobit, Judith, the Wisdom of
Solomon, Sirach, 2 and 3 Esdras, the Letter of Jeremiah, Baruch and 3 Maccabees, and also the Prayer of Manasseh at the end of 2 Chronicles, as well as
various parts of the book of Esther, Psalm 151, and three fragments from the
book of the Prophet Daniel (3.24–90, 13, 14).

The Protestant Bible does not include the non-canonical books of the
Old Testament, and in this way it differs from the Orthodox just as from
the Catholic Bible. The Catholic Bible includes the non-canonical books
under the category of "deuterocanonical" (this term was coined by the Council of Trent in 1546). For the Orthodox Christian, the difference between the

---

[1]Cf.: Schedrovitsky, *Introduction to the Old Testament: the Five Books of Moses* (MOSCOW: 2001), 26.

canonical and non-canonical books of the Old Testament is of a conventional character inasmuch as the question is not about an Orthodox or Christian canon, but is about the Jewish canon, completed independently from Christianity. In the Orthodox Church, the basic criterion for the specific canonicity of this or that book in the Old Testament is its use in the divine services. In this regard one cannot consider the Wisdom of Solomon and those fragments of the book of Daniel which are absent in the Hebrew canon, but which hold an important place in Orthodox services, to be non-canonical. Sometimes the non-canonical books, from the viewpoint of the Hebrew canon and the "deuterocanonical" Catholic canon, in Orthodox usage are called by the Greek term *anaginoskomena*, ἀναγινοσκώμενα (i.e. acknowledged, recommended reading).

While all of the canonical books of the Old Testament are written in Hebrew, the basis of the Old Testament text in the Orthodox tradition is the Septuagint, a Greek translation by the "seventy interpreters" made in the third to second centuries BCE for the Alexandrian Hebrews and the Jewish diaspora. The authority of the Septuagint is based on three factors. First of all, though the Greek text is not the original language of the Old Testament books, the Septuagint does reflect the state of the original text as it would have been found in the third to second centuries BCE, while the current Hebrew text of the Bible, which is called the "Masoretic," was edited up until the eighth century CE. Second, some of the citations taken from the Old Testament and found in the New mainly use the Septuagint text. Third, the Septuagint was used by both the Greek Fathers of the Church, and Orthodox liturgical services (in other words, this text became part of Orthodox church Tradition). Taking into account the three factors enumerated above, St Philaret of Moscow considers it possible to maintain that "in the Orthodox teaching of Holy Scripture it is necessary to attribute a dogmatic merit to the Translation of the Seventy, in some cases placing it on an equal level with the original and even elevating it above the Hebrew text, as is generally accepted in the most recent editions."[2]

If the Septuagint has served as a *textus receptus* (official, "received" text) in the Eastern Church for many centuries, then the Vulgate (a Latin translation made by the Blessed Jerome, 342–420) has been a comparable text for the Church in the West. The Council of Trent (1546) recognized the Vulgate as

[2]Metropolitan Philaret of Moscow, *On the Dogmatic Worthiness of the Septuagint* (Moscow: 1858).

the official text of the Bible as received in the Catholic Church. The Vulgate text differs from the Septuagint since the latter appeared some centuries before the Vulgate and based itself on a much more ancient Hebrew text. The contents of the Vulgate even differ from the Septuagint, particularly in the presence of 4 Esdras, absent in the Greek language version.

When the question arose of a translation of the Bible into Russian in the beginning of the nineteenth century, translators seemed to be in a difficult situation, insofar as there was not one single opinion on which original should serve as the basis for the translation. The Slavonic translation of the Bible, originating from Sts Cyril and Methodius but repeatedly edited over centuries, was based on the Septuagint. It was the Slavonic text to which the ear of the Russian Orthodox Christian was accustomed, and thus it seemed most logical to make the Russian translation of the Bible from the Greek language. The deciding factor, however, became the voice of the Metropolitan of Moscow Philaret who, with all his respect concerning the dogmatic merit of the Septuagint, nevertheless did not consider it possible to translate the Bible into Russian while ignoring the Hebrew Masoretic text. In accordance with Philaret's recommendations for the translation of the Old Testament into Russian, the Masoretic text was taken as the basis, though it was checked against the Septuagint text. Philaret developed various "conservative rules," insisting on giving preference to the Greek text in those cases when, for example, an Old Testament text cited in the New came from the Septuagint, or when Christian tradition had firmly secured the understanding of a text based on the Septuagint, or when the Masoretic text was thought to have been corrupted. As a result the canonical books of the Old Testament were translated from the Hebrew and occasionally from the Greek, but the non-canonical books were translated from the Septuagint, with 3 Esdras being an exception as it was translated from the Latin (in the Vulgate this is 4 Esdras).

The difference between the Russian and Slavonic Bibles is especially noticeable in the translations of the Psalter. In the divine services of the Russian Orthodox Church the psalms are read in Slavonic, though if the believer should want to understand the meaning of the Slavonic text by checking it against the Russian translation, this will appear to be impossible, since the Russian contains a different text. Thus, for example, Psalm 18.26–27 reads in Slavonic as: "With the pure you show yourself pure; and with the crooked you show yourself perverse. For you deliver a humble people, but the haughty eyes you bring down." However, in the Russian version done from the Masoretic text, the above verses of the psalm acquire a completely different meaning. Similar examples of a divergence in meaning between Russian and Slavonic translations of the Old Testament, contingent upon differences between the Hebrew and Greek texts as well as an incorrect understanding of the Greek text by Slavonic translators,[3] can account for much.

We spoke earlier on the formation of the canon of the holy books of the New Testament in the section on early Christian literature.[4] The contents of the New Testament in Orthodoxy, Catholicism, and Protestantism are one and the same. However, in the Orthodox edition of the Bible, the book of the Acts of the Apostles is followed by the Catholic Epistles, the Pauline Epistles, and Revelation, while in the Catholic and Protestant editions, Acts is followed by the Pauline Epistles and then the Catholic Epistles and Revelation. This difference exists already in early Greek and Latin manuscripts; there is no theological significance to it whatsoever.

There was not one sole opinion concerning the dogmatic meaning and "canonicity" of Revelation in the ancient Church. St. Gregory the Theologian gives the following list of "authentic" books of the New Testament in one of his poems:

> Matthew really did write the miraculous books of Christ for the Hebrews,
> And Mark for Italy,
> Luke for Greece,
> John, that great preacher ascending to heaven, for all.
> After that is the Acts of the Apostles, most wise,
> And the fourteen epistles of Paul,
> And the seven Catholic Epistles, one of which is from James,
> Two from Peter, three for John once again,

---

[3]In this case the argument revolves around the imprecise translation from Greek to Slavonic. The understanding of the Greek text found in the works of the Greek Fathers of the Church bears witness to this in particular: "You justly vouchsafed me your blessing because You are just, with the blessed You can be blessed. For if I were to abide in sin I would give myself over to utter corruption, thus I know that You are truly the Great Judge, for You would have to pronounce Your judgment upon me, according to my sin. But insofar as I keep to Your paths, so You, Who are blessed in the saints and blameless with the blameless, did not keep Your gaze on digressions from what is right, which for a time I was guilty of, but You rendered Your judgment to me for the life I led afterwards and for the deeds which I accomplished in righteousness" (Athanasius of Alexandria *Commentary on Psalm 17*).

[4]See the author's *Orthodox Christianity*, vol. I (Yonkers, NY: St Vladimir's Seminary Press, 2011), 32–33 [hereafter Orthodox Christianity I].

And the seventh from Jude. Now you have them all.
If something else appears apart from this, then it is not
numbered among the genuine (books).[5]

Thus Gregory the Theologian does not recognize Revelation as numbered among the "genuine" books. A younger contemporary of Gregory, St Amphilochius of Iconium (d. after 394), includes in his own list of New Testament writings the four Gospels, Acts of the Apostles, the Pauline Epistles, the Catholic Epistles, and Revelation. In this list however, he notes that some consider the Epistle to the Hebrews to be false; others maintain that among the Catholic Epistles, only three should be accepted–James, 1 Peter, and 1 John. Concerning Revelation, Amphilochius says that "some accept it, but the majority consider it false."[6] Arguments over Revelation concluded with its entering the New Testament canon, intended for home reading, though in the divine services of the Orthodox Church Revelation is never considered to be distinct from the rest of the New Testament books.

How should the Orthodox Church view what is called biblical criticism, the science of the provenance and development of the scriptural text? There is the opinion that the Orthodox Christian ought to reject biblical criticism as a product of primarily a Protestant discipline. This opinion presents itself as rather erroneous, first, because there is no one generally accepted biblical text in the Orthodox tradition (it is enough to point out the differences between the Russian and Slavonic bibles), and second, a reverential attitude towards the Bible by no means excludes a scientific approach towards its text. The collation of ancient manuscripts, the arrangement of variant readings among them and the revelation of the most authoritative text does not at all contradict the Orthodox understanding of Holy Scripture. This concerns not only the Old, but the New Testament, a text which underwent various changes in the manuscript tradition. For this reason the critical edition of the Scriptures, that is to say the edition based on the most authoritative, ancient manuscripts containing a list of the original variant texts, is no less valuable to the Orthodox Christian than to the Catholic or Protestant. Especially valuable are those places in the critical edition of Holy Scripture where a reading known by the Fathers of the Church, but subsequently changed for some reason, is restored.

---

[5]Gregory the Theologian *Dogmatic Verses 12: On the Genuine Books of the God-Inspired Scriptures* PG 37, 474A.
[6]Amphilochius of Iconium *To Seleucus*.

A. V. Kartashev

In the nineteenth century St Philaret of Moscow considered it necessary to approach the text of the Holy Scriptures critically, and the Russian translation of the Bible under his direction was considered a success of biblical criticism of that time. In the twentieth century a number of Orthodox theologians spoke out in favor of the necessity for introducing Orthodox academics to the achievement of contemporary biblical criticism. A. V. Kartashev highlighted the following:

In the inevitable forthcoming missionary campaign of the Russian Church along the vast expanse of the homeland, it is not possible to make do with one singular, obsolete means from the arsenal of our scientific-theological backwardness. In order to defeat the enemy at all his seemingly advanced and scientific positions, one needs to wield the same weapons of the newest scientific technology. But for this one needs, in the first place, to perceive creatively, to master, and to transfigure it in the bosom of church theology and its truth.[7]

Archpriest Sergei Bulgakov also wrote on the positive attitude of Orthodoxy toward biblical criticism:

. . . nothing is hindered by (quite the opposite, it seems fully natural) . . . using those genuine scientific achievements that have been realized in modern times in this society of the western Christian world and, having rectified and applied them accordingly, taking it to the fullness of Church tradition, of course not for abolition, but for the furthest exposure and fulfillment of what exists. The truth is one, but it overtakes people in the discursive process of development. In the Orthodox consciousness there is no basis for fearing biblical criticism nor for being embarrassed by it, because through it the comprehensible paths of God and the activity of the Holy Spirit, working repeatedly and diversely in the Church, are only made more concrete.[8]

[7] A. V. Kartashev, *Old Testament Biblical Criticism* (Paris: 1947), 96.
[8] S. N. Bulgakov, *Orthodox Christianity*, 3rd ed. (Paris: 1989), 60.

The Orthodox Church accepts the present biblical criticism only insofar as it does not contradict the Church's own Tradition. Orthodoxy rejects those excesses of biblical criticism that were characteristic of a broken Protestantism, when the authenticity of this or that other book of the New Testament came under doubt, and those which are present in modern biblical studies. Orthodox tradition views as alien the historical-critical method of R. Bultmann (1884–1976), based on the idea of the "demythologization" of the Gospel (the separation of the essence of evangelical kerygma, or good news, from the proposed latest developments, "myths," which are allegedly found in church tradition). Such a method presents itself in direct contradiction to the understanding of the Gospel as an inalienable component of church Tradition.

Apart from these considerations, the Orthodox Church does not approve of those translations of the Scriptures that distort the holy text simply for the sake of skirting church tradition. The most odious Russian translation of this sort was *The Uniting and Translation of the Four Gospels* by Leo Tolstoy, mentioned above.[9] Speaking on this translation, Archbishop Hilarion (Troitsky) recalls a scene from Goethe's *Faust*, where Faust translates the first verse of the Gospel of John from "In the beginning was the mind" to "In the beginning was the might" to "In the beginning was the act." This scene may seem to be a caricature, but really, asks Archbishop Hilarion, "Was this not played out in the Russian land, in Yasnaya Polyana, where the admirer of good thoughts (only his own!) decided by referencing the Greek lexicon to settle on this translation of the Gospel text: 'In the beginning of all came the meaning of life'?"[10] Such scenes also play out in our own time when free translations of Scripture, noted by their striving to be dissociated from ecclesial usage, appear in a Protestant environment.

However, it is not only in the Protestant world, but also in the Orthodox world of recent times where translations have appeared in which a worthy and lofty ecclesial lexicon is systematically replaced by one that is base and non-ecclesial. Among such translations is one of the Pauline Epistles[11] done by V.N. Kuznetsova and published by the Russian Biblical Society. Below are merely a few quotes from this work:

[9]In *Orthodox Christianity* I, 232–233.
[10]Hilarion (Troitsky), *Holy Scripture and the Church vol. 2* (Moscow: 2004), 166–167.
[11]The Pauline Epistles.

Oh, I wish you could bear with me, even if I am a little foolish! But do bear with me, please . . . I think that I am not in the least inferior to these super apostles. It is possible that I am not a master speaker, but I am knowledgeable . . . I say again, don't take me for an idiot! But if you, then accept me as an idiot so that I can brag a bit! What I say now, of course, is not from the Lord. In this venture I will boast that I am an idiot . . . Let anyone boast as he wish–I still speak as an idiot . . . (2 Cor 11.1–22).

I have gone completely mad! You have driven me to it! You should have been commending me! So you will say I did not burden you, yet I am a dodger and laid hands on you through cunning. Did I ever live off of you through any of those whom I sent to you? (2 Cor 12.11–18).

Food is for the tummy and the tummy for food . . . And you who are part of the body of Christ want to turn it into the body of a hussy? God forbid! (1 Cor 6.13–16).

In such a "translation," one finds a conscious and constant desacralization of the holy text, which is transferred into a vulgar, crude, and low language. The words "idiot," "brag," "venture," "to go mad," "dodger," "to live off of someone," "tummy," and "hussy," and the idioms "master speaker," "laid hands on," and "driven me to it," correspond to the holy text neither in spirit nor in letter; the text deserves to be treated with more reverence than that.

The Orthodox Church cannot approve of scriptural translations deliberately made for an alien, specialized audience, to whose taste the holy text has been artificially tailored. Prevalent in the West are feminine and "politically correct" versions of Scripture that are perceived by the Orthodox Christians as impermissible infringements of the holy text, verging on blasphemy. The Orthodox Church consistently comes out against so-called "gender-neutral" versions of the Bible, in which "inclusive language" is applied to God. This phenomenon occurs primarily in English translations of the Bible, for in that language not many words are morphologically marked for gender. Even so, God is traditionally referred to with the pronoun "he," and not the feminine pronoun "she." Some proponents of feminist theology insist that since God does not appear as a man, it follows that he should be referred to with neutral pronouns or even not be referred to with pronouns at all. Instead of the traditional terms "Father, Son, and Holy Spirit," which contain a rather marked male emphasis, feminists suggest the gender-neutral terms of "Parent, Redeemer, and Sustainer."

The issue, however, is not merely limited to the demand for a correction of terminology. Proponents of feminist theology point out that throughout the course of Holy Scripture preference is given to males, and not to females. The Old Testament speaks of the God of Abraham, Isaac, and Jacob (Ex 3.16), and not the God of Sarah, Rebecca, and Rachael; the commandments of Moses are made to men, not to women ("Thou shalt not covet thy neighbor's wife"); in the Wisdom of Solomon the author addresses a male reader, whereas he speaks of women in the third person. In the New Testament the addressees of the moral commandments also seem to be primarily males (Mt 5.31–32; Lk 18.29; 1 Cor 7.27–28); women are excluded in the recollections of those present (Mt 14.21: "Those fed were around five thousand men, besides women and children;" Cf. Mt 15.38); even those numbered among the 144 thousand who are saved are only men (Rev 14.4: "These are the ones who were not defiled with women"). In the Pauline Epistles the inequality between men and women is repeatedly highlighted (1 Cor 11.3–16; 1 Cor 14.34–35; Col 3.18; 1 Tim 2.11–15). From the point of view of feminist theology, the presence of so many texts either excluding or degrading women explains the cultural and societal standards of the patriarchal era in which the authors of the Old and New Testaments lived and, consequently, the given texts should be updated. However, such an update would be intolerable in the Orthodox Church, since it would not only radically destroy the text of Holy Scripture but also in many cases it would lead to a revision of those moral directives which were so characteristic of the early Church and which are kept in the Orthodox Tradition.

4

The Contents and Authority of Tradition.
The Legacy of the Holy Fathers

APART FROM THE HOLY WRITINGS of the Old and New Testaments, the content of Tradition in the Orthodox Church includes other written sources, among which are the texts of the divine services, the orders of the Sacraments, the resolutions of the ecumenical and local councils, the works of the Fathers and readings of the ancient Church. What authority do these texts have for the Orthodox Christian?

This absolute and indisputable authority is used in the dogmatic decisions of the ecumenical councils, proceeding from what the Church has received. Above all is the Niceno-Constantinopolitan Creed, which presents itself as a summary version of Orthodox dogma, taken from the First Ecumenical Council (325) and supplemented by the second council (381). Another point is the other dogmatic decisions of the councils that enter into the canonical compilations of the Orthodox Church. These decisions are not subject to change and are universally applied to all members of the Church. That which really concerns the disciplinary canons of the Orthodox Church (amongst the compilation of canons in the Orthodox Church one finds, in addition to the decisions and canons of the seven ecumenical councils, the "Apostolic Canons" and the canons of the local councils of the Eastern Church of the fourth century to the ninth), is their application, which defines the real life of the Church in each historical period of its development. Some canons, established by the Fathers in antiquity, are still maintained in the Orthodox Church, while others have passed out of use.[1] A

---

[1]So, for example, all the resolutions of the ancient Church dealing with the wives of bishops (Ap 5.51; I Nic 3) are not used in present times since the Orthodox Church no longer allows a married episcopate. The canon which prescribes excommunication for clerics who have dined at a restaurant (Ap 54) is no longer observed, nor is the one which excommunicates laymen who, having entered the church and having listened to the reading of the Scriptures, do not stay for the end of the service or do not receive communion of the Holy Mystery (Ap 9). Many other canons that prescribe a severe

Council of the Twelve Apostles.
Constantinople, beg. of the
14th c.

review and renovation of the code of canonical regulations is one of the Orthodox Church's most pressing assignments.

The liturgical Tradition of the Church is certainly used as an absolute authority. In their dogmatic irreproachability, the texts of the divine services of the Orthodox Church serve as do Holy Scripture and the faithful decrees of the councils. These texts are not only works issued by theologians and poets, but are a part of the liturgical experience of many generations of Christians. In the Orthodox Church, the authority of the texts of the divine services is founded on reception, the process these texts underwent over many centuries, when they were read and sung everywhere in every Orthodox temple. Throughout these centuries, all that was false and alien that could creep into the texts by misunderstanding or oversight was eliminated by church Tradition itself. The texts became pure and irreproachable theology, covered in the poetic forms of church hymns. That is why the Church acknowledged the texts of the divine services among the ranks of the "Rules of Faith," in the ranks of the infallible dogmatic sources.

It stands to reason that the next place in the hierarchy of authority is occupied by the works of the Fathers of the Church. For an Orthodox Christian, the main significance of the holy Fathers' legacy is the work of the church fathers of the ancient Church before any schism, in particular the eastern fathers who had a decided influence on the formation of Orthodox dogmatics. The opinions of western fathers in agreement with the teachings of the Eastern Church are organically intertwined with Orthodox Tradition, which contains within itself both a western and eastern theological legacy. Those opinions of the western Fathers that are found to be in direct contradiction to the teachings of the Eastern Church are not considered authoritative for the Orthodox Christian.

The legacy of the holy Fathers has always played a special role in Orthodox Tradition. St John of Damascus defined the Tradition of the Church as

canonical penance for various divergences from the norms of Christian morality are no longer observed, or at least are applied only with a significant softening.

"a boundary that our holy Fathers received."[2] St Athanasius of Alexandria spoke of the "original Tradition" and of "the faith of the Universal Church, which the Lord granted, the apostles passed down, and the Fathers preserved."[3] Faith, as professed by the Eastern Church, is defined as the "apostolic faith, the patristic faith, the Orthodox faith."[4]

It is understandable why the Christian faith should be "apostolic": handed down by the incarnate Word of God himself, faith was entrusted to the apostles like a talent that needed to be multiplied, so that it might bring forth fruit ten, fifty, or a hundredfold in the history of many peoples. It is understandable why faith should be "Orthodox," for having the right mind concerning God is necessary for salvation, just as a false understanding of God brings one to spiritual death. But why should faith be "patristic"? Perhaps it all comes down to some sort of inevitable stylization of Orthodoxy under a "patristic antiquity." Or perhaps Orthodox Christianity should always be concerned with the past and not live in the present, nor work toward the future. Or perhaps it is ideal that the Orthodox Christian should remain in some kind of "Golden Age" in which the great Fathers of the Church lived and to which the present Church should orient itself. Or, perhaps, the issue is that the formation of Orthodox theology and church tradition was concluded in the "patristic age" and, consequently, nothing new is needed in Orthodox theology, nor for that matter in the life of the Orthodox Church in general.

If this is the case—and many truly think so—then the fundamental task of the Orthodox Church consists of keeping watch over a Byzantine legacy, vigilantly guarding Orthodoxy from the infectious spirit of these new times. Some act just so, disowning the calls of modernity and linking any creative interpretation of Tradition to the age of "general apostasy," since all has already been interpreted and laid out by the Fathers in previous centuries; they spend all their strength conserving what they understand to be within the traditional teaching of the Orthodox Church. As a rule, these adherents to the "preservation of Orthodoxy" love to quote the "teachings of the holy Fathers," but in actuality they do not know the patristic teaching: they are accustomed to the thoughts of individual fathers to prove their theories and

[2]John of Damascus *Treatises Against Those Decrying the Holy Images* 3.41.
[3]Athanasius of Alexandria *On the Holy Spirit* 1.28.
[4]The Synodikon of the Sunday of Orthodoxy.

ideas, but they do not study patristic theology in all its many forms and in its totality.

If the Orthodox Christian ought to concern himself only with the protection and conservation of that which was accumulated by the holy Fathers in antiquity, then there is no higher purpose beyond that. If, however, it is necessary for him to put the talent of the patristic legacy in circulation, then his task is not simply to study the works of the holy Fathers, but also to interpret these works in the light of contemporary experience and, moreover, to interpret contemporary experience in the light of the teachings of the Fathers. It is not enough to study the works of the Fathers; one must learn to think patristically, to live patristically. In this last point lies the task that stands before the Orthodox Christian.

The works of the Fathers are not a museum exhibit, nor should the "patristic faith" be taken exclusively as a legacy from a bygone age. Now there is the widespread opinion that the holy Fathers are theologians of the past, but the past itself is dated in different ways. In the estimation of some, the Patristic Age came to an end in the eighth century, when John of Damascus wrote *An Exact Exposition of the Orthodox Faith*, summing up a few centuries' worth of theological disputes. In others' minds, it ended in the eleventh century with the final schism between the first and the second Rome, or in the middle of the fifteenth century with the fall of the "Second Rome" (Constantinople), or in 1917 with the fall of the "Third Rome" (Moscow) as the capital of an Orthodox empire. Correspondingly, there is now a return to "patristic sources," to be understood precisely as an embrace of the past and a restoration of either the eighth, fifteenth, or nineteenth centuries.

Such an understanding, however, ought to be questioned. According to Archpriest Georges Florovsky, "The Church does not now hold less authority than it did in previous centuries, just as the Holy Spirit does not live in it less than it did in a past age"; this is why it is not permissible to limit the "age of the Fathers" to some time in the past.[5] Metropolitan Kallistos (Ware) of Diokleia says, "The Orthodox must not simply know and quote the Fathers; they must enter more deeply into the inner spirit of the Fathers and acquire a 'patristic mind,' and must treat the Fathers not merely as relics of the past, but as living witnesses and contemporaries." Metropolitan Kallistos does not

---

[5]Georges Florovsky, *Saint Gregory Palamas and the Traditions of the Fathers* (Moscow: 1995), 383–384.

think that the age of the holy Fathers was concluded in the fifth century, nor in the eighth, but that the patristic age continues in the Orthodox Church to this very day: "Indeed, it is dangerous to look on 'the Fathers' as a closed cycle of writings belonging wholly to the past, for might not our own age produce a new Basil or Athanasius? To say that there can be no more Fathers is to suggest that the Holy Spirit has deserted the Church."[6]

In this way, confessing the "patristic faith" means not only studying the patristic writings, not merely striving to embody the commandments of the Fathers in life, but it means believing that the present age is no less patristic than any other. The "Golden Age," beginning with Christ, the apostles, and the ancient Fathers, continues in the theological works of the contemporary Church fathers. It will continue so long as the Church of Christ stands on the earth and the Holy Spirit acts in it.

In the works of the Church fathers it is necessary to differentiate what is within time and what is eternal: on the one hand, what preserves value forever and has an immutable significance for the Christian today, and on the other hand, what has worth within history, what has been born and has died within the context in which its given ecclesial author lived. For example, many views on natural science contained in Basil the Great's *Homilies on the Hexaemeron* and in John of Damascus' *An Exact Exposition of the Orthodox Faith* are obsolete, whereas the theological interpretations of the creation of the cosmos by these authors still have significance in our own time. Another similar example is the anthropological views of the Byzantine fathers who believed, like everyone in the Byzantine era, that man's body was made up of four elements, that the soul was divided in three parts (reason, desire, and appetite). These views, dependent on an antiquated anthropology, are now outdated, but much of what these noted Fathers said about man, about his soul and body, about the passions, about the ways of thoughts and spirits, has not lost its significance in our own day.

Furthermore, it is worth differentiating in the patristic writings what is said by its authors on behalf of the Church and what is conveyed by general ecclesial teaching, from personal theological ideas (*theologoumena*, θεολογού-μενα).[7] Personal opinions should not be cut off for the creation of certain

---

[6] *The Orthodox Church*, 204.

[7] This difference was first introduced by the Russian church historian V. V. Bolotov (1853–1900), who applied the term *theologoumenon* to the Roman Catholic teaching of the Filioque.

simplified "theological summaries," for the removal of a certain "common denominator" of Orthodox dogmatic teaching. At the same time though, personal opinion, even if its authority is founded on the name of a person placed by the Church amongst the ranks of Fathers and teachers, so long as it is not consecrated by the communal reception of ecclesial wisdom, cannot be placed on the same level with the ideas that this reception allows. A personal opinion, as soon as it is conveyed by the Church fathers, though not as yet judged to be universal, enters into the realm of the permissible and possible, but it is not considered absolutely necessary for the Orthodox faithful.

In the next place after the patristic writings are the compositions of those known as the teachers of the Church, theologians from antiquity who have exerted influence on the formation of ecclesial teachings, but for some reason or other have not been elevated to the rank of Father by the Church (numbered among these, for example, are Clement of Alexandria and Tertullian). Their ideas are authoritative insofar as they agree with wider Church teachings.

The only apocryphal literature that can be considered authoritative is those texts that are received in a direct or mediated form by church consciousness, specifically those found to be reflected in theology or in hagiographic literature. Those apocrypha that were rejected by the mind of the Church have no authority for the Orthodox.

Individual compositions on dogmatic themes deserve to be mentioned, those which appear in the sixteenth to nineteenth centuries and are sometimes called the "symbolic books" of the Orthodox Church. The very name "symbolic books" is taken from Protestantism, where this name refers to normative dogmatic documents (for example, the Large and Small Catechism of Martin Luther, the Augsburg Confession of 1530). In response to the Protestant symbolic books, Roman Catholics began to compile rather similar documents. Concerning Orthodox dogmatic documents of this period, they had mainly a polemical character and were directed either against Catholicism or against Protestantism. Particular documents of this kind to note are: "The Answers of Patriarch Jeremias II to the Lutherans" (1573–1581), "The Confession of Faith of Metropolitan Metrophanes of Alexandria" (1625), "The Orthodox Confession of Peter Moghila" (1642), "The Confession of Faith of Patriarch Dositheus of Jerusalem" (1672): these make up the line of anti-Catholic and anti-Protestant letters of the Eastern patriarchs from the seventeenth to the first half of the nineteenth century; "The Epistles of the Eastern Patriarchs to Pope Pius IX" (1848); and "The Answer of the Constantinopolitan Synod to Pope Leo XIII" (1895).

As far as the dogmatic significance of these texts goes, the period between the sixteenth and nineteenth century was not necessarily considered to be the most positive for Orthodox theology: the development of theology in the Greek East was severely curtailed by provisos issued under Turkish rule, while both in Greece and in Russia, the discipline of theology found itself under a Western, primarily Catholic influence. This influence manifests itself in the theological character of the aforementioned compositions, in which the Orthodox authors frequently use Protestant arguments in direct polemic with Catholic ones, or vice versa. In the opinion of Archbishop Vasily (Krivoshein), these compositions:

> Cannot be considered authoritative and necessary symbolic texts, equated with a canon of an ecumenical council, as their origin is not of a general ecclesial character, but is usually a low-level theological notion and frequently a divergence from patristic and liturgical Tradition, while carrying traces of a formal, sometimes actual, influence of Roman Catholic theology. They preserve their own worth only as a historical witness of ecclesial and theological self-consciousness and its position in the major annals of church history. In this sense they deserve full respect and attention, all the more so if they are true to the Orthodox Faith, though they did not especially successfully wrap it in heterodox "clothing." For this reason their authority is secondary or auxiliary in nature.[8]

Finally, it is necessary to speak about the authority of the works of contemporary Orthodox theologians on dogmatic issues. The same criteria can be applied to these texts as were applied to the compositions of the ancient teachers of the Church: they are authoritative insofar as they correspond to church Tradition, insofar as they reflect a patristic form of reason. Orthodox authors of the twentieth century have made an essential contribution to the matter of interpreting various aspects of Orthodox Tradition, to the development of Orthodox theology and its freedom from outside influences, and to the elucidation of the fundamentals of the Orthodox Faith in the face of

---

[8]Vasily (Krivoshein), *Symbolic Texts in the Orthodox Church* (Nizhny Novgorod: 2004), 214.

heterodox Christians. Many works of modern Orthodox theologians have become an inalienable part of Orthodox Tradition, by re-stocking the treasury in which, in the words of Irenaeus of Lyons, the apostles received "all that related to the truth"[9] and which in the passing of time has been enriched with an increased number of fresh texts on theological themes.

[9]Irenaeus of Lyons *Against Heresies* 3.4.

PART TWO

GOD

5

The Revelation of a Personal God.
Theology and Knowledge of God

C HRISTIANITY, TOGETHER WITH JUDAISM AND ISLAM, belongs to the group of monotheistic religions also known as "Abrahamic." All three religions go back to a revelation by God to Abraham that is recorded in the Old Testament. Christianity confesses that God is one, that he is the Father of all people, that he is the Creator of the material and spiritual worlds.

According to Christian understanding, God is not an abstract beginning, a faceless spiritual force, an impersonal being. The Christian God is the Personal God, the Living God. He reveals himself to man through a personal relationship, a personal experience, and a personal encounter. At the same time God is transcendent to man, he is incomprehensible, indescribable, and invisible. In this is the primordial paradox of religious experience—the paradox that is impossible to explain to an unbeliever or agnostic, so far removed from religion.

In Christianity, the empirical experience carries with it a decisive meaning. It is impossible to prove the existence of God to him who has not felt God's essence in his own life. All attempts to prove the existence of God undertaken throughout history were evidence enough for those who wanted to believe them. Thus, for example, Thomas Aquinas set out five proofs for the existence of God in his *Summa Theologica*: 1) from motion (*ex motu*); 2) from the nature of the efficient cause (*ex ratione causae efficientis*); 3) from necessity (*ex possibili et necesario*); 4) from the degrees found in living things (*ex gradibus rei*); and 5) from the governance and order of things (*ex gubernatione rerum*). The first proof comes from the notion that everything in nature is moving, and all movement has something else as its cause, consequently it is necessary to access some kind of "first-mover," who himself is not moved by something else: God is the "first-mover." Along the same lines, the second proof, through the understanding of cause and effect, comes to the acknowledgement of the first reason of all, which is God. The third proof is based on the fact that there is the possibility for all subjects in this world to be or not to be, but there should be one necessarily existing being: this being is God. The fourth proof dispenses with the notion that things in the world can be more or less perfect, but there is necessarily a higher perfection that could be the reason for all that is good and perfect: this is God. Finally, the fifth proof comes from the knowledge that subjects devoid of reason, submitting themselves to expediency, are rulers of their conscious will: "Therefore some intelligent being exists by whom all natural things are directed to their end; and this being we call God."[1]

Not one of these proofs, based on the philosophy of Aristotle, will be able to convince a non-believer of the existence of God. This is precisely why the patristic theology of the Eastern Church in the first millennium (and after it, Orthodox theology in the second millennium) refrained from making attempts to prove God's existence with the help of rational arguments and logic problems. As St Maximus the Confessor maintains, God's being is perceived by faith, and this faith is "more worthy than any piece of evidence," inasmuch as it is true knowledge, "exceeding both thought and reason."[2]

Some Orthodox authors of more recent times have used rational proofs of God's existence borrowed from Western scholasticism, in academia or for apologetic purposes, though such proofs were alien and unnecessary for the ancient theological intuition of the Eastern Church. Rejecting them or refraining from them, Orthodox Tradition is based on the idea that rational acknowledgement of God's existence is not at all identical to faith in God, for faith is an experiential knowledge of God, an encounter with the Living God, and such an encounter is generally impossible by way of rational knowledge. Religious experience transcends reason, and its expression demands another means aside from utilizing philosophic discourse.

In Orthodox tradition the very understanding of "theology" is least of all linked to rational thought, and theology is not perceived as a science, as an abstract theorization. The theologians of the ancient Church were not men who sat behind a desk surrounded by books, dictionaries, reference books, and academic textbooks. The overwhelming majority of church fathers were bishops or monks: they either actively studied church functions or worked in

---

[1] Thomas Aquinas *Summa Theologica* 2.3.
[2] *Chapters on Theology and Oikonomia* 1.8–9.

a monastery. Their theology was born from an inner mystical, enriching experience, coming into contact daily with Church Tradition through the liturgical services, prayer, the reading of Scripture, and relationships with the people of God. The classical formula of Evagrius of Pontus (fourth century) says: "If you are a theologian, then you will pray sincerely, and if you pray sincerely, then you are a theologian."[3] In this definition the border between theology and the knowledge of God, between theology and prayerful experience, fades away completely: theology is not what is other, but like an experience of a mystical encounter with God in prayer, it is an experience of relationship with God.

Concerning theology as an experiential encounter with the Living God, V.N. Lossky writes in his *Mystical Theology of the Eastern Church*:

> God is not a scientific subject, and theology differs from philosophical thought in radical forms: a theologian does not seek God as one researches any other subject, but God himself takes possession of the theologian, just as another's personality can seize control of us. This is exactly why God first found the theologian, exactly why God went out to meet him in his revelation, so that it would seem possible to seek God as we all search for our own existence, and consequently for our mind, for any kind of presence. The God of theology—this "you," is the living God of the Bible. Of course, this is the Absolute, but a personal Absolute, whom we call "you" in prayer.[4]

The Fathers of the Eastern Church warned against the profanation and desecration of theology, of its transformation into a subject of dispute, and as the object of terrible fights. Theology is not an activity for the marketplace, stressed St Gregory of Nyssa, exposing his contemporaries, not without sarcasm, for their excessive partiality for arguments on theological themes:

> Everywhere, in the public squares, at crossroads, in the streets and lanes, people would stop you and discourse at random about the Trinity. If you asked something of a moneychanger, he would begin discussing the question of the Begotten and the Unbegotten. If you questioned a baker about the price of bread, he would answer that the Father is greater and the Son is

---

[3] *On Prayer* 61.
[4] (Moscow, 1991), 200.

subordinate to him. If you went to take a bath, the Anomoean bath atten-
dant would tell you that in his opinion the Son simply comes from nothing.[5]

In the words of St Gregory the Theologian, "to philosophize about God,"
that is, to theologize, can only be done by one who leads a contemplative
way of life and who purifies himself for God; not everyone can participate in
theological discussions—only those who do these things diligently. Finally,
not every theological subject can be discussed aloud:

> Discussion of theology is not for everyone, I tell you, not for everyone—
> it is no such inexpensive or effortless pursuit. Nor, I would add, is it for
> every occasion, or for every audience; neither are all its aspects open to
> inquiry. It must be reserved for certain occasions, for certain audiences,
> and certain limits must be observed. It is not for all people, but only for
> those who have been tested and have found a sound footing in study,
> and, more importantly, have undergone, or at the very least are undergo-
> ing, purification of body and soul. . . . What aspects of theology should
> be investigated, and to what limit? Only aspects within our grasp, and
> only to the limit of the experience and capacity of our audience. . . . Yet
> I am not maintaining that we ought not to be mindful of God at all times.
> . . . It is more important that we should remember God than that we
> should breathe. . . . So it is not continual remembrance of God I seek to
> discourage, but continual discussion of theology. I am not opposed either
> to theology, as if it were a breach of piety, but only to its untimely prac-
> tice, or to instruction in it, except when this goes to excess.[6]

St Gregory the Theologian considers purification as the necessary condition of theologizing: "It is a great thing to speak about God, but it is an even
greater thing to cleanse yourself for God."[7] Purification is not opposed to theology in this saying: in essence, theology is a kind of spiritual cleansing that is
done necessarily for the knowledge of God. A pure word, a word about that
which is beyond words, reason, and hearing, should be born of silence:

> You do not know what a divine gift silence is, not needing to speak every
> word, but keeping it within ourselves as masters over speech as well as

[5] *De Deitate Filii et Spiritus Sancti*, PG 46.556.
[6] Gregory the Theologian *Oration* 27.3–4 (Crestwood, N.Y.: SVS Press, 2002), 26–28.
[7] *Oration* 32.12.

silence. For by nature every word is feeble and inadequate . . . but speech about God is so much more, a subject so much loftier, the fervor stronger, the risk more intense. But what are we afraid of, and what do we hope for? For intellect, speech, or hearing, if danger threatens all three? For it is difficult to comprehend God, it is impossible to explain,[8] and to attain a pure understanding is the most difficult of all.[9]

Jacob's Ladder. Palatine chapel. Palermo. Twelfth century.

The theme of silence is a leitmotif of Eastern Christian theology. As one may recall, the Holy Martyr Ignatius the God-Bearer said two centuries before St Gregory that whoever possesses the word of Christ "can ever hear his silence."[10] St Isaac the Syrian would say three centuries after Gregory that "silence is the sacrament of the coming age, but speech is the essential tool of this world."[11] The Fathers of the Eastern Church realized sharply how inadequate and ill-suited human language is for the expression of divine reality. This is why the patristic tradition has counterbalanced what is called cataphatic (positive, affirmative) theology with the apophatic (negative). Cataphatic theology strives to describe God with the aid of human speech, to endow God with this or that quality that corresponds to a human one. Apophatic theology, by negative means saying what God is not, brings to mind God's incomprehensibility, his absolute transcendence. Apophatic theology corresponds to the way of knowledge about God by putting away rational thought and by being silent before the mystery, in order to express what human speech is incapable of expressing.

The essence of cataphatic and apophatic theology was most fully expressed by Dionysius the Areopagite in the treatise *Mystical Theology*. After Gregory the Theologian and Gregory of Nyssa, the author of this treatise compares the path of knowledge about God with the ascent of Moses to Mount Sinai from the entry "into the thick darkness where God was" (Ex 20.21). God is known through darkness, or the haze of ignorance, that is,

---

[8]Cf.: Plato *Timaeus* 28C.
[9]Gregory the Theologian *Oration* 32.14.11–21.
[10]Ignatius the God-Bearer *Epistle to the Ephesians* 15.2.
[11]Isaac the Syrian *Oration* 42.

through the renunciation of all rational and discursive knowledge, maintains Dionysius. The final aspect of the theologian is to find himself "in this radiant twilight and by means of blindness and ignorance to see and understand that which is above contemplation and knowledge, that which is impossible to see and to know."[12] According to Dionysius, this aspect of the apophatic method approaches the truth more than the cataphatic. Consequently, by rejecting all that God is not, the theologian reaches a claim on the complete incomprehensibility of the First Principle of all essence:

> We therefore maintain that the universal Cause transcending all things is neither impersonal nor lifeless, nor irrational nor without understanding: in short, that it is not a material body, and therefore does not possess outward shape or intelligible form, or quality, or quantity, or solid weight; nor has it any local existence which can be perceived by sight or touch. . . . Once more, ascending yet higher we maintain that it is not soul, or mind, or endowed with the faculty of imagination, conjecture, reason, or understanding; nor is it any act of reason or understanding; nor can it be described by reason or perceived by understanding, since it is not number, or order, or greatness, or littleness, or equality, or inequality, and since it is not immovable in motion, or at rest, and has no power, and is not power or light, and does not live, and is not life; nor is it personal essence, or eternity, or time; nor can it be grasped by understanding since it is not knowledge or truth; nor is it kingship or wisdom . . . nor can reason attain to it to name it or to know it; nor is it darkness, nor is it light, nor error, nor truth; nor can any affirmation or negation apply to it; for while applying affirmations or negations to those orders of being that come next to it, we apply unto it neither affirmation nor negation, inasmuch as it transcends all affirmation by being the perfect and unique Cause of all things, and transcends all negation by the preeminence of its simple and absolute nature—free from every limitation and beyond them all.[13]

The gnosiology of Dionysius the Areopagite introduces a classical model of Christian mysticism. According to the Areopagite, the way to knowledge of God is "the way of rejection and renunciation, the way of simplification

---

[12]Dionysius the Areopagite *Mystical Theology* 2.
[13]Ibid. 4–5.

and silence";[14] God is known only in peaceful ignorance, which is higher knowledge. Mystical ignorance is none other than ecstasy—a frenzy, an exodus of man from himself into divine reality, an exodus from the sphere of reason and an entrance into the sphere of the incomprehensible:

> Hence God is known in all things and apart from all things; and God is known through Knowledge and through Unknowing; and on the one hand he is reached by Intuition, Reason, Understanding, Apprehension, Perception, Conjecture, Appearance, Name, etc; and yet, on the other hand, he cannot be grasped by Intuition, Language, or Name, and he is not anything in the world nor is he known in anything. He is All Things in all things and Nothing in any, and is known from all things unto all men, and is not known from any thing unto any man. 'Tis meet that we employ such terms concerning God, and we get from all things (in proportion to their quality) notions of him who is their Creator. And yet on the other hand, the Divinest Knowledge of God, that which is received through Unknowing, is obtained in that communion which transcends the mind, when the mind, turning away from all things and then leaving even itself behind, is united to the Dazzling Rays, being from them and in them, illumined by the unsearchable depth of Wisdom. Nevertheless, as I said, we must draw this knowledge of Wisdom from all things; for wisdom it is (as saith the Scripture) that hath made all things and ever ordereth them all, and is the Cause of the indissoluble harmony and order of all things, perpetually fitting the end of one part unto the beginning of the second, and thus producing the one fair agreement and concord of the whole.[15]

The ecstasy (*ekstasis*, ἔκστασις) of man from his very self is not necessary for an encounter with God, just as an exodus (*proodos*, πρόοδος) is not necessary for God to come to man. The same mystical experience with God becomes, in this way, the fruit of synergy, together with the action of man and God uniting with each other in the harmony of oneness. In the process of the mystical ascent to God, cataphatic theology, operating under positive understanding, has a rather auxiliary meaning: it serves only as a trampoline for thought, which ought to gather speed and achieve free flight to the heights of the knowledge

---

[14]Georges Florovsky, *Eastern Fathers of the Fifth to Eighth Centuries* (Paris, 1937), 103.
[15]Dionsyius the Areopagite *On the Divine Names* 7.3.

of God. In the process of flying, reason all the more renounces all earthly knowledge, whether it be cataphatic or apophatic. In the end, having reached the highest level possible of putting off thought and ignorance, reason enters the place where rational ideas cease their functioning, as man, going beyond the limits of specifics, names, words, and understanding, is united with him, "Who is higher than every name, every word, and every meaning."[16]

In the seventh century St Maximus the Confessor, a follower of and commentator on Dionysius the Areopagite, began his *Chapters on Theology and Oikonomia of the Incarnation of the Son of God*, a series of contradicting and mutually exclusive claims of an apophatic and cataphatic character. The contradiction of these claims, however, is intentional, for it serves to demonstrate the relativity of every human understanding applied to God:

> God, as far as it merits us to say, is not in and of himself a beginning, a middle, or an end; nothing is, which does not follow from him, contemplating essential forms. For God is endless, immovable, and infinite, so he endlessly surpasses all essence, force, and action.
>
> God is not made up of stuff. . . . God is not a possibility. . . . God is not an action. . . . But God is a builder of matter and the supersubstantial Original Being; he creates force and is the all-powerful Founder; finally, he is the eternal and acting Existence of all action. In short, God is the Creative Reason of matter, strength, and action, that is, of beginning, middle, and end.
>
> God . . . includes in himself the sum total of all authentic being and, at the same time, surpasses this being. If this is so, then in general nothing that is meant by the word "being" can exist, not having existence in the genuine sense of the word. Even generally, nothing is apart from God in essence, not having contemplated together with him from eternity, nor from a century, nor from a moment, nor as those natures that live in them. For authentic and inauthentic being are by no means combined one with the other.
>
> By no means does every beginning, middle, and end negate the category of relationship. God, existing in infinite eternity, surpasses every relationship and, essentially, is not a beginning, nor an end, nor a middle. For he is not some sort of thing from which it is possible to contemplate a category of relationship.

[16]Ibid. 12.3.

God is the Beginning, the Middle, and the End of all beings, just as he acts, but does not suffer. He is also everything we name him. For God is the Beginning as Creator, he is the Middle as Provider, and he is the End as Judgment. For the apostle says: "For from him and through him and to him are all things (Rom 11.36)."[17]

The apophatic method of theology has an advantage over the cataphatic, for it brings to mind that to which God corresponds not in words, but in the absence of words, in reverential and trembling silence. At the same time the apophatic method has one serious inadequacy: the absence of words does not always provide real communion for man, for an encounter with the Living God. For such people to be led to God, it is necessary to speak about him, according to Gregory the Theologian. Moreover one cannot just speak in the negative, but also in assertions, never mind that there is no assertion about God that can be settled. The cataphatic method of theology is only a kind of supplement to the apophatic method, though without such a supplement the apophatic method would go nowhere:

> An inquirer into the nature of a real being cannot stop short at saying what it is not but must add to his denials a positive affirmation (and how much easier it is to take in a single thing than to run the full gamut of particular negations!). The point of this is that comprehension of the object of knowledge should be affected both by negation of what the thing is not and also by positive assertion of what it is. A person who tells you what God is not but fails to tell you what he is, is rather like someone who, asked what twice five are, answers "not two, not three, not four, not five, not twenty, not thirty. . . ." He does not deny it is ten, but he is also not settling the questioner's mind with a firm answer. It is much simpler, much briefer, to indicate all that something is not by indicating what it is, than to reveal what it is by denying what it is not.[18]

Such reasoning can prove to be an unworthy claim, even if "the nature of a real being" is not the same as twice five; and if the question "what twice five equals" has only one positive answer, then the question of the nature of God cannot and will not have such an answer. However, Gregory the Theologian does not maintain that a conclusive answer can be given as regards the divine

[17]1.2; 1.4; 1.6; 1.7; 1.10.
[18]Gregory the Theologian *Oration 28.9*.

nature. He merely considers that a positive assertion on the nature of God can stop man short of thinking about God, just as an uninterrupted series of negations can lead one away from God.

Gregory compares the way of theology and knowledge about God to a descent into the bottomless depths: the lower one allows the intellect to go, the more the darkness thickens about oneself; in this one does not at all approach even one aspect, just as the bottom does not exist. The immersion into the abyss of the divine has no end, and is conditional on the limits of human reason and speech, which are not strong enough to penetrate the mysteries of the essence and judgments of God:

> All truth, all philosophy, to be sure, is obscure. . . . Now theology is fuller, and so harder. . . . So it was with Solomon. . . . The more he entered into profundities, the more his mind reeled. He made it a goal of his wisdom to discover just how far off it was. Paul tries to get there—I do not mean to God's nature (that he knew to be quite impossible) but only to God's judgments. Paul found no way through, no stopping-place in his climb, since intellectual curiosity has no clear limit and there is always some truth left to dawn on us. . . . I share his feelings as he closes his argument with impassioned wonder at the sort of thing he calls "the wealth and depth of God" in acknowledgment of the incomprehensibility of God's judgments. His language is almost the same as David used. David at one point calls God's judgments a "great abyss," fathomless by sense; at another point he says that the knowledge even of his own make-up was "too wonderful" for him, "too excellent" for him "to be able to grasp."[19]

The way to knowledge about God concludes in surprise and amazement before wonder—in this situation all discursive thought ceases; speech is silenced. This situation is not an understanding of God, it is the silencing of all human knowledge before the face of the divine limitlessness and fathomlessness. Understanding God's essence is not accessible to man, inhabiting a body, speaking in an earthly tongue, thinking in earthly categories. All cataphatic theological terminology, collected over the passage of time, is merely a witness to "the inertia of our speech and the weakness of our thoughts before the mysterious face of God, who himself is transcendent to all creation."[20]

[19]Ibid. 52–53.
[20]V. N. Lossky, *Theology and the Vision of God*, 13–14.

6

God in the Old Testament

THE NAME OF GOD AND THE GLORY OF GOD

IN THE BIBLE, a name is thought of as the complete and true expression of a given subject. In the language of the Bible, a name is not merely a conventional indication of this or that person or subject: a name points to a fundamental characteristic of the bearer, revealing his or her deep essence. To find out someone's name meant to enter into a connection with the bearer of that name, to know his or her inner being. To bestow a name on something or someone meant to possess it. In the context of this perception of names, to find out the name of God would signify a knowledge of God's essence. This is why God appears in the Bible as an Essence both nameless and mysterious. In the biblical narrative of Jacob's fight with God, Jacob asks for God's name, but does not find out what it is:

Jacob was left alone; and a man wrestled with him until daybreak. When the man saw that he did not prevail against Jacob, he struck him on the hip socket; and Jacob's hip was put out of joint as he wrestled with him. Then he said, "Let me go, for the day is breaking." But Jacob said, "I will not let you go, unless you bless me." So he said to him, "What is your name?" And he said, "Jacob." Then the man said, "You shall no longer be called Jacob, but Israel, for you have striven with God and with humans, and have prevailed." Then Jacob asked him, "Please tell me your name?" But he said, "Why is it that you ask my name?" And there he blessed him. So Jacob called the place Penuel,

Jacob wrestling with the Angel.
Monastery of Chora.
Constantinople. 14th c.

63

saying, "For I have seen God face to face, and yet my life is preserved" (Gen 32.24–30).

This story, which is interpreted in various ways in Christian exegesis,[1] speaks of the namelessness of God. It is characteristic that all of Jacob's inter-action with God comes through the sphere of names: God blesses Jacob by giving him a new name, which signifies Jacob's entry into a closer interrela-tionship with God; Jacob blesses God by naming the place where God's pres-ence became visible to him. However, Jacob does not receive an answer to his question asking the name of God. At the same time, Jacob does speak about the fact that he has seen God "face to face" in naming the place of sighting "Penuel," which means "the face of God."

The notion of God's name as inaccessible to man is present in many other accounts in the Old Testament, in particular the narrative in Judges of the appearance of the angel to Manoah: "Then Manoah said to the angel of the Lord, 'What is your name, so that we may honor you when your words come true?' But the angel of the Lord said to him, 'Why do you ask my name? It is too wonderful . . . ' And Manoah said to his wife, 'We shall surely die, for we have seen God' " (Judg 13.17–22). The last words of Manoah indicate that it was God who appeared to him, not an angel. It follows that the refusal to give out his own name belongs to God himself.

Equal to the notion of God's namelessness, which acts as a leitmotif throughout the whole Bible, is the idea that in the Old Testament, God is called by many names and specifications: scholars count no fewer than one hundred such names for God in the Bible.[2] The God of the Old Testament is *El* (God), or *Elohim* (God in the plural), the Creator of heaven and earth (Gen 1.1). He is "the Lord," *Adonai* (literally "my Lord" in the plural), the Lord and Master of the universe, the Lord of all people, who are his slaves. He is *El Shaddai*, the All-Powerful (literally "God on the mountain," Lofty, the Most High): God revealed himself to Abraham with these names (cf. Gen 17.1; 35.11). He is the Lord of Hosts, *Sabaoth*, the Founder and Originator of the angelic world.[3] The plural used in the names *Elohim* and *Adonai*, in the

---

[1]The most prevalent interpretation being that he who fought with Jacob is understood to be the Son of God. Cf., for example: Justin Martyr *Dialogue with Trypho 125*.

[2]Cf. Serge Verkhovskoy, "On the Names of God," *Pravoslavnaya Mysl'* 6 (1948): 37–55.

[3]Etymologically, the name *Sabaoth* is not entirely clear: it is possible it has something to do with the angelic hosts, but it may have something to do with the host of Israel.

opinion of some researchers, presents itself as the grammatical formula of *pluralis majestatis*[4] (a plural of greatness), or *pluralis divinitatis* (a plural of divinity): this form is used to highlight the greatness of the given subject.

Every one of God's names found in the Old Testament indicates one or another quality of God: his power, righteousness, holiness, fairness, love, wisdom, or mercy. Above all, the all-powerfulness of God is reflected in his names, he who creates all that he desires whether in heaven or on earth. His power is revealed particularly in the fate of the people of Israel. He is the leader of the host of Israel, he fights in battle on Israel's side; he rules the people of Israel "with a strong hand and an outstretched arm" (Ps 136.12). God is "the Shepherd and Rock of Israel" (Gen 49.24), he is the "help and shield" of the house of Israel and all those who fear him (Ps 33.20).

The God of the Old Testament is the Living God (1 Sam 17.26, 17.36; 2 Kg 19.16). The expression "as the Lord God lives" (1 Kg 17.1, 17.12; 18.10, 18.15, etc.) was one of the most prevalent forms of remembering God in a vow or greeting: remembering God, it is as if man has brought God as a witness to the truthfulness of his words. The Lord himself, embracing the people of Israel, says: "I live" (Ezek 5.11). God is always alive and acting, He "will neither slumber nor sleep" (Ps 121.4), "He does not faint nor grow weary" (Is 40.28). His living presence is felt by the whole people of Israel and by every member of this people. Nature responds to his presence: before the face of God "the sea . . . fled; Jordan turned back. The mountains skipped like rams, the hills like lambs" (Ps 114.3–4).

The Old Testament God is the God who is "Holy" (Is 57.15), his name is "holy and awesome" (Ps 111.9; 99.3). No other people can stand before the Holy God (cf. 1 Sam 6.20), but the people of Israel stand before God's holiness with fear and trembling. A covenant has been made between God and the people of Israel, ratified by God's holiness. This is why the people call God "the Holy One of Israel" (Ps 71.22; Is 5.24) while God, embracing the people, calls himself "the Holy One in your midst" (Hos 11.9).

The Old Testament God is the "Judge of all the earth" (Gen 18.25); "He is entering into judgment with all flesh, and the guilty He will put to the sword" (Jer 25.31). "God is a righteous judge, and a God who has indignation every

---

[4]Pluralis majestatis: a grammatical formula, prevalent in various languages. In English it can be seen in the use of the pronoun "we" in place of the first person singular (for example, in royal manifestos or patriarchal letters).

day" (Ps 7.11); he is seated on his throne and pronounces judgment (Ps 9.4); he "executes judgment, putting down one and lifting up another" (Ps 75.7); he "gives to the proud what they deserve" (Ps 94.2). The fairness of God is expressed when he generously rewards righteousness and severely chastises sins. Yahweh is "a God merciful and gracious, slow to anger, and abounding in steadfast love and faithfulness, keeping steadfast love for the thousandth generation, forgiving iniquity and transgression and sin, yet by no means clearing the guilty, but visiting the iniquity of the parents upon the children and the children's children, to the third and fourth generation" (Ex 34.6–7).

The God of the Old Testament is the One and Only God: "Before me no god was formed, nor shall there be any after me. I, I am the Lord, and besides me there is no savior" (Is 43.10–11). God is named "Jealous"[5] (Ex 34.14; 20.5), not allowing the worship of other gods, accepting the people of Israel as his own bride (cf. Isa 54.5; Jer 2.2) and Israel's every turning to idol-worship is like adultery and fornication (Ex 34.15–17; Is 1.21; Ezek 16.1–43). There will come a time, God says in the book of the prophet Hosea, when the people of Israel will reject the worship of false gods and will adhere to the truth of Yahweh as a wife to her husband:

> On that day, says the Lord, you will call me, "My husband," and no longer will you call me, "My Baal." For I will remove the names of the Baals from her mouth, and they shall be mentioned by name no more . . . And I will take you for my wife forever; I will take you for my wife in righteousness and justice, in steadfast love, and in mercy. I will take you for my wife in faithfulness; and you shall know the Lord . . . And I will sow him for myself in the land. And I will have pity on Lo-ruhamah, and I will say to Lo-ammi, "You are my people"; and he shall say, "You are my God" (Hos 2.16–23).

In Old Testament texts God frequently appears as a man-like being, with arms and legs, eyes and ears, a heart and mouth. It is said that God walks (cf. Gen 3.8), rests (cf. Gen 2.2), remembers (cf. Gen 8.1; 19.29; 13.22) and forgets (cf. Ps 9.18), hates (cf. Ps 11.5; Isa 61.8; Jer 44.4; Am 5.21; Zech 8.17), rejects (cf. 2 Kg 17.20; Ezek 23.18), is wrathful and repentant (cf. Gen 6.6), sleeps and wakes up (cf. Ps 44.23). Sometimes God's presence is associated with a certain

[5]In the sense of "jealous," and not "zealous."

place: Moses and Aaron see "the standing-place of the God of Israel,"[6] after which the Lord says to Moses: "Come up to me on the mountain" (Ex 24.12). At the base of this anthropomorphism lies the experience of man's encounter with the Living God, and the experience that the authors of the biblical books described in concrete and simple language, far from philosophic abstraction. Many names of God in the Old Testament bear a stressed anthropomorphic character, for example: "the Lord is a warrior" (Ex 15.3).

Out of all the names of God enumerated above, it makes sense to set aside the holy name Yahweh (He Who is), the name with which God revealed Himself to Moses (in some editions of the Bible this name, along with *Adonai*, is replaced with the word "the Lord," or sometimes with "God" or "Jehovah"). God Himself gives the name Yahweh a special significance when he says: "'I am the Lord [Yahweh]. I appeared to Abraham, Isaac, and Jacob as God Almighty [*El Shaddai*], but by name "the Lord" [Yahweh] I did not make myself known to them'" (Ex 6.2–3).

The cult of the holy name Yahweh occupies an exclusive place in the Bible. The book of Exodus connects the revelation of this name with Moses, to whom God appeared on Mount Horeb, when Moses saw the bush that burned yet was not consumed:

> God called him out of the bush, "Moses, Moses!" And he said, "Here I am." Then He said, "Come no closer! Remove the sandals from your feet, for the place on which you are standing is holy ground . . ." Then the Lord said, "I have observed the misery of my people who are in Egypt . . . So come, I will send you to Pharaoh to bring my people, the Israelites, out of Egypt . . ." But Moses said to God, "If I come to the Israelites and say to them, 'The God of your ancestors has sent me to you,' and they ask me, 'What is his name?' what shall I say to them?" God said to Moses, "I AM WHO I AM [*ehyeh asher ehyeh*]." He said further, "Thus you shall say to the Israelites, 'I AM has sent me to you.'" God also said to Moses, "Thus you shall say to the Israelites, 'The Lord, the God of your ancestors, the God of Abraham, the God of Isaac, and the God of Jacob, has sent me to you': This is my name for ever, and this my title for all generations" (Ex 3.4–15).

---

[6]In the Septuagint the word "standing-place" is omitted.

Moses at the burning bush.
Sinai. Beginning of the 13th c.

Understanding the exact thought behind this passage can be a bit difficult. It deals with the fact that the Hebrew phrase *ehyeh asher ehyeh* used here is translated as "I AM" (literally "I AM WHO I AM"): this can be understood as a formula indicating the desire not to answer the question directly. In other words, this account could be understood not as a revelation of God's personal name, but as an assertion that no human language has the words that could be the name of God in the Hebrew understanding, i.e., a certain all-embracing symbol, the fullness of which is characterized by its bearer. God's answer to Moses' question concerning his name, in this way, is in the same vein as his refusal to name himself to Jacob.

If indeed one understands the holy name Yahweh as the personal name of God, then the etymology of the name remains unclear. Even the vocalization of the four consonants that make up its letters is hypothetical. The issue is that after the Babylonian captivity, or in any case sometime after the third century B.C.E., Hebrews generally stopped pronouncing the holy name of God, out of reverence. Rather, once, on the Day of Atonement (Yom Kippur), the high priest entered into the Holy of Holies in order to utter this holy name. In all other cases they changed the name to *Adonai* or other names, though in script they indicated the four consonants YHWH (the so-called holy tetragrammaton), which, however, they did not pronounce. Over the centuries the correct pronunciation of this name was finally forgotten. Since the sixteenth century the West has used the artificial vocalization Jehovah, the result of adding the vowels of the name *Adonai* to the consonants YHWH, and only in the middle of the nineteenth century did scholars come to the mind that the tetragrammaton should be read as Yahweh.[7] Although such a vocalization of the name YHWH is generally accepted in biblical studies, there is a significant difference of opinion amongst scholars as to the interpretation of this name. The majority of researchers nevertheless agrees with the idea that this name is

---

[7]In contemporary Judaism the restriction on pronouncing the name YHWH is maintained, although the vocalization of the four consonants is considered known: *Yihoweh* (a famous rabbi from Jerusalem informed the author of this book of this vocalization).

connected with the verb *hayah*, which means "to be," "to exist," "to have being," and that the actual name means "I am," or "I am what I am."

The peak of Mount Sinai.

In the book of Exodus, the story about God's revelation of the name Yahweh to Moses on Mount Sinai plays a central role. On Sinai, the people of Israel receive from God, through Moses, a code of law, beginning with the Ten Commandments. The first commandment is an extended interpretation of the name Yahweh, while the second commandment speaks directly of this name:

> I am the Lord [Yahweh] your God, who brought you out of the land of Egypt, out of the house of slavery; you shall have no other gods before me. You shall not make for yourself an idol, whether in the form of anything that is in heaven above, or that is on the earth beneath, or that is in the water under the earth. You shall not bow down to them or worship them; for I the Lord your God am a jealous God, punishing children for the iniquity of parents, to the third and the fourth generation of those who reject me, but showing steadfast love to the thousandth generation of those who love me and keep my commandments. You shall not make wrongful use of the name of the Lord your God, for the Lord will not acquit anyone who misuses his name (Ex 20.2–7).

In the first commandment of the Mosaic Law the name of God is received in historical context: Yahweh is that same God who played a decisive role in the history of the people of Israel, leading them out from Egypt. The God Yahweh is distinguished from other gods. The second commandment prohibits taking the name of God in vain. The idea behind this prohibition is that just like glory, the usage of the name of God ascends to God himself, so the dishonoring of God's name indicates an insult to God himself. The name Yahweh is practically identified here with Yahweh himself.

Though the meaning of the name Yahweh remains hidden and the name itself does not describe God, it is precisely this name which has been accepted as the personal name of God in the Hebrew tradition: all other names of God are considered interpretations of the holy name Yahweh. The narrative in the book of Exodus concerning the appearance of God to Moses on Mount Sinai bears witness to this:

Thus the Lord used to speak to Moses face to face, as one speaks to a
friend . . . Moses said, "Show me your glory, I pray." And he said, "I will
make all my goodness pass before you, and will proclaim before you the
name, 'the Lord' [Yahweh]; and I will be gracious to whom I will be gracious, and will show mercy on whom I will show mercy. But," he said,
"you cannot see my face; for no one shall see me and live." And the Lord
continued, "See, there is a place by me where you shall stand on the rock;
and while my glory passes by I will put you in a cleft of the rock, and I
will cover you with my hand until I have passed by; then I will take away
my hand, and you shall see my back; but my face shall not be seen . . ."
And he [Moses] rose early in the morning and went up on Mount Sinai,
as the Lord had commanded him . . . The Lord descended in the cloud
and stood with him there, and proclaimed the name, "the Lord." The
Lord passed before him, and proclaimed, "The Lord [Yahweh], the Lord
[Yahweh], a God merciful and gracious, slow to anger, and abounding in
steadfast love and faithfulness, keeping steadfast love for a thousand generations, forgiving iniquity and transgression and sin, yet by no means
clearing the guilty, but visiting the iniquity of the parents upon the children and the children's children, to the third and fourth generation." And
Moses quickly bowed his head towards the earth, and worshipped. (Ex
33.11, 18–23; 34.4–8)

At first this account says that God spoke to Moses "face to face," but then
God says that man cannot see the face of God and live. Moses sees God's
"back," and at the utmost moment of revelation God proclaims the name
Yahweh (Jehovah), i.e., his own name. All other names that come after the
name Yahweh ("Lover of Mankind," "Merciful," and others) are merely interpretations of this holy name, as if they add overtones to its basic sound.

Yet another key understanding of the Old Testament is contained in the
excerpt cited above, indisputably connected with the understanding of God's
name: the glory of God or the glory of the Lord (the *kabod* of Yahweh). If the
highest moment of revelation of this glory is the proclamation of the name
Yahweh, then what is this so-called glory of God? It is difficult to translate
this meaning adequately into contemporary language: in the Old Testament
it is included above all as an understanding of the mysterious presence of
God that appeared in visible images (for example, in the image of a cloud or

fire). The glory of God appeared to the people of Israel in a cloud when the people cried out to the Lord (cf. Ex 16.9–10); the glory of God descended in the form of a cloud on Mount Sinai and remained there over the course of six days (cf. Ex 24.16): "Now the appearance of the glory of the Lord was like a devouring fire on the top of the mountain in the sight of the people of Israel" (Ex 24.17).

The glory of God frequently seems to be localized in a concrete place or connected with this or that other holy object: the cloud of the glory of God fills the tabernacle of the covenant (cf. Ex 40.34–35); it even appears on the golden cover of the mercy-seat (cf. Lev 16.13). The glory of God and the mercy-seat are closely related; losing the mercy-seat means the loss of the glory of God (cf. 1 Sam 4.21–22). The cover of the mercy-seat, or more accurately, the space above it, was the place of the particular presence of the glory of God: "There I will meet you . . . from above the mercy-seat" (Ex 25.22). Subsequently in *targumim* literature, the presence of God above the cover of the mercy-seat would be known by the term *Shekhina*, meaning "the presence of God."[8]

In the book of Deuteronomy, the commandment of God, given to Moses, is repeated: "You shall not make wrongful use of the name of the Lord your God, for the Lord will not acquit anyone who misuses his name" (Deut 5.11). A threat of punishment is conveyed to those who do not have fear before the name Yahweh: "If you do not . . . [fear] this glorious and awesome name, the Lord your God, then the Lord will overwhelm both you and your offspring" (Deut 28.58–59). Fear before God is an inalienable component of Old Testament religion. In biblical understanding, insofar as God is identified with his name, the fear of Yahweh, or "the fear of the Lord" (*pahad* Yahweh), develops into a religious reverence for the name Yahweh, to whom one is ordered to act with fear and trembling.

In Deuteronomy, the expression "the name of Yahweh" (*shem* Yahweh) acquires a meaning closer to the notions of "the glory of God," "the might of God," or "the presence of God." This expression is used in Deuteronomy not only and not so much as a synonym of Yahweh himself as an indication of the appearance, the presence, of the activity of Yahweh. If Yahweh himself inhabits the heavens, then "the name of Yahweh" is present on earth: it is his

---

[8]Concerning *Shekhina*, see Louis Bouyer, *On the Bible and the Gospel* (Brussels, 1988).

earthly representative. Such a usage results in the appearance of the representation of the Name (Shem) in later Judaism as a force all its own, a kind of mediator between Yahweh and people.

The Old Testament religious cult is full of the fear before Yahweh and his name. The passage in the First Book of Kings on the construction of Solomon's temple witnesses to this phenomenon with particular clarity:

> And when the priests came out of the holy place, a cloud filled the house of the Lord, so that the priests could not stand to minister because of the cloud; for the glory of the Lord filled the house of the Lord. Then Solomon said, "The Lord has said that he would dwell in thick darkness. I have built you an exalted house, a place for you to dwell in for ever." Then Solomon stood before the altar of the Lord in the presence of all the assembly of Israel, and spread out his hands to heaven. He said . . . "But will God indeed dwell on the earth? Even heaven and the highest heaven cannot contain him, much less this house that I have built! Have regard to your servant's prayer and his plea . . . that your eyes may be open night and day towards this house, the place of which you said, 'My name shall be there,' that you may heed the prayer that your servant prays towards this place. When your people Israel, having sinned against you, are defeated before an enemy but turn again to you, confess your name, pray, and plead with you in this house, then hear in heaven, forgive the sin of your people Israel . . . Likewise . . . when a foreigner comes and prays towards this house, then hear in heaven your dwelling-place, and do according to all that the foreigner calls to you, so that all the people of the earth may know your name and fear you . . . so that they may know that your name has been invoked on this house that I have built." (1 Kg 8.10–13, 22, 23, 27–29, 33, 34, 41–43)

The whole life of the Solomonic temple is centered around the worship of the name of God: the temple is called by the name of the Lord, the name of the Lord dwells in the temple, people come to the temple upon hearing of the name of the Lord, and they confess the name of the Lord in the temple. The holy name of Yahweh defines the whole liturgical construction of the temple. Even after the first temple was destroyed and a second temple was built in its place, it was perceived as the place where the name of God dwelt, as in former times (1 Esd 6.12). Even when it came to pass that speaking the name Yahweh was forbidden and it was referred to by other names in spoken speech, once a year a priest would enter the sanctuary for the specific task of uttering this holy name in a whisper (with fear and trembling) over the cover of the mercy-seat.

In the Old Testament, God appears as a Being great and terrible, who reveals himself to man in the storm and cloud, in thunder and lightning, and with whom impotent man is at law. The book of Job contains an extensive passage in which Job, struck with sickness and grief, accuses God of his bad fate in a conversation with his friends. Unexpectedly, God himself enters the conversation and answers Job "out of the whirlwind":

> Who is this that darkens counsel by words without knowledge? Gird up your loins like a man, I will question you, and you shall declare to me. Where were you when I laid the foundation of the earth? Tell me, if you have understanding. Who determined its measurement—surely you know! Or who stretched the line upon it? On what were its bases sunk, or who laid its cornerstone when the morning stars sang together and all the heavenly beings shouted for joy? Or who shut in the sea with doors when it burst out from the womb?—when I made the clouds its garment, and thick darkness its swaddling band . . . Have you commanded the morning since your days began, and caused the dawn to know its place? . . . Have you entered into the springs of the sea, or walked in the recesses of the deep? Have the gates of death been revealed to you, or have you seen the gates of deep darkness? Have you comprehended the expanse of the earth? Declare, if you know all this. (Job 38.2–9, 12, 16–18).

The Lord does not respond to even one of Job's accusations. The subtext of the Lord's answer to Job is something like, "How can you, a weak man, hope to fight with me, your Creator?" Shocked and overwhelmed before the majesty of the Lord, Job answers God: "I know you can do all things, and that no purpose of yours can be thwarted . . . I had heard of you by the hearing of the ear, but now my eye sees you; therefore I despise myself, and repent in dust and ashes" (Job 42.2, 5–6). This story, just like the story of Jacob's struggle with God, of God's appearance to Manoah, of God's appearance to Moses, speaks of a direct vision "face to face," a vision that was accessible to the Old Testament elect of God, in spite of the abyss separating man from God.

Thus on the one hand the Old Testament maintains that God is name-less, though on the other hand it calls him by name. On the one hand Yah-weh is "a God who hides Himself" (Isa 45.15), it is impossible to see his face and live, though on the other hand, the righteous see him face to face. God is "near by . . . and not a God far off" (Jer 23.23). There exists between Holy God and man an insurmountable distance, but at the same time, God sur-mounts this distance when he wants to reveal himself to man.

THE SPIRIT OF GOD, THE WORD OF GOD, THE WISDOM OF GOD

The "Spirit of God" appears as an important theological understanding of the Old Testament. At the time of the foundation of the world "a wind from God [God's Spirit] swept over the face of the waters" (Gen 1.2). The Spirit of God formed man (Job 33.4) and lives in his nostrils (Job 27.3). The Spirit of God, or the Spirit of the Lord, is "the spirit of wisdom and understanding, the spirit of counsel and might, the spirit of knowledge and the fear of the Lord" (Is 11.2). It descends on kings, priests, and prophets, putting them in service, revealing to them the mysteries, appearing in visions. The Spirit of God in the Old Testament is devoid of personal attributes; it is more like the breath of God, his energy, his creative and life-giving power.

The understanding of the "word of God" also plays an essential role in the Old Testament. The word of the Lord exists eternally (Isa 40.8); it is for-ever fixed firmly in the heavens (Ps 119.89). It is the force through which God directs nature and the universe: "Praise him, you highest heavens, and you waters above the heavens! Let them praise the name of the Lord, for he com-manded and they were created. He established them for ever and ever; he fixed their bounds, which cannot be passed. Praise the Lord from the earth, you sea monsters and all deeps, fire and hail, snow and frost, stormy wind fulfilling his command" (Ps 148.4–8). The word of the Lord is not like man's word: "Is not my word like fire, says the Lord, and like a hammer that breaks a rock in pieces?" (Jer 23.29). "So shall my word be that goes out from my mouth; it shall not return to me empty, but it shall accomplish that which I purpose, and succeed in the thing for which I sent it" (Is 55.11); "not one thing has failed of all the good things that the Lord your God promised concern-ing you" (Josh 23.14). The word of God acts without delay: "For he spoke, and it came to be; he commanded, and it stood firm" (Ps 33.9). The word of God possesses healing power (cf. Ps 107.20). At the same time the "all-powerful word [of God is like] . . . a stern warrior" (Wis 18.15) with a sword in hand, an instrument of God's judgment and punishment.

The word of God is linked to the Spirit of God: "The spirit of the Lord speaks through me, his word is upon my tongue" (2 Sam 32.2). During the foundation of the world, the Word and Spirit work together: "By the word of the Lord the heavens were made, and all their host by the breath of his mouth" (Ps 33.6). This psalm verse drew special attention from Christian interpreters, who were surprised by the indication that all three Persons of the Holy Trinity participated in the creation of the world.

The indication of a threefold Godhead can be seen in those Old Testament texts where God speaks of himself in the plural (cf. Gen 1.26; 3.22; 11.7. Isa 6.8) and in the name *Elohim*, taken from the plural for *El* (God), although grammatically this is explained by a usage of *pluralis majestatis* (a plurality of greatness) or *pluralis divinitatis* (a plurality of divinity).

In the narrative of the appearance of the three men to Abraham (cf. Gen 18) the plural alternates with the singular. The context of the account allows as an explanation that sometimes Abraham is relating to all three men and sometimes to one, and that sometimes all three answer him, but sometimes only one–the chief one. This chief of the three is identified as the Lord, while the two others are identified as angels (Gen 18.33; 19.1). However, in Christian theological tradition, in the most prevalent reflection of the account in Orthodox iconography (in particular, in the icon of the Holy Trinity by St. Andrei Rublev), the whole narrative is perceived as a mysterious indication of the triune Godhead.

The notion of the Wisdom of God also plays an essential role in the Old Testament. Sometimes the Wisdom is described as one of the qualities of God: "With God are wisdom and strength; he has counsel and understanding" (Job 12.13), "with him are strength and wisdom" (Job 12.16), "he is wonderful in counsel, and excellent in wisdom" (Isa 28.29). However, in three biblical books (Proverbs, Wisdom of Solomon, and Sirach) the Wisdom is presented as a power of God, bestowing characteristics of live spiritual existence:

> I learned both what is secret and what is manifest, for wisdom, the fashioner of all things, taught me. There is in her a spirit that is intelligent,

holy, unique, manifold, subtle, mobile, clear, unpolluted, distinct, invulnerable, loving the good, keen, irresistible, beneficent, humane, steadfast, sure, free from anxiety, all-powerful, overseeing all, and penetrating through all spirits that are intelligent, pure, and altogether subtle. For wisdom is more mobile than any motion; because for her pureness she pervades and penetrates all things. For she is a breath of the power of God, and a pure emanation of the glory of the Almighty; therefore nothing defiled gains entrance into her. For she is a reflection of eternal light, a spotless mirror of the working of God, and an image of his goodness. Although she is but one, she can do all things, and while remaining in herself, she renews all things; in every generation she passes into holy souls and makes them friends of God, and prophets; for God loves nothing so much as the person who lives with wisdom. She is more beautiful than the sun, and excels every constellation of the stars. Compared with the light she is found to be superior, for it is succeeded by the night, but against wisdom evil does not prevail. She reaches mightily from one end of the earth to the other, and she orders all things well. She glorifies her noble birth by living with God, and the Lord of all loves her. For she is an initiate in the knowledge of God, and an associate in his works. (Wis 7.21–30; 8.1, 3–4)

Wisdom is symbolically described in the form of a woman that has a house (cf. Prov 9.1; Sir 14.25) and servants (cf. Prov 9.3). She has slaughtered the sacrifice, mixed her wine, prepared a feast and called all to her: "Come, eat of my bread and drink of the wine I have mixed. Lay aside immaturity, and live, and walk in the way of insight" (Prov 9.5–6). In Christian tradition this passage is perceived as a foreshadowing of the Eucharist, though biblical Wisdom is not identified with the Son of God. In the words of the apostle Paul, Christ is "the power of God and the wisdom of God" (1 Cor 1.24). Despite the fact that Wisdom is called "spirit" and "breath," it is not identified with the Holy Spirit in Christian tradition. The very book of the Wisdom of Solomon makes a distinction between the Holy Spirit and the Wisdom of God: "Who has learned your counsel, unless you have given wisdom and sent your holy spirit from on high?" (Wis 9.17).

Prophecy of the Messiah

As has already been mentioned, Christianity views the Old Testament through the prism of the New Testament revelation of Christ. In connection with those many places in the Old Testament in which Jewish tradition perceives something relating either to the people of Israel, or to King David, or to the expected Messiah, in Christianity it is all interpreted as an indication of Jesus Christ. According to scholars' calculations, the Old Testament contains more than 450 prophecies concerning Christ. Of these, no fewer than 100 are contained in the Psalter.[9] The psalms in which the Son of God is mentioned are particularly important among messianic prophecies:

> The Lord said to my Lord, Sit at my right hand, until I make your enemies your footstool. The Lord shall send out a rod of power for you out of Zion: rule in the midst of your enemies. With you is dominion in the day of your power, in the splendours of your saints: From the womb, before the morning star, I have begotten you. The Lord has sworn, and will not repent, You are a priest for ever, after the order of Melchisedek. The Lord at your right hand has dashed in pieces kings in the day of his wrath. He shall judge among the nations, he shall fill up the number of corpses, he shall crush the heads of many on the earth. He shall drink of the brook in the way; therefore shall he lift up his head. (Ps 110)

Some psalms speak of the Son of God as a King and anointed Messiah. Messianic interpretation was firmly secured through these designations in Christian tradition:

> Why did the heathen rage, and the nations imagine vain things? The kings of the earth stood up, and the rulers gathered themselves together, against the Lord, and against his Christ; saying, Let us break through their bonds, and cast away their yoke from us. He that dwells in the heavens shall laugh them to scorn, and the Lord shall mock them. Then shall he speak to them in his anger, and trouble them in his fury. But I have been made king by him on Zion his holy mountain, declaring the ordinance of the Lord: the Lord said to me, You are my Son, this day have I begotten your. Ask of me, and I will give you the heathen as your inheritance,

[9] Cf. W.C. Kaiser, *The Messiah in the Old Testament* (Carlisle, 1995), 92; J. Barton Payne, *Encyclopedia of Biblical Prophecy* (New York, 1973), 257.

and the ends of the earth as your possession. You shall tend them as a shepherd, with a rod of iron; you shall dash them in pieces, like a potter's vessel. Now therefore understand, O kings: be instructed, all you who judge the earth. Serve the Lord with fear, and rejoice in him with trembling. Accept correction, lest at any time the Lord be angry, and you perish from the righteous way: whenever his wrath is suddenly kindled, blessed are all they that trust in him. (Ps 2.1–12)

Psalm 22 is perceived in Christian tradition as speaking on the passion of Jesus Christ on the cross:

O God, my God, why have you forsaken me? the account of my transgressions is far from my salvation. . . . All who saw me mocked me: they spoke with their lips, they shook their heads, and said, He hoped in the Lord: let him deliver him, let him save him, because he takes pleasure in him. . . . I am poured out like water, and all my bones are loosened: my heart in the midst of my belly has become like melting wax. My strength is dried up like a potsherd; and my tongue is glued to my throat; and you have brought me down to the dust of death. For many dogs have surrounded me: the assembly of the wicked has beset me round round about: they pierced my hands and my feet. They counted all my bones; and they observed and looked upon me. They parted my garments among themselves, and for my raiment they cast lots. But you, O Lord, do not remove my help far off: be ready for to come to my aid. Deliver my soul from the sword; my only-begotten one from the power of the dog. (Ps 22.1, 7–8, 14–20)

Prophecies on the coming Messiah are contained in many other psalms. In particular, psalm 15.10 is considered an assertion of the three-day death and resurrection of Christ. The first part of psalm 45 (verses 2–9) is perceived as relating to Christ, while the second part (verses 10–16) as relating to the Holy Theotokos. Various verses of psalms 69 and 118 are interpreted as depicting Christ's passion. Psalm 72 is interpreted as relating the justness of the Messiah's judgment. Psalm 109 (especially verses 6–20) is seen as a prophecy on the traitor Judas. Many verses of psalm 119 are perceived in Christian tradition as written from the point of view of Christ.

The majority of prophecies concerning the Messiah is contained in the prophetic books of the Old Testament. The most "messianic" of these is the book of the prophet Isaiah; it is widely used in Orthodox divine services in connection with various events from the life of Christ. Isaiah prophesies that "the virgin is with child and shall bear a son" (Isa 7.14) and that, being born, the Child is named "Wonderful, Counsellor, Mighty God, Everlasting Father, Prince of Peace" (Isa 9.6). The Spirit of the Lord rests on the Child whose hand the Lord holds, and "he will bring forth justice to the nations. He will not cry or lift up his voice, or make it heard in the street; a bruised reed he will not break, and a dimly burning wick he will not quench; he will faithfully bring forth justice" (Isa 42.1–3). The Lord protects him and gives him "as a covenant to the people, a light to the nations, to open the eyes of the blind, to bring out the prisoners from the dungeon, from the prison to those who sit in darkness" (Isa 42.6–7). The Spirit of the Lord has anointed him and sent him "to bind up the broken-hearted, to proclaim liberty to the captives, and release the prisoners; to proclaim the year of the Lord's favor" (Isa 61.1–2).

The Prophet Isaiah. Monastery of Nea Moni. Chios. 11th c.

The prophecy of Isaiah concerning the passion and death of the Messiah is read in the services of Holy Week in Orthodox churches:

> As many shall be amazed at you, so shall your form be dishonored by men, and your glory by the sons of men. Thus shall many nations wonder at him; and kings shall keep their mouths shut: for they to whom no report was brought concerning him, shall see; and they who have not heard, shall consider. . . . O Lord, who has believed our report? and to whom has the arm of the Lord been revealed? We brought a report as of a child before him; he is as a root in a thirsty land: he has no form nor glory; and we saw him, but he had no form nor beauty. . . . He bears our sins, and is pained for us: yet we accounted him to be in trouble, and in suffering, and in affliction. But he was wounded on account of our sins, and was bruised because of our iniquities: the chastisement of our peace

was upon him; by his bruises we were healed. All we as sheep have gone astray; every one has gone astray in his way; and the Lord gave him up for our sins. And he, because of his affliction, opens not his mouth: he was led as a sheep to the slaughter, and as a lamb before the shearer is dumb, so he opens not his mouth. . . . And I will give the wicked for his burial, and the rich for his death; for he practised no iniquity, nor dishonesty with his mouth. (Isa 52.14–15; 53.1–2, 4–7, 9)

The first generation of Christians already recognized these prophecies as relating to the passion on the cross and death of Jesus Christ, and, following Christian tradition, this thought has been precisely and strictly maintained. In the words of the Apostle Peter, the Spirit of Christ prophesied through the prophets "when it testified in advance to the sufferings destined for Christ and the subsequent glory" (1 Pet 1.11).

Messianic prophecies are sprinkled throughout the corpus of the Old Testament; many of them are cited in the New Testament as having been fulfilled in Jesus Christ. "All this took place to fulfill what had been spoken by the Lord through the prophet" (Mt 1.22)—similar expressions are frequently found in the Gospel of Matthew and other New Testament writings. Christ himself saw his mission as a fulfillment of Old Testament prophecies (cf. Mt 26.54; Lk 24.47).

7

God in the New Testament

I N CHRISTIAN UNDERSTANDING, the New Testament
was a continuation and fulfillment of the revelation that God gave to the people of Israel in the Old
Testament. Jesus Christ saw his ministry as being
exactly that. He rejected the accusation that his
teaching contradicted the Old Testament law, insisting on the immutability of the law: "Do not think
that I have come to destroy the law or the prophets;
I have come not to destroy but to fulfill. Amen I say
to you, till heaven and earth pass away, not one jot
or tittle shall by any means pass from the law until
all is fulfilled" (Mt 5.17–18). In his own words, Jesus
repeatedly appealed to the law, though he gave the
commandments of the law a new interpretation, frequently surprising his disciples. The entirety of the
Sermon on the Mount consists of interpretations of Old Testament statutes,
to which Jesus grants new meaning: "You have heard that it was said by those
of olden times . . . But I say to you . . ." (Mt 5.21–22, 27–28, etc.).

Christ PANTOKRATOR. *Hagia Sophia. Constantinople. 13th c.*

THE NEW TESTAMENT: A NEW REVELATION OF GOD

Not rejecting the Old Testament revelation of God, the New Testament
reveals God in a different way, in a new fullness. If the Old Testament was the
revelation of the invisible God, the God whose face man could not gaze
upon and live, then in the New Testament the Incorporeal One became incarnate, the Invisible One became visible. In the Old Testament God appeared
in thunder and lightning, and only special chosen ones were worthy to see

his "back," while in the New Testament all mankind saw God's face in the flesh. In the Old Testament God frequently appears as an anthropomorphic essence, and his presence is linked to a concrete place or thing: Mount Sinai, Jerusalem, the Ark of the Covenant, and the Temple. In the New Testament both the spiritual nature of God and the spiritual character of the interrelation between God and man are highlighted: "The hour is coming when you shall worship the Father neither on this mountain nor yet at Jersusalem . . . God is spirit, and those who worship him must worship in spirit and truth" (Jn 4.21, 24). In the Old Testament, the image of the God of Judgment dominated, punishing the children for the crimes of their fathers to the third and fourth generation, but in the New Testament the image of God the Savior prevails, wishing not to judge people, but to have mercy and save them. "For the Father judges no one, but has committed all judgment to the Son," Christ says, giving witness to the Father (Jn 5.22). Concerning himself he says: "I came not to judge the world, but to save the world" (Jn 12.47).

One of the leitmotifs of the Old Testament is the theme of God's righteousness, rewarding virtue and punishing sins. The leitmotif of the New Testament is the theme of the forgiveness of sins by the merciful God. God "is kind to the unthankful and the evil" (Lk 6.35); he "makes his sun rise on the evil and on the good, and sends rain on the just and on the unjust" (Mt 5.45). In the sayings of Jesus, God is presented not as a punisher of sins, but as a forgiver of them: in this in particular is the basic idea of the parables of the lost sheep, the lost coin, and the Prodigal Son (Lk 15.1–32). The God of the New Testament is he who leaves to search for the lost sheep and, finding it, places it on his shoulders; he who rejoices at finding the one coin that was lost; he who patiently waits for the return of the prodigal son and, when he returns, does not punish him, but calls him worthy to be his son. Being God incarnate, Jesus himself gives his own examples of divine forgiveness. He does not judge the woman seized for adultery, but answers her accusers: "He that is without sin among you, let him first cast a stone at her" (Jn 8.7). Stretched out on the cross, he turns to the Father with a prayer of forgiveness for those who crucified him: "Father, forgive them; for they know not what they do" (Lk 23.34).

The Old Testament only rarely remembers God as Father (Deut 32.6; Isa 63.16, 64.8; Mal 1.6, 2.10), and the feeling of the tender love of a son towards God was not characteristic for the ancient Hebrews: more characteristic was the feeling of a servant's fear and trembling before God. The theme of God's paternity is central in the New Testament. Relating to God through prayer, Jesus calls him Father: fifty-one examples of this type of relation can be found in the Gospels. Sometimes the evangelists translate this relationship as "Abba Father" (*abba ho patēr*, ἀββᾶ ὁ πατήρ) (Mk 14.26), using the affectionate form of the Hebrew word for "father," indicating a special closeness of Son to Father. Jesus wants to share this closeness with all believers, teaching them to begin prayers to God with the words: "Our Father'" (Mt 6.9; Lk 11.2). In the mind of the apostle Paul, the right to relate to God as "Abba, Father" is evidenced by the adoption of Christians by God: "And because you are sons, God has sent forth the Spirit of his Son into your hearts, crying, 'Abba! Father!' Wherefore you are no more a servant, but a son; and if a son, then an heir through Jesus Christ" (Gal 4.6–7).

The Old Testament sometimes speaks of God's love for his people Israel (e.g., Jer 31.3), though this love manifests itself above all as jealousy in relation to other gods: Yahweh does not allow worship of other gods because he is a jealous God. In the New Testament God's love toward man is revealed as a sacrificial love, not a mandatory reciprocation. God loved man before man loved God, and without dependence on man's love of God. God's love for the race of man reached the highest level in the descent into the world of the Son of God, who was incarnate, suffered, and died for the people:

> In this was manifested the love of God toward us, because God sent his only begotten Son into the world, that we might live through him. Herein is love, not that we loved God, but that he loved us, and sent his Son [to be] the propitiation for our sins. And we have known and believed the love that God has for us. God is love; and he that dwells in love dwells in God, and God in him. We love him, because he first loved us. (1 Jn 4.9–10, 16, 19)

God not only uncovers himself as merciful and compassionate in the New Testament, but also as suffering for the sake of man's salvation. Being equal to God, the Son of God made himself like man (Phil 2.6–7). "Wherefore in all things it behoved him to be made like his brethren, that he might be a merciful and faithful high priest in things pertaining to God, to make reconciliation for the sins of the people" (Heb 2.17). God's death on the cross became the highest manifestation of God's solidarity with man, of God's desire to share man's sufferings, even unto the abandonment of God. While on the cross, Jesus called out to his Father with the words of Psalm 22, conveyed by the Evangelist in the Hebrew language: "*Eli, Eli, lama sabachthani? that is to say, 'My God, my God, why have you forsaken me?'*" (Mt 27.46; Mk 15.34). This cry of Jesus does not mean that God abandoned him at the moment of his suffering on the cross, but that he experienced the torment of abandonment as it is characteristic to man. By this, according to the teaching of the Church, even in the moment of abandonment he was God, and his Divinity was not even for a moment separated from his humanity.

The Old Testament was the revelation of the One God, but the New Testament became the revelation of the One God in Three Persons. According to the Synoptic Gospels, when Jesus Christ came out of the water after being baptized by John, "suddenly the heavens were opened to him and he saw the Spirit of God descending like a dove and alighting on him. And a voice from heaven said, 'This is my beloved Son, in whom I am well pleased'" (Mt 3.16–17). In the Gospels of Luke and Mark the Father relates directly to the Son: "You are my beloved Son, in whom I am well pleased" (Mk 1.11; Lk 3.22).

The voice of the Father is heard in two other gospel accounts: the Transfiguration of the Lord and Christ's conversation with the people. In the first case the Gospels say that when Christ was transfigured, a bright cloud overshadowed the disciples and a voice proclaimed from the cloud: "This is my beloved Son: hear him!" (Mk 9.7; Lk 9.35; Mt 17.5). The second case speaks of the time when Jesus is conversing with the people, when he relates to the Father: "Father, glorify your name." Then a voice came from heaven, "I have both glorified it, and will glorify it again." The crowd . . . said that it was thunder. Others said, "An angel spoke to him." Jesus answered, "This voice came not because of me, but for your sakes" (Jn 12.28–30).

In the three accounts in which the voice of God the Father is heard, the most important for the development of the Christian teaching of One God in Three Persons is that of the Baptism of the Lord. In Christian tradition, what is described of the event is perceived as a simultaneous appearing of the three Persons of the Holy Trinity (the Father, the Son, and the Holy Spirit): the Son appeared to the people in his human form, the voice of the Father bore witness to the Son, and the Spirit descended on the Son in the form of a dove. In the Orthodox Church the feast of the Lord's Baptism is called Theophany ("God's appearing," or Epiphany). The troparion of this feast says: "When thou, O Lord, wast baptized in the Jordan, the worship of the Trinity was made manifest. For the voice of the Father bore witness to thee, and called thee his beloved Son, and the Spirit, in the form of a dove confirmed the truthfulness of his word."[1]

Apart from the story of the Lord's baptism, another important and influential text for the Christian teaching of the Triune God was the words of Christ addressed to his disciples: "Go therefore and teach all nations, baptizing them in the name of the Father, and of the Son, and of the Holy Spirit" (Mt 28.19). It is precisely these words that became the baptismal formula of the ancient Church. The Trinitarian faith of the Church was based on this formula even before the teaching of the Trinity had received its final terminological formulation.[2]

The Trinitarian formulae referring to God the Father, the Lord Jesus Christ, and the Holy Spirit are found in the Epistles of the apostles Peter and Paul: "Elect according to the foreknowledge of God the Father, through sanctification of the Spirit, unto obedience and sprinkling of the blood of Jesus Christ: Grace unto you, and peace, be multiplied" (1 Pet 1.2); "The grace of the Lord Jesus Christ, and the love of God, and the communion of the Holy Spirit be with you all. Amen" (2 Cor 13.13). However, the Apostle Paul hails the addressees in his Epistles much more frequently in the name of God the Father and the Lord Jesus Christ. This is explained not so much by an unworthy elaboration of Trinitarian terminology of its time (the teaching of the equality of the three Persons of the Holy Trinity and of the single essence of the Father, the Son, and the Holy Spirit, was finally formulated only in the fourth century), as it is by a Christological trend of his epistles. It is precisely the proclamation of Jesus Christ "who was made of the seed of David according to the flesh and declared to be the Son of God with power, according to the spirit of holiness, by resurrection from the dead" (Rom 1.3–4) that was the main component of all the Pauline Epistles.

---

[1] *The Festal Menaion*, Theophany, Great Vespers, Troparion.

[2] In the First Epistle of the Apostle John the Theologian there is a verse that intends to support the Trinitarian faith of the ancient Church: "There are three that testify in heaven: Father, Word, and Holy Spirit, and these three . . ." are one (1 Jn 5.7). However, this verse is not in critical editions of the New Testament, as it is not in ancient Greek manuscripts. It is found only in Latin New Testament manuscripts that were borrowed from Latin writers, though in later times is was included in printed Greek editions of the New Testament. In the interpretations of the Greek Fathers of the Church, including the interpretation of Blessed Theophylact the Bulgarian, this verse in the First Epistle of John is absent.

JESUS CHRIST—GOD INCARNATE

The Nativity of Christ.
Monastery of Osios Loukas.
Greece. 11th c.

The New Testament was the revelation of the God who became incarnate, of the God who became man. From the point of view of Christianity, the dogma of the Incarnation was the completion and justification of the Old Testament history. At the center of the New Testament proclamation is the identity of Jesus Christ, through whom the salvation and redemption of man is perfected. According to the gospel teaching, Jesus is the Messiah himself, whose arrival was foretold by the prophets.

The key question of whether or not one accepts Christianity is the question of Christ's divinity. Monotheistic religions answer this question in different ways. Judaism considers the acceptance of Jesus Christ as contradictory to the Old Testament revelation of the One God. Islam accepts the historical Jesus, although it considers him one of the prophets, whose teaching was subsequently corrupted by Christians. Only Christians, whether Orthodox, Catholic, or Protestant, view Jesus Christ as God and Savior.

It is necessary to note that before the fourth century there was not one single understanding of Christ's divinity within Christianity. In particular, the Arians rejected Christ's divinity and were condemned for this in the First and Second Ecumenical Councils. In later times Christ's divinity was rejected in various forms in art, literature, philosophy, theology, and biblical criticism. A painting in the Renaissance period, representing Christ as a humanitarian, as become man, was an implicit rejection of his divine nature. Philosophical systems in the Enlightenment and German idealism in the nineteenth century had no place for faith in the God-Man. In the nineteenth and twentieth centuries, multiple attempts were made at creating an image of the "historical" Christ, as in the works of Ernest Renan and Leo Tolstoy, or the "alternative" Christ as in *Judas Iscariot* by L. N. Andreev and *Master and Margarita* by Mikhail Bulgakov. The artistic worth of these works varies, but they are joined in one thing: the rejection of the divinity of Jesus Christ, the perception of Christ as only a human being.

What do the Evangelists and authors of the apostolic Epistles say of Christ's divinity? What is the basis of the Christian faith that Jesus Christ is

God and Savior? Also, how does this faith correspond to the strict monotheism that runs throughout the Old Testament?

Jesus, referring to himself in the third person, calls himself most often the "Son of Man": this name is encountered in the four canonical gospels around eighty times. "Son of Man" is a phrase that, in the Aramaic language, does not merely mean something along the lines of "human." It could be supposed that, calling himself Son of Man, Jesus intentionally calls attention to his humanity instead of his divine provenance. However, the Son of Man of whom Jesus speaks is by no means an ordinary person: he is "the one who came down from heaven" (Jn 3.13), "for him God the Father has sealed" (Jn 6.27), the angels of God ascend and descend toward him (Jn 1.51). The Son of Man came down from heaven (Jn 3.13) so as to save the souls of mankind (Lk 9.56). He "has power on earth to forgive sins" (Mt 9.6); the faithful should eat his body and blood so as to have life in themselves (Jn 6.53). He rises from the dead (Mk 9.9) and ascends to heaven (Jn 3.13) "where he was before" (Jn 6.62). His coming will be unexpected (Mt 24.44, 25.13ff.), like lightning, flashing at one edge of the sky and shining from another (Lk 17.24). He will come "in the glory of his Father with the holy angels" (Mk 8.38), and will sit forever on the throne of his glory and will seat the apostles on twelve thrones "judging the twelve tribes of Israel" (Mt 19.28), and all the people will be gathered before him, and he will separate the sheep from the goats among them (Mt 25.31–33).

Jesus is frequently called the Son of God (Mt 14.33), the Son of the Living God (Mt 16.16; Jn 6.69), and he accepts these names (Lk 22.70). To the question of the high priest, "Are you the Christ, the Son of God," Jesus answers, "You have said so [in other words, "yes, I am the Son of God"]. But I tell you, from now on you will see the Son of man seated at the right hand of power and coming in the clouds of heaven" (Mt 26.64). In referring to himself, Jesus uses the names "Son of Man" and "Son of God" as synonyms:

> And no man has ascended up to heaven, but he that came down from heaven, even the Son of man who is in heaven. And as Moses lifted up the serpent in the wilderness, even so must the Son of man be lifted up: that whosoever believes in him should not perish, but have eternal life. For God so loved the world, that he gave his only begotten Son, that whosoever believes in him should not perish, but have everlasting life.

For God sent his Son into the world not to condemn the world; but that the world through him might be saved. He that believes in him is not condemned: but he that does not believe is condemned already, because he has not believed in the name of the only begotten Son of God. (Jn 3.13–18)

Amen, amen, I say to you: The hour is coming, and now is, when the dead shall hear the voice of the Son of God: and those who hear shall live. For as the Father has life in himself, so he has given to the Son to have life in himself; and he has given him authority to execute judgment also, because he is the Son of man. (Jn 5.25–27)

The biblical name "son of God" does not necessarily in and of itself indicate the divinity of its bearer, especially when it is used in the plural. The book of Genesis speaks of "sons of God" who saw "the daughters of men" (Gen 6.1–4). The angels are named sons of God, including Satan (Job 1.6, 2.1). The people of Israel are called sons of the Lord God (Deut 14.1). However, in the New Testament the expression "Son of God" carries with it a special meaning as applied to Jesus Christ. Jesus is the Only-begotten Son of God (Jn 3.16, 3.18; 1 Jn 4.9), Only-begotten from the Father (Jn 1.14), "who is in the bosom of the Father" (Jn 1.18). In conversations with the disciples and with the Jews described in the Gospel of John, Jesus repeatedly bears witness to his oneness with the Father:

But Jesus answered them, "Amen, amen, I say to you, the Son can do nothing of himself, but what he sees the Father do; for whatever things he does, these also the Son does likewise. For the Father loves the Son, and shows him all things that he himself does; and he will show him greater works than these, that you may marvel. For as the Father raises up the dead, and gives them life, even so the Son gives life to whom he will. For the Father judges no man, but has committed all judgment to the Son, that all should honor the Son, even as they honor the Father. Whoever does not honor the Son does not honor the Father who sent him. Amen, amen, I say to you: He who hears my word, and believes in him who sent me, has everlasting life, and shall not come into condemnation, but has passed from death to life. . . . I can of myself do nothing; as I hear, I judge; and my judgment is just, because I seek not my own will, but the will of the Father who has sent me. (Jn 5.19–24, 30)

For I came down from heaven, not to do my own will, but the will of him who sent me. (Jn 6.38)

As the Father knows me, even so I know the Father. (Jn 10.15)

The works that I do in my Father's name bear witness to me . . . I and my Father are one. (Jn 10.25, 30)

Jesus said to him, "I am the way, the truth, and the life: no man comes to the Father but by me. If you had known me, you would have known my Father also: and from henceforth you know him, and have seen him." Philip said to him, "Lord, show us the Father, and it suffices us." Jesus said to him, "Have I been with you for so long a time, and yet you have not known me, Philip? He who has seen me has seen the Father; and how do you say, 'Show us the Father'? Do you not believe that I am in the Father, and the Father in me? The words that I speak to you I speak not of myself, but the Father who dwells in me, he does the works. Believe me that I am in the Father, and the Father in me." (Jn 14.6–11)

At the Last Supper, having prayed for all those who believe in him, Jesus asks the Father to preserve that unity between them that connects him with the Father:

The Last Supper. Cathedral of Monreale. Sicily. 12th c.

Father, the hour is come; glorify your Son, that your Son also may glorify you. . . . I have glorified you on the earth: I have finished the work which you gave me to do. And now, O Father, glorify me with your own self with the glory which I had with you before the world was. I have manifested your name to the men whom you gave me out of the world: they were yours, and you gave them to me; and they have kept your word. . . . I pray for them: I pray not for the world, but for them whom you have given me; for they are yours. And all mine are yours, and yours are mine; and I am glorified in them. . . . Nor do I pray for these alone, but for those also who shall believe in me through their word; that they all may be one; as you, Father, are in me, and I in you, that they also may be one in us. (Jn 17.1, 4–6, 9–10, 20–21)

Although Jesus repeatedly calls himself the Son of God and bears witness to his unity with the Father, nowhere in the gospels does he call himself God. Moreover, when someone called him "good teacher," Jesus said to him: "Why do you call me good? There is none good but one, that is, God" (Mt 9.17; Mk 10.18; Lk 18.19). Jesus' answer can be understood in the sense that he is rejecting his own divinity, contrasting himself with God. However, Jesus' words can be understood in another way: "Calling me good, you acknowledge my divinity." In Christian tradition, the interpretation of Jesus' words as a reproach to the youth, that he did not acknowledge his divinity, received a wide dissemination. St Gregory the Theologian understood this position in much the same way: "The words, 'None is good' are a reply to the lawyer who was testing him and had borne witness to his goodness as man. Consummate goodness, he meant, belongs to God alone, though the word 'good' can be applied to man."[3]

In the Gospels and Epistles the name "God" (*Theos*, Θεός) is used mainly in reference to the Father, whereas when referring to Christ, the name "Lord" is used. The Acts of the Apostles speaks of the fact that "God has made [him] . . . both Lord and Christ," this Jesus whom the Jews crucified (Acts 2.36). "God has . . . raised up the Lord," says the Apostle Paul (1 Cor 6.14). One frequently encounters in the apostolic Epistles the expression "the God and Father of our Lord Jesus Christ" (1 Pet 1.3; Rom 15.6; 2 Cor 1.3, 11.31; Eph 1.3, 17; Col 1.3) or "God our Father and the Lord Jesus Christ" (e.g., Rom 1.7), and other similar formulae.

[3] *Oration 30.13, 104.*

The word "Lord" (*Kyrios*, Κύριος) does not indicate divinity in and of itself: it signifies "master." However, this word was already being used in the Septuagint as a translation for the name of God Yahweh (Jehovah, Lord, God) and *Adonai* (Lord), but in the New Testament the name Lord (Κύριος) is gradually used to reference God the Father side by side with the name God (Θεός). In the community of Christ's disciples, the application of the name "Lord" to Jesus absolutely indicated an acknowledgment of his divinity. The Apostle Thomas uses the words "Lord" and "God" synonymously when he confesses the resurrection of Christ with the words: "My Lord and my God" (Jn 20.28). In the words of the Apostle Paul, "no one can say that Jesus is the Lord but by the Holy Spirit" (1 Cor 12.3). In Paul's Epistles, the names "God," "Lord," and "Christ" are frequently used synonymously: Paul speaks of God's Church and Christ's Church, God's Kingdom and Christ's Kingdom, God's goodness and Christ's goodness, God's Spirit and Christ's Spirit. In the mind of John Chrysostom, the name "God" is no greater than the name "Lord," and the name "Lord" is not inferior to the name "God," inasmuch as God the Father is continually called Lord in the Old Testament.[4]

The clearest support of the faith of the early Church in Jesus Christ's divinity is the prologue of the Gospel of John, in which Christ is identified as the Word of God:

> In the beginning was the Word, and the Word was with God, and the Word was God. The same was in the beginning with God. All things were made by him; and without him was not any thing made that was made. In him was life; and the life was the light of men. And the light shines in darkness; and the darkness comprehended it not. . . . That was the true Light, which enlightens every man that comes into the world. He was in the world, and the world was made by him, and the world knew him not. He came unto his own, and his own received him not. But as many as received him, to them he gave power to become the sons of God, even to them that believe in his name: who were born, not of blood, nor of the will of the flesh, nor of the will of man, but of God. And the Word was made flesh, and dwelt among us, and we beheld his glory, the glory as of the only begotten of the Father, full of grace and truth. (Jn 1.1–5, 9–15)

[4]CJohn Chrysostom *Against the Anomians* 5.2.

This gospel passage is read in the Orthodox Church in the main liturgical service of the year: the Divine Liturgy on the night of Holy Pascha, when the Resurrection of Christ is celebrated. These words manifest exactly the faith of the ancient Church in the divinity of Jesus Christ, a faith that the Church considers to be the cornerstone of its being. The prologue of the Gospel of John contains the explicit acknowledgment that the Word of God, the Only-begotten Son of God, is God. This Word of God existed from the beginning "with God" (the Greek phrase *pros ton theon*, Gr: πρὸς τὸν θεόν, is more precisely translated as "toward God"), that is, it was always with God the Father; there was not one moment when the Only-begotten Son was not with the Father. The Word of God became flesh, it became incarnate, was made man, and lived among men. It is precisely God becoming man that is the good news that is brought to the world by the evangelists and apostles of Christ. Precisely in this news lies the novelty of Christianity as the New Covenant between God and men.

The prologue of the Gospel of John ends with the words: "No one has seen God at any time, the Only-begotten Son, who is in the bosom of the Father, he has declared him" (Jn 1.18). Contemporary critical editions of the New Testament put this text into various redactions: instead of "Only-begotten Son" (*monogenēs hyios*, μονογενὴς υἱός) is "Only-begotten God" (*monogenēs theos*, μονογενὴς θεός). This reading is based on the most ancient manuscripts (whereas the reading "Only-begotten Son" is found only in a few manuscripts, beginning in the fourth century). The authenticity of this reading is supported as well by the use of the phrase "Only-begotten God" in Basil the Great,[5] Amphilochius of Iconium,[6] Gregory of Nyssa,[7] and many other Eastern Christian authors. The phrase "Only-begotten God" is another confirmation of the belief in the ancient Church of Christ's divinity.

THE NAME OF JESUS

The evidence of the faith of the early Church in the divinity of Jesus Christ is that Christ's disciples turned the Old Testament cult of the name of God into the worship of the name of Jesus Christ. This transformation is evident

---

[5]Cf.: *Letter 38.4.*
[6]Cf.: *On the True Faith.*
[7]Cf.: *Great Catechetical Oration 39*; *To Ablabius.*

in the pages of all four Gospels, in the Acts of the Apostles, in the corpus of apostolic Epistles, and in Revelation.

The theme of Jesus' name occupies an important place in the Gospels. In conversations with disciples and other people, Jesus often speaks about his name. Taking a child, he placed it in the midst of his disciples and said, "Whoever receives one such little child in my name receives me'" (Mt 18.5; Mk 9.37; Lk 9.48). He warns the disciples that they will be persecuted because of his name: "They shall lay their hands on you . . . [and you shall be brought] before kings and rulers for my name's sake. . . . And you shall be hated by all men for my name's sake" (Lk. 21.12, 17; Mt 10.18, 22, 24.9; Mk 13.13). Having appeared to his disciples after his resurrection, he reminds them, "Thus it is written, and thus it behoved Christ to suffer, and to rise from the dead the third day: and that repentance and remission of sins should be preached in his name among all nations, beginning at Jerusalem" (Lk 24.46–47).

The Synoptic Gospels constantly speak of the miraculous power of the name of Jesus. John turns to Jesus with the question: "And John answered him, saying, Master, we saw one casting out devils in your name, and he does not follow us: and we forbade him, because he does not follow us. But Jesus said, Do not forbid him: for there is no man who does a miracle in my name, that can lightly speak evil of me" (Mk 9.38–39). Jesus sends out seventy disciples to evangelize; upon their return they joyfully tell him: "Lord, even the devils are subject to us through your name. And he said to them, Notwithstanding, do not rejoice that the spirits are subject to you; but rather rejoice, because your names are written in heaven" (Lk 10.17–20). However, Jesus stresses that it is not merely calling the name of God, for accomplishing miracles in Jesus' name is not salvific for a man if he does not bring forth good fruit or if he performs unlawful deeds:

> Not every one who says to me, "Lord, Lord," shall enter into the kingdom of heaven; but he that does the will of my Father who is in heaven. Many will say to me in that day, "Lord, Lord, have we not prophesied in your name? and in your name have cast out devils? and in your name done many wonderful works?" And then will I profess to them, "I never knew you: depart from me, you who work iniquity." (Mt 7.21–23)

In the Gospel of John, the theme of Jesus' name appears as a leitmotif. This Gospel already mentions in the prologue that "to as many as received him, those who believed in his name, he gave power to become sons of God" (Jn 1.12). Further on it is recalled that many had believed in his name in Jerusalem during the Passover (Jn 2.23). In a conversation with Nicodemus, Jesus speaks of the condemnation of those who have "not believed in the name of the Only-begotten Son of God" (Jn 3.18). Thus, to believe in the name of the Son of God is to believe in the Son of God, that is, to recognize him as the Son of God, sent from the Father.

In his last conversation with the disciples, Jesus thrice exhorts his disciples to ask "in his name" when asking of the Father. The insistence exhibited when he speaks on the subject shows that he bestows special meaning on this commandment:

> Whatever you shall ask in my name, I will do, that the Father may be glorified in the Son. If you ask anything in my name, I will do it. (Jn 14.13–14)

> You have not chosen me, but I have chosen you, and ordained you, that you should go and bring forth fruit, and that your fruit should remain: that whatsoever you ask of the Father in my name, he may give it you. (Jn 15.16)

> And on that day you shall ask me nothing. Amen, amen, I say to you, Whatsoever you ask the Father in my name, he will give to you. Hitherto you have asked nothing in my name: ask, and you shall receive, that your joy may be full. . . . On that day you shall ask in my name: and I do not say to you that I will pray the Father for you: For the Father himself loves you, because you have loved me, and have believed that I came out from God. (Jn 16.23–24, 26–27)

The story of Jesus' earthly life ends in the Gospel of Mark with the last exhortation of Jesus:

> And he said to them, Go into all the world, and preach the gospel to every creature. He who believes and is baptized shall be saved; but he who does not believe shall be damned. And these signs shall follow those who believe; In my name they shall cast out devils; they shall speak with new tongues; they shall take up serpents; and if they drink any deadly thing, it shall not hurt them; they shall lay hands on the sick, and they shall recover. (Mk 16.15–18)

Christ says to his disciples in the Gospel of Luke: "Thus it is written, and thus it behoved Christ to suffer, and to rise from the dead the third day: and that repentance and remission of sins should be preached in his name among all nations" (Lk 24.46–47). As then in the Gospel of John, its account of Christ's resurrection is completed with the words: "These are written, that you might believe that Jesus is the Christ, the Son of God; and that believing you might have life through his name" (Jn 20.31).

In the Acts of the Apostles, various themes are linked with the name of Jesus: 1. repentance, forgiveness of sins, and baptism in the name of the Lord Jesus; 2. salvation in the name of Jesus; 3. suffering for the name of Jesus; 4. faith in the name of Jesus; 5. miraculous power through the name of Jesus. Typical is the account of Peter and John's conversation with the priests, elders, and Sadducees, after they healed the lame man:

> The next day their rulers, and elders, and scribes, and Annas the high priest, and Caiaphas, and John, and Alexander, and as many as were of the kindred of the high priest, were gathered together at Jerusalem. And when they had set [the apostles] in their midst, they asked, "By what power, or by what name, have you done this?" Then Peter, filled with the Holy Ghost, said to them . . . "By the name of Jesus Christ of Nazareth, whom you crucified, whom God raised from the dead: by him does this man stand before you whole . . . for there is no other name under heaven given among men, by which we must be saved." (Acts 4.5–12)

Later on, the passage recounts how the elders and scribes decided threateningly to forbid Peter and John to "speak from then on to anyone in this name" (Acts 4.17). However, the apostles did not follow the elders' decree "not to speak at all nor teach in the name of Jesus" (Acts 4.18), and continued to preach and perform miracles, praying to God: "Grant to your servants, that with all boldness they may speak your word, by stretching forth your hand to heal; and that signs and wonders may be done by the name of your holy Son Jesus" (Acts 4.29–30). The apostles were summoned again to the Sanhedrin, where the high priests reminded them: Did we not give you strict orders not to teach in this name?" But Peter and the apostles answered, "We must obey God rather than men" (Acts 5.28–29). After the dispute with the apostles the high priests once again forbade them "to speak in the name of Jesus." As they left the council, the apostles "rejoiced

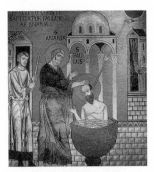

The baptism of Saul by the apostle Ananias. Palatine chapel. Palermo. 12th c.

that they were counted worthy to suffer shame for the sake of his name" (Acts 5.40–41).

A very interesting narrative is that of Saul's conversion, who met the Lord on the road to Damascus. After this encounter, the Lord appeared to Ananias and ordered him to go to Saul in order to heal him of his blindness. Ananias answered: "Lord, I have heard from many about this man, how much evil he has done to your saints at Jerusalem: And here he has authority from the chief priests to bind all that call on your name." But the Lord said unto him, "Go thy way: for he is a chosen vessel to me, to bear my name before the Gentiles, and kings, and the sons of Israel" (Acts 9.13–15). Ananias then found Saul, who accepted baptism and then began immediately in Damascus to speak "boldly in the name of Jesus." And after arriving in Jerusalem, similarly there he "spoke boldly in the name of Jesus." (Acts 9.27–28)

Thus all actions of the apostles are linked to the name of Jesus: this is the name they preach, for which they suffer, which they consider to be saving, in which they work miracles, in which they baptize. A few cases of baptism "in the name of the Lord Jesus" in Acts of the Apostles are a result of the apostles' preaching. Thus, after Peter's preaching in Jerusalem, the people, being moved in their hearts, ask Peter, "What shall we do?" Peter answers: "Repent, and be baptized every one of you in the name of Jesus Christ for the remission of sins, and you shall receive the gift of the Holy Spirit" (Acts 2.38). Preaching in the house of Cornelius, Peter speaks concerning Christ: "All the prophets witness to him, that whoever believes in him shall receiver remission of sins through his name." And he commanded them to be baptized in the name of the Lord Jesus" (Acts 10.43, 48). In Ephesus, Paul baptizes "in the name of the Lord Jesus" those who earlier were baptized with John's baptism (Acts 19.5).

The Catholic Epistles speak of Jesus' name, in particular those written by Peter and John:

If you are reproached for the name of Christ, blessed are you! (1 Pet 4.14)

I am writing to you, little children, because your sins are forgiven you for his name's sake. (1 Jn 2.12)

And whatever we ask, we receive from him, because we keep his commandments and do those things that are pleasing to him. And this is his commandment, that we believe in the name of his Son Jesus Christ, and love one another, as he commanded us. (1 Jn 3.22–23)

I have written these things to you who believe in the name of the Son of God, that you may know that, believing in him, you have eternal life. (1 Jn 5.13)

In the Epistles of the Apostle Paul, the theme of the name of Jesus Christ occupies a rather prevalent place. In particular, the First Epistle of Paul to the Corinthians opens with an exhortation to the Corinthian Church, "with all of those who call on the name of our Lord Jesus Christ" (1 Cor 1.2) regarding divisions that exist among them:

I beseech you, brethren, by the name of our Lord Jesus Christ, that you all speak the same thing, and that there be no divisions among you . . . For I have heard that among you there are those who say, "I am of Paul"; and , "I am of Apollos"; and, "I am of Cephas"; and, "I am of Christ." Is Christ divided? Was Paul crucified for you? Or were you baptized in the name of Paul? I thank God that I baptized none of you . . . lest anyone should say that I baptized in my own name. (1 Cor 1.10–15)

Later in the same epistle the Apostle Paul speaks of the members of the Corinthian Church who were washed, sanctified, and "were justified in the name of the Lord Jesus Christ and by the Spirit of our God" (1 Cor 6.11). In the Epistle to the Colossians, Paul speaks about the necessity to "do all in the name of the Lord Jesus" (Col 3.17), and in the Epistle to the Romans he speaks on grace and apostleship, receiving them from Christ "so that all nations might be obedient to the faith through his name" (Rom 1.5). Here the words of the Prophet Joel: "Whoever calls on the name of the Lord[8] shall be saved" (Joel 2.32), refer to those who confess the name of the Lord Jesus Christ (Rom 10.9–13). Paul attributes to the name of Jesus the same understanding with which the Old Testament invested the name Yahweh.

In the Epistle to the Philippians we find one of the most meaningful New Testament Christological texts that speaks about the name of Jesus:

---

[8]In the original this reads "the name of Yahweh."

Who, being in the form of God, did not think it robbery to be equal with God, but made himself of no reputation, and took upon himself the form of a servant, and was made in the likeness of men: And being found in fashion as a man, he humbled himself, and became obedient unto death, even the death of the cross. Wherefore God also has highly exalted him, and given him a name which is above every name, that at the name of Jesus every knee should bow, of things in heaven, and things on earth, and things under the earth, and every tongue should confess that Jesus Christ is Lord, to the glory of God the Father. (Phil 2.6–11)

The name that God the Father gave to the Son appears to be, from the context, the name "Lord" (*Kyrios*, Κύριος). But the Greek word *kyrios*, as has already been mentioned, is no more than one of the translations of the Hebrew names for God Yahweh and *Adonai*. Therefore, Jesus Christ is identified as the God of the Old Testament, and the name of Jesus Christ is connected with the holy name of God. The theme of the above text from the Apostle Paul is the deification of Christ's human nature: Jesus Christ as a man, having submitted to death on the cross, elevated human nature to the glory of God, thanks to the fact that his name, the Lord Jesus Christ Lover of Mankind, possesses a universal significance, having become the object of veneration (worship) not only by human beings, but also by the angels and by the demons.

The cult of the name of Jesus occupies a special place in Revelation. This book, the most mysterious and enigmatic of all the books in the biblical canon, returns us to the world of Old Testament prophecy, images, and symbols. Revelation is permeated with mystical names and numbers and on this plane can be considered as a continuation of the ancient Hebrew theological tradition, even though it is written in Greek. Specifically, all basic aspects of the worship of God's name, converted in the Christian Church to the worship of the name of Jesus, were reflected in the pages of this book.

Revelation opens with an appeal from the person of the Son of Man to the angels at the seven Asian churches, while three of the churches receive praise for believing in his name. Thus, to the angel of the church at Ephesus the Son of Man says: "You have endured much and have had patience, and that for my name's sake you have labored and have not grown faint" (Rev 2.3); to the angel of the church at Pergamum he says: "I know where you live,

The Last Judgment. The angel twisting the heavens. Monastery of Chora. Constantinople. 14th c.

even where Satan's throne is, and that you hold fast to my name and have not denied my faith" (Rev 2.13); to the angel of the church at Philadelphia he says: "I know your works. Lo, I have opened a door before you, and no one can shut it; for you have not much strength, and you have kept my word, and you have not denied my name" (Rev 3.8).

The fundamental theme of Revelation is the battle between God and the devil, between Christ and the antichrist, between the Lamb and the beast, the fight in which some of the people will fall under the power of the beast, while others will conquer him. The result of the victory over the antichrist is the reception of a secret new name, which will not be blotted out of the book of life. This was spoken of in the addresses to the angels of the churches at Pergamum and Sardis: "To the one who conquers I will give of the hidden manna, and I will give him a white stone, and on the white stone a new name written that no one knows except the one who receives it" (Rev 2.17). In the address to the angel of the church at Philadelphia, the name received by man is identified with the name of God: "The one who conquers I will make a pillar in the temple of my God, and he shall not go out of it again. I will write on him the name of my God, and the name of the city of my God, which is New Jerusalem, which comes down out of heaven from my God. And I will write upon him my new name" (Rev 3.12). The new name of Jesus is this secret name that no one knows aside from its bearer:

> And I saw heaven opened, and behold, a white horse; and he who sat upon it was called Faithful and True, and in righteousness he judges and makes war. His eyes were as a flame of fire, and on his head were many crowns; and he had a name written, that no one knew, but he himself. And he was clothed with a robe dipped in blood. And his name is called The Word of God. . . . And he has on his robe and on his thigh a name written: "King of kings and Lord of lords." (Rev 19.11–13, 16)

The mysticism of the name plays an essential role in the descriptions of the eschatological glory of the righteous. Below are some of the most impressive visions of the author of Revelation, described in the concluding chapters of the book:

> And I saw a new heaven and a new earth: for the first heaven and the first earth had passed away; and there was no more sea. And I John saw the holy city, new Jerusalem, coming down from God out of heaven, prepared as a bride adorned for her husband. And I heard a great voice out of heaven saying, Behold, the tabernacle of God with men, and he will dwell with them, and they shall be his people, and God himself shall be with them, and be their God. And God shall wipe away all tears from their eyes; and there shall be no more death, neither sorrow, nor crying, neither shall there be any more pain: for the former things are passed away. . . . And he carried me away in the spirit to a great and high mountain, and showed me that great city, the holy Jerusalem, descending out of heaven from God, having the glory of God. . . . It had a wall great and high, *and* had twelve gates, and at the gates twelve angels, and twelve names written on them, which are the names of the twelve tribes of Israel. . . . And the wall of the city had twelve foundations, and in them the names of the twelve apostles of the Lamb. . . . And I saw no temple therein: for the Lord God Almighty and the Lamb are its temple. And the city had no need of the sun, neither of the moon, to illumine it: for the

glory of God illumined it, and the Lamb is its light. . . . And nothing unclean shall intrude there, and nothing given over to defilement and lying, but only those who are written in the Lamb's book of life. . . . And there shall be no more curse: but the throne of God and of the Lamb shall be in it; and his servants shall serve him: And they shall see his face; and his name shall be on their foreheads. And there shall be no night there; and they shall need no candle, nor the light of the sun; for the Lord God gives them light: and they shall reign for ever and ever. (Rev 21.1–4, 10–14, 22–23, 27; 22.3–5)

All the biblical theology of the name is concentrated in these descriptions. At the center of all is the Lamb, who has the secret name, unknown to everyone besides himself, though he has also such other names as: "Word of God," "King of kings," and "Lord of lords." Around the Lamb are his servants, who have his name written on their foreheads, and they sing out his name. The attributes of the Old Testament cult are present in this description, but in a renewed and transfigured form. Instead of the old Jerusalem is a new Jerusalem, descending from heaven and filled with the glory of God. Instead of the Old Testament tabernacle is a new tabernacle of God with his people. Instead of the Old Testament temple of God's name is God himself and the Lamb. Instead of the Ark of the Covenant is the altar of God and the Lamb. The names of the twelve tribes of Israel written on the gates of the new Jerusalem symbolize the Old Testament chosen people of God. The names of the twelve apostles of the Lamb symbolize the New Testament redemption of mankind by Christ, written in the book of life of the Lamb.

Revelation is the concluding book of the Bible, and in this sense it can be thought of as the result of the worship of the name of God in the Bible. If, in the Old Testament, abusing the name of God resulted in death, then in Revelation a "second," or final death is spoken of for those who profane the name of God and whose own names are not written in the book of life (Rev 20.13–15). If God reveals himself as Yahweh in the Old Testament, then in the New Testament Jesus receives the name "Lord," so that Revelation speaks of the eschatological "new name" of the Lamb, which no one knows but the Lamb himself.

The Holy Spirit

The Lord's baptism.
The Russian North. 14th c.

As we have already noted, mentions of the Spirit of God can already be found in the Old Testament. However, it is in the New Testament that the Spirit of God is revealed not just as a mysterious power, acting from the name of God, but as a divine being, possessing personal characteristics. Furthermore, the New Testament reveals the indissoluble bond that exists between the Son and the Spirit.

In the course of his earthly life, Jesus Christ is constantly accompanied by the Holy Spirit. Even before his birth, the angel appears to Mary and says: "The Holy Spirit will come upon you, and the power of the Most High will overshadow you; therefore that holy one who will be born of you will be called the Son of God" (Lk 1.35). Jesus is born of the Virgin Mary and the Holy Spirit (Mt 1.18–20). The forerunner of Jesus "will be filled with the Holy Spirit" (Lk 1.15) even before his birth. He baptizes people "with water for repentance" but he says, "he who is coming after me will baptize . . . with the Holy Spirit and fire" (Mt 3.11; Mk 1.8; Lk 3.16). At the moment of Jesus' baptism, the Holy Spirit descends from heaven in the form of a dove and rests upon him (Lk 3.22). Then after his baptism, "Jesus, full of the Holy Spirit, returned from the Jordan and was led by the Spirit into the wilderness" (Lk 4.1) to be tempted by the devil.

Jesus speaks repeatedly in his preaching of the activity of the Holy Spirit. He predicts that his disciples will be persecuted for him, but exhorts them not to consider what to say ahead of time, for it will not be they who speak, but the Holy Spirit (Mt 10.20; Mk 13.11; Lk 12.12). Jesus warns that, "whoever speaks against the Holy Spirit, it shall not be forgiven him, neither in this age or in that to come" (Mt 12.32; Mk 3.29; Lk 12.10).

While Jesus was not yet glorified his disciples did not have the Holy Spirit (Jn 7.39). The death and resurrection of Christ were necessary conditions for his disciples to receive the Holy Spirit. Jesus speaks of this in his parting words with the disciples, as one of the leitmotifs that appear in the sending down of the Comforter:

And I will ask the Father, and he shall give you another Comforter, that he may abide with you for ever, even the Spirit of truth, whom the world cannot receive, because it neither sees him nor knows him. But you know him, because he dwells with you, and he shall be in you. (Jn 14.16–17)

When the Comforter comes, whom I will send to you from the Father, the Spirit of truth who proceeds from the Father, he will testify about me. (Jn 15.26)

Nevertheless, I tell you the truth: it is expedient for you that I go away, for if I do not go away, the Comforter will not come to you; but if I depart, I will send him to you. And when he comes, he will reprove the world of sin, and of righteousness, and of judgment: of sin, because they do not believe in me; of righteousness, because I go to my Father and you will see me no more; of judgment, because the prince of this world has been judged. I have yet many things to say to you, but you cannot bear them now. But when the Spirit of truth comes, he will guide you into all the truth; for he shall not speak on his own account, but whatever he hears, that he will speak; and he will declare to you the things that are to come. He shall glorify me, because he will take from what is mine and declare it to you. All things that the Father has are mine. For this reason I said that he will take from what is mine and declare it to you. (Jn 16.7–15)

After his resurrection, Jesus appears to his disciples and through a breath sends the Holy Spirit to them, saying: "Receive the Holy Spirit. Whose soever sins you remit, they are remitted them; whose soever sins you retain, they are retained" (Jn 20.22–23). At the same time he commands the disciples that they should not depart from Jerusalem, but to wait for the promise of the Father, which, he said, "you have heard of from me; for John truly baptized with water, but you shall be baptized with the Holy Spirit not many days hence . . . But you shall receive power after the Holy Spirit has come upon you; and you shall be witnesses to me in Jerusalem, in all Judea, and in Samaria, and unto the uttermost ends of the earth" (Acts 1.4–5, 8).

The descent of the Holy Spirit on the Apostles. Monastery of Osios Loukas. Greece. 11th c.

The event Jesus foretold came to pass on the day of Pentecost, when tongues of fire descended on the apostles, and "they were all filled with the Holy Spirit and began to speak in other tongues, as the Spirit gave them utterance" (Acts 2.4). In Jerusalem, many people were gathered together for the feast, and each heard the apostles speaking in his own native tongue, and a few suspected that they were drunk on wine (Acts 2.7, 12). Peter turned to preach to the people from among the apostles; he said:

> Men of Judea and all who dwell in Jerusalem, be this known to you, and listen to my words. For these men are not drunk, as you suppose, for it is but the third hour of the day. But, this is what was spoken by the prophet Joel: "It shall come to pass in the last days, God declares, that I will pour out of my Spirit upon all flesh, and your sons and your daughters shall prophesy, and your young men shall see visions, and your old men shall dream dreams . . . Then whoever calls on the name of the Lord shall be saved" [Joel 2.28–32]. Men of Israel, hear these words: Jesus of Nazareth, a man approved of by God among you by miracles and wonders and signs that God did by him among you, as you yourselves also know–him, being delivered by the determinate counsel and foreknowledge of God, you took, and by wicked hands crucified and slew by the hands of lawless men. But God raised him up, having loosed the pains of death, because it was not possible for him to be held fast by it. . . . Being therefore exalted at the right hand of God, and having received from the Father the promise of the Holy Spirit, he has poured out this that you now see and hear . . ." Now when they heard this, they were cut to the heart and said to Peter and to the rest of the apostles, "Men and brethren, what shall we do?" Then Peter said to them, "Repent, and be baptized every one of you in the name of Jesus Christ for the remission of sins; and you shall receive the gift of the Holy Spirit." (Acts 2.14–17, 21–24, 33, 37–38)

Pentecost marked the beginning of the mission of the Christian Church, which has continued up to now and in which the Holy Spirit plays a central role. It is precisely the action of the Holy Spirit that is perceived in the Church as a guarantee that Christ's teaching has not undergone any distortion, that his service will be continued by his disciples and followers, that Christ will remain the living and acting Head of the Church, accomplishing its governance through the aid of the Holy Spirit. The Holy Spirit is that person that Christ left in his Church instead of himself: He is "another Comforter" who, unlike Jesus, will not ascend to heaven, but will remain with his disciples forever (Jn 14.16). He will not speak on his own, but in the name of Christ (Jn 16.13–14).

If the Synoptic Gospels are dedicated primarily to the narrative of Christ's ministry on earth, and the Gospel of John and the apostolic Epistles to the theological understanding of this ministry, then the book of Acts of the Apostles is above all a witness to the blessed activity of the Holy Spirit in the founding of Christ's Church. It is not accidental that the reading of the book of Acts in the Orthodox Church begins at the Paschal liturgy, and is concluded on the feast of Pentecost.

The action of the Holy Spirit on the faithful in Acts of the Apostles is described with the help of the phrase "filled with the Holy Spirit" (Acts 4.8, 4.31, 9.17, 13.9, 13.52) and "receiving the Holy Spirit" (Acts 8.15, 8.17); It is also spoken of in the descent of the Holy Spirit on the faithful (Acts 8.39, 10.44, 11.15). The sign of the descent of the Holy Spirit often manifests itself in speaking in tongues, to which the following passage in particular bears witness:

> While Apollos was in Corinth, Paul after passing through the upper regions, came to Ephesus. And finding certain disciples, he said to them, "Have you received the Holy Spirit, when you believed?" They said to him, "We have not even heard that there is a Holy Spirit." Then he said to them, "Into what then were you baptized?" And they said, "Into John's baptism." Paul said, "John indeed baptized with the baptism of repentance, saying to the people that they should believe in the one who was to come after him, that is, in Christ Jesus." When they heard this, they were baptized in the name of the Lord Jesus. And when Paul had laid his hands on them, the Holy Spirit came upon them, and they spoke in tongues and prophesied (Acts 19.1–6).

In this passage, the Holy Spirit descends on the disciples not in the moment of baptism, but directly after it, at the laying on of hands of the Apostle Paul. Baptism and the laying on of hands were independent rites of initiation, to which the narrative of the descent of the Holy Spirit on the Samaritans bears witness. The apostles sent Peter and John to them so that, having come and prayed for them, they might receive the Holy Spirit. "For as yet he had descended on none of them; they were only baptized in the name of the Lord Jesus. Then they laid their hands on them, and they received the Holy Spirit" (Acts 8.16–17).

The presence of the Holy Spirit in the early Christian Church is similar in many ways to the presence of God Yahweh in the midst of the people of Israel. The Holy Spirit takes a lively and direct part in the life of the Christian community. He speaks with the disciples (Acts 13.2, 21.11), sends them to preach (Acts 13.14), and places them in ministry (Acts 20.28). Making this or that decision, the apostles feel the Holy Spirit acting, and they announce the decision with the words: "For it has seemed good to the Holy Spirit" (Acts 15.28). Subsequently, this formula began to be used in the decisions of the ecumenical councils.

If the presence of God in the Old Testament instilled above all reverential trembling and fear, then the activity of the Holy Spirit in the New Testament Church filled its members with joy and inspired them to speak "the word of God with boldness" (Acts 4.31). At the same time, sometimes the action of the Holy Spirit through the apostles brought all "great fear" (Acts 5.5, 11), as happened after the sudden death of Ananias and Sapphira. As told in the book of Acts, in the first Christian community, all "were together" and "had all things in common." They sold all their possessions and distributed the profit to all those in need (Acts 2.44–45). This is why "there was not a needy person among them" (Acts 4.34). However, one couple, Ananias and Sapphira, having sold their possessions, decided to hide a part of the proceeds from the community. When Ananias came and laid the money at the feet of the apostles, Peter said to him:

> Ananias, why has Satan filled your heart to lie to the Holy Spirit and to keep back part of the price of the land? While it was unsold, was it not your own? And after it was sold, was not the money in your power? You have not lied to men, but to God! On hearing these words, Ananias fell down and died. . . . And it was about three hours later, his wife came in, not yet knowing what had happened, and Peter said to her: "Tell me whether you sold the land for so much." She answered, "Yes, for that much." Then Peter said to her, "How is it that you have agreed together to put the Spirit of the Lord to the test? Lo, the feet of those who have buried your husband are at the door, and they will carry you out." Immediately she fell down at his feet and died. (Acts 5.1–10)

Characteristically, "to lie to the Holy Spirit" and "to lie to God" are syn-onyms for the Apostle Peter, which supports the apostles' belief in the divin-ity of the Holy Spirit. No less characteristic is the uncompromising nature that the apostles have in relation to matters of faith: they do not accept a par-tial, incomplete attitude toward Christ; they do not accept a lie regarding the general rules of the community's life.

As unacceptable as hiding the actual price of sold possessions may be, even more so is striving to receive the gift of the Holy Spirit with money. The story that provides proof enough of that concerns Simon Magus, who "when [he] saw that through the laying on of the apostles' hands the Spirit was given, he offered them money, saying, 'Give me also this power so that any-one on whom I lay my hands may receive the Holy Spirit.' But Peter said to him, 'Your money perish with you, because you thought the gift of God may be purchased with money'" (Acts 8.18–20). In the last few centuries the Church has fought tirelessly against "Simonism," the offering of a bribe for the laying on of hands for a holy order. According to the canons, those who received the laying on of hands for money, as well as the bishop who per-formed it, were expelled from the clerical orders.

The Holy Spirit is discussed in the Catholic Epistles, in particular First Peter, where the Holy Spirit is called the "Spirit of Christ" (1 Pet 1.11), "The Spirit of Glory," and the "Spirit of God," worshipped by those who are reviled "for the name of Christ" (1 Pet 4.14). According to the teaching of the Apostle Peter, the very same Holy Spirit sent from heaven, who acted in the prophets, acts in the proclaimers of the Christian faith, the apostles of Christ (1 Pet 1.11–12). Peter calls Christians to purify their souls by "obedience to the truth" (1 Pet 1.22), reminding them that their adornment should "be the inner man of the heart, in that which is not corruptible, even the ornament of a gentle and quiet spirit" (1 Pet 3.4).

According to the teaching of the Apostle John the Theologian, commun-ion with the Holy Spirit is the sign of man dwelling in God: "By this we know that we dwell in him, and he in us, because he has given us of his Spirit" (1 Jn 4.13). The apostle says that Christ came "not by water only but by water and blood. And it is the Spirit that bears witness, because the Spirit is truth" (1 Jn 5.6). Christians are also saved through the Spirit, water, and blood (1 Jn 5.8), that is, through baptism, martyrdom, and communion of the Holy Spirit. Speaking of the necessity of testing souls, the apostle contrasts the

"Spirit of God" with the spirit of the antichrist, acting in false prophets: "By this you know the Spirit of God: Every spirit that confesses that Jesus Christ has come in the flesh is of God, and every spirit that does not confess that Jesus Christ has come in the flesh is not of God; and this is that spirit of antichrist" (1 Jn 4.2–3). Thus the criterion for recognizing the Holy Spirit and for distinguishing it from false spirits is the belief in the incarnation.

The teaching on the Holy Spirit occupies an essential place in the Pauline Epistles. In his theological vision the action of the Holy Spirit is continuously connected with the redemptive feat of Christ. In the Epistle to the Romans, Paul summons Christians to "live according to the Spirit," seeing in this way of life the key to a future resurrection:

> And those who are in the flesh cannot please God. But you are not in the flesh, but in the Spirit, if the Spirit of God dwells in you. Now if any one does not have the Spirit of Christ, he is not of Christ. And if Christ is in you, the body is dead because of sin, but the Spirit is life because of righteousness. But if the Spirit of him who raised up Jesus from the dead dwells in you, he who raised up Christ from the dead shall also give life to your mortal bodies by his Spirit that dwells in you. Therefore, brethren, we are debtors, not to the flesh, to live after the flesh. For if you live after the flesh, you shall die, but if you through the Spirit you mortify the deeds of the body, you shall live. For as many as are led by the Spirit of God are the sons of God. For you have not received the spirit of bondage again to fear, but you have received the Spirit of adoption, by which we cry, "Abba, Father!" The Spirit itself bears witness with our spirit, that we are the children of God; and if children, then heirs, heirs of God, and joint heirs with Christ; and if indeed we suffer with him, that we may also be glorified together [with him]. (Rom 8.8–17)

Already noted above was the Apostle Paul's idea that proper relation with God the Father with the prayer "Abba! Father!" bears witness to the adoption of Christians by God. According to Paul's teaching, when a Christian turns to God in prayer, he prays not just from himself, but the Holy Spirit prays to the Father within him: "For we do not know what we should pray for as we ought, but Spirit itself makes intercession for us with groanings which cannot be uttered. And he who searches the hearts knows what is the mind of the Spirit, because he makes interecession for the saints according to the will of God" (Rom 8.26–27).

In the First Epistle to the Corinthians, speaking of the secret and hidden wisdom of God, the Apostle Paul maintains that God's wisdom reveals spiritual people by means of the Holy Spirit:

> But, as it is written, "Eye has not seen, nor ear heard, nor has it entered into the heart of man, the things which God has prepared for those who love him. But God has revealed them to us by his Spirit: for the Spirit searches all things, indeed, the deep things of God. For what man knows the things of a man, except the spirit of man which is in him? Even so the things of God no man knows, but the Spirit of God [knows]. Now we have received, not the spirit of the world, but the Spirit which is of God, that we might know the things that are freely given to us by God. But the natural man does not receive the things of the Spirit of God, for they are foolishness to him; nor can he know them, because they are spiritually discerned. But he who is spiritual judges all things, yet he himself is judged by no man. For who has known the mind of the Lord, that he may instruct him? But we have the mind of Christ. (1 Cor 2.9–16)

Cautioning the Corinthian Christians against an ungodly life, the Apostle Paul exclaims: "Do you not know that you are the temple of God, and that the Spirit of God dwells in you? If anyone defiles the temple of God, God will destroy him, for the temple of God is holy, and you are that temple" (1 Cor 3.16–17). The Apostle Paul explains the intolerance for sin in that the bodies of Christians are in essence the members of Christ and the temple of the Holy Spirit (1 Cor 6.15–19).

The apostle devotes special attention to the many aspects of the gifts and actions of the Holy Spirit within the Church of Christ. According to his teaching, all ministries in the Church are divided up by the Holy Spirit, and they are all necessary for the preservation of the unity, integrity, and fullness of the church organism:

> Now there are diversities of gifts, but the same Spirit. And there are differences of administrations, but the same Lord. And there are diversities of operations, but it is the same God who works all in all. But the manifestation of the Spirit is given to every man to profit from it. For to one is given by the Spirit the word of wisdom; to another the word of

knowledge by the same Spirit; to another, faith by the same Spirit; to another, the gifts of healing, by the same Spirit; to another the working of miracles; to another, prophecy; to another, discerning of spirits; to another, different kinds of tongues; to another, the interpretation of tongues. But that one and selfsame Spirit works all of these, and he divides them to every man as he will. For as the body is one, and has many members, and all the members of that one body, though many, are one body, so also is Christ. For by one Spirit we are all baptized into one body, whether Jews or Gentiles, whether slaves or free, and we have all been given to drink in one Spirit. (1 Cor 12.4–13)

8

God in the Works of the
Eastern Church Fathers

I N THE WORKS OF the Eastern Church Fathers, the New Testament proclamation of the One God in three Persons received a prolonged and
detailed development. In the Orthodox Church, the teaching on God has
been preserved in the way in which it was formed by the Eastern Fathers. The
foundational milestones in the development of Eastern Christian patristic
teaching on God were: 1) the formation of Christian theology in the works of
the apostolic men, Christian apologists, and teachers of the Church of the
second and third centuries; 2) the Trinitarian disputes of the fourth century
and the teaching of the Cappadocian Fathers of the One God in three
Hypostases; 3) the theological disputes of the fifth through eighth centuries;
4) the anti-Latin polemic, beginning in the eleventh century, regarding the
issue of the procession of the Holy Spirit; 5) the hesychastic disputes of the
fourteenth century and the teaching of St Gregory Palamas on the essence
and energies of God.

The main themes of the Eastern Christian patristic teaching on God are
the incomprehensibility of God, the oneness of God, God as Trinity, the
names of God, the qualities of God, God's love, the essence and energies of
God, and the procession of the Holy Spirit. These themes will appear below
as the foundation of the works of the Fathers of the Eastern Church from the
second to the fourteenth centuries. Special attention will be paid to Gregory
the Theologian (in the exposition of teachings on the incomprehensibility of
God, the oneness of God, the Trinity, and the divine light), Gregory of Nyssa
and Dionysius the Areopagite (concerning the examination of the divine
names), Isaac the Syrian (on the exposition of teachings on God's love),
Symeon the New Theologian (on the exposition of teachings on the divine
light), Gregory Palamas (concerning the examination of the issue of God's

essence and energies), and Mark of Ephesus (for the analysis of the procession of the Holy Spirit), as well as Maximus the Confessor and John of Damascus (for the examination of various issues).

THE INCOMPREHENSIBILITY OF GOD

The point of departure for the theologizing of the Church Fathers in the East
and in the West was the understanding of God's incomprehensibility, inherited from Holy Scripture. In the words of St Maximus the Confessor, "God
is one, without beginning, incomprehensible and possessing with all strength
the totality of being; he . . . is inaccessible to all beings and is not known by
even one created being in his natural manifestation."[1] St John of Damascus
begins *An Exact Exposition of Orthodox Faith* with the chapter "That the Deity
is Incomprehensible":

> No one hath seen God at any time; the Only-begotten Son, which is in
> the bosom of the Father, he hath declared him (Jn 1.18). The Deity, there-
> fore, is ineffable and incomprehensible. For no one knoweth the Father,
> save the Son, nor the Son, save the Father (Mt 11.27). And the Holy Spirit,
> too, so knows the things of God as the spirit of the man knows the things
> that are in him (1 Cor 2.11). Moreover, after the first and blessed nature
> no one, not of men only, but even of supramundane powers, and the
> Cherubim, I say, and Seraphim themselves, has ever known God, save he
> to whom he revealed himself.[2]

The theme of God's incomprehensibility occupied a central place in the
theology of the Eastern Fathers of the Church in the fourth century, because
of the necessity to counteract the heresy of Eunomius. This man claimed,
among other things, that God's essence was comprehensible for man: "God
knows nothing more of his own nature than we do; it is not permissible to say
that it is more known to him, and less to us";[3] "I know God as God knows his
own self."[4] Eunomius' teaching was an attempt at the rationalization of Christianity, in which nothing ought to remain cloaked in mystery, exceeding the

---

[1] *Chapters on Theology and on Oikonomia* 1.1.
[2] 1.1.
[3] Socrates Scholasticus *Church History* 4.7.
[4] Gregory of Nyssa *Sermon on the Divinity of the Son and Spirit.*

potential of human thought. "Religion is only within the bounds of reason," as the European rationalists of the nineteenth century (Kant, Renan, Tolstoy, and others) tried to establish, though in fact this idea was already formed fifteen centuries before them.

According to Eunomius, the assertion of God's incomprehensibility is none other than atheism, a rejection of the existence of God. According to the Fathers of the Church, on the other hand, the claim that God is comprehensible in his essence is the height of atheism and blasphemy. Such a claim, in the words of John Chrysostom, is "the root of all evil":

Christ between two angels.
Church of San Vitale.
Ravenna. 6th c.

And just how is this the root of all evil? . . . Man dared to say: I know God as God knows himself. Is it truly necessary to denounce this? Is it truly necessary to prove it? . . . This is obvious madness, an inexcusable recklessness, the most novel form of dishonor; no one ever dared either to think or to pronounce in speech anything of the like. Think, O unhappy and pitiable one, who you are and who [it is that] you examine? You are a man, and yet you examine God? . . . Is it true, tell me, that you examine God, without beginning, unchanging, without end, imperishable, omnipresent, surpassing all and higher than all creation? . . . But you will say: I am a man, honorable in freedom. You are not honorable in order to use freedom for opposition, but in order to use this honor for hearing the Most Honorable One. God honored you not so that you would offend him, but so that you would glorify him; he who offends God is he who scrutinizes his essence.[5]

The Christian theologian humbly knows that whatever concerns a mystery is beyond any possible intellectual comprehension, contrary to a rationalist, pretending that he knows God no worse than God knows himself. The claim of St Gregory the Theologian became a theological axiom of the Church Fathers: "The Godhead is incomprehensible for the human mind, and it is wholly impossible to imagine it as it is."[6] Why then does God remain incomprehensible? One cannot know the reason for God's incomprehensibility,

[5] *Homilies against the Anomoians and on the Incomprehensible Nature of God* 2.3–5.
[6] *Oration* 28.11 (ad hoc translation–*ed.*).

answers Gregory, though one does know that between man and God stands man's "corporeal gloom," as there was between Israel and Egypt (Ex 10.22).[7] In other words, while man inhabits a material body, he cannot reach God's essence, just as the material remains a barrier between man and God. Turning to the exclusive sphere of corporeality, it is impossible to emerge to that level on which genuine knowledge of God occurs. God's essence is ever evading man's speech and reason, as if they were not trying to describe or grasp God:

> Yet we "prisoners of the earth," in divine Jeremiah's phrase (Lam 3.34), pent in this gross portion of the flesh, know this: you cannot cross your own shadow however much you haste—it is always exactly ahead of your grasp. . . . No more can embodied beings keep incorporeal company with things ideal. Some corporeal factor of ours will always intrude itself, even if the mind be most fully detached from the visible world and at its most recollected when it attempts to engage with its visible kin. . . . This way our mind tires of getting past bodily conditions and companying with things sheerly incorporeal, and meanwhile it gazes in impotence at what lies beyond its powers.[8]

Does it follow from this that man will come to know God's essence when he is freed from the body? Gregory leaves the question open, however, he himself yields in order to give a positive answer. The knowledge of God will become possible in the state of adoration, when man's mind will be united with that which bore him, that is, with God:

> No one has yet discovered or ever shall discover what God is in his nature and essence. As for a discovery some time in the future, let those who have a mind to it research and speculate. The discovery will take place, so my reason tells me, when this God-like, divine thing, I mean our mind and reason, mingles with its kin, when the copy returns to the pattern it now longs after. This seems to me to be the meaning of the great dictum that we shall, in time to come, "know even as we are known" (1 Cor 13.12). But for the present what reaches us is a scant emanation, as it were a small beam from a great light.[9]

[7]Ibid. 28.12.
[8]Ibid. 28.12–13 p. 46–47.
[9]Ibid. 28.17 p. 49–50.

Unity and Trinity

The cornerstone of Christian theology is the biblical understanding of God's unity. "Both the Old Testament and New Testament Scriptures teach that the beginning of all was in unity, the God of all and Father of our Lord Jesus Christ," writes Theodoret of Cyrus.[10] "God according to nature is always in the genuine meaning of the word One and Only,"[11] says Maximus the Confessor. In the words of John of Damascus, "that God is one, and not many gods, is not subjected to doubt in the true Divine Scripture."[12]

The appearance of the Holy Trinity to Abraham. Theophanes the Greek. Church of the Transfiguration. Novgorod. 14th c.

The teaching of the unity of God is expressed in the opening words of the Niceno-Constantinopolitan Creed: "I believe in one God." Cyril of Alexandria sees in these words of the Creed an assertion not only of unity, but of a transcendent God, whose nature is above all created nature:

> The Fathers declared this: "We believe in one God"—with the aim, in the very basic, or deepest sense, to break the mind of the nations, which . . . served the elements of the world, having thought up not just many gods, but countless gods. For this reason the Fathers called God one, for the eradication of the delusion of paganism, departing not at all from Holy Scripture, and clearly showing the beauty of truth to all living things in the universe. . . . For this reason the all-praised Fathers gave a firm foundation to the faith, that is, precisely, that one should know and confess that God is one and united in essence and truth. As they said perfectly: "We believe in one God."[13]

Christian authors of the second century proved the unity of God in countering the pagan nations and the gnostic heretics. "Our teaching identifies the one God, the Creator of this world, who himself is not formed, for that which is truly existing does not receive being, but only that which is not true

---

[10] *An Exact Exposition of Divine Dogma* 1.
[11] *Chapters* . . . 1.6.
[12] *An Exact Exposition* 1.5.
[13] *On the Holy Symbol.*

being,"[14] wrote Athenagoras of Athens. Characteristically, the main accusation of pagans toward Christians was the charge of godlessness, atheism, for Christians did not accept the pagans' gods. Responding to this accusation, Athenagoras wrote: "We are not godless when we identify the one God without beginning, eternal, invisible and impartial, unbounded and immeasurable, comprehended by one thought and mind, filled with light and beauty, by spirit and indescribable might, who by his Word crafted and formed all and rules all."[15]

The one God of Christianity is God the Creator. In the words of Irenaeus of Lyons, he "created heaven and the earth and all that is in them. . . . There is nothing higher nor lower than him. . . . He is the one God, one Lord, one Creator, one Father, and the one who rules all and gives being to all."[16] As Cyril of Alexandria writes, "by calling him 'Creator of everything in heaven and on earth,' the Fathers allow us to understand his relation not with just any kind of work, because nothing can compare the differences between Creator and creation, between the unbegotten and the begotten, between subordinate, servile nature and nature which is adorned in majestic worthiness, having divine and otherworldly glory."[17]

In the fourth century, when the Church was torn by Trinitarian disputes, the Church Fathers were confronted by accusations not of atheism, but of tritheism, believing in three gods: this accusation against the Church was levied by the Arians. In their opinion, the teaching on the single nature of the Father, the Son, and Holy Spirit divides the belief of the one God and the understanding of the "monarchy," the unified rule of God the Father, introducing instead three independent beings, gods equal to one another. The idea of the "monarchy" of the Father was, for Arius, foundational. Arius rejected the claim of a Son coeternal with the Father precisely because he interpreted it as a violation of the principle of the Father's one rule. It seemed to him that placing the origin of the Son outside of time, in eternity, Orthodox Christians introduced "two unbegotten origins."[18]

In carrying on polemics with the Arian understanding of "monarchy," Gregory the Theologian claimed that the term refers not to the Hypostasis of

[14]*Apology* 4.
[15]Ibid. 10.
[16]*Against Heresies* 2.1.1.
[17]*On the Holy Symbol.*
[18]Epiphanius *Panarion* 69.6.

God the Father, but to the Deity as a whole, to all three Hypostases in totality. For him, this understanding is connected not with the sole rule of the Father, but with the unity of the Deity, which is preserved in the confession of three equal, coeternal Hypostases in one essence:

> The opinions about deity that hold pride of place are three in number: atheism, polytheism, and monotheism. With the first two the children of Greece amuse themselves. Let the game go on! Atheism with its lack of a governing principle involves disorder. Polytheism, with a plurality of such principles, involves faction and hence the absence of a governing principle, and this involves disorder again. Both lead to an identical result—lack of order, which, in turn, leads to disintegration, disorder being the prelude to disintegration. Monotheism, with its single governing principle, is what we value—not monotheism defined as the sovereignty of a single person (after all, self-discordant unity can become a plurality) but the single rule produced by equality of nature, harmony of will, identity of action, and the convergence towards their source of what springs from unity—none of which is possible in the case of created nature. The result is that though there is numerical distinction, there is no division in the substance. For this reason, a one eternally changes to a two and stops at three—meaning the Father, the Son, and the Holy Spirit.[19]

The idea of the extension of the monad into a diad and the diad into a triad is expressed to highlight the primordial unity of God, not to violate the dogma of the Holy Trinity. A similar idea was encountered in the third century by St Dionysius of Rome: "We broaden the divine unity to a triad and, paradoxically, we bring the triad together, not lessening it in its unity."[20] These words show that in Christianity, God's unity is not understood statically, but dynamically. This is the difference between Christian monotheism and the monotheism of Judaism and Islam, where any notion of the plurality of God is perceived as a contradiction to the revelation that God gave to Abraham. From the Christian point of view, the teaching of the One God in three Persons, based on the revelation of the New Testament, does not contradict the Old Testament revelation, but rather completes and fulfills it.

---

[19] *Oration* 29.2 p. 70.
[20] Athanasius of Alexandria *On the Exposition of Dionysius.*

Speaking on the unity and trinity of the Deity, Gregory the Theologian uses the term "Oneness," relating it to the One God, from whom proceeds and to whom returns "that which is from the Oneness." Gregory refutes the opinion that Christians believe in three gods:

> "If," it is asserted, "we use the word 'God' three times, must there not be three Gods? . . ." We have one God because there is a single Godhead. Though there are three objects of belief, they derive from the single whole and have reference to it. They do not have degrees of being God or degrees of priority over against one another. They are not sundered in will or divided in power. . . . To express it succinctly, the Godhead exists undivided in beings divided. It is as if there were a single intermingling of light, which existed in three mutually connected Suns. When we look at the Godhead, the primal cause, the sole sovereignty, we have a mental picture of the single whole, certainly. But when we look at the three in whom the Godhead exists, and at those who derive their timeless and equally glorious being from the primal cause, we have three objects of worship.[21]

According to the teaching of Gregory the Theologian, the unity and threefold nature in God do not contradict one another, but are continually connected:

> The three are God when known together, each God because of the consubstantiality, one God because of the monarchy. When I first know the one I am also illumined from all sides by the three; when I first distinguish the three I am also carried back to the one. When I picture one of the three I consider this the whole, and my eyes are filled. . . . I cannot grasp the greatness of that one. . . . When I bring the three together in contemplation, I see one torch and am unable to divide or measure the united light.[22]

God's threefold nature is not only an abstract idea: this is truth, uncovered through the reflection of God. The mystical unity in trinity was revealed to people in order that they learn to live in unity in peace and love. Jesus Christ himself prayed that the example of unity between him and the Father might influence his disciples to care for the preservation of unity: "That they

---

[21] *Oration* 31.13–14 p. 127–128.
[22] *Oration* 40.41 p. 137.

all may be one, as you, Father, are in me and I am in you, may they also be in us" (Jn 17.21).

The unity of the three Hypostases is a mystery, going beyond the bounds of human perception. For this reason no comparison, no analogy from life in the created world is capable of representing this unity. The Church Fathers, speaking on the unity of the Trinity, resorted to comparisons, but only in order to make this teaching clearer, more accessible to the simple believer. They always stipulated that similar comparisons were conventions and did not settle the mystery of the Trinity. The human family, in the mind of a few Fathers, was an image of the Holy Trinity: as Seth was begotten by Adam, and Eve was taken from Adam's rib, so is the Son begotten of the Father, while the Holy Spirit proceeds from the Father.[23] Other images include: spring, source, and river;[24] sun, ray, and light; the reflection of a sunray that moves along a wall so quickly that it is in multiple places at the same time.[25]

However, there is an essential shortcoming in all these images. The first image suggests an idea of movement within God and reduces the unity of God to an arithmetical unity. The second conceives the divinity as something complicated, and having attributed all essence to the Father, makes the two other Persons dependent. In the third the presence is too obviously set in motion, while the more primary things of God are absent, yet in general motion and variation are not connected with the Godhead. For this reason, concludes Gregory the Theologian, "I resolved that it was best to say 'good-bye' to images and shadows, deceptive and utterly inadequate as they are to express the reality. I resolved to keep close to the more truly religious view and rest content with some few words. . . . To the best of my powers I will persuade all men to worship Father, Son, and Holy Spirit as the single Godhead and power."[26]

The understanding of the unity of God in patristic theology is connected to the idea of the simplicity of God's nature. St Gregory of Nyssa in particular expresses this notion: "Divine nature, blessed and above all other nature, is simple."[27] By "simple," God's nature is understood to be devoid

---

[23]Cf.: Gregory the Theologian *Dogmatic Verses 3: On the Holy Spirit*; Gregory of Nyssa *Oration on the Meaning of "In the Image."*

[24]Cf.: Athanasius *On the Holy Spirit* 1.19; Basil *Against Eunomius* 5.

[25]Cf.: Gregory the Theologian *Oration* 31.31–32.

[26]Ibid. 31.33 p. 143.

[27]*Against Eunomius* 1.

of complication, of divisibility into parts: "Divine nature, as if it were not of essence, is one; it is something simple, single in form, and uncomplicated, and is in no way conceived of as some kind of multi-faceted multiplicity."[28] The threefold Persons in God do not infringe upon the simplicity of the divine nature, just as this nature remains as one for the three Persons—Father, Son, and Holy Spirit.

As one may recall, the being of each of the Persons of the Holy Trinity was described by the Cappadocian Fathers with the term "hypostasis" (*hypostasis*, ὑπόστασις), which they used side by side with the term "face" (*prōsopon*, πρόσωπον). God is one in "essence" (*ousia*, οὐσία), they said, but One in three Persons, or Hypostases. The word "God" points out the unity of God's essence, stresses St Gregory of Nyssa:

> If the name "God" served as a sign of the Persons, then in naming three Persons we would not necessarily have named three gods. If the name "God" signifies an essence, then confessing one essence of the Holy Trinity, not without a foundation in the glory of the One God, because the word "God" is the one name of the one essence. For this reason, in conformity with both essence and name, there is one God, and not three gods. For we do not recall "God and God and God" as we name "Father and Son and Holy Spirit" as names, indicating persons, adding the conjunction "and," because the Persons are not one and the same, but are different, varying one from the other by virtue of the name . . . God the Father, God the Son, and God the Holy Spirit. . . . But as an essence—the Father, an essence—the Son, and an essence—the Holy Spirit, are not three essences, so God—the Father, God—the Son, and God—the Holy Spirit, are not three gods. For there is one God and he is one and the same, just as there is one essence, and it is one and the same.[29]

The terminology of "hypostasis" and "essence" is borrowed from the language of ancient Greek philosophy and was necessary for explaining the teaching of the Trinity in that historical stage of development in the Church, when intellectuals actively used this language. However, the Fathers of the fourth century realized that all the conventions of language in abstract understanding as applied to God underscore that God is above all definitions and

[28]Ibid. 2.
[29]Gregory of Nyssa *To the Greeks*.

cannot be explained by any philosophical term. In this vein, the author of the *Corpus Areopagiticum* (fourth century) calls God "the one who is beyond all essence and understanding."[30] The First Principle of all essence, in the words of the Areopagite, is not essence: "It is not something from non-essence, nor is it something of essence; nor do things of essence know what it is, or how it is, nor does it know things of essence according to existing knowledge."[31] Commenting on these words, St Maximus the Confessor (seventh century) says:

> Do not be confused by these chapters, and do not think that this godly man blasphemes. His goal is to show that God is not made out of some sort of stuff, but that he is higher than existing things. Even if he, having created, brought all into being, how can he somehow be of those things created? . . . Nothing from the existing things knows God as he is; it has to do with his unknowable and super-essential nature, or by the state of being in which he is. . . . Not even God knows the things of essence according to existing knowledge, in other words, he cannot approach perceptible things perceptibly, or material things as material, for these things are not like God. . . . Existing things, or creation, cannot go beyond their nature in their thought. Naturally, those things that gaze at themselves cannot know Divine Nature when it appears. . . . No one knows the Most Blessed Trinity as it is; in other words . . . there is nothing like it, no way to know it as it truly is. Do we not know that human nature understands itself, inasmuch as we are people? We do not know what kind of form of existence recognizes itself as the Holy Trinity.[32]

The teaching on God, One in three Persons, is the cornerstone of Orthodox theology, an indisputable part of Church Tradition. It was reflected in the Creed, in the theological treatises of the Church Fathers, in liturgical texts, and in Christian poetry. One of the many examples of liturgical exposition on Trinitarian dogma is the *sticheron* (liturgical verse) sung at Vespers on the day of Pentecost:

> Come, O people, let us worship the Godhead in three Persons: the Son in the Father, with the Holy Spirit. For the Father timelessly begot the

[30]Dionysius the Areopagite *Mystical Theology* 1.
[31]Ibid. 5.
[32]*Scholia on Dionysius* 5.

Son, who is co-eternal and co-enthroned with him; and the Holy Spirit was in the Father and is glorified with the Son. We worship one Power, one Essence, one Godhead, and we say: "Holy God, you created all things through your Son with the cooperation of the Holy Spirit. Holy Mighty, through you we know the Father; through you the Holy Spirit came to dwell in the world. Holy Immortal, comforting Spirit, you proceed from the Father and rest in the Son. O Holy Trinity, glory to you!"[33]

The teaching of the Trinity was set in poetic form in the eleventh century by St Symeon the New Theologian who, addressing God in one of his hymns, wrote:

> You are a Unique Being.
> But this Unique Being is unknown to all nature.
> He is invisible and ineffable. . . .
> This Divine Being is a Unity in three hypostases,
> One Kingdom, one Divinity, one power,
> for the Trinity is a Unique Being.
> For my God is a Unique Trinity, not three beings,
> Because the one is three according to hypostases.
> They are connatural, one to the other according to nature.
> Entirely of the same power, having the same essence,
> United without confusion in a way that transcends any human
>   intelligence.
> Yet they are mutually distinct without being separated. . . .
> In the One are the Three and in the Three are the One,
> Or rather, the Three are as One to me and One again as Three.
> Thus, think of this mystery, adore and believe now and forever.[34]

THE TRINITY: FORMATION OF DOGMA

The Christian teaching on the Trinity took shape over the course of more than three centuries and reached its final formulation only towards the end of the fourth century. At the foundation of this teaching lay the stated higher

[33]Pentecostarion, Pentecost, Great Vespers, *Sticheron* at the Doxastichon.

[34]St Symeon the New Theologian, *Hymns of Divine Love*, George A. Maloney, S.J., tr. (New Jersey: Dimension Books), 233.

teaching of the New Testament concerning the Only-begotten Son of God, who was sent by the Father for the salvation of the world, and concerning the Holy Spirit, who proceeds from the Father and pours itself out on Christ's Church through the Son. As was already said, the baptismal formula given by Christ ("Go therefore and make disciples of all nations, baptizing them in the name of the Father and of the Son and of the Holy Spirit") became the most important formative factor in Christian triadology. From this formula sprang up baptismal creeds, one of which, the Niceno-Constantinopolitan, became the expression of faith universally accepted in the Church over the course of

The visitation of Abraham by the three men. Church of Santa-Maria Maggiore. Rome. 5th c.

many centuries up to and including the present day. The interpretation of the Creed became the mission of catechists, who prepared catechumens for baptism. Thus, the dogma of the Holy Trinity was present in the baptismal practice of the Church considerably earlier than theologians formulated it in the fourth century.

Trinitarian dogma has been an inseparable part of Christian theology from the very first centuries of Christianity's existence. All of the basic prayers of a liturgical nature, in particular those that arose from the *Apostolic Tradition* of St Hippolytus of Rome (third century), conclude with a doxology to the Father, Son, and Holy Spirit. The Trinitarian formulae in the Apostolic Epistles were adopted by liturgical Church Tradition from the earliest times, to which the extant texts of the ancient liturgy bear witness. The words of the Apostle Paul "the grace of our Lord Jesus Christ, and the love of God the Father, and the communion of the Holy Spirit, be with you all" entered into the Christian Eucharistic liturgy. Considering the fact that life in the early Christian Church was defined first of all by the Eucharist, but not at all by theological treatises, the presence of Trinitarian terminology in all liturgical rites makes it impossible to underestimate this as a formative factor of the Orthodox teaching on the Trinity.

Heresies became the direct occasion for the working out of Trinitarian terminology, when they arose in the Church in the second through the fourth centuries and alerted the Church Fathers to search for the most precise expressions of the teaching on the Trinity, as implicitly contained in the New Testament. The very term "Trinity" (Gr. *trias*, τριάς) was first encountered in texts of the second century. The first of the famed Eastern Church Fathers to use it was St Theophilus of Antioch. The first western writer applying this term (Lat. *trinitas*) was Tertullian. In the third century the term "Trinity" was already widely used by Christian authors, in particular by Origen, who also introduced into use the formula "One God in three Hypostases."[35] In the fourth century, the term "Trinity" became one of the basic Christian terms, applied in relation to God as one of the main "names of God."

St Gregory the Theologian, discussing the dogma of the Holy Trinity at the end of the fourth century, says that this dogma is part of Tradition, hailing from the early Fathers of the Church: "O, if only we would confess to the last breath and with much boldness that dear pledge of the holy Fathers, who are closer to Christ and the original faith."[36]

Reflecting on how the mystery of the Trinity was uncovered in history, Gregory the Theologian advances the idea of a gradual development of Church dogma, which arises thanks to what he calls "additions," that is, thanks to a gradual elaboration and enrichment of theological language. In the mind of Gregory, God already revealed himself to man in the Old Testament, though the unity of God was the key element of revelation, unity which was asserted in contradistinction to paganism; for this reason God the Father was the object of revelation. The New Testament revealed the Son to man, while the present period is the era of the action of the Holy Spirit, when dogmatic truths receive their final expression. Thus Gregory the Theologian does not consider the New Testament revelation to have settled all theological problems, nor does he consider that the answer to any question can be found in the Holy Scripture of the New Testament. On the contrary, the New Testament is only one of the stages of the "ascent" of Christian theology "from glory to glory." This ascent, in Gregory's opinion, will continue until the close of the age:

> There have been two remarkable transformations of the human way of life in the course of the world's history. These are called two "covenants. . . ." The first was the transition from idols to the law; the second, from the law

[35]Origen *Interpretation of John* 2.6.
[36]*Oration* II. 6.

to the Gospel. . . . In this way, the old covenant made clear proclamation of the Father, a less definite one of the Son. The new covenant made the Son manifest and gave us a glimpse of the Spirit's Godhead. At the present time, the Spirit resides amongst us, giving us a clearer manifestation of himself than before. It was dangerous for the Son to be preached openly. . . . It was dangerous, too, for the Holy Spirit to be made . . . an extra burden, when the Son had not been received. . . . No, God meant it to be by piecemeal additions, "ascents" (Ps 84.6) as David called them, by progress and advance from glory to glory, that the light of the Trinity should shine upon more illustrious souls. . . . Thus do I stand, thus may I stand, and those I love as well, on these issues, able to worship the Father as God, the Son as God, the Holy Spirit as God–"three personalities, one Godhead undivided in glory, honor, substance, and sovereignty."[37]

This most important text for the understanding of the whole history of Christian theology contains a few key ideas: 1) God's revelation, begun in the Old Testament period, did not conclude in the New Testament, but continues to this day; 2) the revelation comes not by way of coercion, but by way of conviction, for that is a necessary and defined tactic from the point of view of God as Pedagogue; 3) the tactic is concluded in that the revelation is accomplished gradually and by phase, by way of uncovering and further elucidating these or other dogmatic truths; 4) The Bible is not the last word in Christian dogmatics, only a specific stage in its development; 5) Christ himself did not say in the Gospel everything that is necessary for a Christian to know about God: Christ continues to reveal God to people through the Holy Spirit, that is, the New Testament revelation continues in the Church. Such is the dynamic understanding by Gregory of the development of Orthodox dogmatics and the revelation, in phases, in history of the mystery of the Trinity. His argument does not involve introducing new dogmata, but a gradually fuller uncovering of those dogmata, which in the form of "allusions" (Gr. *hypodeiksis*, ὑπόδειξις), is contained in Scripture.

Gregory the Theologian expressed here the traditional (for Eastern Christian theology) idea of the holy Tradition of the Church as a main source of the faith. It was previously discussed that eastern theology did not know of the opposition of Scripture and Tradition that was characteristic for the

---

[37] *Oration* 31.25–28 (Crestwood, N.Y.) 136–139.

Church in the West. In the eastern understanding, Scripture is a part of Tradition: Scripture grew out of Tradition and reflects a specific stage in the
development of Tradition—a development that has not yet been concluded
in this stage. "Mystical knowledge," that is, Christ's teaching, is not entering
into the New Testament canon, does not appear in the fabrications of the
Gnostics: it exists, but it exists not in them, but in Church Tradition. It is
Christ who entrusted this knowledge to the Church, and in the experience of
the Church, in its theology, fundamental truths of the Christian faith continue to be uncovered.

It fell to the lot of the Cappadocian Fathers to formulate a Trinitarian
dogma in the age when the Church was most in need of it. In opposition to
the Arian notion of hierarchical subordination of the Son to the Father, they
cultivated the teaching on the Trinity as a union of three equal Hypostases in
one nature. The Cappadocians continued the line of the Council of Nicaea
and St Athanasius of Alexandria, though they introduced a more precise differentiation of the understanding between "hypostasis" and "nature." This
word usage helped the Cappadocians effectively to beat off the Arian attacks,
accusing them either of Sabellianism or Modalism. Aside from this, the Cappadocians logically applied the term "birth" to the description of the provenance of the Son from the Father, and the term "procession" to the
description of the Holy Spirit's provenance from the Father:

> In a serene, non-temporal, incorporeal way, the Father is parent of the
> "offspring" and originator of the "emanation"—or whatever name one can
> apply when one has entirely extrapolated from things visible. We shall not
> venture, as a non-Christian philosopher rashly did, to talk of an "over-
> flowing of goodness," "as though a bowl had overflowed"—these were the
> plain terms he used in his disposition on primary and secondary causes.[38]
> We ought never to introduce the notion of involuntary generation (in the
> sense of some sort of unrestrained natural secretion), which is completely
> out of keeping with ideas about the Godhead. This is why we limit our-
> selves to Christian terms and speak of "the Ingenerate," "the Begotten,"
> and (as God the Word himself does in one passage) "what Proceeds from
> the Father" (Jn 15.26).[39]

[38]Cf.: Plotinus *Enneads* 5.1, 6; 5.2, 1. According to Plotinus, the One is the "first principle," the
Being is the "second principle."

[39]Gregory the Theologian *Oration* 29.2 (Crestwood, N.Y.) 70.

According to the teaching of the Cappadocian Fathers, God the Father appears in the Trinity as the "Beginning" (Gr. *archē*, ἀρχή) of the Son and the Holy Spirit. The term "beginning" is one of the basic Trinitarian terms of the fourth century. Both Orthodox and Arians utilized it, but they invested it with different meaning. The Arians considered God only to be without beginning: all that has a beginning is not God, so it follows that the Son is not God. "We are persecuted because we assert that the Son has a beginning, since God is without beginning,"[40] said Arius. The Cappadocians also asserted that the Son has a beginning, though they did not consider the Father's lack of a beginning to be synonymous with his divinity. Being without beginning, according to Gregory the Theologian's teaching, is a characteristic of the Father, differentiating him from the Son; however, both the Son and the Father possess the fullness of divinity. The Son is not without beginning in relation to the Father, though he is without beginning in relation to time.[41] The birth of Christ is coeternal with the Father's being; between the Father and the Son there is no sort of interval, no sort of succession, no sort of inequality.[42]

Another term applied to God the Father by the Cappadocians was the term "principle" (Gr. *aitia*, αἰτία): The Father is the Principle of the Son and the Spirit. The terms "beginning" and "principle" were frequently used as synonyms:

> It would not do to love the Father so much as to take away his fatherhood from him, for whose Father would he be if the Son were part of creation and estranged from him in essence? Nor would it do to love Christ so much as not to conserve his Sonship, for whose Son would he be if he did not ascend to the Father as Principle? Nor would it do to decrease the characteristics in the Father as Father and Parent worthy to be the origin, in order not to seem to be the origin of something base and unworthy, if he is not the divine Principle, contemplated in the Father and Spirit. It follows, on the contrary, to confess the One God in three Hypostases, that is, three Persons, of which every one has personal traits.[43]

---

[40] Arius *Epistle to Eusebius* (taken from: Epiphanius of Cyprus *Panarion* 69.6).
[41] Cf.: Gregory the Theologian *Oration* 20.7.
[42] *Oration* 20.10.

If the central point in the dispute between Arians and Orthodox in the first half of the fourth century was the issue of the Son's divinity, then in the second half of the century, the object of dispute became the divinity of the Holy Spirit. One of the *Theological Orations* of Gregory the Theologian is wholly devoted to the defense of the teaching of the Holy Spirit's divinity. As already spoken of in detail, in the consecrated history of the Church,[44] the fourth century question of the Holy Spirit did not carry a terminological discrepancy just between Arians and Orthodox, but also among the Orthodox themselves. Specifically, some Orthodox authors refused to name the Holy Spirit as God, limiting to it the application of the term "Lord" (similar to how the apostle Paul applied the term "God" to the Son of God). Gregory the Theologian, coming from his idea of gradual elucidation of dogmata by way of the development of dogmatic terminology, considered it necessary to apply the term "God" not only in relation to the Son, which in his time had become generally accepted among Orthodox, but also in relation to the Holy Spirit.

The Arians, in the dispute with the Orthodox, insisted that belief in the divinity of the Holy Spirit was not based in Scripture. In response to this Gregory first asserts that the denial of the use of extra-biblical terms signifies nothing other than the full stagnation of dogmatic theology. Second, Gregory expounds his theory of the gradual uncovering of Trinitarian dogma, which was already seen above. Third, he refers to the baptismal practice of the Church:

> Were the Spirit not to be worshipped, how could he deify me through baptism? If he is to be worshipped, why not adored? And if to be adored, how can he fail to be God? One links with the other, a truly golden chain of salvation. From the Spirit comes our rebirth, from rebirth comes a new creating, from a new creating a recognition of the worth of him who effected it.[45]

Fourth, Gregory refers to the Bible and proves that the Scripture bears witness to the divinity of the Holy Spirit. Christian faith is not a teaching of some kind of "strange, unscriptural [Gr. *agraphon*, ἄγραφον] 'God.'"[46] On the

---

[43]Ibid. 20.6.
[44]Cf.: *Orthodox Christianity Volume I*, 46.
[45]*Oration* 31.28 (Crestwood, N.Y.) 139.
[46]Ibid. 31.1 p. 117.

contrary, the Scripture clearly shows that the Spirit is God and that the Spirit is inseparably connected to the Son: "Christ is born, the Spirit is his forerunner; Christ is baptized, the Spirit bears him witness; Christ is tempted, the Spirit leads him up [in the desert]; Christ performs miracles, the Spirit accompanies him; Christ ascends, the Spirit fills his place."[47] The names of the Spirit used in Scripture bear witness to his divinity, and the qualities by which he is endowed in Scripture are also characteristic of God, but not of created essence:

> He makes us his temple, he deifies [us], he makes us complete, and he initiates us in such a way that he both precedes baptism and is wanted after it. All that God actively performs, he performs. Divided in fiery tongues, he distributes graces (Acts 2.3; 1 Cor 12.11), makes apostles, prophets, evangelists, pastors, and teachers.[48]

THE NAMES OF GOD

One of the key Eastern Christian patristic teachings on God was the theme of the names of God. This theme was developed throughout the Arian controversies of the fourth century and found its classic expression in the Areopagite's treatise *On the Divine Names*.

In the works of the fourth century church fathers, God is not only incomprehensible, but un-nameable. God's anonymity bears witness, in the opinion of Gregory the Theologian, to that reverence with which ancient Israel surrounded the name of "the Existing One": in writing it is expressed by the holy tetragrammaton, but in the period after the Babylonian captivity it ceased to be pronounced at all. Gregory saw in this a direct indication that the nature of God surpasses every name:

> Our starting-point must be the fact that God cannot be named. Not only will deductive arguments prove it, but the wisest Hebrews of antiquity, so far as can be gathered, will too. The ancient Hebrews used special symbols to venerate the divine and did not allow anything inferior to God to be written with the same letters as the word "God," on the ground that

---

[47]Ibid. 31.29 p. 139.
[48]Ibid. 140.

the divine should not be put on even this much of a level with things human. Would they ever have accepted the idea that the uniquely indissoluble nature could be expressed by evanescent speech? No man has yet breathed all the air; no mind has yet contained or language embraced God's substance in its fullness.[49]

Gregory divides the names of God into three categories: those that show his essence, those that show his power on earth, and finally, those that show his "economy," or any kind of action for the good of man. Applied to the first category are the names Existing One, God, and Lord.[50] In the second category are the names All-Powerful, King of glory, King of the ages, King of might, King of kings, Lord of Sabaoth (Lord of hosts), Lord of might, and Lord of lords. In the third category are the names God of salvation, God of vengeance, God of peace, God of righteousness, God of Abraham, Isaac, and Jacob, and other names linked to God's actions in the history of the people of Israel. To this category may be added the names of God after the incarnation, i.e. the personal name of Jesus. God is primarily called, before other names, Peace and Love.[51]

Every name of God characterizes one or another trait of his. However, these names are so relative and incomplete that not one of them can, on its own or even in totality, offer the possibility to imagine what God is in his nature. If one were to gather all of God's names and the forms with which God is connected in the Scriptures, and stick them together to make one whole, one would achieve a kind of artificial, speculative construction—more idol than God.

Every simplified, partial, one-sided, cataphatic conception of God is akin to idol-worship. It subjects God to the category of a human idea. Those anthropomorphic notions of God that are found in Holy Scripture should be understood as allegory: through the "letter" of Scripture one can penetrate its "inner contents."[52] There are things that are named in Scripture, though they do not exist in actuality (biblical anthropomorphisms belong in this category). It is said of God in Scripture that he sleeps, wakes, grows angry, walks,

[49]Ibid. 30.17 p. 107.
[50]Ibid. 6.12
[51]Cf.: Ibid. 6.12.
[52]Ibid. 31.21. Gregory recalls the traditional (for the Alexandrian school) concept of the presence of various levels of meaning in Scripture: "the letter" and "the spirit."

and has Cherubim as his throne. "This is a non-factual, mental picture. We have used names derived from human experience and applied them, so far as we could, to aspects of God," clarifies Gregory the Theologian. If God, for whatever reason, does not provide visible signs in his care for us, we begin to think that he is sleeping; if there suddenly appears some kind of blessing, then he awakes. He punishes, and we think that he is angry; he acts here, and then there, and it appears to us that he is walking. God moves quickly—we call this a flight (Ps 18.10); he looks upon us and we call this his face (Ps 34.16); he gives us something and we name it his hand (Ps 145.16). "Indeed every faculty or activity of God has given us a corresponding picture in terms of something bodily."[53]

The idea of God's anonymity is a leitmotif of St. Gregory of Nyssa'a treatise *Against Eunomius*. According to the author of the treatise, God, being incomprehensible and ineffable, is higher in essence than all names:

> The simplicity of the true faith assumes God to be that which he is, viz., incapable of being grasped by any term, or any idea, or any other device of our apprehension, remaining beyond the reach not only of the human but of the angelic and of all supramundane intelligence, unthinkable, unutterable, above all expression in words, having but one name that can represent his proper nature, the single name of being "above every name."[54]

> For by what name can I describe the incomprehensible? By what speech can I declare the unspeakable? Accordingly, since the Deity is too excellent and lofty to be expressed in words, we have learned to honor in silence what transcends speech and thought.[55]

> When Manoah asks to know his name, that, when the promise has come actually to pass, he may by name glorify his benefactor, he says to him, "Why dost thou ask this? It also is wonderful" (Judg 13.18); so that by this we learn that there is one name significant of the Divine Nature—the wonder, namely, that arises unspeakably in our hearts concerning it.[56]

---

[53]Ibid. 31.22 p. 134.
[54]I.42.
[55]Ibid. 3.5.
[56]Ibid. 8.1.

Christ Pantokrator.
Theophanes the Greek.
Church of the Transfiguration.
Novgorod. 14th c.

For this reason the title "Angel" is placed before that of the "Self-Existent," the Son being termed "Angel" as the exponent of his Father's will, and the "Existent" as having no name that could possibly give a knowledge of his essence, but transcending all the power of names to express. Where also his name is testified by the writing of the apostle to be "above every name" (Phil 2.9), not as though it were some one name preferred above all other, though still comparable with them, but rather in the sense that he who verily *is* is above every name.[57]

The names of God contained in Scripture, including those that were first pronounced by God himself, are in human words—a product of the act of human thought, considers Gregory of Nyssa. If God uses these words, it is not because he invented them or needed them, but because man cannot understand God in any other way. God condescends to man's weakness and speaks in human language since he cannot speak in any other language. Since one cannot call another a deaf-mute just because one is able to communicate with a deaf-mute through sign language, so one cannot attribute human words to God on the basis that he condescended to use human speech.[58]

What is the origin of the divine names? According to St Gregory of Nyssa, God receives names in accordance to his activities (energies) in his relations with people:

> He who is above every name has for us many names, receiving them in accordance with the variety of his gracious dealings with us a "tower of strength" (Ps 61.3) and a "city of encompassing," and a fountain, and a rock, and a vine, and a physician, and resurrection, and all the like, with reference to us, imparting himself under various aspects by virtue of his benefits toward us.[59]

> God is not speech, nor does he have being in voice or sound. Nor can he be summoned by naming what he is, for the essence of the Existing One

[57]Ibid. 11.3.
[58]Cf.: Ibid. 12.
[59]Ibid. 10.1.

is ineffable, but, as we believe, he receives naming from activities that concern our life.[60]

Does what Gregory says signify that the divine names have lost that understanding of the right-worship of the holy names of God that permeated the Old Testament? By no means. The Old Testament theme of the divine names is transformed in Gregory of Nyssa (just as in the other two Cappadocian Fathers) into the theme of God's anonymity. Moreover, all that Gregory said about the names of God in opposition to Eunomius is related to those man-made names that consist of sounds and letters and, by their very nature, are inadequate for characterizing God's essence. At the same time Gregory does

*The Savior. Andrei Rublev.
15th c.*

not omit the possibility of the existence of a certain hidden name that might signify the divine essence. However, he insists that this name is unknown to man and that, in any case, it cannot be verbally expressed:

> We are taught the fact that of [the Divine Nature's] existence, while we assert that an appellation of such force as to include the unspeakable and infinite Nature, either does not exist at all, or at any rate is unknown to us. Let him then leave his accustomed language of fable, and show us the names which [sic] signify the essences, and then proceed further to divide the subject by the divergence of their names. . . . So long as we say and believe these things, how like is an argument that promises any comprehension and expression of the infinite Nature, by means of the significance of names, to one who thinks that he can enclose the whole sea in his own hand! For as the hollow of one's hand is to the whole deep, so is all the power of language in comparison with that Nature which is unspeakable and incomprehensible.[61]

God's anonymity is the initial point of Dionysius the Areopagite's treatise *On the Divine Names*. This treatise presents itself as the most complete and systematic (this in distinction from the anti-Eunomian compositions of the Cappadocian Fathers in that it lacks a polemical edge) exposition of the

[60]Ibid. 12.
[61]Ibid. 7.4.

theme of the divine names in all of Eastern Christian patristics. The God-head, in Dionysius' words, "transcends every word and thought and resides above every mind and essence, encompassing, uniting, combining, and enveloping all existing things beforehand," it is "completely impossible to grasp, not by perception and not by feeling, not by expression or discern-ment, not by name or word, not by contact or recognition." One can speak about the divine names only as a basis for the activities of God, his manifes-tations in the world. God cannot be identified by even one human concept, but, being the Reason for everything that exists, he can be exalted as "pro-ceeding from their every origin, that in him everything may rejoice, and he exists before all, and everything exists in him, and his being is the reason for the appearance and the existence of all."[62]

This is precisely why, continues Dionysius, "theologians proclaim him both as nameless and as conformable to all names."[63] The anonymity of God, like his calling, is based on the witness of Holy Scripture:

> For instance, they call it nameless when they say that the Supreme God-head itself, in one of the mystical visions whereby it was symbolically manifested, refuted him who said: "What is thy name?" and, as though bidding him not to seek by any means of any name to acquire a knowl-edge of God, made the answer: "Why askest thou thus after my name see-ing it is secret?" (Gen 32.29). Now is not the secret name precisely that which is above all names and nameless (Phil 2.9), and is fixed beyond every name that is named, not only in this world but also in that which is to come (Eph 1.21)? On the other hand, they attribute many names to it when, for instance, they speak of it as declaring: "I am that I am," or "I am the Life," or "the Light," or "God," or "the Truth," and when the inspired writers themselves celebrate the Universal Cause with many titles drawn from the whole created universe, such as "Good," and "Fair," and "Wise," as "Beloved," as "God of gods," and "Lord of lords. . . ." Thus, then, the universal and transcendent Cause must both be nameless and also possess the names of all things in order that it may truly be an uni-versal Dominion, the Center of creation on which all things depend, as on their Cause and Origin and Goal.[64]

[62]1.5.
[63]Ibid. 1.6.
[64]Ibid. 1.6–7.

According to Dionysius the Areopagite, theologians borrow names for the Cause of all "from universal or from particular or providential activities, but sometimes they have gained their images from certain heavenly visions (which in the holy precincts or elsewhere have illuminated the Initiates or the Prophets), and, ascribing to the super-luminous nameless Goodness, titles drawn from all manner of acts and functions, have clothed it in human (fiery or amber) shapes or forms." From here come many anthropomorphic descriptions of God in the Bible, in which God appears as having eyes, ears, hair, a face, arms, a back, wings, feathers and legs, as having formed a crown, a throne, a mixing bowl, a cup, and other "such mystical conceptions."[65]

Accounting for the teaching on God's namelessness and naming, Dionysius the Areopagite divides the divine names into two categories: undifferenced and differentiating. "Undifferenced" names relate to all three Persons of the Holy Trinity, among which are the names "Super-Excellent," "Super-Divine," "Super-Essential," "Super-Vital," and "Supra-Sapient," expressing the superiority of the Trinity over all created beings; all negative names that indicate the excesses of the Trinity before all creation; all those names that have a "casual sense," like "Good," "Fair," "Existent," "Lifegiving," "Wise," and all other cataphatic names for God that are taken from his actions. Concerning the "differentiating" names are those that separate one Person of the Trinity from the other: above all, this concerns the names "Father," "Son," and "Holy Spirit," as well as the name "Jesus" and all other names attributed to the Son of God.[66]

The source of the divine names, according to Dionysius the Areopagite, is found in the "beauty of the processions [*proodoi*, πρόοδοι] of the supreme Godhead from without."[67] These "processions" (the term can also be translated as "emanations" or "appearances") are understood as the manifestations of God outside his own essence. Here the Areopagite follows the characteristic (in Eastern Christian tradition) difference between, on the one hand, the essence of God, and on the other, the activities or actions manifested by God *ad extra* (from without). This difference, already encountered in the Cappadocian Fathers, acquired a final dogmatic expression in the works of St Gregory Palamas, which will be discussed below.

[65]Ibid. 1.8.
[66]Ibid. 2.1–3.
[67]Ibid. 2.10.

Thus the names of God are the divine names of "processions," but not the names of God's essence.[68]

The main part of Dionysius the Areopagite's treatise presents itself as a theological interpretation on the names of God. God is called Good because he is "Super-Excellent Goodness," extending goodness to all existing beings, from him everything arises and is, he attracts everything to himself. This Good One is the intellectual Light, which gathers into itself and embraces all that sees, moves, glorifies, warms, who purifies the intellectual eyes of man from the darkness of ignorance, enlivens them and opens them. The Good One is called Wonderful and Fair, because from him beauty communes with all existing things, because he is the reason for good works and grace. In him all that is good preexists in its Principle. He is Love, which "allowed [it] not to remain unfruitful [it]self, but moved [it] to exert the abundance of [its] powers in the production of the universe."[69]

In the interpretation of names, "Existing One," occupies a central position in the Old Testament. The Areopagite proceeds from the meaning that this name has in the Greek version, that is, he is not interpreting the Hebrew Yahweh, but the Greek *ho ōn* (ὁ ὤν). All of his interpretation revolved around the understanding of the "essence" (*ousia*, οὐσία), which is regarded as a philosophical category that is applied to God only insofar as God's essence appears from without. According to the Areopagite, God is called "Existing One" because, being greater than every existing thing, he is the source of all essence, of all that exists:

> The Existent God is, by the nature of his power, super-essentially above all existence; he is the substantial Cause and Creator of Being, Existence, Substance and Nature, the Beginning and the Measuring Principle of the ages; the Reality underlying time and the Eternity underlying existences; the time in which created things pass, the Existence of those that have any kind of existence, the Life-Process of those which in any way pass through that process. From Him-that-is come eternity, essence, being, time, life-process; and that which passes through such process, the things which inhere in existent things and those which under any power whatever possess an independent subsistence. For God is not existent in any ordinary

<hr/>

[68]Ibid. 2.11.
[69]Ibid. 4.1–10.

sense, but in a simple and undefinable manner embracing and anticipating all existence in himself. Hence he is called "King of the ages," because in him and around him all being is and subsists, and he neither was, nor will be, nor hath entered the life-process, nor is doing so, nor ever will, or rather he doth not even exist, but is the essence of existence in things that exist; and not only the things that exist but also their very existence comes from him that is before the ages. For he himself is the Eternity of the ages and subsists before the ages.[70]

The Areopagite's logical apophasis brings one to the paradoxical claim that God "neither was, nor will be." Such a claim would be unthinkable in the language of the Bible (indeed, it would be taken for blasphemy), inasmuch as the biblical understanding of relationship between the word-name and the reality for which it stands would eliminate the possibility of a similar type of claim. In the language of speculative philosophy that the Areopagite uses, this claim, on the contrary, looks like it is the entirely persuasive end of a logical step of the rejection of all that is not God. If God is not "being" and "essence" in the human understanding of these terms, which only fit the descriptions of reality in the created world, but not the descriptions of divine being, consequently, the verbs "to be" and "to exist" that come from them also do not fit descriptions of God's being and existence, who possesses "in a transcendent manner pre-existence and pre-eminence."[71] As the terms "being" and "non-existence" are equally far from God, to say that "God is" is just the same as saying "God is not."

Dionysius the Areopagite follows the same path as Gregory of Nyssa in the latter's polemic *Against Eunomius*, though he reaches the same limit in striving to prove the relative character of human speech. In this work he widely uses Greek speculative philosophy as a tool. Moreover, it would have been a big mistake to see in the Areopagite's treatise *On the Divine Names* an attempt to contradict rational Greek philosophy with the mysticism of the biblical proclamation. The cultural and linguistic context of Dionysius, just like the context of the other Greek Fathers, sharply contrasts from the biblical, though his theological vision is deeply mystical: this is by no means stark philosophic rationalism, put into service for Christianity. On the contrary, in

[70]Ibid. 5.1–5.
[71]Ibid. 5.5.

Dionysius, the described process of ascent to God, speculative thought, gradually gives way to mystical contemplation.[72]

The treatise *On the Divine Names* ends with a solemn claim of the complete inadequacy of the names of God, as far as the recognized ones are expressed:

> When we speak of the all-transcendent Godhead as an Unity and a Trinity, it is not an Unity or a Trinity such as can be known by us or any other creature, though to express the truth of its utter self-union and its divine fecundity we apply the titles of "Trinity" and "Unity" to that which is beyond all titles, expressing under the form of Being that which is beyond being. But no Unity or Trinity or number or oneness or fecundity or any other thing that either is a creature or can be known to any creature, is able to utter the mystery, beyond all mind and reason, of that transcendent Godhead which super-essentially surpasses all things. It has no name, nor can it be grasped by reason. . . . These intelligible names we have collected and endeavored to expound, though falling short not only of the actual meaning . . . nor yet merely of such utterance as angels would have given concerning them . . . nor yet do we merely fall behind the teaching of the sacred writers thereon or of the ascetics.[73]

Dionysius the Areopagite takes the traditional Eastern Christian antinomy of the naming and namelessness of God to its logical conclusion. Besides, though the theme of God's names is sufficiently and specifically developed by preceding authors, particularly by the Cappadocian Fathers, no one before Dionysius was able so clearly to show its significance for the mystical life of the Christian. One may note that after Dionyius, not one of the eastern fathers said anything new in principle on the given subject, and that his treatise has been in circulation for many centuries in the East, and, for that matter, his exposition is considered normative in the West as well.

The teaching on the names of God by the great Cappadocian Fathers and Dionysius the Areopagite was noticed by St Isaac the Syrian. In his words, all that is known to us about God is based on what God himself revealed to us through his divine names, written in Holy Scripture:

---

[72]Cf.: Lossky, *Dogmatic Theology*, 34.
[73]Dionysius 13.3–4.

That thing that can know about God by means of intellectual thought—and precisely, those things that by love he perceived in himself for the sake of our own advantage—consists in the image of sensory indications, for by means of them the Holy Scripture shows our senses what may be understood relating to the world beyond the senses, although these indications, as a matter of fact, appertain to him. The question is, in particular, about what God said to Moses: "I appeared to Abraham, Isaac, and Jacob as God Almighty [and

The Image Not Made by Hands. Novgorod. 12th c.

He Who Is], but by my name 'The Lord' I did not make myself known to them" [Ex 6.3]. The difference between "Almighty" and "He Who Is" is concluded in the course of study: it is the difference between what our knowledge may claim, and the actual reality of this knowledge.[74]

In this difficult-to-understand text, Isaac speaks of the different levels of divine names: there are some names, like "Almighty," which indicate the activity of God in relation to the created world, and then there are names such as "He Who Is," which speak to the very reality of divine being, of God in and of himself. However, these and other names are the essence of only certain mystical indications of reality, exceeding every human name and word. For this reason, as Isaac emphasizes, "there was a time when God did not have names, and there will be a time when he will not have any sort of name."[75] All the names by which we know God are accepted by him in his love for us, so that we might come to know God through them and commune with him. God is in and of himself "far above . . . every name that is named, not only in this world but also in the world to come" (Eph 1.21).

The theme of God's namelessness and the names of God has firmly entered into Christian poetry. One of Gregory the Theologian's poems relates to God as to the bearer of all names, and at the same time to him who is above every name, to him whom the whole world glorifies in speech and in silence:

---

[74]Isaac the Syrian *Chapters on Knowledge* 4.3.
[75]Ibid. 3.1.

O you who are on every side! For what else can be sung of you?

How can a word proclaim you? For you are inexpressible by any
    word!

How can the mind gaze at you? For you are incomprehensible for
    any mind!

You are the one who is ineffable, for you bore all by a word.

You are the one who is unknowable, for you brought forth all
    knowledge.

Every speaking and unspeaking thing proclaims you.

Every wise and dumb thing honors you.

Every wish, every care is directed at you!

Everything prays to you.

Everything, understanding your command, sends up unceasing
    hymns to you.

All exist through you the first being. The whole totality strives to be
    with you.

You formed all, you who are One, and All, and No-one,

And yet not one, not all. O All-Named one!

How can I call you, the One who is not named? Will some
    heavenly mind pierce through the veiled clouds?

Be merciful O you who are on every side!

For what else can be sung of you?[76]

This inspirational hymn of Gregory clearly has something to do with
Dionysius the Areopagite when he said that "theologians" proclaim God "as
nameless and the bearer of every name."[77] As one may recall, in the Byzantine tradition, the one they called "theologian" above all was Gregory, whose
works were perceived as the standard of theological precision.

Another author that has received the title "theologian," Symeon the New
Theologian, has also proclaimed the Divine Goodness, the One in the three
Persons, as possessing many names:

For this reason we do not call him by one name only but several.

He is light and peace and joy,

life, food and drink, clothing, a robe, a tent, and a divine dwelling.

[76]*Dogmatic Verses* 29.
[77]*On Divine Names* 1.6.

He is the East, the resurrection, repose, and a bath,
fire, water, river, source of life and a flowing stream.
Bread and wine, the new delight of believers,
the banquet, the pleasure which we enjoy in a mystical way,
sun, indeed, without any setting, star always shining,
lamp that burns inside the dwelling of the soul.[78]

THE QUALITIES OF GOD. GOD AND EVIL. DIVINE PROVIDENCE

The theme of God's names is tightly linked to the patristic understanding of the qualities of God. It is necessary to note that eastern patristics did not form a harmonious teaching on the properties or qualities of God, similar to the Latin scholastic teaching of the divine attributes. In a few transformative ways the Latin teaching of God's attributes entered into later (eighteenth and nineteenth centuries) Orthodox dogmatic textbooks, such as *Dogmatic Theology* by Metropolitan Macarius (Bulgakov), where the qualities of God are divided into general qualities of God's essence (incomprehensibility, one in essence and three in Persons), private qualities of God's essence (originality, independence, immeasurability, omnipresence, eternality, unalterability, all-powerful), qualities of God's mind (all-seeing, highest wisdom), and qualities of God's will (freedom, holiness, goodness, righteousness). However, such a division was alien in eastern patristics. The Fathers of the Eastern Church preferred to talk about the names or energies of God, and not about his properties or qualities, for they did not dare conceive of God as a sum of attributes, and they generally shied far away from the theological rationalism so characteristic of scholasticism.

Nevertheless, quite conditionally, some sayings of the Eastern Fathers about God could be grouped in the general theme of "qualities of God." One can attribute to this theme, in particular, the given higher notions of the Fathers on the incomprehensibility and unity of divinity, on the namelessness of God and the divine names, on the simplicity of the divine nature. Here one may also include the teaching of the Fathers concerning the spiritual nature of God, on God's eternity without beginning and without end, on God's goodness, on his all-powerful and all-seeing nature, and on God's love.

[78] *Hymn* 45 233–234.

One of the chapters in *An Exact Exposition of the Orthodox Faith* by John of Damascus is called "On the Properties of the Divine Nature." Here the Damascene defines God as the Essence "uncreated, without beginning, immortal, infinite, eternal, immaterial, good, creative, just, enlightening, immutable, passionless, uncircumscribed, immeasurable, unlimited, undefined, unseen, unthinkable, wanting in nothing, being his own rule and authority, all-ruling, life-giving, omnipotent, of infinite power, sanctifying and moving, [containing] and maintaining [all] and making provision for all."[79]

God is called uncreated in the patristic tradition because he was formed by no one; he does not have an outward cause for his being, he himself being the Creator and Fashioner of all existence. God is without beginning insofar as he does not have a beginning in time. However, the term "beginning" can be understood in the sense of "cause," as well as in the sense of a chronological beginning. If the term is understood in the first sense, then the question regards only the Father as without beginning, but if in the second sense, then it concerns all three Persons of the Holy Trinity. Gregory the Theologian says: "The Father is a father and without origin, for he is not from anyone. The Son is a son and not without origin, for he is from the Father. But if you take it to mean an origin in time, he is also without origin; for he is Creator of time, not subject to time."[80]

Being outside of time, God is immortal and eternal, inasmuch as he does not have a beginning or end within time. He is changeless, inasmuch as change is linked with existence in time. God is his own authority and rule in that he does not have an outside impetus, an outer motive to call him into action. God abides outside of space because he is described as uncircumscribed, immeasurable, and unlimited. Being perfect, God is in no way insufficient or in need. God is all-powerful; for him nothing is impossible. God possesses omniscience; nothing can be hidden from him. These and other divine properties are known through God's actions in relationship with man, but it is impossible to reduce God to any one of these properties or even to their totality.

According to Christian dogma, God is a bodiless Essence: "God is spirit" (Jn 4.24; 2 Cor 3.17). The term "spirit" (Gr. *pneuma*, πνεῦμα) is applied to God in a general sense in patristic theology, when the question is on the spiritual, immaterial nature of God, as well as on the Holy Spirit. The immateriality

---

[79]1.14.
[80]*Oration* 39.12 (Crestwood, N.Y.: 2008) 88.

and incorporeality of God separates him from man, clothed in the body. As Symeon the New Theologian writes:

> For God is uncreated; we all are creatures.
> He is incorruptible, we are corruptible and dust.
> He is spirit and above every spirit
> as the Creator of spirits and their Master.
> We are flesh made from dust, earthly substance.[81]

According to the patristic teaching, God is the Essence that is good, just, and omnipotent, that is, possessing exclusively creating power. In *A Conversation on God Not Being Capable of Evil*, Basil the Great says that denying God's goodness is tantamount to denying God's existence. But if God is the sole creator only of good things, then from whence comes evil? God is not the creator of evil things, answers Basil, but the potential for evil is rooted in the free will of rational nature. God created the good angels, but some of them, thanks to their directing their own wills toward God's, preserved goodness, while others inclined to sin and turned themselves into demons. In the same way man is the cause of both good and evil when, voluntarily, under his own will, he commits sins. Similar to sickness, Basil says, sins are not primordially inherent in man's nature, but appeared as a consequence of the Fall: "God formed the body, but not illness. In the same way, God created the soul, but not sin." What then of natural disasters, of the idea that they are sent by God for punishment and correction; they "stop the increase of sin" and "stop the handiwork of true evil."[82]

Christian tradition always rejected the teaching of a duality of evil and goodness, of the presence in the world of two equal origins—one divine and the other demonic. Athanasius of Alexandria summarized these teachings in the following words: "Now certain of the Greeks, having erred from the right way, and not having known Christ, have ascribed to evil a substantive and independent existence. In this they make a double mistake: either in denying the Creator to be maker of all things, if evil had an independent subsistence and being of its own; or again, if they mean that he is maker of all things, they will of necessity admit him to be maker of evil also."[83]

---

[81] *Hymn* 42, 219.
[82] 2–5.
[83] *Oration Against the Gentiles* 6.

The Gnostic and Manichean conceptions of evil as coeternal and equal to God from the beginning, as creator of everything material and corporeal, finding itself in constant battle with God, were resolutely refuted by the Church from the second to fourth centuries. Gregory the Theologian is in complete accordance with Church tradition when he says:

> And you, evil Manichean shade, were not primordially
> Equal in power to the most exalted Light. If you were God,
> Then you would not be shadow. For evil could not place itself
>   in equality with God.
> If you were darkness, you would not know God. You could not
>   adhere to him in a single mind (with evil);
> If the two would enter into battle, he who is stronger would win;
>   but if they were equal in strength,
> Who would be the third to bring them to unity in his wisdom
>   and halt the fight?[84]

St Isidore of Seville banishes a demon. Cathedral of San-Marco. Venice. 14th c.

According to Eastern Christian tradition, evil is not an essence, but is merely the absence of good, just as darkness is the absence of light. Evil is not hypostatic, it is "nothing."[85] A section of the Areopagite's treatise *On the Divine Names* is dedicated to the question of the origin of evil. The treatise's author claims that evil does not possess actual being in and of itself: "Unto evil we can attribute but an accidental kind of existence. It exists for the sake of something else, and is not self-originating."[86] There is an absolute Good One, who is God, the source of every good thing. But there is not absolute evil; there is no evil that has completely departed from the Good One. Evil is "imperfect goodness,"[87] it is a "waning" that fights with the Good One.[88] Evil is

---

[84]*Dogmatic Verses* 4.
[85]Cf.: Origen *Interpretation on John* 2.3; Athanasius of Alexandria *Oration Against the Gentiles* 6; Gregory of Nyssa *On the Life of Moses*; *Great Supplicatory Oration* 5.
[86]4.32.
[87]Ibid. 4.20.
[88]Ibid. 4.29.

Synaxis of the bodiless Heavenly Hosts. The laying low of Lucifer.
Monastery of Dionysiou. Athens. Beginning of the 17th c.

is not in God, nor is it in any kind of existing thing: not in angels, not in demons, not in souls, not in bodies, not in dumb beasts, not in matter.[89] The demons come from the good angels, but they "changed their nature,"[90] and for this reason evil is in them.

According to the Areopagite's teaching, evil itself lacks creative capabilities. It has this capability only insofar as it is connected with the Good One:

> Evil (being evil) causes no existence or birth, but only debases and corrupts, so far as its power extends, the substance of things that have being.

[89]Ibid. 4.22–28.
[90]Ibid. 4.23.

And if anyone says that it is productive, and that by the destruction of one thing it gives birth to somewhat else, the true answer is that it does not so being destructive. Being destructive and evil it only destroys and debases; but it takes upon it the form of birth and essence through the action of the Good. Thus evil will be found to be a destructive force in itself, but a productive force through the action of the Good. Being evil it neither has being nor confers it; through the action of the Good, it has being (yea, and a good being) and confers being on good things.[91]

Evil is never a result of God's actions, but can result from his "permission." In the words of John of Damascus, "it is the custom in the Holy Scripture to speak of God's permission as his energy,"[92] from which one can get the impression that God initiates evil. Thus, for example, it is said in the Bible that God hardened the heart of Pharaoh (Ex 4.21; 7.3; 14.4); he sent an evil spirit into Saul (1 Sam 16.14; 19.9); he gave the people "commandments that were not good" (Ezek 20.25); he "gave them up to degrading passions" and "a debased mind" (cf. Rom 1.24–32), he "has closed them all up in unbelief" (Rom 11.32), and "gave them a spirit of slumber, eyes that they should not see, and ears that they should not hear" (Rom 11.8). All similar places in Holy Scripture "must be understood not as though God himself were causing them, but as though God were permitting them." The word "evil" has a double meaning: "sometimes it means what is evil by nature, and this is the opposite of virtue and the will of God: and sometimes it means that which is evil and oppressive to our senses, that is to say, afflictions and calamities. Now these are seemingly evil because they are painful, but in reality are good. For to those who understand they became ambassadors of conversion and salvation. The Scripture says that of these God is the author."[93]

The world is guided by Divine Providence, to whose energy is subject not only the good taking place in the world, but evil as well. Divine Providence (God's care, or attention) "is the will of God through which all existing things receive their fitting issue." But that which pertains to Providence is "partly according to the good will and partly according to permission," or tolerance, that is, related to the will of God, while God merely allows the other. For example, God may allow a righteous person to fall into unhappiness for

[91]Ibid. 4.20.
[92]An Exact Exposition . . . 4.19.
[93]Ibid.

educational purposes. God allows the committing of sins, but the choice of whether it be done resides entirely in the power of man, and responsibility for sin lies completely in man, not in God.[94]

John of Damascus makes a distinction between the foreknowledge of God and predestination. God knows everything beforehand; nothing is unknown to him. But the fact that God knows the sins committed by people in advance does not mean that people were "predestined" to fulfill these acts:

> God knows all things beforehand, yet he does not predetermine all things. For he knows beforehand those things that are in our power, but he does not predetermine them. For it is not his will that there should be wickedness nor does he choose to compel virtue. So that predetermination is the work of the divine command based on foreknowledge. But on the other hand, God predetermines those things which are not within our power in accordance with his prescience. For already God in his prescience has prejudged all things in accordance with his goodness and justice. . . . Virtue is a gift from God implanted in our nature. . . . But we have it in our power either to abide in virtue and follow God, who calls us into ways of virtue, or to stray from paths of virtue, which is to dwell in wickedness, and to follow the devil who summons but cannot compel us. For wickedness is nothing else than the withdrawal of goodness, just as darkness is nothing else than the withdrawal of light.[95]

The patristic tradition refutes the notion that man is predestined ahead of time to this or that fate, to commit this or that act. The teaching of fate, inherited from Greek mythology, is definitively rejected by the Fathers of the Church.[96] There are no people wittingly predestined to destruction; all people are predestined to salvation. In the words of the Damascene, God wishes in advance for all to be saved and to be made heirs to his Kingdom: he created people not in order to punish them, but so that they might become partakers of his goodness. If then he punishes them, his just judgment demands it.[97] But sin serves as the reason for punishment, committed by man according to man's own will, and not by predestination.

[94]Ibid. 2.29.
[95]Ibid. 2.30.
[96]Cf.: For example, Gregory of Nyssa's treatise *Against the Teaching of Fate.*
[97]Cf.: *An Exact Exposition . . .* 2.30.

THE LOVE OF GOD

Of all the names of God, the one that held special meaning in eastern patristics was the name "Love": Gregory the Theologian considers this name "more
fitting for God than any other name."[98] Many Church Fathers wrote on God
as Love, including the Cappadocian Fathers, Maximus the Confessor, John
of the Ladder, and Symeon the New Theologian.

St Isaac the Syrian takes an exceptional interest in the teaching of God as
Love. In his understanding, God is above all measureless and ineffable Love,
which is beyond the limits of man's understanding and higher than every
spoken description. This Love, according to Isaac, can be recognized through
the examination of God's actions in relation to the created world and man:
"Among his actions there is not a one that is not filled with mercy, love, and
compassion: this makes up the beginning and end of his relationship with
us."[99] The divine love was the chief reason for God's forming the world and
his coming in the flesh; it is the chief mover of the force of created being:
"The only reason for the creation of the world and the coming of Christ into
it was to enter into the abundant love of God, which brought both into being.
The strength of God's love in relation to creation is reflected in Christ's coming into the world."[100] In forming the world, the love of God manifests itself
in all its fullness:

> To what can this Being be likened, which is invisible, without beginning
> in its nature, which is one in itself, which in its essence is beyond the
> knowledge, intellect, and senses of creation, which is outside time and
> age, which is the Creator of all this. . . . Let us think now, how rich in its
> abundance is the ocean of God's creation and how many works belong
> to God and how in his compassion he bears all, he calls on all, he both
> cares for [all] and rules all; and how he with his immeasurable love came
> to the created world and origin of creation; and how God is compassion-
> ate and how patient his Spirit, and how he loves this creation, and how
> he bears it, and how he is lenient toward its vanities, sins, and other evil
> works, its unbelievably blasphemous demons, and evil people.[101]

[98]*Oration* 22.4.
[99]*On the Divine Mysteries: Conversation* 39.22.
[100]*Chapters on Knowledge* 4.79–80.
[101]*On the Divine Mysteries: Conversation* 10.18–19.

God's love is the continuous and never-ending revelation of the Divinity in his creative energies. Love lies at the foundation of the world, it guides the world, and it even brings the world to its glorious end, when it will be totally "swallowed up" by divinity:

> O, what deep riches, what a great design and what lofty wisdom God has! O, what compassionate mercy and rich goodness the Creator has! He created this world and brought it into being with such thought and such love! . . . He brought the world into being through love; he brings his timely form of essence to it through love; he brings his marvelous change to it through love, and the world will be swallowed up in this great mystery of him who created it all; the outcome of the whole history of existing creation is love.[102]

God is not only the Demiurge and First-Mover in relation to the universe; he is "the true Father of spoken essence, which he bore himself through his charge so that they might become heirs of his glory in the coming age, so that his riches might be to them an unending joy."[103] God, according to Isaac, is that only "true Father, who in his immeasurably great love surpasses all other fatherly love."[104] For this reason his relation to the created world is characterized by continual providential care for all who abide in him: for angels and demons, for man and animals. Divine Providence is for all and is extended to all.[105] Not one being is excluded from the realm of the all-loving Divine Providence, but the love of the Creator is devoted to each one in equal measure: "How can the Creator not know one of his creation, which would sooner or later, albeit in his eternal consciousness, be brought into being by him. . . . Thus not one is ahead or behind in his love for them: he does not have "more" or "less" in general. On the contrary, as his knowledge is equal and continual, so is his love equal and continual."[106]

All living essences were located in God's mind before their creation. Even before they were brought into being, every one of them received a place in the hierarchical order of the universe. This place is not taken away even in the case of a falling away from God:

[102]Ibid. 38.1–2.
[103]*Chapters on Knowledge* 1.1.
[104]*Oration* 25.
[105]*Oration* 67.
[106]*On the Divine Mysteries: Conversation* 38.3.

Every thing has its very own place of love in his consciousness connected to the image that he saw of them before, with which he formed them and all the rest of creation, before which he planned the creation of the world. He, whose love is without beginning, possessed primordially in the beginning the incentive for creating the world. He has one order of perfect, impartial love for all of them, and he has one and the same Providence for those who fell and those who did not fall.[107]

Nothing coming from creation can influence the nature of the Creator, who is lofty, majestic, glorious, and filled with love.[108] The providential care of God and his love are extended to the angels, who were the first product of God's creative act, including those who fell from God and became demons. According to Isaac, the Creator's love is not lessened towards the fallen angels after their fall, and is no less than the fullness of the love that he has for the other angels.[109] To say that God's love lessens or disappears as a result of the fall of created nature means to reduce the nature of the Creator to powerlessness and changeability.[110] For:

We know, and every person is persuaded, that the Creator is not changeable, nor does he have some kind of earlier or later purpose, nor does he have hate or indignation in his nature, nor more or less love for one thing or another, nor is anything first or last in his knowledge. For if every person believes that creation came into being through his goodness and his love, then they[111] never lessened or changed within the Creator's nature as a result of the disorderly progression of creation.[112]

God loves the righteous and the sinners equally, not differentiating between them: "He has one love towards us and the holy angels. He loves the sinners as he loves the righteous. The incarnation is the proof of this."[113] Before creating man, God already knew about his sinful life—and nevertheless he formed him.[114] God knew all people before they became righteous or

[107]Ibid. 40.3.
[108]Ibid. 10.23.
[109]Ibid. 40.2.
[110]Ibid. 38.4.
[111]Note: his goodness and love.
[112]Isaac the Syrian *On the Divine Mysteries: Conversation* 38.5.
[113]*Chapters on Knowledge* 4.87.
[114]*On the Divine Mysteries: Conversation* 5.11.

sinners, and his love was not changed by their being subject to change.[115] Even many reprehensible acts of man are accepted by God in his mercy, "and the perpetrators are forgiven, without any judgment, by God, who knows all, to whom all is known beforehand, how it happens, and who knew the needs of our nature before he created us."[116]

When God punishes man, he does it out of love and for the sake of salvation, not for the sake of retribution. God respects man's free will and does not want to do anything contrary to it:

> God teaches with love; he does not take revenge—may this never be so!— but, on the contrary, he wants to raise his image in man. He is not enraged in those cases where correction is not possible, for God does not seek to take vengeance on himself! Here is the goal of love: the punishment of love is for correction, not for the purposes of retribution. . . . He who prefers to think of God as vengeful, and who supposes that in this he bears witness to the fairness of God, charges God with insufficient goodness. But let it not be that there might be in this Fountain of love and this Ocean, filled with goodness, some kind of image of vengeance![117]

The image of God's judgment is hidden in the perception of Isaac the Syrian by the image of the God of Love and Mercy. Mercy, considers Isaac, is incompatible with just judgment:

> Mercy is opposed to just judgment. Just judgment is the leveling of exact measures, because to each is given what is deserved . . . but mercy is pity, arousing blessings and giving in to all with compassion: whoever deserves evil, it is not rendered to him, and whoever deserves blessings, they are doubly given. And if it is obvious that mercy belongs to the realm of righteousness, then fairness belongs to the realm of evil. As hay and fire cannot be found in the same place, so too can mercy and fairness not coexist in one spirit.[118]

For this reason one should not speak of God's fairness, but one may speak only of mercy, surpassing all fairness:

[115]Ibid. 38.3.
[116]Ibid. 14.5.
[117]*Oration* 45 (according to the Syrian edition).
[118]Ibid. 85.

As a grain of sand does not balance out a large quantity of gold, so do the demands of God's just judgment not maintain the balances in comparison with God's love. Like a handful of sand thrown into a great sea is the sin of all flesh in comparison with Providence and the mercy of God. And as a spring abundant in water is not blocked by a fistful of dust, so is the mercy of the Creator not conquered by the vices of creation.[119]

Rejecting, with such resolve, the idea of a fair rendering of payment, Isaac teaches that the Old Testament concept of God as the chastiser of sinners, punishing children for the iniquity of parents, "to the third and fourth generation" (Ex 20.5; Num 14.18), does not coincide with the revelation we receive through Christ in the New Testament. In Isaac's mind, if God revealed himself in the Old Testament as Judge and Lord, then it was done for pedagogical purposes. As a matter of fact, God always wanted to be the Father to his people. God's fatherhood found its utmost expression in the divine incarnation:

After the Fall, God appeared to his people as the Judge, but in the later revelations, as Lord, as in the cases of Noah, Abraham, and those who came after him. . . . From the coming of Christ onwards, revelations began showing the levels of fatherhood, that he indeed is the Father, and does not want to act toward us as a lord or a judge.[120]

Though David calls God just and fair in the Psalms (Ps 119.137), the Son of God showed that he is more good and blessed, emphasizes Isaac. Christ confirms God's "injustice" and his goodness with the parables of the Vinedressers and the Prodigal Son (Mt 20.13–15; Lk 15.20–22), but even greater is his redemptive feat, completed for the salvation of sinners. "Where is this righteous judgment of God? In that we are sinners, yet Christ died for us?"[121] asks Isaac. In another place he says decisively: "Nowhere in Christ's teaching does he recall anything regarding a just judgment."[122]

In Isaac's opinion, it does not serve to understand literally those Old Testament texts that speak of God's fury, wrath, hate, or jealousy. All of those are feeble names, not corresponding to the greatness and goodness of the Creator: "The names and labels of passions, such as anger, wrath, and judgment, do not

---

[119]Ibid.
[120]*Chapters on Knowledge* 1.17.
[121]*Oration* 90.
[122]Ibid. 50 (according to the Syrian edition).

correspond and are highly inadequate when used in reference to God."[123] If any similar anthropomorphic terms are found in Scripture, they are used in a transferrable sense, for God never does anything out of anger, hate, or jealousy: all of this is alien to God's nature. Just as the New Testament revelation brought us closer to a correct understanding of God, we should read between the lines of the Old Testament and see the hidden and guiding Divine Providence, and not perceive everything literally as written.[124] "Fear God out of love, not because he is considered cruel,"[125] says Isaac.

In God there is no hate, wrath, or jealousy in relation to this one or that one, there is only all-encompassing love, not distinguishing between righteous and sinners, between a friend of the truth and an enemy of the truth, between angels or demons. Every created being is precious to God, for he cares for each one in his consciousness, and all resides in him, the loving Father. If we leave God, he will not leave us: "If we are faithless, he remains faithful—for he cannot deny himself" (2 Tim 2.13). So that no one in mankind and nothing from creation would remove itself far away from God, God remains faithful in his love, which one cannot and does not want to reject.

THE ESSENCE AND ENERGIES OF GOD

In the theological tradition of the Orthodox Church special attention is given to the teaching on the essence and energies of God, enumerated by Gregory Palamas in the dispute against Akyndinos and Varlaam and supported by the Constantinopolitan councils in the middle of the fourteenth century. This teaching set the goal of giving a theological basis to the Christian understanding of God as simultaneously incomprehensible and comprehensible, transcendent and immanent, nameless and named, ineffable and utterable, communicable and incommunicable. We trace the given paradox beyond the example of Dionysius the Areopagite's teaching of God as nameless while possessing every name. The Christian teaching on divine visions of God can serve as another example of such a paradox, in that God is invisible in his essence and at the same time reveals himself to those deemed worthy: "No one shall see [God] and live" (Ex 33.20), and at the same time individual

---

[123] *Chapters on Knowledge* 4.85.
[124] *On the Divine Mysteries: Conversation* 39.19.
[125] *Oration* 90.

chosen ones of God see him "face to face" (Gen 32.30; Ex 33.11; Deut. 34.10), they see God "as he is" (1 Jn 3.2). The teaching on the knowledge of God can serve as yet another example: that God is incomprehensible is the only thing about him that is comprehensible.[126]

One of the ways to explain the given paradox in the Eastern Christian tradition is to employ the notion of the "activities," or energies (Gr. *energiai*, ἐνέργιαι) of God, which differ from the essence of God. If God's essence is invisible, the energies can be seen; if the essence is nameless, the energies can be named; if God's essence is incomprehensible, then the energies can be intellectually comprehended. In the words of St Basil the Great, "we know our God by his energies, but we do not pretend that we can draw near to his essence; for his energies descend to us, but his essence remains inaccessible."[127] In the teaching on the divine names, as one may recall, the understanding of the energies-activities had a key significance: according to Gregory of Nyssa, God "receives a name from an action, which . . . revolves around our life."[128] Dionysius the Areopagite spoke out against such an idea, naming the activities of God *ad extra* (from without) "emanations," "appearances" (*proodoi*, πρόοδοι): the names of God do not describe the divine essence, but "emanations" of God from without.[129]

St Gregory Palamas' contribution is concluded by his being able to explain, theologically, the difference between God's essence and his energies, to reveal the correlation between the essence and energies, to show what is different and what is shared between them, and to describe the nature of the divine energies. Above all he showed that the divine energies are a connecting link between God and the created world:

> If there are those who commune with God, but also a supersubstantial nature of God that is not communicable, that means there is something between the incommunicable nature and the communicants, through which they commune with God. You took away that between the incommunicable and the communicants—O, what injury!—and you severed us from God, having thrown away the key link and having placed a great and impassable wasteland between the Foundation and the origin and the

[126]Cf.: Gregory the Theologian *Oration* 38.7.
[127]*Epistle* 234.
[128]*Against Eunomius* 12.
[129]Cf.: *On the Divine Names* 2.11

structure of those who are rising. . . . Thus, there is something between that which has risen and the incommunicable parts of the Supersubstance, and not only one, but many. . . . But it . . . does not exist in and of itself: these are the forces of the Supersubstance, one and united in the form of that which all the countless multitude of communicants has anticipated, in whom it is multiplied by emanations and, by all that is communicable, inescapably holds itself incommunicable and alone. . . . It came to be incommunicable, and God himself is communicable, but incommunicable as the Supersubstance, communicable as having creative power and an all-transfiguring and all-perfecting energy.[130]

At the same time, Palamas constantly stresses that the presence of energies in God is in no way contingent upon the existence of the created world—they are coeternal with God's essence:

Foreknowledge, will, Providence, self-reflection, and all other similar acts of God are without beginning and before time; but if contemplation, Providence, and foreknowledge, then predestination and will are God's acts without beginning, and this means this is a virtue, because virtue and existence are in all of that which is enumerated, because existence precedes not only essence, but also all that exists, being primary. Then, are not will and predestination truly virtues? It is known perfectly well in divinity, says Maximus, that "existence, and life, and holiness, and virtue are the acts of God, not made within time"[131]; and so that no one would think that they exist in the age, though they are not within time,[132] he continues: "There was never a time when there was not virtue, goodness, holiness, and immortality."[133] They allow self-communing, but they are already as acts of the essence without beginning to those communicants, and are completed within the time of the act.[134]

The divine energies, besides, are not emanations of the divinity in the Plotinian sense: they are not partial manifestations of God, but God himself in

---

[130]*Triads 3* 2.24–25.
[131]Maximus the Confessor *Chapters on Theology . . .* 1.48.
[132]Here Gregory Palamas voices the traditional (for Eastern Christian patristics) difference between age and time: the term age (Gr. *aiōn*, αἰών) in patristic language always indicates a certain kind (form, level) of created being, but it is not at all necessary for a certain period.
[133]Maximus the Confessor *Chapters on Theology . . .* 1.50.
[134]Gregory Palamas *Triads 3* 2.7.

his activity and revelation to the world. Each energy of God, being inseparable from God's essence, contains God himself:

> The supersubstantial essence of God is not uncreated goodness, not eter-
> nal glory, and not life and other similar things, for God is the Cause from
> which they come. We name him Life, Good, and similar things only by
> the revealed energies and powers of his higher being. . . . Therefore God
> is totally present in each God-befitting energy, in each one of them by
> which we name him.[135]

> That which is or can be understood, or can become communicable, is not
> a part of God . . . but by some form he is all and is manifest or not [man-
> ifest], and is comprehended or not comprehended, and is communicable
> and remains non-communicable.[136]

According to Palamas, "every (divine) power or every energy is God
himself."[137] In this sense the divine energy is the link between God and the
created world, but it is not a "mediator" between the created and the uncreated, between the human and the divine: it is not some kind of intermediate nature, differing from the divine and human.[138] All of God's energies
are uncreated and divine, they are all God himself, all divine in his outward
manifestation: "As if they were not named—by grace, by the divine life, by
light, by illumination—energies, or divine activities, belonging to the existing God himself; they present his existence for us. This means that it is not
only just, but necessary, to use in reference to him his personal descriptions
of divinity: they are God (*Theos*, Θεός) in the Divinity (*Theotēs*,
Θεότης)."[139]

The last two terms used by Palamas are really synonyms: they both signify the divine energy. As Protopresbyter John Meyendorff notes, there is a
consensus among the eastern fathers that asserts that the term "God" signifies etymologically the divine energy, and not the essence.[140] This same word
is related to the term "Divinity," the use of which is applied to God's energy

---

[135] Ibid.
[136] *On the Worship of Communion.*
[137] *Epistle to John Gavras.*
[138] *Against Akyndinos* 4.3.
[139] John Meyendorff, *The Life and Works of St Gregory Palamas* (St Petersburg: 1997), 295.
[140] Ibid.

and was sanctioned by the Council of Constantinople in the year 1341, in the fifth anathema against Varlaam, which proclaims:

> Philosophizing and saying that the divine name, related only to the divine essence, and not confessing, in accordance with the divinely inspired theology of the holy and devout philosophers of the Church, that this is applied to the divine energy, and thus to all the ways insisting upon the one divinity of the Father, the Son, and the Holy Spirit, if only as one of the divine bearers of the mystery called either their essence divine, or their energy, on this we proclaim a threefold anathema.[141]

Every name, word, and term, including the term "God" and "Divinity," can be applied in reference to God's essence only conditionally: Dionysius the Areopagite already called God "beyond divine,"[142] while John of Damascus spoke of the "beyond divine Divinity,"[143] thereby emphasizing the relativity of the understandings of "God," "Divinity," and "Divine," applied to him who surpasses all understanding, word, and name. After the Areopagite, Gregory Palamas calls God "beyond divine,"[144] showing that, since God's essence is higher than every name, all the names of God signify this or that other activity of God, but not God's essence.[145] For us, nothing in God is accessible besides the energies; speaking of "God" and the "Divinity," we can have an idea of the energies of God, while God's essence is beyond the reaches of our understanding and perception.

The account above of Gregory Palamas' teaching, asserted by the Constantinopolitan councils in the middle of the fourteenth century, raises an issue in the age-old development of the Eastern Christian teaching of God, finally formulizing a notion of the namelessness of God's essence and the naming of God's energies. All the names of God, including the names "God" and "Divinity," are names of the energies, and not the essence, of God. They can be applied in relation to the essence, though only in a conditional sense, for the essence of God is nameless, beyond name, and above all names and comprehension.

---

[141]Greek text cited in: S. V. Troitsky, "Athonite Troubles," *Additions to Church Statements* 20 (1913): 893.

[142]Cf.: *On the Divine Names* 2.3.

[143]Cf.: *An Exact Exposition . . .* 1.12.

[144]*Triads* 2 3.37.

[145]*Against Akyndinos* 5 17.13–21, 26.3–27.

Besides this, the Palamite teaching on the essence and energies of God raises, on a new level, the question of the relativity of human language as applied to God. Every word, name, and term, being part of human language, is suited to the description of created reality, but cannot hold in itself the reality of the uncreated divine being. Although the names of God are the names of God's energies, they have only a conditional significance as applied to the energies: possessing all characteristics of God's essence, the energies possess namelessness. We name God only by his energies and in no way do we name him by his essence, but even in relation to the divine energies, such as the divine light, human names are conditional and inadequate.

THE DIVINE LIGHT

The difference between the essence and energies of God, formulated by Gregory Palamas, helps in understanding the Eastern Christian patristic teaching on God as light, as well as the mystical phenomenon on which this teaching is based.

The first Christian writer to declare that "God is light" was the holy Apostle and Evangelist John the Theologian. In his own words, he heard this truth from Jesus Christ himself: "This then is the message that we have heard from him, and declare to you, that God is light, and in him is no darkness at all" (1 Jn 1.5). The last phrase presents itself, probably, as one of the *logia Iēsou* (λόγια Ἰησοῦ)–aphorisms of Jesus, which were remembered by Christ's disciples and partially entered into the New Testament canon, partially into the apocryphal writings, and partially were preserved over quite a long time in oral tradition. Jesus said concerning himself: "I am the light of the world" (Jn 9.5). For John the Theologian, Jesus was the light that "shines in the darkness" and that "enlightens every man that comes into the world" (Jn 1.5, 9). The teaching of Christ as "Light of Light" entered into the Nicene Creed; it also found reflection in the theology of the Orthodox Church.[146]

The theme of the divine light was a leitmotif in the works of Gregory the Theologian. One of Gregory's favorite images when speaking of God was the image of the sun.[147] Gregory uses this image in particular when speaking of the innate striving of man to God as to the utmost goodness:

[146]Cf.: For example, the hymn "Joyous Light." The theme of light particularly developed in the liturgical feasts of Pascha, Transfiguration, and Theophany.

[147]Cf.: *Oration* 21.1; 28.30; 40.5; 40.37; 44.3.

For many and great as are our blessings . . . which we have and shall have from God, this is the greatest and kindliest of all, our inclination and relationship to him. For God is to intelligible things what the sun is to the things of sense.[148] The one lightens the visible, the other the invisible, world. The one makes our bodily eyes to see the sun, the other makes our intellectual natures to see God. And, as that, which bestows on the things which see and are seen the power of seeing and being seen, is itself the most beautiful of visible things; so God, who creates, for those who think, and that which is thought of, the power of thinking and being thought of, is himself the highest of the objects of thought,[149] in whom every desire finds its bourn, beyond whom it can no further go. For not even the most philosophic, the most piercing, the most curious intellect has, or can ever have, a more exalted object. For this is the utmost of things desirable, and they who arrive at it find an entire rest from speculation.[150]

Gregory emphasizes the Trinitarian character of the divine light. God as Trinity is light, and every one of the Persons of the Holy Trinity is light, says Gregory, quoting the Evangelist John:

"He was the true light that enlightens every man coming into the world" (Jn 1.9)–yes, the Father. "He was the true light that enlightens every man coming into the world"–yes, the Son. "He was the true light that enlightens every man coming into the world"–yes, the Comforter (Jn 14.16, 26). These are three subjects and three verbs–he was and he was and he was. But a single reality *was*. There are three predicates–light and light and light. But the light is one, God is one. This is the meaning of David's prophetic vision: "In your light we shall see light" (Ps 36.10). We receive the Son's light from the Father's light in the light of the Spirit: that is what

---

[148]Cf.: Plato *Republic* 6

[149]Cf.: Plotinus *Enneads* 6.7.16: "The sun, cause of the existence of sensing-things and of their being seen, is indirectly the cause of sight, without being either the faculty or the object: similarly this Principle, the Good, cause of Being, and Intellectual-Principle, is a light appropriate to what is to be seen there and to their seer; neither the Being nor the Intellectual-Principle, it is their source and by the light it sheds upon both makes them objects of Intellection. This filling procures the existence; after the filling, the being; the existence achieved, the seeing followed: the beginning is that state of not yet having been filled, though there is, also, the beginning which means that the Filling Principle was outside and by that act of filling gave shape to the filled."

[150]Gregory the Theologian *Oration* 21.1.

we ourselves have seen and what we now proclaim—it is the plain and simple explanation of the Trinity.[151]

The most complete teaching of Gregory on God as light is revealed in a sermon on the holy feast of the Lord's baptism, called by the liturgical calendar of the Eastern Church the "feast of lights." Gregory speaks here of the light of the Holy Trinity, which, on the one hand, is beyond the grasp of all sense and comprehension, but on the other hand, is at the head of the whole hierarchy of lights from the spiritual to the material. The light of the Holy Trinity transcends created being absolutely, at the same time penetrating into the created world so that every existing thing, at some different level, participates in this light:

> The highest light is God, unapproachable and ineffable, neither grasped by the mind nor expressed in language. It illumines every reason-endowed nature. It is to intelligible realities what the sun is to sense-perceptible realities. To the extent that we are purified it appears, to the extent that it appears it is loved, to the extent that it is loved it is again known. It both contemplates and comprehends itself and is poured out but a little to those outside itself. I speak of the light contemplated in the Father and Son and Holy Spirit, whose wealth is the confluence and the leaping forth of this radiance. A second light is the angel, a kind of emanation or participation in the first light, toward which it inclines and by whose help it possesses illumination. I do not know if the illumination is apportioned according to the rank in which each stands, or if each receives its rank according to the measure of its illumination. A third light is the human being, and this is also clear to those outside the church. For they name the human being a light[152] because of the power of reason in us, and in addition the name is given to those of us who are more deiform and approach more closely to God. I also know another light, by which the primordial darkness was driven away or cut off, the first thing brought into existence of the visible creation, which shines upon the circular orbit of the stars and the whole universe, the beacon fire on high.[153]

---

[151]*Oration* 31.3 p. 118.

[152]A similar etymology (Gr. *phōs*, φώς—man, from *phōs*, φῶς—light) can be found in Clement of Alexandria *Pedagogue* 1.6.

[153]Gregory the Theologian *Oration* 40.5 p. 101–102.

Apart from the hierarchy of lights, there exist, according to Gregory, other forms of light: the issue is one concerning the appearances of the divine light in human history. The whole Bible, the whole life of the Church up to the entry into the eschatological Kingdom of God could be considered as a revelation of the divine light. This revelation is given to individual people, to whole peoples, to all Christians, and finally—in the coming age—to the entirety of those saved:

The first precept given to the first-created human being was also a light (Gen 2.16–17). . . . The written law is a light that is typological and proportionate to those receiving it, sketching the truth and the mystery of the great light, though indeed the face of Moses was also glorified by it (Ex 34.29–35). And, to add more lights to our discourse, it was a light that appeared to Moses from the fire, when the bush burned but was not consumed (Ex 3.2), in order to show forth its nature and make known its power. It was a light that in a pillar of fire guided Israel and tamed the desert (Ex 13.21). It was a light that carried off Elijah in the chariot of fire and did not burn up the one being carried (2 Kg 2.11). It was

The Lord's Transfiguration.
Church of the Dormition.
Daphne. Constantinople. 11th c.

a light that flashed like lightning around the shepherds, when the timeless light was mingled with what is in time (Lk 2.9). It was a light of the star hastening to Bethlehem, among other reasons to guide the magi and to escort the light above us that has come to be with us (Mt 2.9). It was a light, the divinity that showed itself upon the disciples, a little too strong for their eyesight (Mt 17.2). It was a light, the vision that flashed like lightning around Paul and wounded his eyesight, healing the darkness of his soul (Acts 9.3–9). It is a light, the radiance hereafter for those who have been purified here, when the just will shine forth like the sun (Mt 13.43), when they will be gods and kings (Ps 82.1) and God will stand in their midst, determining and distinguishing the ranks of the blessedness there. A light in the proper sense, beyond these, is the light of baptism . . . [that] encompasses a great and wondrous mystery of our salvation.[154]

[154]*Oration* 40.6 p. 39.

The theme of the divine light united the three spiritual writers on whom the Orthodox Church bestows the title "Theologian": the Apostle John the Theologian, Gregory the Theologian, and Symeon the New Theologian. For Symeon, this theme had special meaning, since his theology was based on his personal mystical experience of contemplation of the divine light—an experience that he so clearly described in his orations and hymns. After Gregory the Theologian, Symeon spoke of God as light that disappears as soon as it is shown to man, as soon as he reaches it:

> By having the light, you do not have it;
> for you have it, since you see,
> but you cannot keep it
> or grasp it in your hands.
> It seems to you that you hold nothing.
> You open your palms
> and the sun shines on them
> and you imagine you possess it. . . .
> Suddenly, you close your hands,
> the light stays outside your grip.
> Hence, in one way, you have nothing.[155]

Symeon reproduces the teaching of Gregory the Theologian on the world as a hierarchy of lights, going back to the source of light—God:

> God is light, and light is limitless and incomprehensible. . . . The Father is light, the Son is light, the Holy Spirit is light. They are one light, simple, uncomplicated, timeless, coeternal, equal in honor, equal in glory. In addition, that which is from him is light, given to us by the Light. Life is light; immortality is light; the source of life is light; the living water is light; love, peace, truth, the door to the Kingdom of Heaven—are all light. The marriage hall is light, the palace, garden, enjoyment of the garden, the gentle earth, the crowns of life, the very robes of the saints—are light. Jesus Christ, the Savior and King of all, is light. The bread of his most precious flesh—is light, the wine of his honorable blood—is light. His resurrection is light, his face is light. His hand, finger, and mouth, are light, his eyes are light. The Lord is light, his voice is glorious light from light. The

---

[155]*Hymn* 23 p. 118–119.

Comforter is light. The pearl, the mustard seed, the righteous vinedresser, the leaven, hope, and faith, are all light. . . . For God is One in the Father, Son, and Holy Spirit, a light inaccessible and pre-eternal . . . as I learned in the very experience of this teaching.[156]

Symeon continually returns to the idea that God the Trinity is one incomprehensible light. This thought is the cornerstone of his theology and mysticism. Symeon describes all the divine qualities in terms of light. He speaks of the light of divine glory, the light of divine goodness, the light of Christ's face, the light of divine love, the light of knowledge, the light of Holy Scripture, the light of eternal life, the light of immortality, passionlessness, and the divine commandments.

Symeon frequently compares God with the sun, using the analogy that is traditional in the works of the holy fathers. Developing Gregory the Theologian's concept on the two suns and two worlds,[157] Symeon writes:

God created two worlds from the beginning, one visible and the other invisible. . . . In the two worlds, there accordingly shine two suns, one perceptible, and the other intellectual. What is seen and perceptible is the sun, therefore what is invisible and intellectual is God. . . . One of the two worlds, that is, the perceptible one and that which is in it, is illumined by the perceptible and visible sun, while the other, that is the intellectual and which is in it, is illumined and lit up by the intellectual Sun of truth.[158]

Symeon regards the whole history of the world, in total, as one continuous revelation of divine light. The divine light formed the angels,[159] those "second lights."[160] Although the divine light is absolutely transcendent to the visible world, God did not leave this world without any light, but created the sun, moon, and lights.[161] Man was made in the image and likeness of God and clothed in the "light bearing and divine raiment" with which he subsequently identified himself.[162] The Son of God became man so that we,

---

[156] *Theological Oration* 3.137–166.
[157] Cf.: Gregory the Theologian *Oration* 21.1.
[158] *Chapters* 2.22.
[159] *Hymn* 38.37–40.
[160] Ibid. 50.150–152; *Moral Oration* 1.5, 79–83.
[161] *Hymn* 38.66–69.
[162] Ibid. 45.63.

through our conformity and participation, might become "second lights," similar to the first Light.[163]

In the understanding of Symeon the New Theologian, the divine light is not an angel, nor is it some kind of created essence or manifestation.[164] According to Symeon, the divine light is God himself in his revelation to man: "Your light is you, my God," he said.[165] As with Gregory the Theologian, with Symeon the light can at times be identified with the Holy Trinity,[166] in other cases, with the Holy Spirit.[167] Symeon also speaks rather frequently of the visions of Christ as light.[168]

The light described by Symeon is not a physical or material phenomenon: Symeon defines it as "immaterial,"[169] "simple and formless, perfectly uncomplicated, incorporeal, and indivisible."[170] With the aid of apophatic expressions, Symeon stresses that the divine light is beyond the bounds of any material category or form, just as it is beyond the reaches of human speech and understanding. This "treasury is inexpressible, unspeakable, not qualitative, without quantity, inconspicuous, immaterial, without form, formed only for inexpressible beauty, everything as simple, the light that is above every light."[171] The latter expressions show that Symeon does not bestow on the term "light" a literal meaning: this term only symbolically indicates the reality, surpassing every human word from afar.

Being immaterial, the divine light is an "intellectual" light: it appears in the mind, it shines in it, it lights it up, it purifies it, it envelops the mind in its mystical ascent to God. The divine light is invisible for the bodily eyes, but it may be seen by the mind, or, more precisely, by what Symeon calls "the mind's eye," "the intellectual eyes of the heart," "the eyes of the soul." At times Symeon even claims that the divine light is "inaccessible for the intellectual eyes of the heart";[172] in other places he affirms the

---

[163]Ibid. 42.189–192.

[164]Ibid. 17.238.

[165]Ibid. 45.6.

[166]Ibid. 12. 19–23 ("One Light, Father, Son, and Spirit, Three Are Seen by Me"); Ibid. 1.226; 2.86–94; 21.147; 24.248; 25.33–48; 33.1.

[167]Ibid. 44.114 ("Spirit, Shining in Unseen Light"); Ibid. 17.36; 22.177.

[168]Ibid. 51.15; 25.145–151; *Moral Oration* 4.263.

[169]*Hymn* 38.64; 51.141; *Moral Oration* 11.176.

[170]*Hymn* 13.41–42.

[171]*Moral Oration* 11.174–177.

[172]*Hymn* 38.84.

opposite, saying that the Inaccessible is accessible for the intellectual eyes.[173]

Speaking on the divine light, Symeon uses images that are traditional for Eastern Christian theological literature in such a way that they are characteristic only for the light itself. He uses the traditional image of the sun constantly: he speaks of the vision of God as the sun, of a sun shining in his heart, of a sun shining in his hands, of a rational sun, of a never-setting sun, of a sparkling sun, of a sunny circle, of a sunbeam, of the beauty of the sun, of a light higher than the sun. In Symeon's works, the image of the moon is only rarely encountered; frequently there arises an image of the stars, of a lamp, of a glow, of a light-reflecting cloud. Sometimes the different images are brought together in one description of the divine light: "I see you, as the sun, I contemplate as a star, I consider as a lamp burning inside a vessel, and I carry you inside, like a pearl."[174] In other cases the different images point out different stages in the vision of light: "You are visible in the distance, as a rising star, expanding bit by bit . . . and you are seen, like the sun."[175]

The teaching of God as light, hidden in the works of Gregory the Theologian and Symeon the New Theologian, received the most extensive development in the theology of St Gregory Palamas. He uncovered the theme of the divine light within the context of his teaching of the essence and energies of God. Speaking on the nature of the divine light, Gregory Palamas emphasizes that this light, on the one hand, is uncreated and divine; on the other hand, it is by no means the essence of God. The divine light, according to Palamas, is an energy of God, changing and transfiguring man. Contemplating the divine light, man sees God himself, and by this, God continues to remain invisible:

Of course, no one has seen God (Jn 1.18) nor will see him, not man, nor an angel, but only inasmuch as angel and man see with the senses or intellectually. Having been placed by the Spirit and seeing in the Spirit, how can he not see like in like, according to the expression of the theologians?[176] Moreover, even in the very vision in the spirit, the divine light that surpasses everything is hidden in a yet more perfect measure. For

---

[173]Ibid. 15.52–53.
[174]Ibid. 42.85–87; 17.325; 22.5–9.
[175]Ibid. 51.35–38.
[176]Cf.: Clement of Alexandria *Stromata* 5.1; Gregory of Nyssa *On the Protomartyr Stephen* 1; Basil the Great *Conversation on Psalm 48*, 8.

what being from creation would be able to hold the whole infinite strength of the Spirit, in order, thanks to it, to consider everything that relates to God? And what do I refer to here by this hiddenness? The same brightness of this light, incomprehensibly used in a material glance of the onlooker, becoming keener through the single spiritual eye and making it far more possible to contain itself, never in its eternity ceasing to light it up with increasingly brighter rays, to fulfill the more hidden light and brighten what was dark in the beginning. Moreover, and because theologians call it the never ending light through which, after the quieting of every known power, God will become visible to the saints by the power of the Spirit, uniting with them as God with gods and visible things, that having turned to nothing better thanks to the better one in communion and, according to the prophetic word, being renewed in strength (Isa 40.31), they cease all action of body and spirit, so that they themselves contemplate only the light.[177]

There are no names in human language for describing the divine light. All names, comparisons, and analogies can be used only in a conditional sense, since the divine light is nameless:

God is not only higher than knowledge, but that which is unknowable, just as his provenance is also hidden—he is supremely divine and at the same time most exceptional. The divine visions, even if they are symbolic, are unattainably unknowable; they are revealed as some kind of other order, as something else in relation to the divine, and in relation to human nature—if it may be said thus—beyond us while in us—so that there is no way to precisely express the names. This is shown in the words of him who answered Manoah's question, "What is your name?" with "It is Wonderful" (Judg 13.17-18); so then his vision would also be wonderful, being not only incomprehensible, but nameless. Moreover, if the vision is higher than the denial, then the word interpreting this vision remains lower than the negative ascent, moving by way of comparisons and analogies, and not coincidentally are the names and titles here frequently accompanied by the particle "like," carrying the meaning of a likening, since the vision is invisible and beyond naming.[178]

[177] *Triads* 2 3.31.
[178] *Triads* 1 3.4.

Being invisible, beyond naming, nameless, and incomprehensible, that is, possessing all the qualities of God himself, the divine light is not at the same time the essence of God:

> The light is seen in light, and in a similar light are the seers. If there is not any kind of other action, then the seers, departing from all else, become light completely and used by that which is visible, or more precisely, united with him without confusion, being light and seeing light by means of light: when he looks at himself, he sees light; if at this one, what he sees is all light; whether on this one, through what he sees is light both here and there. In some way there is a unity, so that all of this might be one, so then the seer does not recognize what is seen, what it watches, what this is, only that he became light and sees light, different from all of creation. . . . As the divine Maximus says: "The existent in God left behind itself all that was after God";[179] and also: "All works, names, and worthiness, being after God, will be lower than those who will be in God through good action"[180] . . . for the essence of God is higher than the non-essence, surpassing the existent things; he is not for nothing both "super-divine" and in excellence "non-existing," seen spiritually by intellectual senses, though not in the least as the essence of God, but the glory and the brightness that are inseparable from his nature and through which he is united only with those worthy, of angels and men.[181]

The divine light is not sensory or symbolic, but it is rather the Divinity itself in its revelation to man. It is an energy of God, that is, God himself in his manifestation *ad extra*. Being a divine energy, the divine light may be called God:

> When contemplation comes, by the pouring out of its impartial joy, by the intellectual peace and by the kindling flame of love toward God, the seer truly knows that this is the divine light. . . . But he does not at all consider that he has been vouchsafed to see God's nature directly. . . . The light is born in the God-bearing soul out of the implanting of God within it, although the unity of the all-powerful God with the worthy is nevertheless higher than this light, because in its supernatural might God

---

[179] *Chapters on Theology and Oikonomia* 1.54.
[180] *Ambigua.*
[181] Gregory Palamas *Triads* 2 3.36–37.

Transfiguration of the Lord.
Theophanes the Greek. 14th c.

simultaneously abides totally in himself and lives totally in us, granting us therefore not his nature, but his glory and radiance. This is the divine light, and the saints justly call it divine, for it surely deifies; and if this is so, then it still is not simply [the Divinity], but it is in and of itself divine nature,[182] that is, God. "This seems to be the division and complication of the One God, for God is surely equally well the First God, and the Lofty God, and the Super Principle";[183] he is one in his united divinity, but the First God, and the Lofty God, and the Super Principle because in him is the foundation of this divine adoration. . . . Rising to these heights of contemplation, they know that they are seeing the light with intellectual senses, and that the light is God.[184]

The stated teaching on the divine light, equally with the teaching on the essence and energies of God, is one of the cornerstones of Orthodox theology. The sources of this teaching are already contained in the New Testament; western theological tradition shares this teaching on one or another level. However, it is in the Orthodox East that the teaching on the divine light was worked out in such detail and thought out from all sides. This teaching was reflected not only in the theology of the Orthodox Church, but also in its liturgical services, as well as in its iconographic art. The icon of the Lord's transfiguration by Theophanes the Greek, penetrated by rays of light, like many other Byzantine and Russian icons of the twelfth to sixteenth centuries, bears witness to how deeply rooted the teaching of the divine light is in Orthodox Tradition.

THE PROCESSION OF THE HOLY SPIRIT

By virtue of historical circumstances, the theme of the procession of the Holy Spirit from the Father occupies an important place in the Orthodox teaching

---

[182]Cf.: Dionysius the Areopagite *On the Divine Names* 11.6.
[183]Ibid. 2.11.
[184]Gregory Palamas *Triads* I 3.22–24.

on God. "There is not one medieval Byzantine theologian who did not in any event participate in the never-ending dispute on the procession of the Holy Spirit,"[185] notes Protopresbyter John Meyendorff. This dispute arose as a result of the addition to the Creed made in the Roman Catholic West, according to which the Holy Spirit proceeds not from the Father, but from the Father and the Son (the Filioque).

The premises of the teaching of the Filioque are contained in the triadology of Blessed Augustine. In his treatise *On the Trinity*, the starting-point becomes not the "monarchy" of God the Father, as this was accepted in the East, but the unity of the divine nature: the three Persons (*personae*) of the Holy Trinity act as "one beginning" (*unum principium*), one Creator and one Lord.[186] According to Augustine, they are in essence one beginning in relation to the Holy Spirit, who is a "general gift" of the Father and the Son, being a link between the Father and the Son and the love that they pour out into our hearts.[187] It is namely Augustine's Trinitarian doctrine that predetermined the appearance of the claim in the Latin Creed of the procession of the Spirit from the Father and the Son, a claim that became one of the reasons for the split between East and West. Although the split occurred decidedly later, one can verify that the western conceptual model of the Trinity that received its complete, final form in Augustine, already differed in essence from the eastern model by the fourth century.

As one may recall, the Roman teaching on the Filioque was noticed in the Christian East before the Great Schism in 1054. The first of the eastern fathers to bring up the issue of the procession of the Holy Spirit from the Father and the Son was Maximus the Confessor, although he did not see the initial differences between the eastern teaching of the procession of the Spirit from the Father through the Son and the western teaching of the procession of the Spirit from the Father and the Son. More significant was the sharper position taken by Patriarch Photius, who saw signs of Sabellianism in the Filioque. After the Great Schism in 1054, the polemics became yet more pointed. Among others, Sts Gregory II of Cyprus, Patriarch of Constantinople (1283–1289), Gregory Palamas, and Mark of Ephesus introduced their contribution to the formatioin of an Orthodox position on the issue of the Filioque.

---

[185]Meyendorff, *The Life and Works . . .* 309.
[186]Augustine *On the Trinity* 5.14.
[187]Cf.: Ibid. 5.11; 5.14–16; 8.1.

In the course of the polemics, the Greek fathers brought forward varied responses against the western teaching of the Filioque. These can be brought together into five fundamentals:

1. The very fact of the addition of a word to the Niceno-Constantinopolitan Creed is an impermissible innovation.

2. The teaching of the Filioque contradicts Holy Scripture.

3. The teaching of the Filioque contradicts the writings of the eastern fathers of the Church, whose authority is supported by the ecumenical councils.

4. The teaching of the Filioque infringes on the principle of the "monarchy," of the single beginning of the Trinity, bringing to it a "second beginning."

5. The pre-eternal procession of the Holy Spirit from the Father is not identified as his being sent down at the time from the Son.

Some contemporary Orthodox theologians add their own expression to these against the Filioque, formulated in the patristic age. V.N. Lossky, for example, linked the Filioque to the teaching of papal primacy and proved that the insertion of a change into the dogma of the Trinity led to ecclesiological corruption in the Latin West. On the other hand, V.V. Bolotov related the teaching of the Holy Spirit's procession from the Father and the Son to a number of theologoumena (personal theological opinions), based on the authority of the western fathers, and did not consider the Filioque an insurmountable obstacle for unity between the Orthodox and Catholics. Neither this, nor the other view allows for the complete recognition of the accordance with such an understanding of the problem that is found in the works of the eastern fathers of the Church. The latter was uncharacteristically not exaggerated, nor did it underestimate the significance of the Filioque as a factor of division. The eastern fathers of the Church, as far as one can judge, did not try to consider the Filioque in an ecclesiological context; they objected to the papal pretensions of a universal jurisdiction irrespective of the issue of the Filioque. At the same time, they did not at all consider the Filioque as an expression of a private theological opinion, but perceived it as an invasion of the realm protected by Holy Tradition, of the realm of God-revealed dogma.

We shall consider the expressions of the eastern fathers against the western teaching of the procession of the Holy Spirit from the Father and the Son in order. Above all, the teaching of the procession of the Holy Spirit from the

Father was, as Patriarch Photius emphasizes, maintained by six ecumenical councils: "The second of the seven holy and ecumenical councils defined precisely that the Holy Spirit proceeds from the Father; this [teaching] was accepted by the third [ecumenical council], supported by the fourth, the fifth agreed [with this teaching], the sixth preached it, and it was imprinted with pure, unclouded feats of victory by the seventh."[188] The insertion of would-be changes into the Creed, which is supported by the authority of the ecumenical councils, was impermissible from the point of view of the eastern fathers. St Gregory Palamas, directing himself to the Western Church, writes:

How can you say that which was not boldly spoken by the proclaiming truth, which the Spirit did not announce, the proclaimer of all truth, to which he did not bear witness and which he did not relay, he who notified all his friends about all that he heard from the Father, who came so that he might bear witness to the truth? How can you introduce an alien addition to the specific creed, which was written jointly by the chosen Fathers who, gathered together spiritually for this, wrote the Creed from a sincere opinion of the Father and the Son and the Holy Spirit and gave it as a touchstone of the true knowledge of God and an immutable confession of faith for all of the elect to direct the word of truth? . . . In our opinion, at first your addition needs to be taken away, and then to consider whether the Holy Spirit is from the Son or not, and to maintain whether or not it corresponds to the extant decision of the God-bearers.[189]

St Mark of Ephesus refers to the decision of the Fourth Ecumenical Council about the Niceno-Constantinopolitan Creed: "This holy and divinely blessed Creed suffices for the full knowledge of worship and the assertion, for it teaches perfectly about the Father and the Son and the Holy Spirit." This council decided that "no one else would be allowed to submit another creed, whether he writes, fabricates, studies, or submits it. Whoever has boldness enough to write or fabricate another creed, such a one, whether bishop or cleric, alienates his episcopal rank from the episcopacy and his clerical rank from the clergy. But if he is from the laity, he is anathema." The Seventh Ecumenical Council decided: "We maintain the laws of the Church; we keep to the definitions of the Fathers; we anathematize anyone who adds to

---

[188] *Mystagogy of the Holy Spirit* 5.
[189] *Apodictic Treatise* 1.

or lessens something of the Church. . . . If anyone despises church Tradition, written or unwritten, let him be anathema." Commenting on these conciliar decrees, Mark of Ephesus said at the Council of Florence-Ferrara:

> Do you really not break with the written tradition of the Fathers by this that you introduce, this novelty? How can you not blush, pronouncing in other respects the whole Creed as the Fathers formed it, while inserting one word of your own? For to add or to remove words is a heretical act by which you wish to strengthen your heresy. Would you truly accept such a thing with respect to the Gospels or Epistles or one of your teachers? . . . Are you truly not ashamed to add to these other scriptures, already formed and ruling in all the universe, your own words and by them to arouse such temptation in the churches?[190]

The teaching on the Filioque, in the opinions of the eastern fathers, contradicts Christ's words that the Holy Spirit "proceeds from the Father" (Jn 15.26). Indeed, Christ also says: "The Holy Spirit, whom the Father will send in my name" (Jn 14.26), "I will send to you from the Father" (Jn 15.26); but the Apostle Paul calls him the Spirit of Christ (Rom 8.9), the Spirit of the Son of God (Gal 4.6) and "the Holy Spirit . . . [that] he poured out on us richly through Jesus Christ our Savior" (Tit 3.5–6). However, not one of the scriptural texts speaks of the procession of the Holy Spirit as being from the Father and the Son; they only speak of his descent on people by the Son or the Father in the name of the Son.

The teaching of the Filioque contradicts the multitude of evidence of the Fathers of the Eastern Church concerning the procession of the Holy Spirit from the Father. Set out here is only some of such evidence, dating to the fourth century:

> The [Holy] Spirit, who proceeds from the Father, and, belonging to the Son, is from him given to the disciples and all who believe in him.[191]

> He is called the Spirit of God (Mt 3.16), and the Spirit of truth who proceeds from the Father.[192]

---

[190]Mark of Ephesus *The Dialogue Known as "to the Latins," or Additions to the Creed.*
[191]Athanasius of Alexandria *On the Holy Spirit* 1.2.
[192]Basil the Great *On the Holy Spirit* 9 (Crestwood, N.Y.: 1980) 42.

"By the Word of the Lord the heavens were established, and all their host by the Spirit of his mouth" (Ps 32.6 LXX). The Word is not merely air set in motion by the organs of speech, nor is the Spirit of his mouth an exhalation of his lungs, but the Word is he who "was in the beginning with God . . . and was God" (Jn 1.1), and the Spirit of God's mouth is the Spirit of truth who "proceeds from the Father" (Jn 15.26).[193]

I know the Spirit with the Father, though I know that the Spirit is not the Father; I received the Spirit with the Son, although it is not named the Son. But I recognize its relationship with the Father because it proceeds from the Father, and its relationship with the Son.[194]

The Holy Spirit in the form of a dove. Detail of a mosaic in the baptistery dome. Ravenna. 5th c.

And the Son came from the Father, and the Spirit proceeds from the Father; but the Son was begotten in his form from the Father, while the Spirit is from the Father in a speechless form.[195]

Thus, then, the Holy Spirit, from whom all the supply of good things for creation has its source, is attached to the Son, and with him is inseparably apprehended, and has its being attached to the Father, as cause, from whom also it proceeds; it has this note of its peculiar hypostatic nature, that it is known after the Son and together with the Son, and it has its subsistence from the Father.[196]

Learn to confess the One Holy Spirit, who comes from or proceeds from the Father.[197]

The Holy Spirit is the Spirit who proceeds from God, but is not a son, and is not begotten, but proceeds.[198]

---

[193]Ibid. 16 p. 62–63.
[194]*Conversation against the Sabellians.*
[195]Ibid.
[196]*Epistle 38.4.*
[197]Gregory the Theologian *Oration 25.15.*
[198]Ibid. 39.12.

One finds in the eastern fathers the notion of the Son as a crucial link between the Father and the Holy Spirit. In particular, Gregory of Nyssa writes on this subject:

> While we confess the invariable character of the nature, we do not deny the difference in respect of cause, and that which is caused, by which alone we apprehend that one Person is distinguished from another—by our belief, that is, that one is the Cause, and another is of the Cause; and again in that which is of the Cause we recognize another distinction. For one is directly from the first Cause, and another by that which is directly from the first Cause; so that the attribute of being Only-begotten abides without doubt in the Son, and the interposition of the Son, while it guards his attribute of being Only-begotten, does not shut out the Spirit from his relation by way of nature to the Father.[199]

Proceeding from such an understanding, some eastern fathers spoke of the procession of the Holy Spirit "from the Father through the Son." Similar expressions are encountered especially in Cyril of Alexandria:

> Christ calls the Comforter the Spirit of Truth, that is, he himself says that it proceeds from the Father. This is because it is like the Son's own Spirit, naturally existing in him and proceeding though him, just like the Spirit of the Father.[200]

> This is the Spirit of God the Father, and at the same time it is the Spirit of the Son, this that in essential form pertains to both, that is, poured out from the Father through the Son.[201]

Maximus the Confessor's *Letter to Marinus* is an interesting document devoted to the question of the procession of the Holy Spirit and ancestral sin. The authenticity of the letter is disputed by some scholars,[202] although the majority of contemporary scholars acknowledge the work as Maximus'.[203] In this letter, Maximus considers it possible to place a mark of equality

[199] *On Not Three Gods.*
[200] *Interpretation on John* 10.2.
[201] *On the Worship in the Spirit and Truth* 1.
[202] Cf.: in particular, the critical observations of Bishop Basil (Karayannis): Basil Karayannis, *Maximus the Confessor: the Essence and Energies of God* (Paris: 1993), 88–90 (note 142).
[203] For more detail on the authenticity of the letter, see Jean-Claude Larchet, *Maximus the Confessor: Mediator between East and West* (Moscow: 2004), 38–43.

between the Eastern Christian understanding of the procession of the Holy Spirit from the Father through the Son and the Latin teaching of the procession of the Holy Spirit from the Father and the Son:

> Those of the Queen of Cities[204] have attacked the synodal letter of the present very holy Pope, not in the case of all the chapters that he has written in it, but only in the case of two of them. One relates to the theology [of the Trinity] and according to this, says "the Holy Spirit also has his procession from the Son." The other deals with the divine incarnation. With regard to the first matter, they [the Romans] have produced the unanimous evidence of the Latin fathers, and also of Cyril of Alexandria, from the study he made of the Gospel of St John. On the basis of these texts, they have shown that they have not made the Son the cause of the Spirit—they know in fact that the Father is the only cause of the Son and the Spirit, the one by begetting and the other by procession—but that they have manifested the procession through him and have thus shown the unity and identity of the essence.[205]

Thus, Maximus the Confessor posits that the Romans acknowledge the Father as the one Cause of the Son and Spirit. Moreover, at the Council of Florence-Ferrara, the Romans insisted that the Holy Spirit proceeds from the Father and the Son as from one origin. The papal bull of Eugene IV, "*Laetentur coeli*," signed by the Greeks at the Council of Florence-Ferrara, proclaimed:

> We have determined that the Holy Spirit exists eternally from the Father and the Son and that it has its own essence and its own subsistent being simultaneously from the Father and the Son and proceeds eternally as from One just as from the Other, as from one beginning and one breath. We declare that which the holy fathers and teachers said, that the Holy Spirit proceeds from the Father through the Son, which gives understanding to what it means that the Son, like the Father, is, according to the Greeks, the Cause, but according to the Romans, the origin of the subsistence of the Holy Spirit.[206]

[204]Constantinople.
[205]*Letter to Marinus.*
[206]*Christian Dogmatics: Dogmatic Texts of the Teaching of the Catholic Church from the Third to the Twentieth Centuries* (Saint Petersburg: 2002), 129.

Thus, the Romans maintained that the western "from the Father and the Son" was identical to the eastern "from the Father through the Son," as Maximus the Confessor thought in his own time. However, the interpretation of these expressions demanded further elaboration in light of the Roman teaching on the Father and the Son as one beginning. One participant of the Council of Florence-Ferrara who did not subscribe to its documents was St Mark of Ephesus, who considered that the expressions "from the Father through the Son" and "from the Father and the Son" were not identical at all. The expression "the Holy Spirit proceeds from the Father through the Son" is used in the sense that "proceeding from the Father through the Son, it is made present or is known, or enlightens or is known, as showing" the Son. The Holy Spirit "is not another kind of relationship to the Son, as if it is only known by him, as in relation to the Father—that he does not have being apart from him. Thus, the Holy Spirit does not proceed from the Son and does not have being from him." It is precisely for this reason that "no one will find anywhere that it is said that the Spirit proceeds through the Son without remembering the Father, and so it is said: from the Father through the Son."[207]

According to the teaching of Gregory Palamas, Mark of Ephesus, and other fathers of the late Byzantine period, the opinion on the procession of the Holy Spirit from the Father and the Son "as from one origin" disturbed the traditional Eastern Christian patristic understanding of the "monarchy" of the Father, of the Father as the only Cause of the being of the Son and Spirit. As was already mentioned above,[208] according to the teaching of the eastern ecclesial writers, the quality of being without beginning and the Cause, or Principle, of the Son and Spirit belongs only to God the Father. In the course of polemics with the Roman Church the teaching of the Father as the only cause of being of the Son and Spirit acquired a significance of the first order, and the eastern fathers guarded it zealously. In the words of Gregory of Cyprus, "The Spirit is the Holy Spirit of the Father, since proceeding from the Father, and the Spirit of the Son, being not from him, but as proceeding through him from the Father, the Father is therefore the only cause."[209] Gregory Palamas wrote: "Saying that the Son is the cause of the

---

[207]Mark of Ephesus *Confession of the True Faith.*
[208]Cf.: "The Trinity: Formation of Dogma."
[209]*On the Procession of the Holy Spirit.*

Divinity denies the Son, since it says in the Gospel, 'the Father is greater than I' (Jn 14.28), not only as man, but as God, as the cause of the Divinity." The Father is greater than the Son not as God, but as the Cause, and according to his divinity, the Son is equal to the Father, whereas according to "cause" they are not equal. For this reason "we recognize the equality of the Son with the Father in nature, and confess the excellence of the Father as principle, which encompasses both the begetting and the procession."[210] If the expression "proceeds through the Son" would indicate the Son as cause of the Holy Spirit, and not that he enlightens through him and is in general together with him proceeding and accompanying him, then each theologian in succession would not have taken away so emphatically the cause of being of the Holy Spirit from the Son, and would not have prescribed it only to the Father, asserts Mark of Ephesus.[211]

The teaching of the Filioque, from the point of view of the eastern fathers, inevitably brings to mind "two causes" and "two principles" in the Trinity. If the Holy Spirit truly proceeded from the Father and the Son, then it would proceed from them "either as from two Hypostases, or as from their general essence, or from their spent strength," says Mark of Ephesus. But in all three cases there would be two causes at hand, two principles, and two dispensers in the Holy Trinity.[212]

Finally, it is worth discussing the difference between the pre-eternal procession of the Holy Spirit from the Father and its descent within time through the Son. This difference was not precisely formulated in the compositions of the theologians of the ecumenical councils. Thus, for example, Maximus the Confessor wrote: "By nature, the Holy Spirit is in accordance with its essence essentially proceeding through the begotten Son."[213] According to John of Damascus, the Father "was eternally having from within himself his Word, and through his Word the Holy Spirit, proceeding from him."[214] In both cases the idea is about the pre-eternal procession of the Holy Spirit from the Father through the Son.

St Photius, patriarch of Constantinople, introduced the difference between the pre-eternal procession of the Holy Spirit from the Father and its

---

[210] *Apodictic Oration* 1.
[211] Cf.: *Confession of the True Faith*.
[212] *Syllogistic Chapters against the Latins* 1.
[213] *Questions to Thalassius* 58.
[214] *Dialogue against the Manicheans* 5.

descent in time through the Son into theological practice for the first time: "The Spirit of Christ does not come from God but from man, and realized (from the Son) not primordially and pre-eternally when it is from the Father, but when the Son perceived human confusion."[215]

In the mind of Mark of Ephesus, the descent of the Holy Spirit into the world through the Son corresponds to that phase of divine revelation that followed after the New Testament (here St Mark reproduces the teaching of the gradual revelation of the Holy Trinity, first formulated by Gregory the Theologian):

> The Father is recognized in the Old Testament, while the Son becomes known in the New. For this reason the sending of the Son is as if he appeared in the world as the Father. After that, when the Son was recognized, the Holy Spirit became known; for this reason it is said that it is from the Father and the Son, already foreknown, it is sent, that is, it appears. For what else could the sending off and dispatching of the omnipresent God and the totally unchanging nature of his place signify? For this reason Christ says: "If I go, I will send him to you" (Jn 16.7). It is completely obvious that this does not speak of the eternal procession.[216]

According to the teaching of Gregory Palamas, the Holy Spirit is sent worthily from the Father and the Son, but proceeds only from the Father:

> When his [the Father's] Word, through flesh, spoke [entered into relation] with us, we learned excellence from the Father by the name of the Spirit's existence. And this occurred not only from the Father, but from him himself. He truly said: "The Spirit of Truth, who proceeds from the Father" [Jn 15.26]. . . . For truly the Holy Spirit is the pre-eternal joy of the Father and the Son, a common possession for both, since it is worthily sent from both, but existing in essence only from the Father. Thus from him only it proceeds in essence.[217]

However, Gregory Palamas introduces an important clarification into Orthodox triadology, taking the difference between essence and energy to a triadic dogma. He claims that all the places in the works of the Fathers of the

---

[215] *Mystagogy of the Holy Spirit* 93.
[216] *Syllogistic Chapters against the Latins* 4.
[217] *Natural Chapters* 36.

Church that speak of the descent of the Holy Spirit on people should be understood in the sense that the energy of the Holy Spirit, its activity, its gift bestowed to people, is by no means a Hypostasis of the Holy Spirit. Hypostatically, the Holy Spirit proceeds only from the Father, while the Holy Spirit's energy is transferred to people from the Father through the Son, or from the Son. "The Holy Spirit belongs to Christ in essence and energy, because Christ is God; However, in essence and hypostasis it belongs to him, but does not proceed from him, while at the same time it belongs to him according to energy, and proceeds from him,"[218] writes Gregory. If the eastern fathers ever spoke of the procession of the Holy Spirit from the Father and the Son, then the argument was not about the pre-eternal procession of the Spirit, but about the sending down of the Spirit on people, within time. Gregory Palamas interprets precisely those texts of Cyril of Alexandria that speak of the procession from the Father through the Son:

> When you hear that the Holy Spirit proceeds from both, for it proceeds essentially from the Father through the Son, you ought to understand its teaching in the following sense: that which is poured out is the power of God and essential energies, but is not the divine Hypostasis of the Spirit.[219]

> The hypostasis of the All-Holy Spirit does not proceed from the Son; it is not given nor is it received by anyone; [it is received and given] only by the grace of God and the divine energy.[220]

> For if the procession of the Spirit for them [the Father and the Son] is always in common—as [a procession] from them—then the Spirit will only be an energy, and not a hypostasis, for it is only an energy—this is that which is common for them.[221]

Thus, the procession of the Holy Spirit from the Father has a pre-eternal and hypostatic character, while the sending down of the Spirit through the Son has an energetic character. Such is the Orthodox understanding of the procession of the Holy Spirit as it was formed in the fourteenth to fifteenth centuries.

[218] *Apodictic Oration* 2.
[219] Ibid.
[220] Ibid.
[221] Ibid.

PART THREE

THE WORLD AND MAN

9

Creation

THE IDEA OF THE CREATION is a cornerstone of Christian cosmology. Christian tradition has always been against "godless heretics," who deny the existence of the Creator. Such people, in the words of Cyril of Jerusalem, "while seeing with bodily eyes, lack spiritual vision."[1] The holy fathers rejected the notion that the universe could be propagated by itself, without the participation of a higher Power, and that anyone could correct it:

> After all, what could be more pitiful and more stupid than people coming up with arguments like this, claiming that beings get existence of themselves, and withdrawing all creation from God's providence? How could you have the idea . . . that so many elements and such great arrangement were being guided without anyone to supervise and control it all? Surely no ship ever managed to navigate the waves of the sea without a pilot, or soldier do brave deed with no general in command, or house stand firm with no householder in charge—whereas this immense universe and the design of all these elements could happen simply by chance without anyone present with the power to guide it all, controlling and maintaining all things in existence from his innate wisdom—is this feasible?[2]

The Christian idea of the creation is founded on the Old Testament revelation of God as the Creator of the world and on the New Testament teaching that God made the world through the mediation of his Son, supplemented by the notion that the Holy Spirit also participated in creation. The formation of the world, therefore, is perceived in the Christian tradition as a creative act of the Triune God, an act in which all three Persons of the Holy Trinity took part.

[1] *Catechetical Sermon* 9.4.
[2] John Chrysostom *Homily on Genesis* 3.13, http://www.scribd.com/doc/63012934/Homilies-on-Genesis-Saint-John-Chrysostom; repunctuated.

The fullest idea of the creation is expressed in the first two chapters of the book of Genesis, where God is represented as the Creator of heaven and earth, the waters and the dry places, the plants and the trees, the sun, the moon, and the stars, the creeping things, the fish, the animals, and man. This passage was known to the authors of the other biblical books in which the thought of God as Creator of the world and man stood out:

For in six days the Lord made heaven and earth. . . . And on the seventh day he rested. (Ex 20.11, 31.17)

You are the only God in all the kingdoms of the earth; you have made heaven and earth. (2 Kg 19.15)

For all the gods of the nations are devils, but the Lord made the heavens. (Ps 96.5; 1 Chr 16.26;)

You are the only Lord; you made heaven, and the heaven of heavens, with all their order, the earth and all things that are in it, the seas and all things in them. To all of them you give life, and the hosts of heaven worship you. (Neh 9.6)

The sea is his, for he made it, and his hands formed the dry land. (Ps 95.5)

Know that the Lord is God. He made us, and not we ourselves; we are his people, and the sheep of his pasture. (Ps 100.3)

He appointed the moon to mark the seasons; the sun knows its time for setting. (Ps 104.19)

Your hands have made and fashioned me. (Ps 119.73)

Let them praise the name of the Lord, for . . . he commanded and they were created. (Ps 148.5)

O Lord of hosts, God of Israel, who are enthroned above the cherubim, you alone are the God of every kingdom of the world; you have made heaven and earth. (Isa 37.16)

Lift up your eyes on high and see: Who has displayed all these things? He who brings forth his host by number; he shall call them all by name by his great glory, and by the power of his might; nothing has escaped you. (Isa 40.26)

Thus says the Lord who redeems you, and who formed you in the womb: I am the Lord, who made all things, I alone stretched out the heavens, and established the earth. (Isa 44.24)

I made the earth, and man upon it; I with my hand established the heavens, and I gave commandment to all their stars. (Isa 45.12)

For thus says the Lord, who made the heavens, this God who created the earth and made it; he marked it out, he made it not in vain, but formed it to be inhabited: I am the Lord, and there is no other. (Isa 45.18).

It is the Lord that made the earth by his strength, who set up the world by his wisdom, and by his understanding stretched out the sky (Jer 10.12; 51.15).

O ever-living Lord! You made the heaven and the earth by your great power, and with your high and lofty arm: nothing can be hidden from you. (Jer 32.17)

It is he that makes all things, and changes them, and turns darkness into morning, and darkens the day into night, who calls for the water of the sea, and pours it out on the face of the earth, the Lord is his name. (Am 5.8)

The teaching of God's creation of the world and man is often repeated in the New Testament (Mt 19.4; Mk 10.6; Acts 4.24, 7.50, 14.15, 17.24; Rev 4.11, 10.6). However, one can add to this New Testament teaching the notion that God created everything through the mediation of his Word: "All things were made by him, and without him not one thing was made that has been made" (Jn 1.3). The Apostle Paul says about God that he "created all things by Jesus Christ" (Eph 3.9), "whom he appointed heir

The days of creation. Cathedral in Monreale. Sicily. 12th c.

of all things, by whom also he made the worlds" (Heb 1.2). With regard to the teaching of the Holy Spirit's participation in creation, it experienced a development after the New Testament epoch, although it was based on the claims in the Bible that, at the creation of the world, "the Spirit of God moved upon the face of the waters" (Gen 1.2) and that "the Spirit of God has made" man (Job 33.4). The following verse, in the minds of Christian interpreters, asserts the participation of the Holy Spirit in creation: "By the word of the Lord were the heavens established, and all the host of them by the breath of his mouth" (Ps 33.6).

Basil the Great says concerning the participation of the three Persons of the Holy Trinity in creation that:

> When you consider creation I advise you to first think of him who is the first cause of everything that exists: namely, the Father, and then of the Son, who is the creator, and then the Holy Spirit, the perfector. So the ministering spirits that exist by the will of the Father, are brought into being by the work of the Son, and are perfected in the work of the Spirit. . . . And let no one accuse me of saying that there are three unoriginate persons, or that the work of the Son is imperfect. The Originator of all things is One: he creates through the Son and perfects through the Spirit.[3]

The Father, therefore, is the first cause and source of all created things, the Son is he by whose hands the Father brings the world into being, and the Holy Spirit concludes the creative process, bringing it to completion. Gregory the Theologian says concerning God's forming of the angelic world: "And the thought was action, accomplished by the Word and perfected by the Spirit."[4] John of Damascus echoes Gregory: God "creates by thought, and this thought, brought to fulfillment by the Word and perfected by the Spirit, becomes deed."[5]

The Christian teaching on the creation received a final formulation in the theological thought of the Fathers of the Church from the fourth to the eighth centuries. Before the fourth century, Christian writers did not always make an exact differentiation between the being and appearance of God *ad*

---

[3] *On the Holy Spirit* 16 (Crestwood, N.Y.) 62.
[4] *Oration* 38.9 p. 67.
[5] *An Exact Exposition* . . . 2.2.

extra (from without), but the biblical notion of the creation of the world sometimes joined with the ancient notion of eternity and fluctuation of the cosmos.

A characteristic example of such a vision appears in Origen, who considered that if God was always Lord, Creator, and Almighty, then this signified that the cosmos always existed, since he would have to rule over something. If someone could think of what was in ancient times when creation was not yet created, then this would signify that throughout the course of that particular age, God was not Creator nor Almighty, and that he became such only afterwards, with the appearance of the visible world. But as far as God, being the highest perfection, cannot further improve himself, it is necessary to acknowledge that he "always had that which he ruled over and subjected to his control as King and Head."[6] Among the eternal works of God, according to Origen's teaching, was the Only-begotten Son of God, since God was always the Father of the Only-begotten.[7] "The logical link between the birth of the Son and the genesis of the world are still unbroken in the works of Origen," notes V. V. Bolotov.[8]

This link was broken by the theologians of the fourth century, who insisted on the necessity of carefully differentiating between ontological and cosmological aspects in God's being, between God in and of himself and God as Creator of the visible world. God the Father pre-eternally bears the Son and sends forth the Holy Spirit: the act of the Son's begetting and the Spirit's procession are manifestations of God's essence. The creation of the world, on the other hand, occurred in time and is the consequence of God's activity, of his energy. Being the Almighty and Creator of the visible world, God cannot suffer any sort of change to his essence, no kind of "development," because the creation of the world was exclusively the result of his action, his will.

The world is not coeternal with God and is not immanent to him. As Athanasius of Alexandria stressed, creation "is in no way similar in essence to its Creator, but is located outside of him."[9] Gregory the Theologian says: "If God, then not creation. . . . If creation, then not God, for it received its

---

[6] *On First Principles* 1.2.10.
[7] Ibid. 1.2.2–3.
[8] V. V. Bolotov, *Origen's Teaching of the Holy Trinity* (Saint Petersburg: 1879), 380–381.
[9] *To Adelphius* 1.20.

beginning in time. And if it received a beginning, then there was a time when it was not."[10]

God always existed and could not somehow not exist, since creation could then not exist.[11] In this is the cardinal difference between the pre-eternal generation of the Son from the Father and the creation of the world within time. "For generation means that the begetter produces out of his essence offspring similar in essence. But creation and making mean that the creator and maker produces from that which is external, and not out of his own essence, a creation of an absolutely dissimilar nature."[12] Athanasius of Alexandria, disputing with the Arians, emphasizes that the generation of the Son was not one of the acts of creation, and that the Son was generated not for the sake of the world's creation, though the formation of the world could not occur without the mediation of the Son:

> The Word of God did not receive being for our sake, quite the opposite, we, thanks to him, received being and all was formed by him (Jn 1.3). Not by our infirmities did he, as mighty, receive being from the one Father, so that the Father might create us as a tool for him. . . . If it [had] pleased God not to form creation, nevertheless the "Word was with God" (Jn 1.1), and the Father was in him. It was impossible for creation to receive being without the Word, for this reason it received being from him. . . . Since the Word is the Son of God by nature, since he is from God and in God, as he himself flowed out over everything, then it would be impossible for those things formed not to receive being through him.[13]

The ontological gulf between God and the created world is conditional upon God's existence in eternity. Though creation is formed out of nothing, God exists outside of time, and the existence of the visible world is connected to time, while God is changeless, though the existence of the world "began with change."[14] The same crossing from non-existence into being "is a certain kind of change, thanks to those non-existing things that God brings into being by his might."[15] Thus, that which began with change will then

---

[10]*Oration* 42.17. A play on the Arian phrase "there was a time when [the Son] was not."
[11]Cf.: Athanasius *To Adelphius* 1.20.
[12]John of Damascus *An Exact Exposition* . . . 1.8.
[13]*To Adelphius* 2.31.
[14]Gregory of Nyssa *Great Catechetical Oration* 6.
[15]Ibid. 21.

"necessarily be subject to further changes."[16] Linked to the understanding of change and corporeality, that is, materiality, is the understanding of time: "Time moves where there are actions of bodies; wherever bodies are not, change is not; where there is no change, there is no time."[17]

The biblical expression "In the beginning God created the heavens and the earth" (Gen 1.1) is understood in the patristic tradition as an indication that the world received its existence within time. However, this "beginning" about which the Bible speaks, according to the thought of Basil the Great, is not something consisting of sections, nor is it continuous: "As the beginning of a path is not a path, and the beginning of a house is not yet a house, so the beginning of time is not yet time, nor is it the smallest fraction of time."[18] In other words, being exists in time, but it is a participant in eternity only insofar as it is a creation of the eternal God. A "beginning" is nothing more than a fraction of eternity, an "implantation" in time and present in it like leaven in dough. Created time is transcendent to the eternal God, but, being made by him, it communes with him by the very act of creation. It is precisely thanks to this that God offered a "beginning" to all, having manifested all time, all movement, all hierarchy, and all materiality.

In the book of Genesis, creation is presented in the form of a gradual process, proceeding step by step throughout the course of six "days," that is, six temporal segments. The biblical narrative on the creation is sometimes presented as contradicting contemporary scientific theories, according to which the universe came into being billions of years ago. However, it is necessary to note, first of all, that one generally accepted point of view on the age of the universe does not exist in science: by this reckoning there is a multitude of different, often mutually exclusive, theories. Secondly, in the language of the Bible, the word "day" does not at all indicate a twenty-four hour calendar period: this word often signifies a prolonged period of time. The Psalmist calls the Hebrews' forty year wandering in the wilderness "the day of temptation in the wilderness" (Ps 95.8). Another psalm says: "For a thousand years in your sight are as yesterday which is past" (Ps 90.4). These words are repeated by the Apostle Peter, who says: "One day is with the Lord as a thousand years, and a thousand years as one day" (2 Pet 3.8). Thus, already contained in the Bible,

---

[16]John of Damascus *An Exact Exposition . . .* 1.3.
[17]Isaac the Syrian *Chapters on Knowledge* 1.17.
[18]*Conversation on the Hexaemeron* 1.6.

there are implicit indications that the narrative on the creation of the visible world in six days by God is not necessarily to be understood literally.

There are also indications in Christian tradition, particularly patristic theology, that the biblical days of creation do not follow the notion of a calendar day absolutely. Speaking of the first day of creation, Basil the Great notes that this day is not called "the first day" in the Septuagint, but "day one," which, in his opinion, allows for the placing of an equal sign between the biblical understandings of "day" and "age." Scripture frequently speaks of the "age of ages" or "ages of ages," indications of that "eighth day" that is none other than eternity. This is that "never-setting, without succession, and never-ending day," which is located beyond the bounds of time. For this reason, "whether you call it day or age, you choose one or the other understanding, whether you say this day or this condition, it is always one and not many, whether you name it age, it will be one, and not repeated."[19] Under this understanding, the whole history of mankind up until now corresponds to the seventh day on which God "rested from all the work that he had done" (Gen 2.3). But if the seventh day lasts for thousands of years, then why could the previous "days" of creation not be periods of time numbering in the thousands or even millions of years?

The question of the time of the appearance of the visible world was never raised to the level of dogma in the Church. Both Byzantium and Rus' used the dating system "from the creation of the world," according to which the generation of Adam occurred 5508 years before the birth of Jesus Christ. This dating system was one of many, used both in ancient times and the Middle Ages, and it was never dogmatized by the Orthodox Church. It indicates not so much the age of the universe as it does the age of human civilization. From the Orthodox point of view, an understanding of the first six days of creation that presents these days as temporal segments of a significant length is fully permissible. In such a case, the period before man in the history of the universe could stretch for thousands, millions, even billions of years. Only from the consciousness of the first man, Adam, does the time of the existence of human civilization begin to be counted, which scholars do not consider to exceed seven and a half millennia.[20]

---

[19]Basil the Great *Conversation on the Hexaemeron* 2.8.

[20]The most ancient of the known civilizations, the Sumerian, is dated from around fourth to third millennium before Christ.

The Orthodox Church stays away from the contemporary scientific dispute between evolutionists and creationists. The majority of Orthodox theologians reject the theory of evolution as contradicting the Bible (although some Orthodox authors of the twentieth century considered evolution and the Bible to be compatible). An officially developed and supported position of the Orthodox Church on the theory of evolution does not exist at this present moment, and the rejection of Darwinism is not an absolutely conditional assumption in the Orthodox Church. However, Orthodoxy rejects any theory of the origin of the world in which the biblical notion of God as Creator and Artificer is absent. It absolutely rejects the idea of the origin of man from apes or other animals as well. The Bible, it seems, does not say anything of the possibility or impossibility of evolution within individual species of plants and animals, although the biblical narrative of the creation of the world does not leave room for speculations on the origin of man from another type of animal.

Days of creation. Cathedral in Monreale. Sicily. 12th c.

The theory of evolution is one of the many contemporary hypotheses on the origin of the universe—hypotheses not supported by even one irrefutable fact. Not one scientist has yet been able to come up with convincing evidence for evolution of one form or another, of a transformation of an inorganic material into an organic one, or an ape into man. The relation of Orthodoxy to the theory of evolution is based on the principles formed by Archpriest Vasily Zenkovsky, which relate to Christian cosmology in total:

> The Christian teaching on the world, not rejecting by any means those *factors* that are established by scientific researchers, has, however, the whole foundation relating reservedly and critically to the different hypotheses and general theories, to which comes contemporary knowledge. The Christian teaching on the world, essentially, is not concurrent

with scientific constructions, does not generally pretend to deal with them. But Christianity has *something to say concerning the world*; everything that was said about the world by the Apostle Paul (not to mention the Old Testament teachings) and the holy fathers, now preserves its meaning in strength, notwithstanding all the undisputed successes of knowledge.[21]

The attitude of the Orthodox Church towards contemporary scientific creationism is based on these principles. The striving of the creationists to introduce the universe as a product of God's creation and to bring the scientific explanation of the world to a biblical understanding is seen as absolutely positive. At the same time, an Orthodox Christian cannot discount the fact that scientific creationism is influenced above all by a Protestant understanding of the Bible, granting unlimited freedom for the rationalistic interpretation of biblical prose. In Protestantism, church Tradition as reflected in the works of the Fathers of the Church is not normative. The absence of a respect for the patristic tradition, characteristic in Protestantism as a whole, is a quality of the majority of creationist scientists, who do not lean on the teaching of the holy fathers for the construction of their model of the creation of the world. This compels the Orthodox Church to show a definite restraint with respect to scientific creationism.[22]

What was the reason for the creation of the world and why did God bring it from non-existence into being? According to the teaching of the Fathers, there was no sort of necessity in the creation of the world, and God was not obligated to grant being to every created thing: "[Not] influenced by anyone, but of his own free will, he created all things,"[23] says Irenaeus of Lyons. The reason for creating the world was God's goodness, for which "it was not sufficient for goodness to be moved only in contemplation of itself, but it was necessary that the good be poured forth and spread outward."[24] God, "who is good and more than good, did not find satisfaction in self-contemplation,

---

[21] *The Basics of Christian Philosophy* 2 (Paris: 1964), 5. Italics are the author's.
[22] Insisting on the necessity to consider a patristic approach to the biblical narrative on the creation of the world, the Orthodox Church at the same time by no means makes absolute or dogmatizes those views of the holy fathers that are based on antiquated concepts of natural science. In the section on the holy sources of Orthodox dogma, we already discussed the many views in natural science that are contained in the *Conversations on the Hexaemeron* by Basil the Great and in *An Exact Exposition of the Orthodox Faith* by John of Damascus that are outdated and do not have ecclesial authority only by virtue of their being included in the works of these fathers of the Church.
[23] *Against Heresies* 2.1.1.
[24] Gregory the Theologian *Oration* 38.9 p. 66.

but in fits of exceeding goodness wished certain things to come into existence that would enjoy his benefits and share in his goodness."[25] As Isaac the Syrian writes, God made the worlds because he wanted all to know him, and populated the worlds with intellectual creatures so that they might join in the glory of his divine nature:

> He brought innumerable worlds and infinite natures into being; and he made legions of angels, who are without number, from nothingness. Existing in his own being, he, when no one was who could awake him—for nothing existed—deigned and wished by his own will and by his own goodness that the world would be brought into being, so that all might know him. And he completed creation by his goodness, granting us as well, people, who are formed from the dust of the earth, a quieter nature, and thanks to his creative art raised us up to the state of language, so that we might appear before him and talk with him in prayer, and so that we might communicate, by our minds, in this glory of the divine nature—if our life is worthy of this—and so that we might imitate the example of his bodiless essence on earth.[26]

The created world is hierarchical: there exist in it higher and lower creatures, some closer to God and some less close.[27] According to the teaching of Gregory the Theologian, amongst created beings there are some who are very close to God and even "intimate" with him, but some are very far from him and are alien to him. The former concerns angels, and the latter—animals, and inanimate objects as well. All possible steps of kindred with God or foreignness to him are taken up between these poles:

> Therefore [God] first thought of the angelic and heavenly powers. . . . And since the first world was beautiful to God, he thought a second material and visible world, that which is composed of heaven and earth and the system and composite of realities existing between them. It is praiseworthy because of the good disposition of each thing, but more praiseworthy because of the good connectedness and harmony of the whole. . . . Thus God has shown that he was able to create not only a nature akin

---

[25]John of Damascus *An Exact Exposition* . . . 2.2.
[26]*On the Divine Mysteries: Conversation* 1.72.
[27]Cf.: Gregory the Theologian *Oration* 34.8.

to himself but also what is entirely foreign to him. For the intelligible natures and those apprehended by the sense are entirely foreign to it, and those which are entirely without life or movement are still farther removed.[28]

[28] *Oration* 38.9–10 p. 67.

10

Angels

CREATED BEING CONSISTS OF the invisible world of bodiless spirits and the visible material world. The former deals with angels and demons, the latter–the whole universe, including people, animals, and inanimate objects.

The biblical narrative of the creation of the world does not include how God made the angels. However, the angels are constantly acting entities in many books in the Old Testament as well as the New. The angel of the Lord appears to the Old Testament righteous and speaks with them on behalf of God (Gen 16.7, 21.17, 22.11, 32.1; 1 Kg 19.5–7, etc.). Angels appear to prophets, enter into conversation with them, and enlighten them (Dan 9.21; Zech 1.9–14, etc.). The righteous and the prophets frequently contemplate angels in their visions. Jacob sees a ladder, placed on the earth, but reaching up to heaven, and angels of God are ascending and descending upon it (Gen 28.12). Isaiah sees the Lord sitting on a throne, and around him stand the six-winged Seraphim crying: "Holy holy holy is the Lord of Hosts! The whole earth is full of his glory" (Isa 6.3). One of the Seraphim flies over to the prophet and touches his mouth with a burning coal (Isa 6.6–7).

Angels are described in the Old Testament in the form of warriors, standing on the right hand and left hand of the Lord (1 Kg 22.19). The angels' function is to serve God as autocrat, to be his courtiers, his retinue. The Lord sits on the Cherubim (Ps 18.10, 80.2), and they bear the wheel of the glory of the Lord (Ezek 10.9–19). At the same time, angels are God's messengers and his servants, fulfilling his will and his ordinances with respect to people. In this sense, angels are mediators between God and the race of man. Sometimes angels fulfill the function of destroyer (2 Sam 24.15; 2 Kg 19.35; 1 Chr 21.15–16; 2 Chr 32.21; Isa 37.36), although they protect man much more frequently (Ex 23.20; Tob 3.17; Ps 91.11) and save him (Isa 63.9). Man has a guardian angel that shows him the straight path (Job 33.23).

White angel. Monastery of Mileseva. Serbia. 13th c.

In the New Testament, angels play a no less important role. An angel appears to Zechariah and announces the birth of John the Baptist (Lk 1.13); an angel appears to Mary and announces Jesus' birth from her (Lk 1.26–38). An angel proclaims the birth of the Messiah to the shepherds (Lk 2.8–20); an angelic host cries out at the birth of Jesus: "Glory to God in the highest, and on earth, peace, goodwill among men" (Lk 2.14). An angel twice appears to Joseph in a dream (Mt 1.20, 2.13). Angels minister to Jesus in the desert (Mt 4.11); an angel strengthens Jesus in the garden of Gethsemane (Lk 22.43); an angel proclaims the resurrection of the Savior to the myrrh-bearing women (Mt 28.2–7). An angel appears to Philip (Acts 8.26); one speaks with Cornelius in a vision (Acts 10.3–7); one leads Peter out of prison (Acts 12.7–10). The book of Revelation by John the Theologian is full of passages about angels.

Jesus Christ frequently speaks to his disciples about the angels. In the words of Jesus, every "one of these little ones" has an angel who sees "the face of [the] Father in heaven" (Mt 18.10). Angels rejoice at the repentance of every sinner (Lk 15.10). The day of the last judgment and Second Coming of Christ is unknown to the angels (Mt 24.26). However, at the Second Coming the angels will accompany Christ (Mt 16.27): they will separate the evil from the good (Mt 13.49) and gather the chosen of God from the four winds (Cf. Mt 24.31).

Some angels remembered in Holy Scripture have their own names, for example Raphael (Tob 3.16, 12.15), Gabriel (Dan 8.16, 9.21), and Michael (Dan 10.13, 10.21, 12.1). The angelic ranks have acquired names, among which, beyond Angels, we encounter the Cherubim (Gen 3.24; 2 Sam 6.2; Ps 18.11, etc.), the Seraphim (Isa 6.2), the Archangels (Jud 1.9; 1 Thess 4.16), and the Thrones, Dominions, Principalities, Authorities, and Powers (Col 1.16; Eph 1.21). These biblical names lie at the foundation of the patristic teaching on the nine angelic hierarchies, compiled in the fifth century.

The patristic angelology is based on the biblical concept of the angels, although in some aspects there are meaningful supplements to Holy Scripture. Above all, the Fathers of the Church fill in the silence of the book of Genesis regarding God's creation of the angels. Concerning this, as John of Damascus notes, some authors propose that the angels came before all creation, while others that they came "after the rise of the first heaven." John of Damascus himself holds on to the first opinion,[1] which is the most developed among the eastern fathers of the Church. In particular, Basil the Great, interpreting the words of the book of Genesis "in the beginning God created the heavens and the earth" (Gen 1.1), says:

It appears, indeed, that even before this world an order of things existed of which our mind can form an idea, but of which we can say nothing, because it is too lofty a subject. . . . The birth of the world was preceded by a condition of things suitable for the exercise of supernatural powers, outstripping the limits of time, eternal and infinite. The Creator and Demiurge of the universe perfected his works in it, spiritual light for the happiness of all who love the Lord, intellectual and invisible natures, all the orderly arrangement of pure intelligences who are beyond the reach of our mind and of whom we cannot even discover the names. They fill the essence of this invisible world, as Paul teaches us. "For by him were all things created that are in heaven, and that are in earth, visible and

[1]Cf.: *An Exact Exposition* . . . 2.3.

invisible whether they be thrones or dominions or principalities or powers" (Col 1.16) or virtues or hosts of angels or the dignities of archangels.[2]

Isaac the Syrian proposes that the angels were created by God "in
silence,"[3] which indicates the secret character of their creation. The nine ranks
of the angelic hierarchy were formed "suddenly out of nothing."[4] Isaac says
regarding the meaning of the names of the angelic ranks:

The angelic powers.
Sicily, 12th c.

> The divine Scripture gave these spiritual essences
> nine spiritual names and divided them into three
> sections, with three names in each. The first is
> divided into the great, lofty, and most holy
> Thrones, the many eyed Cherubim, and the six-
> winged Seraphim; the second is divided into the
> Dominions, Powers, and Authorities; the third is
> divided into the Principalities, Archangels, and
> Angels. These ranks are interpreted thusly: the
> Seraphim—from the Hebrew for "burning and con-
> suming"; the Cherubim—"abundant in knowledge
> and wisdom"; the Thrones—"God's support and God's repose"; and these
> ranks are known by these names according to their actions. The Thrones
> are named as worthy of honor, the Dominions—as having power over
> every kingdom, the Principalities—as making ether, the Authorities—as rul-
> ing over peoples and over every man, the Powers—as mighty strength, the
> Seraphim—as consecrating, the Cherubim—as bearing, the Archangels—as
> vigilant guards, and Angels—as messengers.[5]

Isaac the Syrian borrowed the teaching on the nine ranks of the angelic
hierarchy from Dionysius the Areopagite, although Gregory the Theologian
laid down this teaching earlier than Dionysius. According to Gregory, different ranks of angels exist, shining with divine light and placed by God in service to people:

> You see how we become dizzy with the theme and can get no further than
> the stage of being aware of angels and archangels, thrones, dominions,

---

[2] *Conversations . . . 1.5.*
[3] *Oration 25.*
[4] *On the Divine Mysteries: Conversation 10.24.*
[5] *Oration 25.*

princedoms, powers, of glowing lights, ascents, intellectual powers or minds, beings of nature pure and unalloyed. Fixed, almost incapable of changing for the worse, they encircle God, the First Cause, in their dance. . . . He makes them shine with purest brilliance or each with a different brilliance to match his nature's rank. So strongly do they bear the shape and imprint of God's beauty, that they become in their turn lights, able to give light to others by transmitting the stream that flows from the primal light of God. As ministers of the divine will, powerful with inborn and acquired strength, they range over the universe. . . . Each has under him a different part of the Earth or the universe. . . . They hymn God's majesty in everlasting contemplation of everlasting glory.[6]

As one can see, the nine names of the angelic ranks are found in Gregory the Theologian, although he does not attempt to arrange these ranks into a strict, ordered hierarchy. Dionysius the Areopagite undertook the task of the "systematization" of the angelic ranks. In his system, the angelic ranks are precisely divided into three hierarchies: 1) the Thrones, Seraphim, and Cherubim; 2) the Dominions, Powers, and Authorities; 3) and the Principalities, Archangels, and Angels.[7] The nine ranks of the angelic hierarchy, according to Dionysius, correspond to the nine ranks of ecclesial hierarchy, consisting of three sacraments (baptism, the Eucharist, and anointing), three orders of the priesthood (bishop, presbyter, and deacon), and three orders of lay service (monastic, lay, and catechumen).

The division of the angelic world into nine ranks has firmly entered into Orthodox theology and liturgical tradition. However, it was never dogmatized by the Orthodox Church. Moreover, the liturgical tradition has somewhat corrected the speculative construction of the Areopagite, in whose system the Archangels occupy the second place of the lowest angelic hierarchy: in liturgical texts, on the other hand, Archangels are perceived as one of the highest angels, as "Arch-strategists" (leaders of the angelic forces).

In general, the striving to systematize the angelic hierarchy, to give it a conclusive image, was not characteristic for the patristic tradition up until Dionysius the Areopagite. Some Fathers spoke directly about the fact that not all the names of the angelic ranks are known to man:

---

[6] *Oration* 28.31 p. 63.
[7] Cf.: Dionysius the Areopagite *Celestial Hierarchy* 6.

There are Angels and Archangels, Thrones and Dominions, Principalities
and Authorities; but not one of these assemblies exist in the heavens, but
an endless horde and innumerable tribes, which no word can depict.
Where is this known from, that there are many other forces besides these,
which we do not know by name? Paul, having spoken about the first,
refers to the second, expressing himself concerning Christ in this way: he
placed him "far above all rule and authority and power and dominion,
and above every name that is named, not only in this age but also in the
age to come" (Eph 1.21). Can you not then see that there are some names
that will be known there, and others unknown?[8]

The speculative character of the teaching on the nine ranks of hierarchy
developed by the Areopagite is sufficiently obvious: its weakest spot is its
striving to bring together all the angelic and ecclesial ranks into a definite
symbolic quantity. However, the very idea of a hierarchy as a holy order,
layer, or rank is an inseparable part of the Tradition of the Church in relation
to the ecclesial hierarchy, just as with respect to the angelic hosts. A hierarchy, in the words of Dionysius, presents itself as "a certain holy regulation,
an image of primordial beauty, a most holy action that by means of ranks,
and primordial knowledge, and the sacrament of its own vision, becomes like
its Principle to the extent that it is accessible."[9] The goal of a hierarchy is
assimilation of God and union with him.[10] The higher ranks of the angels
receive illumination directly from God himself, while the lower ranks receive
it by means of the higher.[11]

Patristic tradition did not have just one opinion concerning the corporeality or incorporeality of the angels. The generally-accepted term "bodiless
spirits" indicates the angels' difference from man more than it does a comparison of the angels' nature with the immaterial, divine nature. Although
the angels do not have material bodies similar to man's, they do, in the
opinion of some Christian authors, possess a certain "slight corporeality." In
the words of Macarius of Egypt, "Every created thing—both angel, and spirit,
and demon, according to its own, personal nature, has a body; because,
although they are refined, in their essence, according to their distinguishing

---

[8]John Chrysostom *Homilies Against the Anomoians* 4.3.
[9]*Celestial Hierarchy* 3.
[10]Ibid. 3.
[11]Ibid. 7.3.

characteristics and image, they are accordingly of a refined nature; the essence of their body is slight, whereas our body is crude in its essence."[12] John of Damascus considered that the bodiless and immaterial angelic nature is called thus "in comparison with us," whereas in comparison with God everything "seems crude and material, since there is only one Divinity that is indeed immaterial and bodiless."[13] The seventh ecumenical council called the angels "not completely bodiless," but "having a slight body, like air and flame."[14]

According to John of Damascus' teaching, an angel is an essence, bestowed with an intellect and free-will. An angel is immortal, though not by nature, but by blessing; "For all that has had beginning comes also to its natural end." God is the only one who is ever-existing, or rather: he is beyond eternity, for the Creator of time is not found to be dependent on time, but beyond it. Following after Gregory the Theologian,

Angels of the Lord. Detail of a mosaic of the Theophany. Palatine chapel. Palermo. 12th c.

the Damascene calls angels "second lights," "derived from that first light which is without beginning." Angels do not have need of language or hearing, relating to one another without means of words. Angels are boundless, since "they are not hemmed in by walls and doors, and bars and seals." However, they do not possess the omnipresence that is characteristic of God: "When they are in heaven, they are not on earth, and when they are sent by God to earth, they do not remain in heaven."[15]

In appearing to people, angels take on an aspect "that corresponds to how the viewer may see them."[16] Thus, for example, Isaiah gazed upon the Seraphim in the form of some existing thing with six wings: "With two they

---

[12] *Spiritual Homily* 4.9.

[13] *An Exact Exposition . . .* 2.3.

[14] "Acts of the Ecumenical Councils" 4 (Saint Petersburg: 1996), 494. The dispute of the corporeality of the angelic nature was resumed in the nineteenth century. In this dispute, Ignatius Brianchaninov defended the opinion on the slight corporeality of the angels and souls (cf.: his "Homily on Death"). Theophan the Recluse appeared against the above opinion, maintaining that "souls and angels are not bodies, but spirits" (see his essay of the same name).

[15] *An Exact Exposition . . .* 2.3.

[16] Ibid.

covered their faces, and with two they covered their feet, and with two they flew" (Isa 6.2). Ezekiel saw the Cherubim with a multitude of eyes, a back, hands, and wings (Ezek 10.12). However, angels are represented most frequently as a human-like being with wings, sometimes with a sword in hand (1 Chr 21.16). All of these variations regarding the outward form of the angels are found both in the liturgical and iconographical traditions of the Orthodox Church.

According to Basil the Great, "the business of the angels is to glorify God; there is but one duty of the heavenly hosts—to proclaim the glory of the Creator."[17] In much the same way as Basil, John of Damascus claims that angels live in heaven and that their main task is to sing praises to God.[18] Isaac the Syrian also speaks of this, for according to his teaching, the chief assignment of the angels consists in "raising praise to God in that great silence that spills out across all the world, in order that through it, the glorious nature of the Trinity might be brought to the contemplation of the world, and that it might reside in amazement, seeing the greatness of this ineffable glory."[19] The angels are in continual amazement and delight of those mysteries and revelation that descend on them from the divine nature.[20]

In the words of John of Damascus, the angels "are mighty and prompt to fulfill the will of the Deity, and their nature is endowed with such celerity that wherever the divine grace bids them they are straightway found." Angels "are the guardians of the divisions of the earth: they are set over nations and regions, allotted to them by their Creator: they govern all our affairs and bring us succor."[21] The idea that angels protect individual countries, and that each country and city has its own Guardian Angel, is based on the witness of Holy Scripture (Dan 10.13–21). In accordance with this concept, Gregory the Theologian says that each one of the angels "has under him a different part of the Earth or universe."[22]

A large part of Christian tradition received the teaching of the presence of a Guardian Angel for every concrete human being. The teaching, once again, is based on the testimony of Holy Scripture (Mt 18.10) and is already encountered in such early works such as *The Shepherd* by Hermas (second

[17] *Homily on Psalm 28* 7.
[18] Cf.: *An Exact Exposition* . . . 2.3.
[19] *On the Divine Mysteries: Conversation* 12.1.
[20] Cf.: Ibid. 8.6.
[21] *An Exact Exposition* . . . 2.3.
[22] *Oration* 28.31 p. 63.

century). This apocryphal composition says that two angels are bestowed upon every person—one good, one evil. The good angel is "quiet and humble, gentle and peaceful": entering into the heart of a person, it instills in one "fairness, chastity, purity, gentleness, leniency, love, and piety." But the evil angel instills "malice, wrath, and recklessness, and its actions are evil and they corrupt the servants of God."[23] In the ensuing years, the concept of an evil angel (demon) specially assigned to man disappeared from Christian tradition, whereas the concept of the Guardian Angel was developed and strengthened in theological literature as well as in liturgical texts. One of the supplicatory petitions in the Divine Liturgy says: "An angel of peace, a true guardian, a protector of our souls and bodies, let us ask of the Lord."

The angels, in the understanding of Christian writers, have a light and agile essence. John of Damascus asserts their "lightness and the ardor, and heat, and keenness and sharpness with which they hunger for God and serve him."[24] Isaac the Syrian emphasizes the dynamism, mobility, and lightness of the angels, saying that God made them like:

Innumerable higher worlds, boundless forces, legions of light-filled Seraphim, terrible and quick, marvelous and mighty, endowed with power and fulfilling the will of almighty Providence, simple spirits, light-bearing and bodiless, speaking without mouths, seeing without eyes, hearing without ears, flying without wings, acting without hands, accomplishing all the functions of the members without having those members. They do not tire and they do not grow faint, they are quick to action, not lagging behind, they are terrible to see; their ministry is marvelous, they are rich in revelations, sublime in contemplation; they gaze at the place of the invisible *Shekhina*;[25] glorious essences, and holy, ordered in nine ranks formed by the Wisdom that made everything. . . . They are fiery in their movements, with sharp minds, entrancing in knowledge, becoming like God inasmuch as this is possible.[26]

While there is no mention in the Bible of the creation of the angels in the image and likeness of God, such an idea is present in patristic works.

---

[23]Hermas *The Shepherd* 2.6.2.

[24]*An Exact Exposition . . .* 2.3.

[25]Lit.: "the *Shekhina* of invisibility." *Shekhina* (Heb.) is the presence of God, the glory of God; it is one of the most important concepts of biblical theology.

[26]*On the Divine Mysteries: Conversation* 10.24.

Gregory the Theologian calls angels "rays of the perfect Light."[27] John of
Damascus claims that God formed the angels "according to his image."[28]
Isaac the Syrian speaks of God's likeness in the angels: "There is a likeness
in them, as much as this is possible, to the very one who formed being itself—
the Creator who is above all."[29] The angels' god-likeness consists, above all,
in the absence of a material body: they are "lofty and immaterial, they are
closer to God than we, they are formed as secondary beings after God, lights
from the Light, servants of the King, fiery orders, arranged in front of the
palace, ready to fulfill his will; flesh does not hinder their ability to see
clearly the mysteries of his sanctuary; they are not subject to passions and
are likened to God."[30]

It is said in the Bible concerning the quantity of angels that they are "a
thousand thousand" and "myriads of myriads" (Dan 7.10; Rev 5.11). In the
patristic tradition, there is a generally accepted idea that angels significantly
outnumber all people who have ever lived, are living, and who are yet to be
born. Cyril of Jerusalem understands the ratio of the angels to people to be
ninety-nine to one, based on the gospel parable of the lost sheep (Mt 18.12–13),
by which is to be understood all mankind:

> Reckon, therefore, how many are the Roman nation; reckon how many
> the barbarian tribes now living, and how many have died within the last
> hundred years; reckon how many nations have been buried during the
> last thousand years; reckon all from Adam to this day. Great indeed is the
> multitude; but yet it is little, for the angels are many more. They are the
> ninety and nine sheep, but mankind is the single one. . . . The whole earth
> is but as a point in the midst of the one heaven, and yet contains so great
> a multitude; what a multitude must the heaven which encircles it con-
> tain? And must not the heaven of heavens contain unimaginable num-
> bers? And it is written, "Thousand thousands ministered unto him, and
> ten thousand times ten thousand stood before him" (Dan 7.10); not that
> the multitude is only so great, but because the prophet could not express
> more than these.[31]

[27] *Oration* 6.12.
[28] *An Exact Exposition . . .* 2.3.
[29] *On the Divine Mysteries: Conversation* 20.8.
[30] *Chapters on Knowledge 4* 86.
[31] *Catechetical Lecture 15* 24.

The angelic world, according to the teaching of Basil the Great, is permeated with the presence of the Holy Spirit. Without it, the angels could not live, neither could they act, nor contemplate God, nor praise him:

> If we agree that the Spirit is subordinate, then the choirs of angels are destroyed, the ranks of archangels are abolished, and everything is thrown into confusion, since their life loses all law, order, or boundary. How can the angels cry, "Glory to God in the highest" (Lk 2.14), unless the Spirit enables them to do so? "No one speaking by the Spirit of God ever says, 'Jesus be cursed!' and no one can say 'Jesus is Lord' except by the Holy Spirit" (1 Cor 12.3). . . . Not even Gabriel could have announced events to come, unless the Spirit gave him foreknowledge—since one of the gifts distributed by the Spirit is prophecy. . . . How can one explain the blessed life of thrones, dominions, principalities, or powers, if these spirits do not behold the face of the Father who is in heaven (Mt 18.10)? One cannot see the Father without the Spirit! . . . How can the Seraphim sing, "Holy, holy, holy" (Isa 6.3), without the Spirit teaching them to constantly raise their voices in praise? If all God's angels praise him, and all his host, they do so by cooperating with the Spirit. Do a thousand thousands of angels serve him? Do ten thousand times ten thousand stand before him? They accomplish their proper work by the Spirit's power. All the indescribable harmony of the heavenly realm, whether it be the praise of God or the mutual concord of the bodiless powers, would be impossible without the authority of the Spirit.[32]

---

[32] *On the Holy Spirit* 16.38 p. 63–64.

II

The Devil and Demons

Angels binding Satan. Detail of an icon of the Lord's resurrection. Dionysius. 15th c.

S ATAN, OR THE DEVIL, is not frequently mentioned in the Old Testament. A serpent figures prominently in the narrative of the book of Genesis concerning the Fall of the first people (Gen 3.1–15), which Christian tradition identifies as Satan. Such an understanding was already characteristic for the book of the Wisdom of Solomon, where it says that "through the devil's envy death came into the world" (Wis 2.24). Satan appears in the book of Job in the capacity of one of the "sons of God," who regularly stand before the Lord (Job 1.6, 2.1). God enters into dialogue with him and asks whether he had taken notice of Job's righteousness. Satan answers that Job is righteous because God has "put a hedge around him and around his household and all his possessions" (Job 1.10). At first God delivers all of Job's possessions and all of his children into Satan's hands, and they perish one after the other, and then his body is also given over, which breaks out in sores (Job 2.7). In the book of the Prophet Zechariah, Satan opposes the high priest Joshua (Zech 3.1–3). The first book of Samuel repeatedly mentions "an evil spirit from God" or "an evil spirit from the Lord" (1 Sam 16.14–16, 23, 18.10, 19.9), which descends on Saul and forces him to be possessed. In the first book of Kings, the Lord permits a "lying spirit" to enter the mouth of the prophets of Ahab (1 Kg 22.21–23). Finally, one of the psalms of David turns to God with a request concerning punishment of an offender: "Set a sinner against him; let the devil stand at his right hand" (Ps 109.6).

In the books of Job, 1 Samuel, and 1 Kings, Satan, or the evil spirit, acts as if he were sent by direct wish or order by God. The Old Testament does not attempt to answer the question of Satan's origin, nor his interrelation with God. However, the beginning of the book of Job shows that in the understanding of the Old Testament author, Satan was one of the sons of God, found to be in personal relationship with God. Satan acts within the limits set by God, and he cannot act outside of them. He inflicts harm on man, and God allows him to do so.

The New Testament mentions the devil and the evil-spirits (demons) repeatedly. The Synoptic Gospels contain the story of the temptation of Jesus in the wilderness by the devil (Mt 4.1–11; Mk 1.13; Lk 4.1–13). In the Gospel according to Luke, Jesus, turning to Peter, says: "Simon, Simon, behold, Satan has wanted you, that he may sift you like wheat, but I have prayed for you that your faith may not fail" (Lk 22.31–32). In both cases the devil is introduced as something that exists, having direct access to Jesus and entering into dialogue with him (just as Satan enters into dialogue with God in the book of Job).

Jesus mentions the devil in parables and in conversations with the Jews. In one of the parables, the devil is compared to a sower who sowed tares (Mt 13.39). In another place Jesus speaks about the devil as one who carries away the word of God from the heart of a man in which it had been sown (Lk 8.12). Jesus says to the Jews: "You are from your father the devil, and you will to do your father's lusts. He was a murderer from the beginning, and did not abide in the truth, because there is no truth in him. When he speaks a lie, he speaks on his own, for he is a liar and the father of lies" (Jn 8.44). Speaking of the last judgment, Jesus mentions the eternal fire, prepared "for the devil and his angels" (Mt 25.41).

The Synoptic Gospels contain many accounts of Jesus casting out demons from the possessed. Some witnesses of these acts of exorcism said that Jesus cast the demons out by the power of "Beelzebul, the prince of the devils" (Mt 12.24).[1] However, Jesus rejects this: "If Satan casts out Satan, he is divided against himself; how then shall his kingdom stand? If I by Beelzebub cast out devils, by whom do your children cast them out? . . . But if I cast out devils by the Spirit of God, then the kingdom of God has come upon you" (Mt 12.26–28). Jesus endowed his disciples with the power to cast out evil spirits (Mt 10.8; Mk 3.15, 6.13). When the disciples, sent by Jesus to preach, return to him, they say: "Lord, even the devils are subject to us through your name." And he answers: "I beheld Satan as lightning fall from heaven. Behold . . . I

[1]The name Beelzebul can be found in 2 Kings (chapter 1), where this name is called "the god of Ekron," that is, one of the idols of the nations.

have given you power to tread on serpents and scorpions, and over all the power of the enemy; and nothing shall by any means hurt you" (Lk 10.17–19).

The Apostolic Epistles contain exhortations to stand against the devil (Jas 4.7), to "resist [him], steadfast in the faith" (1 Pet 5.9), not to give him room (Eph 4.27), to stand "against the snare of the devil" (Eph 6.11), not to fall "into reproach and the snare of the devil" (1 Tim 3.7). "Be sober, be vigilant; for your adversary the devil goes about like a roaring lion, seeking someone to devour," warns the Apostle Peter (1 Pet 5.8). "Everyone who commits sin is of the devil; for the devil sins from the beginning. For this purpose was the son of God manifested, that he might destroy the works of the devil," says the Apostle John the Theologian (1 Jn 3.8). The Apostle Paul says that the Lord accepted flesh and blood for himself "so that through death he might destroy him who had the power of death, that is, the devil" (Heb 2.14).

The book of the Revelation of John the Theologian relates the overthrow of the devil by Michael and his angels: "And there was war in heaven: Michael and his angels fought against the dragon; and the dragon fought and his angels, and did not prevail; neither was their place found any more in heaven. And the great dragon was cast out, that old serpent, called the devil, and Satan, who deceives the whole world: he was cast out onto the earth, and his angels were cast out with him" (Rev 12.7–9). The angel, descending from heaven, binds for a thousand years "the dragon, that ancient serpent, who is the devil and Satan," throws him into the abyss, and locks and seals it over him (Rev 20.2–3). The final victory of God over the devil, or "the second death" of the devil (Rev 20.14), comes when the devil is cast into a lake of fire, where he will be "tormented day and night for ever and ever" (Rev 20.10).

Biblical demonology became the foundation on which the Fathers of the Church built their own teaching on the devil and demons. Placed before the Fathers above all was the question of the origin of the devil and demons. Some early Christian authors, dispensing with the biblical recollection of the "sons of God" who "took to themselves wives of all whom they chose" (Gen 6.2), spoke out against the opinion that demons came about as a result of copulation between angels and women.[2]

However, the generally accepted answer to the question posited above became the teaching that God created a good angel, but he opposed God and fell away from him, turning into the devil. Gregory the Theologian calls the

[2]Cf.: Justin *Second Apology* 5.

angel who fell away from God "the first light-bearer," who carried other angels away with him and turned them into demons:

> O first light-bearer, you extolled yourself so highly,–
> For he dreamt of the kingly honor of the great God,
> Having himself the primary glory,–he destroyed his radiance,
> He fell from there in dishonor, having made himself not a god,
>   but a shade.
> Though he is light in nature, however, he fell to the vile earth.
> Since that time he hates the good and wise and obstructs every
> Path to heaven, irritated by his loss.
> He does not want them to go to that divinity from which he fell,
> Approaching creation, but not wanting it to be the norm for
>   him, and wanting the dead to
> Become sin and darkness. This jealous one cast out from
>   paradise
> Those who wished to have glory equal to God's.
> Thus, extoling himself, he descended from the heavenly realm;
> But he did not fall alone, but, since his pride was destroyed,
> He threw down many–all who learned sin. . . .
> From thence came the subterranean bearers of evil–
> The demons, followers of the evil king and man-slayer,
> Powerless, dark, evil phantoms of night.[3]

Athanasius of Alexandria calls the first angel that opposed God "one of the Cherubim,"[4] while St Cyril of Jerusalem called it an archangel who was created good, but then fell from God.[5] John of Damascus considers that he who fell from God was:

> He who from among these angelic powers was set over the earthly realm, and into whose hands God committed the guardianship of the earth. . . . He was not made wicked in nature but was good, and made for good ends, and received from his Creator no trace whatever of evil in himself. But he did not sustain the brightness and the honor which the Creator had bestowed on him, and of his free choice was changed from what was in

[3] *Dogmatic Poems 6: On Rational Beings.*
[4] *On the Holy Spirit* 1.26.
[5] *Catechetical Lecture* 2 4.

harmony to what was at variance with his nature, and became roused against God who created him, and determined to rise in rebellion against him: and he was the first to depart from good and become evil.

There followed after him, and fell together with him, "an innumerable host of angels subject to him." Possessing equality with the angelic nature, these fallen angels "became wicked, turning away at their own free choice from good to evil."[6]

Thus, the devil fell away from God "according to his autocratic will," that is, as a result of the action of free will. The issue of the reason for the devil's falling away from God is connected, in the patristic tradition, to the question of the origin of evil and is examined in the context of the teaching on free will. A distinguishing quality of freedom, according to the opinion of Gregory of Nyssa, is concluded in freely electing that which is desired, and for this reason one guilty of evil is not God, being of a "nature that is independent and not servile," but it is folly for him who chooses evil instead of good.[7] Being intelligent, angels were formed as free, emphasizes John of Damascus. But for created nature, freedom signifies the possibility to choose between good and evil. "This in fact is made plain by the devil who, although made good by the Creator, became of his own free-will the inventor of evil, and by the powers who revolted with him, that is the demons, and by the other troops of angels who abided in goodness."[8]

The falling away from God of the devil and the demons is perceived in the patristic tradition as an event that occurred once and will not be repeated in the future. Although the angels, the devil, and the demons maintain their free will, the fall of the devil and the demons is final and irreversible, just as the angels abiding in goodness remain in it steadfastly. In the words of Basil the Great, "Gabriel is an angel, and always will be. Satan is an angel and fell from his own rank absolutely. The former was preserved in celestial will, while the latter was thrown down by his own will. The former could have become an apostate, and the latter could not pass up the opportunity. But the insatiable love for God saved one, while the other was made an outcast and sent away from God."[9]

---

[6] *An Exact Exposition* . . . 2.4.
[7] Cf.: *The Great Catechism.*
[8] *An Exact Exposition* . . . 2.27.
[9] *Homily 9* 8.

The temptation of Christ in the wilderness. Monastery of Chora. Constantinople. 14th c.

The devil and the demons are "of the same nature as the angels,"[10] considers John of Damascus. However, according to the idea of Gregory of Sinai, the demons lost their immateriality and narrowness after the falling away from God, and were clothed in a body: "They were never with minds, but, falling away from that immateriality and narrowness, each one of them acquired a certain material crudeness, becoming bodily in rank and action."[11]

The devil and demons "have no power or strength against anyone except what God in his dispensation hath conceded to them ... But when God has made the concession they do prevail, and are changed and transformed into any form whatever in which they wish to appear."[12] As an example of God's tolerance concerning the demons' activity, the Damascene brings up the story of Job and the evangelistic prose on the evil spirits that come out of the Gadarene demoniac and enter the herd of swine (Mt 8.32). As for the question of why God allows demonic activity, the general answer is that God directs evil actions of the devil to good consequences and allows temptation from the devil for the examination and spiritual success of man.

While the demons are indeed permitted to attack man, "they have not the strength to overpower anyone: for we have it in our power to receive or not to receive the attack."[13] It is said of Anthony the Great that the Lord appeared to him and said: "The devil cannot depose anyone. He does not have any more power after I, having perceived human nature, shattered his rule. But man falls all by himself, when he gives in to recklessness."[14]

The devil does not have authority over man, however, he can entice, lure, and deceive him. The fundamental method of his action is to lie (Jn 8.44). Being a shade, "Satan masquerades as an angel of light" (2 Cor 11.14). He covers his evil beneath a good guise: "He frequently hides his bitter taste under a veil of sweetness, so as not to be exposed."[15]

---

[10] *An Exact Exposition* ... 2.4.
[11] *Chapters on the Commandments and Dogma* 123.
[12] John of Damascus *An Exact Exposition* ... 2.4.
[13] Ibid.
[14] Anthony the Great *Exhortations to Monks.*
[15] *Instruction on the Life in Christ* 32.

Neither angels nor demons know the future, "yet they make predictions. God reveals the future to the angels and commands them to prophesy, and so what they say comes to pass. But the demons also make predictions, sometimes because they see what is happening at a distance, and sometimes merely making guesses: hence much that they say is false and they should not be believed, even although they do often . . . tell what is true."[16]

The devil and demons (evil spirits) are characters that are constantly acting in the Eastern Christian ascetical literature, which is filled with descriptions of demonic temptations, demonic "barbs," and demonic "terrors." The description of demonic temptations occupies a significant portion of *The Life of St Anthony the Great* by Athanasius of Alexandria. In the compositions of Evagrius of Pontus and other Egyptian hermits of the fourth century, in the works of Mark the Ascetic, Abba Isaiah, John of the Ladder, Symeon the New Theologian, Gregory of Sinai, and other authors, great attention is given to the action of the devil and his demons toward monks. Evagrius' classic composition *On Prayer* describes the devices used by the devil to hinder one's attention on prayer:

> The demon is very malignant towards any person who prays, and it employs every means to defeat his purpose. It does not cease moving thoughts of matter through the memory and stirring up all the passions through the flesh, so as to be able to impede his excellent course and his departure to God.
>
> When, despite all his efforts, the malevolent demon is unable to hinder the prayer of one who is earnest, it lets up for a time and then takes its revenge when he finishes praying. It either: enflames him with anger, thus ruining the excellent state that, through prayer, has been welded together in him; or it entices him to some irrational pleasure and so commits an outrage on the *nous*.
>
> The whole war between us and the unclean demons concerns nothing other than spiritual prayer, because it is very hostile and burdensome to them, while it is salvific and very soothing for us.
>
> If demons threaten to appear suddenly to you out of the air to terrify you and snatch away your *nous* or to harm your flesh like wild beasts, do not let them fluster you, do not pay any attention at all to their threats.

---

[16]John of Damascus *An Exact Exposition* . . . 2.4.

They are trying to frighten you, to test whether you are taking any notice of them or whether you ignore them totally.[17]

The Ladder frequently speaks of evil spirits as of a collective enemy of the ascetic, but sometimes this or that passion is associated with a concrete demon standing behind it. John of the Ladder, in particular, mentions the demon of "wandering and pleasure,"[18] the demon of despair,[19] the demon of avarice with "countless heads,"[20] the demon of cowardice,[21] the demon of despondency,[22] and the demon of vainglory.[23] Sometimes two, or even a few, demons act in tandem; sometimes, quite the opposite occurs, and "one devil is cured by another,"[24] that is, one passion casts out another. In his descriptions of demonic snares, St John, like Evagrius, displays the psychological power of observation so characteristic of ascetic writers in the monastic circle:

> Do not be so fooled by the spirit of conceit that you confess your sins to your director as though they were someone else's. Lay bare your wound to the healer. Only through shame can you be freed from shame.[25]

> God is merciful before a fall, inexorable after—so the demons say.[26]

> It is the murdering demons that push us into sin. If they are balked here, they get us to pass judgment on those who are sinning, thereby smearing us with the stain we are denouncing in others.[27]

> Be sure to laugh at the demon who, when supper is over, says that in the future you should eat later, for you may be sure that at the ninth hour he will change the arrangements made on the previous day.[28]

---

[17]47, 48, 50, 99; translation by Luke Dysinger, O.S.B., http://www.ldysinger.com/Evagrius/03_Prayer/00a_start.htm.
[18]*The Ladder of Divine Ascent* 3.5.
[19]Ibid. 5.29.
[20]Ibid. 16.1.
[21]Ibid. 21.9.
[22]Ibid. 13.8.
[23]Ibid. 22.18; 3.27.
[24]Ibid. 9.7.
[25]Ibid. 4.63.
[26]Ibid. 5.31.
[27]Ibid. 10.11.
[28]Ibid. 14.13.

I have seen the demon of vainglory suggesting thoughts to one brother, revealing them to another, and getting the second man to tell the first what he is thinking and then praising him for his ability to read minds.[29]

I have seen a demon harm and chase away his own brother. Visitors from the outside world came just at the moment when a brother got angry and the wretched man gave himself over to vainglory. He was unable to serve two passions at the one time.[30]

Someone who is occupied with some task and continues with it at the hours of prayer is being fooled by the demons, for these thieves aim to steal one hour after another from us.[31]

St John of the Ladder devotes special attention to the activity of the demons during dreams, saying that "the demons of vainglory are as prophets in dreams": while they do not know anything about the future, they can conclude what may happen in the future from present circumstances and predict them to us, so that when these foretold things are fulfilled, we might get a false notion of their prophetic abilities. For example, seeing that someone will die, a demon predicts this in a dream to someone who is weak in faith. In the words of St John, "To the credulous, a devil is a prophet; and to those who despise him, he is just a liar." Demons can transfigure themselves into angels of light or into the form of the martyrs and appear to us in dreams as if we should go to them, but upon waking they will grant us unholy joy and conceit. "If we start to believe in the devils of our dreams, then we will be their playthings when we are also awake. The man who believes in dreams shows his inexperience, while the man who distrusts every dream is very sensible," concludes St John of the Ladder.[32]

The works of Symeon the New Theologian contain many accounts of demonic temptation and discussions on the nature and activities of the devil. Symeon names conceit and self-importance as the reason for the fall of the devil and his demons. The angels, he says, "Grew in fear and knowledge and redoubled their fear, seeing Satan falling and his companions carried off by presumption. That is the only thing that all those who fell, slaves of their

---

[29]Ibid. 22.19.
[30]Ibid. 22.27.
[31]Ibid. 28.35.
[32]Ibid. 3.27–28.

pride, forgot."[33] After the fall of the devil and his angels, they lost their light-
bearing quality and found themselves in darkness: "The prince (the devil),
after being defeated, was at once deprived of the light and thrown into darkness. And with him there are all those who fell with him from Heaven into
darkness. And he reigns there—I mean in the darkness—over those demons
and humans held in captivity."[34]

Since the irreconcilable enmity between the devil and man began, the
devil used every means available to him so as to gather as many people as
possible into his fate.[35] The devil has acquired great authority over the world.
Symeon calls the devil "the prince of darkness," who "rules over the earth by
evil, ruling over all the oceans and waters and toys with the world, as one
might play with a little bird."[36] Man's struggle with the devil is not cut short
by even a minute:

> This war is endless, and Christ's warriors should always bear arms. There
> is no rest from this war, neither in day nor in night. . . . We have bodiless
> enemies that stand before our faces interminably, though we do not see
> them; they vainly leave their footprints behind, whether or not one of our
> members is laid bare so that they can plunge their arrows into us and kill
> us. And no one can hide behind physical walls or fortresses. . . . One can-
> not save oneself by fleeing, nor can one man take up the fight for another,
> but every man must carry himself into the fray and either gain victory and
> remain alive, or be defeated and finally die.[37]

Symeon compares man's life to a king's highway: along both sides of it
are forests, precipices, cliffs, and canyons, but also plains and beautiful
places, in which, however, "a great multitude of wild beasts and regiments of
thieves and murderers" are hidden. If we go down this path, imitating those
saints that went down it before, and not paying attention to the hidden enemies, especially if we have a guide and good traveling companions, then not
one of them will dare to attack us blatantly.[38]

---

[33] *Hymn 2* 119–124 p. 19.
[34] *Hymn 33* 26–30 p. 183.
[35] *Catechetical Lecture 7* 55–59.
[36] *Catechetical Lecture 23* 180–183.
[37] *Catechetical Lecture 3* 330–346.
[38] *Catechetical Lecture 7* 246–262.

The devil and the demons have power only in darkness, but they lose it at the slightest proximity to the Light of life:

> Every soul who does not see the light of life shining radiantly day and night is punished by the devil, is wounded, subjugated, is dragged and chained, and is pierced continually by the arrows of pleasures. . . . Still with great sweat, fatigue, pain, and sorrow, it carries on a perpetual war, made by the demon with never the possibility of ending it. But every soul that contemplates the divine light, wherever the evil one has fallen, it despises him, and . . . it tramples under foot the prince of darkness, as leaves falling to the earth from a high tree. It is in darkness that he has power and might, but in the light he is only a fallen cadaver.[39]

Symeon describes, in detail, various tricks used by evil spirits in battle with people. Sometimes, he says, they stand afar off, sometimes they come closer; sometimes they frighten man and watch with "bloodthirsty eyes," while in another instance they flatter with their tongues as if it were a friendly conversation or inviting one to try some sweets, some good fruits, and to rest from hard labor. "Thus they rise up against us day and night, and not only when we are vigilant, but also while we sleep."[40] Sometimes they assail and threaten with death, thinking to bring one down that road. "Some of them show us that it is impossible to remove all the labors of this way, others show what vanity [these ways] are and how they bring no kind of benefit to the laborers; still others say how this way will never have an end, showing some of those who were not corrected and, although much time was spent in ascetical efforts, not one received benefit."[41] Finally, they bring down that road those who went along it willfully or proudly. "But how can I relate to you," concludes Symeon, "or how can I estimate . . . the snares of our enemy the devil and his evil spirits?"[42]

Symeon teaches all of the illusions and deceptions the devil can offer man. If he "takes the form of an angel of light," then it is imagined; if he offers man pleasure, then it is not genuine: "Being shadow, he is transfigured into an angel of light, but not in actuality, just as a phantasm; he does not

---

[39]*Hymn 33* 31–49.
[40]*Catechetical Lecture 7* 262–274.
[41]Ibid. 275–285.
[42]Ibid. 292–295.

have and cannot give anything that is delightful, joyful, free, tranquil, rational feeling, or spiritually instructive."[43] Offering man imaginary blessings, the devil deprives him of actual blessings:

> By showing me the visible life, it tears away from me the life of the spirit. Through the sensation of actual goods, it robs me and it plunders the rich of future blessings. Quite another is its external appearance and quite another what it conceals. . . . What will not the inventor of evil do? How will he not lead astray, especially the young? How will he not fool those who are innocent, without any experience, without any guile, he who by choice is Satan, the artful one, the one who invents all ruse with skill?[44]

[43] *Catechetical Lecture 15* 88–93.
[44] *Hymn 24* 151–163 p. 129.

12

Man

THE ORTHODOX TEACHING ON MANKIND is based mainly on two sources—the Bible and the works of the church fathers. The Fathers' anthropology, in its turn, absorbed not only the biblical teaching on man, but many elements of ancient Greek philosophical anthropology as well. The patristic teaching of the creation of man, his fall, and atonement, is wholly based on the Bible. The teachings of man as a microcosm, of the four elements of the human body, and of the tripartite construction of the soul, on the other hand, are borrowed from ancient Greek philosophy and medicine. Some ideas that are characteristic for patristic anthropology come from both sources.

Patristic theology considers man to consist of three aspects, or three states. First, it speaks of the primordial man, formed in the image and likeness of God. Second, it speaks of fallen man, whose nature is distorted by sin. Third, it speaks of the redeemed man, moving along the path to deification. In the present section the question concerns the first two aspects in Orthodox anthropology above all.

PRIMORDIAL MAN

Commenting on the biblical passages concerning the creation of man, the church fathers place special attention on the words: "And God said, 'Let us make man according to our image and likeness'" (Gen 1.26). When God created the heavens, the earth, the lights, the plants, and the animals, he did not consult with anyone. But before the passage relating the creation of man, the flow of the biblical narrative is suddenly cut off, and the author slightly reveals the mystery of the inner relation of the

The creation of man. Palatine chapel, Palermo. 12th c.

Trinity, for in the biblical "let us make," patristic theology sees an indication synonymous to the conference of the three Persons of the Holy Trinity: "In the beginning," says St Basil the Great, "before the creation of the world, we see that God converses with the Son and the Spirit. . . . For to whom does he say 'let us create' if not to the Word and Only-Begotten Son, through whom, according to the word of the evangelist, 'All things came into being,' and to the Spirit, of whom it is written: 'The Spirit of God, who has formed me'?"[1]

In Eastern Christian theology and liturgical tradition, the conference of the three Persons of the Holy Trinity before the creation of man received the title "Pre-eternal Council." St John of Damascus calls it the "Pre-eternal and Changeless Council" of God.[2] Maximus the Confessor says: "The Great Council of the God and Father is accompanied by silence and an unknown mystical economy. The Only-Begotten Son revealed and fulfilled it through the incarnation, having become the Herald of the great and Pre-eternal Council of God the Father."[3] One of the *stichera* on the feast of the Annunciation of the All-Holy Mother of God begins with the words: "Revealing to you the Pre-eternal Council, Gabriel stood before you, O Maiden." The news that the Theotokos received from the angel was in keeping with a divine decision made at the Pre-eternal Council of the Holy Trinity, the decision that God should become incarnate and himself become man, for the salvation and deification of mankind.

At the Pre-eternal Council the issue was about the fate of man and about what God's answer to the possibility of man's deviation from God's will would be. Man is formed in the image and likeness of God: this means that he will have in his nature those traits characteristic of the Trinitarian God; he will possess qualities that only God has in the highest degree, including free will. However, if, for God, freedom signifies an endless and unshakeable will for good, then for man it can signify the right to choose between good and evil. The freedom made by God for man is so unlimited, that man, if he so desires, can separate himself from God and live just as he wants to, to be in direct contradiction to God's will and Divine Providence.

In the words of V. Lossky, included in this possibility of man's to deviate from God's will was "the risk of creation," for, "creating identity, the Divine

---

[1] *Against Eunomius* 5.
[2] *Apologetic Treatises against Those Decrying the Holy Images* 1.10.
[3] *Chapters on Theology and Oikonomia* 2.23.

Almighty brought about a kind of radical 'intrusion,' something totally new: God forms beings that, like him (here we recall the Divine Council in the book of Genesis), can decide and choose." But this risk is a "paradoxical form that joins itself to the all-powerfulness of God":

> The height of the divine all-powerfulness hides within itself as if it were a weakness of God. . . . God becomes powerless before human freedom, he cannot constrain it because it proceeds from his power. . . . The will of God will always submit itself to the prodigals, the deviants, and even to the rebellious of the human will, in order to bring it to free concord. Such is Divine Providence.[4]

Having made man free, God linked his own life to that of man, for he took responsibility for man's fate. The necessity of the incarnation flows from the very act of creation, since without God's becoming man, man could not become god. But man's salvation and deification are not only the actions of the Son of God: all three Persons of the Holy Trinity participate in them. It is said in the gospel: "For God so loved the world that he gave his only begotten Son, that whoever believes in him should not perish but have everlasting life" (Jn 3.16). This means that God the Father loved man so much that he gave his Son over to death for the sake of man's salvation. Christ even says concerning himself that he came to fulfill the Father's will (Jn 6.38). But the Father's will is that no one should die, not even one person made by him. Christ says concerning the Holy Spirit: "If I do not go away, the Comforter will not come to you; but if I depart, I will send him to you" (Jn 16.7).

The foundation for these words of Christ can be reconstructed (of course, on a conditional, symbolic plane) as that which came from the Pre-eternal Council. God the Father, wishing to create man in his image and likeness, turns to the Son, asking him if he is ready to take responsibility for man's fate until he himself should become man and share in the fate of mankind. The Holy Spirit participates in this meeting as well, and the descent of the Holy Spirit upon people, his presence in the world, is set in place by direct dependence on the incarnation of the Son of God. In other words, the Pre-eternal Council signifies the accord of all the Persons of the Holy Trinity in taking responsibility for mankind's fate.

---

[4] *The Mystical Theology of the Eastern Church* (Moscow: 1991), 243–244.

The All-Holy Trinity.
St Andrei Rublev. 15th c.

The theme of the Pre-eternal Council found a resonance in Russian religious art. It is expressed in literary form by the Archpriest Avvakum in the first chapters of his famous *Life*:

And this glance into God was before even Adam was created, before he was even imagined. The Father said to the Son, "Let us make man according to our image and likeness." And the Second answered, "We shall make him, O Father, and he will transgress." And again he said, "O my Only-Begotten! O my Light! O Son and Word! O my radiant glory! If you consent to our creation, it will befit you to put on rotting man, it will befit you to walk upon the earth, to take on flesh, to struggle and to accomplish all." And the Second answered, "May your will be done, Father." And thus Adam was created.[5]

The image of the Holy Trinity painted by the hand of St Andrei Rublev is the iconographer's portrayal of the Pre-eternal Council. Three angels are represented in this icon, bowing to one another in silent conversation, while the middle angel indicates with his finger the chalice with the sacrificial lamb. The three angels symbolize the three Persons of the Holy Trinity, while the chalice symbolizes the divine incarnation and the sacrificial death on the cross of the Son of God. There is no disagreement or contradiction between the three interlocutors: they reside in harmonious and inviolable unity. Love reigns among them, that same divine love that became the reason for the creation of the world and man, and the reason for the divine incarnation.

Thus, only after it was decided that God himself would become the redeeming guarantor of man's salvation, "God made man, according to the image of God he made him, male and female he made them" (Gen 1.27). Speaking of the creation of mankind in the image and likeness of God, Gregory of Nyssa likens God to an artist, and man to a painting that reflects the perfection of the Creator:

It is true, indeed, that the divine beauty is not adorned with any shape or endowment of form, by any beauty of color, but is contemplated as

[5] *Life of Avvakum* (Moscow: 1960), 58–59.

excellence in unspeakable bliss. As then painters transfer human forms to their pictures by the means of certain colors, laying on their copy the proper and corresponding tints, so that the beauty of the original may be accurately transferred to the likeness, so I would have you understand that our Maker also, painting the portrait to resemble his own beauty, by the addition of virtues, as it were with colors, shows in us his own sovereignty: and manifold and varied are the tints, so to say, by which his true form is portrayed: not red, white, or the blending of these, whatever it may be called, nor a touch of black that paints the eyebrow and the eyes, and shades, by some combination, the depressions in the figure, and all such arts which the hands of the painters contrive, but instead of these, purity, freedom from passion, blessedness, alienation from all evil, and all those attributes of the like kind which help to form in men the likeness of God: with such hues as these did the Maker of his own image mark our nature.[6]

The theme of God's image is one of the central themes in the anthropology of the Fathers of the Church. Various understandings of God's image in man exist in the patristic tradition. The majority of the Fathers perceived God's image to be in the human soul[7] or in its higher faculties—the intellect.[8] In the words of St Gregory the Theologian,

> There was a time when the lofty Logos of the Mind, serving the
> great Mind of the Father,
> Founded the world that did not exist until that moment.
> He spoke—and all that he willed was accomplished. But when all
> this—
> Land, sky, and sea—comprised the cosmos,
> Became necessary, and the contemplative of Wisdom, the
> mother of all,
> The reverential king of all the earth. Then the Logos. . . .
> Taking part in the newly-formed earth,
> Formed my image with immortal hands,
> To whom he gave something out of his life, since he sent to it

---

[6] *On the Making of Man* 5.
[7] Cf.: Gregory the Theologian *Dogmatic Verses 8: On the Spirit*; Maximus the Confessor *Chapters on Theology* 1.11; *Mystagogia* 7.
[8] Cf.: John of Damascus *An Exact Exposition . . .* 3.18.

The Spirit, who is the spirit of the invisible Divinity.
Thus from dust and breath man was formed, the image of the
Immortal One,
While the nature of the mind rules in both.
For this reason I am attached to this life, from my earthly origin,
But out of a part of the Divinity, I bear in my breast love for
God.[9]

Sometimes the Fathers saw God's image in man's free will.[10] Some
Fathers also made a distinction between the "image" and "likeness": the
image is that which was given to man in the very moment of his creation; the
likeness though, that is, similarities to God, is something man must reach as
a result of moral perfection and good works.[11]

Some Christian authors saw the divine image as having sway over the
position that man occupies in the universe,[12] as well as in man's immortality[13] and in his creative power.[14]

St Gregory of Nyssa, moreover, spoke about the fact that man was formed
in the image of the Tri-Hypostatic God. Gregory saw in the first human family—Adam, Eve, and their sons—the image of the Father, the Spirit, and the
Son.[15] God did not create just one man, not a singular, mutually exclusive
monad, not a unity, but "man and woman," whom he commanded "to bear
fruit and multiply" (Gen 1.27–28). As God is one in three Hypostases, so is
man comprised of a multi-hypostatic essence. Adam, Eve, and their descendants, are the entire human race, humankind. All people have one nature and
one essence, but at the same time, every person thinks of him or herself as a
unique hypostasis, and individual.

Speaking of man as an image of the Holy Trinity, Anastasius of Sinai offers
the following interpretation: the image of the Holy Trinity is soul, wisdom,
and intellect. By this reckoning, the soul "is unbegotten and has no origin, in

[9]*Dogmatic Verses 8: On the Spirit.*
[10]Cf.: Maximus the Confessor *Chapters on Theology* 1.11.
[11]Cf.: Irenaeus of Lyons *Against Heresies* 5.6.1; Clement of Alexandria *Stromata* 2.22; Origen *On
First Principles* 3.6.1; Diadochos of Photiki *Ascetical Oration* 89; Maximus the Confessor *Chapters on Love*
3.25; John of Damascus *An Exact Exposition . . .* 2.12.
[12]Cf.: John Chrysostom *Homilies on Genesis* 8.2–3.
[13]Cf.: Tatian *Address to the Greeks* 7; Cyril of Jerusalem *Mystagogical Catechesis* 4.18.
[14]Cf.: Theodoret *Difficult Passages of Divine Scripture.* Photius of Constantinople *To Amphilochius*
253.
[15]Cf.: *Oration on What Is Meant by "in the Image."*

the seal of God the Father who is unbegotten and has no origin," and wisdom then is born of the soul in the image of the Son of God, while the intellect proceeds from the soul according to the image of the Holy Spirit.[16]

In the words of the Apostle John the Theologian, "God is love" (1 Jn 4.16). God does not simply *possess* love, directed to something dear to him: he is, within himself, in his very being, love. But God would not be love if he were not a Trinity, for something that is isolated and closed within itself cannot be love. This is precisely why man could not love, nor could he partake of love, if he remained alone, if his personal potential were not realized in contact with other people. Man becomes man thanks to social interaction with people. And it is precisely through people that he experientially joins with love.

Man was thought up and created by God as an essence, chosen to realize this potential of love that is pledged to him from the moment of his creation. In his youth he reaches out for his mother, and the bonds of love unite him with her, with the closest companionship, with the closest family bond, in the indissoluble image. Upon growing up, man enters into the union of marriage, and there occurs what is said in the Bible: "Therefore a man shall leave his father and his mother and shall cleave to his wife" (Gen 2.24). The child becomes the fruit of love between a man and a woman, and they pour out their parental love on it. Therefore, it is love that is the main motivating force in human history, a force handed down from generation to generation as a legacy that is divine and never grows scarce.

God created man "from the dust of the earth, and breathed upon his face the breath of life" (Gen 2.7). The church fathers most frequently understand "the breath of life" to mean the soul that God granted to man. St Gregory the Theologian calls the soul "the breath of God."[17] Received from the mouth of God, this divine breath elevates man above the whole universe and places him in direct proximity to the Creator.

Having created man, God endowed him with the right to grant names: he introduced all the animals and birds to man "to see what he would call them; and whatever the man called any living creature, that was its name. And the man gave names to all the cattle, and to the birds of the sky, and to all the wild beasts of the field" (Gen 2.19–20). Having given man the right to name the creatures, God placed man above them, he made him their master,

---

[16]*On the Creation of Man* 1.3.
[17]*Dogmatic Verses 8: On the Spirit.*

for in the understanding of the Bible, granting a name to any kind of created being means to rule it.[18] For the animals themselves remained nameless, but the word of man bestows names on them, and thus man guides them on a higher level than they guide themselves.[19] As St John Chrysostom says, the names are bestowed by man "so that the mark of rule might be seen in the naming of them." Chrysostom likens this custom to people changing the names of slaves after their purchase; "so God made Adam, as master, give names to all the dumb creatures."[20] Moreover, the right to grant names indicates man's ability to see the essence of things clearly, thereby becoming like God and participating in the divine creation. In the words of Basil of Seleucia, by giving man the right to name the animals, God is somehow saying to Adam: "Be the creator of names, so long as you cannot be the creator of the creatures themselves. . . . We will share the glory of creative wisdom with you. . . . Give names to all the things to which I gave being."[21]

The creation of woman.
Palatine chapel. Palermo. 12th c.

Having made Adam from earthly material, God forms Eve from Adam's rib. Why would God create a helper for man? St Theophilus of Antioch offers this explanation: he created her so that there might be love between the two of them.[22] Blessed Augustine answers: for parenthood.[23] This brings into consideration the question of the supposed means of human propagation in a scenario in which they did not fall into sin. The Eastern theological tradition proceeds from the fact that "innocence flourished in paradise," and the words "be fruitful and multiply" did not signify an obligatory marital union, "for God had power to multiply the race in different ways as well, if they kept the precept unbroken to the end."[24] St Gregory of Nyssa considers that people could have multiplied just like the angels.[25] Western theology has supported the view of Blessed Augustine, who says that the marital union should have been fulfilled

[18]Louis Bouyer, *On the Bible and the Gospel* (Brussels: 1998), 23.
[19]Hans Urs von Balthasar, *A Theology of History* (Moscow: 2001), 248.
[20]*Conversation on Genesis* 14.5.
[21]*Oration 2: On Adam.*
[22]*To Autolycus* 2.28.
[23]*On the Book of Genesis* 9.3.
[24]John of Damascus *An Exact Exposition . . .* 4.24.
[25]*On the Creation of Man* 17.

absolutely, but people could not enter into it, finding themselves in paradise, because "right after the forming of woman, before they entered into union, the crime occurred for which they were cast out of that blessed place."[26]

According to biblical revelation, man was formed as having dominion over the universe (Gen 1.26). John Chrysostom emphasizes that "man is the most excellent of all the visible animals; everything was created for him alone: the heavens, the earth, the sea, the sun, the moon, the stars, the creeping things, the livestock, and all the dumb animals."[27]

The first-formed man, according to the teaching of the Church, abided in harmony with himself, with nature, and with God his creator. In the words of Macarius of Egypt, Adam was God's friend, he abided in purity, he ruled over his thoughts and was in a state of bliss. The Word resided in Adam, and he had the Spirit of God within himself: "The Word, having resided in him, was everything—knowledge, feeling, legacy, and learning."[28] Adam's closeness to God was very great: "Angels trembled, the Cherubim and Seraphim did not dare to stare directly at God, whereas Adam conversed with him as with a friend."[29]

At the same time, the first-formed man was not so fortified in goodness that he did not have the possibility of falling into sin. For this reason God planted in paradise "the tree of the knowledge of good and evil" (Gen 2.9), "as a kind of test,"[30] and gave man an order, so that fulfilling it, he might practice good things. "For it was no profit to man to obtain incorruption while still untried and unproved,"[31] since in this case, the risk remained that he might fall into pride and become twisted unto the condemnation of the devil.

The first man was formed so that there would be someone "to till" the ground (Gen 2.5). One may observe in this an indication as to the vocation of man within creation. God is introduced in the Bible as Creator-Demiurge-Maker: "My Father is working even until now, and I am working" (Jn 5.17). Man also becomes a maker, and although different from God, he can nevertheless create "out of nothingness," he can take God's gifts and complete

---

[26] *On the Book of Genesis* 9.4.
[27] *Conversation on Genesis* 8.2.
[28] *Spiritual Homilies* 12.7.
[29] John Chrysostom *Homily in the Church of the Apostle Thomas* 3.
[30] Ibid.
[31] John of Damascus *An Exact Exposition . . .* 2.30.

them, bringing them to an even greater beauty and harmony. Man can make a house from trees, a sculpture from rocks, and a pitcher from clay. In creating, man imitates the Creator and becomes like him. Man enters into the material universe as a mediator between God and creation, as a priest of the whole universe. Like a priest saying "thine own of thine own" during liturgy, returning God's own gifts back to him with thanksgiving, man was called to possess this world for the purpose of ruling over it, to lead the world to perfection and adoration. Man should have returned the world to its own Creator through fulfillment of the law, to the Creator who placed him as lord and king over the universe.

The Fathers of the Church speak of man as God's highest creature, as the crowning of the Creator's creative process. In the words of St Irenaeus of Lyons, "The glory of God is living man."[32] Gregory the Theologian echoes Irenaeus: "Your glory is man, whom you put here as an angel, to sing of your radiance."[33] In another place Gregory speaks of man as of a temple of God and as a "created god":

> If you would think narrowly of yourself, (then remember), that
> you are Christ's creation
> And breath, a venerable part (of him), and therefore are
> heavenly,
> And earthly; you are a created god, an unforgettable work (of
> the Creator),
> Going to the imperishable glory through the suffering of Christ.
> . . .
> For man is the temple of the great God; and this makes him
> such (a temple),
> Who is renounced from the earth and goes continuously to
> heaven.
> I command you to preserve this temple with sweet-smelling
> fragrance
> From your deeds and words, always keeping God within
> yourself.[34]

[32] *Against Heresies* 4.20.7.
[33] *Autobiographical Poems 38: A Hymn to Christ after the silence at Pascha.*
[34] Ibid.

The main purpose and vocation of man is to rise from the earthly things to the heavenly, from the human to the divine. God, according to Gregory the Theologian, formed man so that he might attain great glory, and "replacing within himself the earthly with the heavenly . . . like God, he might go from here towards God."[35] Being god in his potential, man ought to attain such a step so as to be god-like, by which he might become wholly deified. The goal of human life is "to turn oneself into god and spirit . . . to become a rank of the radiant angelic choir, having received for great efforts an even greater reward."[36] By this claim Gregory puts faith in all of the Eastern Christian tradition that defines the goal of man's life in terms of "deification" or "theosis."[37]

BODY, SOUL, AND MIND

If the Divinity is "simple and uncomplicated,"[38] then man, on the contrary, is thought of as some kind of composite, a "mixture"[39] of various elements. A material element can be discerned in man, which is called a "body" or "flesh," and a spiritual side, expressed in terms of "spirit," "soul," or "mind." The Fathers of the Church sometimes speak of a twofold composition of man (body and soul), and sometimes of a threefold composition (body, soul, and mind, or less commonly, body, soul, and spirit). In the last case mind, or spirit, is not thought of as a higher form of the soul, but as an independent element in man.

The Bible repeatedly highlights this dichotomy, this dual-composition of man. In the book of Job, Satan says to God: "But put forth your hand and touch his bones and his flesh," but God responds, "Behold, he is in your hands; only save his life" (Job 2.5–6). The Psalmist distinguishes between the soul and the flesh in man: "My soul thirsts for you; my flesh pines for you" (Ps 63.1). Sometimes the flesh is opposed to the spirit: "The Egyptians: human, and not God; their horses: flesh, and not spirit" (Isa 31.3). This opposition is further developed in the gospels: "The spirit indeed is willing, but

---

[35] *Dogmatic Verses 8: On the Soul.*
[36] *Autobiographical Poems 45: Weeping for the Sufferings of His Own Soul.*
[37] For more on theosis see chapter 20.
[38] John of Damascus *An Exact Exposition* . . . 1.8.
[39] Ibid. 2.12.

Christ with the soul of the Most Holy Theotokos. Detail of the icon of the Dormition. Theophanes the Greek. 14th c.

the flesh is weak" (Mt 26.41); "It is the spirit that gives life; the flesh profits nothing" (Jn 6.63).

The tripartite view of man is inherited, rather, from ancient philosophy. There are relatively few texts within Holy Scripture that can be interpreted as being tripartite in this way. An example of a text like this can be found in the words of the Apostle Paul: "May your spirit and soul and body be kept in all integrity, without flaw" (1 Thess 5.23). The Apostle Paul opposes the "intellectual" man to the "spiritual" (1 Cor 2.14–15). He also speaks about the word of God, "piercing even to the sundering of soul and spirit" (Heb 4.12). However, the dual opposition of body and spirit is found much more frequently in the Apostle Paul (Rom 8.10), or of flesh and spirit (Gal 5.7; Col 2.5), or of flesh and mind (Rom 7.25).

The Eastern Christian tradition defines man as a rational, living essence (*zōon logikon*, ζῶον λογικόν), consisting of a soul and body:

For what is man, if not consisting of a soul and body as a rational living thing? Therefore, is the soul in and of itself man? No, the soul is not man. Would you call the body man? No, but it is called the body of man. Therefore neither one of the two is in and of itself man, but the union of the two is indeed called man.[40]

For man is an essence made up of flesh and soul, wisdom and blood, elements and many other kinds (of matter). . . . Man is a living essence, possessing intellect and a way of learning.[41]

This is what man is: a living essence both dead and immortal, visible and invisible, sensory and mental, capable of seeing visible creation, and grasping thought.[42]

---

[40]Justin Martyr *Fragments*. The phrase "rational living thing" (or "living reason") is borrowed from Aristotle and Sextus Empiricus.
[41]Athanasius of Alexandria *Definitions* 3.
[42]Symeon the New Theologian *Chapters* 2.23.

Emphasized in all of these definitions is antinomy, the dual nature of man consisting of soul and body: in body he is mortal, visible, and sensory, but in spirit, he is invisible, immortal, and mental.

Speaking on the primordial dichotomy of human nature, some fathers of the Church refer to the classical idea of "microcosm," according to which man understands himself as a "small world," uniting within himself those very same elements from which the universe is made.[43] However, if the classical philosophers spoke of man as a "small world," then for Gregory the Theologian, it is precisely the material world that is "small" in comparison to the macrocosm-man, since man consists of both realities: material and spiritual, while at the same time the world possesses only one material existence":

> The Creator Word also makes one living creature out of both, I mean invisible and visible natures, that is the human being. And having taken the body from the matter already created, he breathed in breath from himself, which is surely the intelligent soul and the image of God of which the Scripture speaks. The human being is a kind of second world, great in smallness, placed on the earth, another angel, a composite worshiper, a beholder of the visible creation, an initiate into the intelligible, king of things on earth, subject to what is above, earthly and heavenly, transitory and immortal, visible and intelligible, a mean between greatness and lowliness. He is at once spirit and flesh.[44]

How then are the two polar elements, material and spiritual, united in man? Long before the rise of Christian theology, classical thinkers and eastern mystics pondered over this. To Plato, the soul and body were presented as elements so alien and hostile to one another that he called the body a "dungeon,"[45] where the soul was kept as if against its will. Plato divided the dissemination of notions in his time into the pre-existence of souls and into their migration from one body to another, including from humans to animals.

The teaching of metempsychosis (the transmigration of the soul) was rejected by all early church traditions. In the second century, Theophilus of Antioch wrote:

[43]This idea is found in Democrates, Galen, Philo of Alexandria, and others.
[44]*Oration* 38.11 p. 68.
[45]*Phaedo* 82e–83a.

Did not Plato, who spoke so much of the unity of God and of the soul of man, asserting that the soul is immortal, himself afterwards find, inconsistently with himself, that some souls pass into other men, and that others take their departure into irrational animals? How can his doctrine fail to seem dreadful and monstrous—to those at least who have any judgment—that he who was once a man shall afterwards be a wolf, or a dog, or an ass, or some other irrational brute? Pythagoras, too, is found venting similar nonsense.[46]

Polemicizing with classical philosophers and Gnostics, Irenaeus of Lyons decisively rejected the idea of the transmigration of the soul already in the second century:

We may subvert their doctrine as to transmigration from body to body by this fact, that souls remember nothing whatever of the events which took place in their previous states of existence. For if they were sent forth with this object, that they should have experience of every kind of action, they must of necessity retain a remembrance of those things which have been previously accomplished, that they might fill up those in which they were still deficient, and not by always hovering, without intermission, round the same pursuits, and spend their labor wretchedly in vain.[47]

Origen rejected the idea of the soul's transmigration in the third century in a number of exegetical and polemical compositions of the later period:

But now according to our ability let us make investigation. . . . Lest I should fall into the dogma of transmigration, which is foreign to the Church of God, and not handed down by the Apostles, nor anywhere set forth in the Scriptures. . . . For if because of sin it [the soul] should be twice in the body, why should it not be thrice, and repeatedly in it, since punishments, in respect of this life, and of the sins committed in it, shall be rendered to it only by the method of transmigration? But if this be granted as a consequence, perhaps there will be no place for the corruption of the world, at which "the heavens and the earth shall pass away."[48]

---

[46] *To Autolychus* 3.7.
[47] *Against Heresies* 2.33.1.
[48] *Commentary on the Gospel According to Matthew* 13.1.

If we should cure those who have fallen into the folly of believing in the transmigration of souls through the teaching of physicians, who will have it that the rational nature descends sometimes into all kinds of irrational animals, and sometimes into that state of being which is incapable of using the imagination?[49]

Origen, in his early treatise "On First Principles," did not seem to be free from the influence of Platonic ideas. In the original version of this composition, the entirety of which is preserved only in the Latin translation, Origen developed the theory in which God is the Creator of multiple worlds: there existed other worlds before this present one, and after the conclusion of the history of the world there will be yet more new worlds. This theory, in combination with the idea that people's souls are for the "cooling" of minds, sent into the body for punishment, provided the foundation for some of the subsequent critics of Origen, especially Gregory of Nyssa and the Blessed Jerome, to claim that he taught the transmigration of souls. Refuting Origen, Gregory of Nyssa directly correlated his idea of the pre-existence of souls to the teaching of metempsychosis:

Some of those before our time who have dealt with the question of "principles" think it right to say that souls have a previous existence as a people in a society of their own, and that among them also there are standards of vice and virtue, and that the soul there, which abides in goodness, remains without experience of conjunction with the body. . . . Those who stand by the former doctrine, and assert that the state of souls is prior to their life in the flesh, do not seem to me to be clear from the fabulous doctrines of the heathen which they hold on the subject of successive incorporation: for if one should search carefully, he will find that their doctrine is of necessity brought down to this. They tell us that one of their sages said that he, being one and the same person, was born a man, and afterwards assumed the form of a woman, and flew about with the birds, and grew as a bush, and obtained the life of an aquatic creature; and he who said these things of himself did not, so far as I can judge, go far from the truth: for such doctrines as this, saying that one soul passed through so many changes, are really fitting for the chatter of

---

[49] *Against Celsus* 3.75.

frogs or jackdaws, or the stupidity of fishes, or the insensibility of trees. And the cause of such absurdity is this—the supposition of the pre-existence of souls.[50]

Other church writers of the fourth century refuted the idea of the transmigration of souls. Basil the Great called for all to "avoid the nonsense of those arrogant philosophers who do not blush to liken their soul to that of a dog; who say that they have been formerly themselves women, shrubs, fish." As Basil sarcastically notes, "Have they ever been fish? I do not know; but I do not fear to affirm that in their writings they show less sense than fish."[51] John Chrysostom puts the Christian anthropology expressed in the Gospel according to John in opposition to the "embarrassing" teaching of the Greek philosophers on metempsychosis:

> As for doctrines on the soul, there is nothing excessively shameful that [Plato and Pythagoras] have left unsaid; asserting that the souls of men become flies, and gnats, and bushes, and that God himself is a soul; with some other the like indecencies. . . . But this man's[52] [writings] shine brighter day by day. For from the time that he (was) and the other fishermen, since then the (doctrines) of Pythagoras and of Plato, which seemed before to prevail, have ceased to be spoken of. . . . Neglecting to teach men anything useful, [Pythagoras] taught that they might as well eat the heads of those who begot them, as beans. And he persuaded those who associated with him, that the soul of their teacher had actually been at one time a bush, at another a girl, at another a fish. . . . Plato assert[s] . . . sometimes that [God] is intellect, sometimes that he is a soul; for these things are far removed from that divine and unmixed Nature which has nothing in common with us, but is separated from any fellowship with created things, I mean as to a substance, though not as to relation.[53]

The idea of metempsychosis was officially rejected by the Church in the sixth century, at the Council of Constantinople in 543, and at the fifth ecumenical council, and at the council against John Italos in 1082. The Fathers of the Church opposed this idea with the teaching that every person comes

---

[50] On the Making of Man 28.
[51] Homilies on the Hexaemeron 8.2. Also Gregory the Theologian Dogmatic Verses 8: On the Soul.
[52] The Apostle John the Theologian.
[53] Homilies on the Gospel According to St John 2.3, 5, 7.

into being with one unrepeatable identity in which the soul is continuously united with the body. "As each one of us receives his body through the skillful working of God, so does he also possess his soul," says Irenaeus of Lyons, "For God is not so poor or destitute in resources, that he cannot confer its own proper soul on each individual body, even as he gives it also its special character."[54] In the words of Athenagoras of Athens, "The soul and the body make up one living creature in man, who can feel his own soul and his own body."[55] As Cyril of Jerusalem emphasizes, the body is not "alien" clothing, borrowed by man for the time being, but is "his," received for eternity:

> We do nothing without the body. We blaspheme with the mouth, and with the mouth we pray. With the body we commit fornication, and with the body we keep chastity. With the hand we rob, and by the hand we bestow alms; and the rest in like manner. Since then the body has been our minister in all things, it shall also share with us in the future the fruits of the past. Therefore, brethren, let us be careful of our bodies, nor misuse them as though not our own. Let us not say like the heretics, that this vesture of the body belongs not to us, but let us care for it as our own; for we must give account to the Lord of all things done through the body.[56]

There is a generally accepted idea in patristics, according to which the soul is the element of the loftier things in man, while the body is the element of those baser things. Accordingly, the body should be found to be in hierarchical subordination in relation to the soul. Some authors liken the soul to a mistress and the body to a maidservant. In the Middle Ages, the popular work *The Diopter* of the Byzantine author Philip the Hermit (eleventh century), in the form of a dialogue between the soul and the flesh, was built on this traditional contrast. The maidservant Flesh turns to the mistress Soul: "You rule over me . . . you direct me as a rider guides a horse. . . . You are wise, and immortal, and you come from the higher heavenly world. . . . But I am base-born, I am a slave from that fickle and iniquitous world, and I consist of all its four elements." However, the unbreakable link between Soul and Flesh is emphasized: "Without the aid of my organs, O mistress, you would not be

[54] *Against Heresies* 2.33.5.
[55] *On the Resurrection of the Dead* 13.
[56] *Catechetical Lectures* 18.19–20.

Christ with the soul of the Most Holy Theotokos. Detail of the icon of the Dormition. Novgorod. 13th c.

able to glorify your Creator and God. . . . Without me you would not be able to offer up thanksgiving to your Creator as his creature, nor repent from sins with tears. . . . If I were not formed, you would not have been formed together with me."[57]

There exists a false notion that Christians characteristically relate to the body and the flesh scornfully. As a matter of fact, such an attitude was characteristic of the Platonic and Neo-Platonic traditions, which Christianity approached critically. As already mentioned, Plato likened the body to a dungeon or prison in which the soul was held captive.[58] Plotinus compared the body to a house in which the soul found timely asylum: there will come a time when the soul will no longer need this house and when it will find its genuine native land.[59] In the words of Porphyrius, Plotinus' biographer, the latter "always tested the shame of the other that lived in bodily form"; because of this he never spoke of his parents and motherland, he never posed for a painter or sculptor, he did not go to the baths nor did he take medicine.[60]

The Platonic concept of the body as a prison seemed to be an influence for some Christian writers, Origen in particular. However, his teaching that souls appeared in the body as a result of "cooling," was subjected to severe criticism as early as the third century, when St Methodius of Olympus wrote the special anti-Origenist treatise *On the Resurrection*, where he refuted the idea that man's body is the source of sin. Since the nature of the resurrected body after the universal resurrection is the basic theme of the treatise, it will be discussed in greater detail in the chapter dealing with Orthodox eschatology.[61]

---

[57] *Third Oration.* Cited in G. M. Prokhorov, *Memorials of Russian and Translated Literature of the Fourteenth and Fifteenth Centuries* (Leningrad, 1987), 215, 217, 223.

[58] Cf.: Plato *Phaedo* 82e–83a.

[59] Cf.: Plotinus *Enneads* 2 9, 15.

[60] Cf.: Porphyrius *The Life of Plotinus.* Cited in: Diogenes Laertius, *Lives and Opinions of Eminent Philosophers* (Moscow: 1979), 462.

[61] Cf.: Chapter 6.3.

For Christianity, which preaches the God who has appeared in the flesh, any spiritualism, whether it be Platonic, Neo-Platonic, Origenist, Gnostic, or Manichean, is alien. On the contrary, as a Christian author of the second century wrote, "We ought to preserve the flesh as the temple of God."[62] Around the second and third centuries, Tertullian said that the flesh is a glorious creation of God, "the labor of his own hands, the care of his own thoughts, the receptacle of his own spirit, the queen of his creation, the inheritor of his own liberality, the priestess of his religion, the champion of his testimony, the sister of his Christ."[63] "Why then, O soul, should you envy the flesh?" asks Tertullian, "There is none, after the Lord, whom you should love so dearly; none more like a brother to you, which is even born along with yourself in God."[64]

According to Tertullian's thought, God, in forming human flesh, created it not only for man, but also for his own Son, having in mind his future incarnation:

A great matter was in progress, out of which the creature under consideration was being fashioned. So often then does it receive honor, as often as it experiences the hands of God, when it is touched by them, and pulled, and drawn out, and molded into shape. Imagine God wholly employed and absorbed in it—in his hand, his eye, his labor, his purpose, his wisdom, his providence, and above all, in his love, which was dictating the lineaments (of this creature). For, whatever was the form and expression that was then given to the clay (by the Creator), Christ was in his thoughts to become man one day, because the Word, too, was to be both clay and flesh, even as the earth was then.[65]

In the words of the Blessed Theodoret, man's body is God's creation, in which all the members coexist in a harmonious unity:

As now by the will of the Creator a fetus is being built up in the maternal womb and nature follows order in the beginning to his specifications, so and then according to his desire humankind was formed out of the earth and dust became flesh, blood, skin, fat, sinews, veins, beating heart,

[62]Clement of Rome *Second Epistle to the Corinthians* 9. Modern academic critics contest the authorship of this epistle.
[63]*On the Resurrection of the Flesh* 9.
[64]Ibid. 63.
[65]Ibid. 6.

brains, and digestive fluids; and a bone structure formed, and eyelids, clear pupils, spiraled passages for hearing, the sense of smell and the organ of the mouth for speech, in which the teeth serve instead of strings, the tongue like a bow, and the mind as the right hand of a musician.[66]

Admiration for the expediency of the construction of man's body was characteristic for many church writers. The Apostle Paul commenced the start of this theme in Christian tradition, when he wrote: "Now there are many members, yet but one body. . . . But God has tempered the body together by giving more abundant honor that part which lacked, that there should be no schism in the body, but that the members should have the same care one for another" (1 Cor 12.20–25). In the construction of the body, emphasizes Gregory of Nyssa, all is expedient, all of the bodily organs are formed for the sake of one of three purposes: for life, for a good (blessed) life, or for the continuation of the race. The mind, the heart, and the liver are necessary for man to live; the sensory organs are so that man might live well and join in the joy of life; the genitals are for the creation of descendants.[67]

In those cases when the holy Fathers speak of the enmity of the body and the soul (this theme also comes from the Apostle Paul), it is worth thinking of it more on an ascetic plane, rather than an ontological antinomy in philosophical thought. By "mortification of the flesh," Christian tradition understands freeing the flesh from sinful passions.

In accordance with the patristic teaching, the body is the house of the soul, and the soul uses the bodily senses as windows through which it can come into contact with the material world. The body is called the chariot of the soul, the organ of the soul. It is necessary to care for the body because it is the soul's instrument.[68]

Patristic tradition never received a definitive answer to the question of whether or not the soul can be located in some part of the body, or whether it permeates throughout the whole body, or finally, whether it mixes the body in with itself. Nemesius of Emesa expresses the latter point of view, for he suggests that the body is not capable of containing the soul within itself, because the soul is not constrained by space, but rather, on the contrary, the soul contains the body within itself, which is included in the soul as a

[66] *A Brief Exposition of Divine Dogma* 8.
[67] Cf.: *On the Making of Man* 30.
[68] Cf.: Barsanuphius and John *Direction for the Spiritual Life* 518.

vessel.[69] Leontius of Byzantium maintains the even more widespread point of view, claiming that the soul nevertheless is contained by the body.[70]

Is there some kind of organ in the body that can be considered the center of spiritual strength, or is it that all the members serve the soul equally? Usually the organ of the intellect is considered to be the brain,[71] but the basic organ of the other spiritual powers is the heart.[72] However, the soul permeates all the members of the body; some are specially destined to be the "abodes" of the spiritual senses: Organs of sight serve the nerves of the brain and eyes, those of hearing serve the brain and the ears, those of smell serve the nostrils, those of taste serve the tongue and the palate, those of touch serve the whole human nervous system.[73]

Those who spoke especially much of the heart as the center of man's spiritual life were those writer-ascetics who struggled with the theory and practice of the intellectual prayer of the heart. They perceive the heart as an organ of the mystical perception of God.

> The divine Grace writes the laws of the Spirit and heavenly mysteries on the tablets of the heart. The heart commands and rules over all the bodily organs. And if the Grace pierced the depths of the heart, then it rules over all the bodily organs and over all its thoughts. For the intellect is located there and all the thoughts of the soul and its hope.[74]

The most important events of spiritual rebirth take place in the heart: the inspiration of its soul, contact with the higher realm, an encounter with God. Together with these events, "evil thoughts, murders, adulteries, fornications, thefts, false witness, [and] blasphemies" (Mt 15.19) arise and proceed forth from the heart, that is, all that is sinful in man is conceived within its depths, in its "abyss." Here is the task of the ascetics—to purify the heart, to free it from sinful inclinations.

In Christian anthropology, the term "soul" signifies the invisible part of man's composition, in contrast with the body. In the Bible, this term some-

---

[69]Cf.: *On the Nature of Man* 3.
[70]Cf.: *Against Nestorius and Eutychius* 1.
[71]Cf.: John of Damascus *An Exact Exposition . . .* 2.19.
[72]On the heart as the spiritual-mystical center of the human organism, see B. Vysheslavtsev, *The Heart in Christian and Indian Mysticism* (Paris: 1929).
[73]Cf.: John of Damascus *An Exact Exposition . . .* 2.18.
[74]Macarius of Egypt *Spiritual Homilies* 15.20.

times designates every living creature in general (Gen 2.19, 9.12), in other cases a certain vital principle or source of life contained within the flesh (Gen 9.4), and even blood (Lev 17.11). The word "soul" is also used in these ways in the New Testament.

In Eastern patristics, the soul is defined as "the intellectual, bodiless, passionless, immortal essence [*ousia*, οὐσία]"[75]; "it is a created, living, intellectual being, with the power, as long as it is provided with organs, of sensuous perception";[76] "the soul, accordingly, is a living essence, simple, incorporeal, invisible in its proper nature to bodily eyes, immortal, reasoning and intelligent, formless, making use of an organized body, and being the source of its powers of life, and growth, and sensation, and generation."[77]

In understanding the structure of the soul, the Fathers of the Church proceeded from the generally accepted (in Socratic-Platonic psychology) division of the soul into three parts: reason (*logos*, λόγος), feeling (*thymos*, θύμος), and desire (*epithymia*, ἐπιθυμία). The names of the three parts are sometimes translated as ruling, incensive, and appetitive. In the words of Symeon the New Theologian, the soul is "an intellectual workshop, in the midst of which, like the heart, is mixed intellectual power, and together with the ruling, the incensive, and the appetitive."[78]

What is the origin of the soul? Was the soul of each person formed before the body, or simultaneously with the body? Is it formed "mature," or does it develop, like the body? In the opinion of Gregory of Nyssa, God forms the soul simultaneously with the body, not before the body. Like the measure of the body, the soul also "develops and grows." From the beginning, at the moment of the creation of the body, there is in the soul only one "power of growth and nutriment," similar to a root buried in the ground. Then, when the plant emerges into the light, "the gift of sensibility blossoms" in the soul. When the sprout ripens, "the power of reason begins to shine forth like a fruit, not appearing in its whole vigor all at once, but by care increasing with the perfection of the instrument, bearing always as much fruit as the powers of the subject allow."[79]

---

[75] Athanasius of Alexandria *To the Bishop of Antioch* 16.
[76] Gregory of Nyssa *On the Soul and the Resurrection.*
[77] John of Damascus *An Exact Exposition . . .* 2.12.
[78] *Moral Oration* 4 392–394.
[79] *On the Making of Man* 29.

Is the soul incorporeal in nature? The soul can be called incorporeal only in relation to the body, but not in relation to God. As John of Damascus stresses, God is the only one who is bodiless in essence; even the angels, demons, and souls are bodiless only by grace.[80] There was widespread opinion among the writers of the ancient Church that the soul has some kind of bodily shell, or "narrow body." Tertullian in particular insists that the soul is corporeal, "possessing a peculiar kind of solidity in its nature, such as enables it both to perceive and suffer."[81]

The teaching on the immortality of the soul is generally accepted in Christian tradition. However, this immortality is not understood as absolute and ontological, but rather as relative and "iconographic," residing completely in the power of God. God is the only one who is absolutely immortal; the soul is immortal insofar as it communes with the divine being and the divine immortality. Justin Martyr says, "The soul partakes of life, since God wills it to live. Thus, then, it will not even partake [of life] when God does not will it to live."[82] Theophilus of Antioch considers man not to be immortal by nature, but capable of becoming immortal.[83]

The understanding of the "mind" (Gr. *nous*, νοῦς) plays an important role in Christian anthropology. This term, frequently used by the Apostle Paul, comes from classical anthropology.[84] The nous is not synonymous with the soul: in the words of Anthony the Great, "The mind is not the soul, but is rather a divine gift, saving the soul. The mind pleasing to God goes before the soul and advises it to despise that which is within time, material, and perishable, but to love that which is eternal, imperishable, and immaterial goodness, so that man, finding himself within a body, might think with the mind and contemplate that which is heavenly and divine. The God-loving mind is the benefactor and salvation of the human soul."[85] The soul finds itself in the world, as one begotten, but the nous is outside the world, as one unbegotten.[86] The nous not only rules over the soul, but it "deifies the soul."[87] The

---

[80]Cf.: *An Exact Exposition . . .* 2.12.
[81]*On the Resurrection of the Flesh* 17.
[82]*Dialogue with Trypho* 6.
[83]Cf.: *To Autolycus* 2.27.
[84]This term is not found in the Greek text of the Old Testament (the Septuagint); used instead are the concepts of "mind" (*dianoia*, διάνοια) and "discernment" (*fronēsis*, φρόνησις).
[85]*Teachings on Good Morals* 94.
[86]Ibid. 136.
[87]Ibid. 135.

nous is covered by the secret places of the heart, deeply hidden in the depths of the soul and cannot appear in any way in normal life, being replaced by the spiritual mind. Man will recognize that the spiritual mind lies within him only when he enters onto the path of ascetical efforts, the goal of which is the revelation of the spiritual mind and the inspiration of the soul. When the fullness of the spiritual mind is revealed in man in all its radiance and god-likeness, this is a sign that man has reached perfection:

> Such is God's specification, that by the standards of the flesh, the soul is filled with the nous, so that man might choose freely between good and evil. The soul then that does not choose good does not have a nous. For this reason, though every body has a soul, it can be said that not every soul has a nous. For the god-loving nous abides in chastity, saintliness, justice, purity, goodness, mercy, and piety. The presence of the nous is an aid for (man) (in his relationship) with God.[88]

The nous is the instrument of spiritual sight: "The eye sees the visible, but the nous comprehends the invisible."[89] The organ of the intellect is the brain, but the organ of the nous is the heart. Because of this, "he who has a god-loving nous has an enlightened heart, and he sees God in his nous."[90] Symeon the New Theologian calls the nous the "eye of the heart."[91] In the process of the mystical ascent to God, the nous is the hegemonic leader; it follows directly after God, who elevates it. The soul follows after it: "The nous comes to know the Creator through the majesty and beauty of creation that call it back to contemplation of him, and it kindles the soul's contemplation of the Creator."[92] The soul, in its turn, rules over the body. However, only the nous can ascend to contemplation. "Man . . . [is] endowed with reason amidst creatures without reason, for he is double, composed of one and the other, sensible and intellectual. He is the center of all creatures. He alone knows God and, for him only, God is perceptible in an imperceptible manner to his mind, he lets himself be seen in an invisible manner and be possessed without being possessed."[93]

---

[88]Ibid. 126.
[89]Ibid. 128.
[90]Ibid.
[91]*Catechetical Oration* 1.12.420.
[92]Ibid. 6.252–255.
[93]*Hymn 23* 70–79.

Man's nous possesses a natural radiance: "Strive to preserve the radiance of your nous's sovereignty unharmed,"[94] says John of Karpathos. The ancient ascetics, at the highest stages of mystical sight, saw the light of their own nous. According to the teaching of Evagrius of Pontus, there are two lights: first, there is the "blessed light of the Holy Trinity,"[95] and second, there is the light of man's own nous, his own radiance.[96] There exists a kinship between the divine light and the light of man: inasmuch as the nous is created in the image of God, the light of the nous is also "related to him."[97] During prayer, a person's nous, having reached a state of passionlessness, becomes capable of contemplating its own primordial condition of radiance, becoming "like light,"[98] "a shining star,"[99] and "like a sapphire and heavenly flower."[100]

The nous can be guided toward God just as it can be guided toward the opposite side. The holy fathers, especially those who spoke on "intellectual activities," proceeded from the notion that the nous acquires a different tinge depending on what side and to what objects it is guided. Just as the world consists of many diverse and heterogeneous elements, so the nous, guided to the subjects of the world, loses its simplicity and becomes many and, on the other hand, returning to God, contemplating the Unity, itself becomes one.[101] St Maximus the Confessor speaks on the various states of the nous: "The nous, guided to God by prayer and by love, becomes wise, strong, a lover of mankind, merciful, or, simply put, has in itself all the characteristics of God, translated into material things, becoming alive and crude."[102] The nous, having lost its unity of vision and its spirituality, is in no way different from spiritual intellect. From the depths of the heart it supplants the cerebral brain, divided into a multitude of thoughts on worldly things, forgetting God. For the nous to remember God, it is necessary for it once again to be brought together into the heart and to "settle" there.

Memory is one of the most mysterious capabilities of man. Is it that memory is related to the region of the nous or is it summoned by the ability of

[94]John of Karpathos *Exhortatory Chapters* 82.
[95]*On Tempting Thoughts* 42.
[96]*The Knower* 45. Cf. also: *On Prayer 74.*
[97]*Skemmata* 2.
[98]*Gnostic Chapters* 5.15.
[99]*On Tempting Thoughts* 43.
[100]Ibid. 39.
[101]Cf.: Kallistos Katafygiotis *On Unity with God.*
[102]*Chapters on Love* 52.

the intellect? John of Damascus, evidently, attributes it to the intellect: "Memory is a fantasy that is left behind from some sensation and thought manifesting itself in action."[103] Sensation and thought are abilities of the soul; they are taken in by the soul for the sake of preserving memory. Here, however, the argument concerns the so-called "earthly memory," including in itself recollections of all events and appearances of the material world.

There is a side of memory that relates to the realm of the nous and the heart, this "memory of God." Mental memory is concentrated in the mind, it is varied and diverse, because mixed within itself are many things and manifestations. The noetic memory is contained in the heart; it is one and simple because it has as its own subject the one God. When the memory of God is revealed in man, it gradually supplants mental memory. In the words of Isaac the Syrian, "memory of God, when it masters the pasture within the soul, destroys the memory of all that is visible within the heart."[104]

THE FALL AND PREDESTINATION TOWARD SALVATION

The teaching that the primordial God-ordained nature of man was subjected to perversion as a result of the Fall, a consequence which affected the whole human race, plays an important role in Christian anthropology.

According to the biblical account, man did not fall away from God by his own will: he was tempted by the serpent, of whom it is said in the Bible that he was "the most crafty of all the wild beasts" (Gen 3.1). This deals with the same "old serpent, called the Devil and Satan, who deceives the whole world" of whom Revelation speaks (Rev 12.9).

When God formed man, evil already existed, and it was personified in the devil and the demons. Having created man, God placed him in a world where there was not only light, but darkness; not only good, but evil; not only blessings, but struggles; not only life, but death. For this reason God showed man the tree of the knowledge of good and evil, from which it was forbidden to eat: "For in whatsoever day you eat of it, you shall surely die" (Gen 2.17). Man should have obeyed this divine commandment and avoided the forbidden tree. He could have enjoyed the fruits of the other trees, among which was

---

[103] *An Exact Exposition* . . . 2.20.
[104] *Oration* 85.

the tree of life, meaning he might have been immortal. But he should have restrained himself from the knowledge and taste of evil, because as soon as he tasted evil, as soon as he (if only for a moment) fell away from love for God, he would immediately lose all that he possessed that was formed in the image of God.

Why did the tempting advice of the serpent turn out to be so corrupting?

In the words of Gregory the Theologian, the devil deceived man "with the hope of divinity,"[105] that is, he played with the most hidden aspirations of man, using those things closed up within man that strive to reach the state of god-likeness. God invited man on the journey to deification through obedience to the divine commands. But the devil "ensnared [man] with the hope of divinity" when he said to Adam and Eve: "You will be like God" (Gen 3.5). Both God and the devil promised Adam and Eve that they would be like gods. But God says to people: if you fulfill my commandments, if you keep faith in me, then I will make you so great in blessings as I am by nature. But the devil says: if you break God's commandments, you will become just like God, because God has forbidden you to taste of the tree of the knowledge of good and evil out of envy. The devil never uncovers his base intentions, but masks them under the guise of a good purpose. In order to corrupt man, to deceive him, he parodies God, promising man exactly what God already promised him.

Eve was the first to fall into temptation: she tasted of the tree of the knowledge of good and evil, thereby breaking God's commandment. We read in the Bible: "And the woman saw that the tree was good for food, and that it was pleasant to the eyes" (Gen 3.6). She felt that the fruit would be sweet, and preferred the sweetness of the forbidden fruit to the sweetness of fulfilling God's commands. She believed that there were values outside of God and apart from God. She decided to scorn God's commandment, to have a taste of that which was outside of God. After Eve, Adam tasted of the tree of the knowledge of good and evil. Immediately their nakedness was

*The Fall.
Cathedral of Monreale.
Sicily. 12th c.*

---

[105] *Oration* 39.13 p. 89.

revealed to them, they saw that which they had not noticed earlier. They understood that besides good there can also be evil; that besides beauty, there can be ugliness and nakedness; besides joy, there can be shame; and besides truth, there can be lies.

Having heard the voice of God coming to paradise, Adam wanted to hide himself from God. Having broken God's commandment, man, in one moment, lacked that whole, integral knowledge of God, that innate intuition and wisdom, which he possessed from the moment he appeared on the earth. Earlier, man knew that hiding himself from God would be impossible, that God exists everywhere. Having broken the commandment, he lost that knowledge. Going away from God, he immediately received a distorted concept of God. Earlier he did not know and could not even grasp that it served to fear God, that God could punish him. Earlier it would not even have entered Adam's head to run from God and to hide himself from him. Now, though, he tries to hide himself, he seeks refuge because the command was broken, the link between man and God weakened.

But Adam is not successful in hiding himself from God, and he encounters God face to face. The encounter, which earlier was a source of blessing and joy, now becomes a source of suffering and shame. Having seen Adam, the Lord pronounces his sentence: man should be driven out of paradise, and not because God wants this, but because there is no place for evil in paradise, no place for disobedience and unfaithfulness. Man, having tasted of the tree of the knowledge of good and evil, already cannot be found in paradise, he has become foreign to it. The expulsion of Adam from paradise becomes a natural consequence of breaking God's commandment: this is a sentence that man prescribed for himself.

St Melito of Sardis, in his second century poem *On Pascha*, recounts the narrative of Adam's fall and his being cast out of paradise in poetic form:

> God, in the beginning, having made the heaven and the earth
>   and all in them through the Word,
> formed humanity from the earth and shared his own breath.
> He set him in the garden in the East, in Eden, there to rejoice.
> There he laid down for him the law, through his
>   commandment:
> "Eat food from all the trees in the garden yet eat not from the

> tree of the knowledge of good and evil;
> on the day that you eat you shall die."
> The man was susceptible by nature of good and evil,
> as a clod of earth may receive seed of either kind,
> and he consented to the wicked and seductive counselor,
> and stretched out for the tree and broke the commandment and
> disobeyed God.
> For this he was thrown out into this world, condemned as
> though to prison.[106]

As a result of the Fall, the cooperation of man's free will with the will of God changed in radical form. The first-formed man did not have a propensity to sin: his free will was found to be in obedience to God's will and in harmony with it. However, after man tasted of "the tree of the knowledge of good and evil," that is, after he experimentally communed with evil and sin, his free will turned out to be placed continually before the choice between evil and good. In each concrete moment in life, man must make this choice; however, so that the choice might be made on the right side, it is necessary to guide his will consciously to good. St Maximus the Confessor speaks of the presence of a "natural will" in man, or essentially what is inherent in all people, and "free choice" (or gnomic will), signifying the choice between good and evil and assumed responsibility for one's own actions. There was a natural will in Jesus Christ, but there was no wavering between good and evil, whereas in fallen man, free will frequently results in conflict with divine will.[107]

The Fall of Adam and Eve was not simply one independent act: it had consequences for all of humanity. For elucidation on the form of sin the ancestors of man transmitted to the human race, Maximus the Confessor introduces the understanding of two sins: the first sin belonged to Adam's crime, and the second was those that followed, which that first sin brought for all of mankind. The first sin that occurred "was culpable, when his free choice willfully rejected the good," but the second, having as its cause the first sin, "was innocent, since human nature unwillingly put off its incorruption." The first sin, that is the voluntary fall from good to evil, is worthy of blame, but the second is "the innocent transformation of human nature from

---

[106] 47–48, Alistair Stewart-Sykes (Crestwood, NY: St Vladimir's Seminary Press, 2001), 49–50.
[107] For more detail on "gnomic will," see Chapter 15 on the two wills of Christ.

incorruption to corruption."[108] These formulations have much meaning for the understanding of the Orthodox attitude toward the Latin teaching on original sin, about which the argument will continue below.

One of the consequences of original sin became the extension of sin to the whole race of man. In the words of Melito of Sardis, sinfulness, corruptibility, and death were those things that Adam left as an inheritance to his descendants:

> As an inheritance he left his children:
> not purity but lust,
> not incorruption but decay,
> not honor but dishonor,
> not freedom but bondage,
> not sovereignty but tyranny,
> not life but death,
> not salvation but destruction.[109]

Sin and death are indissolubly connected: sin is a "collaborator of death." For this reason, when people's souls fell under the influence of sin, their bodies inevitably became the spoils of death:

> Sin rejoiced in all of this, working together with death,
> making forays into human souls and preparing the bodies of the
>   dead as his food.
> Sin set his sign on every one and those on whom he etched his
>   mark were doomed to death.
> All flesh fell under sin,
> and every body under death,
> and every soul was plucked from its dwelling of flesh,
> and that which was taken from the dust was reduced to dust,
> and the gift of God was locked away in Hades.
> What was marvelously knit together was unraveled,
> and the beautiful body divided.
> Humanity was doled out by death,
> for a strange disaster and captivity surrounded him;

[108] *On the Cosmic Mystery of Jesus Christ: Ad Thalassium* 42 Paul M. Blowers and Robert Louis Wilken, trans., (Crestwood, N.Y.: St Vladimir's Seminary Press, 2003), 119.
[109] *On Pascha* 49 p. 50.

> he was dragged off a captive under the shadow of death,
> and the father's image was left desolate.[110]

The sin of Adam, in the words of John Chrysostom, became the reason for the "general decay" of human nature.[111] As Cyril of Alexandria emphasizes, "in the likeness of Adam's crime, all mankind is clothed in corruption," being sprouts from one damaged root.[112] Macarius of Egypt speaks of the sinful "leaven," in which all partake in succession as descendants of Adam.[113] According to Macarius' teaching, "when man turned aside from the commandment . . . sin took him as its citizen and, like a certain bitter abyss, narrow and deep, entering inside, it took possession of the soul's pasture up to its deepest recesses. . . . Sin . . . appeals to habit and predisposition, in each person it grows up from youth and educates and teaches him evil."[114] Being descendants of Adam and having inherited his nature, every person participates in sin with each moment of his or her appearance on earth:

> We are all born as sinners out of Adam's trespass, as criminals out of his criminal nature, as slaves to sin out of a slave to sin, as cursed and dead out of one who is cursed and dead; we are born out of the one who gave consent to the devil, laboring for him and losing free will, so we are his children, over whom the devil lords and rules in his tyranny.[115]

The consequences of the Fall inform the whole spiritual-bodily composition of man. Man was created with a light, pure, incorruptible, and immortal body, but after the Fall the body lost these characteristics and became material, corruptible, and dead. Disease entered into the life of man. The majority of ancient church writers shared the opinion that the reasons for all of the diseases are rooted in sinful human nature. If "sin, when it is perfected, brings forth death" (Jas 1.15), or in other words, death appears as a result of sin, then disease is found between sin, out of which it comes, and death, which it precedes. The interrelationship between sin and disease can manifest itself in various ways. Sts Barsanuphius and John say that sometimes

---

[110]Ibid. 54–56 p. 51–52.
[111]*Conversation on Romans* 10.1.
[112]*Interpretation of Romans.*
[113]Cf.: *Spiritual Conversations* 24.2.
[114]Ibid. 41.1.
[115]Symeon the New Theologian *Catechetical Oration* 5.406–413.

disease is a direct result of some kind of sin: "Diseases coming from negligence and disorder occur in natural forms. . . . It depends on you to be negligent or live uncleanly and fall into them unless, of course, you right yourself." In other cases disease is sent from God as a punishment for sin "for our benefit, so that we might repent."[116] Some diseases come "from bile," that is, from physiological causes, and still others "from demons."[117] Finally, "disease can be a test, and tests lead to skill."[118]

The Fall informed the spiritual composition of man. After the Fall, the soul served the body and, "having united itself with the body, lies in the darkness of the body."[119] All of the soul's qualities and capabilities turned out to be dark and sick. In the words of Isaiah the Recluse, it is natural for the soul to strive for God, but the enemy changed it to shameful lust; zealousness for God was changed in people to unnatural jealousy and envy of one another; the ability to be angry at the devil, without which it would be impossible to reject his temptations, was turned into wrath toward one's neighbor because of everything that is not needful and useless.[120] The powers of the soul were made to be sick and deranged, as Gregory Palamas writes:

> The soul is tripartite and can be seen in three faculties—the intellectual, the irritable, and the desirable; the soul is sick in all of them. . . . The appetitive serves as food for the incensive; both of them arouse the soaring of the ruling; for this reason you will never see a healthy incensive part of the soul, if you do not heal the appetitive part first, while the ruling part must be cured before these two.[121]

It is worth noting that the holy fathers treat the falling away from God as a movement from the simple to the complex, from unity to plurality, from integration to disintegration, from association to disassociation. The Blessed Diadochus speaks of the primordial unity and the ensuing divisions of the soul's senses: "The natural sense is one . . . but because of Adam's transgression it was divided into two activities";[122] for this reason the impassioned part

[116]*Guidance toward the Spiritual Life* 521 Book 251.
[117]Ibid. 517 Book 250.
[118]Ibid. 613 Book 293.
[119]Anthony the Great *Instructions on Good Morals* 117.
[120]Cf.: *Oration* 2.2.
[121]*To the Most Reverend Nun Xenia.*
[122]Diadochus of Photiki *Ascetical Oration* 25.

of the soul is sometimes drawn to it, that is, to the appetitive and incensive parts, and then it strives for the worldly blessings, but sometimes it inclines toward the ruling and delights in heavenly beauty.[123] St Gregory of Sinai asserts the "division of the one vision and simple memory," with the result that "the simple is made complex, from a single vision to many forms."[124] The process of disassociation, therefore, deals with every part of human composition.

The expulsion from paradise. Cathedral of Monreale. Sicily. 12th c.

The Fall of Adam was reflected in the mental components of man's nature. There came to pass a darkening of the mind, which "having been separated from its own primordial dwelling place, forgot its own radiance."[125] Man's fallen mind, incapable of standing firm in the "simple and unified vision" of the memory of God, reaches out for the prodigal themes of the outside world. Man immerses himself in the knowledge of his surroundings and the multitude of subjects more and more, while the knowledge of God grows dim before these things. The condition in which the nous finds itself after the Fall is called "suspension" (*meteōrizmos*, μετεωρισμός) in the ascetical tradition. In this condition, the nous is not capable of concentration, prayer, or mystical experiences, but floats along, distracted by various thoughts and images.

Having lost its original wholeness, it is as if the nous divided itself into two parts, one of which St Anthony the Great calls "the general worldly nous," driven both to good and to evil, fickle, and inclined toward material things, and the other he calls "the God-loving nous," which fights against evil.[126] St Gregory the Theologian speaks on the coexistence of these two minds in one man: "There are two minds within me: one is good, and it follows all that is wonderful, but the other is bad, and it follows after evil; one nous goes to the light and is ready to submit itself to Christ, but the other nous is of flesh and blood, and it covers itself in darkness and agrees to give itself as a captive of Belial."[127] Macarius of Egypt also speaks of this:

[123]Ibid. 29.
[124]*Chapters on the Commandments and Dogma* 60.
[125]Elias of Crete *Anthology* 89.
[126]*Instructions on Good Morals* 7.
[127]*Poem on Himself 45: Lament for the Suffering of One's Soul.*

The nous is distinguished from the nous. . . . There is a nous, embracing and flowing toward heaven and embarking on the path of purifying its thoughts and reaching for its paths and trails, preparing itself for holiness in the heavens. And there is another nous, groveling along the earth and creeping on the paths of the flesh. There is a fleshly nous and there is a spiritual nous, and the spiritual nous is distinguished from the fleshly one.[128]

The Fall of Adam and Eve, according to the Church's teaching, had consequences not only for the human race, but for the whole created world. According to the teaching of the Apostle Paul, accepted by the Eastern Christian tradition, creation "was made subject to vanity, not willingly" but as a result of the Fall of man: together with man it "groans and travails in labor pains together until now," but it awaits freedom "while we wait for the adoption, the redemption of our body" (Rom 8.20–23). Interpreting these words of the apostle, John Chrysostom says: "What is the meaning of 'the creation was made subject to vanity?' Why, that it became corruptible. For what cause, and on what account? On account of thee, O man. For since thou hast taken a body mortal and liable to suffering, the earth too hath received a curse. . . . Yet it has had no wrong done it. For incorruptible will it be for thy sake again."[129] In other words, creation will become incorruptible as soon as man becomes incorruptible.

The teaching of the Fall, based on the third chapter of the book of Genesis and having received development on all sides in patristics, is common in all Christian confessions—Orthodox, Catholic, and Protestant. However, in Christian societies of Western traditions this teaching is linked with the concept of "Original Sin" (peccatum originale), or "original guilt," coming from the Blessed Augustine. According to Augustine's teaching, Adam's sin led to the root corruption of human nature. Since the whole human race comes from Adam, then Adam's sin was transmitted as an inheritance through the body, or more precisely, through fleshly copulation. Humanity was transformed, in Augustine's words, into a "mass of the condemned" (massa damnata).[130] After the Fall, "vanquished by the sin into which it fell by its volition, nature has lost liberty," and sin became "the hard necessity" for all people.[131] Adam's

[128]New Spiritual Conversations 4.2
[129]Homilies on Romans 14.
[130]Cf.: The City of God 21.12.
[131]Concerning Man's Perfection in Righteousness 4 (9).

fault, transmitted to all of his descendants, made them "children of wrath." They needed the Intercessor for their redemption, he who calms God's wrath, offering himself as a sacrifice for the sin of all mankind.[132]

Augustine, who was the most prominent theologian of the West, wrote about the mysteries of the faith in juridical terms, and this legalism has forever left an imprint on the subsequent development of Western theology. The concept of original guilt entered into the flesh and blood of Western theology: not even the theology of the Reformation could be saved from this legalistic understanding. In fact, Augustinian legalism and the deepest pessimism in view of fallen human nature were only intensified by theologians of the Reformation, especially by Luther and Calvin, who claimed that Original Sin in its fullness deprived mankind of free will. According to Calvin, after Original Sin people were so completely depraved and incapable of good works that they consequently lost divine blessings. The *Formula of Concord*, incorporated in the year 1577 and the normative dogmatic book of Lutheranism, proclaims:

> We believe, teach, and confess that original sin is not a slight, but so deep a corruption of human nature that nothing healthy or uncorrupt has remained in man's body or soul, in his inner or outward powers.[133]

It is said in the extensive exposition of this formula that "because of Adam and Eve's disobedience we now find ourselves in God's disfavor" and are "the offspring of wrath." Original Sin signifies the absence of an inherited righteousness and of the divine image, according to which man was created in the beginning, and also an "incapability and uselessness toward that which comes from God." Instead of just a lost image of God in man, there occurs a "deep, depraved, repulsive, fathomless, incomprehensible, and inexpressible corruptness of all nature and all its abilities and powers, but especially the highest, fundamental abilities of the soul in the realm of understanding, feeling, and will, so that now, after the Fall, man inherits a congenital, depraved inclination, and an inner impure heart, toward evil lusts and passions."[134]

In Orthodox tradition, based on the theological legacy of the Eastern fathers, the concept of Original Sin as an inheritance of guilt is alien. Better

---

[132] *On the Trinity* 13.22.
[133] *Formula of Concord, Epitome* 1.
[134] *Formula of Concord, Solid Declaration* 1.

corresponding to an Orthodox understanding of the Fall is the view given above by St Maximus the Confessor, according to whom the only sin that is reprehensible is the sin that Adam committed by his own free will, that is, the sin of disobedience, whereas the consequences of sin expressed by the corruption and death of human existence are not reprehensible. Adam's descendants inherit corruption and a mortal nature, that is, the consequences of sin that are not blameworthy. In this context it is difficult and even impossible to speak of how, from the Orthodox point of view, the guilt of Adam's sin can be transmitted to other people. Every person is guilty only of one's own personal sins, those that are committed by one's own voluntary consent, and not of sins committed by parents, ancestors, or the first-made man, Adam. It is precisely the personal sin of a person that is reprehensible, and not the general sinfulness of the race of man, of which each person is a participant by virtue of being born, but for which one cannot bear personal responsibility.

The Orthodox Church does not share the extreme pessimism of Catholicism and especially Protestantism with regard to the fallen nature of man. According to the Orthodox understanding, the image of God in fallen man is occluded, but not fully eliminated: man remains in the image of God even in his sinful condition. One of the funeral hymns of the Orthodox Church says: "I am the image of your inexpressible glory, even though I bear the wounds of sin."[135]

The Orthodox do not consider that man, in his fallen state, has fully lost his free will and is incapable of good deeds. Basing itself on the works of the Eastern fathers, especially Maximus the Confessor, the Orthodox Church teaches that man's free will can be guided entirely to sinful acts, but not that it inevitably must be. God's kindness toward man was not lost after the Fall, just as man's striving for God was not lost. Man preserves the ability to perform good works, which are accomplished *with the help* of divine goodness, but *not exclusively* thanks to divine goodness, as the Protestants think.

Another concept alien to Orthodox tradition is the notion that after the Fall of man the relationship with God changed, that God took away his grace from man as a punishment of sin, that mankind is completely devoid of divine grace and is a mass of condemned sinners. People's attitude toward

[135]Cf.: Ware, *The Orthodox Church*, 224.

God changed, but not God's attitude toward people: God's love for the race of man remained unchanged. Amongst the ranks of the other Eastern fathers, St Isaac the Syrian spoke about this with the greatest fervor.[136]

The difference in the approach toward the teaching of the Fall between the East and the West was affected by the way that the predestination of mankind to salvation is understood in the two Christian traditions. The proceeding point in the given question appears in the Apostle Paul's writings: "For those whom he foreknew he also predestined to be conformed to the image of his Son. . . . And those whom he also predestined he also called; and those whom he called he also justified; and those whom he justified he also glorified" (Rom 8.29–30). The Blessed Augustine understood this text in the sense that God predestined some people for salvation from the beginning, but others for condemnation, while man's free will does not play any sort of role in the act of salvation. Those who are predestined to salvation are all those whom God has given faith, but if God does not give it, then man's will cannot oppose it. God teaches faith to some, but not to others: he teaches the former by his lovingkindness, but the latter do not learn of his righteous judgment.[137] Since all people come from Adam, they received a just judgment, but this would not be some kind of reproach of God, even if not one person were delivered from condemnation.[138] In other words, if God were to save no one, it still would not be permissible to reproach him in this. If the question is why God chooses some, and not others, then it does not serve to seek the answer to this question, in view of the scriptural passage, "how unsearchable are his judgments and his ways past finding out" (Rom 11.33).[139]

Flowing from these views of Augustine is the idea that those who are not saved and cannot be saved, indeed who are not predestined to salvation, are those who do not hear the preaching of the Gospel, those who do not respond to this preaching, and unbaptized youths. Those who are saved are only those who are wittingly predestined to salvation and who by the power of predestination are vouchsafed with the gift of faith and saving grace:

> Both those who have not heard the Gospel, and those who, having heard it and been changed by it for the better, have not received perseverance,

---

[136]Cf.: See above Chapter 2.4: The Love of God.
[137]Cf.: Augustine *A Treatise on the Predestination of the Saints* 8 (14).
[138]Ibid. (16).
[139]Ibid.

and those who, having heard the Gospel, have refused to come to Christ
.., and those who by their tender age were unable to believe, but might
be absolved from original sin by the sole laver of regeneration, and yet
have not received this laver, and have perished in death: are not made to
differ from that lump which it is plain is condemned, as all go from one
into condemnation. Some are made to differ, however, not by their own
merits, but by the grace of the Mediator; that is to say, they are justified
freely in the blood of the second Adam. . . . We ought to understand that
from that mass of perdition which originated through the first Adam, no
one can be made to differ except [him] who has this gift, which whosoever has, has received by the grace of the Savior. . . . Those, then, are
elected, as has often been said, who are called according to the purpose,
who also are predestined and foreknown.[140]

*The parable of the Last
Judgment. Basilica of
Sant'Apollinare Nuovo.
Ravenna. 6th c.*

The teaching that in fairness all people ought to
be condemned and that some appear to be chosen
for salvation only by God's mercy was developed
by the theologians of the Reformation. The concept of a "dual predestination" became the cornerstone of the theological doctrine of Luther and
Calvin. Calvin asserted that Adam "stumbled
because it was decreed by God," although he also
stumbled "because of his own prophecies."[141] Like
Calvin, Luther also rejected the presence of free will
in fallen man and its possibility to influence a person's salvation. Speaking on the feats of the mar-
tyrs, Luther claimed that the reason for their steadfastness was exclusively
the grace of God, and not their own free will: "There is not any kind of freedom here, nor free will, it is impossible to change yourself, to desire something else, so long as the spirit and grace of God are not strengthened in
man."[142] The battle for each person's soul unfolds not within the person,
but outside, between God and the devil. A person's will, like a pack animal,
finds itself between God's will and Satan's will: if God takes possession of
the person, then she or he follows after God, but if Satan takes hold, that

[140]*Treatise on Rebuke and Grace* 12–14.
[141]*Instruction in the Christian Faith* 3.23.8.
[142]*On the Slavery of the Will.*

person follows Satan.[143] Therefore the person remains only a passive viewer of his or her own salvation or condemnation.

Orthodox tradition, again basing itself on the theological legacy of the fathers of the Eastern Church, speaks differently of man's predestination toward salvation. From the Orthodox point of view, those who are predestined for salvation are all the people created by God; there is no one who is wittingly predestined for destruction, condemnation, or damnation. St Symeon the New Theologian in particular speaks of this in the interpretation of Romans 8.29–30. Relating the words of the apostle to someone who "misconstrues their own perdition" and says "what use is it for me to bear these many labors, to show an appeal to damnation, if I am not predestined by God for salvation?" Symeon writes:

> Do you not hear the Savior crying out every day: "I live and do not want the death of a sinner, but rather that he should turn to me and live"? Do you not hear how he says: "Repent, for the Kingdom of Heaven is at hand"? Perhaps he said to one: "Do not repent, because I will not accept you," but to others, to those who are predestined: "Repent, because I knew you before"? No! But every day in every church he calls out to the whole world: "Come to me, all who labor and are heavy laden, and I will give you rest." Come, he says, you who are burdened with sins, to him who takes the sins of the world on himself![144]

Every person is chosen for salvation and predestined for deification, and consequently, anyone who wishes can be acquitted and glorified. God wishes, without exception, for all people to be made gods by grace:

> The grace of the Holy Spirit strives to become inflamed in our souls, in order that . . . coming nearer the flame (either each one separately or, if possible, all together) they might catch fire and be radiant like gods. . . . I think that this is how it actually is, that this is precisely what God's will for us consists of.[145]

For seven centuries before Symeon the New Theologian, and for eleven centuries before Calvin, the Eastern Christian tradition, in the person of John Chrysostom, chose its view on predestination and calling: "If all sinned, then

[143]Ibid.
[144]*Moral Oration* 2.12–25.
[145]Symeon the New Theologian *Catechetical Oration* 34.235–245.

why are some saved and others perish? Because not all want to come, even though all are saved by God's will, since all are called."[146] In other words, all are predestined and called to salvation without exception, but only those who willingly respond to God's invitation are saved; those who reject God's summons are not saved.

Salvation, according to Orthodox dogma, is the fruit of "synergy" between God and man. Man's free will plays a role of the utmost importance in this synergy, as it can be guided either to the good, or to the bad. If it is guided to evil, then it is not because God predestined it so, but because the person has made a free choice on behalf of evil. But if it is guided to the good, then this occurs because of the action of God's grace, yet again not without the participation of that very person. The battle for salvation unfolds within man, not without. The devil can influence a man by various means, but man is capable of opposing him. The will of the devil cannot destroy a person: in the final account the deciding factor of a person's fate is precisely the direction of his or her free will toward good or evil.

This does not mean that the Orthodox disparage the meaning of predestination, calling, and the action of God's grace in man's salvation. It only means that the notion of God as punisher is alien, he who in his justice should have destroyed all people after they succumbed to sin, and who saves some only by mercy. The Orthodox Church, after the Apostle Paul, believes that God "will have all men to be saved and to come to the knowledge of the truth" (1 Tim 2.4). The salvation of every person is a result of God's love for the whole human race, and not a consequence of God removing his inexpressible lovingkindness from the "mass of the condemned" of these or those transgressors, to whom he grants salvation despite his own fairness.

God can save every person and wishes to save each and every person. However, he cannot save someone without the participation and accord of that person. As Maximus the Confessor emphasized, every person has the right to reject salvation. Salvation is not to be forced or coercive: those who wish to follow Christ will be saved.[147] It is in man's compliance with the will of God concerning his own salvation, in the voluntary keeping of the divine commandments, and in the inclusion of that synergy about which Orthodox theology speaks.

[146]*Homilies on Romans* 16.5.
[147]Cf.: Maximus the Confessor *Ad Thalassium* 63.

PART FOUR

CHRIST

The All-Powerful Lord. Church of the Dormition. Daphne. Constantinople. 11th c.

C HRISTOLOGY IS THE PRIMARY POINT of the theology of the Christian Church. Precisely in the teaching of Christ as God-man and Savior lies the cardinal difference between Christianity and the other monotheistic religions.

At the foundation of Orthodox theology is the teaching of Christ, contained in the New Testament, in the dogmas of the ecumenical councils, and the works of the Fathers, above all the Eastern ones. This teaching is subdivided into several themes, which will be looked at throughout the coming chapter: the dogma of the incarnation; the teachings on the two natures, the two energies, and two wills of Christ; the passion and death of the Savior; the Cross of the Lord; Christ's descent into Hades and the resurrection; and the atonement and deification.

13

The Incarnation

The nativity of Christ. Palatine Chapel. Palermo. 12th c.

WE WILL EXAMINE THE THEME of the incarnation through the example of the teaching of some of the most authoritative fathers of the Eastern Church: Athanasius of Alexandria, Gregory the Theologian, Isaac the Syrian, Maximus the Confessor, and Symeon the New Theologian. A survey of the views of these authors on the dogma of the incarnation will offer a sufficiently comprehensive picture of its understanding in the Orthodox Church.

Athanasius of Alexandria's treatise *On the Incarnation of the Word* became the classical expression of the Eastern Christian teaching on the incarnation. The author, speaking in this exposition of the reasons for the incarnation, turns to the biblical concept of God's image. The image of God was occluded in fallen man, similar to a depiction of a person on a panel, which, covered with layers of stains, ceases to be visible. For this depiction to be renewed, one cannot simply throw out the panel. For this to happen it is necessary for the one from whom the portrait was done to come, and to draw the face on the old panel anew. This is precisely what the Son of God accomplished: "Being the image of the Father, [he] came to our realm to renew man once made in his likeness."[1]

But God's image in man could not be renewed without the abolition of death and corruption. For this reason it was necessary for the Word of God to take on a mortal body, so that by its aid death might be destroyed[2] and the image of God might be renewed in people.[3] However, the Son of God did not immediately become a sacrifice for all through the incarnation,

---

[1] Athanasius of Alexandria *On the Incarnation of the Word* 14.1.
[2] For the patristic understanding of the abolition of death by Christ's resurrection, see below, in the section on the holy resurrection of Christ.
[3] Athanasius of Alexandria *On the Incarnation . . .* 13.

giving his body over to death.[4] First he, as a man, lived amongst people and taught them the knowledge of his Father, so that they might leave idol worship and come to worship God.[5] And only after he proved his divinity through his deeds "did he hand his own bodily temple over unto death as a sacrifice for all, in order to free all from the debt of the ancient crime."[6]

Gregory the Theologian, in his treatise on the dogma of the atonement, emphasizes the love of God, which was the chief reason for the incarnation. The Only-begotten Son of God was sent into the world by the Father in order to heal the injury of sin in man's nature. Sin entered into the life of man after the Fall: the punishment for sin was death. But this very same punishment was the manifestation of God's love, and a divine act was hidden in death itself, since it blocked the way to the propagation of sin. Over the course of many centuries God taught mankind in different ways, though sin continued to be transmitted from generation to generation. There needed to be a much stronger "medicine," which ended up being the incarnation of the Word of God:

> He who is comes into being, and the uncreated is created, and the uncontained is contained, through the intervention of the rational soul, which mediates between the divinity and the coarseness of the flesh. . . . What is the wealth of his goodness? What is this mystery concerning me? I participated in the divine image, and I did not keep it; he participates in my flesh both to save the image and to make the flesh immortal. He shares with us a second communion, much more paradoxical than the first; then he gave us a share in what is superior, now he shares in what is inferior. This is more godlike than the first; this, to those who can understand, is more exalted.[7]

Thus, the incarnation became the pivotal point in the fate of mankind: in its own significance, as Gregory considers, it surpasses even the creation of man. Speaking on the incarnation, Gregory employs the terms "impoverishment" and "draining," or "emptying" (*kenōsis*, κένωσις). This term, coming from the words of the Apostle Paul, became a classic expression of Eastern

[4]Ibid. 16.
[5]Ibid. 15.
[6]Ibid. 20.
[7]Gregory the Theologian, *Oration 38* 13 (Crestwood, NY: 2008), 71.

Christology, for it explains that the Son of God "emptied (*ekenōsen*, ἐκένωσεν) himself, taking the form of a servant, and was made in the likeness of men, and being found in fashion as a man" (Phil 2.7). Citing the Apostle Paul, Gregory writes:

> He was actually subject as a slave to flesh, to birth, and to our human experiences; for our liberation, held captive as we are by sin, he was subject to all that he saved. What does the lowliness of man possess that is higher than involvement with God, than being *made* God as a result of this intermingling, than being so "visited by the dayspring from on high" (Lk 1.78) that "the holy thing which is born" has been called "Son of the most high" (Lk 1.35) and that there has been "bestowed on it the name which is above every name. . . ." What of the "bowing of every knee" to one who "was made empty on our account," who blended the "divine image" with a "slave's form" (Phil 2.9–10).[8]

The teaching of the divine emptying is a leitmotif of St Gregory the Theologian's Christology:

> The one who enriches becomes poor; he is made poor in my flesh, that I might be enriched through his divinity. The full one empties himself; for he empties himself of his own glory for a short time, that I may participate in his fullness.[9]

> God descended from his heavenly throne, having emptied his glory into a mortal womb and having intermingled himself with mortality, and united God and man together.[10]

> Christ was impoverished in crude flesh, being of the highest intellect and of the first nature of the mind.[11]

> God, having become man, suffers like man, and condescends to accept flesh for himself, so that all might become deified by his condescension.[12]

---

[8]*Oration 30* 3 (Crestwood, NY: 2002), 94–95.
[9]*Oration 38* 13 (Crestwood, NY: 2008), 71.
[10]*Poems on Himself 13: On Bishops.*
[11]*Moral Poems 10: On Virtue.*
[12]*Oration 44* 4.

The nativity of Christ.
Monastery of Hosios Loukas.
Greece. 11th c.

Being the path of humble leniency and of divine emptying, the incarnation of the Word became at the same time a path of man's ascent to the heights of deification. The Divine Word, coeternal and of one essence with the Father, remained such as he was even after taking on himself in the incarnation that which he was not–human nature. Preserving his divinity whole, the Word accepted humanity wholly for himself; remaining one in essence with the Father in divinity, the Son of God became one in essence with us in humanity; being God and Master, Christ became our brother.[13] Therefore, no change occurred in God at the moment of the incarnation: his essence remained as it had been. The change occurred in us, for everything in our essence and in our fate changed by that cardinal image. Addressing his Arian opponents, Gregory says:

> He whom presently you scorn was once transcendent, over even you. He who is presently human was incomposite. He remained what he was; what he was not, he assumed. No "because" is required for his existence in the beginning, for what could account for the existence of God? But later he came into being because of something, namely your salvation, yours, who insult him and despise his Godhead for that very reason, because he took on your thick corporeality. Through the medium of the mind he had dealings with the flesh, being made that God on earth, who is man: man and God blended. They became a single whole, the stronger side predominating, in order that I might be made God to the same extent that he was made man. He was begotten[14]–yet he was already begotten–of a woman. And yet she was a virgin. That it was from a woman makes it human, that she was a virgin makes it divine. On earth he has no father, but in heaven no mother. All this is part of his Godhead.[15]

In the teachings of the Greek fathers on the incarnation, the term *oikonomia* (οἰκονομία) is widely used, which is translated literally as "economy" (the

---

[13]Cf.: *Oration 44* 7.

[14]In other words he was born as a man from the Virgin Mary, but as God he was begotten eternally from the Father.

[15]*Oration 29* 19 (Crestwood, NY: 2002), 86–87.

management of the household) or sometimes as "leniency." This term traditionally demonstrates the saving act of the Son of God in relation to the race
of man, that is the nativity, earthly life, passion, and death of Christ. Gregory
the Theologian opposes the "nature" of God to divine "economy" when he
says that it is necessary to understand the multitude of New Testament texts
that in some way speak on the inequality between the Father and the Son. In
Gregory's opinion, there are expressions in Scripture that point out Christ's
divinity, and there are those that relate to his economy:

> In sum: you must predicate the more sublime expressions of the God-
> head, of the nature which transcends bodily experiences, and the lowlier
> ones of the compound, of him who because of you was emptied, became
> incarnate and (to use equally valid language) was "made man." Then next
> he was exalted, in order that you might . . . learn . . . to ascend with the
> Godhead and not linger on in things visible but rise up to spiritual reali-
> ties, and that you might know what belongs to his nature and what to
> God's plan of salvation.[16]

This hermeneutical principle can be applied to the names of Christ found
in the New Testament. These names, according to Gregory, are divided into
two categories, belonging "to him on both levels, the transcendent and the
human," and belonging to "those that are distinctively human and
belong[ing] to what he assumed from us."[17] Of the first rank are the names
Son, Only-begotten, Word, Wisdom, Power, Truth, Image, Light, Life, Right,
Hallowed, Atonement, and Resurrection. The names of the second rank are
those that relate to the saving plan of salvation and point out Christ's human
nature: Man, Son of Man, Christ, Way, Door, Shepherd, Sheep, Lamb, Archpriest, and Melchizedek.[18] All of these names make up the ladder by which
man must ascend to reach deification:

> There you have the Son's titles. Walk like God through all that are sub-
> lime, and with a fellow-feeling through all that involve the body; but even
> better, treat all as God does, so that you may ascend from below to
> become God, because he came down from above for us. Above all, keep

---

[16] *Oration 29* 18 (Crestwood, NY: 2002), 86.
[17] *Oration 30* 21, III.
[18] Ibid. 27.

hold of this truth and apply it to all the loftier and lowlier names and you will never fail.[19]

Isaac the Syrian, who lived three centuries after Gregory, also writes on the names, or titles, of Christ. Like Gregory, Isaac relates some names to Christ's divinity or Godhead, and others to his humanity:

Christ the Lord is both the First-begotten and the Only-begotten. One and the other do not coexist in one nature, for "first-begotten" supposes many siblings, whereas "only-begotten" does not suppose any other kind of being born before or after him. These two names are confirmed in God and in man, united in one hypostasis, while the qualities of both natures are not mingled by virtue of this union.[20]

St Isaac the Syrian.
Russian icon. 15th c.

Isaac the Syrian develops the theme of the divine economy as well, emphasizing that the saving plan of salvation is a mystery, going beyond the boundaries of the human intellect: "A great mystery, concealed in the economy of our Lord: it is loftier than the remission of sins and the destruction of death."[21]

In the theological view of Isaac the Syrian, divine love occupies such a central place that in his treatise on the incarnation other traditional Christian themes emanate from the second plan, such as the expiation of sins and the victory over death. Isaac, for instance, considers that the Son of God became incarnate not for the sake of the remission of sins and the destruction of death, nor for people's deliverance from sin, but for the sake of God's love being made manifest to man:

If he was sufficiently zealous for the correction of people, why did God clothe himself in flesh, in order to bring the world back to his Father with

[19] *Oration 30* 21, 112.
[20] *Chapters on Knowledge I* 49.
[21] *Chapters on Knowledge IV* 84.

the help of meekness and humility? And why was he hung on the cross for the sake of sinners, having given his holy body for the world? I say that God did all this for no other reason than to manifest his love to the world, the love that he possesses. His goal was so that when we come to know it, our love might grow within us and we might be captives of his love.[22]

Isaac highlights that God's incarnation occurred without any kind of request from people. It was initiated by God and as a consequence of his immeasurable leniency toward the human race:

When the totality of creation let go of and forgot God, having perfected itself in every evil, he descended into their homes and lived amongst them in their body by his own will and without request,[23] as one of them, and with love that is beyond the comprehension and words of all creation, he entreated them to turn to him. . . . He forgave them all their sins that they had committed before, and confirmed the truth of this reconciliation by means of persuasive signs and miracles and revelations of his mysteries to them; after all this he humbles himself to such humility[24] that he wants sinful nature (dust of the earth, despicable people, flesh, and blood) to call him Father. Could this ever come to pass without great love?[25]

The incarnation of the Son of God, according to Isaac, became a new revelation of God to be compared with the Old Testament. In the Old Testament age, the tribe of Israel was neither capable of hearing God's voice nor of seeing divine revelation; but after the incarnation all of this becomes possible:

Creation could not gaze upon him unless he accepted a part from it and therefore began to converse with it; it could not hear the words of his mouth uttered face to face. For this reason the sons of Israel could not hear his voice when he spoke to them from the cloud (Deut 5.25). . . . The sons of Israel purified themselves by Moses' command for three days, preparing themselves and restraining themselves in order to be made worthy to hear God's voice and to see God's revelation (Ex 19.15); but when the time came, they could not bear the sight of his light nor the might of

---

[22]Ibid. 78.
[23]Meaning without request from people.
[24]Word for word in the original.
[25]Isaac the Syrian *On the Divine Mysteries: Conversation* 40.14.

his thundering voice. But now, when he poured out his own grace on the world by his coming, he was not in the earthquake, not in the fire, and not in the terrible and powerful whirlwind (1 Kg 19.12), but he was "like rain that falls on the mown grass" and like drops that gently fall on the earth (Ps 72.6), so was he seen conversing with us in a different form, that is, when, as if in a treasury, he concealed his majesty beneath a veil of flesh (Heb 10.20), and spoke amongst us and with us while wrapped in it, having fashioned it for his own purpose and will in the Virgin's womb.[26]

Isaac the Syrian emphasizes the universal significance of God's coming to earth and taking on human flesh for himself. The incarnation is directly related to the fate of the whole cosmos and of each individual person:

O wonder! The Creator in human clothing entered into the house of publicans and prodigals, and when they . . . turned to him, he persuaded them, giving them confidence in their reconciliation with him through his teachings. And he sealed the word of truth by sincere witnesses through powers and signs. And through his beautiful visage and love, the whole universe was drawn to a unified confession of God, the Lord of all, and the knowledge of the one Creator was sown in every person.[27]

The teaching on the reasons for the incarnation contained in the works of Maximus the Confessor brings up special interest by virtue of its originality, just as in view of what it has in common with treatises on the incarnation found in medieval Western theologians.[28] In the West, beginning with Rupert of Deutz (d. 1129), the question became whether the Son of God would still have become incarnate had Adam not sinned. In other words, could the incarnation be considered a consequence of Adam's fall, or would it have occurred independently of it? Honorius of Autun (d. 1152) maintained that the reason for the incarnation was not the sin of Adam, but "the predestination of the deification of man," which existed from the beginning of time. In Honorius' words, it was necessary for Christ "to become incarnate so that man might become deified. It does not follow here that sin was the reason

---

[26] *Oration 53.*
[27] *On the Divine Mysteries: Conversation* 11.28.
[28] H. U. von Balthasar was the first to pay attention to the parallel thoughts between Maximus and the Western theologians: Balthasar, *Liturgie Cosmique.* Moreover, this issue was examined by Protopresbyter Georges Florovsky in the article "Cur Deus Homo?"

for the incarnation, but rather that sin could not change God's decision concerning man's deification."[29] In John Duns Scotus's (d. 1308) understanding, the incarnation of the Son of God was the chief reason for the creation of the world. It "was not thought up accidentally, as God's foreknowledge had this goal from time immemorial."[30] Even if not one angel nor one man fell, Christ would nevertheless have become man, though in this case the passion and redemptive feat would not have been necessary: he would have immediately appeared as the glorified Christ.[31]

Similar ideas can be found in the works of Eastern fathers. Maximus the Confessor in particular returns to the notion repeatedly in his compositions that the incarnation was the ultimate purpose for creation:

[The incarnation] is the great and hidden mystery, at once the blessed end for which all things are ordained. It is the divine purpose conceived before the beginning of created things. . . . This mystery is the preconceived goal for which everything exists, but which itself exists on account of nothing. With a clear view to this end, God created the essences of created beings, and such is, properly speaking, the terminus of his providence and of the things under his providential care. Inasmuch as it leads to God, it is the recapitulation of the things he has created.[32] It is the mystery which circumscribes all the ages, and which reveals the grand plan of God, a super-infinite plan infinitely preexisting the ages. The Logos, by essence God, became a messenger of this plan when he became a man and, if I may rightly say so, established himself as the innermost depth of the Father's goodness while also displaying in himself the very goal for which his creatures manifestly received the beginning of their existence. Because of Christ . . . all the ages of time and the beings within those ages have received their beginning and end in Christ. For the union between a limit of the ages and limitlessness, between measure and immeasurability, between finitude and infinity, between Creator and creation, between rest and motion, was conceived before the ages. This union has been manifested in Christ at the end of time.[33]

[29] *The Eighth Book of Question on Angels and Man* 2.

[30] *Opus Oxoniense* 3.19.

[31] Cf.: John Duns Scotus *Reportata Parisiensa III* 7.4.2.

[32] These words reflect the theory of "Recapitulation" developed by Irenaeus of Lyons. For more on this theory, see the following section of this chapter.

[33] *Ad Thalassium* 60 (Crestwood, NY: 2003), 124–125.

The nativity of Christ.
The Dark Church in Göreme.
Cappadocia. 11th c.

In the above text the incarnation is linked not with Adam's sin, but with the creation of the world: the whole world, in Maximus' mind, was created for the sake of the ultimate goal of the incarnation. Man was created for deification, and this divine goal remained immutable after the Fall. The given teaching was reflected in the historic-philosophical views of Maximus, who had considered it possible to divide the whole history of the divine economy into two periods: the first includes the ages that relate to "the mystery of the divine incarnation," and the second is the age relating to "the grace of human deification."[34] The incarnation, therefore, is considered a pivotal point in the history of mankind and the whole created world: all was brought into being for the sake of this event, and this event marked the beginning of the way of creation to that purpose that was preordained by the Creator at the Pre-eternal Council.

Therefore there is some degree of proximity between the views of Maximus the Confessor on the incarnation and the teaching of John Duns Scotus. At the same time it is necessary to emphasize that Eastern patristics never placed the question for the reason of the incarnation in such a perspective as the issue was placed in the West, and the hypothetical possibility of the existence of another world, which exists now, was never scrutinized by the Eastern fathers. In accordance with this, neither redemption nor deification stood out in the character of independent themes from the general context of the teaching of the divine economy—or plan—of salvation. This saving plan was considered the only indissoluble act, and redemption was never placed in opposition to deification.[35]

In the works of Symeon the New Theologian, redemption and deification appear as two purposes for the incarnation, inseparable from one another. Symeon repeatedly says that the aim of the incarnation was man's deliverance

[34]Ibid. 22, p. 115.

[35]As V. Lossky considers, "if our deification had had its own absolute condition, independent of the Fall and by which the necessary redemption was called, God would have given man both this absolute condition and the incarnation of the Son of God, who created the world, i.e., above all he would have become incarnate, not leaving his creation 'incomplete,' incapable of reaching communion with God." V. N. Lossky, "Dispute on Sofia," *Theology and Seeing God: A Collection of Articles* (Moscow: 2000), 454. Lossky's given claim advances the polemic with Protopresbyter Sergius Bulgakov, whose views on the incarnation were notably influenced by Western Medieval theology.

from slavery to the devil. Just as man served the devil from his very birth throughout the course of his whole life, so the Lord proceeded through every age, so that the devil was conquered in each stage of man's development: Christ "became incarnate and was born . . . sanctifying conception and birth and, as he continued growing bit by bit, blessed every age . . . making himself a servant, taking the form of a servant, and the Lord once again led us slaves to worthiness and made us lords and rulers over the devil himself, who before was our tyrant."[36]

Symeon presents the idea of deification as the goal of the incarnation with no less persistence. Almost repeating the classic formula of Irenaeus of Lyons, Symeon says: "Why did God become man? So that man might become God."[37] Deification is the miraculous unification of God with man, similar to the oneness between the Father and the Son:

He promises that, if we so desire, he will have with us the same unity by grace that he himself has with the Father by nature. . . . O awesome promise! The glory that the Father gave the Son, the Son gives to us by grace, if we desire it. . . . For the love with which God, the Father of the Only-Begotten Son and our God, loves, is the same, it is said, and will be in us, and the Son of God will be in us.[38]

Symeon emphasizes the personal character of the incarnation, thanks to which man becomes a sibling and "co-inheritor" of the Lord. Christ becomes incarnate not for some abstract "mob" of people, but for each and every concrete human person: "God sent his Only-Begotten Son to earth for you and for your salvation, because he knew you before and predestined you to be his kin and co-inheritor."[39]

God becomes so close to man in the incarnation that this proximity is compared to a familial bond: "Having become once our kinsman by flesh and having made us co-communicants of his divinity, he made all his kinsmen. . . . As Eve was taken from the flesh and bones of Adam, and they were both one flesh, so Christ teaches us to be partakers of his very flesh and bones."[40] Symeon portrays the kinship between Christ and people with the

---

[36] *Catechetical Oration* 5.413–425.
[37] *Moral Oration* 5.31–34.
[38] Ibid. 1.6.57–76.
[39] Ibid. 2.160–163.
[40] Ibid. 1.6.76–139.

aid of the following metaphor: "The house of David is us as his[41] kin, for you yourself, the Creator of all, made yourself his Son, but we are your children by grace. You are our kinsman in the flesh, but we are yours by your divinity. . . . Uniting ourselves, we all become one house, that is, we are all kin, we are all your siblings."[42]

According to Symeon's teaching, one receives justification through Christ and the whole history of man in a final and absolute thought, including the Fall and the expulsion from paradise, from which the first father and mother "received not shame, but great benefit,"[43] because the Lord readied them in advance for something greater than the original paradise–the Kingdom of Heaven. Having become man, Christ healed the consequences of Adam's crime, he delivered people from the servitude of the devil, from condemnation and damnation; he reconstituted, smelted, and renewed the nature of man, distorted by sin.

The incarnation of the Son of God and his salvific act were not an intrusion into man's free will, were not a rupture of the "autonomy" granted to him. Symeon always insists that the fruits of Christ's redeeming sacrifice– that is: union with God, brotherhood and kinship with Christ, and finally, deification–are adopted by us only on the condition that we want them. Christ is the Shepherd and Master for those wishing to follow him, but for others, while he is Creator and God, he is neither their King nor their Shepherd, because they are the offspring and vessels of the enemy.[44] Christ does not coerce man, but rather waits for his voluntary and conscious entry onto the path toward salvation.

Symeon notes that by virtue of the incarnation of Christ, people, "although they became siblings and relatives of him by flesh, but being dust, they remained so and were not made immediately into sons of God."[45] This signifies that deification, as the goal of Christian life, is not attained instantly, but is built up in a gradual process in the continual spiritual growth of a person. The attainment of the goal of Christian life in large part depends on the strength of that very person, however his salvation is in the hands of God. Therefore, salvation is an act of synergy between God's creation and man.

[41]David's.
[42]Symeon the New Theologian *Hymn 15* 118–125.
[43]*Catechetical Oration* 5.379–380.
[44]*Moral Oration* 43.27–56.
[45]*Hymn 13* 152–155.

14

Christ: The Second Adam

T HE THEME OF CHRIST AS THE SECOND ADAM
occupies an important place in the Christology of the Eastern Church. This theme comes
from the teaching of the Apostle Paul on the first
and second man:

> The first man, Adam, was made a living soul;
> the last Adam was made a life-giving spirit. . . .
> The first is of the earth, earthy; the second man
> is the Lord from heaven. As is the earthy, so are
> they that are also earthy; and as is the heavenly,
> so are they also that are heavenly. And as we
> have borne the image of the earthly, we shall
> also bear the image of the heavenly (1 Cor
> 15.45–49).

*The Lord and Adam. Palatine
chapel. Palermo. 12th c.*

Developing the teaching of the Apostle Paul, in the second century the
holy martyr Irenaeus of Lyons worked out a theory, according to which all
the events of Christ's life are regarded as a repetition of the events of Adam's
life, only their effect is reversed. The idea behind this theory is as follows:
everything that Adam should have fulfilled but did not, Christ fulfilled for
him; every mistake Adam made was corrected by Christ; every sin Adam
committed was healed by Christ. In academic literature this teaching of Irenaeus received the name "recapitulation" (Lat. *recapitulatio*, Gr.
anakephalaiōsis, ἀνακεφαλαίωσις), since the given term used by Irenaeus literally means something like a "reverse table of contents," that is an enu-
meration of chapters listed in reverse order. The list of actions subject to
this recapitulation consists of all the acts that Adam either should have performed or not performed, or that he performed in a way that God had not

commanded. Christ becomes the new Adam for the correction and healing of what was broken by our forebears:

> The Lord was manifestly coming to his own things . . . and was making a recapitulation of that disobedience which had occurred in connection with a tree, through the obedience which was [exhibited by himself when he hung] upon a tree. . . . For in the same way the sin of the first created man receives amendment by the correction of the First-begotten, and the coming of the serpent is conquered by the harmlessness of the dove, those bonds being unloosed by which we had been fast bound to death.[1]

The first created people, Adam and Eve, according to Irenaeus' teaching, found themselves in a state of spiritual immaturity; they were not instructed in the perfect image of life.[2] The reason for the first sin of Adam and Eve is rooted in this ignorance. However, the Son of God came into the world, "restoring [lit. recapitulating] all in himself."[3] In Irenaeus' words, "The Son of God, although he was perfect, passed through the state of infancy in common with the rest of mankind, partaking of it thus not for his own benefit, but for that of the infantile stage of man's existence, in order that man might be able to receive him."[4] Christ's obedience to God the Father in his passion on the cross was the solution for Adam's disobedience.[5]

St Gregory the Theologian develops this very theme in the fourth century when, following Irenaeus, he emphasizes that each event from the life of Christ corresponds to an analogous event from Adam's life. Christ proceeded consecutively through all the stages of human life so that sin might be cured at each stage. The second Adam settles the debts of the first Adam individually:

> So all became one for the sake of all, and for the sake of one, our progenitor, the soul because of the soul which was disobedient, the flesh because of the flesh which cooperated with it and shared in its condemnation, Christ, who was superior to, and beyond the reach of, sin, because of Adam, who became subject to sin. This is why the new was

---

[1] *Against Heresies* 5.19.1.
[2] Cf. Irenaeus of Lyons *Against Heresies* 4.38.1.
[3] Ibid.
[4] Ibid. 4.38.2.
[5] Ibid. 5.16.3.

substituted for the old, why he who suffered was for suffering recalled to life, why each property of his, who was above us, was interchanged with each of ours, why the new mystery took the place of the dispensation, due to loving kindness which deals with him who fell through disobedience. This is the reason for the generation and the virgin, for the manger and Bethlehem; the generation on behalf of the creation, the virgin on behalf of the woman, Bethlehem because of Eden, the manger because of the garden, small and visible things on behalf of great and hidden things. . . . This is . . . why tree is set over against tree, hands against hand,[6] the one stretched out in self-indulgence, the other in generosity; the one restrained, the others fixed by nails, the one expelling Adam, the other reconciling the ends of the earth. This is the reason of the lifting up to atone for the fall, and of the gall for the tasting, and of the thorny crown for the dominion of evil, and of death for death, and of darkness for the sake of light, and of burial for the return to the ground, and of resurrection for the sake of resurrection.[7]

For Gregory, the incarnation is the greatest mystery, not subject to the paradox of human wisdom, of the wondrous union of that which is impossible to unite: God and man. Adam's salvation, brought about as a result of the incarnation, is also a mystery:

An innovation is made to natures, and God becomes human, and he who "has mounted upon the heaven of heavens at the dawn"[8] of his own glory and splendor, is glorified at the sunset of our cheapness and lowliness, and the Son of God accepts both to become Son of a human being and to be called such; not changing what he was, for he is immutable, but assuming what he was not, for he loves humankind. . . . For this reason unmingled realities are mingled, not only God with generation, or mind with flesh, or the atemporal with time, or the uncircumscribed with measure, but also childbirth with virginity, and dishonor with what is above all honor, and suffering with the impassable, and the immortal with the corruptible. For since the deceptive advocate of evil[9] thought he was unconquerable as he

---

[6] In other words, instead of Adam's hand, audaciously reaching for the forbidden fruit, are Christ's hands, stretched out on the cross.

[7] *Oration 2 23–25.*

[8] Cf. Ps 67.34 (LXX).

[9] I.e., the devil.

ensnared us with the hope of divinity, he was ensnared by the obstacle of flesh. Just as when he meant to attack Adam he encountered God, so also by the new Adam the old was saved and the condemnation of the flesh was abolished, since death was put to death by flesh.[10]

It is impossible not to recognize in this text echoes of Gregory of Nyssa's theory, according to which the devil was defeated by the lure of the flesh, not having seen that God was inside it.[11] Gregory the Theologian uses a similar image,[12] however in distinction from Gregory of Nyssa he does not develop the foundation of his soteriological theory, which would attempt to explain the mystery of redemption. A ransom was truly offered, the devil was truly deceived, and man was truly saved by the incarnate God; but Gregory the Theologian does not want to go beyond these assertions: "The greater part will be revered by silence."[13]

The theme of Christ as the second Adam is central in the Christology of St Symeon the New Theologian. Using the words of the Apostle Paul on the first and second man as a springboard, Symeon stresses that, having taken on the fullness of human nature and having made himself perfect man, the Son of God did not depart from the Father and remained perfect God:

He is God from God, without beginning of the Father's eternal Origin, bodiless from the bodiless, incomprehensible from the incomprehensible one, eternal from the eternal one, unapproachable from the unapproach-able one, immortal from the immortal one, invisible from the invisible one, the Word of God and God, through whom all came into being, everything in heaven and on earth. . . . Being such and existing in the Father and having the Father exist in him, not separating from him and absolutely not leaving him, he descended to earth and became incarnate of the Holy Spirit and the Virgin Mary and became man, having become . . . equal to us in everything except sin, so that, experiencing all that is ours, he might reconstitute and renew that first man, and through him and all that are born and are being born, all might be like his parent.[14]

---

[10] *Oration 39* 13 (2008), 89.

[11] For more on this theory, cf. Chapter 4.4.

[12] *Dogmatic Verses 9: On the Commandments and Manifestations of Christ*: Christ appeared "wrapped from every quarter in a curtain . . . for he needed the serpent, considering itself to be wise, approaching Adam, unexpectedly to meet God instead of Adam and have God's fortress smash his malice."

[13] *Oration 45* 22 (2008), 182.

[14] *Moral Oration 13* 76–89.

Symeon asserts repeatedly and with great persistence that God foresaw Adam's fall and his following repentance even before the creation of the world, and because of this he predetermined man's salvation through Christ before the ages. The divine predestination was expressed after the Fall, when Adam became corruptible and mortal, and creation already did not want to obey and bow down to him, and God compelled it into submission, having made it corrupt and mortal like man, though it was not guilty of sin. But creation should be restored, as the Apostle Paul says: "For the earnest expectation of the creation waits for the manifestation of the sons of God. For the creation was made subject to vanity, not willingly, but by reason of him who has subjected it in hope, because the creation itself also shall be delivered from the bondage of corruption in to the glorious liberty of the children of God" (Rom 8.19–21). Therefore the future restoration of creation and its predestined freedom from slavery to corruption should come through man:

*The Fall. Palatine chapel.
Palermo. 12th c.*

> Knowing before the construction of the world that Adam would break the commandment, he predestined his life and reconstruction from a new birth through the Only-Begotten Son of God born in the flesh. . . . He wants creation to remain in submission, serving man for whom it was created, having become corrupt for the corrupted, so that when it again becomes renewed and spiritual, incorruptible, and immortal, then it, being freed from slavery . . . might be co-renewed together with man and might become incorruptible and somehow spiritual. For the All-Merciful God and Lord preordained this before the construction of the world.[15]

Symeon stresses that the incarnation of the Son of God brought man an endlessly greater blessing than that which he lost through the Fall. In the very expulsion of Adam from paradise God's grace and love for mankind is already manifest: "If they [Adam and Eve] repented while still in paradise,

[15]Ibid. *1* 2.78–94.

then they would have received again only that same paradise, and nothing more."[16] But the Lord prepared the Heavenly Kingdom for them:

> See how great God's love toward man is! Descending to Hell and having resurrected them, he did not restore them again to the same paradise from which they had fallen, but led them to the heaven of heavens itself. . . . Can you see to what heights he elevated them for their repentance, humility, grief, and tears? . . . God did not only cleanse and glorify Adam, but also . . . all his sons who imitated him in his confession, repentance, and tears.[17]

Symeon is reminiscent of Isaac the Syrian in these words, for Isaac claimed that God cast Adam out of paradise "under the guise of wrath," although in this very casting out, just as in the establishment of death, "the economy is already present, perfecting and leading everything to that original purpose of the Creator." The Creator's true intention was "our transfer to that delightful and glorious world" that is the Kingdom of Heaven. Death and the expulsion from paradise, in Isaac's opinion, had only the look of condemnation, but in actuality they were God's blessing and boon on the race of man. Even if the first man and woman had not broken the commandment, they would not have been left to remain interminably in paradise in any case.[18]

Speaking on the comparisons between the first and second Adams, it is necessary to answer the following question: what kind of human nature did Christ take for himself—that of the first-formed Adam or that of fallen Adam?

On the one hand, it would seem, the answer to this question is sufficiently obvious: many pronouncements of the Eastern fathers, including Irenaeus of Lyons, Athanasius of Alexandria, Gregory of Nyssa, Cyril of Alexandria, and Gregory Palamas, leave no doubt that these fathers considered Christ's human nature, with the exception of sin, to be like the nature of fallen man. It is from the fallen, and not the first-formed Adam, that Christ inherited a corrupted, mortal, and impassioned nature:

> The Word has saved that which really was humanity which has perished.[19]

---

[16] *Catechetical Oration* 5.340–341.
[17] Ibid. 5.348–362.
[18] Cf. Isaac the Syrian *On the Divine Mysteries: Conversation* 39 4.
[19] Irenaeus of Lyons *Against Heresies* 5 14.2.

If, then, any one allege that in this respect the flesh of the Lord was different from ours, because it indeed did not commit sin . . . he says what is the fact. But if he pretends that the Lord possessed another substance of flesh, the sayings respecting reconciliation will not agree with that man. For that thing is reconciled which had formerly been in enmity. Now, if the Lord had taken flesh from another substance, he would not, by so doing, have reconciled that one to God which had become inimical through transgression.[20]

He was made man so that we might be deified in him; he became man from a woman and was born of the Virgin so that he might take on our lowly birth into sin and make us a holy race, partakers of the divine nature (2 Pet 1.4).[21]

The Word was kind enough to take on human generation and creation, weakened by sin, corruption, and death, in order to restore and renew the image in himself.[22]

Why has God been reduced to beggary? So that he might take upon himself the beggarly nature and set it in his own righteousness.[23]

We say that the Only-Begotten God, having by his own agency brought all things into being, by himself has full power over all things, while the nature of man is also one of the things that were made by him: and that when this had fallen away to evil, and come to be in the destruction of death, he by his own agency drew it up once more to immortal life, by means of the man in whom he tabernacled, taking to himself humanity in completeness, and that he mingled his life-giving power with our mortal and perishable nature, and changed, by the combination with himself, our deadness to living grace and power. And this we declare to be the mystery of the Lord according to the flesh, that he who is immutable came to be in that which is mutable, to the end that altering it for the better, and changing it from the worse, he might abolish the

---

[20]Ibid. 14.3.

[21]Athanasius of Alexandria *Against the Arians* 4.

[22]*Against Apollinarius* 1.5. Contemporary patristic scholars doubt the authenticity of both books titled *Against Apollinarius*, though they think them to be written by some of Athanasius' disciples around the year 380. Cf. J. Quasten, *Patrology* 1–3, *5th* ed. (Westminster, MD: 1990), 29.

[23]Ibid. 2.11.

evil which is mingled with our mutable condition, destroying the evil in himself.[24]

The Pure and Whole One accepts for himself the impurity of man's nature, bearing the entirety of our poverty, even unto the trial of death.[25]

For if the body had come down from heaven and had not partaken of our nature, what would have been the use of his becoming man? For the purpose of God the Word becoming man was that the very same nature, which had sinned and fallen and become corrupted, should triumph over the deceiving tyrant and so be freed from corruption.[26]

Not only does the Existing One of one essence with the Father on high wrap himself in fallen nature by his birth, and not only does he receive this extreme poverty, being born in a cavern, but he immediately, even while still in his Mother's womb, accepts the sentence passed on our nature, and is numbered and enrolled among slaves.[27]

The logic of the above patristic sayings is abundantly clear and fits in the immortal Christological aphorism of Gregory the Theologian (brought out in the context of the polemic with the heretic Apollinarius): "The unassumed is the unhealed."[28] The nature of the first-formed Adam did not need healing, since it was not damaged: the nature of fallen Adam was damaged and was in need of healing. For this reason Christ accepts human nature for himself, making himself "hostile" to God because of the crime, so as to reconcile him with God; he accepts a nature that is "reduced to beggary," "trespassing," "fallen into sin," "damaged," and "corrupted," in order to renew it in himself; he accepts an "impure human nature" in order to cleanse mankind of it.

The liturgical texts of the Orthodox Church also speak synonymously of the fact that God the Word was clothed in corruptible, mortal, impassioned, and fallen human nature:

Christ, the divinely existing Life, as compassionate God, thou hast clothed thyself with my corruptible form. Thou didst descend to the dust of death. (*Octoechos*. Sunday. Tone One. Canon. Ode Three.)

[24]Gregory of Nyssa *Against Eunomius* 5.4.
[25]*On Bliss* 1.
[26]John of Damascus *An Exact Exposition* . . . 3.12.
[27]Gregory Palamas *Homilies*.
[28]*Letter 101* 5 (Crestwood, NY: 2002), 158.

Thou, O Christ, who art impassable in thy immaterial Godhead, wast passable and mortal in thy human nature, and hast raised the dead. (*Octoechos*. Sunday. Tone Two. Canon. Ode Five.)

He was shown to be the Conqueror, smitten by death whom he vanquished. For putting on passable flesh, he wrestled with the tyrant. (*Octoechos*. Sunday. Tone Three. Canon. Ode One.)

In a mortal body thou hast shared in death . . . O Life. (*Octoechos*. Sunday. Tone Three. Canon. Ode Four.)

In thy compassion thou hast come down to earth, O Lord, and hung upon the wood of the cross: thou hast exalted the fallen nature of man. (*Octoechos*. Sunday. Tone Four. Canon. Ode Five.)

Thou hast bent down to the pit, O Giver of Life, without danger of falling. Thou hast raised me up from there, bearing with my evil-smelling corruption, O Christ, while thou didst remain untouched. (*Octoechos*. Sunday. Tone Five. Canon. Ode One.)

In the liturgical texts, Christ is called not only Adam's descendant, but also the descendant of Abraham who, of course, possessed the nature of fallen man.[29]

On the other hand, the question of how much of fallen man's nature is identified in Christ's nature was never developed in the Greek fathers' theology to its fullest extent.[30] The fact that Christ was born not from the normal "mingling," but from the Holy Spirit and a pure virgin, makes his nativity stand out from the sequence of usual human generation. It is precisely this fact, in the opinion of Gregory Palamas, which made Jesus the "new Man," capable of containing within himself the fullness of the Godhead:

If it [had] been conceived from seed, then after having been born he would not have become the new Man, without sin, the Savior of sinners. . . . If God's conception came from seed, then he would not be the new Man, the head of the new and by no means of the old life; for if he had not been . . . the inheritor of that ancestral sin, he could not have carried

---

[29]Cf. Nativity of Christ, Matins, Canon 2, Ode 6: "For our sakes he has come forth from the loins of Abraham . . . into the darkness of sin that bowed [us] to the earth."

[30]Cf. John Meyendorff, *Byzantine Theology* (Minsk: 2001), 224.

in himself the fullness of the pure Godhead and have made his flesh an inexhaustible font of blessing.[31]

The human nature of fallen Adam was in Christ, however, insofar as he was simultaneously God and man; his human nature, by virtue of "qualities of intermingling," was deified from the beginning. Christ inherited Adam's nature, although he did not inherit that predisposition toward sin nor any kind of participation in sin at all that was characteristic of all of Adam's descendants. Not participating in sin, Christ, in the words of the Apostle Paul, "made him[self] to be sin,"[32] in order to lead mankind out of sin. Speaking of the changes of human nature "from incorruption to corruption following the fall of Adam, Maximus the Confessor points out:

> Having originally been corrupted from its natural design, Adam's free choice corrupted along with it our human nature, which forfeited the grace of impassability. . . . In turn, just as through one man, who turned voluntarily from the good, the human nature was changed from incorruption to corruption to the detriment of all humanity, so too through one man, Jesus Christ, who did not turn voluntarily from the good, human nature underwent a restoration from corruption to incorruption for the benefit of all humanity. . . . For our sake he became a human being naturally liable to passions, and used the "sin" that I caused to destroy the "sin" that I commit. . . . He became the "sin" that I caused, in terms of the passibility, corruptibility, and mortality, and he submitted voluntarily to the condemnation owed me in my nature, even though he himself was blameless in his freedom of choice, in order to condemn both my deliberate "sin" and the "sin" that befell my nature.[33]

Discussing this theme in another place, Maximus the Confessor says that "the divine Logos assumed our human nature without altering his divinity, and became perfect man in every way like us save without sin. He appeared like the first man Adam in the manner both of his creaturely origin and his birth." The first man was free from corruption and sin, "for God did not create either of these," but since the breaking of God's commandment, passion and sin began to be added to the process of man's creation. Therefore, sin

[31] Homilies 14.
[32] Cf. 2 Cor 5.21
[33] To Thalassius 42 (Crestwood, NY: 2003), 119–121.

became a kind of natural property of man's essence, which became impassioned. No one was without sin due to this passion, for every person in nature is subject to the law of birth. And since sin is transmitted by inheritance, an increase in the population of man meant that sin increased, and there was no hope of salvation for man.[34]

Thus, continues Maximus, "the only-begotten Son and Logos of God became perfect man, with a view to redeeming human nature from this helplessness in evil. Taking on the original condition of Adam as he was in the very beginning, he was sinless but not incorruptible, and he assumed, from the procreative process introduced into human nature as a consequence of sin, only the liability to passions, not the sin itself."[35] These words of Maximus, serving as a contemporary Orthodox commentator, understand creation in the sense that by "taking on" Adam the Word of God accepted human nature in its original wholeness—as God made it. By "being born" the Word "adopted human nature in its fallen condition, which came about as a result of Adam's sin and which each one of us inherits from birth." The Word of God accepted corruptibility, mortality, and passion from the nature of fallen Adam, but without the sinfulness by which this passion is marked.[36]

Here it is necessary to recall Maximus' teaching on the two sins of Adam—one reprehensible, and the other not.[37] Christ, in Maximus' reckoning, was not a participant in the reprehensible sin, which is one that is arbitrary. Christ did inherit the non-reprehensible sin though, which consists of passion, corruption, and mortality, as a descendant of Adam.

To understand the logic of the Christological discourse of St Maximus it is necessary to dwell on how the concepts of "passion," "corruption," and "mortality" were used in Byzantine theology.

The word "passion" (*pathos*, πάθος) has a double meaning in the Greek (and Slavonic) language: it can indicate a sinful passion, but it can also signify a struggle or natural infirmity of man's nature. According to the teaching of the Byzantine fathers, especially Maximus the Confessor and John of Damascus, Christ was a participant in the "natural and innocent passions," though he was devoid of sinful passion by nature. The Damascene notes that

[34]*To Thalassius 21* (2003), 109–110.
[35]Ibid., 110–111.
[36]Cf. Jean-Claude Larchet, *St Maximus the Confessor—Mediator between East and West* (Moscow: 2004), 140.
[37]See Chapter 3.4.

Christ's descent into Hades.
Church of the Twelve Apostles.
Thessalonika. 14th c.

the natural passions "are those which are not in our power, but which have entered the life of man owing to the condemnation by reason of the transgression; such as hunger, thirst, weariness, labor, the tears, the corruption, the shrinking from death, the fear, the agony with the bloody sweat, the succor at the hands of angels because of the weakness of the nature, and other such like passions which belong to every man." Christ took on all of these passions in order to sanctify them and to give our nature the strength to conquer the enemy "in order that nature which was overcome of old might overcome its former conqueror by the very weapons wherewith it had itself been overcome."[38]

The term "corruption" (*phthora*, φθορά), according to John of Damascus' explanation, has a dual meaning as well: it can indicate the subjection of human nature to the passions, but it can also indicate the decomposition of the body after death, its destruction. The human nature of Christ can be called corruptible in the sense that Christ endured hunger and thirst, suffered on the cross, and that his soul was separated from his body after his death, but not in the sense that it was subject to decay.[39] The Damascene disproved the view of Julian of Halicarnassus that Christ's body was incorruptible in the sense that it was not subject to passion:

For if it were incorruptible it was not really, but only apparently,[40] of the same essence as ours, and what the Gospel tells us happened, viz. the hunger, the thirst, the nails, the wound in his side, the death, did not actually occur. But if they only apparently happened, then the mystery of the dispensation is an imposture and a sham, and he became man only in appearance, and not in actual fact, and we are saved only in appearance, and not in actual fact. But God forbid, and may those who so say have no part in the salvation. But we have obtained and shall obtain the true salvation.[41]

---

[38] *An Exact Exposition . . .* 3.20.
[39] Ibid. 3.28.
[40] In other words, only in outward form.
[41] *An Exact Exposition . . .* 3.28.

In regard to the "mortality" of Christ's human nature, John of Damascus elaborates that "the Lord's flesh, hypostatically united with God the Word himself, did not lose its natural mortality, but, because it was hypostatically united to the Word, was made life-giving."[42] In other words, the human nature of Christ was mortal, though it became life-giving by virtue of its being deified from the beginning, i.e., by virtue of the "qualities of intermingling."

According to the witness of the Gospel and the teaching of the Church contained in the Niceno-Constantinopolitan Creed, the Son of God became incarnate "of the Holy Spirit and the Virgin Mary." In other words, his birth was not preceded by the bodily union of his parents. In Western theology, the teaching that Christ was removed from Original Sin from the very beginning arose from this basis. As we remember, Original Sin was perceived in the West above all as an inheritance of guilt, transmitted from Adam to all his descendants. Besides this, after Augustine, the notion that Original Sin was transmitted through fleshly union strengthened in the West. Since the God-man Christ was not born from a physical union of man and woman, but was born from the Holy Spirit and the Virgin, and since he did not bear any kind of inherited guilt, he did not have Original Sin.

Such an arrangement of accents is only possible in Western theology. Within the framework of Eastern theology, the question of whether or not Christ was subject to Original Sin generally cannot be asked, since the very notion of Original Sin in the sense of an original guilt is practically non-existent in the East. Such a question was asked in the age of the "Western Captivity" of Orthodox theology (the eighteenth to nineteenth centuries), and the Orthodox answered it exactly as the Catholics would, that Christ was freed from Original Sin.[43] It stands to reason, if Original Sin is understood exactly as it is in the West (as an inheritance of guilt), that the Orthodox theologian would agree that Christ is wholly and completely free from it. Following after the Fathers of the Eastern Church, the Orthodox theologian would also maintain that Christ does not participate in any kind of *personal* sin, from which flows the necessity of an "evil inheritance." Christ was free from this inheritance: he was not an "heir of ancestral sin."[44] Maximus the

---

[42]Ibid. 3.21.

[43]Cf., for example: N. Malinovsky, *Study of Orthodox Dogmatic Theology. Sergiev Posad, 1911* (Moscow: 2003), 404–405.

[44]Cf. the above citation from Gregory Palamas' *Homilies* 14.

Confessor interpreted the Latin teaching of Original Sin in this sense: "[The Lord] did not have any capacity for the sin with which Adam struggled previously, neither were the movements nor the energies of evil that came from sin in his body."[45]

However, if freedom from Original Sin is understood in the sense that the human nature of Christ was the nature of the first man Adam, and not the nature of the fallen Adam, then such an interpretation serves to identify the contradictions of Orthodox tradition. There can be only one Orthodox answer to the question of which nature Christ inherited from Adam: the same nature that needs healing. For "what is not assumed is not healed."

---

[45] *Letter to Marinus.*

15
Two Natures, Two Energies, Two Wills

A CCORDING TO THE TEACHING of the Orthodox Church, Jesus Christ is both God and man at the same time, of one essence with the Father in divinity and with us in humanity. The divine and human natures coexist in joint and inseparable unity in the person of Jesus Christ.

The Christian Church, from the very first years of its existence, lived in the belief that Jesus Christ was at the same time God and man. However it was only in the age of the Christological controversies (the fifth and sixth centuries) that such theological formulae were discovered, which allowed the union of the divine and human natures of Christ to be described in such a way that was devoid of heretical interpretation of this phenomenon.

The Christological controversies of the fifth century unfolded mainly between the proponents of the Alexandrian and Antiochene theological schools: the former stressed the unity of the two natures in Christ, the latter the differences between the two. The third ecumenical council expressed the theological teaching in terms of the Alexandrian Christology, based on the teachings of St Cyril of Alexandria on the unity of Christ's God-man nature. The fourth ecumenical council, on the other hand, equipped itself with the Antiochene Christological tradition and its emphasis on Christ's "two natures." Neither the best proponents of the Alexandrian nor those of the Antiochene traditions subjected the fullness of divinity and the fullness of humanity in Christ to doubt; both claimed that Christ is "of one essence with the Father in his divinity and of one essence with us in his humanity." But one or another truth concerning the fullness of divinity or humanity in Christ was expressed differently by the two theological traditions, while both terminological expressions seemed Orthodox in their essence.

Of course, there were divergences from Orthodox teaching owing both to Alexandria and to Antioch. In the Alexandrian camp, the most clearly expressed divergence became the teaching of Eutychius, who spoke of a complete absorption of Christ's humanity by his divinity: before the incarnation there were two natures, and after, one. The extreme Antiochene Christology was expressed in the teaching of Nestorius, who perceived Christ cut into "two hypostases," "two identities," and "two sons." However, the great theologians of both traditions fled from deviations and extremes, utilizing theological terminology characteristic of their tradition, expressing Orthodox Christological teaching.

A few decades before the beginning of the Nestorian disputes, Gregory the Theologian, among other great fathers of the fourth century, formulated a principle of communication of properties of the two natures in Christ (*communicatio idiomatum*) that was accepted as the foundation of the Council of Chalcedon in the fifth century. It is thanks to this interrelationship that the deification of the human nature in Christ occurred, and together with it, the deification of every human nature. God, according to Gregory's figurative expression, "raised mortal man to divinity" and died "for those who fell to the earth and died in Adam."[1] The latter signifies that the saving death of Christ spread to all of humanity: the entire nature of Adam is deified in Christ.

The entire Gospel witnesses that Christ was at the same time God and man. Every one of his actions, every event from his life can support this. The hermeneutical principle that Gregory uses consists of the fact that some of Christ's energies can be considered characteristic of mortal man, while others can be considered as appertaining to the immortal God:

> He was mortal, but God. He is born of David, but created Adam.
> He is a bearer of flesh, though outside the body.
> He is the Son of the Mother, but a virgin one; we can describe it,
>   but not measure it.
> He was placed in a manger, but a star led the Magi to him;
> They came with gifts and bended knees.
> As mortal he struggled, but as the Invincible One he conquered
> The three-sided battle of the tempter. He ate food,
> But fed thousands and turned water into wine.
> He was baptized, but he cleansed sins, and with a loud voice
> The Spirit confirmed him as Son of the One Without Beginning.

[1] *Poems on Others: To Vitalius.*

Praying at Gethsemane. Church of the Mother of God Perivlepta. Ochrid. Macedonia. 13th c.

As mortal he tasted sleep but as God he calmed the sea.
He tired along the way, but he gave strength and generations to
    mortals.
He prayed, but who pays attention to the prayers of the doomed?
He is Sacrifice, but Archpriest; Worshipper, but God.
He offered blood to God, yet he cleansed the whole world.
He hung on the cross, and yet he nailed sin to the cross. . . .
If one person witnessed the poverty of a mortal man,
Then another might witness the divinity of the Bodiless One.[2]

The mystery of the union of the two natures in Christ can be approached from various sides, all attempting to select the terminology and images by which this mystery can be expressed. One such image is the curtain: God unites two natures, one hidden, another seen by people, and it appears to people to be covered by a curtain of the flesh.[3] Another image is anointing: God the Father anointed the Son "with the oil of gladness beyond [his] fellows" (Ps 45.7), having anointed humanity with divinity so that one may be made from two;[4] accepting human nature, having made it one and the same

---

[2]*Dogmatic Verses 2: On the Son.*
[3]Cf.: Gregory the Theologian *Dogmatic Verses 2: On the Son.*
[4]*Oration 10* 4.14–15.

by the Anointing, he became "one with God."[5] Gregory also uses the image of a temple, in which God is implanted.[6] This image, based on John 2.21 ("He spoke of the temple of his body"), was widely used by theologians of the Antiochene tradition.

Making a clear difference between the two natures of Christ, Gregory nevertheless emphasizes that they are inseparably united in him, and that is why he decidedly rejects the view of "two sons," that is, two independent identities in Jesus Christ:

> He teaches, now on a mountain; now he discourses on a plain; now he passes over onto a ship; now he rebukes the surging waves. And perhaps he goes to sleep, in order that he may bless sleep also; perhaps he is tired that he may hallow weariness also; perhaps he weeps that he may make tears blessed. He removes from place to place, he who is not contained in any place; the timeless, the bodiless, the uncircumscript, the same who was and is; who was both above time, and came under time, and was invisible and is seen. He was in the beginning and was with God, and was God (Jn 1.1). "The word was" occurs the third time to be confirmed by number. What he was he laid aside; what he was not he assumed; not that he became two, but he deigned to be one made out of the two. For both are God, that which assumed, and that which was assumed; two natures meeting in one, not two Sons (let us not give a false account of the blending).[7]

In the fifth century, the teaching of "two sons" was charged to Nestorius, who failed to prove that the accusation was unfounded. Significant in this is that Gregory the Theologian's Christological insights and his theological terminology, in essence, anticipated the controversies of the fifth century, in this case concerning the term "Theotokos." Nestorius rejected this term on the basis that "Mary did not give birth to the Godhead." Half a century before the Third Ecumenical Council, which condemned Nestorius, Gregory the Theologian passed judgment regarding the heretical deviations in the exposition of Christological doctrine:

> Whoever does not accept Holy Mary as the Mother of God has no relation with the Godhead.

[5] *Oration 45* 13 (Crestwood, NY: 2008), 172.
[6] *Poems on Others 7: To Nemesius.*
[7] *Oration 37* 2.7–20.

Whoever says that he was channeled, as it were, through the Virgin but not formed within her divinely and humanly ("divinely" because without a husband, "humanly" because by law of conception) is likewise godless.

Whoever says the human being was formed and then God put him on to wear him is condemned. . . .

Whoever imports two "sons," one from God the Father, a second from the mother, and not one and the same Son, loses the adoption promised to those who believe aright. Two natures there are, God and man . . . but not two "sons" or two "Gods". . . . In sum: the constituents of our Savior are different *things* . . . but not different *people*–God forbid! The pair is one by coalescence, God being "in-manned" and man deified.

Whoever speaks of "activation by grace" as happens in a prophet, but does not speak of "joining" and "being joined" is devoid of the higher kind of action and full, rather, of its contrary.

Whoever does not worship the Crucified One is to be anathema and ranked with the God-slaughterers.

Whoever says he was made perfect by his works, or that . . . he was deemed worthy of adoption after his baptism or after his resurrection from the dead, is to be anathema.

Whoever says that his flesh descended from heaven, but had no source here among us, is to be anathema.[8]

Enumerated in this text are all the foundations of Christological views that were subsequently condemned by the Church. One cannot avoid marveling at Gregory's vigilance, able to diagnose dangerous digressions from Orthodox Christology long before they became the subject of painful disputes. Having sharply defined the boundaries outside which the theologian risks falling into heresy, Gregory created his own balanced and harmonious Christological doctrine. It is no accident that the Fathers of the third and fourth ecumenical councils turned to his writings, seeing in them an example of a pure and undamaged Orthodox teaching on the two natures in Christ.

The works of the fourth century fathers directed against the heresy of Apollinarius of Laodicea held great significance for the development of Orthodox Christology. First among these is again Gregory the Theologian.

[9]Gregory the Theologian *Letter 101* (Crestwood, NY: 2002), 156–158.

As we recall, Apollinarius considered that the Divine Logos existed in place of a mind in Christ: this Logos fulfilled those functions in Jesus that a mind and a soul usually fulfill in a person. Rejecting the presence of a human soul and mind in the incarnate Word, Apollinarius rejected the wholeness of Christ's human nature that Gregory had recognized.

Gregory accused Apollinarius with the charge that, according to his teaching, only half of man was saved in Christ, and not the whole man: if not all of man is assumed, then "not all is saved, although all fell and is condemned for the disobedience of the first man."[9] Adam's Fall affected all the elements of human nature, including the body, soul, and nous. If Christ then assumed only the human body, and not the body and mind at the same time, then only that which is united to God is saved, for "the unassumed is unhealed."[10] If Christ was God, having assumed human nature for himself as a kind of mask, then he was not fully human, and all that he accomplished as a man was some sort of "hypocritical theatrical performance." On the contrary, if the incarnation occurred with the complete destruction of sin and the salvation of mankind, then like would have been sanctified by like, and consequently, "he [Christ] required flesh (because flesh had been condemned), and likewise a soul (because the soul had been condemned), then he needed a mind too: because the mind not only fell in Adam, but it was the 'protopath.'"[11]

The union of God and man in the person of Jesus Christ was not an artificial and temporary union of two opposite natures. God assumed human nature for himself forever, and Christ did not throw off the flesh after his resurrection: his body did not turn into the sun, as the Manicheans thought, nor was it smote by the air, nor did it decay, but it remained with him who assumed it for himself. The Second Coming of Christ, according to Gregory, will be the manifestation of the Lord in a human body, but in such a body as appeared to the disciples on the mountain, that is, transfigured and deified.[12]

In the first half of the fifth century, the clearest articulator of Orthodox Christology was St Cyril of Alexandria, who exposited his teaching in many polemical works dedicated to the refutation of Nestorianism. Above all, Cyril emphasized the unity of the Hypostasis of Jesus Christ—from God and

---

[9] *Oration 22* 13.1–15.
[10] *Letter 101*.
[11] Ibid., 161.
[12] Ibid.

man. From this unity flows the essential type of the naming of the Virgin Mary as Theotokos, for she bore not Jesus the man, different from God the Word, but she bore the very Son of God, begotten of the Father before the ages:

Having been born of the Holy Virgin we acknowledge both perfect God and perfect man, bestowed with an intellectual soul. For this reason we call the Holy Virgin the Theotokos and say that God the Word actually—not merely theoretically, but in actual fact—dwelled in her and that he, when he was two or three months old, was the Son of God and Son of Man at the same time. Especially then, ascribing to the Divine Scripture, his human essence and his divine power were united in him as one identity by our conversion. He was one and the same, when he slept and when he subdued the sea and winds by his almighty power; one and the same when he grew fatigued along the road and when he traveled along the sea and passed through the wilderness by his power. Thus, without any doubt, he was God together with man.[13]

Cyril of Alexandria put down his Christological teaching into anathemas directed at the heresy of Nestorius, but also at other more widespread fourth and fifth century heretical interpretations on the union of the two natures in the Hypostasis of the God-man Christ:

If anyone does not confess that Emmanuel is God in truth, and therefore that the holy virgin is the mother of God (for she bore in a fleshly way the Word of God become flesh), let him be anathema.

If anyone does not confess that the Word from God the Father has been united by hypostasis with the flesh and is one Christ with his own flesh, and is therefore God and man together, let him be anathema.

If anyone divides in the one Christ the hypostases after the union, joining them only by a conjunction of dignity or authority or power, and not rather by a coming together in a union by nature, let him be anathema.

If anyone distributes between the two persons or hypostases the expressions used either in the gospels or in the apostolic writings, whether they are used by the holy writers of Christ or by him about himself, and ascribes some to him as to a man, thought of separately from the Word

---

[13]Cyril of Alexandria *On the Incarnation*.

from God, and others, as befitting God, to him as to the Word from God the Father, let him be anathema.

If anyone dares to say that Christ was a God-bearing man and not rather God in truth, being by nature one Son, even as "the Word became flesh," and is made partaker of blood and flesh precisely like us, let him be anathema.

If anyone says that the Word from God the Father was the God or master of Christ, and does not rather confess the same both God and man, the Word having become flesh (Jn 1.14), according to the Scriptures, let him be anathema.

If anyone says that as man Jesus was activated by the Word of God and was clothed with the glory of the Only-begotten, as a being separate from him, let him be anathema.

If anyone dares to say that the man who was assumed ought to be worshipped and glorified together with the divine Word and be called God along with him, while being separate from him (for the addition of "with" must always compel us to think in this way), and will not rather worship Emmanuel with one veneration and send up to him one doxology, even as "the Word became flesh," let him be anathema.

If anyone says that the one Lord Jesus Christ was glorified by the Spirit, as making use of an alien power that worked through him and as having received from him the power to master unclean spirits and to work divine wonders among people, and does not rather say that it was his own proper Spirit through whom he worked the divine wonders, let him be anathema.[14]

It is difficult for someone today to comprehend why Christian doctrine had to be expressed in the form of anathemas. The reason the holy fathers' used this genre so frequently consisted in the fact that the main mobilizing force of their polemical writings was the struggle to expose and neutralize heresies. Moreover, the union of the two natures in Christ is one of the theological mysteries more suited to explanation through apophatic, rather than cataphatic, language. Not incidentally, the formulas of the Council of Chalcedon spoke of the union of the two natures in Christ as "joint, changeless, indivisible, inseparable." In other words, the fathers of the council could say

[14] *The Twelve Chapters.*

only how the two natures were *not* united, but they did not attempt a positive explanation of the manner of their union.

The general trend in Cyril's anathemas is defined by their striving to emphasize the unity of the two natures within Christ, as well as their fullness. Contrary to Arianism, Cyril maintains that Jesus Christ is not a deified man, but rather the incarnate God: he is God the Word in truth, descended from heaven and become incarnate for the salvation of mankind. Contrary to Nestorianism, Cyril maintains the inseparability of the two natures in Christ: they are not united by a "union of merit," but essentially, hypostatically. One cannot speak of God the Word and the man Jesus as two subjects: that which in the Gospel refers to Christ as man may not be dissociated from what refers to Christ as God the Word. Veneration is rendered unto the one God-man Christ, and not to the man Jesus *together with* God the Word. All that pertains to the man Jesus, pertains to God the Word as well: Jesus' flesh is the flesh of the incarnate God (this claim plays a role of utmost importance in the formation of the Orthodox teaching on the Eucharist). The Holy Spirit is not a foreign power to Jesus, which he might use for the performance of miracles: the Holy Spirit pertains to Christ as "one of the Trinity."

However, the union of natures in Christ does not signify their merging into one of the natures, whether it be the divine, as Eutychius proposed, or the God-man, as was frequently expressed by Cyril. The contribution of the Council of Chalcedon was that it not only condemned Eutychian monophysitism, but it clarified Cyril of Alexandria's terminology, rejecting, in particular, the formula "one nature of God the Word incarnate" that he employed. In using this formula, Cyril did not fill it with heretical contents: in his theological language it only stressed the unity of the natures in Christ. However, when Eutychian monophysitism declared that the human nature in Christ was completely swallowed up by the divine after the incarnation ("I confess two natures before the incarnation, one after it," said Eutychius), terminological precision became necessary.

If the Council of Ephesus (the Third Ecumenical Council) emphasized the unity of the two natures, then the Council of Chalcedon (the fourth) highlighted the fact that each of Christ's natures is fully complete: at the union of the divine and human natures, neither did the former weaken or suffer any kind of damage or loss, nor did the latter seem in any way incomplete. Neither Cyril nor the great fathers of the fourth century doubted this,

ORTHODOX CHRISTIANITY

although it was at the Council of Chalcedon where it was decreed in full strength. And it was a theologian at Chalcedon who brought the idea of "communication of properties" (*communicatio idiomatum*) to its logical conclusion, according to which the properties of the divine nature in Christ cannot be separated from the properties of the human nature. As John of Damascus writes:

> A single Christ, a single Lord, one and the same who is both Son of God and Son of Man, at once completely God and completely human, the whole God and a whole human being, one composite individual [formed] from two complete natures, divinity and humanity, and [subsisting] in two complete natures, divinity and humanity. You are not simply God or merely human, but one who is both Son of God and God enfleshed, God and human at the same time; you have not undergone confusion or endured division, but you bear in yourself the natural qualities of two natures essentially distinct, yet united without confusion and without division in your concrete existence: the created and the uncreated, the mortal and the immortal, the visible and the invisible, the circumscribed and the uncircumscribed.[15]

The controversy of the two natures of Christ that concerned the Church in the fifth century, was expressed in the seventh century via the controversy of the energies and wills in Jesus Christ. The monergism and monothelitism of the seventh century, on the one hand, were motivated by the attempt to reach a political reconciliation between rival patriarchs by way of a dogmatic compromise; on the other hand, they were an attempt to explain how the human nature of Christ differed from the human nature of fallen Adam. We saw how the Fathers of the Church, insisting on the identity of Christ's nature as fallen Adam's nature, simultaneously stressed that Christ was like man in every way except for sin. What is actually meant by "except for sin"? Surely not that Christ did not have his own will distinct from the Father, or his own independent energy distinct from the Father's? Could it be said that Christ had a human will and a human energy, and that both the one and the other were forever and wholly subject to the will and energy of the Father? The Church, above all in the person of St Maximus the Confessor, for-

---

[15]John of Damascus, *On the Dormition of Mary: Early Patristic Homilies: On the Dormition of the Holy Mother of God*, Brian E. Daley, tr. (Crestwood, NY: St Vladimir's Seminary Press, 1998), 186.

mulated the teaching that Christ possessed a human will and human energy: if this was not so, then Christ would not have been fully man. If Christ did not have an independent human will and independent energy, then "the unassumed is the unhealed": the will and energy of fallen man remain unhealed. As Maximus the Confessor says, if Christ had one will, then it would have been only either divine, or angelic, or human. But in that case Christ would not have been the God-man, but would have been either only God, or angel, or man.[16]

Christ's human will was found to be at the same time in full harmony with the will of God the Father, and there was no contradiction or conflict between the two. The absence of contradiction or conflict between Christ's human will and the divine will is explained by the fact that the will and energy of Christ, just like all of his human nature, were fully deified. Maximus the Confessor interprets this with the aid of the difference between physical and the gnomic wills. The physical, or natural, will belongs to all of human nature. The gnomic, or "will of choice" (from the Greek *gnōmē*/γνώμη–"choice, purpose"[17]) belongs to every individual identity. If Christ had possessed "the will of choice," then he would have been "a simple man like us, predisposed to reasoning, ignorance, doubting, and possessing contradiction."[18] The human will in Christ was in complete submission to the divine will, and for this reason it could be said that there was no conflict or contradiction between the two wills: "Just as one and the same was completely God together with man, and the same one completely man together with God, he himself, as a man, subjected the human elements to the God and Father in himself and through himself, having granted us himself as a more perfect prototype and example for imitation."[19]

Echoing Maximus the Confessor,[20] John of Damascus explains: it is not one and the same to will in general, that is to possess the capability of willing, as it is to will in some defined way (i.e., to wish for something specific). To will in general, just like seeing in general, is an essential faculty, for this

---

[16]Cf.: Maximus the Confessor *Dispute with Pyrrhus*.

[17]The term has a larger spectrum of meaning. Maximus the Confessor asserts that Holy Scripture and the works of the Fathers reveal eighteen definitions of this term. Maximus the Confessor *Dispute with Pyrrhus*.

[18]Ibid.

[19]Ibid.

[20]Ibid.

is associated with all people. But to will something specific is a faculty that is not from nature, but from our free choice (gnomic will). That very same thing applies to energy: the ability to act belongs to all human nature, but this or that concrete manner of energy is a faculty only of concrete human identity.[21]

It is precisely on the level of "free choice" (gnomic will) in man where the choice and wavering between good and evil occurs, and Christ was primordially free from this wavering: his will, being deified, never inclined and could not have inclined to evil. It is impossible to speak of free choice in the Lord, claims John of Damascus (again following after Maximus), for free choice is a decision made on the basis of exploration and consideration of this or that subject, after conferring with and judging it. Christ then, being not merely man, but God at the same time, and being omniscient, had no need either for "consideration or exploration, for conferring or judging": he, by nature, was inclined to good and refused evil. The prophet Isaiah speaks of this: "For before the child shall know good or evil, he refuses evil to choose the good" (Isa 7.16).[22] The word "before" shows that he is not as we are, owing to exploration and pondering; but being God who is hypostatically united with flesh, by virtue of his being divine and omniscient, he possessed grace by his nature.[23]

Summarizing Maximus the Confessor's teaching on the union of the two wills in Christ, St Anastasius of Sinai wrote:

I do not at all support . . . [the presence of] two wills warring with each other within Christ; I do not generally speak of a fleshly, impassioned, and evil will, for not even the demons dare say this with regard to Christ. But since he assumed the whole man in order that all might be saved, since he is perfect in his humanity and divinity, then for this reason we name a divine will in Christ, mastering the care of his wills and commandments, but beneath the human will within him we dwell on the willful power of the intellectual soul, which is in the image and likeness of God, given and inspired by God. . . . If then Christ's soul is deprived of an intellectual, willful, discerning, creative, acting, and wishful power, then it will

---

[21]Cf.: John of Damascus *An Exact Exposition* . . . 3.14.
[22]John of Damascus cites Isaiah using the LXX translation, provided here.
[23]Cf.: John of Damascus *An Exact Exposition* . . . 3.14.

cease to be genuine according to God's image and one in essence with our own souls. . . . In that case one cannot say that Christ is perfect in his humanity. For this reason Christ, "in the form of God" (Phil 2.6), possesses a ruling will by his divinity, which is the will common to the Father and the Son and the Holy Spirit; but "taking the form of a servant" (Phil 2.7), he has both a reasoning will and his pure soul, which, being in God's image and likeness, fulfills the will of the Master.[24]

[24]*The Guidebook* 1.2.

16

The Passion and Death of the Savior. The Dogma of the Redemption

THE TEACHING OF THE TWO NATURES, two wills, and two energies in Jesus Christ has decisive significance for the Orthodox understanding of the Savior's passion and death on the cross. If Christ were not fully man, if his human nature were swallowed up by the divine, as Eutychius thought, then his passion on the cross would not have been real, but would have been an illusion, imagined. If Christ did not have a human will, but fully substituted it with a divine one, then his suffering would not have been voluntary, meaning he would not have achieved any sort of moral feat. Finally, if Christ did not have a human energy, but only the divine one to lead him to the cross, this would mean once again

The Crucifixion.
Dionysius. 16th c.

that his suffering on the cross would be of no personal service: he would only have needed to fulfill that which his Father prepared for him.

Christ's moral feat consisted in the fact that he, being man, with all the qualities inherent in man, took human suffering upon himself, accepted to do this voluntarily, though it was in obedience to the Father. Christ himself spoke of this to his disciples: "For this the Father loves me, because I lay down my life that I might take it up again. No one takes it from me, but I lay it down of myself. I have power to lay it down, and I have power to take it [up] again. This command I have received from my Father" (Jn 10.17–18). The combination of free will with complete obedience was a consequence of Christ's human will and his human energy being fully deified.

The voluntary character of the Savior's passion, according to the teaching of the Eastern fathers, was evidence of his divine nature. Arguing with the Arians, who rejected Christ's divinity on the grounds that he suffered in the flesh, Gregory the Theologian writes:

> Do you bring as a charge against God his good deed? Is he small because he is humble for your sake? Do you accuse the Good Shepherd because he went to the one who strayed, he who laid down his life for the sheep (Jn 10.11)? . . . If so, one must also blame the physician for bending over one who is ill and enduring the stench to give health to one who is sick. . . . For indeed Scripture says that he was given up (Rom 4.25), but it is also written that he gave himself up (Eph 5.2, 25); and he was raised and taken up to heaven by the Father (Acts 3.15, 1.11), but he also resurrected himself and ascended there again (1 Thess 4.14; Eph 4.10). For one is the Father's good will, the other is his own power. You speak of what belittles him, but you overlook what exalts him; you recognize that he suffered, but you do not add that it was voluntary.[1]

The teaching that he who suffered on the cross, Jesus, was God himself, is central to the understanding of Christ's passion in Orthodox tradition. The given teaching was a belief of the Church from the beginning, to which the poem *On Pascha* by the holy martyr Melito of Sardis, which can be dated to the second century, bears witness. In this poem, prescribed to be read in the church on Holy Friday, it is said that God himself was killed in Jerusalem:

> Listen all you families of the nations and see:
> A strange murder has occurred in the middle of Jerusalem. . . .
> And who had been murdered? . . .
> He who hung the earth is hanging.
> He who fixed the heavens in place has been fixed in place.
> He who laid the foundations of the universe has been laid on a
>   tree.
> The master has been profaned.
> God has been murdered.[2]

---

[1] *Oration 38* 14–15 (Crestwood, NY: 2008), 72–74.
[2] *On Pascha* 94–96 (Crestwood, NY: 2001), 63–64.

Gregory the Theologian also found it possible to speak of "God's suffering and death."[3] The Eastern fathers of the fifth century, above all Cyril of Alexandria, insisted in the dispute with the Nestorians that "God suffered in the flesh," "God died on the cross": in academic literature this teaching received the term "theopaschism" (from the Greek *theos*/θεός–God, and *paschō*/πάσχω–to suffer). Addressing Emperor Theodosius during the proceedings of the Council of Ephesus in the year 431, Cyril of Alexandria exclaimed: "We, O Christ-loving emperor, proclaim the death not of an ordinary man, but of the incarnate God, who having suffered, as it is written, for us in the flesh, is alive, as God, and exists impartial in his essence."[4]

The descent from the cross. Icon from the Novgorodian school. 15th c.

Cyril maintains that God is impartial in essence, following after the preceding Greek fathers. However, in his economy, having become man, he accepted human suffering along with human flesh:

> The Only-Begotten Son himself, begotten of God the Father, of his very Word incarnate and become man, suffered, died, and arose from the dead on the third day. Without doubt the Word of God, by his own nature, is inaccessible to suffering. No one, of course, would be so thoughtless as to think that the nature that is above all natures could be capable of suffering. But just as he made himself man, having adopted flesh for himself from the Holy Virgin, so he held on to the teachings of the saving plan, and so we assert that he suffered in his own human flesh, he who as God is beyond all suffering.[5]

The very idea that he who suffered on the cross was not a deified man, but rather God incarnate, the Creator of heaven and earth, is a leitmotif of the theology of Holy Week. In the antiphons sung in the Orthodox Church on Holy Friday, one finds images and ideas similar to those in Melito of Sardis' poem *On Pascha*:

[3] *Oration 45* 19.
[4] *Defense to the Emperor Theodosius.*
[5] *On the Holy Creed.*

Today he who hung the earth upon the waters is hung upon the
tree.
He who is King of the angels is arrayed in a crown of thorns.
He who wraps the heavens in clouds is wrapped in the purple of
mockery.
He who in the Jordan set Adam free receives blows upon his
face.
The Bridegroom of the Church is transfixed with nails.
The Son of the Virgin is pierced with a spear.
(Holy Friday. Matins. Service of the Twelve Gospels. Antiphon
Fifteen.)

Like Melito, the authors of the liturgical texts of Holy Week use theopas-
chite expressions such as "God crucified," "God, dead and naked," "the
shamed God," and speaks of "the hidden God," that is his divinity was covered by human nature:

He who clothes himself in light as in a garment, stood naked at the judgment; on his cheek he received blows from the hands which he [had]
formed. The lawless people nailed to the Cross the Lord of Glory. Then
the veil of the temple was rent in twain and the sun was darkened, for it
could not bear to see such outrage done to God, before whom all things
tremble. (Holy Friday. Matins. Service of the Twelve Gospels. Antiphon
Ten)

Thy cross, O Lord, is life and resurrection to thy people; and putting all
our trust in it, we sing to thee, our crucified God: have mercy upon us.
(Holy Friday. Matins. Service of the Twelve Gospels. Antiphon Fifteen)

The disciples' courage failed, but Joseph of Arimathea was more bold; for
seeing the God of all a corpse and naked, he asked for the body and
buried him. (Holy Saturday. Matins. Canon. Ode Eight)

Through a tree Adam lost his home in paradise, and through the tree of
the cross the thief made paradise his home. For the one, by eating, trans-
gressed the commandment of his Maker; but the other, crucified at thy
side, confessed thee as the hidden God. (Holy Friday. Matins. Service of
the Twelve Gospels. Verses at the Beatitudes.)

The liturgial texts of the Orthodox Church repeatedly emphasize that neither during the passion, nor at the time of Christ's death, nor during the descent into Hades, did his divinity become separated from his humanity:

> Thou wast torn but not separated, O Word, from the flesh that thou hadst taken. For though thy temple was destroyed at the time of thy passion, yet the Person of thy Godhead and of thy flesh is but one; in both thou art one Son, the Word of God, both God and man. (Holy Saturday. Matins. Canon. Ode Six)

> In hell and in the tomb and in Eden, the Godhead of Christ was indivisibly united with the Father and the Spirit. (Holy Saturday. Matins. Canon. Ode Seven)

> In the tomb with the body, in hell with the soul as God, in paradise with the thief, and on the throne with the Father and the Spirit, wast thou, O boundless Christ, filling all things. (The Pascha of the Lord. Hours. Troparion)

The cited texts contain echoes of the theological disputes of the fourth century, in the course of which the question was posed: how could Christ be simultaneously in the depths of the earth, in paradise with the thief, and in heaven together with his Father? Answering this question, Gregory of Nyssa compares three sayings of Christ: "Son of Man shall be three days and three nights in the heart of the earth" (Mt 12.40), "Today you shall be with me in paradise" (Lk 23.43), and "Father, into your hands I commend my spirit" (Lk 23.46). It would be simplest above all, says Gregory, to explain this with the fact that God "is everywhere and there is no place where he is not." However, St Gregory offers another explanation, based on the idea of the duality of the human essence and presence of the divine in his body and soul. During the time of Christ's earthly life, the divinity present in him was made manifest in the performance of miracles, moreover the divinity in Christ's soul was made present by the motivation of his will, but its manifestation in his body was his touch, by which he healed the sick. "Having changed the whole man into a divine nature through mingling with him," God did not yield up his body or his soul at Christ's passion and death.[6]

---

[6]Gregory of Nyssa *On Holy Pascha* 1.

Christ in the tomb.
Icon from the Novgorodian
school. 15th c.

Following this logic then, John of Damascus claims that although Christ died as a man and his soul was separated from his body, the divinity remained undivided one from the other, and the one Hypostasis of the Word of God was not fragmented. For "although the soul was separated from the body topically, yet hypostatically they were united through the Word."[7] It is precisely this understanding that is reflected in the liturgical texts of Holy Week.

The unique quality of the Holy Week services is that Christ's death is not experienced as an end to the drama in the Gospels, but rather as the beginning of a new life, perceived of not as a defeat, but as a victory: it does not become a source of shame, but a source of joy and amazement before the great redemptive feat of the Lord and Savior.

The service of Holy Friday, when the Church recalls the crucifixion and death of Christ, does not concentrate so much on the psychological experience of the Savior's passion as much as on the spiritual contemplation of the divine glory that was manifest in the incarnate God's sufferings. St Andrew of Crete speaks of this "glory on the cross": "The cross is the glory of Christ; it was the goal defined for him before the ages. . . . Though he had the Father's glory even before all ages, as God and Son of God, equal in essence to the Father; but the holy passion of his most pure flesh imputes glory to him as the principle of the universal salvation."[8]

The service of Holy Saturday, when Christ's sojourn in the tomb and descent into Hades is remembered, is permeated with the expectation of the resurrection and the experience of God's victory over death and Hell. "The death of God" reveals the way to the resurrection, and the tomb of the Savior becomes "a life bearing tomb," the source of life for all mankind, redeemed through Christ.

As Protopresbyter John Meyendorff notes, the theological premises of the Holy Saturday service are found in the "theopaschism" of Cyril of

[7] *An Exact Exposition . . .* 3.27.
[8] *Oration 8: On the Resurrection of Lazarus.*

Alexandria. If Cyril's opponents refused to speak of "the death of God," then for Cyril salvation itself is conditioned precisely on the fact that "one of the Trinity suffered." Only God can save: in order to save man, he voluntarily "reduced himself not merely to man as such, but to the very depths of fallen man, to the very lowest level of disintegration—to death itself." For death is inseparably connected to sin: it makes man enslaved to sin, swallowed up by itself, forcing him to fight for the necessity of his own existence, frequently offering up the life of others as a sacrifice. Not partaking in sin, the incarnate God accepted death for himself, becoming the consequence of sin so that by it he might break the flogging circle of sin and death. "In the world, in which battle for survival at the cost of others has become the law, he became death as a greater manifestation of love for others. And when this greater manifestation of love was perfect God himself, a new life truly entered the world."[9]

The liturgical texts say that Christ's death on the cross had a salvific and redemptive meaning for all humanity:

> Thou hast redeemed us from the curse of the Law by thy precious blood: nailed to the cross and pierced by the spear, thou hast poured forth immortality upon mankind. O our Savior, glory be to thee. (Lenten Triodion. Holy Friday. Matins. Troparion)

But how is one to understand this redemption accomplished by the incarnate God? From what "curse of the Law" did Christ free mankind by being hanged and dying on the cross?

The term "redemption" (Gr. *lytrōsis*, λύτρωσις), when found in the Bible, literally means "setting free" or "ransom," that is payment made for a slave's freedom. Linked with this understanding of "redemption" in the Old Testament above all is God's deliverance of the people of Israel from bondage in Egypt, and from the Babylonian captivity as well (Ps 74.2; Mic 6.4). "Redeemer" is one of God's names in the Old Testament, particularly in the book of the Prophet Isaiah (Isa 41.14, 43.14, 47.4, 48.17, 49.26, 59.20, 63.16). In the New Testament, the concept of "redemption" indicates the salvation and justification of mankind by Jesus Christ, who poured out his blood and died on the cross for the sake of the salvation of all (Mt 20.28; Mk 10.45; Rom 3.24; Gal 3.13, 4.5; Eph 1.7; 1 Tim 2.6; Heb 9.12, 15; Rev 5.9).

---

[9]John Meyendorff, "The Time of Holy Saturday," *Moscow Patriarchate Journal* 4 (1992): 33–34.

The literal meaning of the verb *lytroō/*λυτϱόω ("to redeem") forced the early Christian theologians to ponder exactly to whom Christ paid the ransom for mankind. Origen, especially, claimed that at the moment of the Savior's death on the cross, his spirit was given up to the hands of the Father, but the soul was given to the devil as the ransom price for people:

> To whom did the redeemer give his own soul for the redemption of many? Not to God, but . . . to the devil. . . . The soul of the Son of God was offered up as a ransom for us, but not his spirit, for he had already given it to his Father with the words: "Father, into your hands I commend my spirit" (Lk 23.46); likewise not the body, because we do not find anything like this in the Scriptures.[10]

According to the teaching of Gregory of Nyssa, man was found to be in servitude to the devil as a result of the Fall; in order to be redeemed from this, it was necessary to pay a compensation to the devil, a ransom; the man Jesus Christ was offered as the ransom; the devil accepted him in exchange for mankind, although under the "bait" of Christ's human nature lay the "hook" of the Godhead, which the devil could not grasp: thus God deceived the devil.[11]

Basil the Great adhered to a similar view concerning the devil's right to compensation, although his theory was a bit different: the "ransom" necessary for mankind's deliverance from slavery to the devil could not have been limited to mere man, since slave cannot redeem slave and man cannot deliver himself; there needed to be something greater than man, someone who surpassed human nature–the God-man Christ; he who poured out his blood for the people paid the ransom simultaneously to the devil and to God.[12]

Neither one nor the other treatise on redemption gained the sympathies of Gregory the Theologian, who considered that speaking of the death of the Son of God as a sacrifice to the devil was shameful. But one cannot say that the Son of God offered himself as a ransom to the Father and that the Father could wish for the death of his own Son:

> To whom was the blood poured out for us, and why was it poured out, that great and renowned blood of God, who is both high priest and

[10]*Commentary on Matthew* 16.8.
[11]Cf.: *Great Catechetical Oration* 22–24.
[12]Cf.: *Homily on Psalm 7* 2; *Homily on Psalm 48* 3.

victim? For we were held in bondage by the Evil One, sold under sin, and received pleasure in exchange for evil. But if the ransom is not given to anyone except the one holding us in bondage, I ask to whom this was paid, and for what cause? If to the Evil One, what an outrage! For the robber would receive not only a ransom from God, but God himself as a ransom, and a reward so greatly surpassing his own tyranny that for its sake he would rightly have spared us altogether. But if it was given to the Father, in the first place how? For we were not conquered by him. And secondly, on what principle would the blood of the Only-begotten delight the Father, who would not receive Isaac when he was offered by his father but switched the sacrifice, giving a ram in place of the reason-endowed victim?[13]

Gregory emphasizes that God accepted the sacrifice of his Son not because he had need of it, but out of leniency, so that man might be blessed by the human nature of the incarnate God.[14] As opposed to Cyril of Jerusalem, who considered that the Son of God, having become redemption for the sins of the people, delivered humanity from God's wrath,[15] Gregory the Theologian insisted that the Savior's sacrifice on the cross was necessary not for God the Father, but for us, and it was the result of the love, not the wrath, of the Father: "For God so loved the world that he gave his only begotten Son, that whoever believes in him should not perish, but have everlasting life" (Jn 3.16).

John Chrysostom speaks of the fact that the Son of God's sacrifice on the cross was a consequence of God's love, not anger: "Why did God not spare his only-begotten Son but surrendered the only Son he had? It was to reconcile to himself those who hated him and to make them a people of his own possession (Tit 2.14)."[16] It was not God who hated man, but man who hated God. For this reason the Son of God's sacrifice was a sacrifice of reconciliation, but once again it was not God who was reconciled to man thanks to this sacrifice, but man to God.

Isaac the Syrian speaks of God's love for the race of man as the chief reason for the Savior's suffering on the cross:

---

[13] *Oration 45* 22 (Crestwood, NY: 2008), 182.
[14] Ibid.
[15] Cf.: Cyril of Jerusalem *Catechetical Lecture 13* 2.
[16] *On the Priesthood 2* 1, Graham Neville, tr. (Crestwood NY: St Vladimir's Seminary Press, 1977), 53.

He offered up his own Son to death on the cross in his love for creation. ... This was not because he could not redeem us by other means, but he taught us through the abundance of his love; he brought us closer to himself through the death of his Only-Begotten Son. Yes, if he had anything more precious he would have offered it for us so that he might gain back our race. And by his great love he was not disposed to restrain our freedom, although he was capable of doing so, but by his love of our own intellect he had the kindness to let us draw near to him. He took on profanation and grief for himself by his love for us and by the obedience of Christ to his Father.[17]

The teaching of the Savior's redeeming sacrifice as gratification of God the Father's wrath, while found in individual Eastern authors, did not receive much serious support of any kind in the Christian East. However, it was precisely this understanding of redemption that was celebrated and preserved over many centuries in the Latin West. Anselm of Canterbury, in the famous eleventh century treatise *Cur Deus Homo?* (*Why Did God Become Man?*), formulated the theory by which Christ's death was the gratification of the outraged justice of God the Father. Since God is righteous, and he is outraged by the Fall of man, his righteousness requires satisfaction: the Son of God offers himself as a sacrifice to the Father and his blood calms the wrathful God. This theory was developed from medieval concepts of the necessity of gratification for bruised honor, and it is very far removed from the theological speculations of the Eastern fathers of the Church.

The controversies that developed in the local councils of 1156–1157 in Constantinople became an echo of this juridical theory of the redemption in the Orthodox East. The words of one of the prayers in the rite of the Divine Liturgy addressed to Christ: "For thou art the one who offers and the one who is offered, the one who receives and the one who is received," served as the grounds for the beginning of the polemic. These words are based on the understanding of the ancient Church of the Savior's sacrificial death, formulated by John Chrysostom especially: "The victim of this sacrifice is unusual because it is extraordinary and unprecedented. In this case, one and the same was both sacrifice and priest: the sacrifice was flesh, but the priest was the spirit. One and the same offered and was offered in the flesh."[18]

[17] *Oration 48.*
[18] *Homily on the Cross and the Thief* 1.

In the dispute heating up in the Byzantine capital in the middle of the twelfth century, one side claimed that the redeeming sacrifice of the Son of God was offered by the whole of the Holy Trinity and that Christ, in accord with the words of the prayer, was both the offered sacrifice and the acceptor of it. The other side insisted that if Christ was both the offerer and the offered, then this consequently introduces two independent hypostases. Sotericus Panteugenicus voiced the second opinion, saying that in view of the impure, darkened sin of humanity, the Son of God offered his blood instead of ours as a salvific propitiation as reconciliation with the Father, who rewarded us with sonship.[19] Since Sotericus' theory had some outward similarity with that of Anselm of Canterbury, they named him the "Latin Sage."

In relation to the various understandings of the meaning of the Savior's redeeming sacrifice were two different concepts of the meaning of the Eucharistic offering: some claimed that the Eucharist is offered to God the Father, while others that it is offered to all the Holy Trinity.

Having examined both understandings of Christ the Savior's redeeming sacrifice, the Council of Constantinople (1157) came to the following conclusion:

> Christ the Master voluntarily offered himself as a sacrifice, he brought himself in his humanity and he himself accepted the sacrifice as God together with the Father and Spirit. . . . At the time of the masterful passion, the Word, the God-man at first brought himself as a salvific sacrifice to the Father, to himself, as God, and to the Spirit, by whom man was brought out of nothingness into being, whom he angered by breaking the commandment, with whom reconciliation occurred through Christ's suffering. Likewise bloodless sacrifices are now offered to the all-perfect Trinity, and it accepts them.[20]

The dogmatic definitions of the Council of Constantinople (1156–1157) remain equally little-known not only beyond the boundaries of the Orthodox Church, but within it as well. Meanwhile, they preserve their significance in the capacity of alternatives to the Western legal theory of the redemption and as an attempt to explain the dogma of the redemption in categories that are more customary for theological ideas in the Orthodox East.

---

[19]Cf.: Pavel Cheremukhin, "The Council of Constantinople (1157) and St Nicholas, Bishop of Mephon," *Theological Works* 1 (Moscow, 1960), 85–110, 91.

[20]Ibid., 93.

Do not lament, O Mother.
Icon of the Novgorodian school.
15th c.

It is generally preferred in the East not to think of the term "redemption" in its literal meanings, and a discussion of who was actually offered by the Savior as a ransom by suffering and dying on the cross never left the first plan, either in theological discourse, or in the liturgical tradition. It is characteristic that the liturgical texts of Holy Week work around this issue in silence, preferring to concentrate on the meaning of the universal significance of the Savior's sacrifice through the cross for all mankind.

Theologians of the Eastern Church emphasize the universal character of the death on the cross. Paraphrasing the Apostle Paul (1 Cor 9.22), Gregory the Theologian said that Christ became "all for all, in order to save all."[21] Offering himself as a sacrifice, he cleanses not just a small part of the universe for a small stretch of time, but he cleanses rather the whole world for eternity.[22] Thanks to the Savior's sacrifice through the cross, all mankind is united under one Head–Christ:

> Having stretched out his holy body to the ends of the world,
> He drew together all the dead from all the ends,
> He united them in one man
> And laid the one Godhead in their hearts,
> Purifying all impurity with the blood of the Lamb,
> Purifying the way from earth to heaven that was barred by
>   death.[23]

The Savior's palms, outstretched on the cross, embrace all the ends of the universe and unite all people into "one man," which the Savior lays "in the heart of the one Godhead"; that is, he unites it to God and deifies it. We find a similar image in Cyril of Jerusalem: "He stretched out his hands on the cross so as to grasp the ends of the universe."[24] But in the liturgical texts of Holy Week it is said: "Thou hast stretched out thine arms and

[21] *Oration 37* 1.7–8.
[22] *Oration 45* 13.
[23] *Moral Poems 37: Another Prayer on Successful Travel.*
[24] *Catechetical Oration* 13.28.

united all that before was separated";[25] "Stretched out upon the tree, thou didst gather man."[26]

The redemptive feat of the Savior, according to the teaching of the Orthodox Church, has a direct relationship with every person. Christ dies not for the abstract "masses," not for the cast out and now brought in "Adam," but for every person, for every concrete Adam. Like many theologians of the Eastern Church, Gregory the Theologian considers that salvation has an immediate relationship to everyone personally: Christ, he says, "accepted the form of a servant, tasted death and found a second life, being God, in order to deliver me from slavery and death."[27] Gregory examines all events connected with the suffering and death of Christ as having a direct relation to his own salvation: "I direct you to the remembrance of Christ and his exhaustion for our sakes, of the passion of the Passionless One, the cross and nails by which I was delivered from sin, and the ascension . . . and forms of my salvation."[28]

In Gregory the Theologian's perceptions, reflecting a characteristic approach for the Eastern Church, the mystery of the redemption is not an object for the construction of theological theories: it more closely resembles a prayerful meditation. In the Savior's redemptive feat, Gregory sees a most wonderful mystery, which serves not so much for consideration in the pages of a theological composition, as much as for crying out:

> We needed a God made flesh and made dead, that we might live. We were made dead with him that we might be purified. We have risen with him since we were made dead with him. We were glorified with him since we rose with him. Many indeed are the wonders of that time: God crucified; the sun darkened and again rekindled . . . the veil split; blood and water pouring forth from his side . . . the earth shaken, rocks broken in pieces for the sake of the Rock; dead people raised . . . the signs at the tomb and after the tomb. Who can adequately sing their praise? Yet none is like the wonder of my salvation: a few drops of blood re-create the whole world . . . binding and drawing us together into one.[29]

---

[25]*Lenten Triodion.* Holy Saturday. Matins. Canon. Ode Three.
[26]Ibid. Praises.
[27]*Poems on Himself 45: Mourning for the Passions of the Soul.*
[28]*Oration 17* 12.
[29]*Oration 45* 28–29 (Crestwood, NY: 2008), 189.

17

The Cross of Christ

Veneration of the cross. The reverse of the icon "Imager Made Without Hands." Novgorod. 12th c.

T HE VENERATION OF THE CROSS as an instrument of execution that has become the instrument of redemption and a symbol of the victory over death, occupies an important place in Eastern Christian tradition. The cult of the cross is a rather natural symbol that has grown out of the Orthodox teaching of the expiation of sins.

There are a few views on the depiction of the cross in Orthodox tradition. A widely disseminated one is the simple four-pointed cross (or *crux immissa*, in which the vertical beam sticks out beyond the crossbeam), consisting of two beams: it is this type of cross that was most frequently used in the ancient Church. The eight-pointed cross received wide diffusion in the Russian tradition, where the upper cross-beam symbolizes the sign with the inscription "Jesus of Nazareth, King of the Jews," and the lower one represents the support for the Savior's feet. Sometimes such a cross is represented on "Golgotha," the dual-staged stand: to the left of the viewer is the spear that pierced the Savior's side, and to the right is the reed with the sponge that was raised to his lips. Beyond these symbolic representations of the cross, it is not uncommon to find the "crucifixion" in churches, the representation of the Savior on the cross.

There are several days throughout the course of the year when the Orthodox Church commemorates the veneration of the cross. Above all is the Week of the Cross (the third week of Great Lent), the feast of the Elevation of the Cross of the Lord, as well as series of other feasts that hallow the cross. Canons that are devoted to the cross of Christ are read during the services of every Friday and on the days of Holy Week. Many prayers read during the divine services of the Orthodox Church are directed not only to Jesus crucified on the cross, but at the very cross of the Lord itself.

The Orthodox Church preserved the ancient custom of making the sign of the cross in liturgical and private prayer. This custom comes from the early Christian Church: Basil the Great bears witness to this as an inseparable part of ancient Church Tradition.[1] Believers make the sign of the cross over themselves during prayer, as well as before the beginning of any task. A priest's blessing is expressed by making the sign of the cross over the person approaching him. The transformation of the bread and wine into the Body and Blood of the Savior, the blessing of the water at the sacrament of baptism, and many other important priestly actions are accomplished by the aid of the sign of the cross.

The veneration of the cross in Orthodox tradition has a theological basis beneath it that is many hundreds of years old. The cross is recalled repeatedly already in the Epistles of the Apostle Paul. Paul calls the propagation of the Savior's crucifixion the "message about the cross," which is "to those who are perishing, foolishness; but to us who are saved it is the power of God" (1 Cor 1.18). Paul speaks of the "offence of the cross" (Gal 5.11), of the persecution "for the cross of Christ" (Gal 6.12), of the enemies of the cross of Christ (Phil 3.18). Paul writes concerning himself: "But God forbid that I should glory, save in the cross of our Lord Jesus Christ, by whom the world is crucified to me, and I to the world" (Gal 6.14). According to Paul's teaching, Christ "who for the joy that was set before him endured the cross, despising the shame . . . has sat down at the right hand of the throne of God" (Heb 12.2). Christ reconciled man to God "in one body by the cross, having slain the enmity by it" (Eph 2.16; Col 1.18–20). Christ destroyed "the record of ordinances that was against us" and nailed it to the cross (Col 2.14). All creation, heavenly and earthly, was reconciled to God through Christ, "having made peace through the blood of his cross" (Col 1.20). In every case that is recalled, the "cross" is a synonym of the crucifixion, of the Savior's death upon the cross.

The holy martyr Ignatius the God-bearer speaks of the cross in this sense. Addressing the Christians in Ephesus, he writes: "Drawn up on high by the instrument of Jesus Christ, which is the cross, making use of the Holy Spirit as a rope, while your faith was the means by which you ascended, and your

[1]Cf.: Basil the Great *On the Holy Spirit* 27.

love the way which led up to God."[2] In the same epistle Ignatius speaks of his own reverence before the cross of Christ: "Let my spirit be counted as nothing for the sake of the cross, which is a stumbling block to those that do not believe, but to us salvation and life eternal."[3] In the *Epistle to the Trallians*, Ignatius says that the very cross of "Christ invites you to [share in] his immortality . . . inasmuch as ye are his members."[4]

If in the first and second centuries the word "cross" was used as a synonym for the Savior's death on the cross, then no later than the fourth century the cult of the Lord's cross arose and the cross was then written of as a sacred object, possessing special power. A significant portion of Cyril of Jerusalem's *Catechetical Lectures*, which are addressed to those preparing to accept the sacrament of baptism, is dedicated to this theme. Here, St Cyril speaks of the power of the sign of the cross, accompanying man along every step of life's way:

> Let us not then be ashamed to confess the Crucified. Be the cross our seal made with boldness by our fingers on our brow, and on everything; over the bread we eat, and the cups we drink; in our comings in, and goings out; before our sleep, when we lie down and when we rise up; when we are in the way, and when we are still. Great is that preservative; it is without price, for the sake of the poor, without toil, for the sick; since also its grace is from God. It is the sign of the faithful, and the dread of devils: for he "triumphed over them in it, having made a show of them openly" (Col 2.15); for when they see the cross they are reminded of the Crucified; they are afraid of him, who bruised the heads of the dragon. Despise not the seal, because of the freeness of the gift; but for this rather honor thy Benefactor.[5]

Further on Cyril refutes the view of the Docetists, who claim that Christ's passion on the cross was illusory, or imagined:

> If any say that the cross is an illusion, turn away from him. Abhor those who say that Christ was crucified to our fancy only; for if so, and if salvation is from the cross, then is salvation a fancy also. If the cross is fancy,

[2]*Epistle to the Ephesians* 9.
[3]Ibid. 18.
[4]11.
[5]13.36.

the resurrection is fancy also; but "if Christ be not risen, we are yet in our sins" (1 Cor 15.17). If the cross is fancy, the ascension also is fancy; and if the ascension is fancy, then is the second coming also fancy, and everything is henceforth unsubstantial. Take therefore first, as an indestructible foundation, the cross, and build upon it the other articles of the faith.[6]

Cyril reminds his listeners about the foundational events of the last days of the Savior's life and of the main protagonists of the gospel story of Christ's passion. The whole narrative bears witness to the crucifixion, which the Christian should never renounce. The wide distribution of Christians over all the world bears witness to the cross, and the very fact that people come to Christ can be explained by its power:

> Thou hast twelve apostles, witnesses of the cross; and the whole earth, and the world of men who believe on him who hung thereon. Let thy very presence here now persuade thee of the power of the crucified. For who now brought thee to this assembly? What soldiers? With what bonds wast thou constrained? What sentence held thee fast here now? Nay, it was the trophy of salvation, the cross of Jesus that brought you all together . . . . This, that to this day heals diseases; that to this day drives away devils, and overthrows the juggleries of drugs and charms.[7]

John Chrysostom repeatedly speaks of the cross of the Lord in his compositions. The cross for him is above all the sign of Christ's victory over the devil and death. Following after Irenaeus of Lyons, Gregory the Theologian, and other preceding authors, Chrysostom traces the parallel between the tree of the knowledge of good and evil, the harbinger of mankind's death, and the tree of the cross, bringing life:

> Can you see the divine victory? Can you see the actions of the cross? . . . Whatever victory the devil achieved, Christ surmounted it; Having seized his instrument, he gained the victory over him. . . . A virgin, a tree, and death were the signs of our abasement: the virgin was Eve, since she had still not known Adam. But here is again a Virgin, a tree, and death, these signs of abasement now made to be signs of victory. Instead of Eve, Mary; instead of the tree of the knowledge of good and evil, the tree of the cross;

[6]Ibid. 37–38.
[7]Ibid. 40.

instead of the death of Adam, the death of Christ. Can you see how that by which the devil gained a victory has now itself been conquered by that very thing? The devil defeated Adam through a tree; Christ bested the devil through the cross; so then the tree overthrew Hades, this is the tree that extricated those who departed from there. And again that tree stole away the naked captive, the tree that revealed the naked Conqueror to all from the heights. Likewise death: they were condemned to death who lived after it, while this death resurrected those who lived before it. . . . Through death we were made immortal: such are the actions of the cross.[8]

The Cross, according to Chrysostom's teaching, is the universal symbol of victory, given to us by Christ without any kind of merit or effort on our part:

We did not stain our arms with blood, we did not stand in the lines, we did not receive wounds, and we did not see battle, but we did receive the victory; the deed is the Master's, but the crown is ours. . . . This is what the cross accomplished for us; the cross is the trophy against the demons, the weapon against sin, the sword with which Christ pierced the serpent; the cross is the will of the Father, the glory of the Only-Begotten, the joy of the Spirit, the adornment of the angels, the foundation of the Church, the praise of Paul, the stronghold of the saints, the light of the whole world. As in a house enveloped in darkness, when someone, having lit a lamp and having put it in a sconce, drives the darkness away, so does Christ do for the whole universe, which is enveloped in darkness, having erected the cross as a kind of lamp, and having raised it high, he scattered all the darkness from the earth. And as a lamp contains light overhead and it extends to the upper parts, so too does the cross extend the mighty Sun of righteousness to the outer reaches of the world.[9]

In a homily dedicated to the ecclesial celebration in honor of Christ's cross, Chrysostom speaks not of sufferings and death, but of the victory over death:

Today our Lord Jesus Christ is on the cross, and we celebrate so that you might know that the cross is a holiday and a spiritual wonder. Before, the

[8] *Homily on the Cemetery and the Cross.*
[9] Ibid.

cross served as a sentence of punishment, but now it has become an object of worship; before it was a symbol of condemnation, but now it is the sign of salvation. In fact, it became for us the principle of innumerable blessings: it freed us from error, it enlightened those who sat in darkness, it reconciled us, who were previously at enmity with God, it made the estranged friends, it made those who were far off to be close. The cross is the destruction of the enemy, it is the defense of the world; it became for us a treasury of innumerable blessings. Thanks to the cross we are no longer prodigals in the wilderness, because we have now recognized the true path, we no longer dwell outside the kingdom, because we have found the door, we do not fear the fiery darts of the devil because we have seen the source. Thanks to the cross we are no longer widowed because we have received the Bridegroom, we do not fear the wolf because we have the good Shepherd. . . . Thanks to the cross we do not tremble before the tyrant because we are near the King. This is why we celebrate the memory of the cross.[10]

The crucifixion. Icon of the Moscow school. 14th c.

Chrysostom adds that on Golgotha, Christ was both sacrifice and priest, but the cross was the altar of sacrifice. Why then was he offered in sacrifice on the heights of a stage, and not under a roof? In order to purify aerial nature and all the earth on which the blood of the Lamb dripped. But why was the sacrifice offered outside the walls of the city? "So that you would know that it was a general sacrifice, offered for the whole world, so that you would know that the purification was public, not private, as it is with the Jews." To the Jews, clarifies Chrysostom, "God commanded to abandon all the land and to offer sacrifice and prayer in one place, because all the earth was unclean, since above it hovered smoke, ash, and every other stench from the Gentile sacrifices. But now for us, since the coming Christ purified the whole universe, every place has become a place of prayer."[11]

---

[10]*Homily on the Cross and the Thief* 1.
[11]Ibid.

The cross of Christ opened paradise, which had been closed, and led the wise thief into it, returning him to the ancient fatherland.[12] The Lord did not allow the cross to remain on earth, but raised it to heaven, and at the Second Coming the cross of Christ will appear with him. Like that which heralds the entrance of a king into a city, preceding his forces, carrying his banners, so will Christ appear in the procession of the cross. At the Last Judgment, Christ will process with his cross and his wounds, in order to show that he truly is the one who was crucified.[13]

In some cases when speaking on the might of Christ's cross, Chrysostom equates the energy of this might to the energy of the names of Jesus Christ. In the cross, as in the names of Christ, Chrysostom sees not their own strength, but God's strength, equal in form to these two salvific instruments:

> For we have, we surely have, spiritual charms, even the name of our Lord Jesus Christ and the might of the cross. This charm will not only bring the serpent out of his lurking places, and cast him into the fire, but even wounds it healeth. But if some that have said this name have not been healed, it came of their own little faith, and was not owing to any weakness in what they said. For some did throng Jesus and press him, and got no good therefrom. But the woman with an issue, without even touching his body, but merely the hem of his garment, stanched a flux of blood of so long standing. This name is fearful alike to devils, and to passions, and to diseases. In this then let us find a pleasure; herewith let us fortify ourselves.[14]

John Chrysostom claims that by the might of the cross of the Lord and by the power of the name of the one who was crucified, Christianity was spread to the whole world, conquering paganism and giving people true knowledge of God:

> The cross wrought persuasion by means of unlearned men; yea, it persuaded even the whole world: and not about common things, but in discourse of God, and the godliness which is according to truth, and the evangelical way of life, and the judgment of the things to come. And of

[12]Cf.: Ibid. 2.
[13]Ibid.
[14]*Homily on Romans 8.*

all men it made philosophers: the very rustics, the utterly unlearned. Behold how "the foolishness of God is wiser than men," and "the weakness stronger" (1 Cor 1.25). How stronger? Because it overran the whole world, and took all by main force. . . . For what did not the cross introduce? The doctrine concerning the immortality of the soul; that concerning the resurrection of the body; that concerning the contempt of things present; that concerning the desire of things future. Yea, angels it hath made of men, and all, everywhere, practice self-denial, and show forth all kinds of fortitude.[15]

The words cited above of Cyril of Jerusalem and John Chrysostom bear witness to the fact that the veneration of the cross of Christ was widespread in fourth century Byzantium. But the cross served as an object of veneration and religious worship beyond the limits of the Byzantine Empire, particularly among the Syrian Christians. One of the homilies of Isaac the Syrian, named *On the Contemplation of the Mystery of the Cross; and What Strength it Bears Invisibly in its Visible Form, and on the Many Mysteries of God's Saving Plan, which Was Accomplished from of Old; and the Totality of This in Christ Our Lord; and how the Totality of This Bears in Itself the Almighty Cross*, bears witness to this.

Beginning the exposition on the theme, Isaac emphasizes that there is no special strength in the cross that differs from that strength that is eternal and without beginning, which brought the world into being and which guides all creation in cooperation with the will of God. That same divine power lives in the cross, that power that lived in the ark of the covenant (Ex 26.10–22), surrounded by such trembling and worship:

> The immeasurable strength of God lives within the cross, just as it lived in the incomprehensible image of the ark to which the people[16] bowed down with great reverence and fear, which lived, accomplishing in it wonders and terrible signs amongst those who were not ashamed even to call it God (Num 10.35–36), that is who gazed at it in fear, as if at God himself. For the honor of the most worthy names of God was in it. It was not only the people who worshipped him by these names, but also other hostile peoples: "And the Philistines feared, and said, These are the Gods that are come to them into the camp" (1 Sam 4.7). That same power that was in

[15] *Homily on 1 Corinthians 4* 6.
[16] The people of Israel.

the ark lives, as we believe, in that worshipper of the image of the cross, which we consider in great conscience to be the presence of God.[17]

What then was in the ark of the covenant that made it so terrible and full of almighty power and signs? Isaac answers that they worshipped the ark because the *Shekhina* lived within it—the invisible presence of God:

> Did not Moses and the people submit themselves before the ark with great fear and trembling? Did not Joshua the son of Navi lie before it from morning until evening, falling to the ground on his face (Josh 7.6)? Did not fearful revelations of God appear in it, calling them out to worship it? For the divine *Shekhina* lived within it, that very essence that lives now in the cross: it went out from there and secretly made its abode in the cross.[18]

Therefore, the ark of the covenant was a foreshadowing of the cross, similar to how the whole Old Testament was a foreshadowing of the New Testament. The Old Testament cult, with all its miracles and signs, was not capable of destroying sin, whereas the cross destroyed the power of sin. The cross destroyed the power of death as well: "And if death was so fearful to man's nature then, now even women and children laugh at it. Death, which ruled over all, now not only seems easier for a child of faith, but the fear of it dwindled even for the Gentiles when compared to what was before."[19] In other words, the religion of the cross brought the world a different relationship with death: no one fears it any longer as they feared it in the pre-Christian era. Does this text of Isaac contain a link to the age of martyrs, when women and children manfully met death for Christ? Christian peace before the face of death, according to Isaac, proved to be an influence on the Gentile world: the relationship with death became less dramatic.

Returning to the Old Testament image, Isaac asks the reason why a wooden structure, built by the hands of carpenters, would be given "worship, filled with fear," despite the fact that the first commandment of the law of Moses says: "You shall not make for yourself an idol, whether in the form of anything that is in heaven above, or that is on the earth beneath" (Ex 20.4; Lev 26.1; Deut 5.8). Because, answers Isaac, there was in the ark of the

---

[17] *On the Divine Mysteries: Conversation 11* 3–4.
[18] Ibid. 5.
[19] Ibid. 8.

covenant, in contrast to Gentile idols, the power of God in visible form, and because the name of God was imprinted on it.[20]

Speaking on the veneration of the cross, Isaac rejects the accusation of idolatry–that same charge that was brought against the defenders of icon worship in Byzantium in the eighth and ninth centuries. Although the context of the Byzantine polemic with the iconoclasts was a bit different, Isaac's ideas on the presence of the Godhead in material subjects resonate with what the Byzantine iconodules wrote at that time with respect to God's presence in the icons. In particular, Isaac speaks of the fact that if the cross had not been prepared in the name of "the Man, in whom the Godhead lives," that is the incarnate Son of God, the charge of the iconoclasts would have been correct.[21] He also refers to the interpretations of the "Orthodox fathers," according to whom the golden mercy-seat, placed above the Old Testament ark (Ex 25.17), foreshadowed Christ's human nature.[22]

Isaac emphasizes that the divine presence of the *Shekhina* accompanies the cross forever, from the very moment of its preparation: "For immediately, as soon as its outline is traced along a wall or on a board, or made out of any kind of gold or silver or something like it, or is cut out from some wood, at that moment it takes on divine power, which dwelt there,[23] and fills it and becomes the place of the divine *Shekhina*."[24] These words reflect the practice of the ancient Church, which did not know special prayers for the consecration of a cross: it was considered that the cross, as soon as it was formed, became the source of purification for people and the place of divine presence. For this reason, "when we gaze at the cross while at prayer, or when we bow down before its portrayal, which has the image of the Man who was stretched out upon it, we receive divine power through it, and help, salvation, and ineffable blessings in this world and in the coming world that is being prepared. All this is through the cross."[25]

Isaac persistently stresses the cross's surpassing of the Old Testament symbols of God's presence:

[20]Cf.: Ibid. 11.
[21]Ibid. 13.
[22]Ibid. 15.
[23]In the ark of the covenant.
[24]Isaac the Syrian *On the Divine Mysteries: Conversation* 11 12.
[25]Ibid. 13.

The New Testament, as a service before God, is more meet and right than that which was in the Old Testament, as is the difference between Moses and Christ, as the service that Jesus received is better than that which was given through Moses, as man's glory is greater and more wonderful in creation than the glory of dumb objects, just so is this image,[26] which now exists so much greater in honor because of that Man who from us took divinity into his own dwelling, and by reason of the divine goodwill that was in this Man, who had become fully his temple (Jn 2.19–21),[27] the goodwill different from that foreshadowing goodwill that was in dumb objects in ancient times, foreshadowing, like a shade, the future blessing in Christ.[28]

The Old Testament cult demanded a reverential and trembling relationship to the holy objects. When a priest entered into the tabernacle, he did not dare raise his eyes and gaze at the mercy-seat of the ark of the covenant, "for so terrible was the *Shekhina* of the Godhead on it, and even more frightening and deserving of honor was its visage than that of the other objects consisting of that part of the service." If the foreshadowing was so frightful, then how much more reverence does "the Foreshadowing to which belong the mysteries and images" deserve? At the same time, Isaac notes that the worship surrounding the Old Testament priestly objects was summoned out of fear of punishment, to which every person was submitted who dared to act disrespectfully toward them. Even in the New Testament "blessing is poured out without measure, and strictness is swallowed up by softness, and boldness appears . . . but boldness usually drives away fear, thanks to God's great mercy, which is poured out on us at all times."[29]

For this reason we do not consider the cross as a fearful punishment, but as reverential trembling before Christ, who accomplished our salvation by means of the cross. Contemplating the cross, Christians see the Savior himself:

Truly, the sight of the cross is no small thing for believers, for the whole mystery is understood through it. But every time they raise their eyes and look at it, it is as if they glance at the face of Christ, and so they express

---

[26]The image of the cross.

[27]The theological language of this excerpt corresponds to the traditional Christology of the Church of the East to which Isaac the Syrian belonged.

[28]Isaac the Syrian *On the Divine Mysteries: Conversation 11* 12.

[29]Ibid. 15–16.

Apostles at the cross. Detail of a mosaic in a baptistery cupola. Ravenna. 5th c.

their reverence toward him: the sight of him is precious for them and fearful, and longed for at the same time. . . . And every time we draw ourselves near to the cross, we somehow draw near to the body of Christ: so
it is made known to us by faith in him. And through our proximity to
him and gazing at him we immediately, consciously raise our thoughts to
heaven. As if thanks to some invisible and elevated sense of vision and
respect in relation to the humanity of our Lord, our hidden sight is swallowed up by a kind of contemplation of the mystery of the faith.[30]

We consider the cross in Christ's name and for the sake of Christ.[31] In
general, everything that pertained to Christ as a man, should be considered
by us to be elevated to God, who wished for the Man-Christ to participate in
the glory of the Godhead. All of this became manifest for us on the cross,
and through the cross we received precise knowledge of the Creator.[32]

The cross, foreshadowed by the ark of the covenant, is in its own turn a
foreshadowing of the eschatological Kingdom of Christ. The cross somehow

[30]Ibid. 17–19.
[31]Ibid. 21.
[32]Cf.: Ibid. 21–22.

unites the Old Testament with the New, and unites the New Testament with "the future age" in which all material symbols will be annulled. Christ's saving plan, having begun in Old Testament times and continuing until the end of the age, is concluded in the symbol of the cross:

> For the cross is Christ's raiment, just as Christ's humanity is the clothing of his divinity. As the cross serves the image, anticipating the time when the true Prototype will appear: then those objects will not be needed. For the divinity lives inseparably in man, without end, and forever, that is without border or limit. For this reason we look at the cross as the place of the *Shekhina* of the Most High, the sanctuary of the Lord, the ocean of mysteries of God's saving plan. This image of the cross is the mystery of the two Testaments to our eye. . . . For this is also written in our Savior's saving plan. Whenever we look at the cross in this way, with quiet thoughts, the recollection of the saving plan of our Lord is collected and stands before our inner eyes.[33]

The "theology of the cross" laid out by Isaac the Syrian can be summarized in the following theses: 1) The *Shekhina*, the presence of God, lives in the cross, transferred into it from the ark of the covenant; 2) the Old Testament ark was a foreshadowing of the cross; 3) the veneration of the cross is not idol worship, since Christ's presence is in the cross and because veneration is given to him, not to the material object; 4) the cross is a symbol of God's saving plan for humanity; 5) the cross prefigures the reality of the coming age, in which all material symbols will be abolished.

The theological knowledge of the mystery of the cross is contained in Gregory Palamas' homily *On the Honorable and Life Creating Cross*, dedicated to the interpretation of the Old Testament foreshadows of the Lord's cross. According to Palamas' teaching, the cross was the instrument of salvation even before it was erected on Golgotha and Christ stretched out upon it, for many Old Testament righteous were saved by the might of the cross. The words of Christ himself, uttered before the crucifixion, bear witness to the saving power of the cross before Christ's crucifixion: "And the one who does not take up his cross and follow me is not worthy of me" (Mt 10.38). It is necessary for Christians to "ascend to the heights of the cross" themselves, by means of ascetical struggle. How is one to do this? Through fulfillment of the

---

[33]Ibid. 24–26.

gospel commandments that call man "to gain the victory through infirmity, to be raised up through humility, to become rich through poverty."[34]

According to the Palamite's teaching, the sign of the cross is "divine and worthy of praise, being holy and imbued with honor, consecrated and perfectly given by God to the human race as an ineffable blessing of the highest essence, consuming cursing and condemnation, abolishing corruption and death, granting eternal life and blessing." The cross is the "saving tree, the royal scepter, the divine trophy over the visible and invisible enemies." The cross of the Lord "is the proclamation of the whole saving plan of the Coming One in the flesh and concludes in itself the whole mystery relating to this and extending to all the ends and borders: that which is above, that which is below, that which is on the periphery, and that which is in between."[35] As in Chrysostom, these words of Gregory Palamas present the cross as the universal symbol of salvation.

The cited witness of the Eastern fathers of the Church from the fourth to the fourteenth centuries surprisingly shows that the veneration of the cross and bowing down to the cross remained an inseparable part of the theology and spirituality of the Orthodox Church over the centuries. Respect for the cross was indissolubly connected to the Lord and Savior who was crucified on it, and the theological texts tightly interweave the themes of the cross, the passion, the crucifixion, and the resurrection. At the same time, the cross by itself possessed significance as the main Christian symbol, to which worship is given, to which is ascribed miraculous power, before which prayer is offered.

Moreover, there was a widely developed practice of prayerfully addressing the cross of Christ in the Byzantine age. Quite a few of these addresses are contained in the liturgical texts dedicated to the cross, especially in the texts of the Week of the Veneration of the Cross:

> Hail life-giving cross, the fair paradise of the Church, tree of incorruption that brings us the enjoyment of eternal glory. (*Lenten Triodion*. Week of the cross. Great Vespers. *Sticheron* at "Lord, I Call")

> Hail, life-giving cross, unconquerable trophy of the true faith, door to paradise, succor of the faithful, rampart set about the Church. Through

[34]Gregory Palamas *Homilies 11*.
[35]Ibid.

thee the curse is utterly destroyed, the power of death is swallowed up, and we are raised from earth to heaven. (*Lenten Triodion.* Week of the cross. Great Vespers. *Sticheron* at "Lord, I Call")

O mighty cross of the Lord, manifest thyself: show me the divine vision of thy beauty. . . . For I speak to thee and embrace thee as though thou wast alive. (*Lenten Triodion.* Week of the cross. Matins. Canon. Ode 1)

The above texts, especially the last one, can suggest the notion that the cross is considered to be a living thing in Orthodox tradition, capable of hearing prayers and answering them (the Russian theologian and priest Pavel Florensky came to such a conclusion).[36] However, it is worth noting that a similar type of "spiritualization" of the cross, its transformation into a living essence, was not characteristic of the theologians and Fathers of the Church. The Orthodox Church has age-old experience in terms of respect for the cross and venerating it. This experience, reflected both in theological literature and in liturgical texts, includes within one of the prayers to the cross, "as though thou wast alive." This experience shows that the cross of Christ is a source of healing: it casts out demons; the faithful are granted divine blessing through it. However, the power that acts through the cross is not some kind of autonomous power, existing in the cross as such. The power of God, the energy of God, acts through the cross, that same energy that is included in the names of God. The prayer addressed to the cross of Christ ascends to him who was crucified on it; the power that comes from the cross, comes from the Lord himself. And the salvation that flows from the cross does not have as its principle the cross itself, but the One who was stretched upon it, the Savior of the whole world, Christ.

[36]Cf.: Pavel Florensky, from "Theological Legacy," *Theological Works* 17, 91.

18

The Descent into Hades

T HE SAVIOR'S DEATH ON THE CROSS became the crowning achievement of
the outpouring-kenosis that began with Christ's birth from the Virgin
and continued over the course of his whole earthly life. But in order to save
fallen Adam, it was necessary for Christ to descend not just to earth, but to
the lowermost depths of the earth, where the dead languished in expectation
of him. The liturgical texts of Holy Saturday speak thus of this:

> To earth thou hast come down, O Master, to save Adam: and not finding
> him on earth, thou hast descended into hell, seeking him there. (*Lenten
> Triodion*. Holy Saturday. Matins. Troparia at the "Praises")

The teaching of Christ's descent into Hades is one of the most important
themes of Orthodox Christology.[1] It is characteristic of Byzantine and
ancient Russian icons of the resurrection of Christ that the resurrection itself,
Christ's exit from the tomb, is never actually depicted. Depicted instead is
"Christ's descent into Hades," or, more precisely, Christ's exodus from
Hades. Christ, sometimes with the cross in his arms, is represented as leading Adam, Eve, and the other righteous from biblical history, out from Hell;
beneath the feet of the Savior, against a background of a black abyss of the
nethermost regions, are keys, locks, and shards of the gate that no longer bars
the way to resurrection for those who have died.

Christ's descent into Hades is one of the most mysterious, puzzling, and
difficult to explain events of the New Testament story. This event is understood in various ways in the contemporary Christian world. Liberal Western
theology generally denies any possibility of speaking of Christ's descent into
Hades in literal terms, claiming that the texts of Holy Scripture dedicated to
this theme are to be understood metaphorically. Traditional Catholic dogma

---

[1]For more on this subject, see: Hilarion (Alfeyev), *Christ the Conqueror of Hell: The Descent into
Hades from an Orthodox Perspective* (Crestwood, N.Y.: St Vladimir's Seminary Press, 2009).

The descent into Hades. Monastery of Chora. Constantinople. 14th c.

insists that Christ, after his death on the cross, descended to Hell to lead out the Old Testament righteous exclusively. A similar understanding is fairly widespread amongst Orthodox Christians.

On the other hand, it is already said in the New Testament that Christ's preaching in Hades was addressed to those sinners who had not repented (1 Pet 3.18–21), and the liturgical texts of the Orthodox Church repeatedly stress that, descending into Hell, Christ opened the way to salvation for all people, not just for the Old Testament righteous. Christ's descent into Hades is perceived as an event of cosmic significance, pertaining to all people, without exception. Besides, it is said of Christ's victory over death, of the complete devastation of Hell, that after Christ's descent no one remained there besides the devil and the demons.

How can these two points of view be reconciled? What was the original belief of the Church? What do the Eastern Christian sources tell us about the descent into Hades? It is important to dwell on these questions and to present them in detail.

Christ's descent into Hades is not spoken of in even one of the canonical Gospels. However, in the Gospel according to Matthew, in the narrative of the Savior's death on the cross, it is recalled that "the graves were opened, and many bodies of the saints who slept arose, and came out of the graves after his resurrection, and went into the holy city and appeared to many" (Mt 27.52–53). The same Gospel presents Christ's words on the Savior's three day dwelling in the bowels of the earth: "For as Jonah was three days and three nights in the whale's belly, so shall the Son of Man be three days and three nights in the heart of the earth" (Mt 12.40). In Christian tradition, the story of the Prophet Jonah will come to be considered as a foreshadowing of Christ's descent into Hell.

The belief that Christ descended into the abyss of Hades after his death on the cross is clearly expressed in the Acts of the Apostles, where the Apostle Peter gives a speech after the descent of the Holy Spirit upon the apostles on the day of Pentecost (Acts 2.22–24, 29–32). However, the most important New Testament text that speaks directly of Christ descending into Hell is the First Epistle of the Holy Apostle Peter, where this theme is covered in the context of the teaching on baptism. Here the apostle speaks not only of Christ's time spent in the hellish "darkness," but also of his homily given to the souls found there:

> For Christ also suffered once for [your] sins, the just for the unjust, that he might bring you to God; being put to death in the flesh, but made alive by the Spirit, by which also he went and preached to the spirits in prison; who sometime were disobedient, when once the longsuffering of God waited in the days of Noah, while the ark was being built, in which a few, that is, eight souls, were saved through water. And baptism, which was thereby prefigured, now saves us . . . by the resurrection of Jesus Christ (1 Pet 3.18–21).

In the same First Epistle of Peter we read: "For this cause was the gospel preached also to them that are dead, that they might be judged according to me in the flesh, but live according to God in the spirit" (1 Pet 4.6). The above words laid the foundation of the teaching that Christ suffered for the "unrighteous," and his address in Hades dealt with those of whom it was said in the Old Testament that "every one in his heart was intently brooding over evil continually" (Gen 6.5). Judgment was once imposed upon "man's flesh," condemned and destroyed by God who, in the Bible's phrasing, "was sorry" that he had created man (Gen 6.6), but these people did not perish totally: descending to Hades, Christ gives them all another chance for salvation, preaching the gospel of the Kingdom to them so that they might live "in the spirit as God does."

Among other New Testament texts that relate to the theme of the descent into Hell, one may refer to the words of the Apostle Paul, that Christ "descended first into the lower parts of the earth" (Eph 4.9; Rom 10.7), and on Christ's victory over death and Hell (1 Cor 15.54–57). The teaching of Christ as the Conqueror of Hell, of the overthrow of the devil, death, and Hell into "the lake of fire and sulphur" (Rev 20.10, 14), is one of the fundamental themes of the Revelation of John the Theologian. Christ says of himself in Revelation: "I am the first and the last, and he who lives, and was dead; and behold, I am alive for evermore (Amen); and I have the keys of Hades and of death" (Rev 1.17–18). The theme of the "keys of Hades" receives its own development both in iconography and in the literature of liturgical poetry.

The theme of Christ's descent into Hades is covered in much greater detail in the early Christian apocrypha than it is in texts coming from the New Testament canon. These are texts such as *The Ascension of Isaiah*, *The Book of Asher*, *The Testaments of the Twelve Patriarchs*, *The Gospel of Peter*, *The Epistle of the Apostles*, *The Shepherd of Hermas*, and *The Epistle of Bartholomew*. The most developed exposition of Christ's descent into Hades is contained in the *Gospel of Nicodemus*, which has proven to be a key influence on the formation of church teaching on the question. It is recounted here how those who found themselves in Hell languished, awaiting the coming of the Savior, and how John the Baptist proclaimed the coming deliverance.[2] Later in the scene Adam and Seth appear: the latter tells his father and the other "patriarchs and prophets" of the promise he received from the angel of the incarnate Son of God.[3] After that there ensues a dialogue between Satan and Hades: "If thou bring him [Jesus] unto me he will set free all that are here shut up in the hard prison and bound in the chains of their sins that cannot be broken," says Hades, "and will bring them unto the life of his Godhead forever." At this moment a voice like thunder rings out: "Remove, O princes, your gates, and be ye lift up, ye everlasting doors, and the King of glory shall come in" (Ps 23.7[4]). Hades tries to resist Christ's coming and commands its demons: "Shut ye the hard gates of brass and put on them the bars of iron and withstand stoutly." But the resistance is in vain—the King of glory bursts into Hell, binds Satan and commits him to Hell with the words: "Satan the prince shall be in

[2]Cf.: *The Gospel of Nicodemus* 18.
[3]Ibid. 19.
[4]LXX.

thy power unto all ages." Receiving Satan, Hades says to him: "Behold now, this Jesus . . . hath broken the strong depths of the prisons, and let out the prisoners *and loosed them that were bound.*"[5]

The leading of the dead out of Hades by the incarnate Christ is described in the *Gospel of Nicodemus* in the following way:

> And the Lord stretching forth his hand, said: "Come unto me, all ye my saints which bear mine image and my likeness. Ye that by the tree and the devil and death were condemned, behold now the devil and death condemned by the tree." And forthwith all the saints were gathered in one under the hand of the Lord. . . . But Adam, casting himself at the knees of the Lord entreated him with tears and beseechings, and said with a loud voice: "I will magnify thee, O Lord, for thou hast healed me; Lord, thou hast brought my soul out of hell. . . ." In like manner all the saints of God kneeled and cast themselves at the feet of the Lord, saying with one accord: "Thou art come, O redeemer of the world. . . ." And the Lord stretched forth his hand and made the sign of the cross over Adam and over all his saints, and he took the right hand of Adam and went up out of hell, and all the saints followed him. . . . And all the saints answered, saying: "Blessed is he that cometh in the name of the Lord. God is the Lord and hath shown us light. Amen, Alleluia. . . ." But the Lord holding the hand of Adam delivered him unto Michael the archangel, and all the saints followed Michael the archangel.[6]

If in the beginning of this excerpt it says that Christ began to lead out all the dead from Hades, then later on it speaks only of "all the prophets and saints," of "the patriarchs, prophets, martyrs, and forefathers," but also of "all the righteous."

The Gospel of Nicodemus contains in itself the whole complex of ideas and images used in Christian literature of subsequent centuries in representing Christ's descent into Hades: Christ not only descends to the abyss of Hell, he *invades* it, overcoming the resistance of the devil and the demons, shattering the gates and bursting asunder its lock and bolts. All these images are summoned in order to illustrate one fundamental idea: Christ descended to Hades not as a usual victim of death, but as the Conqueror of death and Hell,

[5] *The Gospel of Nicodemus* 20–23. Emphasis is the author's.
[6] Ibid. 24–25.

before whom the powers of evil turn out to be impotent. Precisely such an understanding will be characteristic for the literature of liturgical poetry dedicated to this theme, as well as for Eastern Christian patristic literature.

We do not find a systematic and detailed, developed teaching of Christ's descent into Hades in the Fathers themselves: this theme is most frequently touched on in connection with the dogma of redemption or in the context of the teaching of Christ's resurrection. The theme of the descent into Hades has found a much fuller reflection in the literature of liturgical poetry than in theological treatises. Nevertheless, the following review is necessary in order to understand what is contained in ecclesial hymnography and in the prose that is dedicated to the theme in which we are now interested.

We encounter references to Christ's descent to Hell and to his resurrection from the dead in such Greek authors of the second and third centuries as Polycarp of Smyrna, Ignatius the God-Bearer, Justin Martyr, Melito of Sardis, Hippolytus of Rome, Irenaeus of Lyons, Clement of Alexandria, and Origen.

A few references to Christ's descent to Hades can be found in the works of Irenaeus of Lyons. In *On the Apostolic Preaching*, preserved in the Armenian language, Irenaeus says that Christ's descent to Hades "was for the salvation of the dead."[7] In his composition *Against Heresies*, he says:

> The Lord descended into the regions beneath the earth, preaching his advent there also, and [declaring] the remission of sins received by those who believe in him. Now all those believed in him who had hope towards him, that is, those who proclaimed his advent, and submitted to his dispensations, the righteous men, the prophets, and the patriarchs, to whom he remitted sins in the same way as he did to us, which sins we should not lay to their charge, if we would not despise the grace of God.[8]

The teaching of Christ's descent to Hades found a sufficiently well-rounded exposure in the *Stromata* of Clement of Alexandria, who claimed that Christ's preaching in Hades dealt not only with the Old Testament righteous, but also with the Gentiles who lived outside the true faith. Commenting on 1 Peter 3.18–21, Clement expresses confidence in the fact that Christ addressed everyone who was in Hell and who was capable of believing in Christ:

[7] 78.
[8] 4 27.2.

Do not [the Scriptures] show that the Lord preached the Gospel to those that perished in the flood, or rather had been chained? . . . And, as I think, the Savior also exerts his might because it is his work to save; which accordingly he also did by drawing to salvation those who became willing, by the preaching [of the Gospel], to believe in him, wherever they were. If, then, the Lord descended to Hades for no other end but to preach the Gospel, as he did descend; it was either to preach the Gospel to all or to the Hebrews only. If, accordingly, to all, then all who believe[9] shall be saved, although they may be of the Gentiles, on making their profession there.[10]

Clement especially notes that the righteous are among those of the true faith and among the Gentiles, and that those people who did not believe in him during their lives, but whose virtuous lives made them capable of accepting Christ's preaching and that of the apostles in Hell, could indeed turn to God. In Clement's words, the disciples in Hades should be imitators of the Lord, "so that he should bring to repentance those belonging to the Hebrews, and they the Gentiles; that is, those who had lived in righteousness according to the Law and philosophy, who had ended life not perfectly, but sinfully." As Clement maintains, salvation is possible not only on earth, but in Hell, since those, "though found in another place, yet being confessedly of the number of the people of God Almighty, should be saved."[11]

References to Christ's descent in Hades are found repeatedly in the works of another Alexandrian theologian, Origen. In particular, in the composition *Against Celsus*, Origen's main apologetic treatise, we read:

"You will not, I suppose, say of him, that, after failing to gain over those who were there." But whether he [Celsus] like it or not, we assert that not only while Jesus was in the body did he win over not a few persons merely, but so great a number, that a conspiracy was formed against him on account of the multitude of his followers; but also, that when he became a soul, without the covering of the body,[12] he dwelt among those souls which were without bodily covering, converting such of them as were

---

[9]I.e., those who believe in him in Hades.
[10]6.6
[11]Ibid.
[12]Lit. "bared from the body."

willing to himself, or those whom he saw, for reasons known to him alone, to be better adapted to such a course.[13]

All the prominent writers of the "golden age of patristic writing" dealt with the theme of Christ's descent into Hades in one way or another. Just like their predecessors, the fathers of the fourth century revisited this theme above all in the context of the teaching of redemption.

Athanasius of Alexandria references the descent into Hades in the dispute with the Arians. Proving the divinity of the Son to his opponents and emphasizing the unity between the Father and the Son, Athanasius writes:

> Neither can the Lord be forsaken by the Father, who is ever in the Father.
> ... Nor is it lawful to say that the Lord was in terror, at whom the keeper's of hell's gates shuddered and set open hell, and the graves did gape, and many bodies of the saints arose and appeared to their own people.[14]

Apart from the Arians, other opponents of Athanasius included those who considered that the divine Logos turned itself into flesh. Correcting their opinion, Athanasius writes on the Logos' descent into Hades:

> This body it was that was laid in a grave, when the Word [Logos] had left it, yet was not parted from it, to preach, as Peter says, also to the spirits in prison (1 Pet 3.19). And this above all shows the foolishness of those who say that the Word was changed into bones and flesh. For if this had been so, there were no need of a tomb. For the body would have gone by itself to preach to the spirits in Hades. But as it was, he himself went to preach, while the body Joseph wrapped in a linen cloth, and laid it away at Golgotha. And so it is shown to all that the body was not the Word, but body of the Word.[15]

We find in Eusebius of Caesarea, the collector of "patristic tradition" and church history, a narrative of a sermon of the Apostle Thaddeus to King Abgar of Edessa on the Savior's ascension. Addressing the king, the apostle says "how he [Jesus] humbled himself, and died and debased his divinity and was crucified, and descended into Hades, and burst the bars which from eternity had not been broken, and raised the dead; for he descended alone, but rose

[13]2.43.
[14]*Discourse Against the Arians* 3 29.56.
[15]*Letter to Epictetus* 5–6.

with many, and thus ascended to his Father."[16] Eusebius says in another place: "He came for the salvation of the souls dwelling in Hades for many ages, awaiting his coming and, having descended, he shattered the gates of brass and broke the iron bars and led all who had been chained in Hell to freedom."[17]

The teaching of the descent into Hades received development in the compositions of Basil the Great of Cappadocia. Basil speaks of the descent into Hades as a continuation of the pastoral ministry of Jesus Christ in his interpretation of Psalm 48 (49):

"They are laid in hell like sheep: death shall feed upon them" (Ps 48.15[18]). He, who carries away into captivity those who are beastlike and who are compared to senseless herds, like the sheep, which have neither the intelligence nor the ability to defend themselves, since he is an enemy, has already cast them down into his own prison and has handed them over to death to feed. For, death tended them from the time of Adam until the administration of Moses, until the true Shepherd came, who laid down his own life for his sheep (Jn 10.15) and who thus, ma[de] them rise together and le[d] them out from the prison of hell to the early morning of the Resurrection.[19]

We find repeated references on Christ's descent into Hades in the works of Gregory the Theologian. In the famous *On Holy Pascha*, which has become an inseparable part of paschal theology over the course of many centuries, Gregory says: "If he [Christ] descends into Hades, go down with him. Know also the mysteries of Christ there: what is the saving plan, what is the reason for the twofold descent, to save everyone absolutely by his manifestation, or there also only to those who believe."[20] Speaking on the "twofold descent," Gregory has in mind the *katavasis* (κατάβασις) of the Son of God to earth (the incarnation) and his κατάβασις to Hades: in early Christian literature these two themes were closely interwoven.

It is interesting that the question posed by Gregory somewhat hangs in the air, going unanswered. No less curious is the fact that some later authors

---

[16]Eusebius of Caesarea *Church History* 1.13.

[17]*Commentary on the Gospel* 10.

[18]LXX. The translation of the Masoretic text is: "Like sheep they are appointed for Sheol; death shall be their shepherd" (Ps 49.14).

[19]*Homily 19: Interpretation of Psalm 48* 9.

[20]*Oration 45* 24 (Crestwood, NY: 2008), 185.

approached the question of which of those found in Hades did Christ save with much less trepidation. Theophylact of Bulgaria (twelfth century) refers to Gregory the Theologian on these grounds, although he alters the text in this way: "Christ, having appeared to those in Hell, does not save all without exception, but only those who believe."[21] That question which Gregory posed but to which he left no clear answer, seemed to a theologian of the twelfth century to be an obvious fact.

On all counts, the tragedy *Christ the Sufferer* pertains to Gregory the Theologian, written "in the style of Euripides" and preserved in many manuscripts in his name. The opinions of academics relating to the authorship and dating of the tragedy differ, although its weighty reason and logic suggest it is Gregory's genuine work. Supporting this notion is its poetic style, very near in style to Gregory's other poems, as well as carrying in it a mimicking character. The uniqueness of the text in question consists in the fact that we do not have a work of liturgical poetry, but a text for the theater, in which individual phrases and whole strophes from Euripides' tragedies are artificially interwoven into a religious drama with Christian content. The author of such a tragedy could only be a man who completed a course of study in the leading technical antique poetic style of the day: such people were rare in Byzantium, and Gregory absolutely belonged to their number.

The main dynamic character in the tragedy is the Theotokos; other protagonists include Christ, the angel, an anonymous theologian, Joseph of Arimathea, Nicodemus, Mary Magdalene, the youth sitting at the tomb, the high priests, the guard, Pilate, and the choirs. The plot of the tragedy is on the last days, crucifixion, death, burial, and resurrection of Christ. The theme of Christ's descent into Hades is one of the leitmotifs of the piece. It appears in various contexts and in speeches of various protagonists. Addressing Christ, the Theotokos asks him: "O Son and King of all, how has the death of our forebears now led you to dwell in Hades?"[22] In another place the Theotokos cries out: "O Son and Almighty Lord, you have caused so much suffering in my soul while you lived, and when you descended to Hades."[23] Through the mouth of the Theotokos, the poet includes the following highly important (in the dogmatic sense) text:

[21] *Commentaries.*
[22] *Christ the Sufferer* 878–879.
[23] Ibid. 1338–1339.

You descend, O beloved Child, to the dwelling of Hell,
In order to cover yourself in the asylum in which you desire to be
    covered,
But, descending into the lower depths of Hades,
You reduced it to the sorriest pity.
You descend to the prison of the dead and to the gates of darkness,
Hoping to sanctify and enlighten the race [of man],
To resurrect Adam, the father of the dead,
For the sake of whom you, having assumed it, bear the image of the
    dead one (1 Cor 15, 49).
You descend into the dark depths of the shadow of Hell,
Having accepted death from the enemy, but your Mother is left
    unhappy.
But the goodwill of the Father mortifies you,
So that you might bring salvation to others.
The grace of the Father led you to death.
O bitter lamentation! The earth accepts you, O my Child,
Descending to the dark gates of Hades,
In order to pierce it with the sharpest arrow.
For you are the only one who descends there
In order to take death on yourself, but not to be taken by death,
And in order to deliver all, for you alone are free.
For you are the only Man capable of such humanity,
You are the one who suffers for the nature of the dead.
But the struggle that you have endured is now ended,
And you gained the victory over your adversaries,
And by your might put to flight Hades, the serpent, and death. . . .
Having carried the race [of man out from Hell], you now will exit
    in glory,
O King, immortal King, remaining God,
But who united his own image to man's nature.
And now you descend into the dwelling of Hades,
Striving to sanctify and enlighten the darkness.[24]

---

[24]Ibid. 1505–1538.

The author of the tragedy *Christ the Sufferer* perceives the descent into Hades as a redemptive feat accomplished by Christ for the sake of the salvation of all mankind, and not for some specific group of people. Descending into the "dwelling of Hades," Christ enlightens it with his divinity and destroys it, enlightens the whole race of man and resurrects Adam, personified by his own fallen humanity. Exiting Hades, Christ returns to earth[25] in order to bring witness of the truth of the resurrection to the Theotokos, to the myrrh-bearing women, and to the apostles.

The compositions of Gregory of Nyssa also touch upon the theme of the descent into Hades. For this author, the given theme is interwoven with the context of the theory of the "divine deception," on which he constructed his teaching on the redemption. This is the idea that Gregory of Nyssa develops in one of his paschal homilies: *Oration on the Three Day Period of Christ's Resurrection*. In it, Gregory poses the question of why Christ was "for three days and three nights . . . in the heart of the earth" (Mt 12.40). This period was necessary and sufficient, he claims, so that Christ could "expose the foolishness" of the devil, that is out-wit, mock, and deceive him:

> O Almighty Wisdom, you dwelt in the heart of the earth, for this small period of time was sufficient, in order to show the foolishness of that great intellect that lives there. For so the prophet names him when he calls it "great mind" and "Assyrian" (Isa 10.12–13[26]). But since the heart of some forms is the dwelling of the mind, for they think that dominion dwells in the heart, so the Lord visits the heart of the earth, which is the dwelling place of that great mind, in order to reveal the foolishness of its counsels, as the prophecy says (Isa 19.11[27]), in order to seize its craftiness and to place it in opposition to its clever tricks.[28]

Among the authors of the fourth century who developed the theme of the descent into Hades, one cannot neglect to mention John Chrysostom, who continually returns to it in various compositions. In *Homily on the Cemetery and the Cross*, Chrysostom, addressing the image of the "gates of brass" referred to in the book of the Prophet Isaiah and the Psalter, speaks of how

---

[25]Ibid. 2188–2189.
[26]LXX.
[27]LXX.
[28]*On Holy Pascha* 1.

Christ descended into Hades and enlightened it with his light, turning it into heaven:

> Today every place in Hell avoids our Lord; today he shattered the gates of brass, today he broke the iron bars (Isa 45.2; Ps 106.16[29]). Pay attention to the precision of the phrase. It did not say that he "opened the gates of brass," but that he broke them, so that the place where souls were kept in chains would be made useless. He did not lift the bars, but broke them, so that the guards were made powerless. Where there is neither door nor bar, if someone enters, he or she cannot be restrained. Thus, when Christ broke them, who could possibly repair them? For it says that what God has broken, who can then right it? . . . Desiring to show that death is at an end, he broke the gates of brass. They were not called brass because they were made of actual brass, but to show the strictness and implacability of death. . . . You wish to know how it was severe, implacable, and hard, like diamond? Over the course of so much time not even one person who was held by them was able to be freed, until the Master of the Angels descended to Hades, though he did not have to. For from the beginning he bound the strong man, and then he plundered his vessels, as the prophet adds: "Dark treasures, hidden and unseen ones" (Isa 45.3[30]). . . . Was not this place of Hell dark and joyless, and there was never one ray of light; for this reason they are called dark and unseen. For they were truly dark, so long as the Sun of righteousness did not descend there, not enlightening Hades and making it heaven. For where Christ is, there heaven is also.[31]

Further on Chrysostom speaks of how Christ, descending to Hades, freed the whole race of man, bound Hades, and conquered death:

> As a certain king, finding the leader of a den of thieves that has fallen upon the city, committing robberies everywhere, hiding the riches in a covered cave, binds this leader of thieves and sentences him to imprisonment, and transfers the treasure to the royal coffers, so did Christ act: he sentenced to death the leader of thieves and dungeon overseer, that is the devil and death, and transferred the riches, that is the race of man, to the

[29]LXX.
[30]LXX.
[31]*Homily on the Cemetery and the Cross* 2.

royal coffers. . . . The King himself came to those who were in chains, not being ashamed of the darkness or the prisoners–he could not possibly be ashamed of those whom he created–and shattered the gates, broke the bars, appeared before Hades, left the guards to be alone and, having bound the dungeon overseer, entered and came to us. The tyrant is taken captive, the strong man is bound; death itself having thrown down its arms, runs naked to the feet of the King.[32]

The theme of the descent into Hades is one of those central in the Syrian theological tradition. Of the Syrian authors who delve into this theme, it is worth noting the "Persian Sage," Jacob Aphrahat (fourth century) above all. Aphrahat dedicated the following highly expressive text to the descent into Hades, in which personified death enters into a dialogue with Christ:

When Jesus, the slayer of death, came, and clothed himself in a body from the seed of Adam, and was crucified in his body, and tasted death; and when [death] perceived thereby that he had come down unto him, he was shaken from his place and was agitated when he saw Jesus; and he closed his gates and was not willing to receive him. Then he burst his gates, and entered into him, and began to despoil all his possessions. But when the dead saw light in the darkness, they lifted up their heads from the bondage of death, and looked forth, and saw the splendor of the King Messiah. Then the powers of the darkness of death sat in mourning, for he was degraded from his authority. Death tasted the medicine that was deadly to him, and his hands dropped down, and he learned that the dead shall live and escape from his sway. And when he had afflicted death by the despoiling of his possessions, he wailed and cried aloud in bitterness and said, "Go forth from my realm and enter it not. Who then is this that comes alive into my realm?" And while death was crying out in terror (for he saw that his darkness was beginning to be done away, and some of the righteous who were sleeping arose to ascend with him), then he made known to him that when he shall come in the fullness of time, he will bring forth all the prisoners from his power, and they shall go forth to see the light. Then when Jesus had fulfilled his ministry among the dead, death sent him forth from his realm, and suffered him not to remain there. And to devour him like all the dead, he counted it not pleasure. He

[32]Ibid.

had no power over the Holy One, nor was he given over to corruption.[33]

Ephraim the Syrian devotes even more attention to the theme of the descent into Hades. One of his *Heavenly Hymns* contains an expansive monologue from death's point of view, which says that no one ever escaped from its power, not prophets, not priests, not kings, not warriors, not rich men, not poor men, not wise men, not fools, not the old, and not the young. It is only missing two people—Enoch and Elijah—in whose search it descended "there where Jonah descended,"[34] but it did not find them

The descent into Hades. The golden gates. Suzdal. 12th c.

there. Death's monologue unexpectedly breaks up the picture of the resurrection of the dead by Christ's descent into Sheol:

> Death ceased its arrogant speech,
> and the voice of our Lord rang out in Sheol,
> and he exclaimed and smashed the graves, one after another.
> He seized death trembling;
> Sheol, which was never blessed,
> The guards[35] shone radiantly,
> who entered into it in order to lead out
> the dead to meet him,
> who was dead and gives life to all.[36]

Further on it describes death's resistance, hurrying to shut the gates of Sheol in front of Christ. Death is amazed that unlike other people who strive to leave Sheol, Christ instead attempts to enter it. "The venom of life came into Sheol and revived the dead," says death (we found the image of venom poisoning Sheol in Jacob Aphrahat, above). Addressing Christ, death acknowledges its surprise and asks him, after he had taken Adam to himself, to cast him to the ends of Sheol and enter into heaven. The hymn concludes in praise of Christ's victory over death:

---

[33] *Oration 22* 4.
[34] Ephraim the Syrian *Nisibene Hymn* 36.3.
[35] The angels.
[36] Ephraim the Syrian *Nisibene Hymn* 36.11.

Our King of life descended [into Sheol]
and exited from it as Conqueror.
He increased the ruin of those found on his left hand:
the evil spirits and demons, he—the source of wrath,
Satan, and death—suffering, sin, and Hades—grief.
But to those who were on his right hand,
he returned to the present joy.[37]

Therefore a very clear doctrine is laid out in the hymn: death tries to forbid Christ to enter into Sheol, though in vain; entering into Sheol, he resurrects all those found there and leads them away; Sheol is emptied, there are no more dead in it; only the evil spirits (the demons), Satan, death, and sin remain together in Sheol in expectation of the Second Coming of Christ. On the day of the Second Coming, death will lead out to Christ all those who became its victims, with its own hand. Thus in this hymn, Ephraim does not make the righteous or prophets stand out, but says that Christ, descending to Sheol, has saved and resurrected all who were found there.

The approach presented by St Maximus the Confessor on the teaching of Christ's descent into Hades is highly original. Interpreting the words of the Apostle Peter on the proclamation of the gospel to the dead (1 Pet 4.6), Maximus claims that the focus of the text is not on the Old Testament righteous, but on those sinners who even during their earthly life received requital for their evil acts:

Some say that the Scriptures call "dead" those who died before the coming of Christ, for instance, those who were in the time of the flood, at Babel, in Sodom, in Egypt, as well as others who in various times and ways received the varied penalties and terrible afflictions of the divine judgments. These men were punished not so much for their ignorance of God as for the outrages they imposed on one another. It was to them, according to [St Peter], that the great message of salvation was preached when they were already judged as men in the flesh, that is, when they received, through life in the flesh, punishment for crimes against one another so that they could live according to God, in the spirit, that is, the soul; being in Hades, they accepted the preaching of the knowledge of God, believing in the Savior who descended into Hades to save the dead.

[37]Ibid. 36.18.

So in order to understand [this] passage in [Holy Scripture] let us take it in this way: the dead, judged in the human flesh, were preached to precisely for the purpose that they may live according to God by the spirit.[38]

In order to appreciate the novelty of Maximus' approach to the teaching on the salvation of those in Hell through Christ, it is necessary to recall John Chrysostom's view that Christ destroyed the power of death by his descent to Hades, but he did not extirpate the sins of those who died before his coming: the Old Testament sinners, "yet they did also suffer here the most extreme punishment, nevertheless not even this will deliver them."[39] Moreover, Chrysostom asserted that in Old Testament times, it was not faith in Christ that was necessary for salvation, but confession of the one God. Maximus the Confessor, as we can see, places emphasis in a different way. He maintains that the punishments born by sinners "in human flesh," were necessary in order that they might live "by God in the spirit." Consequently, perhaps one can assume that these punishments—whether misfortune and poverty in earthly life or torture in Hell—had an instructional and corrective intent. Moreover, Maximus emphasizes that the sentences passed by God were applied not with a religious, but with a moral criterion: people were punished "not so much for disobedience to God, as much as for offenses committed against one another." In other words, the decisive role was played not by the religious persuasions or world-view of each concrete human being, as much as by his or her actions in relation to the neighbor.

In *An Exact Exposition of the Orthodox Faith*, John of Damascus brings up the point of development of the theme of Christ's descent into Hades in the Eastern patristic writings of the second and third centuries:

The soul [Christ's] when it was deified descended into Hades, in order that, just as the Sun of Righteousness rose for those upon the earth, so likewise he might bring light to those who sit under the earth in darkness and shadow of death (Isa 9.2): in order that just as he brought the message of peace to those upon the earth, and of release to the prisoners, and of sight to the blind (Lk 4.18–19; Isa 61.1–2), and became to those who believed the Author of everlasting salvation and to those who did not believe a reproach of their unbelief, so he might become the same to

---

[38] *To Thalassius* 7.
[39] *Homilies on Matthew* 36 3–4.

those in Hades: that every knee should bow to him, of things in heaven, and things in earth and things under the earth (Phil 2.10). And thus after he had freed those who had been bound for ages, straightway he rose from the dead, showing us the way of resurrection.[40]

According to the Damascene, Christ preached to all those in Hades, although his preaching did not turn out to be salvific for all, since not all were capable of responding to it: for some it could only be the "unmasking of unbelief," but not the cause of salvation. Christ reveals to all the way to paradise, he invites all to salvation, but the answer to Christ's call can be an accord to follow after him just as it can be a voluntary refusal of salvation. In the final analysis, all depends on the person, on his or her free will. God does not save anyone by force, but all are called: "Behold, I stand at the door, and knock; if any man hear my voice, and open the door, I will come in to him" (Rev 3.20). God is knocking on the door of the human heart, but he does not break into it.

In Western tradition, the theme of the descent into Hades has been covered in abundant detail from the time of Blessed Augustine. Augustine's teaching on Christ's descent into Hades is rather contradictory. In some cases he allows that the Old Testament righteous awaiting Christ's coming could be in Hades.[41] However in other cases Augustine claims that the Old Testament righteous were in the "bosom of Abraham," moreover, in contrast to Jerome, he is not at all inclined to identify the "bosom of Abraham" with Hades.[42] Augustine is sharply inclined to show that the "bosom of Abraham" is none other than the third heaven, or paradise, that is "the place where the blessed souls are found."[43] Speaking of Christ freeing those contained in Hades, Augustine stresses that those freed were only those who "deserved to be saved by divine and hidden just judgment,"[44] in other words, only those predestined to salvation.

One of the letters of Blessed Augustine presents itself as a treatise on the theme of the descent to Hades. In this letter, Augustine rejects the traditional and widely accepted understanding of 1 Peter 3.18–21. First, he is not sure that

[40]3.29.
[41]Cf.: City of God 20.15.
[42]Cf.: On the Book of Genesis 12.33.
[43]Ibid. 12.34.
[44]Ibid.

the argument concerns those who truly fell in this life, and not the spiritually dead, those who did not put their faith in Christ. Second, he expresses the highly unexpected idea that Hades does not remember Christ's presence there after he leaves it. Consequently, the descent into Hades was a "one-time" event, relevant only for those who were there at that very moment. Third, and finally, Augustine generally denies any possibility for those people who did not believe in Christ on earth to believe in him in Hades, calling this idea "absurd."[45]

The teaching that Christ did not lead everyone out from Hades, but only those chosen, was developed in the sixth century by St Gregory Dialogus. He claimed that Christ, descending to Hades, did not mortify it, but only "wounded" (lit. "stung") it, that is he gained a certain partial, incomplete victory over it. There is already present here an essential divergence between Gregory Dialogus and the traditional early Christian concept:

St Gregory Dialogus.
St George–Staro Nagoricane.
Macedonia. 14th c.

The chosen [to be resurrected by Christ] are those who although they were dwelling in repose, though contained by the chains of Hades, now are led to the enjoyment of paradise. . . . He drew all into himself (Jn 12.32), for he did not leave even one of his chosen ones in Hades (Hos 13.14[46]). He led all [out of Hades], especially the chosen ones. For the resurrected Lord prepared even some of those who were unbelieving and who were sentenced to eternal punishment for their crimes for pardon, but released from the chains of Hades those who by faith and deed acknowledged his own. For this reason he righteously says though Hosea: "I will be your death, O death; I will be your poison,[47] O Hades. . . ." Thus, since he decisively slew death in his chosen ones, he ended death by death. Since he led out a part from Hades, but left another part, he did not slay Hades decisively, but only wounded it.[48]

---

[45]*Letter 164* IV 10–13.
[46]In the Vulgate.
[47]In Latin, *morsus* literally means "bite" or "sting" (like that of a snake or insect).
[48]*Homilies on the Gospel II* 22.6.

The teaching that Christ, descending to Hades, "led out a part . . . but left another part," is not encountered either in early Latin or in Eastern Christians authors. It said in Greek just as in Latin patristics that either Christ led *all* out of Hades, or else he led *some* (the righteous, the saints, the patriarchs and the prophets, the chosen ones, Adam and Eve, etc.), but it is never specified whom he *did not* lead out from Hades. Gregory Dialogus took the Augustinian teaching on Christ's deliverance of "the chosen ones" to its logical end.

How far such an approach is from the traditional Eastern Christian understanding, can be judged from the correspondence between Gregory Dialogus and Patriarch Cyriacus of Constantinople on the grounds of two Constantinopolitan clerics, Gregory the presbyter and Theodore the deacon, who claimed that Christ, descending into Hades, "saved all those who confessed him as God, and freed them from slavery to punishment." Refuting the Constantinopolitan clerics, Gregory Dialogus says that Christ led out from Hades just those who not only believed in him, but who kept his commandments when they were alive. Gregory claims that the believers who did not perform good works were not saved. If then unbelievers, who did not manifest good works during their life, were saved in Hades, then the lot of those who lived before the incarnation is luckier than the fate of those who were born after the incarnation. Therefore those who were saved were only those who, living in the flesh, were preserved "in faith and a virtuous life" by God's grace.[49]

The teaching of the partial victory of Christ over Hades became generally accepted in the Roman Church after Gregory Dialogus. It was supported by the Council of Toledo in the year 625.

Thomas Aquinas contributed the final form of this teaching in the thirteenth century. In his *Summa Theologica*, he divides Hades into four parts: 1) purgatory (*purgatorium*), in which sinners suffer through purifying punishment; 2) the Hades of the patriarchs (*infernum patrum*), in which the Old Testament righteous are found until the coming of Christ; 3) the Hades of the unbaptized youths (*infernum puerorum*); 4) the Hades of the condemned (*infernum damnatorum*). Responding to the question of to which Hades did Christ descend, Thomas Aquinas allows for two possibilities: Christ either descended to all parts of Hades or only to the one that contained the Old

[49]*Letter VII* 5.

Testament righteous, whom he then must lead out from there. In the first case, "going down into the hell of the lost he wrought this effect, that by descending thither he put them to shame for their unbelief and wickedness: but to them who were detained in Purgatory he gave hope of attaining to glory: while upon the holy Fathers detained in hell solely on account of original sin, he shed the light of glory everlasting." In the second case Christ's soul "descended only into that part of hell wherein the just were detained," though his presence was perceptible in some form in other parts of Hades.[50]

According to Thomas' teaching, Christ freed only the Old Testament righteous from Hades, contained there by reason of Original Sin.[51] What happened to the sinners found in the "Hades of the condemned," then, is that since they were either unbelievers or believers who did not possess virtue in likeness to the suffering Christ, they were not cleansed of sins, and Christ's descent into Hades did not bring them freedom from the tortures of that place.[52] Also not set free from Hades are the children who died in a state of Original Sin, since "by baptism children are delivered from original sin and from hell, but not by Christ's descent into hell"; it is only possible to accept baptism in actual life, not after death.[53] Finally, Christ did not free those who were found in Purgatory: their suffering was called for because of their personal defects (*defectus personalis*), while "the deprivation of God's glory" was a general defect (*defectus generalis*) of all human nature after the Fall; Christ's descent into Hades returned God's glory to those who were deprived of it by virtue of the general defect of nature, but no one was saved from the torments of Purgatory who was called there by the personal defects of people.[54]

The scholastic understanding of Christ's descent into Hades formulated by Thomas Aquinas was the official teaching of the Roman Catholic Church for many centuries. In the age of the Reformation this concept was subjected to steep criticism from the side of the Protestant theologians. Many contemporary Catholic theologians are highly skeptical of this teaching as well.[55] It is not necessary to speak of how far Thomas Aquinas's teaching is from the

[50]IIIa.52.2.
[51]Cf.: Ibid. IIIa.52.5.
[52]Ibid. 6.
[53]Ibid. 7.
[54]Ibid. 8.
[55]Cf., for example: Balthazar, Grillmeier, *Le Mystère Pascal*, 170 (the Aquinian understanding of Christ's descent into Hades is called "foolish theology").

Eastern Christian teaching on Christ's decent into Hades. Never has even one father of the Eastern Church allowed himself to specify who was left behind in Hades after Christ's descent there; not one of the Eastern fathers spoke of how unbaptized youths were left in Hell.[56] The division of Hades into four parts and the teaching of Purgatory are foreign to Eastern patristics. Finally, the scholastic approach itself, by which the most secret events of holy history are subjected to detailed analysis and rational explanation, is unacceptable for the Eastern Christian theologians.

Christ's descent into Hades remains, for theologians, poets, and mystics of the Eastern Church, above all a mystery that can be praised in hymns, on the grounds of which one may express various suppositions, but of which nothing may be considered definite or conclusive. It is precisely because of this that the theme is given comparatively little attention in theological treatises, but it occupies an exclusive place, in terms of meaning, in liturgical texts. According to the consideration of academics, the descent into Hades is referred to more than fifty times during the services of Holy Friday and Holy Saturday, more than 200 times during the festal period of Pentecost, and more than 150 times in resurrectional and festal hymns over the course of a whole year.[57]

In the *Octoechos*–the liturgical book that contains the hymns of the week and the resurrectional services–Christ's descent into Hades is a central theme. This theme is interwoven in the *Octoechos* with the theme of the Savior's death on the cross and his resurrection, so it is not so simple to separate one from the other. In the services of the *Octoechos*, leitmotifs continue to be the concept of Christ's victory over Hell, death, and the devil; of the "abolition" of the devil's might; and of people's deliverance from the power of death and Hades by virtue of the Savior, resurrected from the dead:

> The gates of death opened to thee from fear, O Lord. When the guards
> of Hell saw thee they were afraid, for thou didst demolish the gates of
> brass and smash the iron chains. (Saturday Tone Two. Vespers. *Sticheron* at
> "Lord, I Call")

---

[56]The teaching on the fate of unbaptized youths contained in St Gregory of Nyssa's *On Infants' Early Deaths*, is opposite that of Thomas Aquinas.

[57]Cf.: Nicholas Vassiliades, *The Mystery of Death* (Holy Trinity-Sergius Lavra: 1998), 166–167.

When thou didst descend to death, O Life Immortal, thou didst slay Hell with the splendor of thy Godhead. (Saturday Tone Two. Vespers. Troparion)

Thou art most blessed O Virgin Theotokos, for through the Son of God who was born of thee Hell has been captured and Adam recalled, the curse has been annulled, and Eve set free, death has been slain and we are given life. (Sunday Tone Two. Matins. Sedalen)

Hell has been made empty and helpless through the death of the One. (Sunday Tone Two. Matins. Canon. Ode Six)

After the evil serpent had lifted thee upon the wood, O Lover of man, he was utterly cast down on the earth, overthrown, he lay as a silent corpse. (Thursday Tone Two. Vespers. *Sticheron* at "Lord, I Call")

The *Octoechos* gives some variations of an answer to the question of who was led out from Hades by the resurrected Christ. The first of them is that Christ led out (resurrected, saved) from Hades all those awaiting his coming (all the honorable, the righteous, the saints). This variant is found fairly seldom in the *Octoechos*, about five times out of 100. Even rarer—two to three cases out of 100—is the notion that Christ granted salvation to the "faithful" (that is, those who were believers) in Hades.

The *Octoechos* much more frequently emphasizes the universal character of the Savior's death on the cross and resurrection. It is said, in particular, that Christ resurrected and led out from Hades the first formed Adam (or Adam and Eve); moreover Adam is understood not so much as a concrete identity, as much as a symbol of all of fallen humanity:

On this day thou didst rise from the tomb, O merciful One, leading us from the gates of death. On this day Adam exults and Eve rejoices. With the prophets and patriarchs, they unceasingly praise the divine majesty of thy power. (Sunday Tone Three. Matins. Kontakion)

The authors of the liturgical texts fairly often identify themselves (and within their identity, the whole Church or even all mankind) with those themes to which the saving act of Christ has been extended. The idea that the salvation of the dead, their being led out from Hades by Christ, is an event that is not "one time only," taking place in the past and in no way connected to the present, can be traced through these texts. Rather, the character of this event is outside time, and its fruits are spread not only to those who were found in Hades at the very moment of Christ's descent there, but to all subsequent generations of people. The all-worldly, beyond time, universal meaning of Christ's descent into Hades and victory over death is emphasized:

> Today is salvation come into the world, let us sing to him who rose from the tomb, the author of our life; for, destroying death by death, he has given us the victory and great mercy. (Sunday Tones One, Three, Five, and Seven. Matins. Troparion at the Doxology)

The most common (approximately forty cases out of 100) liturgical texts of the *Octoechos*, when the question concerns whom Christ resurrected from the dead and whom he led out from Hades, speak of either "the dead," "the mortal ones," "the people of the earth," without any kind of elaboration, or of "the race of man," "the race of Adam," "the world," or "the universe."

Finally, the liturgical texts of the *Octoechos* speak very frequently (maybe thirty five times out of 100) about the fact that Christ resurrected (saved, led out from Hades) *all* the people held there:

> For the sake of the misery of the poor and the sighing of the needy, thou, O Life in mortal flesh, didst converse with death. Destroying the destroyer, O glorified One, thou didst raise up all with thyself, O only Lover of man. (Sunday Tone Three. Matins. Canon. Ode Four)

> Counted among the dead thou didst bind the tyrant, delivering all from the bonds of Hell by thy resurrection. (Sunday Tone Four. Liturgy. Verses at the Beatitudes)

> At thy descent, O Creator of all, hell, the fool, gave up all those who of old had been slain by deceit. (Sunday Tone Five. Matins. Canon. Ode Eight)

> Having risen from the grave, thou didst raise together with thyself all the dead found in Hell. (Sunday Tone Eight. Matins. Canon. Ode Four)

> Having risen from the grave as if from sleep, thou, O merciful One, didst deliver all from corruption. (Sunday Tone Eight. Matins. Canon. Ode Seven)

The company of angels was amazed seeing thee, O Savior, numbered among the dead. For destroying the power of death, thou didst raise Adam with thyself, setting all men free from Hell. (Resurrectional Troparia at the Evlogitaria)

If the above texts are added to those that say that Christ's victory over Hades meant the abolition of Hades, that after Christ's descent Hades was left empty, since there was not one dead person left, then it becomes clear that the authors of the liturgical texts perceived Christ's descent into Hades as an event of universal character, bearing significance for *all* people without exception. Sometimes the texts refer to this or that category of the dead (for example, "the pious" or "the righteous"), but nowhere do they say that people relating to other categories are left outside the "field of action" of Christ's descent into Hades. Nowhere in the *Octoechos* do we find the notion that Christ preached to the righteous, but left the sinners without his saving message, that he led the holy forefathers out of Hades, but left all others there. Nowhere does it say that anyone was excluded from the Divine Providence of the salvation of the people who were there in death and in the resurrection of the Son of God.

If Christ, descending to Hell, had mercy only on the Old Testament righteous who were awaiting his coming, what exactly made this a miracle? If Christ had freed only the righteous from Hades, leaving the sinners there, at what would the "angelic choir" be amazed? As it says in one of the prayers upon lying down to sleep, ascribed to St John of Damascus, "for to save a righteous man is no great thing, and to have mercy on the pure is nothing wonderful, for they are worthy of thy mercy."[58] If Christ had saved only those to whom salvation belongs by right, this would not have been so much an act of mercy as a fulfillment of obligation, a restoration of justice. "For if thou shouldst save me for my works, this would not be grace or a gift, but rather a duty,"[59] as it says in one of the morning prayers.

It is precisely because liturgical texts return again and again to the theme of Christ's descent into Hades, precisely because church hymnography expresses praise and amazement at this event, that common human concepts of fairness, of retribution, of the fulfillment of debts, of reward for the righteous and punishment for the guilty, are not included. Something

[58]*Kanonnikon*, 283.
[59]Ibid. 298.

extraordinary has happened, something that compelled the angels to tremble and be amazed: Christ descended into Hades, destroyed the "stronghold" and the "gate-posts" of Hell, opened its gates and "blazed a path of
salvation to all," that is he revealed the way to paradise for all the dead—all,
without exception.

It seems that we have a sufficient foundation to assert that "according to
the teaching of almost all the Eastern fathers, the Savior's preaching extended
to all without exception and salvation was offered to all the souls that had
fallen asleep throughout the ages, whether Jews or Greeks, righteous or
unrighteous."[60] Christ preached a message of deliverance and salvation not
only to the righteous, but also to the unrighteous, not a message of "denunciation of unbelievers and wicked," as it seemed to Thomas Aquinas. The
whole context of the First Epistle of the Apostle Peter, where he recounts
Christ's preaching to those in Hades, "speaks against the notion of Christ's
preaching as a kind of condemnation and denunciation."[61]

Another question: did all incline to Christ's preaching, did all follow after
him, were all, in the end, saved? We find a direct answer to this in the liturgical texts. It follows from these texts that the possibility of believing or not
believing in Christ remained with those in Hades and that all those who
believed in him followed him to paradise. But did all believe in him? If the
answer is yes, then truly not one of the dead was left in Hades, then Hell was
truly destroyed, since it was voided of all its prisoners. But if Christ preached
to all, and there were some who did not incline to his preaching, even if he
opened the doors for all, even so these would not have followed him. Therefore, of course, those who wished to remain there by their own free will
would be there still.

---

[60]I. N. Καρμίρις, ῾Η εἰς ἄδου κάθοδος ᾽Ιησοῦ Χριστοῦ (᾽Αθῆναι: 1939), 119.
[61]Grigorii (Yaroschevsky), *Explanation of Difficult Passages in the First Epistle of the Holy Apostle Peter* (Simferopol': 1902), 10.

19

The Resurrection of Christ

I N THE ANCIENT CHURCH, Holy Friday—the day dedicated to the remembrance of the suffering and death on the cross of Jesus Christ—is called "Passover crucifixion," in contrast to the "Passover resurrection" that is celebrated on the "day of the sun." The link connecting the two Passovers—the crucifixion and resurrection—was Holy Saturday, the day of remembrance of Christ's descent into Hades. The image of Christ being crucified, dying, and descending into Hell was inseparable from the image of Christ resurrected in the consciousness of early Christians. All three events—the crucifixion on the cross, the descent into Hades, and the resurrection—were perceived as links on one chain, as steps of the one divine saving plan of salvation. For this reason all three themes are interwoven in the theological treatises of the Eastern fathers and in the liturgical texts of the Orthodox Church, and it is practically impossible to separate them.

The life and witness of the first Christians were permeated by paschal joy and the knowledge of the central meaning of Christ's resurrection for the salvation of mankind. The Orthodox Church preserves this joy and this knowledge until the day to which the whole liturgical structure witnesses, oriented to Christ's resurrection, and not his nativity or any other kind of feast day. If the feast of Christ's nativity acquired significance in Western Christianity as the main feast day in the ecclesial year, then in the East the "Feast of feasts" has always been Pascha, the celebratory victory over death by Christ who was resurrected from the dead, resurrecting the whole race of man with himself.

Christ's resurrection was such an indisputable fact for early Christians and there was such deep meaning associated with this event, that the Apostle Paul could, without hesitation, say to the addressees of his epistles: "If Christ be not risen, then our preaching is vain, and your faith also is vain" (1 Cor 15.14). The whole apostolic preaching was built on the witness of Christ's resurrection—a witness that was so surprising that the apostles said concerning it: "We

Christ appearing to the Myrrh-Bearing Women. Miniature. Novgorodian Chludov Psalter. 14th c.

have seen with our eyes," that "which we have looked upon and our hands have handled" (1 Jn 1.1).

And though not one of the apostles saw the very moment of Christ's resurrection, they all saw the risen Christ, who repeatedly appeared to them, strengthening them in faith. Even those who did not see the risen Christ with their physical eyes, like the Apostle Paul and all the subsequent generations of Christians, for instance, saw his resurrection with the eyes of the soul, and their confidence in Christ's resurrection was as strong as that of the apostles.

The Church has preserved indubitable and unshakeable faith in Christ's resurrection to this day. On the night of holy Pascha, and on every day of resurrection throughout the course of the year, the Orthodox Church sings the song: "Having beheld the resurrection of Christ, let us worship the Holy Lord Jesus." Developing the idea behind this church hymn, Symeon the New Theologian asks: why do we not sing "having believed in the resurrection of Christ," but rather "having beheld the resurrection of Christ," since not one of us was a witness of Christ's resurrection, while in fact there was not one witness at the very moment of the resurrection? Does the Church really teach us to lie? No, answers Symeon, it "implores us to speak the truth—that Christ's resurrection comes to pass in each of us, bearing garments of light and shining lightning bolts of immortality and divinity. For the illuminating coming of the Spirit shows us . . . the resurrection of the Master, or even more precisely, it allows us to see his resurrection itself."[1]

Belief in Christ's resurrection, according to the teaching of the Apostle Paul, is a necessary condition for salvation: "That if you confess with your mouth that the Lord Jesus and believe in your heart that God has raised him from the dead, you will be saved" (Rom 10.9). Characteristically, it is said in the Epistles of the Apostle Paul that "God raised" Christ (1 Cor 6.14; 2 Cor 4.14; Col 2.12), and that "Christ has been raised from the dead" (1 Cor 15.20): these two phrases are synonymous for the apostle. In his perception the

---

[1] *Catechetical Oration 13* 105–116.

redemptive act of the Son is inseparable from the grace of God the Father, who in his unspeakable love for mankind gave his Son up to crucifixion and raised him, in order to reveal the path to resurrection for all.

The Apostle Paul emphasizes that the Son of God suffered, died, and rose "for our justification" (Rom 4.25), "a ransom for all" (1 Tim 2.6); the Son of God "became the author of eternal salvation to all those who obey him" (Heb 5.9). This justification, ransom, and salvation occur by acceptance of baptism, through which man becomes a co-struggler of the passion, death, and resurrection of Christ:

> Buried with him in baptism, you are also risen with him through the faith in the operation of God, who has raised him from the dead (Col 2.12).

> Do you not know, that as many of us as were baptized into Jesus Christ were baptized into his death? Therefore we are buried with him by baptism into death: that just as Christ was raised up from the dead by the glory of the Father, even so we also should walk in newness of life. For if we have been planted together in the likeness of his death, we shall be also in the likeness of his resurrection: Knowing this, that our old man is crucified with him, that the body of sin might be destroyed, that henceforth we should not serve sin. For he that is dead is freed from sin. Now if we be dead with Christ, we believe that we shall also live with him: Knowing that Christ, being raised from the dead, dieth no more; death hath no more dominion over him. For in that he died, he died unto sin once: but in that he liveth, he liveth to God. (Rom 6.3–10)

The unbroken link between Christ's resurrection and the baptism "into Christ's death" was expressed in the ancient Church on Holy Saturday, which was the main baptismal day of the year: on precisely this day, the catechumens were brought to the sacrament of baptism. To this day the Holy Saturday and Paschal services of the Orthodox Church follow in the footsteps of this ancient practice.

The link between Christ's resurrection and baptism is also expressed in one of those Old Testament images that the Church perceives to be a foreshadowing of this and another event. Since Christ's crucifixion coincided with the time of the Jewish Passover, the feast of the unleavened bread, dedicated to the remembrance of Israel's exodus from Egypt, this Old Testament event was accepted as a prefiguring of Christ's resurrection. The sacrifice of the Passover lamb symbolized the Savior's death on the cross; the crossing of the Red Sea, the conversion from the sinful way of life to "newness of life" (Rom 6.4); and the eating of the unleavened bread, the purification from the bitterness of sin and a return to a new yeast, "for even Christ our passover is sacrificed for us" (1 Cor 5.7). At the same time, the people of Israel's crossing of the Red Sea was interpreted as a prototype of the sacrament of baptism.

All of this rich typology was developed in patristic works and the liturgical services of the Orthodox Church. It seems important to consider a few theological and liturgical texts in which the Orthodox teaching on Christ's resurrection is expressed to the fullest extent. All of these texts were accepted by the Church in the capacity of classics: they were fulfilled or continue to be fulfilled by the liturgy on the paschal days. The question now is on the poem *On Pascha* by the holy martyr Melito of Sardis, *Oration on Holy Pascha* (*Oration 45*) by St Gregory the Theologian, and the *Catechetical Homily on Holy Pascha* by St John Chrysostom.

Melito of Sardis' poem *On Pascha* has already been cited above. This poetic narrative of a second century author presents itself as an expansive paschal homily, read at the liturgy immediately after the reading from the book of Exodus, dedicated to Israel's exodus from Egypt. Above all, Melito covers the foreshadowing concept of the Old Testament Passover in detail:

> Therefore, well-beloved, understand,
> how the mystery of the Pascha
> is both new and old,
> eternal and provisional,
> perishable and imperishable,
> mortal and immortal.
> It is old with respect to the law,
> new with respect to the word.
> Provisional with respect to the type,
> yet everlasting through grace.
> It is perishable because of the life of the Lord.
> It is mortal because of the burial in the ground,
> immortal because of the resurrection from the dead.
> For the law is old,

> but the word is new.
> The type is provisional,
> but grace is everlasting.
> The sheep is perishable,
> but the Lord,
> not broken as a lamb but raised up as God,
> is imperishable.
> For though led to the slaughter like a sheep,
> he was no sheep.
> Though speechless like a lamb,
> neither yet was he a lamb.
> For there was once a type, but now the reality has appeared.
> For instead of the lamb there was a son,
> and instead of the sheep, a man;
> in the man was Christ encompassing all things.[2]

Pay attention to the strong confidence of the second century writer that the resurrected Christ was God. We remember that the Apostle Paul never called Jesus Christ God, addressing the name "God" to the Father, and the name "Lord" to the Son. However, already in the second century, especially in the context of the development of the Gnostic heresies, the assertion that he who was resurrected from the dead, Christ, was God, becomes a most important point in Christian preaching:

> For the law was a word,
> and the old was new . . .
> and the commandment was grace,
> and the type was a reality,
> and the lamb was a son,
> and the sheep was a man,
> and the man was God.
> For he was born a son,
> and led as a lamb,
> and slaughtered as a sheep,
> and buried as a man,

[2]2–5 (2001), 37–38.

Christ the Lamb. Church of
San Vitale. Ravenna. 6th c.

and rose from the dead as God,
being God by his nature and a man. . . .

He is human in that he is buried.
He is God, in that he is raised up.[3]

Further on Melito recounts the story of the
Egyptian captivity and Israel's exodus from the land
of Egypt in great detail, seeing in these events the
prefiguring of the New Testament Passover—the passion, death, and resurrection of Christ. Melito treats
the very word "Pascha," coming from a calque of the
Hebrew word *pesach* (to pass over), as coming from the word *paschein*/πάσχειν
(to suffer).[4] Such an etymology became widely accepted in Greek patristics.

The narrative on Israel's exodus from Egypt turns into a story of Old Testament prophets awaiting the coming of the Savior. Further, Melito of Sardis
speaks of the redemptive act of Jesus Christ, emphasizing that God himself
was slain on the cross by the Jews (this fragment was quoted above). All of
Christ's earthly life—from the nativity to the crucifixion and resurrection—is
considered by the author of the poem as a single mystery of the Lord,[5] foreshadowed by the events of the Old Testament. Christ became incarnate, suffered, died, and rose from the dead for the sake of our salvation, and for this
reason he is "the Pascha of our salvation":

> This is the one who delivered us from slavery to freedom,
> from darkness into light,
> from death into life,
> from tyranny into an eternal Kingdom,
> and made us a new priesthood,
> and a people everlasting for himself.
> This is the Pascha of our salvation. . . .
> This is the one made flesh in a virgin,
> who was hanged upon a tree,
> who was buried in the earth,
> who was raised from the dead,

[3]7–9 (2001), 38–39.
[4]Cf.: Ibid. 48.
[5]Cf.: Ibid. 58–59.

who was exalted to the heights of heaven.
This is the lamb slain,
this is the speechless lamb,
this is the one born of Mary the fair ewe,
this is the one taken from the flock,
and led to the slaughter.
Who was sacrificed in the evening,
and buried at night;
who was not broken on the tree,
who was not undone in the earth,
who rose from the dead and resurrected humankind from the
grave below.[6]

The concluding verses of the poem contain Christ's monologue, addressed to mankind. Christ, in this monologue, appears as the Victor over Hades and death, as the Redeemer of mankind, granting remission of sins and life eternal:

I set free the condemned.
I gave life to the dead.
I raise up the entombed. . . .
I am he who destroys death,
and triumphs over the enemy,
and crushes Hades,
and binds the strong man,
and bears humanity off to heavenly heights. . . .
So come all families of people,
adulterated with sin,
and receive forgiveness of sins.
For I am your freedom.
I am the Passover of salvation,
I am the lamb slaughtered for you,
I am your ransom,
I am your life,
I am your light,

---

[6]Ibid. 68–71 (2001), 55–56.

I am your salvation,
I am your resurrection,
I am your King.
I shall raise you up by my right hand,
I will lead you to the heights of heaven,
there I shall show you the everlasting Father.[7]

Melito of Sardis' poem turned out to be a great influence on the later development of the Eastern Christian teaching of Christ's resurrection. Its influence can be felt in Gregory the Theologian's *Oration on Holy Pascha*—a work that the Orthodox *Typikon* prescribes to be read at the Paschal Liturgy. This *Oration* is built on the juxtaposition of the Old Testament Passover as a recollection of the crossing of the Red Sea and the New Testament Passover as the celebration of Christ's resurrection. All of the details of the Old Testament Passover are treated by Gregory as foreshadows of the New Testament reality: in this treatise, Gregory follows a tradition that had already taken shape, which reflects Melito of Sardis especially.

The Paschal *Oration* of St Gregory begins with a symbolic description of the vision of the angel, proclaiming Christ's resurrection:

"I will stand on my watch," says the wondrous Habakkuk (Hab 2.1); and I also will stand with him today, by the authority and vision given me by the Spirit, and I will look steadily and observe what will be seen and what will be spoken to me. I have stood and looked steadily, and behold a man mounted upon the clouds, and he was very exalted; and his appearance was like the brightness of an angel (Judg 13.6); and his raiment was like the brightness of lightning; and he was lifting up his hand toward the East and shouting in a great voice. . . . And he said, "Today salvation has come to the world, to things visible and to things invisible. Christ is risen from the dead; rise with him. Christ has returned to himself; return. Christ is freed from the tomb; be freed from the bonds of sin. The gates of Hades are opened, and death is destroyed, and the old Adam is put aside, and the new is fulfilled. If anyone in Christ is a new creation (2 Cor 5.17), be made new."[8]

---

[7]Ibid. 101–103 (2001), 65–66.
[8]1 (Crestwood, NY: 2008), 161.

Gregory speaks of Pascha as the main event of the church year, surpassing all other feasts by its significance. Pascha, just like the Lord's theophany, is a feast of light, which is symbolized by the lighting of candles throughout the whole city on Pascha night:

> The Lord's Pascha, Pascha, and again I will say Pascha, to the honor of the Trinity. It is to us the feast of feasts and the festival of festivals, as far exalted above all—not only for those who are merely human and crawl on the ground but also those who are of Christ himself and are celebrated for him—as the sun is above the stars. Beautiful indeed yesterday[9] were our splendid array and procession of lights, in which we were united both privately and publicly, almost every sort of people and every rank, lighting up the night with plentiful fires. This is a symbol of the great light, both the heavenly light that makes fires from above . . . and equally the light above the heavens . . . in the Trinity, by which every light has been produced, divided off from the undivided light and honored. Yet today is more beautiful and more illustrious, inasmuch as yesterday's light was a forerunner of the great light's rising, and as it were a kind of pre-festal gladness. But today we celebrate the resurrection itself, not as still hoped for but as having already occurred and gathering the whole world to itself.[10]

Having briefly laid out the foundation of the dogma of the Christian faith—on the Trinity, on the creation of the world, on the angels and demons, on the Fall and the incarnation—Gregory completes the etymological excursus "for the lover of science and grace." The word "pascha," he says, means "to pass over" in the Hebrew language: the historical term indicates the flight of the people of Israel from the land of Egypt, but spiritually it is the "passover and ascent from the earthly to the lofty and to the Promised Land." In the Greek language, the word *pascha* is homophonous to the verb *pascho*/πάσχω ("to suffer").[11] Gregory, following after Melito of

Assuring the Apostle Thomas.
Cathedral of Monreale.
Sicily. 12th c.

[9]"Yesterday," that is during the night between Holy Friday and Holy Saturday.
[10]*Oration 45* 2 (2008), 162.
[11]Ibid. 10.

Sardis, sees in this a pointing to Christ's passion, foreshadowed by the sacrificial Passover lamb in the Old Testament.

Speaking on the sacrificial Passover lamb, Gregory the Theologian notes that, according to the law, the lamb ought to be "whole,"[12] symbolizing Christ's wholeness in divinity and humanity; "of the male sex," because it is offered for the whole Adam and because "he bears nothing female, nothing unmanly, in himself"; "one year old" like the Sun of righteousness;[13] without spot and blameless, as the healer of faults and of the damage and defilement coming from evil.[14] The lamb is eaten at evening because Christ's suffering occurred at the end of ages; the lamb should not be boiled, but roasted over the fire, "that our word may have nothing unexamined, nothing watery, nothing easily dissolved, but be entirely firm and solid, and tested by purifying fire"; the lamb should not be left until morning, "because the majority of our mysteries are not carried out to those outside."[15] The lamb is eaten with unleavened bread, since it is impermissible in the Christian life to linger and look back as did Lot's wife (Gen 19.26); with bitter herbs, "because life in accord with God is bitter and arduous"; with a staff in hand, "lest perhaps [we] become forgetful in thought when [we] hear of the blood of God, and his passion, and his death, lest perhaps [we] waver in an ungodly manner when advocating for God. But without shame and without hesitation [we] eat his body and drink his blood . . . neither disbelieving the words about the flesh nor hindered by those about the passion."[16]

A similar type of display of allegorical interpretation of the Old Testament texts is highly characteristic of Clement, Origen, and other representatives of the Alexandrian tradition. The Old Testament only foreshadows the "mysteries" of the New Testament and leads to a better understanding of them. In this sense, the paschal festival of the Christians is a crossing over from the Old Testament to the New, from the Passover of those under the law to the Christian Passover; it is the ascent from earth to heaven, from the earthly to the lofty. But the Christian Passover itself, accomplished in us on earth, is

[12]Cf.: Ex 12.5 ff.
[13]Since the sun completes a full cycle over the course of one year.
[14]Cf.: Gregory the Theologian *Oration 45* 13 (2008), 172–173.
[15]An allusion to the existence of the concept of the "secret teaching" (*disciplina arcana*) in the ancient Church, indicating the impermissible disclosure of the meaning of the Eucharist and other sacraments to non-Christians.
[16]Gregory the Theologian *Oration 45* 16–19 (2008), 175–180.

only a prefiguring of the perpetual Passover, the festival in which the believers in the Kingdom of God participate:

> Such is the feast you are celebrating today. . . . May the mystery of Pascha be such for you. These things the law sketched beforehand; these things Christ fulfilled, the dissolver of the letter, the perfector of the Spirit. . . . "Death, where is your sting? Hades, where is your victory (1 Cor 15.55)?" By the cross you have been overthrown, by the giver of life you have been put to death. You are without breath, dead, motionless, without activity. . . . Now we will participate in a Pascha that is still a type even if more clearly unveiled than the old one, for the Pascha under law, I boldly declare, was a more indistinct type of a type. But a little later, our participation will be more perfect and more pure; when the Word drinks anew with us in the Kingdom of the Father (Mt 26.29), he will reveal and teach that which now he has shown in a limited way.[17]

How does the participation of the faithful occur in the paschal majesty? Through co-participation in Christ's sufferings, through co-survival with those heroes of the gospel stories who are remembered in the accounts of the last days of Jesus' earthly life:

> If you are Simon of Cyrene, take up the cross and follow. If you are crucified with him as a thief, come to know God as kind-hearted. . . . Worship the one hanged for you even if you are hanging. . . . If you are Joseph from Arimathea, ask for the body from the crucifier; let that which cleanses the world become yours. And if you are Nicodemus, the nocturnal worshipper of God, bury him with scented ointments. And if you are a certain Mary or another Mary or Salome or Joanna, weep at daybreak. Be first to see the stone removed, and perhaps the angels and Jesus himself. . . . Become Peter or John; hasten to the tomb. . . . If he descends into Hades, go down with him.[18]

Gregory the Theologian's *Oration on Holy Pascha* has so firmly entered into church tradition that many of its phrases have been borrowed by authors of liturgical texts dedicated to Christ's resurrection. One such text is John of Damascus' "Paschal Canon," which the Orthodox Church uses at Paschal Matins.

[17]Ibid. 21–23 (2008), 181–183.
[18]Ibid. 24, 184–185.

The "Paschal Canon" speaks of Christ's resurrection as the fulfillment of the Old Testament foreshadowings.[19] The Passover lamb is the main one of these foreshadowings, symbolizing the Savior's sacrifice on the cross. However, as John of Damascus emphasizes, Christ was not offered to the Father involuntarily, but "was willingly sacrificed for us all,"[20] "he offered himself willingly to the Father."[21]

The Paschal Canon speaks of Christ's resurrection from an eschatological perspective. Christ's resurrection, according to the author of the canon, prefigures the general resurrection. Pascha night, moreover, is the foreshadow of the bright, shining day of the Kingdom of God, in which believers will communicate with God "more truly"–that is, more fully, more completely than in earthly life.

The last of the texts dedicated to Christ's resurrection that we need to consider is the *Catechetical Oration on Holy Pascha,*[22] attributed to John Chrysostom. This text is read at the liturgy on Pascha night and is an exposition in condensed form of the Orthodox teaching on Christ's resurrection. Christ's victory over Hades and death is the main theme of Chrysostom's *Oration,* which is expressed with special poetic clarity and theological persuasiveness:

Let no one fear death, for the Savior's death has set us free. He that was held prisoner of it has annihilated it. By descending into Hell, he made Hell captive. He embittered it when it tasted of his flesh. And Isaiah, foretelling this, did cry: Hell, said he, was embittered, when it encountered thee in the lower regions. It was embittered, for it was abolished. It was embittered, for it was overthrown. It was embittered, for it was fettered in chains. It took a body, and met God face to face. It took earth, and encountered Heaven. It took that which was seen, and fell upon the unseen. O Death, where is your sting? O Hell, where is your victory? Christ is risen, and you are overthrown. Christ is risen, and the demons are fallen. Christ is risen, and the angels rejoice. Christ is risen, and life reigns. Christ is risen, and not one dead remains in the grave.[23]

[19] Cf.: Paschal Matins. Canon. Ode Four: "Seeing the fulfillment of the figures."
[20] Paschal Matins. Canon. Ode Four.
[21] Ibid. Ode Six.
[22] The *Oration* was an inseparable part of the Paschal Liturgy already by the time of Theodore the Studite (eighth century); see I. Mansvetov, *The Book of Church Order (Typikon): Its Formation and Fate in the Greek and Russian Churches* (Moscow: 1885), 105.
[23] John Chrysostom *Catechetical Oration on Holy Pascha.*

There is an allusion contained in the cited excerpt above of the theory of the "divine deception," formulated by Gregory of Nyssa: Hades was deceived, having accepted Christ as a mere man, but it "swallowed up" God himself. Moreover, the notion of the final descent into Hell and the fall of the demons is expressed in the *Oration*, as well as the idea that there was not one dead person left there after Christ's resurrection: this notion had already existed in the *Gospel of Nicodemus*.[24] However the Synaxarion, prescribed to be read at Paschal Matins after Ode Six of John of Damscus' Paschal Canon,[25] offers the following explanation in terms of what happened at Christ's resurrection:

> Now, having stolen all of human nature from the stronghold of Hades, Christ led it up to Heaven and brought it to its original state of incorruptibility. However, descending, he did not raise up all, but only those who wished to believe in him. He granted all the souls of the saints, held by the power of Hades for ages past, to be freed and to enter into Heaven.[26]

The author of the Synaxarion repeats the notion that we already encountered in examining the theme of the descent into Hades: Christ descended in order to redeem all people ("all of human nature"), but those whom he resurrected were those who "wished to believe in him." Christ did not force anyone to stay in Hell, but he did not save anyone by force: the deciding role in the fate of every person found in Hades was played by each person's own free will, each person's desire or refusal to follow after Christ on the path to salvation and deification.

---

[24]Cf.: *Gospel of Nicodemus* 23.
[25]The author of the Synaxarion is Nicephorus Callistus (fourteenth century).
[26]Paschal Matins. Synaxarion.

20

Salvation as Deification

T HROUGHOUT THE COURSE OF THIS BOOK we have already dealt repeatedly with the themes and terminologies of deification. In the end of the section dedicated to Orthodox Christology, it will be necessary to consider this theme in greater detail, since it is precisely the teaching on deification that contains the main peculiarities of Orthodox Christology and soteriology.

The term "deification" is not found in the Holy Scriptures and bears little meaning for modern man. Much clearer and much more widely used is the traditional Christian term "salvation." This term indicates salvation *from* something: from sin, from the power of the devil, from death and Hell. "Salvation" is the antonym of "downfall," of "death." However, in the Eastern Christian tradition salvation is perceived not only as the correction of the consequences of the Fall, as freedom from the power of the devil, but above all as the realization of that goal to which man was called by being formed in the image and likeness of God. The Eastern fathers used the term "deification" to describe this goal and the means by which it is achieved. The foundation of the teaching on deification is no different from that of the teaching on salvation, only it is expressed in the rhetoric of Eastern Christian theology.

The Lord's transfiguration. Miniature. Thessalonika. 13th c.

The theme of deification has been a central point of the theology, asceticism, and mysticism of the Orthodox East over the course of almost two thousand years, up to the present times. As the holy martyr Hilarion (Troitsky) says, "The Church then and now lives by the ideal of deification, by which it lived in antiquity and for which its theologians and teachers have worked even to the shedding of their blood."[1]

[1]Hilarion (Troitsky), *The Cornerstone of the Church: Works, vol.* 2 (Moscow: 2004), 275.

The theme of deification grows from the roots of the New Testament teaching that people are called to become "partakers of the divine nature" (2 Pet 1.4). At the foundation of the Greek fathers' teaching on deification lie Christ's words as well, by which he called people "gods" (Jn 10.34; Ps 82.6); also the words of John the Theologian on God's adoption of people (Jn 1.12) and the divine image in man (1 Jn 3.2); many texts of the Apostle Paul, in which the biblical teaching on the image and likeness of God in man is examined (Rom 8.29; 1 Cor 5.49; 2 Cor 3.18; Col 3.10); the teaching of God's adoption of people (Gal 3.26, 4.5); and the teaching on man as a divine temple (1 Cor 3.16). The eschatological vision of the Apostle Paul is characterized in terms of the exalted state of humanity after the resurrection, when mankind will be transfigured and raised up by its Head—Christ (Rom 8.18–23; Eph 1.10) and when God will be "all in all" (1 Cor 15.28).

These New Testament ideas received their development from the theologians of the second century. Ignatius of Antioch calls Christians "God bearers"[2] and speaks of their oneness with God, of their partaking of him.[3] We find in Irenaeus of Lyons a formula emphasizing the interrelationship between the likening of God to man in the incarnation and the likening of man to God. The following phrases of Irenaeus lie at the basis of the teaching of deification:

[The Word of God] did, through his transcendent love, become what we are, that he might bring us to be even what he is himself.[4]

For it was for this end that the Word of God was made man, and he who was the Son of God became the Son of man, that man, having been taken into the Word, and receiving the adoption, might become the son of God.[5]

The claim that man becomes god through the incarnation of the Word of God is the cornerstone of the teaching on deification of the subsequent Fathers of the Church. Terminologically, this teaching was developed by theologians of the Alexandrian tradition—Clement, Origen, and Athanasius the Great.

[2] *Epistle to the Ephesians* 9.2.
[3] Ibid. 4.2.
[4] *Against Heresies 5*. Preface.
[5] Ibid. 3 19.1.

The verb *theopoieō*/θεοποιέω ("to make like god," "to deify") is first found in Clement: "The Word deifies man by his heavenly teaching."[6] Clement understands this deification as a moral accomplishment: in his perfect state man becomes "god-seeing and godlike."[7] According to Clement's teaching, we should "always be preoccupied with the heavenly life while here on earth, in which we will one day be deified."[8] Clement considers deification from an eschatological perspective: "Of those who in their proximity to God were pure in heart, await the ascent (into worthiness of adoption) through contemplation of the Invisible One. They will be named gods and co-servitors of those whom the Savior previously numbered among the divine."[9]

The teaching on deification is fully supported in patristic theology by the time of the anti-Arian polemic of the fourth century. Contained in Athanasius is the classic formula expressing the deification of man: "[The Word] became man that we may become God."[10] In another place Athanasius says of Christ: "For he has become man, that he might deify us in himself."[11] For Athanasius, as for the other fathers of the age of the ecumenical councils, the only basis of the deification of man is the incarnation of the Word of God. Athanasius emphasizes the ontological difference between, on the one hand, our adoption by God and deification and, on the other hand, the sonship and divinity of Christ: in the final deification "We too become sons, not as he in nature and truth, but according to the grace of him that calleth."[12]

The idea of deification is present in the works of the great Cappadocian Fathers. Gregory the Theologian put into Basil the Great's mouth the following famous words: "[I cannot], who am the creature of God, and bidden myself to be God, submit to worship any creature."[13] According to Gregory's witness, Basil spoke these words to the prefect of Caesarea in Cappadocia, who demanded that he submit to the emperor and accept the Arian teaching on the Trinity.

The theme of deification occupies a central place in Gregory the Theologian, which has been preserved after him for the course of the whole history

---

[6] *Exhortation to the Heathen* 11.
[7] *Stromata* 6.9.
[8] *Pedagogue* 1.12.
[9] *Stromata* 7.10.
[10] *On the Incarnation* 54.2.
[11] *To Adelphius* 4.
[12] *Against the Arians III* 19.
[13] Gregory the Theologian *Oration* 43 48.

of Byzantine theology. Not one Christian theologian before Gregory used the term deification (*theōsis*/θεώσις) so frequently and consistently as he did; terminologically and consistently, he went far beyond his predecessors in constant use of the term deification.[14]

Already in his first published exposition, the themes of the divine image, adoption by Christ, the adoption by God and deification of man in Christ, become foundational:

> Let us give back to the Image that which is according to the image, recognizing our value, honoring the Archetype, knowing the power of the mystery[15] and for whom Christ died. Let us become like Christ, since Christ also became like us; let us become gods because of him, since he also because of us became human. He assumed what is worse that he might give what is better. He became poor that we through his poverty might become rich. He took the form of a slave, that we might regain freedom. He descended that we might be lifted up, he was tempted that we might be victorious, he was dishonored to glorify us, he died to save us. . . . Let us give everything, offer everything, to the one who gave himself as a ransom and an exchange for us. But one can give nothing comparable to oneself, understanding the mystery and becoming because of him everything that he became because of us.[16]

Gregory says in another place that the goal of the incarnation was "to make man god and a partaker of the higher blessings."[17] Christ deified man by his sufferings, having combined the human image with the heavenly.[18] The leaven of deification made human flesh "a new vintage," and the nous, having taken this leaven into itself, "was combined with God, becoming deified through divinity."[19]

The formulae of Irenaeus and Athanasius arise in Gregory's poetry and prose in various modifications:

[14]Cf.: D. Winslow, *The Dynamics of Salvation: A Study in Gregory of Nazianzus* (Philadelphia: 1979), 179.

[15]In this case the feast of Pascha is understood by "mystery."

[16]Gregory the Theologian, *Oration 1* 4–5 (2008), 58–59.

[17]*Oration 2* 22.

[18]Cf.: *Autobiographical Poems 33: To Christ*.

[19]*Letter 101: The First to Cledonius*.

Being God, you became man, having combined yourself with mortality; you were God from before the ages, but afterwards became man in order to make me god after your becoming man.[20]

[Christ] made me god through his human [nature].[21]

[The Word] was God, but became man like us, so that having mingled himself with earthly things, he might unite us to God.[22]

Even at this moment [the Word] is, as man, making representation for my salvation, until he makes me divine by the power of his incarnate manhood.[23]

The Christ child in the manger. Bas-relief. Byzantine museum. Athens. 5th c.

Since man did not become god, God himself became man . . . in order to reconstruct by means of that which he assumed, to destroy the condemnation of sin, and to mortify mortality by becoming the Mortal One.[24]

Compared with his predecessors, Gregory went quite far in his development of the theme of deification. As in Irenaeus and Athanasius, deification was for Gregory linked to the incarnation. However, Gregory makes an essential elaboration to Athanasius' formula: man becomes god "only to the extent to which" God became man: "Man and God blended. They became a single whole, the stronger side predominating, in order that I might be made God to the same extent that he was made man."[25]

Therefore, a direct link is established not only between God's incarnation and man's deification, but also the *measure* to which God became man and man becomes god. Gregory makes this precision in opposition to the heresy of Apollinarius: if God did not become *fully* human, then man cannot become *fully* god. In one of the poems directed against Apollinarius, Gregory

[20] *Autobiographical Poems 1: Verses on Myself.*
[21] *Moral Verses 13: On the Same.*
[22] *Dogmatic Verses 11: On the Incarnation.*
[23] *Oration 30 14* (2002), 105.
[24] *Dogmatic Verses 10: Against Apollinarius, on the Incarnation.*
[25] *Oration 29 19* (2002), 86.

goes even further and places the incarnation in direct dependence on man's deification: "God became man only insofar as he makes me god from man."[26] The belief in the fullness of Christ's human nature, therefore, presupposes belief in the deification of the entire person, consisting of mind, soul, and body; and vice versa, the idea of deification presupposes faith in Christ as a complete person with mind, soul, and body.

The teaching on the participation of the body in deification is one of the fundamental differences in the Christian idea of deification from its Neo-Platonic duality—the idea of Plotinus on man's striving to become god.[27] In Plotinus' philosophy, the deification of the body is impossible: matter will always remain evil and adversarial to all that is divine. Gregory, on the contrary, asserts that the flesh was deified in Christ by the Spirit: the incarnate God "is united out of two opposites—flesh and spirit, of which one deifies, and the other is deified."[28] Therefore, the body of every person that has attained deification in Christ becomes transfigured and deified as well:

Christ brings me to God in majestic escort by the narrow and difficult path, through the closed gates, impassable for most—god, formed from the earth for, but not begotten of, me, who by death became immortal.

Together with the great image of God[29] he draws in a body, my helper, As a stone magnet tugs at black iron.[30]

The idea of deification permeates Gregory the Theologian's teaching on the Church and the sacraments, its moral and ascetic teaching. According to his words, man's deification occurs in the Church thanks to participation in the sacraments of baptism and the Eucharist. In baptism, man is raised and elevated by the deifying action of the Holy Spirit: "[The Spirit] deif[ies] me through baptism. . . . From the Spirit comes our rebirth, from rebirth comes a new creating. . . . He makes us his temple, he deifies, he makes us complete, and he initiates us in such a way that he both precedes baptism and is wanted after it."[31] In the Eucharist we "partake of Christ, of his sufferings and his

---

[26]*Dogmatic Verses 11: On the Incarnation.*
[27]Cf.: Plotinus *Enneads 1* 2.6: "The intent of man is not only to be without sin, but to be god."
[28]Gregory the Theologian *Oration 45* 9.
[29]With a soul.
[30]Gregory the Theologian *Autobiographical Poems 1: Verses on Myself.*
[31]*Oration 31* 28–29 (2002), 139–140.

divinity."[32] If baptism cleanses man of Original Sin, then the Eucharist makes a person a partaker of Christ's redemptive feat:

> Christ became the direct mediator for two peoples—one far away,
> The other close by,[33]—since he was the common cornerstone for
>   both—
> And he granted a twofold purification to the dead—
> One of the eternal Spirit, through whom is purified in me that
>   injury
> Born in the flesh from of old; another to our blood.
> For my blood is that which Christ emptied, my God,
> For the remission of the passions of the ancestors and for the
> Deliverance of the world.
> Is it not as if I am now not a fickle man, but firm,
> So then only the commandment of the great God was necessary,
> Which kidnapped me, saved me, and led me to greater glory.
> Now though, since God did not make me god,
> But placed in equal weight those who are inclined (either to good,
>   or to evil),
> For this reason he supports me by means of many things,
> One of which is the grace of ablution for the people.[34]

Deification, according to Gregory, occurs thanks to the love man has for God. In his words, "love for God is the path to deification."[35] Union with God is the pinnacle of this way, which is deification: "I am Christ's inheritance; I became the temple and sacrifice, but afterwards I will be god, when my soul is combined with God."[36]

The path to deification lies in active good deeds as well: "If you want to be god, show that you do good, and not evil, by your actions."[37] Doing good is reminiscent of God: being merciful and loving, the superior can become god for the subordinate, the rich for the poor, the healthy for the sick. "Divinity itself is within man—that with which he can do good. . . . Do not neglect

---

[32] *Oration 4 52.*
[33] For the Gentiles and the Jews.
[34] *Dogmatic Verses 9: On the Covenants and Christ's Manifestation.*
[35] *Moral Verses 34.*
[36] *Autobiographical Poems 54: On the Evil One.*
[37] *Moral Verses 33: Thoughts Written in a Quatrain.*

the opportunity for deification."[38] Deification is not only an intellectual ascent; all of Christian life should become a path to deification through the fulfillment of the gospel commandments: "Proclaim rather life than thought. The first deifies, but the second can become the reason for a great fall. Do not make life commensurate with insignificant [things], for even if you ascend those heights, you will still remain below [those things demanded by] the commandments [of God]."[39]

The path to deification, finally, lies through prayer, ascetical struggles, and mystical experience, through the mind's ascent to God, appearing before God in prayerful contemplation. "What do you want to become?' Gregory addresses his soul. 'Would you like to become god, a god standing brilliantly before the great God, singing with the angels? Or going on ahead, spreading your wings and ascending to the heights?"[40] Man, through prayer and the cleansing of the mind, acquires the experience of partial knowledge of God, which becomes even fuller upon approaching the goal—deification:

> The divine draws [us] toward itself, for what is completely ungraspable is unhoped for and unsought. Yet one wonders at the ungraspable, and one desires more intensely the object of wonder, and being desired it purifies, and purifying it makes deiform, and with those who have become such he converses as with those close to him,—I speak with vehement bold-ness—God is united with gods, and he is thus known, perhaps as much as he already knows those who are known to him (1 Cor 13.12).[41]

Ephraim the Syrian developed the concept of deification in the Syrian tradition. According to his words, God, having become man, imbued in him the capability of being "perfect god."[42] Since man turned out to be in no con-dition to fulfill that which was predestined for him, God became incarnate: "The Highest knew that Adam wanted to become god, for this reason he sent his Son . . . in order to grant him the fulfillment of that wish."[43] Ephraim speaks of the "exchange" between God and man in phrases that make one

[38] *Oration 17* 9.
[39] *Moral Verses 33: Thoughts Written in a Quatrain.*
[40] *Autobiographical Poems 88: Iambic Verses to my Soul.*
[41] *Oration 38* 7 (2008), 65.
[42] *Words on Faith* 3.31–32.
[43] *Nisibene Hymn* 69.12.

recall Athanasius' formula of deification: "He granted us divinity; we gave him humanity."[44]

The traditional teaching of the Orthodox East on deification is also widely presented in ascetical literature. Following after Athanasius the Great, Mark the Ascetic says: "God . . . became what we are in order to make us what he is."[45] Diadochus of Photiki advances the following idea in one of his sermons: that which pertains to the incarnate God in his human body, pertains to those who are predestined to become gods, "for God formed people to be gods."[46]

The teaching on deification occupies an important place in the works of Maximus the Confessor. He sees in deification the main destiny and calling of man: "Let us become gods through the Lord, because it is precisely for this reason that man received existence, to be god and lord by nature."[47] Following after Gregory the Theologian, Maximus speaks of the body's participation in deification; when the soul becomes god by co-participating in divine grace, the body is deified along with the soul.[48]

> People wholly participate in the whole God, so that by the form of the soul and the body's union, God makes accessible the soul's participation in him, and by means of the soul and body so that the soul might receive constancy, but the body, immortality, and so that man is wholly made god, deified by God's grace, who had been made man, all–body and soul– remained man in nature, and all–soul and body–becomes god by grace.[49]

Maximus takes as the basis of his understanding of deification the formula of Irenaeus and Athanasius, which he practically repeats: "God the Word, the Son of the God and Father, became man and the Son of Man, so that people might be made gods and sons of God."[50] Stressing the interrelationship between man's deification and God's incarnation, Maximus the Confessor also uses Gregory the Theologian's formula of *tantum-quantum* ("insofar as"):

---

[44] *Hymns on Faith* 5.17.
[45] *Epistle to the Monk Nicholas.*
[46] *Oration on the Ascension* 6.
[47] *Ascetical Oration* 33.
[48] *Chapters on Theology and Oikonomia* 2.88.
[49] *Ambigua.*
[50] *Chapters on Theology and Oikonomia* 2.25.

The hard and true foundation of hope of deification for man's nature is God's incarnation, through which man is made god, in which God himself is made man. For it is manifest that being made man without sin he can deify [human] nature without transforming the divinity, for which reason he called man into himself, for which reason he humbled himself for man's sake.[51]

Moreover, Maximus adds an inverse notion to Gregory the Theologian's formula: God, in his loving kindness, becomes incarnate in the person of Christ and becomes man "insofar as" man is deified and becomes god by love.[52] The interrelationship between the incarnation and deification is emphasized in the following text by Maximus:

Really, the perfect act of love itself predetermines its actions—to allow the individual qualities of those whom it connects . . . to become useful for each other through interrelationship, so that man becomes god, and God is named and is as man.[53]

The theme of deification runs through the liturgical texts of the Orthodox Church,[54] in which the formula of Irenaeus and Athanasius is repeatedly recited:

In order for you to perfect man and make us divine, you, O Christ, became mortal. (Thursday Tone Seven. Vespers. *Sticheron* at "Lord, I Call")

In order to make man god, you, O Lover of Man, became man. (Wednesday Tone Eight. Matins. Canon. Ode Eight)

Today on Mount Tabor Christ changed the darkened nature of Adam, enlightening it and making it god-like. (Transfiguration of the Lord. Little Vespers. *Sticheron* at the *Aposticha*)

Being God the Word, you became all-earthly, blending all of your divinity with human nature in your Hypostasis. (Transfiguration of the Lord. Matins. Second Canon. Ode Three)

---

[51] *Ambigua.*
[52] Cf.: *Ambigua.*
[53] *Epistle 2.*
[54] Cf.: Kiprian (Kern), *Antropologia sv. Grigoriya Palamy* (Moscow: 1996), 394.

Transfiguration of the Lord. The Dark Church in Göreme. Cappadocia. 11th c.

In order to renew Adam, his Creator became incarnate in you O Most Pure One, deifying people. (Sunday. Tone Seven. Nocturns. Canon to the Trinity. Ode Seven. Theotokion)

[You were transfigured] O Christ, making the image that had grown dark in Adam to shine once again like lightning, and transforming it into the glory and splendor of your own Divinity. (Transfiguration of the Lord. Great Vespers. *Sticheron* at the *Aposticha*)

I will be with you in my Kingdom, as God with gods. (Holy Thursday. Canon. Ode Four)

Symeon the New Theologian in particular develops the theme of deification in the late Byzantine period, and it occupies as central a place in him as it does in Gregory the Theologian. It can be said that the idea of deification is at the heart of all the theological thought of Symeon, around which different elements are laid out in a structured system. The teaching of deification influenced the foundations of the theological, anthropological, ecclesiological, ascetical, and mystical ideas of this great Byzantine mystic of the eleventh century.

Symeon almost repeats the formula of Irenaeus and Athanasius word for word when he answers the question "Why did God become man?": "For man to become God."[55] Deification is inseparably linked to the incarnation: this original Christological dimension can be seen in many of Symeon's texts that deal with the question of deification:

> God wants to make gods out of us people. . . . God wants this so badly that . . . leaving the bosom of his blessed Father, he descended and came to earth for our sake.[56]

> I am God become man for your sake, and behold, as you see, I made you god and will so do.[57]

> Christ . . . descended to earth and became man, taking for himself earthly flesh, in order to make us partakers of his Divinity in essence.[58]

Like Ephraim the Syrian, Symeon speaks "a wonderful and new exchange" between God and man: God accepted his human flesh from the Ever Virgin Mary and gave her his own Divinity in return; now he gives his flesh to the saints in order to deify them.[59] Symeon observes this exchange not only in the Theotokos and the saints, but also in himself:

> Dwelling unchangeable in his divinity,
> the Word became man in taking on flesh,
> preserving his humanity unchangeable in his flesh and his soul,
> he made me completely god.
> He took on my condemned flesh and endued me with complete divinity.
> For indeed, baptized, I have put on Christ. . . .
> And how is it that one made god by grace and by adoption

---

[55] *Moral Oration* 5.31–34.
[56] Ibid. 7.598–604.
[57] Ibid. 5.314–316.
[58] Ibid. 4.549–552.
[59] Ibid. 1.10, 118–122.

will not be god in awareness and knowledge and contemplation,
he who has put on the Son of God? . . .
But it is in knowledge, in fact, and in conscious experience,
that God has assumed the whole human nature.
I am entirely god by sharing in God in a conscious awareness
    and by knowledge, not by essence
but by participation, as is absolutely necessary to believe to be
    orthodox.
As indeed God without change became man in body and
    appeared to all,
so likewise ineffably he begot me spiritually
and while I remained a man, he made me god.[60]

Thus, Symeon considers belief in the deification of man an indispensable component of the Orthodox way of thinking. According to Symeon, deification includes in itself both a human initiative and a divine leniency: according to his teaching, the person who would forget the whole world acquires the original whole mind, after which the One God is united with him and through this union deifies him completely.[61] In order to describe how such a deification changes human nature, Symeon uses the traditional image of an iron in the fire: as the fire imparts its qualities to the iron, it does not take on the dark coloring of the iron, just as the Holy Spirit grants people its incorruptibility and immortality, transfiguring them in light and granting full assimilation to Christ.[62] Consequently, deification is the arousal of man's original likeness to God in himself, the God who, in Symeon's words, "is not jealous that mortals should appear equal to himself by divine grace. . . . But rather he is happy and rejoices in seeing all of us . . . become by grace such as he was and is by nature."[63]

By Symeon's thinking, deification is a gradual process, which supposes a path through different consecutive stages. Symeon talks of how man bit by bit reaches the conditions by which sinful thoughts are put aside from his mind and the passions are quelled, all by observing God's commandments; then man possesses humility and sobriety, washing away all anger from his

[60]*Hymn 50* (Denville, N.J.: Dimension Books), 254–255.
[61]*Hymn 29* 254–285.
[62]Cf.: *Hymn 44* 365–383.
[63]*Hymn 44* (Denville, N.J.: Dimension Books), 231–232.

soul, after which the Holy Spirit comes to him.[64] However more zealously a man observes God's commandments, the more so he is purified, enlightened, and sanctified.[65] He receives new eyes and new ears from the Spirit, through which he may see and hear spiritual things: in this state God "becomes everything for him, all that he might desire, and indeed, he does desire him."[66] Man then continually sees God and contemplates the glory of his soul, for it is finally enlightened and consecrated to God.[67]

In another place, linking himself to Gregory the Theologian, Symeon says that the process of deification has no end:

> Perfection has no end,
> there again the beginning is the end.
> How the end? As Gregory the Theologian has said:
> illumination is the end
> of all those who love;
> and the repose of all
> contemplation of the Divine Light.[68]

Thus both Gregory and Symeon consider that deification is above all the shining of the divine light and the participation in it: in this is the end of all desire. Symeon frequently links the two themes of divine light and deification. "Through repentance they become sons of your divine light, but what can light produce if not light? They themselves then are also light, children of God, as it is written, and gods by grace."[69] In another place Symeon addresses his readers: "Hasten . . . to light the spiritual lamp of your soul, so as to become suns which shine in the world . . . so as to become like gods."[70] When the divine light enlightens us, we become god-like and "gods, seeing God."[71] Referring to his own visions of the light, Symeon says that by means of them he is completely renewed, immortalized, and "made Christ."[72]

---

[64] *Catechetical Oration* 14.60–90.
[65] Ibid. 117–119.
[66] Ibid. 123–144.
[67] Ibid. 177–194.
[68] *Hymn 23*, 122.
[69] *Hymn 8*, 30.
[70] *Hymn 13*, 44.
[71] *Hymn 15*.
[72] *Hymn 30*.

Man's deification through the shining divine light and unity with Christ, according to Symeon, is so much fuller and more perfect that it envelops all human nature, including the body and its members:

> We become members of Christ—and Christ becomes our
>   members,
> Christ becomes my hand, Christ, my miserable foot;
> and I, unhappy one, am Christ's hand, Christ's foot!
> I move my hand, and my hand is the whole Christ
> since, do not forget it, God is indivisible in his divinity—;
> I move my foot, and behold it shines like That one!
> Do not accuse me of blasphemy, but welcome these things
> and adore Christ who makes you such,
> since if you so wish you will become a member of Christ,
> and similarly all our members individually
> will become members of Christ and Christ our members,
> and all which is dishonorable in us he will make honorable
> by adorning it with his divine beauty and his divine glory,
> since living with God at the same time, we shall become gods.[73]

The deification of human nature, being completely united to Christ, is the renewal of God's image lost by man in the Fall. Formed in the image of the Holy Trinity, man, through communion with the Godhead, once again acquires this image in all its spiritual and bodily components:

> God is light, and he is united with those in whom he shares his radiance.
> . . . O wonder! Man is united with God spiritually and bodily, for neither
> is the soul separated from the mind, nor the body from the soul, but
> thanks to the essential union, man becomes tri-hypostatic by grace, and
> by adoption—one god from body, soul, and Divine Spirit, with whom he
> communed. And then is fulfilled that which the Prophet David said: "I
> say, 'You are gods, children of the Most High, all of you' " (Ps 82.6). Sons
> of the Most High—that is, in the image and likeness of the Most High.[74]

[73] *Hymn 15*, 54.
[74] *Catechetical Oration* 15.68–80.

PART FIVE

THE CHURCH

Christ the Good Shepherd. Vatican Museum. Rome. 4th c.

O RTHODOX ECCLESIOLOGY WAS FORMED over the course of many centuries, and even to this day it is found in a state of formation. This is
its essential difference from other areas of Orthodox dogma, such as, for
example, Triadology and Christology, formulae that were fully completed as
facts in the age of the ecumenical councils. The relative "lack of development" of Orthodox ecclesiology during the time of the ecumenical councils
is conditioned on the fact that there never arose any kind of heresy on the
issue of the Church as such during this era that demanded a theological
answer. For this reason, the holy Fathers of the first millennium left virtually

no ecclesiological treatises. Not one of the systematic expositions of the Orthodox faith preserved from the first millennium, whether it be Origen's *On First Principles*, Gregory of Nyssa's *Great Catechetical Oration*, Theodoret's *Short Exposition of Divine Dogma*, or John of Damascus' *An Exact Exposition of the Orthodox Faith*, contains a specific chapter on the Church.

As Protopresbyter Georges Florovsky considers, the absence of ecclesiological treatises in the age of the ecumenical councils was not merely an "omission" or an "oversight":

> The Eastern and Western fathers . . . could say much about the Church—and not only could, but did speak of it extensively. However, they never attempted to bring their thoughts on it together into one. Their conjectures and reflections were strewn throughout various compositions, on the whole, exegetical and liturgical in nature, found frequently in sermons, rather than in dogmatic works. One way or another, church writers always had a clear *concept* of what the Church really is—although this "concept" never came to an *understanding*, to a definition.[1]

An intelligible and conclusive definition of the Church is absent in patristic literature, and it is difficult to find an answer to the question of what the Church is in the Fathers and teachers of the Church. St. Philaret of Moscow, in his *Catechesis*, defines the Church as "a society of people established from God, united by the Orthodox faith, God's law, hierarchy, and the sacraments."[2] For all the formal correctness of this definition, it is neither patristic, nor based on Holy Scripture, nor conclusive. The Church is not simply a society of people, united around one faith, one "ideology"; the Church is not simply the totality of clergy and laity, participating in liturgical services and the sacraments. The Church is a reality, the nature of does not lend itself to a verbal definition. The Russian religious philosopher Nikolai Berdiaev speaks of this:

> The Church's ontology is almost completely unrevealed. This is the mission for the future. The Church's existence was not made known and actualized in order to make possible the construction of the ontology of the Church. Would it even be possible to define the Church's nature? It

---

[1] *Christ and His Church*. Found in V. N. Lossky, *Theology and God-Vision* (Moscow: 2000), 600–601. Italics in original.
[2] *Extensive Christian Catechesis*, 43.

is not possible to see and understand the Church fully from without, to define it rationally and fully, to make it penetrable for understanding. One needs to live within the Church. It is comprehensible only within experience. It is not given to us with coercion, like outward reality. And so that which is outward is perceived as the Church, but this is not it in its hidden nature. The Church is not a church building built from stone, it is not spirituality, hierarchy, it is not a society of believers, or a parish made up of people, it is not an institution regulated by right norms, although all of this attends to the Church's being.[3]

Rejecting the formalization of the understanding of "the Church," Berdiaev falls into a different extreme: his vision of the Church's ontological reality suffers from an excessive spiritualization. It defines the Church as an "invisible thing" possessing a spiritual nature. From without, that which is visible is "only stones, only ritual, only the institution, only people, in the form of ecclesial ranks. But the genuine, most objective reality of the Church is hidden, mystically abiding beyond the borders of the outer walls of the stones of the church, of the hierarchy, orders, councils, and all else."[4] Absolutely, the teaching of the "invisible Church" was always one of the teachings making up Christian ecclesiology, although the recognition of the Church's spiritual nature should not lead to the idea of a secondary transfer of "outer" ecclesial attributes. While not merely the totality of a hierarchy, sacraments, orders, and councils, at the same time the Church cannot exist without hierarchy, sacraments, orders, liturgical services, dogma, and conciliarity.

The New Testament repeatedly speaks of the Church, though the authors of the holy books do not make an attempt to specify what exactly the Church is. Jesus Christ describes the reality of the Church with the aid of some metaphors. The Church is a sheepfold, with Christ as the Shepherd and his disciples as the sheep, who hear his voice and whom he calls by name. The sheep come for their own shepherd, but will not for another, because they do not know his voice. The good Shepherd has "other sheep that are not of this fold. Them also [he] must bring. . . . So there will be one flock, one shepherd" (Jn 10.16).

Another metaphor Christ uses: the grape vine and branches. The spiritual unity that the disciples have with their Teacher is likened to the unity that

[3]*Philosophy of the Free Spirit* 2 (Paris: 1927–28), 190.
[4]Ibid. 191.

exists between the vine and the branches: whosoever abides in Christ bears much fruit, but the branch that does not bear fruit will be pruned by the vine-dresser and thrown into the fire (Jn 15.1–7).

We find different metaphors that describe the Church in the Apostolic Epistles, for example, the Body of Christ (Eph 1.22–23; 1 Cor 12.12–13, 27), the bride of Christ (2 Cor 11.2; Eph 5.22–32), the temple of God (2 Cor 6.16), and a spiritual house (1 Pet 2.5). The patristic tradition added another rank of metaphors, such as Noah's ark, or spiritual hospital. Moreover, the Church was described in the Niceno-Constantinopolitan Creed as "One, Holy, Catholic, and Apostolic." Our review of Orthodox ecclesiology will be constructed on the theological interpretations of these definitions and metaphors, which cover the basic characteristics of the Church in a sufficiently comprehensive manner.

21

The Unity of the Church. The Body of Christ

"THE CHURCH BREATHES WITH ONE BREATH," wrote Clement of Alexandria at the beginning of the third century.[1] This formative phrase indicates the spiritual-moral unity that binds the members of the Christian Church. In his epistles, the Apostle Paul repeatedly spoke of the unity of the Church as a Body, the Head of which is Christ, with its members being all Christians:

> [God] has put all *things* under his feet, and gave him *to be* the head over all *things* to the church, which is his body, the fullness of him who fills all in all. (Eph 1.22–23)

> No one ever yet hated his own flesh, but he nourishes and cherishes it, even as the Lord the church, for we are members of his body, of his flesh, and of his bones. (Eph 5.29–30)

> For as the body is one, and has many members, and all the members of that one body, though many, are one body: so also is Christ. For by one Spirit we are all baptized into one body, whether Jews or Gentiles, bond or free; and we have all been made to drink into one Spirit, for the body is not one member, but many. . . . Now you are the body of Christ, and members individually. (1 Cor 12.12–14, 27)

According to the teaching of the Apostle Paul, the Church is one, because being the Body of Christ, it binds all the believers in one faith, baptism, Eucharist, and communion of the Holy Spirit. John Chrysostom numbers these fundamental signs of unity in his interpretation of 1 Corinthians 12.12–13:

> For as the body and the head are one man, so he said that the Church and Christ are one. . . . "As then . . . our body is one thing though it be

---

[1] *Stromata* 7.6.

The Eucharist. St Michael's Golden-Domed Cathedral. Kiev. 12th c.

composed of many: so also in the Church we all are one thing. For though the Church be composed of many members, yet these many form one body". . . . For not in one Spirit was one baptized, and another another. And not only is that which baptized us one, but also that unto which he baptized us, i.e., for which he baptized us, is one. For we were baptized . . . that we might all be one body, into the same were we baptized. So that both he who formed it is one, and that into which he formed it is one.[2]

The teaching of the unity of the Church according to the image of God's unity occupies a most important place in the theology of the Eastern Fathers and teachers of the Church: the Church is one because it was made one. Clement of Alexandria developed this idea:

> The true Church, that which is really ancient, is one, and in it those who according to God's purpose are just, are enrolled. For from the very reason that God is one, and the Lord one, that which is in the highest degree honorable is lauded in consequence of its singleness, being an imitation of the one first principle. In the nature of the One, then, is associated in a joint heritage of the one Church, which they strive to cut asunder into

[2]*Homily on First Corinthians* 30.1–2.

many sects. Therefore in substance and idea, in origin, in preeminence, we say that the ancient and Catholic Church is alone, collecting as it does into the unity of the one faith (Eph 4.13), which results from the peculiar Testaments, or rather the one Testament in different times.[3]

In the fifth century, Cyril of Alexandria developed the teaching that the unity of Christ's disciples in the bosom of the one Church is an image of the unity existing between the Persons of the Holy Trinity. Reflecting on Christ's prayer on the unity of the faithful (Jn 17.20–21), St Cyril writes:

What then, is the manner of his prayer? "That," he says, "they may be one; even as thou, Father, art in me, and I in thee, that they also may be one in us." He asks, then, for a bond of love, and concord, and peace, to bring into spiritual unity those who believe; so that their unitedness, through perfect sympathy and inseparable harmony of soul, might resemble the features of the natural and essential unity that exists between the Father and the Son. But the bond of the love that is in us, and the power of concord, will not of itself altogether avail to keep them in the same unchangeable state of union as exists between the Father and the Son, who preserve the manner of their union in identity of Substance. For the

---

[3] *Stromata* 7.17.

one is, in fact, natural and actual, and is seen in the very definition of the existence of God; while the other only assumes the appearance of the unity which is actual.[4]

For Cyril, the unity of the Holy Trinity provides above all a moral example for Christians:

> We must once more repeat the assertion, that when Christ brings forward the essential unity which the Father has with himself, and himself also with the Father, as an Image and Type of the inseparable fellowship, and concord, and unity that exists in kindred souls, he desires us in some sort to be blended with one another in the power that is of the Holy and Consubstantial Trinity; so that the whole body of the Church may be in fact one, ascending in Christ through the fusion and concurrence of two peoples into one perfect whole. . . . This was, in fact, accomplished; those who believed on Christ being of soul one with another, and receiving, as it were, one heart, through their complete resemblance in piety towards God, and their obedience in believing, and aspiration after virtue. . . . For in what has gone before we rightly maintained that the union of believers, in concord of heart and soul, ought to resemble the manner of the divine unity, and the essential identity of the Holy Trinity, and their intimate connection with each other.[5]

Cyril of Alexandria considers the main factor of church unity to be the holy Eucharist—communion of the Flesh and Blood of Christ, making Christians into one ecclesial body:

> In order, then, that we ourselves also may join together, and be blended into unity with God and with each other, although, through the actual difference which exists in each one of us, we have a distinct individuality of soul and body, the Only-begotten has contrived a means which his own due Wisdom and the Counsel of the Father have sought out. For by one Body, that is, his own, blessing through the mystery of the Eucharist those who believe on him, he makes us of the same Body with himself and with each other. For who could sunder or divide from their natural union with one another those who are knit together through his holy

---

[4] *Commentary on John* II.II.
[5] Ibid.

Body, which is one in union with Christ? For if we all partake of the one Bread, we are all made one Body; for Christ cannot suffer severance. Therefore also the Church becomes Christ's Body, and we are also individually his members.[6]

The unity of Christians through communion of the Body and Blood of Christ is inseparable from their unity through the union in the Holy Spirit:

> With reference, then, to the unity that is by the Spirit, following in the same track of inquiry, we say once more, that we all, receiving one and the same Spirit, I mean the Holy Spirit, are in some sort blended together with one another and with God. . . . For as the power of his holy Flesh maketh those in whom it exists to be of the same Body, so likewise also the indivisible Spirit of God that abideth in all, being one, bindeth all together into spiritual unity. . . . We are all, therefore, one in the Father, and the Son, and the Holy Spirit; one, I mean, both in identity of mental condition (for I think we ought not to forget what we said first), and also in conformity to the life of righteousness, and in the fellowship of the holy Body of Christ, and in the fellowship of the Holy Spirit.[7]

The teaching on the unity of the Church had a decisive significance for the working-out of criteria by which the Church ought to relate to heretical and schismatic groups that had fallen away from it. Such groups existed both in the pre-Constantinian era and in the age of ecumenical councils, and in the course of the following centuries; they exist even now. In the ancient Church, there was no one-way or uniform approach to these groups: the relationships toward them varied between the principle of *akrivia*/ἀκρίβια (strictness, precision) and the principle of *oikonomia*/οἰκονομία (leniency). Some authors identified these schismatic groups as fully devoid of grace, and the sacraments of schismatics and heretics as ineffective. Others allowed that there was some kind of stage of ecclesiality and grace-filled life that had not fully failed in these heretical and schismatic groups, regardless of their being divided from the one Church. The difference in the approach to this problem conditioned the difference in the practice of the reception of those repenting from schism back into the Church, either through baptism or through anointing or through repentance.

[6]Ibid.
[7]Ibid.

The Unity of the Catholic Church, by Cyprian of Carthage, became the classic expression of ecclesial *akrivia* on the issue of the grace of heretical and schismatic groups. As the work of a Western church author, it came about in the age when there was still no sharp theological division between East and West, and the ideas expressed in it corresponded to the theology of the Eastern fathers. At the same time, some of St Cyprian's ideas had a purely Western origin and were subsequently developed among theologians of the western church, but these developments were not received in the East.

Like theologians of the Christian East, Cyprian mentions that the unity of the Church is founded on the unity of the Godhead: "God is one and Christ is one, and his Church and faith are one, and the people are joined together with the glue of concord into the unbroken unity of a body."[8] However, his starting point on the discussion of unity is somewhat different, and his treatise begins with the claim that the unity of the Church is founded on Peter:

The Apostle Peter. Monastery of Chora. Constantinople. 14th c.

The Lord speaks to Peter: "I tell you that you are Peter, and on that rock I will build my Church, and the gates of the underworld will not prevail against her. I will give to you the keys to the kingdom of heaven, and whatever you will bind on earth will have been bound even in heaven, and what you will loose upon earth will have been loosed even in heaven" (Mt 16.18–19). And the same Jesus after his resurrection said to Peter: "Feed my sheep" (Jn 21.17). On one man he builds his Church and, although he assigns to all the apostles after the resurrection equal power with the words: "Just as the Father sends me, also I send you. Receive the Holy Spirit: if you will forgive the sins of anyone, they will be forgiven him; if of anyone you will retain, they will be retained" (Jn 20.21–23). Nevertheless, in order that he might reveal their unity, he ordained by his own authority that the source of that same unity should begin from the one who began the series. The remaining apostles were necessarily also that which Peter was, endowed with an equal partnership

---

[8] *The Unity of the Catholic Church* 23, *On the Church: Select Treatises*, Allen Brent, tr. (Crestwood, NY: St Vladimir's Seminary Press, 2006), 178.

both of honor and power, but the starting point from which they begin is from their unity with him in order that the Church of Christ might be exemplified as one.[9]

The teaching on the primacy of Peter as the basis of ecclesial unity received subsequent development in the Western Church, which developed the theory according to which the role of guarantor of ecclesial unity passed from Peter to the Roman bishop as "preeminent chief of the apostles." Corresponding to this, the schismatics were perceived in the West as not holding "the chair of Peter, which they rend by wicked schism."[10] However, in Cyprian, Peter's service is not absolutely associated with the Roman throne. For him, the guarantor of the unity of the Church is not the bishop of Rome, but the whole episcopacy of the Church, which is charged with the mission of supporting and strengthening this unity:

> Can anyone believe that he himself sticks fast to the faith without sticking fast to this unity of the Church? Can someone be confident that he himself is in the Church if he offers resistance to the Church and opposes her? The blessed Paul teaches this same point and demonstrates the solemn obligation when he says: "There is one body and one Spirit, one hope of your calling, one Lord, one faith, one baptism, one God" (Eph 4.4–6). We, the bishops who preside over the Church, are under the foremost obligation to grasp tightly this unity and to assert our title to it, with the object of proving that the episcopate in itself is one and indivisible. . . . The episcopate is one, an individual share in which individual bishops hold as owners of a common property. The Church is a unity, which extends into a plurality by the widespread increase of her fruitfulness.[11]

The key element in Cyprian's teaching on unity is the claim that there is no salvation outside the Church. This claim held a universal place in all of patristic literature, whether East or West, and was repeatedly supported at ecumenical councils. However, it was Cyprian who was the first church author to dare to formulate this teaching so sharply and laconically:

---

[9]Ibid. 4, 152–153.
[10]Ambrose of Milan *On Repentance* 1.7.
[11]*The Unity of the Catholic Church* 4–5, 153–155.

He cannot have God as his Father who does not have the Church as his Mother. If someone who was outside the ark of Noah could escape, then so could also someone escape who is outside the Church. The Lord warns with the words: "He who is not with me is against me, and he who does not gather with me scatters" (Mt 12.30). He who ruptures Christ's peace and concord acts against Christ. He who gathers elsewhere than in the Church scatters Christ's Church. The Lord says: "I and my Father are one," and, secondly, it is written concerning Father, Son, and Holy Spirit: "And the three are one" (1 Jn 5.8). No one can believe that this unity that proceeds from the Church's stable foundation by God and that is held together by heavenly rites of initiation can be rent asunder in the Church and split by the schisms that result from the clashing of wills. He who does not hold fast to this unity does not hold fast to the law of God, does not hold fast to the faith of Father and of Son, does not hold fast to life and salvation.[12]

The symbol of the Church's unity is the outer garment of the Lord, and every schism tears it; this will become a classic image in Christian ecclesiology:

> This pledge of unity, this bond of a concord that is held together in a way that cannot be split into individual links is demonstrated in the gospel. . . . So truly because Christ's people cannot be torn apart, his tunic, "woven without seam," and holding fast together, has not become divided amongst its owners. The description "unable to be split (united, linked together)," reveals the concord that holds together the unity of our people who have put on Christ. By the sign and seal of the tunic Christ has declared the unity of his Church. Who therefore is so heinously criminal and marked by treachery, who so wild with the frenzy of discord, that he either believes that the Lord's robe, Christ's Church, can be torn asunder, or dares in fact so to tear apart the unity of God?[13]

The Lord speaks of the one flock and the one Shepherd (Jn 10.16), Cyprian further explains. How then can there be many shepherds and many flocks in one place? The rite of the Passover, according to the book of Exodus, demands that a lamb, slain as a type of Christ, be eaten inside one house: "It is not possible to throw the flesh of Christ and the Lord's holy

[12]Ibid. 6, 157.
[13]Ibid. 7–8, 158–159.

sacrament out of doors, neither is there any other home for those who believe except the Church." Only those of one mind live in this house, abiding in openness and love.[14]

Cyprian asserts that kind people cannot be separated from the Church. Only wolves, dogs, and snakes can be separated from the Church. "It is cause for thanksgiving when such persons as these are excluded from the Church in order that they might not take as plunder the doves, Christ's sheep, by their cruel and poisonous contact." Those excluded and separated from the Church are those of whom the Apostle John said: "They went out from us, but they were not of us; for if they had been of us, they would have continued with us. But they went out, that they might be made manifest that they were not all of us" (1 Jn 2.19). In Cyprian's words, "For this reason heresies both have been committed and continue being committed, because a mind that is perverted does not have peace, because bad faith that causes discord does not maintain unity." But the separation of heretics from the Church is none other than the separation of the chaff from the wheat.[15]

Cyprian considers separation from the Church to be self-imposed. Their laying on of hands is ineffectual, and the baptism performed by them is a profanation and defilement of the sacrament:

> The latter [heretics] are those who give themselves precedence, by their own initiative, in ill-considered conventicles, without divine due order, who put themselves in supreme charge without any law of appointment who, when no one grants them the episcopate, take on for themselves the bishop's name. . . . When there cannot be another baptism besides the indivisible one, they think that they are able to baptize. Having forsaken the font of life, they are promising the grace of the water of life and of salvation. These men are not cleansed but rather are soiled, their sins are not purified but, more correctly, piled high. That giving of birth does not produce sons for God but for the Devil.[16]

Cyprian says concerning heretics and schismatics: "The fact is that we did not withdraw from them but they from us." According to the saint's teaching, the Lord is not present in the performance of the holy rites and

---

[14]Ibid. 8, 159–160.
[15]Ibid. 9–10, 160–161.
[16]Ibid. 10–11, 162–163.

sacraments of heretics and schismatics, since they excluded themselves from the Church, from Christ, and from the Gospel.[17] In the *Epistle to Quintus Concerning the Baptism of Heretics*, Cyprian develops in detail the teaching of the absence of baptism in heretical groups:

> [Baptism] is therefore one, because the Church is one, and there cannot be any baptism out of the Church. For since there cannot be two baptisms, if heretics truly baptize, they themselves have this baptism. And he who of his own authority grants this advantage to them yields and consents to them, that the enemy and adversary of Christ should seem to have the power of washing, and purifying, and sanctifying a man. But we say that those who come thence are not re-baptized amongst us, but are baptized. For indeed they do not receive anything there, where there is nothing; but they come to us, that here they may receive where there is both grace and all truth, because both grace and truth are one.[18]

Cyprian of Carthage insists that the sin of schism cannot even be cleansed by martyr's blood:

> To what peace, therefore, do the enemies of the brothers pledge themselves? What sacrifices do the imitators of the priests believe that they themselves celebrate? Do they who are gathered together *outside* Christ's Church think that Christ is with them when they have thus gathered together? Such persons, even if they have been slain whilst confessing the name, their stains will not be washed away with their blood. The blame for discord is serious and cannot be atoned for, and is not purified through suffering. Someone not in the Church cannot be a martyr. Someone who has abandoned the Church that is destined to reign will not be able to arrive at the kingdom of heaven. . . . Those who are unwilling to be of one mind in the Church of God are unable to abide with God. Even though they burn in the flames, and, surrendered to the fire, or exposed to the wild beasts, they should lay down their lives, the latter will not be their crown of faith but the punishment of their bad faith. Their death will enjoy no renown for its religious courage but an annihilation of despair. Such a person can be slain, he cannot be crowned.[19]

[17] Ibid. 12, 164.
[18] *Epistle 70: To Quintus, Concerning the Baptism of Heretics* 1.
[19] *The Unity of the Catholic Church*, 13–14, 166–167.

What does it mean to act against the unity of the Church and how concretely is the schism carried out? According to Cyprian's teaching, since the unity of the Church is based on the unity of the episcopate, to act against the unity of the Church means to act against the episcopate and the clergy, to erect an alternate altar and to make up one's own rite:

> Does someone who works against Christ's priests, who dissociates himself from the community of his clergy and people, think to himself to be with Christ? He is bearing arms against the Church, he is offering resistance to God's ordered arrangement. An enemy of the altar, a rebel against Christ's sacrifice, of bad faith instead of faithfulness, guilty of sacrilege instead of proper religious practice, a disobedient servant, an undutiful son, a brother who is one's enemy, he dares to set up a different altar against the bishops and priests of God whom he has treated despicably and has abandoned. He dares to utter a different prayer in words that are not lawful, to desecrate the truth of the Lord's sacrifice by means of false offerings. Someone who strives against the official appointment of God is not the sort of person to grasp that he is punished by God's divine censure because of the outrageous character of his recklessness.[20]

The teaching set forth here, undoubtedly, differs in proportion and consistency. The basic postulates of this teaching are that there is no salvation outside of the Church; the unity of the Church is secured by the unity of the episcopate; the Church does not lose unity when heretics and schismatics step away from it. These entered forever into the treasury of church Tradition and they underlie Orthodox ecclesiology. The Orthodox Church has always rejected the possibility of the division of its unity into various independent churches, possessing some inner, hidden unity of hierarchy and sacraments. Falling away from the Church is the pruning of the branches from the vine. By this the vine preserves it wholeness, since the pruned branch withers. Such is the fundamental ecclesiological arrangement that flows from Cyprian of Carthage's teaching on the unity of the Church.

At the same time it is impermissible to overlook a few weak points of the doctrine laid out above. Above all, Cyprian does not make a distinction between heretics and schismatics and does not specify exactly what kind of heresies and schisms are liable to such strict judgment. Moreover, the ancient

[20]Ibid. 17, 171.

Church, especially in the East, approached heresy differently, considering some more serious and others less so. Besides this, the Church did not equate heresy with schism. A schism could bear a temporary character, and the motivating force behind a schism was not always a heresy (a theological divergence from the orthodox faith). Quite frequently schisms occurred due to a church administrative issue, and the healing of a schism did not call for a renunciation of heresy, but simply a restoration of the relationship between the hierarchs of the Church and the hierarchs of the ecclesial group that had stepped away from it.

In terms of the attitude of the Christian East, heretics and schismatics were spoken out against less synonymously. The classic document became the canonical letter of Basil the Great to Amphilochius of Iconium, which entered into the code of canons of the Orthodox Church as the first canon of Basil the Great. In this canon Basil, making a connection to ancient practice, speaks of three factions that separate themselves from the Church: heretics, schismatics, and illegal congregations. Basil calls heretics "those who are completely broken off and, as regards the faith itself, alienated"; schismatics are "those at variance with one another for certain ecclesiastical reasons and questions that admit of a remedy," and illegal congregations, "assemblies brought into being by insubordinate presbyters or bishops, and by uninstructed laymen."[21]

By a relatively recognizable baptism and laying on of hands of those persons returning to the Church, Basil lays out the following canon:

> The ancients, accordingly, decided to reject completely the baptism of heretics, but to accept that of schismatics on the ground that they were still of the Church; and as to those in illegal congregations, to join these again to the Church after they had been improved by adequate repentance and change of heart; hence they often received into the same rank, whenever they repented, even those in orders who have gone off with the insubordinate.[22]

In other words, heretics are received into the Church through baptism, and whatever baptism was performed within the heretical group is not accepted

---

[21]*Basil 1.* Cited in: Basil the Great, *The Letters*, R. Deferrari, tr., III (Loeb Classical Library 243, London 1930; reprinted by Harvard University Press), 7–21.
[22]Ibid.

whatsoever by the Church; schismatics are received without baptism, since a baptism performed in schism is still considered valid; but the illegal congregations are reunited through repentance. While Basil shows the whole spectrum of inclusion in this canon, he makes quite an essential reservation:

> Because the beginning of this separation arose through schism, and those who had broken away from the Church no longer had in them the grace of the Holy Spirit; for the imparting of it failed because of the severance of continuity. For those who separated first had ordination from the fathers, and through the imposition of their hands possessed the spiritual gift, but those who had been cut off, becoming laymen, possessed the power neither of baptizing nor of ordaining, being able no longer to impart to others the grace of the Holy Spirit from which they themselves had fallen away. Therefore, they commanded those who had been baptized by them, as baptized by laymen, to come to the Church and be purified by the true baptism of the Church. But since on the whole it has seemed best to some of those in Asia that, for the sake of the discipline of the majority, their baptism be accepted, let it be accepted.[23]

These words of Basil, first, show a different practice of the reception of schismatics into the Church: as through baptism just as without baptism. Secondly, Basil lays out the crucial thesis of the scarcity of the grace Holy Spirit in the schism, resulting in the cessation of the apostolic gifts. Only the first generation of schismatics, who have received the laying on of hands in the true Church, possessed these gifts; leaving the Church and having formed a schism, they lost them, and those of them who have received the laying on of hands within a schism can be considered laymen, not clerics.

Speaking on schismatics, Basil recommends that they be received through baptism. At the same time, Basil admits that demanding reception through baptism can, through its excessive strictness, turn away from the Church those who would wish to return to it. In this case he allows reception into the Church without baptism, through anointing instead. Moreover, Basil refers to the case of the reception of schismatic bishops into their "existing orders," that is without repeating the laying on of hands that, in essence, signifies the Church's acknowledgement of the legitimacy of their hierarchy and sacraments.[24]

[23]Ibid.
[24]Cf.: Ibid.

In the above text, Basil the Great speaks of the necessity "to submit to the canons with precision," but he himself makes provision for a whole slew of circumstances, by which this precision/*akrivia* is exchanged for leniency/*oikonomia*. Such a position was characteristic for the fathers of the Eastern Church. The approach of the Eastern fathers toward the issue of the unity of the Church, perhaps, was not distinguished by such strictness and order as that laid out in the above teaching of Cyprian of Carthage, though he gave greater freedom to the Church in deciding the issue of the reception of heretics and schismatics returning to the Church.

It is necessary to say that Cyprian's teaching was not accepted by all the fathers of the Western Church unreservedly. The Blessed Augustine, who was in agreement with Cyprian in many things, nonetheless considered it permissible to acknowledge the significance of the sacraments of schismatics. Augustine asserts in the treatise *On Baptism* that the Church acts in the sacraments of schismatics: some are born within it, others outside, and it is precisely because a schismatic baptism has significance that the Church perfects it.[25] To the extent to which schismatics preserve the link to the Church, the sacraments are preserved within them.[26]

Augustine introduces the difference between a sacrament and its "efficacy" (*effectus*): the sacraments of schismatics have a place, but they are not efficacious. Augustine considers that each baptism, if it is done in the name of the Holy Trinity, does not merit repeating, since the grace given in that baptism comes from Christ and not from man. It is necessary for heretics (in this case the issue is the Donatists) to return to ecclesial society so that their baptism might become salvific. The sacraments of heretics are not in essence profanations of sacraments: they are genuine sacraments. However, by virtue of their being performed in schism, they are not efficacious, that is they are not salvific, and the grace bestowed through them is "in judgment and condemnation" of those who accept them.[27]

Developing the teaching on the efficacy of the sacraments of schismatic groups, Augustine argues with Cyprian of Carthage:

> The blessed Cyprian was specially conspicuous, that the baptism of Christ could not exist among heretics or schismatics, this simply arose

[25]Cf.: Augustine *On Baptism* 1.15.23.
[26]Ibid. 2.2.3.
[27]Georges Florovsky, *On the Limits of the Church*, 166–167.

from their not distinguishing the sacrament from the effect or use of the sacrament; and because its effect and use were not found among heretics in freeing them from their sins and setting their hearts right, the sacrament itself was also thought to be wanting among them. But . . . since these also who are perverse and lead an abandoned life in unity itself appear to have no power either of giving or retaining remission of sins, seeing that it is not to the wicked but the good sons that it was said, "Whosoever sins ye remit, they are remitted unto them; and whosoever sins ye retain, they are retained," yet that such persons both have, and give, and receive the sacrament of baptism, was sufficiently manifest to the pastors of the Catholic Church dispersed over the whole world, through whom the original custom was afterwards confirmed by the authority of the plenary Council. . . . For the sacrament is equally holy, in virtue of its own excellence, both in those who are unequally just, and in those who are unequally unjust.[28]

Blessed Augustine. Palatine chapel. Palermo. 12 c.

The Augustinian understanding of the "efficacy" of the sacraments was never fully accepted in the Orthodox Church. Such an understanding of the sacraments is unacceptable for Orthodox tradition, for it is an understanding in which the grace inherent within them is considered as autonomous, independent of the Church. The sacraments can be performed only within the Church, and it is the Church that bestows efficacy, reality, and salvation on them. In the Eastern Church, the attitude toward the sacraments of heretics and schismatics varied in different ages depending on the circumstances. The important role of evaluating this or that group that had separated itself from the Church provided a teaching opportunity: they approached most strictly those schisms that had caused the most damage to ecclesial unity.

That very rule acted in relation to heretics as to divergences from general church teachings on dogmatic issues. One of the most important Eastern Christian texts dedicated to this theme is the oration in honor of St Athanasius

[28]*On Baptism* 6.1–2.

of Alexandria, attributed to the hand of Gregory the Theologian. In this text, Gregory tells of the schism that was brewing between the Latin and Greek bishops on the question of triadological terminology and which Athanasius succeeded in preventing. In the course of the exposition, Gregory expresses a few precious ideas on the grounds of dogmatic disputes and schism between different Churches (the argument in this text revolves around the Council of Alexandria in 362, at which the question of the meaning of the triadological terms "hypostasis" and "essence" was raised):

> For as, in the case of one and the same quantity of water, there is separated from it, not only the residue which is left behind by the hand when drawing it, but also those drops, once contained in the hand, which trickle out through the fingers; so also there is a separation between us and, not only those who hold aloof in their impiety, but also those who are most pious, and both in regard to such doctrines as are of small consequence . . . and also in regard to expression intended to bear the same meaning. We use in an orthodox sense the terms one Essence and three Hypostases, the one to denote the nature of the Godhead, the other the properties of the Three; the Italians mean the same, but, owing to the scantiness of their vocabulary, and its poverty of terms, they are unable to distinguish between Essence and Hypostases, and therefore introduce the term Persons, to avoid being understood to assert three Essences. The result, were it not piteous, would be laughable. This slight difference of sound was taken to indicate a difference of faith. Then, Sabellianism was suspected[29] in the doctrine of Three Persons, Arianism in that of Three Hypostases, both being the offspring of a contentious spirit. And then, from the gradual but constant growth of irritation (the unfailing result of contentiousness) there was a danger of the whole world being torn asunder in the strife about syllables[30]. . . . [Athanasius] conferred in his gentle and sympathetic way with both parties, and after he had carefully weighed the meaning of their expressions, and found that they had the same sense, and were in nowise different in doctrine, by permitting each party to use its own terms, he bound them together in unity of action.[31]

[29]In the Greek East.
[30]A danger of a schism between the Greek East and the Latin West.
[31]*Oration 21* 35.

In the above text Gregory, first of all, stresses that the difference in dogmatic terminology does not always signify a discrepancy in the understanding of the same dogmata, and further not all dogmatic disputes arising between Churches are the result of differences in faith; many of them were simply a "slight difference of sound." In other words, not every dogmatic discrepancy is absolutely a heresy. The history of the Church knows many instances when the confession of faith of one local church, translated into another language or concept in the context of a different theological tradition, is perceived as heretical and is rejected by another Church. Schisms arose on these grounds, eucharistic relations ceased between Churches, and their heads conferred anathemas on each other. Then time passed, and people understood that they were speaking in different tongues, yet professed one faith: then ecclesial relations were restored.[32]

No less important is this other thesis: there exist insignificant (lit. "small") dogmata, on the grounds for which discord is permissible. These are dogmata that, in Gregory's opinion, can be "disregarded" for the sake of Church unity.

Now for the third thesis contained in the text just quoted: it is frequently not only "those unfortunate ones" (heretics) who are severed from the Church, but also those "most pious Christians" who either rejected some kind of dogmatic formula suspected of containing heresy, or digressed into an incorrect understanding of one of these "small dogmata." This thesis covers the essential difference between Gregory and Cyprian of Carthage, who considered only "wolves, dogs, and snakes" to be separated from the Church. In Gregory's mind, among those who have separated themselves from the Church are those who remain faithful to it, although they turn out to be outside relationship with it. Not all Christians who separate themselves from the Church are one hundred percent heretics. The theologian demands tactfulness and vigilance in order to define whether or not there is this or that heretical teaching incompatible with general church teaching, or whether there is a discrepancy on the grounds of "small dogmata," permissible within the unity of church tradition, or a "dispute on sounds" in general, arising as a result of misunderstanding and ignorance.

---

[32]One of the sharpest examples is the break between the Alexandrian and Antiochene Churches in 431 and the following reconciliation between Cyril of Alexandria and John of Antioch in 433. The reason for the break in relations was the difference between Alexandrian and Antichiochene Christological terminology.

The fundamental positions of the Orthodox teaching on the unity of the Church were formulated in the age of the ecumenical councils, and the following centuries did not add anything that was new in principle to this teaching. However, schisms of the second millennium placed before the Orthodox Church the mission of making the themes of unity and ecclesial division accessible in a new historical context. After the "Great Schism" of 1054, it became necessary for the Orthodox Church to formulate its own relation to the Catholic Church, and after the rise of the Reformation, to Protestantism.

The relation of the Orthodox Church to the Catholics and Protestants will be spoken of in greater detail in a special section. Concerning the examination of the theme of the unity of the Church, one need only say that the Orthodox Church always identified itself with the One, Holy, Catholic, and Apostolic Church, which is spoken of in the Creed; all the other Christian confessions were considered by it to have fallen away from ecclesial unity.

At the same time, not all Orthodox authors always considered church communities found outside the Orthodox Church to be completely lacking a grace-filled life. In relation to these communities, the principle of *oikonomia* was applied in rather broad strokes—on a theological level just as on the level of ecclesial practice. In particular, the most widespread such application over the course of the centuries was the acceptance of Catholics and Protestants into the Orthodox Church without the performance of the sacrament of baptism.

In the nineteenth century, St Philaret of Moscow, answering the question of whether the Roman Church could be considered true, said: "I would not dare to call any Church believing that Jesus is the Christ to be false. The Christian Church can only be 'purely true' either in confessing the true and salvific divine teaching without the mixture of false and antagonistic views of man, or it can be 'impurely true,' adding to the truth and to the saving faith of Christ's teaching the false and antagonistic views of man."[33] By the purely true Church, Philaret means the Orthodox Church, but the other Christian confessions are referred to as "impurely true."

The ecclesiological self-understanding of the Orthodox Church found reflection in the "Basic Principles of Relation of the Russian Orthodox Church to Non-Orthodox," a document of the Archpriest Council in 2000, containing

[33]Philaret of Moscow, *Colloquy between a True Believer and a Sceptic on the Doctrine of the Greco-Russian Church* (Moscow, 1833), 27–29.

an official position of the Moscow Patriarchate concerning the issue of the unity of the Church and Christian division. This document is based on the teaching of the unity of the Church formulated by the Fathers of the first millennium, although the given teaching was altered for contemporary realities. The document begins with the claim that:

> The Orthodox Church is the true Church of Christ established by our Lord and Savior, the Church confirmed and sustained by the Holy Spirit, the Church of which the Savior himself said, 'I will build my church and the gates of hell shall not prevail against it' (Mt 16.18). She is the One, Holy, Catholic, and Apostolic Church, and the keeper of the holy sacraments throughout the world, 'the pillar and foundation of the truth' (1 Tim 3.15).[34]

In the document's words, the unity of the Church is based on its one Head–the Lord Jesus Christ (Eph 5.23) and the one Holy Spirit who acts in it.[35] Church unity "is inseparable from the sacrament of the Eucharist, in which the faithful, partaking of the one Body of Christ, are really and truly joined into the one and catholic body in the sacrament of Christ's love, in the transforming power of the Spirit."[36] The unity of the Church overcomes barriers and borders, whether racial, linguistic, or social.[37] Hostility and alienation is overcome within the Church, which is united in the love of the image of the consubstantial Trinity for the sinner who has separated himself.[38]

Over the course of centuries, notes the document, Christ's commandment on unity was repeatedly broken, and differences and divisions arose within Christianity. The Church always dealt strictly, and according to principle, with those who appeared against the purity of the saving faith (the heretics), and with those who introduced divisions and sedition into the Church (schismatics).[39] The Orthodox Church always insisted that salvation can be attained only in Christ's Church. At the same time:

> The community that has fallen away from Orthodoxy has never been viewed as fully deprived of the grace of God. The break in communion

[34]"Basic Principles of Relation of the Russian Orthodox Church to Non-Orthodox," 1.1.
[35]Ibid. 1.2.
[36]Ibid. 1.8.
[37]Ibid. 1.4.
[38]Ibid. 1.5.
[39]Ibid. 1.12.

with the Church inevitably leads to damage of life's grace, but not always to its complete disappearance in these separated communities. It is associated with the practice of receiving those coming from non-Orthodox communities into the Orthodox Church without the sacrament of baptism. Despite the rupture of unity, there remains a certain incomplete fellowship which serves as a guarantee of a return to unity in the Church, to catholic fullness and oneness.[40]

It says in the document that "the church position on those who separate themselves does not lend itself to an exact science."[41] The existence of various rites of reception[42] (through baptism, anointing, or repentance) shows that the Orthodox Church approaches non-Orthodox denominations in different ways. The criterion is the degree of preservation of the faith and order of the Church and spiritual standards of Christian life. However, establishing various rites of reception, the Orthodox Church does not assess the extent of damage or the preservation of the life of grace in the non-Orthodox, considering this a mystery of God's providence and judgment.[43]

The presence of schisms and divisions in the Christian world is a historical tragedy of Christianity and goes against Christ's commandment concerning the unity of his Body. "Basic Principles . . ." speaks of this also:

> The results of the violation of the commandment of unity, which led to the historical tragedy of schism, and divided Christians instead of being an example of unity in love in the image of the Blessed Trinity, have become a source of temptation. Christian division was an open and bleeding wound on the Body of Christ. The tragedy of the division has become a serious visible distortion of Christian universalism, an obstacle to peace in the testimony of Christ. For the validity of the evidence of Christ's Church, to a large extent, depends on the realization of its truths preached in the life and practices of Christian communities.[44]

[40]Ibid. 1.15.
[41]Ibid. 1.16.
[42]That is, rites of reception into the Church.
[43]"Basic Principles of Relation of the Russian Orthodox Church to Non-Orthodoxh," 1.17.
[44]Ibid. 1.20.

22

The Holiness of the Church. The Bride of Christ

IN THE EPISTLES OF THE APOSTLE PAUL, the Church is metaphorically described as a pure virgin, betrothed to "one husband . . . Christ" (2 Cor 11.2). Paul develops the image of the Church as Christ's bride in the Epistle to the Ephesians, where he speaks on Christian marriage. Here Christ is presented as the bridegroom of the Church and the Savior of the body, who "loved the church and gave himself up for her, that he might sanctify her and cleanse her with the washing of water by the word, that he might present to himself a glorious church, not having spot, or wrinkle, or any such thing–but that she should be holy and without blemish" (Eph 5.25–27) The Church obeys Christ as a woman obeys her husband, "for no man ever yet hated his own flesh, but he nourishes it and cherishes it, even as the Lord the church, because we are members of his body" (Eph 5.29–30). Citing the words of the Old Testament that "a man shall leave his father and his mother and shall cleave to his wife, and they two shall be one flesh" (Gen 2.24), Paul emphasizes that "this is a great mystery, but I speak concerning Christ and the church" (Eph 5.32).

The crux of the Epistle to the Ephesians revolves around, above all, the unity between Christ and the Church, which Paul likens to a marital union. God was presented as a spouse even in the Old Testament, and the people of Israel were his bride. In the New Testament, the Church as the "new Israel"[1]

---

[1]The theology of the "new Israel" dates back to the Apostle Paul; it opposes the "Israel of God" (Gal 6.16), i.e. the Church, to the "Israel in the flesh" (1 Cor 10.18), i.e. the people of Israel. This theology found reflection in patristic works, including those that were directed against the Jews. In later times that teaching on the Christian Church as the new Israel came to be called a "substitute theology" (in the sense that the Church somehow substituted itself as the people of Israel, chosen by God). Western liberal theology saw signs of anti-Semitism in "substitution theology" and turned away from it. However, from the Orthodox Church's point of view, the teaching on the new Israel did not have any real anti-Semitism, since it is unthinkable to call works of the Fathers of the Church that contain

becomes the bride and spouse of God incarnate, who is presented not just as being jealous of the Church with regard to idols, but as loving, nourishing, and caring for it. The image of the bride, united to a husband through the bonds of marriage, and the image of the body, united to the head, emphasizes the ontological proximity between Christ and his Church.

However, the image of the Church as a pure and spotless virgin is no less important for the understanding of the Church's holiness. According to the Apostle Paul, the Church "is holy and spotless": created by Holy God, it is the bearer of divine holiness. All the members of the Church join in this holiness. It is no accident that the phrase "holy ones" (or "saints") in the book of Acts is a designation for all those who believe in Christ. This word usage is preserved in the Orthodox liturgy, especially in the ancient exclamation of the liturgy "the Holy things are for the holy," which shows that the sacred objects (the Holy Gifts) should be taught only to the holy, that is, the faithful members of the Church. The words "blessed is the entrance of thy saints," pronounced by the senior celebrant at the little entrance, have the same idea: this exclamation indicated that all the faithful enter into the church building with the presider for the accomplishment of the Eucharist. The point here concerns not the personal holiness of each Christian, but rather the Christians who are called to be holy through participation in God's sanctity, submitting to him through the Church, the Eucharist, and the other sacraments, and through the communion of the Holy Spirit.

The Apostle Peter speaks on the calling of Christian society to holiness: "You are a chosen generation, a royal priesthood, a holy nation, a peculiar people, that you should show forth the praises of him who has called you out of darkness into his marvelous light" (1 Pet 2.9). Christians are this "holy nation," but again not by virtue of a personal sanctity, but by virtue of being called to perfection. In the Old Testament, membership in the people of Israel was secured through circumcision, but priesthood was accessible only to those who came from the loins of Levi. In the New Testament, all Christians become a "royal priesthood" and all become a chosen race, the new Israel.

Speaking on the holiness of the Church, Clement of Alexandria stresses that the source of this holiness is God himself, whose receptacle is the Church:

mere disputes with Judaism in them as anti-Semitic. The teaching of the Church as new Israel makes up an inseparable part of the Tradition of the Christian Church and from this perspective it does not merit any further review.

If sacred has a twofold application, designating both God himself and the structure raised to his honor, how shall we not with propriety call the Church holy, through knowledge, made for the honor of God, sacred to God, of great value, and not constructed by mechanical art, nor embellished by the hand of an impostor, but by the will of God fashioned into a temple? For it is not now the place, but the assemblage of the elect, that I call the Church. This temple is better for the reception of the greatness of the dignity of God. For the living creature which is of high value, is made sacred by that which is worth all, or rather which has no equivalent, in virtue of the exceeding sanctity of the latter. . . . Here, too, we shall find the divine likeness and the holy image in the righteous soul, when it is blessed in being purified and performing blessed deeds.[2]

Cyprian of Carthage, developing the image from the Epistle to the Ephesians, sees in this image an indication of the necessity for all Christians to preserve faith in the Church, as the Church preserves faith in Christ. In the Old Testament, idol worship was compared to adultery; in the New Testament, falling away from the Church into schism becomes a spiritual adultery in exactly the same way:

From her womb we are born, by her milk we are nurtured, by her spirit we are given life. It is not possible for the bride of Christ to be counterfeited, there has been no tampering with her, and she is chaste. She knows one home, she guards the sanctity of one bedchamber with a chaste modesty. She watches over us for God, she seals her sons, to whom she has given birth, for the kingdom. Whoever dissociates himself from the Church is joined to a counterfeit paramour, he is cut off from the promises of Christ, and neither will he who abandons Christ's Church attain to Christ's rewards. He is a foreigner, he is deconsecrated, he is an enemy.[3]

How is the Church's holiness expressed? Above all by saying that it infallibly preserves Christ's teaching. Irenaeus of Lyons emphasizes that the guarantees of the Church's theological infallibility are the Holy Spirit acting within it, and the apostolic hierarchical succession:

---

[2] *Stromata* 7.5.
[3] *The Unity of the Catholic Church* 5–6 (2006), 155–157.

The preaching of the Church is everywhere consistent, and continues in an even course, and receives testimony from the prophets, the apostles, and all the disciples—as I have proved—through [those in] the beginning, the middle, and the end, and through the entire dispensation of God, and that well-grounded system which tends to man's salvation, namely, our faith; which, having been received from the Church, we do preserve, and which always, by the Spirit of God, renewing its youth, as if it were some precious deposit in an excellent vessel, causes the vessel itself containing it to renew its youth also. For this gift of God has been entrusted to the Church, as breath was to the first created man, for this purpose, that all the members receiving it may be vivified; and the [means of] communion with Christ has been distributed throughout it, that is, the Holy Spirit, the earnest of incorruption, the means of confirming our faith, and the ladder of ascent to God. . . . For where the Church is, there is the Spirit of God; and where the Spirit of God is, there is the Church, and every kind of grace; but the Spirit is truth.[4]

Whereas the Church infallibly preserves the Christian faith in purity, its individual members can sin and fall into heresy. In this case they fall away from the Church:

"For in the Church," it is said, "God hath set apostles, prophets, teachers," and all the other means through which the Spirit works; of which all those are not partakers who do not join themselves to the Church, but defraud themselves of life through their perverse opinions and infamous behavior. . . . Those, therefore, who do not partake of him, are neither nourished into life from the mother's breasts, nor do they enjoy that most limpid fountain which issues from the body of Christ . . . and drink putrid water out of the mire, fleeing from the faith of the Church lest they be convicted; and rejecting the Spirit, that they may not be instructed.[5]

The sanctity of the Church is expressed not just in that it participates in the holiness of its own Founder and preserves his teaching unharmed. Amongst its members are people who possess personal holiness thanks to their own spiritual efforts and the grace of God, promoting matters of

[4] *Against Heresies* 3.24.1.
[5] Ibid.

spiritual perfection. However, only God is holy in the absolute sense. Even in the angels God "perceives perverseness" (Job 4.18). What is the case then of people when, as it says in a prayer for the departed read in the Orthodox Church, "there is no man who is without sin"? There are no sinless people; there are people who have reached a high level of spiritual perfection, who have overcome within themselves the tug of sin and who have come close to God. The Church calls these people saints.

Holiness is the calling of every person, and the Church promotes personal holiness not just as an ideal, but as the norm. At the same time, the Church never demanded holiness in terms of an absolute condition of membership. Imitating God, who "makes his sun to rise on the evil and on the good, and sends rain on the just and on the unjust" (Mt 5.45), the Church deals with each person in love, the righteous and the sinner alike. Sin is perceived as a sickness, and the Church does not sever the afflicted member, but heals it.

It is no accident that one of the images frequently used by the holy Fathers in exposition of teachings on the Church was the image of hospital. "Have you sinned?" asks John Chrysostom, "Enter a church . . . and repent: this is a hospital, not a courtroom; here they do not torture, but rather forgive sins."[6] The Church of God, Chrysostom says, "is a spiritual market and simultaneously a hospital for souls: consequently, we should, like those going to market, gather up many goods and return home; we should, like those entering a hospital, take here the medicine corresponding to our illness and leave here with it."[7] Anastasius of Sinai asks: "Do you really not see that God's Church is a hospital and refuge? If you leave a hospital while remaining sick, and do not receive healing, then where will you receive it afterwards? If you are in a harbor waiting out a storm, then where will you find silence?"[8]

The contradiction between the holiness of the Church and the sinfulness of its members has occupied the minds of Christian writers throughout the whole course of church history. However, specific disputes never arose in the East on the issue of the Church's holiness. Such disputes arose in the third century in the heart of the Western Church, where two heretical lines arose that brought the question of the holiness of the Church and the sinfulness

---

[6] *Homily on Repentance* 3.4.
[7] *Homily on Genesis* 32.1.
[8] *Oration on the Holy Meeting.*

St Ambrose of Milan.
Basilica of St Ambrose.
Milan. End of the 5th c.

of its members to the forefront. The Novatianists[9] rejected the possibility of repenting from the effects of sins committed after baptism, and excommunicated sinners from church relations. According to the Donatists,[10] the Church is the society of saints and it has a duty to exclude those who fall away during persecutions; the Donatists proclaimed the sacraments performed by unworthy celebrants to be ineffectual.

Such Western authors as Cyprian of Carthage, Ambrose of Milan, Optatus of Milevis, and the Blessed Augustine, were opposed to this heretical trend. Arguing with the Novatianists, St Ambrose turns to the traditional image of the Church as hospital:

Do you then, O Novatians, shut out these? For what is it when you refuse the hope of forgiveness but to shut out? But the Samaritan did not pass by the man who had been left half dead by the robbers; he dressed his wounds with oil and wine, first pouring in oil in order to comfort them; he set the wounded man on his own beast . . . nor did the Shepherd despise his wandering sheep. But you say: "Touch me not. . . ." When, then, you take away all the fruits of repentance, what do you say but this: Let no one who is wounded enter our inn, let no one be healed in our Church? With us the sick are not cared for, we are whole, we have no need of a physician.[11]

Optatus of Milevis (fourth century) expressed important thoughts on the struggle with Donatism.[12] According to his teaching, "the sacraments are holy in and of themselves, not because of people, for God makes everything

---

[9] So named for the Roman priest Novatian, who in 251 usurped the Roman episcopal throne.

[10] This term comes from the name Donatus, who was elected to the Carthaginian episcopate in 312, which Caecilianus occupied. Donatus' supporters claimed that Caecilianus' ordination was ineffectual, since the bishop who performed the laying on of hands on him showed weakness during the persecutions of Emperor Diocletian.

[11] *Concerning Repentance* 1.6.

[12] Cf. Hilarion (Troitsky), *Tvoreniya: V 3 tomakh 1: Ocherki po istorii dogmata o Tserkvi* (Moscow: 2004), 316–323.

pure, not man."[13] Speaking on the sacrament of baptism, Optatus stresses: "The first degree in the completion of a sacramental act pertains to the Holy Trinity, without whom baptism itself is impossible; following after this is the faith of the person being baptized; the person performing the baptism presents himself as something more peripheral, not having equal significance compared to God and the faith of the one being baptized." Optatus comes to the conclusion that "the sacrament cannot depend on the identity of its enactor," since man is changeable, and only the true fulfillment of the sacrament—God—is immutable.[14] Following from here is the conclusion that deals with the holiness of the Church and the sinfulness of its members: "The Church, then, is One, and her holiness is not measured by the pride of individuals, but is derived from the sacrament. It is for this reason that she alone is called by Christ his Dove and his own beloved Bride. The Church cannot be amongst all the heretics and schismatics. It follows that [according to you] she must be in one place only."[15]

Optatus' teaching was received and developed by the Blessed Augustine. Disputing with the Donatists, Augustine compared the Church to a net, in which good fish are mixed in with the bad: it is only possible to make a final separation of sinners from the righteous in an eschatological perspective, while on earth, the righteous coexist with sinners.[16] The Church is like the ark of Noah, in which clean animals are found together with the unclean.[17] The parable of the tares shows as well that until the harvest, the wheat should grow together with the tares.[18] Even if the majority of people within the Church are sinners, nonetheless it does not serve to abuse the Church for this, as the heretics do.[19]

All of these ideas of the Western fathers of the Church were accepted by the Eastern Christian tradition, though with a few highly essential reservations. Above all, as we already noted, the mysteries were never considered in the East as possessing some kind of autonomous, almost magical power, which was preserved even outside the Church. Moreover, the efficacy of the

---

[13] *On the Donatist Schism* 5.4.
[14] Ibid.
[15] Ibid. 2.1.
[16] Cf. Augustine *Psalm against the Donatist Party* 8–20.
[17] *Epistle 108.*
[18] *On the Unity of the Church* 14.35.
[19] Ibid. 13.33.

sacraments in the Orthodox East was never so sharply juxtaposed with the personal quality of the clergyman as it was in the West. At least one liturgical text of the Eastern Church is known that suggests some kind of link between the moral qualities of the priest and the actions performed by them in the sacraments, which is the priestly prayer in the liturgy of Basil the Great: "Do not turn away the grace of thy Holy Spirit from these gifts here offered on account of my sins." There is no direct claim in this text that the sins of the celebrant become hindrances for the action of grace, and consequently, for the efficacy of the sacrament. However, it is possible and it does not exclude this possibility.

In the eleventh century Symeon the New Theologian claimed that the power "to bind and loose" pertains not to all priests, but only to those who "serve the Gospel and live a spotless life in a spirit of humility."[20] Symeon considered it insufficient to receive "the laying on of hands from people"[21]; one needs to be "preordained," that is, called to God by the Holy Spirit.[22]

> Therefore, the power to remit sins is given by God neither to those who have the monastic schema nor to those who are ordained to the ranks of the priesthood, nor to those honored by the office of episcopacy, I mean to patriarchs and metropolitans and bishops, merely because of their ordination and its office. Heaven forbid! Only the performance of services is permitted to them. . . . But the power of remitting sins is given only to those from among the priests and bishops and monks who belong to the rank of the disciples of Christ because of purity.[23]

At first glance such an opinion approaches Donatism, which asserted that sacraments performed by unworthy clerics could not be "efficacious." However, there are various considerations that allow one to see something else from Symeon's point of view, something other than merely a Donatist claim that the efficacy of a sacrament depends on the moral character of the priest who performed it. Above all, in the quoted text, Symeon does not so much put the efficacy of the sacrament performed by an unworthy priest to question, as much as he insists on the need for man to receive a special invitation

---

[20] *Catechetical Oration* 28.263–265.
[21] Ibid. 292–293.
[22] *Moral Oration* 6.428.
[23] *Letter on Confession* 14.

from God before he can take up the service of being a spiritual father; in other words, the power of "binding and loosing" should be "earned" by the priest on the path to moral self-perfection. Moreover, speaking out on similar ideas, Symeon the New Theologian was above all preoccupied with the moral condition of the spirituality of his time. Symeon never made any kind of dogmatic claim, only pointed out that the celebrant should be worthy of his high calling and a performer of the sacraments ought to stand on corresponding spiritual and moral heights.

The issue of the celebrant's moral condition was always a painful one for the Christian Church. How can the Church be Holy, if even amongst the clergy, let alone the simple faithful, there are unworthy, sinful, tainted people? This question was posed particularly sharply in those periods of the Church's history when persecutions ended and the Church became a powerful institution, utilizing the protection of worldly rule. In such times the image of the bishop as shepherd, spiritual leader, and elder, possessing endless authority in the eyes of the sheep by virtue of his high spiritual qualities, could give way to an image of the bishop as high government official, participating in worldly ceremonies, dutifully obeying the decrees of municipal authority not just in matters of church administration, but in dogmatic issues as well. The border between the Church and the world, between "the kingdom of the spirit" and "the kingdom of the Caesar" somehow faded away, and there was great temptation in this not only for the Church, but for those who observed it off to the side.

Yet criticism addressed to celebrants resounds not only from outside the Church, but within it too. Gregory the Theologian sharply criticizes bishops of his time for the reason that they, having received power, do not lead an ascetic way of life and lord themselves over others, being assured that their arch-priestly rank secures for them a theological and moral infallibility:

> There is a danger of the holiest of all offices being the most ridiculous among us. For promotion depends not on virtue, but upon villainy; and the sacred thrones fall not to the most worthy, but to the most powerful. . . . And there is not a physician, or a painter who has not first studied the nature of diseases, or mixed many colors, or practiced drawing: but a prelate is easily found, without laborious training, with a reputation of recent date, being sown and springing up in a moment. . . . We manufacture those who are

holy in a day, and bid those to be wise, who have had no instruction. . . .
[And he] haughtily takes precedence, and raises his eyebrow over his betters,
and does not tremble at his position, nor is he appalled at the sight, seeing
the disciplined man beneath him; and wrongly supposes himself to be his
superior in wisdom as well as in rank, having lost his senses under the influence of his position.[24]

Gregory asserts that rank does not make a man holy, neither does hierarchical position, nor a place on the throne, but a virtuous life. Gregory thinks
it unfair that minions and timeservers turn out to be at the wheel of the
Church's ship, since people who separate themselves through the holiness of
their lives are left in the darkness. He considers that personal holiness should
be the main criterion for elevation to the episcopal throne, and not an influential position in society, administrative capability, or social standing.

Some of Gregory's poems are specially dedicated to the theme of the worthiness of the priestly rank and the unworthiness of its bearers. One of them
contains no small biting invective of their moral character, supported by a
satirical description of the episcopal way of life.

> Gregory no longer dines with an earthly king, as before,
> He no longer indulges his small bag,[25]
> He will not recline amongst those feasting, cast down and silent,
> Barely surviving by breathing and nibbling food, like a slave. . . .
> I will not kiss the hand stained in blood. . . .
> I will not go with a grand retinue
> To the ordination, name-day, funeral, or wedding feast,
> So that all or individual maws can exterminate or let go
> Those in escort. . . .
> And so that at evening I might return again to the loaded ship—
>   the spiritual grave—
> To bring the burdened womb home;
> And so that, barely surviving by surfeit breath, I might hurry to
>   a new heavy laden table,
> Unable to be delivered from the coming feast.[26]

---

[24] *Oration* 43.26.
[25] Body.
[26] *Poems on Himself 17: On the differences of the way of life and of the false priests.*

Another one of Gregory's poems is called *On Oneself and on Bishops*. In it, Gregory speaks of bishops so bitingly that it was decided to omit it in a nine-teenth century Russian translation of the entire corpus of his works. Here Gregory cautions against "foolish bishops" who invite wolves into their sheepfolds:

> You can trust the lion, the leopard can be instructed,
> And even the serpent, possibly, will flee from you, although you
>   fear it;
> But beware of one—foolish bishops,
> Do not be confused by the worthiness of their throne!
> For all have reached a very high position, but not all have grace.
> Employing a penetrating gaze over the sheepfold, watch out for
>   wolves.[27]

Gregory the Theologian's view on the clerics of his time is highly pes-simistic, and his critique can seem excessively severe. Its value, however, is conditioned on the fact that it is from within the Church, not from without—a critique that comes from a man who suffers for the Church, and not one who approaches it with hostility.

Seven centuries later, Symeon the New Theologian addresses the clergy-men of his time with fiery invective in the final hymn from the collection *Hymns of Divine Love*, called *An Instruction Joined with a Reproach to all Men, Kings, Bishops, Priests, Monks, Laity, Presented as Spoken by the Mouth of God*. The hymn begins with an invective against emperors, whom Symeon reproaches for pagan actions and customs. Later there follows a series of invectives against bishops: Symeon rails against their pride, their irreverence toward the holy things, false humility, participation in worldly deeds, their greed, abro-gation of the canons, simony, and enrichment at the cost of church means. Symeon reproaches the clerics of his time for love of glory, love of money, profiting from their priestly rank, and other sins:

> Who among us, the priests of today, had begun to purify
>   himself of his iniquities,
> as to be so completely audacious in exercising his priesthood
> who could say this with full confidence

---

[27] *On Oneself and on Bishops* 33–38.

that he has despised the glory here below
and acts as a priest solely for that glory from above?
Who has loved Christ and him alone
and has scorned all gold and riches?
Who has made himself content with only the bare necessities
and has not cheated in any matter his neighbor?
Who does not have an accusing conscience
because of the gifts pushed upon him to become a priest
or to ordain other priests in buying or selling grace? . . . [28]
Who has never consecrated another bishop
because of a request from those of the world,
from rulers, friends, the rich and the powerful,
without the candidate being worthy?[29]
Really, there is no one today who in these matters has a clean
    heart
and who does not feel a disturbed conscience,
because he has done at least one of the things I mentioned?
But we all have sinned unscrupulously
without making any effort to eliminate the evil,
without engaging in the practice of good.[30]

Symeon threatens with the Last Judgment and eternal torment those clergymen who put material enrichment in the first place and do not watch over
their churches and their families. In the words of Symeon, they will be judged
by God like the man who squanders his wife's dowry, and does not have
money to pay back his debts and is thrown into prison.[31] In Symeon's opinion, the only person who can become a priest is he whose moral life corresponds to holiness and the epitome of service. All other paths to the
priesthood should be closed off:

[28]Simony, i.e. offering money in exchange for the laying on of hands to a priestly rank, became
one of the most widespread blemishes of the higher priesthood in various eras. Apostolic Canon 29
says: "If a bishop, or presbyter, or deacon should receive this honor with the aid of money, let him
and the one who ordained him be cast out and excommunicated."
    [29]A bishop, priest, or deacon, having used "the influence of worldly leaders" in order to receive
a holy rank, according to the ecclesial canons, should be cast out from his rank (Apostolic 30, Nicaea
3).
    [30]*Hymn 58* (Denville, NJ), 291–292.
    [31]Ibid. 294.

> Whoever firstly will not abandon the world
> and will not hate with all his soul the things of the world
> and will not sincerely love only Christ
> and will not lose his soul for him . . .
> such a one through many afflictions and labors
> would not be judged worthy to receive the Divine Spirit . . .
> that such a man would not dare to accept the priesthood
> and the authority over souls or to push himself to accept such![32]

Christ's bride is not only the Church, possessing neither stain nor blemish, but the soul of every Christian. However, Symeon does not see amongst the priesthood of his own time anyone who would trouble over his own soul:

> But who among us priests is concerned
> with the beauty of the soul of the spouse of Christ?
> Show me one and I would be satisfied with him![33]

Symeon's invective against his contemporaries reflects those negative manifestations in the life of the Church, which were on the opposite side of the coin of all the church "renaissances," be it in the fourth or in the eleventh century, be it in the Byzantine or post-Byzantine period. This invective, like the analogous railings of Gregory the Theologian against bishops found above, supports the fact that this critical attitude never left the Church. It always bore witness to its calling to holiness and did not lower the spiritual-moral bar, even if many of its members, including priests, could not reach this bar.

[32]Ibid. 292–293.
[33]Ibid. 294.

23

The Conciliarity of the Church

I N THE CREED, the Church is called Conciliar: this word is translated into the English language from the Greek *katholikē*/καθολική, which literally means "general," "all-encompassing," "universal." For the translation of καθολική into English for academic-theological literature, the word *catholic* is most often used (the Roman Catholic Church obviously uses this word to describe itself). Cyril of Jerusalem clarifies the idea behind the concept of "catholic" in the *Catechetical Lectures*, dedicated to the exposition of the teaching on the Church:

> It is called Catholic then because it extends over all the world, from one end of the earth to the other; and because it teaches universally and completely one and all the doctrines which ought to come to men's knowledge, concerning things both visible and invisible, heavenly and earthly; and because it brings into subjection to godliness the whole race of mankind, governors and governed, learned and unlearned; and because it universally treats and heals the whole class of sins, which are committed by soul or body, and possesses in itself every form of virtue which is named, both in deeds and words, and in every kind of spiritual gifts.[1]

Thus, the Church, according to Cyril's interpretation, is Catholic insofar as it extends to the whole world, is open for every person irrespective of ethnic provenance and social position. The absence of geographical borders in the Catholic Church is highlighted by its comparison to governments, each one of which is bordered by defined territorial boundaries: "The kings of particular nations have bounds set to their authority, [but] the Holy Church Catholic alone extends her power without limit over the whole world."[2]

---

[1]18.23.
[2]Ibid. 18.27.

The term "catholic," moreover, is used to differentiate the true Church from heretical communities. Insofar as heretical assemblies, which would deserve to be called "the Church of the evildoers," call themselves churches, the Creed teaches one to believe "in one Holy, Catholic Church," so that Christians might flee heretical communities and ever dwell in the Holy Universal Church. For this reason, Cyril continues, if you come to whichever city, then do not merely ask "Where is the church of the Lord?" for other dishonorable heretics call their caves churches of the Lord. So do not say "Where is the church?" but, "Where is the Catholic Church?" For it has its own name of "our Holy and general Mother Church, which is the Bride of our Lord Jesus Christ, the Only-Begotten Son of God."[3]

Each local church, that is the Church of a concrete place, enters into the make-up of the Universal Church. Cyprian of Carthage emphasizes this, comparing the Church to the sun from which rays emanate, to a trunk from which branches grow, to a spring from which rivers flow:

> Break a ray from the sun's globe, its unity does not suffer from any division of its light. Snap the bough from a tree, what is snapped off will not be able to produce buds. Cut off the stream from the fountain, so cut off it grows dry. Thus also the Church, when the light of the Lord is poured forth, though she sheds her rays of light throughout the whole world, nevertheless the light is one that is spread everywhere, but the unity is not cut off from the body. She extends her boughs into the whole world with an abundance of fruitful growth, she opens wide her streams that flow forth bountifully, nevertheless one is her head and source, and the one Mother is rich with the offspring of her fertility.[4]

In the interpretation of the First Epistle of the Apostle Paul to the Corinthians, speaking of the Church as the Body of Christ, John Chrysostom stimulates an interest in the words "you are the body of Christ and individually members of it" (1 Cor 12.27). Chrysostom questions what "individually" means. He answers:

> For because he had said, "the body," whereas the whole body was not the Corinthian Church, but the Church in every part of the world, therefore

---

[3]Ibid. 18.26.
[4]*The Unity of the Catholic Church* (Crestwood, NY: 2006), 155.

The Last Supper. Basilica of Sant' Apollinare Nuovo. Ravenna. 6th c.

he said, "severally" [individually]: i.e., the Church amongst you is a part of the Church existing everywhere and of the body which is made up of all the Churches: so that not only with yourselves alone, but also with the whole Church throughout the world, ye ought to be at peace, if at least ye be members of the whole body.[5]

Thus, the local church, whether it be in Corinth, Rome, or some other place, is only a part of the universal Church, which itself possesses all the local churches. This, however, does not signify that the local church has some sort of partial, incomplete character. Each local church, being a member of the one whole, universal, Catholic Church, possesses simultaneously within itself a complete ecclesiology and catholicity. In other words, the universal Church is not just the Catholic Church as the sum total of local churches, but as each local church found in relation with other Churches.

One theory that especially insists upon this is the so-called "eucharistic ecclesiology" cultivated in the second half of the twentieth century by Protopresbyter Nikolai Afanasiev, and further developed by Protopresbyters Alexander Schmemann and John Meyendorff, as well as by Metropolitan John Zizioulas. Eucharistic ecclesiology is an attempt to reconstruct the ecclesiology of the original Church, that is the Church of the apostolic age and of the first post-apostolic generation. The foundational sources for the

[5] *Homily on First Corinthians* 32.1.

construction of this ecclesiology are the epistles of the Apostle Paul, the compositions of Ignatius the God-Bearer and other apostolic men, as well as the works of western authors of the third century, particularly Tertullian and Cyprian of Carthage.

Eucharistic ecclesiology proceeds from the fact that the unity of the original Church consisted of the eucharistic community, united in one place around one celebrant (a bishop or a senior presbyter). As was already mentioned,[6] the first Christian Church was the community of Christ's disciples in Jerusalem: this was the very Holy, Catholic, and Apostolic Church that possessed the whole fullness of church and catholicity. As Christianity spread by degrees to other cities of the empire, other local communities began to arise, though each local community was perceived not just as a part of the universal Church, but as the very Catholic Church in all of its fullness. The guarantee of the catholicity of every local church was the presence in it of one Eucharistic meeting, presided over by the bishop as the chosen leader of God's people, or by a priest, to whom the bishop delegated this presidency.

Speaking on the early Christian ecclesiology, Protopresbyter Nikolai Afanasiev stresses that the experience of catholicity belonged to the members of each local church:

> In empirical actuality, the unity and fullness of God's Church is expressed in a multitude of local churches, of which each reveals not a part, but the whole Church of God. For this reason the multitude of local churches in empirical actuality preserves the unity and fullness of the Church, that is its catholicity. The unity of the local church itself is expressed in its united eucharistic gathering. The Church is one because it had one eucharistic gathering at which the people of God assembled, which consists of priests. . . . However many local churches did not grow, the Church's unity nevertheless remained unbroken, since there were not various eucharistic communities in all of them, but rather one and the same. The unity and fullness were not in the sum total of the local churches, not in their confederation, which never really existed anyway, but in each local church.[7]

[6]Cf. Orthodox Christianity vol. 1 (Crestwood, NY: 2011), 19.
[7]Nikolai Afanasiev, The Church of the Holy Spirit (Paris: 1971), 4–5.

The catholicity, ecumenicity, and universality of the Church, according to Afanasiev's claim, was associated in the minds of the first Christians not with the totality of the Local Churches, but with their own Local Church. Catholicity was perceived as an inner quality of the Church, not only as an outer attribute:

> Being united in all its fullness, the Church ever remained inwardly universal, since each local church contained in itself the rest of the local churches. That which was accomplished in one church was then accomplished in the others, since everything is completed in God's Church in Christ. By virtue of this catholic-universal nature, exclusivity and provincialism were completely foreign to the local churches. Not one church could separate itself from Christ. All were united between each other in love. Each church was the subject of love for all, and all were the subject of love for each.[8]

The basic line of church structure in the ancient Church "went from inner universalism to outer,"[9] considered Afanasiev. In other words, the consciousness of the local church was first, and catholicity was already perceived as a quality of the second degree, existing in all the local churches in totality. This is partly supported by the words of Ignatius the God-Bearer: "Wherever the bishop shall appear, there let the multitude [of the people] also be; even as where Christ is, there does all the heavenly host [the Catholic Church] stand by."[10] The context of St Ignatius' words allows one to claim that he is speaking precisely of a local Church with the bishop at its head. Moreover, the words can be understood in the sense of a comparison of the local church, presided over by the bishop, with the Catholic, universal Church, presided over by Christ.

In what way does the catholicity of the local church correspond to the catholicity of the Church on a universal scale? Protopresbyter John Meyendorff defines the above correlation thusly:

> The idea of a local church, headed by a bishop, who was usually chosen by the whole Church, but takes the form of those charismatic and apostolic functions as a descendant of Peter, is the doctrinal basis of conciliarity, as

[8]Ibid., 5.
[9]Ibid.
[10]*Epistle to the Smyrnaeans* 8.

it has entered into practice since the third century. For Eucharistic ecclesiology suggests that each local church, though the fullness of catholicity
pertains to it, is always found in unity and concord with all the other
churches, as participants of this catholicity. Bishops do not only bear
moral responsibility to this community: they co-participate in the one
episcopal service. . . . Each bishop accomplishes his service together with
the other bishops, because it is identical to the service of the others and
because the Church is one.[11]

Therefore, the local church, while catholic in all its fullness, is not self-sufficient: its catholicity is realized in communion with other local churches. In
resounding support of this is the fact that a bishop cannot appoint his own
replacement: according to ancient canonical practice, the bishop of one local
church (diocese, or eparchy) is chosen by the people of God, but ordained by
bishops of neighboring eparchies. Accordingly, the catholicity of the local
church is guaranteed not only by its being headed by a bishop, but by the
fact that this bishop received the laying on of hands from bishops of other
local cChurches and is in communion with them. The communion of bishops with one another makes up the inseparable trait of catholicity as conciliarity.

Here it is appropriate to mention that the Slavonic word *sobornost'* (from
which "conciliarity" was coined) entered firmly into contemporary ecclesial
language and is used not just in Russian, but in other European languages
(even in Greek) not only in terms of a synonym of catholicity, but in its own
character—as a term that decrees the catholic structure of the Church, its universal direction. The founders of the Russian Slavophile movement posited
such a use of the word "conciliarity," above all A.S. Khomiakov, in an ecclesiology of which this concept had a most important significance. Khomiakov
perceived the Church not only and not so much as an organization bound
by the outward authority of the hierarchy, as much as one conciliar organism, the members of which were bound by the one faith in principles of
equality and freedom:

In issues of faith, it is not the difference between a scholar and an ignora-
mus, between a clergyman and a layman, between a lord and a subject,

---

[11]John Meyendorff, *Orthodoxy in the Modern World* (Klin, 2002), 100–101.

between an overseer and a slave, where, when it is needed, by God's observation, a child receives the gift of sight, a youth is given a word of wisdom, the heresy of a learned bishop is refuted by an illiterate shepherd,
in order that all would be one in the free unity of the living faith, which
is the manifestation of the Spirit of God. Such is the dogma lying in the
depths of the idea of assembly.[12]

The notion of conciliarity as the unity and equality of all the members of
the Church was a most important element of the ecclesiology of A.S. Khomiakov and other Slavophiles. Khomiakov perceived the mystery of salvation in light of conciliarity: "When one falls from us, he falls alone, but no
one is saved alone. He who is saved, is saved in the Church as its member in
union with all of its other members."[13]

In the language of the Slavophiles, conciliarity (*sobornost'*) is not a juridical term, and it relates not so much to church government as it does to the
Church as such, to its inner character. Summarizing A. S. Khomiakov's views
on conciliarity, N.A. Berdiaev writes:

For him, the people were the subject of the Church. The conciliarity of
the people was free unity in love. The conciliarity of the Church, the fundamental idea of all Slavophilism, in which Slavophiles saw the essence
of Orthodoxy, does not conclude in itself formal and rational signs—there
is nothing juridical in conciliarity, nothing reminiscent of governmental
power, nothing outward or coercive. Although Khomiakov himself did
not like to use this word, the conciliarity of the Church is mystical, this
order sacramental. . . . Conciliarity is a living organism, and the people
of the Church live in it. In the proceedings of the ecumenical councils,
the conciliar spirit of the Church was spoken of more resoundingly than
all. Yet the authority of the ecumenical councils is not outward, not formal, not expressed rationally, not translated into juridical language. The
ecumenical councils are authoritative only because the truth of the living
conciliar organism of the Church was revealed in them. The Church is
not authority, the Church is the life of a Christian in Christ, in the body
of Christ, a free life, a grace-filled life.[14]

---

[12] *Izbranniye sochineniya* (NY: 1955), 266.
[13] *Tserkov' odna* (Moscow: 2005), 37.
[14] "Aleksei Stepanovich Khomiakov," *Sobraniye sochinenii* 5 (Paris: 1997), 86.

The teaching of the Slavophiles on the conciliarity of the Church ended up having great influence on contemporary Orthodox theology. It received development by the theologians of the "Paris School." Archpriest Georges Florovsky comes close to the Slavophiles when he claims:

> The catholicity (conciliarity) of the Church—this is not a quantitative or geographical concept. It does not at all depend on the truths scattered throughout the whole world. The Ecumenical Church is the result or manifestation of, and not the reason or basis for, catholicity. The world-wide spread, or universality, of the Church is only an outward sign, more-over it is a sign that is completely unnecessary. The Church was catholic even while Christian communities appeared only as single and rare islets on a sea of faithlessness and paganism. The Church will remain catholic up until the end of time. . . . The Church is not catholic due to its out-ward diffusion, or, in any case, not merely due to this. The Church is catholic not only because it presents itself as a kind of all-encompassing teaching, not only because it unites all its members, all the local churches, but because it is catholic through and through, in any of its smallest parts, in any act and event of its life. The Church's nature is catholic; it is catholic in the very fiber of its being. The Church is catholic, for it is the one body of Christ; it is the union in Christ, the unity in the Holy Spirit, and this unity is great in integrity and fullness.[15]

Florovsky says that in the catholicity of the Church "the injurious dual-ity between freedom and authority is resolved. There cannot be outward authority in the Church. Authority cannot be the source of spiritual life." Within the Church, everyone possesses freedom and is called up not to an official submission to an outer authority, but in order to "restrain one's sub-jectivity, to be freed from psychoses, to raise the level of one's consciousness to its full catholic measure." The Christian should "live in spiritual and con-templative accord with the historical fullness of the ecclesial experience," overcoming subjectivity and particularity. It is necessary to "enter with humility and confidence into the life of the Church and to try to find one-self in it." Trials and doubts of an individual Christian can be resolved "in the united, catholic, and ascetical forces."[16]

---

[15]"The Catholicity of the Church," *Selected Theological Writings* (Moscow, 2000), 143–145.
[16]Ibid., 156–157.

Florovsky relates the idea of catholicity to Eucharistic ecclesiology, cultivated by the theologians of the "Paris School." In Florovsky's words, "the Church recognized its own unity and catholicity and exists above all in Eucharistic sacramental action."[17] The Eucharist is "the spiritual unity of the presiders of the Church, the indivisible conciliarity of prayerful communion."[18] The catholic range and boldness is in liturgical prayer, for it encompasses the whole world. The Eucharistic prayer "with loving care envelops all the fullness and complexity of life's situation and condition, all the complexity of worldly fate": the prayers for the living and the dead at the liturgy are in this vein. The Eucharist is accomplished not only by the person present there in the church, but somehow by the person of the whole Church "in connection with the whole Church."[19]

Pentecost. Byzantium. 12th c.

Orthodox theologians in the twentieth century effectively utilized the teaching on conciliarity in polemics with Catholics. It even turned out to be a tradition to set up Orthodox conciliarity in opposition to Roman papism. Many Orthodox Christians were sure that a council possesses the highest authority in the Orthodox Church, whereas in Catholicism highest authority is attributed to the pope; in Orthodox Christianity, the conciliar mind of the Church is the guarantee of theological infallibility, while in Catholicism infallibility is attained by the Roman bishop.

Such oppositions, however, are subject to infamous simplifications and require substantial clarification on an informative level. The Orthodox categorically reject the idea of papal infallibility, although they do not at all disregard the infallibility of a church council. As we noted when speaking on the significance of the ecumenical councils,[20] there were "robber councils" throughout history, which had all the signs of an ecumenical council, though the Church rejected them post-facto. No outward attribute, as the

[17]"Eucharist and Conciliarity," *Selected Theological Writings* (Moscow, 2000), 75.
[18]Ibid., 76.
[19]Ibid., 77.
[20]*Orthodox Christianity* vol 1, 58.

history of the Church can attest, can guarantee the unimpeded realization of conciliarity.

Observing the history of the ecumenical councils, we arrived at the conclusion that an ecumenical council is by no means the highest organ of guidance in the Orthodox Church: the Orthodox Church has gone on living without ecumenical councils for more than twelve centuries already. And on the level of the local church a council, though desirable, is not at all absolute and not the only way of expressing conciliarity. Over the course of more than 200 years, the entirety of the Synodal period, the Russian Church did not convoke councils of bishops. During this time the Church lived a full-blooded spiritual life, carrying out its salvific mission.

The Church's conciliarity is expressed not only in councils, but in the communion of bishops between one another, in the exchange of letters, in a bishop making two or a few bishops in a region; in the newly established bishop, ascending the episcopal throne, informing a bishop of a neighboring diocese of this news. The same main linking factors and guarantees of conciliarity are precisely the participation of all bishops, clergy, and laymen of various local churches in the Eucharist, which is accomplished in every place, but remains one and indivisible.

Conciliarity, according to the Orthodox understanding, is manifest in that all the bishops, regardless of possible differences in status, calling, and significance, are equal amongst themselves. The head of the local church (the patriarch, metropolitan, or archbishop) is the first among equals: on the sacramental level as on the level of theological infallibility, he is by no means higher or better than other bishops. In this sense, the words of St Cyprian spoken at the Carthaginian Council of 256 are guiding ones for the Orthodox Church: "Not one of us may make himself a bishop of bishops" (*nemo se episcopum episcoporum constituat*).[21]

From the Orthodox point of view, the Roman pope made himself precisely such a "bishop of bishops," officially naming himself "the highest priest of the Universal Church," and this is one of the reasons why the Orthodox do not accept the idea of papal primacy in this form, in which he exists in catholicity and papal infallibility. From the Orthodox point of view, there is not one quality that can be attributed to a bishop that another bishop

---

[21]Cf. the commentary on Cyprian of Carthage's *Epistle 70: To Quintus, Concerning the Baptism of Heretics* in the Patrologia Latina Database. Ed. Chadwyck-Healey. 1993–1995.

would not also possess. If the pope of Rome is infallible when he speaks from his throne, this means that the patriarch of Constantinople, the patriarch of Moscow, or any other diocesan archbishop of any local church should have this infallibility when they speak from their thrones. If the pope of Rome is the "vicar of Christ," then any other bishop should be named vicar of Christ.

Here it is appropriate to recall once more Cyprian of Carthage's words that "the episcopacy is one, and every one of the bishops participates *fully* in it." On the sacramental and theological level, each bishop possesses episcopal authority in its fullness, being equal to that of any other bishop. And each cathedra, be it in Rome, Constantinople, Moscow, Samara, or Vladivostok, is equal to any other cathedra. The primacy among the episcopacy can only be first in honor, but not a judicial primacy, and much less a primacy of theological infallibility. One bishop's acquisition of any kind of special sacramental or theological privilege is, from the Orthodox point of view, a crude rupture and radical perversion of the principle of the Church's conciliarity.

Conciliarity in the Church exists not only on the level of the episcopate, but on the level of lesser clergy and laymen. The Slavophiles connected the conception of conciliarity with the introduction of the people of God as bearers of ecclesial truth, by which laymen were understood to be "people of God." The Slavophiles' ideas influenced Russian hierarchs and theologians at the beginning of the twentieth century to involve laymen in the preparations of the Local Council and participate in its proceedings. Laymen participated in the Local Council of 1917–1918 as delegates with full rights and played a rather substantial role. However, this was clearly an innovation, since all the councils of the ancient Church, whether ecumenical or local, were councils of bishops, and laymen did not participate in them. Exceptions were the emperor as *pontifex maximus* (exalted high priest) and functionaries, appointed for maintaining order, and perhaps secretaries and scribes as well, who would have been present at the councils without the right to vote.

24

The Apostolicity of the Church. Hierarchy and Clergy

O NE WIDESPREAD PHENOMENON in the contemporary Christian world is
known as "anticlericalism." This phenomenon exists in various forms
and is especially noticeable in Protestant circles. Anticlericalists, not rejecting
the Church as such, are against the excessive (in their point of view) concentration of ecclesial power in the hands of the clergy, appealing for as much
authority as possible, in terms of actions in the direction of the Church, to
be given to laymen. Anticlericalism extends its roots back to the Middle Ages,
when lay participation in the Catholic Church was reduced to practically
nothing. The Council of Trent made this situation permanent, proclaiming
a division of the Church into those who teach (the clergy) and those who
learn (the laity).

The history of the early Church does not justify such a sharp division of
the Church into clergy and laity. The "sacramental" priesthood (using contemporary terminology, ill-suited for the consideration of the history of the
ancient Church) arose gradually, and it grew by no means in opposition to
the laity and in no way subjected the laity to an external spiritual authority.
The ministry of bishops and priests became the continuation of the ministry
that Christ entrusted to the whole Church, to all of the "new Israel."

Early Christianity, by Nikolai Afanasiev's observation, was a lay movement.[1] In the Old Testament, the priesthood was closed off outside its own
body: priests came from the offspring of Levi, and access to the priesthood
was closed to the members of the other tribes. Christ himself "sprang out of
Judah, and of that tribe Moses said nothing concerning priesthood" (Heb
7.14). In the Epistle to the Hebrews Christ is presented as "a high priest after
the order of Melchizedek" (Heb 5.10), a priest without father, without mother,

[1] *The Church of the Holy Spirit*, 12.

437

The forefather Melchizedek.
Ferapontov Monastery. Russia.
16th c.

without genealogy (Heb 7.1–3). Christ's priesthood is "not after the law of a carnal commandment, but after the power of an endless life" (Heb 7.16). There were many priests in the Old Testament, "but he, because he continues forever, has an unchangeable priesthood" (Heb 7.24). The Old Testament priests offered sacrifices daily for their sins and for the sins of the people, but Christ "did [this] once and for all when he offered up himself" (Heb 7.27). The Old Testament priesthood was focused around the tabernacle of the covenant in the temple of Jerusalem, but Christ is "a minister of the sanctuary and of the true tabernacle, that the Lord set up, and not man" (Heb 8.2). The Old Testament priests entered the tabernacle, offering the blood of goats and calves, but Christ "neither by the blood of goats and calves, but by his own blood, entered once for all into the Holy Place, having obtained eternal redemption" (Heb 9.12).

The apostles did not have a relation to the Levitical priesthood either, and although in the initial period after Christ's resurrection they continued to attend the Jerusalem temple for participation in the services, this temple did not become the center of their church life. The liturgical life of the first Christians was very quickly dissociated from the Jerusalem temple and was focused around the Eucharist–the breaking of bread, which took place in homes.[2]

The apostles summoned the first Christians to build up spiritual temples and offer spiritual sacrifices. The most important thing in this sense is the following text from the First Epistle of Peter:

> [Come to him], a living stone, rejected indeed by men, but chosen by God, precious. You also, as living stones, are built up into a spiritual house, a holy priesthood, to offer up spiritual sacrifices acceptable to God through Jesus Christ. . . . But you are a chosen generation, a royal priesthood, a holy nation, a peculiar people; that you should show forth the praises of him who has called you out of darkness into his marvelous light. For in time past you were not a people, but now you are the people of God: you had not obtained mercy, but now you have obtained mercy. (1 Pet 2.4–10)

[2]Acts 2.46.

"Let all mortal flesh keep silent." Sretensky Monastery. Moscow. 17th c.

This text has a decisive significance for the understanding of the nature of the priesthood in the New Testament Church. If in the Old Testament, the Levites were devoted to God, called out from the midst of the people of Israel (Deut 10.8; Num 8.15), then in the New Testament those dedicated to God are all Christians. "All of the New Testament people are God's clergy, and each one is a cleric in him," as expressed by Afanasiev.[3] The early Christian Church did not know a division of clergy and laity in the modern understanding.[4] In it, all are stones of the spiritual house, all make up "a royal priesthood, a holy nation," all are dedicated to God.

At the same time, the structure of the ancient Church was not anarchy. From the very beginning there existed in it a ministry of leadership, concentrated in the hands of the apostles—those closest disciples of Christ, witnesses of his life, death, and resurrection. It is exactly belonging to the circle of Christ's disciples that separated the apostles from other believers in Christ, and natural order placed them at the head of ecclesial governance. The apostles' preaching was the witness of what they "have heard, which [they] have seen" (1 Jn 1.1), and it is this that added a special persuasiveness to it. The apostles were those whom the Lord himself chose for ministry (Jn 15.16), to whom the Lord himself bestowed authority to bind and to loose (Mt 18.18): their authority is founded on this above all.

[3] *The Church of the Holy Spirit*, 14.
[4] Ibid., 15.

There are twelve who are numbered among the apostles, whom Christ chose. After Judas' fall Matthias was chosen to take his place. The account of Matthias' choosing (Acts 1.21–26) bears witness to the fact that the apostolic community considered it necessary to take unto itself those functions that pertained to Christ's earthly life. One of those functions became the replenishment of the circle of the apostles, another became celebrating the Eucharist. One of the apostles took the place of Christ at the Last Supper at the first Eucharist celebrated after Christ's resurrection: most likely this was Peter, as the effective leader of the apostolic community.

The circle of the apostles was widened on account of Paul after he embraced Christianity. In contrast to the twelve, he was not with Jesus during his earthly life. He called himself "least of the apostles, not fit to be called an apostle, because I persecuted the church of God." He added, however, comparing himself with the other apostles, "I labored more abundantly than all of them—yet not I, but the grace of God that is with me" (1 Cor 15.9–10). Paul very much insists on his apostleship, which, clearly, was contested by other disciples who considered that only someone who was with Jesus from the time of his baptism by John up to his resurrection, and who was a witness to his resurrection (Acts 1.21–22), could be an apostle. In the Epistle to the Corinthians, whom he brought to Christianity, Paul says: "Am I not an apostle? Am I not free? Have I not seen Jesus Christ our Lord? Are you not my work in the Lord? If I am not an apostle to others, yet doubtless I am to you; for you are the seal of my apostleship in the Lord" (1 Cor 9.1–2). All of Paul's epistles begin with a greeting in which he calls himself an apostle of Jesus Christ.

Speaking of the Church as the body of Christ, the Apostle Paul refers to different ministries in which God has placed members of the Church:

And God has appointed some in the church, first apostles, second prophets, third teachers; after that miracles, then gifts of healing, helping [in various ways], governing, diversities of tongues. Are all apostles? Are all prophets? Are all teachers? Do all work miracles? Do all have gifts of healing? Do all speak with tongues? Do all interpret? (1 Cor 12.28–30)

In this list of ministries, besides apostles and teachers, a whole category of charismatic gifts is enumerated that existed in the ancient Church, but has subsequently been lost or abolished—at least in terms of specific ministries. Among these the ministry of prophets and healers can be noted in particular. Also lost to the modern Church is the gift of speaking in tongues, which was once widespread throughout the ancient Church. The Apostle Paul was already quite critical toward this phenomenon, considering that speaking in a senseless language was not edifying for the Church (1 Cor 14.2–5). "I thank my God that I speak with tongues more than all of you," Paul writes to the Corinthians, "yet in the church I had rather speak five words with my understanding, that I might instruct others also, than ten thousand words in a tongue" (1 Cor 14.18–19).[5] The loss to the Church of the special institutions of prophecy, speaking in tongues, and healing does not signify, from the Orthodox point of view, an impoverishment of the gifts of the Holy Spirit. All these gifts and ministries exist in the Church, just in other forms.

Of all the many ministries that existed in the ancient Church, the oldest and most indispensible has turned out to be that of leadership. In the first years of the Church's existence, the apostles began to ordain presbyters and bishops to lead the local churches, creating an apostolic preaching as a result. Thus was the implementation of apostolic succession in the Church. The apostolic succession of the hierarchy is a key concept of Orthodox ecclesiology: only that Church in which an unbroken succession of the hierarchy exists, coming from the apostles, is the true Church of Christ. If such a succession is absent or somehow broken, the Church cannot be considered true, the hierarchy cannot be considered legitimate, and the sacraments cannot be considered efficacious.

Clement of Rome, one of the earliest writers of the post-apostolic age, says concerning apostolic succession:

> The apostles have preached the Gospel to us from the Lord Jesus Christ; Jesus Christ has done so from God. Christ therefore was sent forth by God, and the apostles by Christ. Both these appointments, then, were made in an orderly way, according to the will of God. Having therefore received their orders . . . they went forth proclaiming that the kingdom of God was at hand. And thus preaching through countries and cities, they appointed the first-fruits [of their labors], having first proved them by the Spirit, to be bishops and deacons of those who should afterwards believe.[6]

---

[5] Speaking in tongues has arisen in contemporary Pentecostal communities, although the Orthodox Church is skeptical of the given phenomenon, by no means considering it necessarily to be a manifestation of the grace-filled gifts of the Holy Spirit.

[6] *First Epistle to the Corinthians* 42.

Clement says in his epistle that it is impermissible to deprive of the dignity of the episcopate those who are worthy of it, those who were "appointed by [the apostles], or afterwards by other eminent men, with the consent of the whole Church."[7] Clement calls these revered men either bishops or presbyters. When observing the canonical structure of the Church, we said already that there was no precise division between the functions of a bishop and a priest in the first century. However, such a division was fully worked out in the second century,[8] and since that time the Church has preserved it without exception.

The concept of apostolic succession is linked with episcopal ministry in the Church. Irenaeus of Lyons developed this concept with the utmost precision in the second century:

> It is within the power of all, therefore, in every Church, who may wish to see the truth, to contemplate clearly the tradition of the apostles manifested throughout the whole world; and we are in a position to reckon up those who were by the apostles instituted bishops in the Churches, and [to demonstrate] the succession of these men to our own times. . . . For they were desirous that these men should be very perfect and blameless in all things, whom also they were leaving behind as their successors, delivering up their own place of government to these men; which men, if they discharged their functions honestly, would be a great boon [to the Church], but if they should fall away, the direst calamity.[9]

Irenaeus offers up the example of the Roman Church as an example of the unbroken line of apostolic succession, preserved in the Church by means of the laying on of hands:

> Since, however, it would be very tedious, in such a volume as this, to reckon up the succession of all the Churches, we do put to confusion all those who, in whatever manner, whether by an evil self-pleasing, by vainglory, or by the blindness and perverse opinion, assemble in unauthorized meetings; [we do this, I say,] by indicating that tradition derived from the apostles, of the very great, the very ancient, and universally known Church founded and organized at Rome by the two most glorious

[7]Ibid. 44.
[8]See *Orthodox Christianity* vol I, 326.
[9]*Against Heresies* 3.3.1.

apostles, Peter and Paul; as also [by pointing out] the faith preached to men, which comes down to our time by means of the succession of the bishops. For it is a matter of necessity that every Church should agree with this Church, on account of its pre-eminent authority, that is, the faithful everywhere, inasmuch as the apostolic tradition has been preserved continuously by those [faithful men] who exist everywhere.[10]

This famous text of Irenaeus of Lyons has been used over the centuries for the defense of the special privileges of the Roman Church, to which every other local church should conform itself, "on account of its pre-eminent authority." According to the Roman Catholic teaching, unity in faith with the Roman Church is the condition for abiding in the Church and the preservation of the true faith, insofar as it is founded on Peter, the prince of the apostles, and it is from Peter that the highest authority over the whole Universal Church is transmitted to the Roman bishops. However, Irenaeus' words do not support this theory. First of all, Irenaeus speaks of the Roman Church as being based on Peter and Paul, not Peter only, and nothing is said of the primacy of Peter. Secondly, he offers the example of the Roman Church as just one of the local churches, specifically saying that he does this so as not to go on too much concerning the transmission of apostolic succession of other Churches. Finally, and this is key, Irenaeus speaks of the Roman Church not as ecumenical and universal, with the other churches as a part of it, but as one of the local churches, although it has "pre-eminent authority" by virtue of its antiquity.

Enumerating the successors of Peter and Paul, Irenaeus traces the line of succession down to his own time:

The blessed apostles, then, having founded and built up the Church, committed into the hands of Linus the office of the episcopate. . . . To him succeeded Anacletus; and after him, in the third place from the apostles, Clement was allotted the bishopric. . . . To this Clement there succeeded Evaristus. Alexander followed Evaristus; then, sixth from the apostles, Sixtus was appointed; after him, Telephorus . . . then Hyginus; after him, Pius, then after him, Anicetus. Soter after succeeded Anicetus, Eleutherius does now, in the twelfth place from the apostles, hold the

---

[10]Ibid. 3.3.2.

inheritance of the episcopate. In this order, and by this succession, the
ecclesiastical tradition from the apostles, and the preaching of the truth,
have come down to us. And this is most abundant proof that there is one
and the same vivifying faith, which has been preserved in the Church
from the apostles until now, and handed down in truth.[11]

Thus Irenaeus sees in the apostolic Tradition not only a guarantee of succession of ecclesial governance, but purity of dogma as well. One of the main
arguments motivating Irenaeus against the Gnostics is the absence of their
apostolic succession. This succession, according to Irenaeus' teaching, is preserved in the Roman Church just as it is in other local churches, in particular in Smyrna and Ephesus:

*The Holy Martyr Polycarp of
Smyrna. Meteora. Greece.
16th c.*

But Polycarp[12] also was not only instructed by
apostles, and conversed with many who had seen
Christ, but was also, by apostles in Asia, appointed
bishop of the Church in Smyrna, whom I also saw
in my early youth, for he tarried [on earth] a very
long time, and, when a very old man, gloriously
and most nobly suffering martyrdom, departed
this life, having always taught the things which he
had learned from the apostles, and which the
Church has handed down, and which alone are
true. To these things all the Asiatic Churches testify, as do also those men who have succeeded
Polycarp down to the present time, a man who was
of much greater weight, and a more steadfast witness of truth, than
Valentinus, Marcion, and the rest of the heretics. He it was who, coming
to Rome in the time of Anicetus caused many to turn away from the
aforesaid heretics to the Church of God, proclaiming that he had received
this one and sole truth from the apostles, that, namely, which is handed
down by the Church. . . . Then, again, the Church in Ephesus, founded
by Paul, and having John remaining among them permanently until the
times of Trajan, is a true witness of the tradition of the apostles.[13]

---

[11]Ibid. 3.3.3.

[12]Polycarp of Smyrna: one of the apostolic men, a disciple of John the Theologian, and author
of the *Epistle to the Philippians*.

[13]Irenaeus of Lyons *Against Heresies* 3.3.4.

At the same time one will notice that Tertullian gives a different genealogy of the bishops of Rome in the third century (claiming that Clement
received the laying on of hands from the Apostle Peter, and not recalling
Linus and Anacletus at all). As for the rest, though, Tertullian is in complete
agreement with Irenaeus, and practically repeats his teaching on apostolic
succession word for word:

> Let [the heretics] produce the original records of their churches; let them
> unfold the roll of their bishops, running down in due succession from the
> beginning in such a manner that [that first bishop of theirs] shall be able
> to show for his ordainer and predecessor some one of the apostles or of
> apostolic men, a man, moreover, who continued steadfast with the apos-
> tles. For this is the manner in which the apostolic churches transmit their
> registers: as the church of Smyrna, which records that Polycarp was placed
> therein by John; as also the church of Rome, which makes Clement to
> have been ordained in like manner by Peter. In exactly the same way the
> other churches likewise exhibit (their several worthies), whom, as having
> been appointed to their episcopal places by apostles, they regard as trans-
> mitters of the apostolic seed.[14]

The most famous fragment of Irenaeus of Lyons' momentous work
Against Heresies is that part that is dedicated to laying out the teaching of apostolic Tradition, preserved undamaged in the Church, as in a treasury:

> Since therefore we have such proofs, it is not necessary to seek the truth
> among others which it is easy to obtain from the Church; since the apos-
> tles, like a rich man [depositing his money] in a bank, lodged in her hands
> most copiously all things pertaining to the truth: so that every man,
> whosoever will, can draw from her the water of life (Rev 22.17). For she is
> the entrance to life; all others are thieves and robbers (Jn 10.8). On this
> account are we bound to avoid them, but to make choice of the thing per-
> taining to the Church with the utmost diligence, and to lay hold of the
> tradition of the truth. For how stands the case? Suppose there arise a dis-
> pute relative to some important question among us, should we not have
> recourse to the most ancient Churches with which the apostles held con-
> stant intercourse, and learn from them what is certain and clear in regard

---

[14]*Prescription Against the Heretics* 32.

to the present question? For how should it be if the apostles themselves had not left us writings? Would it not be necessary, [in that case,] to follow the course of the tradition which they handed down to those to whom they did commit the Churches?[15]

Thus, if there were no Holy Scripture, apostolic Tradition would be sufficient for preserving the true faith unharmed. However, it is necessary to remember that nothing is automatic or magical in the apostolic succession of hierarchy: succession by the laying on of hands is not some kind of autonomous strand, independent of the Church. Bishops and priests were placed by the apostles "with the consent of the whole Church,"[16] and this consent was a factor no less significant than the presence of a lawful ordination. The line of apostolic succession is valid only within the Church: outside the Church, it loses its efficacy and significance. It is precisely for this reason that the Church does not accept the presence of apostolic succession in heretical communities, even if the direct apostolic succession of ordination was never formally broken.

According to the Church's teaching, apostolic succession is transmitted from one bishop to another, and only bishops are successors to the apostles: priests and deacons are not successors as such. There was never a line of succession of priests or deacons in the Church. A bishop receives the laying on of hands by succession from the apostles, but priests and deacons receive it from the bishops. The line of episcopal succession is one and unbroken, but the laying on of hands to the rank of priest or deacon is an event "valid for only one occasion": the laying on of hands of one priest or deacon is in no way connected to the laying on of hands of other priests or deacons; it is connected only to the bishop, a successor of the apostles, through whom the grace of the apostles is transmitted to the lesser clergy.

The above ecclesiological understanding arose by the second century and has remained fundamentally unchanged to this day. Already in Ignatius the God-Bearer, church governance was established in the form of a three-staged hierarchy, consisting of bishops, priests, and deacons. In his words, "[the] bishop presides in the place of God, and . . . presbyters in the place of the assembly of the apostles, along with . . . deacons, who are most dear to me,

---

[15]3.4.1.
[16]Clement of Rome *First Epistle to the Corinthians* 44.

and are entrusted with the ministry of Jesus Christ."[17] Ignatius emphasizes the necessity for unity of the priests to their bishops: "For your justly-renowned presbytery, being worthy of God, is fitted as exactly to the bishop as the strings are to the harp."[18] According to Ignatius' teaching, the people of God should "reverence the deacons as an appointment of Jesus Christ, and the bishop as Jesus Christ, who is the Son of the Father, and the presbyters as the Sanhedrin of God, and assembly of the apostles."[19]

It is characteristic that Ignatius sees the "council" or "assembly of the apostles" in priests, and not in bishops. Ignatius speaks of bishops in the singular, whereas he refers to priests in the plural. This reflects the practice, established in his time, according to which the bishop directed the local church with the assistance of the presbytery, delegating a significant part of his responsibility to the priests. In essence, the ministry of a priest includes within itself all the aspects of the bishop's ministry, with one exception—the laying on of hands performed at an ordination. The priesthood, therefore, is an apostolic ministry to the extent that the priestly functions coincide with the episcopal functions.

In the ancient Church, when there was only one Eucharistic community in each city, the bishop was the spiritual center as head of the Eucharistic community, "sitting in place of God." However, to the extent that the quantity of Eucharistic communities multiplied, their direction was transmitted to the priests; the bishop reserved for himself the direction of the main Eucharistic community of the city or region, watching over the remaining communities, implementing the right of *episcope*/ἐπισκοπή (visitation, observance, oversight). The central place in the life of a parish as a Eucharistic community, headed by a priest, became the priest de facto under this system: it was he who most frequently saw the people of God while "sitting in the place of God," that is as leader in the performance of the Eucharist.

The key role of the priest as the practical chief of each parish is without question the significance that the Fathers of the Church attributed to the priestly ministry. In early Christian patristic literature, there is basically no specific treatise dedicated to the episcopal ministry, but then there are few classic treatises on the priesthood.

---

[17] *Epistle to the Magnesians* 6.
[18] *Epistle to the Ephesians* 4.
[19] *Epistle to the Trallians* 3.

Gregory the Theologian was the first Eastern Christian author to write a special treatise on the priesthood: before him Christian writers only touched on this theme from time to time. Gregory's treatise proved to be a direct influence on many later compositions on this exact theme, such as *Six Homilies on the Priesthood* by John Chrysostom (fourth century), *The Book of Pastoral Rule* by Gregory Dialogus (sixth century), and the homily *To the Pastor* by John of the Ladder (seventh century). In the Orthodox Church, Gregory's treatise remains a reference book for ministers in the Church to this day; future priests study it in seminaries.

According to Gregory's teaching, it is necessary for the priesthood to grow out of the hierarchical structure of the Church, which is the body, united beneath the head of Christ. This idea, coming from the Apostle Paul, influences Gregory to examine order (*taxis*/τάξις) as the basis of the Church's whole being, where, as in the army there are superiors and subordinates, as in the pastures there are shepherds and sheep, as in school there are teachers and students, as on a ship there is a captain and sailors. The hierarchical structure saves the Church from chaotic anarchy; the presence of the presbytery and the episcopate preserves the unity of the Church as an organism in which each member fulfills its function.[20]

The priesthood is above all pastoral in nature; it is caring for the sheep, the management of the flock. Gregory uses an image traditional in biblical theology: in the Old Testament, God is presented as the exalted Shepherd, and the people are his flock (Ps 23.1, 80.2; Isa 40.11; Jer 31.10); the books of the prophets are filled with the denunciations of the unworthy shepherd, to whom God has conferred his sheep (Ezek 34; Jer 23.1–4). In the New Testament, Christ speaks of himself as the "Good Shepherd" (Jn 10.11–16), for whom each sheep is dear: he goes out in search of the lost sheep, and finding it, bears it on his shoulders (Lk 15.4–7). Leaving the earth, he entrusts his sheep to Peter (Jn 21.15–17), and in his stead, other apostles and all future generations of Christian pastors.

Comparing the work of the priest with the work of a shepherd, Gregory the Theologian says that it is much harder to rule over people than it is over livestock. A shepherd need only find a grassy place for his flock so that the sheep and oxen might have sufficient water and food; upon finding such a place, he may tranquilly lounge in the shade, playing on the pipes or singing

[20]Gregory the Theologian *Oration* 2.3–5, 8.

love songs. As a Christian shepherd one needs to instruct people in virtue, so that with difficulty, fallen human nature might be perceived: people are more inclined to evil than to good.[21] The management of an ecclesial flock is not just a profession; it is an art that demands diligence and mastery. "The guiding of man . . . seems to me in very deed to be the art of arts and science of sciences. Any one may recognize this, by comparing the work of the physician of souls with the treatment of the body," notes Gregory.[22]

In this sense the work of a priest is comparable to the work of an artist, who should beware of becoming a "poor painter of the charms of virtue," or, even worse, a bad example for other painters. A priest should not only abstain from evil, but should actively occupy himself with virtuous acts, not only to blot out foolish images from the soul, but to pile up beautiful ones for it[23]; he should "know no limits in goodness or spiritual progress, and should dwell upon the loss of what is still beyond him, rather than the gain of what he has attained, and consider that which is beneath his feet a step to that which comes next."[24] The comparison of the priest to a painter gives perspective to the meaning of the priest in the life of the Church: first of all, he works beyond the form of his own image, never resting on what he has attained and always striving for higher things; secondly, he becomes an icon in the image of that to which every man, being the artist of his own life, can conform his own image. Even the Apostle Paul speaks of the shepherd as an example (*eikōn*/εἰκών) to the believers "in word, in coversation, in love, in faith, in purity" (1 Tim 4.12).

The work of a priest is also compared to the healing arts; although if the latter is guided by the material and temporal, then the former cares for the soul, which is immaterial and divine in its provenance. A doctor prescribes medicine to the sick person, recommends preventive measures, sometimes even cauterizes or uses surgical intervention; however, it is much harder to heal "morals, passions, a way of life, and will," expelling all animalistic and wild things from the soul and placing in it meek and noble things.[25]

The goal of a priest's ministry is the deification of those members of the Church entrusted to him: the priest is called "to make him who belongs to

[21]Ibid. 9–12.
[22]Ibid. 16.
[23]Ibid. 13–14.
[24]Ibid. 14.
[25]Ibid. 16.

the highest order[26] a god, and worthy of great blessing."[27] But in order to bring others to God, one needs to come to him; in order to bring others to perfection, one first needs to make oneself perfect; in order to heal the wounds of others, it is necessary for one's own soul to be healed:

> A man must himself be cleansed, before cleansing others: himself become wise, that he may make others wise; become light, and then give light: draw near to God, and so bring others near; be hallowed, then hallow them. . . . Who can mold, as clay figures are modeled in a single day, the defender of the truth, who is to take his stand with angels, and give glory with archangels, and cause the sacrifice to ascend to the altar on high, and share the priesthood of Christ, and renew the creature, and set forth the image, and create inhabitants for the world above, aye and, greatest of all, be god, and make others to be god?[28]

A priest, according to Gregory's teaching, is a mediator between God and people.[29] This high calling is defined in lofty moral demands directed to the priest. Demanded of him is the experience to know all that he will need to teach his parishioners, and to travel that same path along which he is to lead them. The life of a priest should be a continual and daily spiritual effort: the life of the Apostle Paul and that of the other apostles—and before them, of many Old Testament prophets and righteous—was exactly this.[30] Every holy minister in the Scriptures can be offered up as an example for imitation.

In Gregory's understanding, the main action of the priest is the "distribution of the word"[31]—preaching, teaching, and theologizing. In his eyes the priestly minister is he who correctly conceives of God and is capable of teaching people the dogmata on:

> Such subjects as the world or worlds, matter, soul, mind, intelligent natures, better or worse, providence which holds together and guides the universe. . . . And they are concerned with our original constitution, and final restoration, the types of truth, the covenants, the first and second

---

[26]I.e., one who has accepted holy baptism.
[27]Gregory the Theologian *Oration* 2.21–22.
[28]Ibid. 71, 73.
[29]Ibid. 91.
[30]Ibid. 50–69.
[31]Ibid. 35.

coming of Christ, his incarnation, sufferings and dissolution, with the resurrection, the last day, the judgment and recompense; . . . and, to crown
all, with what we are to think of the original and blessed Trinity.[32]

In order to teach on God in an orthodox manner, it is necessary for the
priest to be morally pure and to be a co-actor with the Holy Spirit, without whom it would be impossible to conceive of, speak with, and listen
to God, "for the pure alone can grasp him who is pure and of the same
disposition of himself."[33]

Other no less important duties of a priest, apart from preaching and teaching, are the actual ministry at the altar, the prayer on behalf of the people, the
accomplishment of the Eucharist. It is in this service that the role of the priest
as mediator between God and people is manifested in its loftiest form; it is
precisely this aspect of priestly service that called out to Gregory as most virtuous, of which he sincerely considered himself unworthy, to offer to God
the bloodless sacrifice. Speaking about this, Gregory uses the image of Moses,
as well as other Old Testament images:

I hear from Moses himself, when God spake to him, that, although many
were bidden to come to the mount . . . the rest were ordered to worship
afar off, and Moses alone to draw near. . . . Moreover, before this, when
the law was first given, the trumpet-blasts, and lightnings, and thunders,
and darkness, and the smoke of the whole mountain, and the terrible
threats that if even a beast touched the mountain it should be stoned, and
other like alarms, kept back the rest of the people, for whom it was a great
privilege, after careful purification, merely to hear the voice of God. But
Moses actually went up and entered into the cloud, and was charged with
the law, and received the tables, which belong, for the multitude, to the
letter, but, for those who are above the multitude, to the spirit. . . . I know
also that not . . . might anyone enter the temple who was not in the most
minute particular pure in both soul and body; so far was the Holy of
holies removed from presumptuous access, that it might be entered by
one man only once a year (Ex 30.10), so far were the veil, and the mercy-
seat, and the ark, and the Cherubim, from the general gaze and touch.

[32]Ibid. 35–36.
[33]Ibid. 39.

Since then I knew these things, and that no one is worthy of the mighti-
ness of God, and the sacrifice, and priesthood, who has not first presented
himself to God, a living, holy sacrifice, and set forth the reasonable, well-
pleasing service (Rom 12.1), and sacrificed to God the sacrifice of praise
(Heb 13.15) and the contrite spirit (Ps 51.19); . . . how could I dare to offer
to him the external sacrifice, the antitype[34] of the great mysteries, or
clothe myself with the garb and name of priest, before my hands had been
consecrated by holy works?[35]

If the episcopate and the priesthood were described quite a lot during the
time of the ancient Church and the age of the ecumenical councils, then the
third level of the clergy, the rank of deacon, it can be said as a general rule,
was described only in passing. There is not one patristic treatise dedicated to
the interpretation of diaconal ministry. Nevertheless, it is possible that the
diaconal rank is actually the most ancient in the Christian Church after that
of apostle. The book of Acts narrates the election and laying on of hands of
seven men, to whom were assigned the care of table serving and the daily distribution of food (Acts 6.1–2). The ministry of the seven was considered to be
the charge of the household needs of the community, of the social aspects of
church life. This service also included an element of charity, especially caring
for widows.

Nowhere in Acts were the seven men chosen and ordained by apostles
called deacons; it was not said anywhere that they could not be, for example,
priests. Their ministry was not generally associated with any term, and they are
referred to only as "the seven,"[36] in distinction from "the twelve," which
referred to the apostles. However, church tradition, beginning with Irenaeus
of Lyons, considered "the seven" to be deacons. Irenaeus calls the Nicolaitans
followers of Nicolas, "one of seven first ordained to the diaconate by the apostles,"[37] and he calls Stephen him "who was chosen the first deacon by the
apostles."[38] In the Orthodox Church, Stephen is venerated as "archdeacon,"

---

[34]The expression "antitype" (*antitypon*/ἀντίτυπον) is found in the liturgy of Basil the Great and
refers to the bread and wine of the Eucharist, which the faithful understand to be the body and blood
of Christ.

[35]Gregory the Theologian *Oration* 2.92, 94–95.

[36]In Acts 21.8, Philip is referred to as "one of the seven." In the Slavonic Synodal translation,
"deacons" is added, but this word is absent in the Greek text.

[37]*Against Heresies* 1.26.3.

[38]Ibid. 3.12.10.

as are the others numbered among "the seven." In the Orthodox rubrics of the diaconal laying on of hands, diaconal ministry is spoken of as a continuation of the service of "the seven."

While church tradition in the West was of one spirit in the definition of the ministry of "the seven" as diaconal, yet in the East there was no such "one spirit." As John Chrysostom notices, in that moment when the apostles chose seven deacons, "there was not even one bishop, only apostles." Chrysostom considers that in Acts, "the designations of deacons and presbyters were not clearly and precisely distinguished." At the least deacons were not only appointed for serving, but were ordained, and they prayed with zeal. According to Chrysostom's supposition, deacons were entrusted both with spiritual gifts and teaching functions.[39] The sixteenth canon of the Sixth Ecumenical Council, linked to Chrysostom's interpretation, speaks of the fact that at the moment of election and ordination of "the seven," neither the name of deacon nor the name of presbyter was known in the Church; in any case, "the seven" were not ministers of the sacraments,[40] that is they did not carry out sacramental functions. Some contemporary researchers, on the contrary, suggest that the ministry of "the seven" was a continuation of the ministry of "the twelve," who delegated all of their authority to "the seven," including the right to preside at the Eucharistic liturgy.[41]

The martyr and archdeacon Lawrence. The church of St Sofia. Kiev. 11th c.

This could not have been the link between the service of "the seven" and the later diaconal ministry, since already during the time of Ignatius the God-Bearer and Justin Martyr, the diaconate existed as a separate ministry, having its own liturgical functions. In particular, deacons administered communion to the faithful at the Eucharistic liturgy, and also brought communion to those who were absent.[42] All the ancient liturgical rubrics that have survived

[39]John Chrysostom *Homily on Acts* 14.3.
[40]Canon 16 of the sixth ecumenical council. Cited in: Nikodim (Milash), *The Canons of the Orthodox Church, together with a Commentary by Nikodim, Bishop of Dalmatia and Istria* 1 (Moscow: 2001), 486–487.
[41]Nikolai Afanasiev, *Tserkov' Ducha Svyatogo*, 196–199.
[42]Justin Martyr *First Apology* 65.

to our time include diaconal exclamations. Deacons served at the Eucharistic liturgy as a link connecting the celebrant and the people: specifically, they summoned the people to prayer, they put into their mouths petitions for the ecclesial and worldly authorities, the country and city, deliverance from natural disasters, those suffering from disease, those traveling, etc.

The diaconal rank almost completely fell out of use over the course of the centuries in the West, yet in the Orthodox East deacons fulfill important liturgical functions to this very day. The deacon unceasingly participates in the hierarchical liturgy, as well as in large parishes. In the case of village parishes or poor parishes, the priest, as a rule, fulfills the deacon's functions.

The diaconate is a ministry of assistance. In distinction from the episcopate and the priesthood, a deacon cannot in and of himself perform the holy services: he can only participate in the liturgical services performed by others—bishops and presbyters. In this sense, diaconal ministry is not a continuation of the apostolic ministry (even if such was indeed the ministry of "the seven"). The deacon receives the laying on of hands from a descendant of the apostles and through this ordination is included in the ranks of the clergy, although his service is qualitatively different from bishops and priests. If the bishop possesses the fullness of church authority according to his succession from the apostles, and a priest receives authority from the archbishop and has, in the bishop's absence, all the rights as performer of all the sacraments except for ordination, then the deacon in general cannot serve liturgically in the absence of the bishop or a priest.

Numbered among the clergy in the Byzantine era, besides bishops, priests, and deacons, were deaconesses, subdeacons, readers, and singers. Thus, for example, among the clergy of the great church of Constantinople (Hagia Sophia) during the time of Emperor Justinian were sixty presbyters, 100 deacons, forty deaconesses, ninety subdeacons, 110 readers, and twenty-five singers—425 people in all. During the reign of Emperor Heraclius, the clergy of the great church increased to 600 people.[43]

The ministry of a deaconess was never identical to that of a deacon, and was not perceived as one of the levels of the priesthood, although in Byzantium deaconesses entered into a clerical rank. Deaconesses were elected from a pool of virtuous virgins or widows. In contrast with the deacons, deaconesses did not participate in the Eucharistic liturgy, and generally, as far as

[43]Nikodim (Milash), 487.

can be seen, did not fulfill any kind of liturgical function. Their role involved preparing women for baptism, assisting the bishop during the baptism of women, conducting catechetical sessions with women, and looking out for the conduct of women in church. It is said in the *Apostolic Constitutions*: "A deaconess does not bless, nor does she do anything else that priests or deacons do; she only guards the doors of the church and assists presbyters with the baptism of women."[44] The First Ecumenical Council (Nicaea, 325) numbers deaconesses among the laity, asserting that they do not receive ordination.[45] However, the Fourth Ecumenical Council (Chalcedon, 451) refers to the laying on of hands, or ordination, of deaconesses.[46] The rank of deaconess disappears in the West in the sixth century; it remains in the East a bit longer, but in the end it disappears there as well.

The teaching on the three levels of ecclesial hierarchy that we find already in Ignatius the God-Bearer is an inseparable component of church Tradition. This teaching received a theological interpretation in the fifth century in Dionysius the Areopagite's treatise *Ecclesiastical Hierarchy*. Dionysius sees a continuation of the nine-ranked angelic hierarchy in church hierarchies, and divides it into nine ranks as well. The first three of them consist of the sacraments of enlightenment (baptism), meeting (Eucharist), and the sanctification of the world (anointing with holy chrism). The second triad consists of the three priestly ranks: bishop, priest, and deacon. The third triad consists of the ranks of those "being raised to holiness," in which therapists (monastics), holy people (laymen), and catechumens are included. The Areopagite is frequently criticized for the artificiality of his constructions.[47] Dionysius' three-staged hierarchy is really formed quite arbitrarily, although this construction is necessary for Dionysius to illustrate his basic idea: the hierarchical church structure, corresponding to the hierarchical structure of the spiritual world.

Dionysius is above all interested in the internal contents of the hierarchical structure of the Church. He bestows a lofty, symbolic, speculative meaning on every ecclesial level. The Areopagite sees a divine establishment in the church hierarchy, the goal of which is guiding people to deification:

[44]*Apostolic Constitutions* 8.28.
[45]Canon nineteen of the First Ecumenical Council.
[46]Canon fifteen of the Fourth Ecumenical Eouncil.
[47]See, for example, John Meyendorff, *Introduction to Patristic Theology* (Klin: 2001), 345–349.

Ours is a hierarchy of the inspired and divine and deifying science, and
of operation, and of consecration. . . . Even Jesus himself . . . illuminates
the blessed beings who are superior to us, in a manner more clear, and at
the same time more intellectual, and assimilates them to his own light, as
far as possible; and by our love of things beautiful elevated to him, and
which elevates us, folds together our many diversities, and after perfecting into a uniform and divine life and habit and operation, holily
bequeaths the power of the divine priesthood; from which by approaching to the holy exercise of the priestly office, we ourselves become nearer
to the beings above us . . . and thus by looking upwards to the blessed
and supremely divine self of Jesus, and reverently gazing upon whatever
we are permitted to see, and illuminated with the knowledge of the
visions, we shall be able to become, as regards the science of divine mysteries, purified and purifiers; images of light, and workers, with God, perfected and perfecting. . . . But the beings and ranks above us . . . are both
incorporeal, and their hierarchy is both intelligible and supermundane;
but let us view our hierarchy, conformably to ourselves, abounding in the
variety of the sensible symbols, by which, in proportion to our capacity,
we are conducted, hierarchically according to our measure, to the uniform deification—God and divine virtue.[48]

Dionysius sees the focus of all the levels of the priesthood in the rank of
bishop, whom he calls "the hierarch." The rank of the hierarch, in the Areopagite's words, "is the first of the God-contemplative ranks; and it is, at the
same time, highest and lowest; inasmuch as every order of our hierarchy is
summed up and fulfilled in it." Like every hierarchy generally concluded in
Jesus, the ecclesiastical hierarchy is "terminated in its own inspired hierarch."
Although priests perform some liturgical rites, "yet never will the priest
effect the holy birth in God without the most divine myrrh;[49] nor will he
consecrate the mysteries of the divine communion, unless the communicat-
ing symbols have been placed upon the most divine altar;[50] and neither will
he be priest himself, unless he has been elected to this by the hierarchical
consecrations." Thus only the rank of hierarch is that "which, full of the

---

[48] *Ecclesiastical Hierarchy* 1.1–2.
[49] I.e., he will not perform the sacrament of baptism without holy myrrh, blessed by the bishop.
[50] I.e., he will not be able to celebrate the liturgy without an antimension, signed by the bishop
and placed on the altar.

perfecting power, pre-eminently completes the perfecting functions of the hierarchy, and reveals lucidly the sciences of the holy mysteries, and teaches their proportionate and sacred conditions and powers."[51]

In terms of "the illuminating rank of the priests," then, in Dionysius' words, they are those "who are being initiated under the rank of the inspired hierarchs to the divine visions of the mystic rites, and in cooperation with it, minister its proper ministrations. Whatever then this rank may do, by showing the works of God, through the most holy symbols, and perfecting those who draw nigh in the divine contemplations, and communion of the holy rites."[52]

In contrast to the diaconal rank, which the Areopagite calls "the rank of the leitourgoi," it is maintained that it is "purifying and separates the unfit, previous to the approach to the ministrations of the priests, [it] thoroughly purifies those who are drawing nigh, by making them entirely pure from opposing passions, and suitable for the sanctifying vision and communion." Deacons remove the clothing from those being baptized before the start of the baptismal sacrament, standing at the doors during the celebration of the Eucharist, fulfilling other liturgical functions.[53]

Dionysius considers the Holy Trinity, out of whom every life and every life's blessing pours, to be the origin and source of every hierarch:

Now the more divine orders know also, together with their own, the sacred sciences subordinate to their own perfection. Nevertheless, since the sacerdotal orderings of the well-arranged and unconfused order of the divine operations are images of divine operations, they were arranged in hierarchical distinctions, showing in themselves the illuminations marshaled into the first, and middle, and last, sacred operations and ranks; manifesting, as I said, in themselves the well-ordered and unconfused character of the divine operations. For since the Godhead first cleanses the minds which he may enter, then enlightens, and, when enlightened, perfects them to a Godlike perfection; naturally the hierarchy of the divine images divides itself into well-defined ranks and powers, showing clearly the supremely divine operation firmly established, without confusion, in most hallowed and unmixed ranks.[54]

[51]Dionysius the Areopagite *Ecclesiastical Hierarchy* 5.5–6.
[52]Ibid. 6.
[53]Ibid.
[54]Ibid. 7.

Dionysius the Areopagites's indisputable contribution is that he saw beyond the ecclesial structure, formed over the course of the first five centuries of Christianity's existence, and saw in the liturgical rites of the Church a deep symbolic meaning. Dionysius inscribed the traditional notion of the three levels of church hierarchy in the context of the patristic teaching on deification. Notions of deification permeate the whole of Dionysius' ecclesiology. In Dionysius' mind the liturgical rites, the sacraments, the hierarchy, every church construct serve one goal—to elevate all to the heights of sanctification and deification. The life of the Church is perceived as a "sacramental rite"—the introduction of spiritual experience into the sacraments, the ascent "to the grace filled and God-created light of Jesus," to the higher stages of the knowledge of God and divine contemplation.

25

The Veneration of the Saints

A CCORDING TO ORTHODOX TEACHING, the veneration of the saints is an inseparable component of church life. Protestants frequently accuse
Orthodox Christians of perceiving the saints as
mediators between people and God, whereas people
can relate to God without mediators. The Orthodox
Church does not reject direct experience when it
comes to divine relation; moreover, it regards this
experience as the foundation of the spiritual life of
every Christian. But it does not consider the veneration of the saints somehow to be a way to hinder
direct relations between man and God. The fundamental part of prayerful petitions, whether sent up

Iconostasis. Icon. Russia. 18th c.

by Orthodox Christians in the church or the home, is addressed to God.
However, Orthodox Christians pray to the Theotokos and the saints along
with these petitions as well. For the Orthodox Christian, the saints are not so
much mediators between a person and God, as much as living bearers of true
Christianity, whose life serves as a higher moral example. Moreover, the
Church believes that the saints do not die, but continue to live in the Church,
and it is by this faith in their living presence that prayers are directed, in communion with them.

The continuity of the Christian experience of holiness, just like the continuity of apostolic succession, consists of a specific character in the Orthodox Church. Likening the hierarchy of the saints to the hierarchy of the
angels, Symeon the New Theologian speaks of the continual stages of Christian holiness, uniting ancient saints with modern ones:

As wise ranks of the highest powers are consecrated in order by God–
from the first original rank to the second, and from this to the next and
so on, so does the divine outpouring of light reach all: the saints, consecrated by the divine angels, connected and united by the link of the Spirit,
becoming as virtuous as the angels, and equal with them. For the saints,
coming from one race to another through doing God's commandments,
have united themselves to those saints who have preceded them in time,
lighting up like those who have received grace from God through communion, and becoming like a sort of golden chain, of which every one of
them is a separate link, forged to the one preceding through faith, deeds,
and love, so that they are one chain in one God, a chain that cannot be
easily broken.[1]

The veneration of the saints in the Orthodox Church is always connected
to the teaching on deification as a goal of Christian life. The link between the
veneration of the saints and the doctrine on deification can be traced to the
works of John of Damascus, who devoted special attention to the theme of
the veneration of the saints in his anti-iconoclast compositions, as well as in
An Exact Exposition of the Orthodox Faith:

> To the saints honor must be paid as friends of Christ, as sons and heirs of
> God. . . . And further, if the Creator and Lord of all things is called also
> King of kings and Lord of lords and God of gods (Rev 19.16; Ps 50.1), surely
> also the saints are gods and lords and kings. . . . Now I mean gods and
> kings and lords not in nature, but as rulers and masters of their passions,
> and as preserving a truthful likeness to the divine image according to
> which they were made (for the image of a king is also called king), and as
> being united to God of their own free-will and receiving him as an
> indweller and becoming by grace through participation with him what he
> is himself by nature.[2]

In the Damascene's words, the saints "are made treasuries and pure habi-
tations of God." Their death is more like a dream (a falling asleep) than death.
They are alive through death and stand before God. God dwelt in the bodies of the saints through the nous, and they became "the living temples of

[1] *Chapters* 3.5.
[2] 4.15.

God, the living tabernacles of God."[3] From here comes the necessity for the veneration of the saints' power as sources of healing and miracles:

The Master Christ made the remains of the saints to be fountains of salvation for us, pouring forth manifold blessings and abounding in oil of sweet fragrance: and let no one disbelieve this. . . . In the law every one who touches a dead body was considered impure, but these are not dead. For from the time when he that is himself life and the Author of life was reckoned among the dead, we do not call those dead who have fallen asleep in the hope of the resurrection and in faith on him. For how could a dead body work miracles? How, therefore, are demons driven off by them, diseases dispelled, sick persons made well, the blind restored to sight, lepers purified, temptations and struggles overcome, and how does every good gift from the Father of lights (Jas 1.17) come down through them to those who pray with sure faith?[4]

The Damascene likens God's union with the bodies of the saints and the presence of the divine grace in their relics to the union of the divine and human natures in Jesus Christ. The result of this union was that Christ's flesh was made completely divine. The same occurs in the bodies of the saints, who, united with God, become permeated with his presence, energy, and grace:

As that which is mixed with fire becomes fire, though not by nature, but by virtue of the mingling, igniting, and partaking, so, I do say, it is with the flesh of the incarnate Son of God. For it, by consequence of hypostatic participation in the divine nature, not changing, was deified, sanctified not by the energy of God, as is each one of the prophets, but by the presence of him who is sanctified. . . . For the saints were full of the Holy Spirit during their life, and in death the grace of the Holy Spirit dwells inexhaustibly in their souls as well, and in their bodies, lying in graves, and in their traits, and in their holy images, not by means of their essence, but as a consequence of grace and the [divine] energy.[5]

The Damascene speaks of the various ways of venerating the saints in the Orthodox Church. Churches are built in their honor and liturgical rites are

---

[3]Ibid.
[4]Ibid.
[5]John of Damascus *Apologetic Treatises Against Those Decrying the Holy Images* 1.20.

composed, days dedicated to their memory become church feast days for spiritual rejoicing. But the glorification of the saints also has a moral signifi- cance—Christians are called to imitate the lives and feats of the saints so that they too might become living temples.[6]

The veneration of the saints differs from the worship that is given only to God in the Orthodox Church. John of Damascus insists on this difference, using two different terms for designating the two kinds of worship: *latreia*/λατρεία (lit. "service") is given only to God, whereas *proskynēsis*/ προσκύνησις ("worship," "veneration") is offered to the angels and deified people, be it the Theotokos or any other saint, as well as to icons, relics, and other holy things. This difference was introduced to combat the charges of idol worship that the iconoclasts levied against the Orthodox in connection to the theme of the veneration of the saints.

The theological basis of the glorification of the saints received its final for- mulation only in the age of iconoclasm, since until that time no heresy arose disputing it. However, the very practice of venerating the saints existed in the Church from the earliest times.

The cult of the apostles and martyrs, widespread throughout the East as well as the West in the second and third centuries, served as the starting point. The Greek word *martys*/μάρτυς, translated as "martyr," literally means "wit- ness." Christ called his disciples by this word, speaking on the mission given to them: "You shall receive power after the Holy Spirit has come upon you; and you shall be witnesses [μάρτυρες] to me both in Jerusalem, and in all Judea, and in Samaria, and to the uttermost parts of the earth" (Acts 1.8). The lives of most of the apostles ended in martyrdom: they bore witness to Christ not only in their preaching, but in their death. After the apostles, thousands of other martyrs filled the martyrologies of the Christian Church, which con- tinue to be filled up until the present time by newer and newer names of wit- nesses to Christ.

Origen calls martyrdom "the full measure of witness," emphasizing that he who publicly confesses God in a time of persecution is united with him in the closest way.[7] Origen considers the age of martyrdom to be "the era of Christian glory."[8] What era, he asks, "is more pleasing to God than when we

---

[6] *An Exact Exposition . . .* 4.15.
[7] Origen *Exhortation of Martyrdom*.
[8] Ibid.

exit life for the Christian faith under duress, before all, in the form of victors rather then prisoners?"[9] Martyrdom is likened to victory on the athletic field, a victory over which the angels rejoice and from which the demons hide themselves.[10] These words reflect the attitude of martyrdom in the ancient Church: death in martyrdom was not at all perceived as a tragedy; on the contrary, it was thought of as a victory over the dread of death and death itself, as an imitation of Christ's martyric struggle, as a co-participation in Christ's passion and in his glory.

St Gregory the Theologian speaks of the significance of the veneration of martyrs in a homily dedicated to the memory of the holy martyr Cyprian of Carthage:

All the saints should be honored, everyone needs readily to open mouth and ear and mind in order willingly to say and hear anything at all regarding them, and so on as to venerate their struggle. For although many serve as guides to a better life for us and many edify in virtue—and wisdom, and the law, and the prophets, and apostles, and the very sufferings of Christ, that first Martyr who ascended the cross and called me up with him, so that my sins might be nailed to it, to triumph over the serpent, to sanctify the tree, to conquer wantonness, to save Adam and raise the fallen image, although by so many and such superb instructors, the martyrs being no less instructive for us—these are verbal whole-burnt offerings, perfect sacrifices, acceptable offerings, this is the preaching of the truth, the exposure of lies, the fulfillment of the spiritual-intellectual law, the destruction of error, the persecution of vice, the drowning of sin, and the purification of the world.[11]

In the ancient Church, the veneration of the martyrs was expressed above all by the fact that their graves became places where the Eucharist was celebrated. Thus, for example, the Roman catacombs served simultaneously as the place of repose for the martyrs and a place for serving the Divine Liturgy: in the catacombs, tombs corresponded to altars. The tradition of placing a particle of a martyr's or saint's relics under the altar of a consecrated church is preserved in the Orthodox Church up to the present day. In the Russian

[9]Ibid.
[10]Ibid.
[11]*Oration* 24.4.

The martyrdom of St George.
Staro Nagoricane. Macedonia.
14th c.

rite, a particle of a saint's relic is also placed in the antimension—a special cloth that is given to a church by the bishop for celebrating the Eucharist.[12] This tradition has its roots in the practice of performing the Eucharist on the graves of martyrs.

The veneration of the martyrs was also expressed in the joyful celebration of the day of their memory. Already by the end of the fourth century, there were quite a lot of days of remembrance of martyrs in the church calendar. The homilies of John Chrysostom given in Antioch especially bear witness to this. He says in one of them: "Yesterday was a day of martyrs, and today is a day of martyrs. O, if only we could always celebrate a day of martyrs!"[13] In another homily on the memory of the martyr Romanus, Chrysostom says: "Again the remembrance of martyrs, and again a holiday and a spiritual celebration. They suffered, and we rejoice; their crown is a general glory, or better yet—the glory of all the Church." Chrysostom compares the struggles of the martyrs to a victory in the Olympic games: one gains the victory, but all rejoice.[14] The martyrs are the treasury of the Church, overflowing with precious stones: material riches pass, clothing unravels, homes are destroyed, "but it is not so in spiritual treasuries, for martyrs remain forever and always in one color and vigor, radiating and shining in the glory of their own light."[15]

Following after the cult of the apostles and martyrs was the rise of the cult of the hierarchs: bishops who were glorified by their deeds in defense of the dogmatic teachings of the Church against various heresies. The cult of the saints received a particularly wide diffusion in the age of the ecumenical councils, when the Church perceived the defense of orthodox teachings as a feat of special importance. The most glorified saints of the age of the ecumenical councils were Athanasius the Great, Basil the Great, Gregory the Theologian, John Chrysostom, and Cyril of Alexandria.

---

[12]Such a tradition is absent in the Orthodox Church of the Greek East.
[13]*Homily on the Martyrs.*
[14]*Oration on the Martyr Romanus* 1.
[15]*Homily on the Martyrs Juventinus and Maximinus.*

The wide extension of the cult of the saints is mostly connected with the development of monasticism in the fourth century and following. One of the most glorified male saints is Anthony the Great, whose life was written of by St Athanasius the Great of Alexandria. Among other Egyptian monastics, special veneration is given to Pachomius the Great, Macarius the Great, and other hermits as well, whose sayings were recorded by their disciples and collected into a special book called the *Sayings of the Desert Fathers* (*Apophthegmata Patrum*). In Palestinian monasteries, the most veneration is given to Hilarion the Great. The Holy Mountain of Athos—the largest center of Byzantine monasticism and the largest breeding-ground of sainthood—gave us a whole plethora of saints at the end of the first millennium and the first half of the second. Many holy fathers were also glorified in the Russian Church over the course of the second millennium.

The cult of devout emperors and blessed princes came about fairly late, compared to the cults of the martyrs and hierarchs. It owes its origin to the role played by the Byzantine emperor in the Church. Not possessing priestly rank, the emperor preserved the title *pontifex maximus* and considered it his duty to prove himself to be a protector of the Church. The Byzantine Church venerated as saints the equal-to-the-apostles Emperor Constantine the Great and his mother Helen, Theodosius the Great, Theodosius the Younger and his wife Eudoxia, Marcion and Pulcheria, Leo the Wise and his first wife Theophano, Justinian and Theodora, Theodora (d. 867), and Irene (d. 1124). The tradition of reckoning emperors and blessed princes in the ranks of the saints was continued in Rus'. In particular, some of the most revered Russian saints are the Great Princess Olga and Great Prince Vladimir, baptizer of Rus'. The life of some of the emperors, kings, and princes venerated in the Orthodox Church is not so far removed from all the aspects that can serve as models for imitation. They are venerated not so much for their high morals, ascetic way of life, or personal piety, as much as for the role they played in the history of the Church. A clear example of this is the Emperor Constantine, who brought the three-centuries-old age of persecution of the Church to an end. His reckoning as a saint was like an act of gratitude on behalf of the Church, rather than an acknowledgment of his personal holiness.

The most unusual type of saint is the holy fool—a person who has voluntarily taken on the identity of one who is insane. Holy fools were decidedly rare in Byzantium. The first famous holy fool is thought to be the Egyptian monk Isidore, about whom Palladius (420) writes in *The Lausiac History*.[16] Among the most revered Byzantine holy fools are Simeon (sixth century) and Andrew (tenth century): the former lived in the Syrian city of Emessa, the latter in Constantinople. Holy fools enjoyed a significantly wider diffusion in Rus' than in Byzantium: they played a large social significance in Muscovite Rus', frequently appearing with loud invective to those in power. The most venerated Russian holy fool is Basil the Blessed (1552).

Lives of the saints—martyrs, hierarchs, venerable ones, and holy fools— were favored reading for Orthodox Christians throughout the centuries. These lives had very different provenances and differed in various degrees of historical authenticity. In some cases—for example, if the life was written by one of the saint's closest disciples, who knew him or her while among us— the life preserves factual characteristics and historical authenticity (for example, the life of St Symeon the New Theologian, written by his disciple Niketas Stethatos, or the life of St Sergius of Radonezh, written by Epiphanius the Most Wise). However, in many cases a life does not even pretend to be historically accurate, just as an icon of a saint does not pretend to be a portrait or facsimile.

The life of a saint is like a literal icon, a kind of idealized image: it is almost always written in correlation with the canon, beyond the bounds of which the author allows himself to venture only in exceptional circumstances. The hagiographic canon is concluded in the fact that one and the same verbal catchphrases, episodes, and miracles occur, translated from one life to another. Thus, for example, there is hardly one hero in hagiographical literature who is not born of pious parents and already manifests signs of special Christian virtue from a young age, who does not flee from common childish games. Practically every saint is diligent in their school lessons, but declines to go on to higher education; they suffer temptations from the devil, but always overcome them; they fight against some kind of heresy and victoriously prevail over it; they perform many miracles and healings.

One can say that it is as if every saint lives three lives in the Church. One is the saint's real life, confined by defined temporal and geographical boundaries. Another is the saint's hagiography. The third is the saint's "posthumous" life, that is, the life in the many-centuries-old experience of the

---

[16]Cf. *The Lausiac History 36: On the Foolish Virgin.*

Church, including various miracles, healings, and cases where the saint has aided people.

Sometimes something is indeed known about the real life of the saint, sometimes very little, and sometimes almost nothing at all. More is usually known about a saint when they leave their own autobiographical compositions (for example, St Gregory the Theologian), or if they perform deeds of which an account is preserved in historical sources (for example, in *Ecclesiastical History* by Eusebius of Caesarea), or, finally, if the saint lived not too long ago and there is still a living memory of him or her among contemporary living people (for example, St Silouan of Mount Athos, and many martyrs of the twentieth century). If a saint did not leave behind personal compositions, an account was not preserved in a historical chronology, and he or she lived a long time ago, then the one literary source from which one can find out about his or her life is the hagiography, written many centuries later and frequently devoid of historical authenticity.

One of the most venerated saints in the Orthodox Church is St Nicholas, bishop of Myra in Lycia. Not very much is known about his true earthly life. His hagiography consists of accounts of various miracles, although some of these accounts are borrowed from the hagiography of another St Nicholas, the bishop of Pinar, who lived in the sixth century. It is recounted in the life of St Nicholas how he participated in the first ecumenical council (325), at which he stuck the heretic Arius, for which he was defrocked, but was eventually restored to the episcopal rank. This episode is absent in the documents of the council that have survived to present times, though not all of the written material from the council has been preserved.

St Nicholas of Myra in Lycia. Sinai. 11th c.

Does this mean that one ought not to believe in the hagiography of St Nicholas and other saints? Not at all. First of all, one cannot demand historical accuracy from hagiographies, seeing as they do not claim it themselves: a hagiography speaks in the first order about the significance of the saint for the Church and its people, drawing a spiritual image of the saint; concerning the historical appearance of the saint, in some cases it remains, in a way, as if "behind the scenes." Secondly, as was said, the saint has, beyond real life and the hagiography, a third life—that which lives beyond him or her in the experience of the faithful over the course of many centuries, after his or her death. This refers to healings and miracles performed before relics or the grave of the saint, of the aid in many forms that is found to come from the saint when he or she is addressed in prayer. The sacramental image of the saint's life in the experience of the Church corresponds to that which one can glean from the hagiography. And the hagiography, devoid of historical authenticity, finds authenticity on a different level. And the miracles described in the hagiography are continuously repeated in the experience of other people.

There was not any kind of procedure for the canonization of saints in the early Christian Church. The cult of this or that saint arose naturally, and no special sanction was demanded for the veneration of a martyr or a saint: the whole community, with the bishop at the head, participated in it. Throughout the course of the whole Byzantine period, the entry of a saint's name into the church calendar and the establishment of his or her memory on a local level was the prerogative of the diocesan bishop. Special decrees were given out by higher church or worldly authorities for relating universal veneration of saints on an individual basis: famous resolutions and decrees came from Patriarch Photius and Emperor Leo the Wise (886–911), dedicated to the glorification of individual saints. However, these decrees had an episodic character, and their presence was not accepted as an absolute condition for the elevation and development of saintly veneration.

Even in the eleventh century, an official sanction of higher ecclesial or worldly authority was not considered necessary for the glorification of this or that person as regards sainthood: the conflict between Symeon the New Theologian and the Constantinopolitan Church bears witness to that. Immediately after the repose of his spiritual father, Symeon the Studite, Symeon the New Theologian established a festal celebration of his memory. There was an icon made of Symeon the Studite as well, and a service composed for him. One of the hierarchs of the Constantinopolitan Church, Metropolitan Stephen of Nicomedia, upon finding this out, began to accuse Symeon of independently glorifying his spiritual father before he was officially reckoned among the saints. However, Symeon so zealously defended the cult of his elder that it served as one of the reasons for his expulsion from Constantinople.

During the time of Symeon the New Theologian, two tendencies existed in the Byzantine Church. On the one hand, the ancient practice of "organic" glorification and veneration of the saints was preserved—this was reflected in the actions taken by Symeon. On the other hand, an effort of codification of the saints was taking place, a systemization and editing of their hagiographies: Simeon Metaphrastes especially involved himself in this work. As a modern researcher of the saints noted, "the contents of Metaphrastes' corpus and . . . the resistance with which it was met by Symeon the New Theologian's attempt to maintain the veneration of his spiritual father Symeon the Studite, show that at the end of the tenth century the Church was officially striving to count the throng of saints of this kind of exclusive association, of which all the places were more or less taken."[17] The above observation, however, cannot be considered true if one takes into account that the reckoning of the ranks of the saints occurred in the Byzantine Church up until the fall of the empire and continued in the post-Byzantine period.

In the Russian Church, from the time of the baptism of Rus' up until the middle of the sixteenth century, the numbering of saints remained for the most part the prerogative of the local bishop, although the veneration of some saints acquired a pan-Russian character (Boris and Gleb, Prince Vladimir and Princess Olga, Anthony and Theodosius of the Kievan Caves). At the Councils of Moscow in 1547 and 1549, thirty-nine saints were canonized for general church veneration, but in the period between these councils and the establishment of the synodal structure, another approximately 130 saints were canonized. Canonization in the synodal period became the exclusive prerogative of the higher ecclesial authorities, and the procedure for canonization became significantly more complicated and formalized. The number of saints canonized in the synodal period is insignificant. The exclusive event in the life of the Church became the canonization in 1903, by the initiative of Emperor Nicholas II, of St Seraphim of Sarov—an ascetic whom all of Russia venerated at that time.

In the Soviet period, up until 1988, the Russian Church was in fact denied the possibility of canonizing a saint. In the 1960s and 1970s, the names of only a few saints were added to the calendar of saints of the Russian Church; these were saints who had either been canonized in other Local Orthodox Churches (John the Russian, Herman of Alaska), or were proposed for canonization by other Churches (Nicholas of Japan, Innocent of Moscow).

<hr>

[17]P. Magdalino, "The Byzantine Holy Man in the Twelfth Century," *The Byzantine Saint* (ed. S. Hackel) (London: 1981), 61.

Many saints venerated throughout the Church, such as John of Kronstadt and Blessed Xenia of Petersburg, could not be canonized because of direct refusal by authorities (John of Kronstadt as a monarchist and as a member of the "Black Hundred," Blessed Xenia as a "hysterical" and "crazy" woman). It is understandable that it was impossible to raise the issue of the glorification of the new martyrs of Russia, since the official authorities rejected the very reality of the Church's persecution.

In 1988, when the 1000-year anniversary of the baptism of Rus' was cele-brated, the Local Council of the Russian Orthodox Church introduced into the ranks of the saints eight pious ascetics for general ecclesial veneration, including those who had been considered local saints in the pre-revolution-ary period. The Council of Religious Affairs approved the candidacy of the saints for the Council of 1988. Furthermore, due to the weakening of the Soviet regime, the influence the authorities had on the canonization process was brought to practically nothing, and already by 1989 the Church was able to canonize Patriarch Tikhon, and by 1990, John of Kronstadt. The canoniza-tion of the names of the new martyrs and confessors of Russia began from 1992, and has continued to this very day. All the Russian new martyrs and confessors, those known by name and those unknown, were brought into the council of the saints at the Jubilee Council in 2000.

The glorification of the new martyrs and confessors of Russia at the coun-cil in 2000 became an event on a widespread ecclesial and national scale. Having numbered the martyrs in the ranks of the saints, the Church gave its appraisal of the most tragic period of Russian history. Such an appraisal has not been given on a political level to this day: politicians argue over the Soviet period, and there are many among them who try to justify the perse-cution, or to prove that the repression and persecution of the faith did not have a widespread character. Having accomplished the glorification of the new martyrs, the Church carried out its judgment and drew a line beneath the terrible period of persecution. It showed by the act of canonization that the period of persecuting the faith brought forth a massive volume of hero-ism from thousands of people, unafraid to confess Christ before the face of godless authority.

It is worth understanding the numbering among the saints of the last Russian emperor Nicholas II and his family in the context of the canoniza-tion of all the new martyrs and confessors of Russia. Many fought over this canonization during the time leading up to the council, since consecrating Nicholas II to sainthood was seen above all in a political aspect. For the Church though, the canonization of the last emperor and his family did not carry a political character with it. This was not the canonization of a monarchy or an acquittal of the political acts of the last tsar: this was above all an acknowledgement of the fact that the royal family shared the fate of its people, turning out to be, just like hundreds of thousands of others, a victim of terror. The Church canonized the last tsar not because he was the tsar, but because he shared the fate of his people and met death with humility as a true Christian and a true righteous person.

The new martyrs of Russia. Hagiographic icon. Moscow. 20th c.

The procedure of the canonization of saints has a most detailed development and most centralized character in the Roman Catholic Church, where from the second half of the twelfth century, canonization becomes the exclusive prerogative of the Roman pope. Since the middle of the seventeenth century, the Catholic Church distinguishes between two levels of sainthood, to which correspond two formal procedures—beatification (the numbering among the blessed ones) and canonization (the numbering among the saints). The process of beatification cannot begin sooner than five years after the repose of the ascetic, although an exception to the rule can be made by decision of the pope (thus, for example, the process of the beatification of Pope John Paul II began, by decree of his successor Pope Benedict XVI, only a few months after his passing). The presence of miracles, accomplished by the prayer of the ascetic and verified by a special committee, is an absolute condition of beatification and canonization. The process of beatification and canonization goes through many levels, although the final decision belongs to the pope. It is he who issues the decision to number this or that person amongst the blessed or the saints, and the decision has the status of "infallibility," like all the other actions of the pope made *ex cathedra*.

Such a specifically developed system of canonization does not exist in the Orthodox Church, and the practice of canonization in one Local Orthodox Church can differ significantly from similar practices in other Churches. Canonization in the Russian Orthodox Church is realized by the episcopal or local council through the presentation of the Committee on Canonization: this committee is given the task of studying the materials and documents of the holy life and deeds of the saints. Names for consideration are submitted to the committee from the diocese, under the signature of the diocesan hierarch. In the Patriarchate of Constantinople, the decision on canonization is accepted by the Holy Synod–there is no special committee on canonization.

If one local church decrees an act of canonization of this or that saint, then the names of the newly canonized saints are, as a rule, sent to the other Orthodox Churches for inclusion in the diptychs (a list of saints). However, the fact that a local church receives a list of newly glorified saints from another Church is not sufficient for the inclusion of those names in the diptychs. For this, a decision of the local church itself is needed, which should acknowledge the canonization that has occurred in the other local church.

26

The Theotokos

I N THE ORTHODOX CHURCH, in contrast with the Catholic Church, there is no "Mariology" as a special component of dogmatic theology. The teaching of the Fathers of the Eastern Church on the Most Holy Theotokos was an inseparable part of their Christology, and it is precisely in the context of the Christological controversies that one can observe the gradual development of the cult of the Theotokos, which occurred in the Christian East, over the whole course of the first millennium.

The New Testament does not give any obvious indication that Jesus' Mother received special veneration in the community of the Savior's disciples during his life or in the first years after his death and resurrection. In the Gospels of Matthew and Luke, the Mother of God is spoken of in detail in relation to Jesus' birth from her (Mt 1.18–25; Lk 1.26–38). The earliest references to Mary the Mother of Jesus in the New Testament bear an episodic character. In the Gospel of Luke, Mary and Joseph are mentioned in the narrative on the twelve-year-old Jesus preaching in the temple (Lk 2.41–51). All three Synoptic Gospels contain the story of how the Mother and brothers of Jesus came to him and asked to meet with him, but Jesus, pointing to those disciples seated around him, said: "Behold my mother and my brothers! For whosoever shall do the will of my Father in heaven is my brother, and sister, and mother" (Mt 12.49–50; Mk 3.31–35; Lk 8.19–21). In the Gospel of John, Jesus' Mother is present at Jesus' first miracle at Cana in Galilee (Jn 2.1–11). The same Gospel says that Jesus' Mother stood before him at the cross (Jn 19.25–27). These conclude the references to the Mother of God in the Gospels. Nothing is said of the Mother of Jesus' role in the community of the apostles either in Acts or in the Apostolic Epistles.

The Mother of God enthroned. Sinai. 6th c.

However, the Virgin Mary becomes an inseparable part of the Christological teaching of the Church by the second century. The writings of Irenaeus of Lyons, in whose teaching on "recapitulation"[1] the Virgin Mary occupies an important place, bear witness to this. As Christ became the new Adam, Mary became the new Eve, so as to correct and heal the disobedience of Eve and to open the way to salvation to man:

> [The effects] also of that deception being done away with, by which the virgin Eve, who was already espoused to a man, was unhappily misled,– was happily announced, through means of the truth [spoken] by the angel to the Virgin Mary, who was [also espoused] to a man. For just as the former was led astray by the word of an angel, so that she fled from God when she had transgressed his word; so did the latter, by an angelic communication, receive the glad tidings that she should sustain God, being obedient to his word. And if the former did disobey God, yet the latter was persuaded to be obedient to God, in order that the Virgin Mary might become the patroness of the virgin Eve. And thus, as the human race fell into bondage to death by means of a virgin, so is it rescued by a virgin; virginal disobedience having been balanced in the opposite scale by virginal obedience.[2]

Church writers of the second and third centuries repeatedly address the theme of the virginity of the Most Holy Theotokos. The dogma of Jesus' virgin birth from Mary is the only Marian dogma founded on the direct witness of the New Testament (Mt 1.18–25; Lk 1.26–35). At the beginning of the second century, Ignatius the God-Bearer refers to Mary's virginity in terms of three mysteries kept hidden from the devil: "Now the virginity of Mary was hidden from the prince of this world, as was also her offspring, and the death of the Lord; three mysteries of renown, which were wrought in silence by God."[3] Justin Martyr, arguing with Trypho the Jew, proves that Christ was born from the Virgin, referencing the Greek translation of the Prophet Isaiah's words: "Behold, the virgin is with child and shall bear a son, and shall name him Immanuel" (Isa 7.14). While Trypho cites the Hebrew text of the Bible where the word *alma* is used, which can mean "young woman" but is

[1] For the teaching concerning this, see Chapter 14.
[2] *Against Heresies* 5.19.1.
[3] *Epistle to the Ephesians* 19.

translated into the Greek as *parthenos*/παρθένος (virgin), Justin insists that this refers precisely to Jesus' birth from the Virgin.[4] In the third century, Origen defended Mary's virgin birth from the attacks of the Gentile Celsus.[5]

The New Testament does not directly speak of Mary remaining Virgin after Jesus' birth. The Gospel of Matthew refers to the fact that Joseph "took her as his wife, but had no marital relations with her until she had born a son" (Mt 1.24–25). The phrase "until" (Gr. *heōs hou*/ἕως οὗ–lit. "as long as," "not yet") indicates that Joseph did not know Mary before Jesus' birth, but nothing is said of her virginity after the birth.

However, the Church glorifies the Theotokos as Ever Virgin (*aeiparthenos*/ ἀειπαρθένος), that is as preserving virginity forever. The council-defined title "Ever Virgin" began to be used starting with the fifth ecumenical council (553), although the teaching that Mary remained Virgin after bearing Jesus was widespread throughout the Christian Church already from the third to fourth centuries. In the fourth century, John Chrysostom said in his commentary on the Gospel of Matthew that Joseph "not even after this, [Mary] having so become a mother, and having been counted worthy of a new sort of travail, and a child-bearing so strange, could . . . ever have endured to know her." Chrysostom considers the proof of Mary's virginity to be the fact that, dying on the cross, Jesus commits her "as unprotected" to his disciple. In the case then of Jesus' "brothers" mentioned in the New Testament, the word "brother" is used in the sense of "kin" or "relative."[6]

One may note that there is not just one opinion concerning "Jesus' brothers" in church tradition: the majority of Eastern and a number of Western church writers (Clement of Alexandria, Origen, Eusebius of Caesarea, Epiphanius of Cyprus, Hilary of Poitiers, Ambrose of Milan), basing themselves on *The Protoevangelion of James*, claim that Jesus' brothers were Joseph's children from his first marriage.[7] Some Western fathers (Jerome, Augustine) considered Jesus' brothers to be his cousins.[8] Church tradition in the East and the West rejected the notion that Jesus' brothers referred to in the Gospels could be legitimate brothers of Christ, born from Mary after Jesus' birth.

[4]Justin Martyr *Dialogue with Trypho* 43; 66–67; 71; 77–78; 84.
[5]Origen *Against Celsus* 1.32.
[6]John Chrysostom *Homily on Matthew* 5.5.
[7]See in particular: *The Protoevangelion of James* 8.3, 9.2, 17.1; Eusebius of Caesarea *Ecclesiastical History* 2.1–2; Epiphanius of Cyprus *Panarion* 7–9.
[8]Jerome *Against Helvidius* 13; Augustine *Seventeen Questions Concerning Matthew* 17.2.

The Ever-Virginity of the Theotokos is one of the important themes of Orthodox liturgy and theology. The liturgical texts of the Orthodox Church say to the Theotokos, "You were a Virgin before birthgiving, and a Virgin as you bore a child, and a Virgin after you had given birth."[9] These phrases pronounce word for word the teaching of John of Damascus on how "the holy, incomparable virgin . . . so longed for virginity that she was transformed into it, as if consumed by the purest fire. Every virgin, after all, loses her virginity in giving birth; but she, who was a virgin before giving birth, remained so during her labors and even after them."[10] In the Damascene's words:

> But just as he who was conceived kept her who conceived still virgin, in like manner also he who was born preserved her virginity intact, only passing through her keeping her closed. The conception, indeed, was through the sense of hearing, but the birth through the usual path by which children come. . . . For it was not impossible for him to have come by this gate, without injuring her seal in any way. The ever-virgin one thus remains even after the birth still virgin, having never at any time up till death consorted with a man. . . . For could it be possible that she, who had borne God and from experience of the subsequent events had come to know the miracle, should receive the embrace of a man? God forbid! It is not the part of a chaste mind to think such thoughts, far less to commit such acts.[11]

The belief of the Church is reflected in these words, that the incarnate God, upon his birth from the Virgin, did not violate her Virginity and kept her womb sealed. In the words of a church hymn, she gave birth while "sealed in purity and preserved in virginity."[12] In the Paschal canon, Jesus' passage through his mother's womb without affecting her virginity is compared to the exit of the resurrected Christ from the tomb without breaking its seal: "Thou didst arise, O Christ, and yet the tomb remained sealed, as at thy birth the Virgin's womb remained unharmed, and thou hast opened for us the gates of paradise."[13]

According to the teaching of the Church, the Most Holy Virgin did not suffer the usual birth-pangs at the nativity of the Savior. In the words of John

[9]*Octoechos*. Sunday. Tone Seven. Theotokion.
[10]*Homily on the Dormition* 2.2 (1998), 204–205.
[11]*An Exact Exposition* . . . 4.14.
[12]*Octoechos*. Sunday. Tone Two. Theotokion.
[13]Pascha. Canon. Tone Six.

of Damascus, the Virgin Mary "brought him into the world without suffering the pains that adhere to our nature,"[14] but she did experience these pains when she stood at the cross of Jesus, seeing "him whom she knew to be God by the manner of his generation, killed as a malefactor."[15]

The Third Ecumenical Council (431), condemning the heresy of Nestorius, triumphantly proclaimed Mary to be "God-bearer" (*Theotokos*/Θεοτόκος). The exact meaning of this term, which has become the basic title of the Most Holy Virgin in Orthodox tradition, has been discussed above.[16] This term was not contrived by theologians. It was born out of the heart of the liturgical life of the Church: at the moment when Nestorius came out against its use, it was already widely used in liturgical services, and it was the renunciation of this term that had become traditional that set off the beginning of the battle with Nestorianism. The Marian dogma was born out of the experience of church prayer: it is through this experience, and not through theological treatises, that the Church came to know that Mary bore the incarnate God, not a deified man.

The term "Theotokos" highlights the significance of Mary as the Mother of God. The name "Theotokos," in John of Damascus' words, "embraces the whole mystery of the dispensation"[17] of mankind's salvation. Elaborating the term "Theotokos," the Damascene writes:

We proclaim the holy Virgin to be in strict truth the Mother of God [Theotokos]. For inasmuch as he who was born of her was true God, she who bare the true God incarnate is the true mother of God. For we hold that God was born of her, not implying that the divinity of the Word received from her the beginning of its being, but meaning that God the Word himself, who was begotten of the Father timelessly before the ages, and was with the Father and the Spirit without beginning and through eternity, took up his abode in these last days (Heb 1.2) for the sake of our salvation in the Virgin's womb, and was without change made flesh and born of her. For the holy Virgin did not bear mere man but true God: and not mere God but God incarnate, who did not bring down his body from heaven, nor simply pass through the Virgin as channel, but received from

[14] *Homily on the Dormition* 2.3 (1998), 207.
[15] *An Exact Exposition . . .* 4.14.
[16] See Chapter 4.3.
[17] *An Exact Exposition . . .* 3.12.

her flesh of like essence to our own and subsisting in himself. . . . Hence it is with justice and truth that we call the holy Mary the Mother of God.[18]

The usage of the term "Theotokos" in relation to the Mother of God, as John of Damascus says further, comes not only from the rejection of Nestorianism, but from the Orthodox teaching on the deification of the human nature in the incarnate Word:

> The holy Virgin is thought of and spoken of as the Mother of God [Theotokos], not only because of the nature of the Word, but also because of the deification of man's nature. . . . For the very Mother of God in some marvelous manner was the means of fashioning the Framer of all things and of bestowing manhood on the God and Creator of all, who deified the nature that he assumed, while the union preserved those things that were united just as they were united, that is to say, not only the divine nature of Christ but also his human nature, not only that which is above us but that which is of us.[19]

The Fathers distinguish between two moments when speaking on the participation of the Most Holy Virgin in the divine plan of salvation: her being pre-elected by the Pre-eternal Divine Council and her personal feat of co-participation in the act of salvation. According to the Church's teaching, the Most-Holy Virgin, foreordained by God before the ages to become his Mother, was prepared and purified beforehand:

> She was chosen from generations of old by the providential will and pleasure of God the Father, who begot you outside of time without alteration and without passion; she gave you birth, made flesh from herself at the end of the ages. . . . The Father predestined her, and the prophets spoke of her through the Holy Spirit. The sanctifying power of the Spirit reposed on her, cleansed her and made her holy; in a certain sense, he fertilized her in advance.[20]

At the same time, the Church had already in the age of the Christological controversies rejected the notion that Christ passed through the Theotokos "as through a channel," that is that she only passively fulfilled the

---

[18]Ibid.
[19]Ibid.
[20]*Homily on the Dormition* 1.3 (1998), 185.

divine predestination, a mute instrument and tool of divine will. The holiness to which the Theotokos attained is, according to the teaching of the Church, not only the fruit of divine pre-election, but also the fruit of her personal spiritual efforts, which she accomplished "as God's helper in accomplishing the act of dispensation."[21]

The Church speaks of this in glorifying the Annunciation of the Most Holy Theolokos. Her humble consent to the will of God, her readiness to accept God incarnate in her womb, were among the conditions of the incarnation. Without the cooperation of the Mother of God, without her voluntary consent to participate in the act of mankind's salvation, this very salvation could not have happened:

The incarnation of the Word was the work not only of the Father, whose good pleasure it was, and of his Power, who overshadowed, and of his Spirit, who descended, but also of the will and faith of the Virgin. For, just as without those three it would have been impossible for this decision to be implemented, so also, if the All-Pure One had not offered her will and faith, this design could not possibly have been brought to fruition. Having in this way taught and persuaded her, God made her

The Annunciation. Detail of an Icon. Sinai. 12th c.

his Mother and borrowed flesh from her with her knowledge and consent, in order that, just as he was conceived voluntarily, it might equally come about for his Mother that she should conceive voluntarily and become his Mother willingly and by her own free decision.[22]

Therefore the incarnation became not only God's initiative, arbitrarily intruding on human history, but an act of synergy between God and mankind. Philaret of Moscow speaks particularly powerfully on this, juxtaposing the creative word of God that brings the world into being to the word of the Most Holy Theotokos, by which she consented to be the Mother of God. It is the phrase "let it be," uttered by the Theotokos, which became the pivotal moment commencing the history of the incarnation:

---

[21]Gregory Palamas *Homilies* 14.
[22]Nicholas Cabasilas *Homily on the Annunciation* 4–5.

In the days of the creation of the world, when God uttered his vivifying and powerful "let there be," the Creator's word brought creation into being; but in this unparalleled day of the world's existence, when the divine Mary uttered the short and obedient "let it be,"–I hardly dare say what happened then–the word of the creature brought the Creator down into the world. And here God utters his word: "You will conceive in your womb and bear a son. . . . He will be great. . . . He will reign over the house of Jacob forever" (Lk 1.31–33). But–another marvelous and incomprehensible thing–the Word of God himself delays his action, waiting for the word of Mary: "How can this be?" (Lk 1.34). Her humble "let it be" was necessary to affect the greatly divine: "let there be." What then is the hidden power in these simple words: "Here am I, the servant of the Lord; let it be with me according to your word" (Lk 1.38), which causes such a rare action? This wonderful power is Mary's most pure and perfect devotion to God, in will, in thought, in spirit, in all essence, in all manner, in all action, in all hope, and in expectation.[23]

As Archpriest Georges Florovsky emphasizes, commenting on these words of the saint, the initiative of the act of mankind's salvation came from God, although "as far as the means of salvation go, as chosen by God, consisting in the union of the divine Hypostasis and human nature, man cannot remain a passive observer in this mystery." By Mary's words the human race "involves itself in the redemptive decision of the divine love."[24]

In the person of the Mother of God, humanity went out to meet God, who wanted to save the race of man. It offers the Virgin Mother as a gift to the incarnate God, as it says in one of the church hymns at the Nativity.[25] Her birth from the holy and righteous Joachim and Anna became the end of the long-lived preparatory period, over the course of which God chose people from the midst of the tribe of Israel, and they answered this election by acts of faith. It is no accident that the Church recalls all the Old Testament righteous leading up to Christ's Nativity, including Abraham, Isaac, Jacob, King David, as those through whom God prepared mankind for the coming

[23]Philaret (Drozdov), *Selected Writings; Letters; Memoirs* (Moscow: 2003), 169–170.
[24]*Dogmat i istoriya* (Moscow: 1995), 174.
[25]See: The Nativity of Christ. Great Vespers. *Sticheron* at "Lord, I Call": "What shall we offer thee, O Christ, who for our sakes hast appeared on earth as man? Every creature made by thee offers thee thanks; the angels offer thee a hymn; the heavens, a star . . . the earth, its cave; the wilderness, the manger; and we offer thee a Virgin Mother."

of the Savior. The last link in this chain of the righteous was the Most Holy Virgin, whose holiness immeasurably surpasses all the Old Testament righteousness and generally every perfection attainable to earthly man.

The Theotokos' holiness, her lack of involvement in sin and the passions, is one of the leitmotifs of patristic preaching and of treatises dedicated to the Theotokos. The idea that the Most Holy Theotokos could partake in any kind of sin is deeply foreign to Eastern patristic tradition. Some church writers proved the presence of faults and weaknesses in the Theotokos that are characteristic for earthly man, though they never called these sins. John Chrysostom in particular comments on the account of how Jesus' Mother and brothers wanted to see him (Mt 12.46–49), saying that the negative response to his Mother and brothers' request was a sign that "their regard for him was towards a mere man, and they were vainglorious."[26] Interpreting the account of the miracle in Cana of Galilee (Jn 2.1–11), Chrysostom asserts that the request of Mother to Son was motivated by the wish "to do them [the guests] a favor, and through her Son to render herself more conspicuous." As Chrysostom notes, "perhaps she too had some human feelings, like his brethren, when they said, 'Show thyself to the world' (Jn 7.4), desiring to gain credit from his miracles." Jesus' sharp response to his Mother ("Woman, what concern is that to you and to me?"), in Chrysostom's opinion, is conditioned on the fact that "she would not readily have chosen even then to be convinced, but would in all cases have claimed the superiority as being his mother."[27]

Chrysostom's sayings cited above bear witness to the fact that the veneration of the Theotokos at the end of the fourth century had not yet reached the great scale that it acquired after the Third Ecumenical Council. The proceedings of this council not only strengthened the veneration of the Mother of God that was already being served in liturgical practice, but also formed the premise for its continued development. The liturgy of the Orthodox Church strengthened the idea of the exclusive holiness of the Mother of God, of her lack of involvement in any sin. The Church named the Mother of God "More Honorable than the Cherubim and more Glorious beyond compare than the Seraphim," that is, immeasurably exalted above angels in her holiness. She came to be known as "Most Holy," literally "height of holiness,"

[26]*Homily on Matthew* 44.2.
[27]*Homily on John* 21.2.

emphasizing the exalted quality of her holiness over the holiness of any other saint. She is remembered in Orthodox services as first among the saints, as the "Most Holy, most pure, most blessed and glorious Lady, the Theotokos and Ever-Virgin Mary."[28]

The holy fathers call the Theotokos "the immaculate Virgin, who never involved herself in earthy passions,"[29] as having "shaken off all the assaults of passion."[30] She "never sinned even in one thought."[31] Her mind "is free from every worldly and base desire," and her life is "an ascent to sanctity," making her "a holy and pure temple, worthy of God Most High."[32] The Theotokos is "the center-point of the divine and human gifts."[33] She is so close to God that she "is the only who is like a border between the created and uncreated essence," that is between the divine and human natures, "and all who know God know her as the Seat of the Uncontainable One; and all who praise God sing praise to her after him."[34] The Theotokos is "the cause of all the blessings and gifts toward the race of man that came before her, and is the Protectress of those now living, and the Mediatrix of the reposed. She is the foundation of the prophets, the source of the apostles, the support of the martyrs, the basis of the teachers. She is the glory of those on earth, the joy of those in heaven, and the adornment of every created thing."[35]

The above formulations of the liturgical texts and patristic treatises bear witness to the exclusive veneration that surrounds the Most Holy Theotokos in the Orthodox Church. It needs to be said that the veneration of the Theotokos throughout the first millennium of Christian history developed in a parallel nature in both East and West. However, in the second millennium, Marian dogma in the Catholic Church was shrouded in such theological forms that made it incomprehensible and alien to Orthodox tradition. The establishment, development, and enforcement of new Marian teachings, unknown to the Fathers of the ancient, undivided Church, was negatively

[28]Petition at the Great and Little Litanies, recited at the Divine Liturgy, Matins, Vespers, and other liturgical services.
[29]John of Damascus *Homily on the Dormition* 2.2 (1998), 205–206.
[30]Ibid. 2.3, 207.
[31]Silouan the Athonite, "On the Mother of God," cited in: Sophrony (Sakharov), *Starets Siluan* (Paris: 1952), 163.
[32]John of Damascus *An Exact Exposition . . .* 4.14.
[33]Gregory of Palamas *Homilies* 14.
[34]Ibid.
[35]Ibid.

received in the Orthodox East and summoned a whole series of anti-Catholic compositions in which these teachings were refuted through critical analysis.

Beginning with John Duns Scotus, the West developed the teaching of the "immaculate conception" of the Mother of God. According to this teaching, the Mother of God was given special privileges by virtue of the future merits of her Son—to be free from Original Sin. In 1854, Pope Pius IX pronounced a teaching, without calling a council, by special bull, of the dogma of the immaculate conception:

> We declare, pronounce, and define that the doctrine which holds that the most Blessed Virgin Mary, in the first instance of her conception, by a singular grace and privilege granted by Almighty God, in view of the merits of Jesus Christ, the Savior of the human race, was preserved free from all stain of original sin, is a doctrine revealed by God and therefore to be believed firmly and constantly by all the faithful.[36]

The rise and development of the teaching of the immaculate conception of the Mother of God was the direct result of the understanding of Original Sin as an inheritance of guilt, which has been asserted in the West since the time of Augustine.[37] In Orthodox circles, this teaching, especially after the official proclamation of its dogma, was sharply rejected. St Ignatius (Brianchaninov) called the new teaching of the Roman Church a heresy, having emphasized that "the papists, acknowledging that the Mother of God is free from Original Sin, recognized her as being free from every sin, totally sinless, and consequently, needing neither redemption, nor the Redeemer."[38] Ignatius maintains, in opposition to the Catholics, that the Mother of God "was conceived and born in sin according to the general law of fallen man"; "the Virgin Mary was conceived and born into perdition, into the Fall, into the bonds of eternal death and sin, was born into the condition common to every member of the human race."[39] Such a stark emphasis on sinfulness connected to the conception of the Mother of God is not characteristic at all of patristic literature. It is dissonant with the liturgical services of the Orthodox Church that are dedicated to the feast of the Conception of the Most Holy Theotokos.

[36]Bull of Pope Pius IX, "Ineffabilis Deus," (December eighth, 1854).
[37]This was discussed in Chapter 12.
[38]Ignatius Brianchaninov, *Writings*, 5 vols., 3rd ed. (St Petersburg: 1905), 410.
[39]Ibid., 406.

A more theologically elevated, although no less biting rejection of the dogma of the immaculate conception, was Vladimir Lossky's position, which above all is concerned with the extreme legalism of the formed dogma. This legalism, in Lossky's opinion, "washes away the true character of the feat of our redemption and sees only an abstract service to Christ, a responsible human figure before the passion and resurrection of Christ, even before his incarnation."[40] If the Most Holy Virgin had been, by virtue of some special privilege, isolated from the rest of humanity, then her freely given consent to the divine will in response to the Archangel Gabriel would have been cheapened. This response would have lost its historical connection to other acts aiding in mankind's preparation throughout time for the coming of the Messiah; "then the succession of the Old Testament holiness would have been broken, which was accumulated from generation to generation, finally resulting in the person of Mary, the Most Pure Virgin, whose humble obedience must cross the last threshold, making our salvation possible."[41] Lossky criticizes the difference between "active" and "passive" conception that the Catholics introduced in order to explain the immaculate conception. The Orthodox Church, devoid of aversion to fleshly nature, will not accept this artificial distinction.[42]

In connection with the "immaculate conception," it is necessary to point out one Orthodox liturgical text which uses this phrase: "We sing the praises of the holy birth and venerate thy conceiving without seed, O Maiden, Bride of God and Virgin."[43] This text from the second canon at the Nativity of the Theotokos is sometimes regarded as an illustration of how the teaching of the immaculate conception of the Mother of God is not foreign to the Orthodox Church. The phrase "thy conceiving," in relation to the norms of the Greek language, can be understood either as referring to the conception of the Most Holy Virgin by Joachim and Anna, or to the conception of the Savior by the Most Holy Virgin. The very fact that the conception is referred to after the nativity, and not before (then it would logically correspond to the following event, which would be the conception of the Theotokos by Joachim and Anna), witnesses in favor of the latter interpretation as a common component

[40]V.N. Lossky, *Theology and the Vision of God: A Collection of Writings* (Moscow: 2000), 339.
[41]Ibid., 341.
[42]Ibid., 343.
[43]Nativity of the Most Holy Theotokos. Matins. Second Canon. Ode Six.

of the canon. Therefore, the hymn in question revolves around the conception of the Savior by the Virgin Mary, coming about by the inspiration of the Holy Spirit: it is precisely this conception, from the point of view of the Orthodox Church, that manifests the full meaning of the word "immaculate."

The Orthodox Church addresses the Theotokos with the words "Most Holy Theotokos, save us," which show the participation of the Theotokos in the act of salvation and redemption (the received formula for saints is "pray to God for us"). However, Orthodoxy will not accept "Co-redemptrix" as a title for the Theotokos, which is used in the Roman

Praise of the Mother of God with Akathist. Moscow school. 16th c.

Catholic Church,[44] since this title lessens the unique redemptive sacrifice of Christ and can create the false notion that Christ and the Mother of God had an equal share in the redeeming act.

The Orthodox and Catholic Churches come much closer in their understanding of the mortal fate of the Most Holy Theotokos, believing that she ascended to heaven together with her body. This belief was confessed by theologians of the East and West over the course of the second half of the first millennium. However, the emphasis in the West was placed not so much on the repose of the Most Holy Virgin, as much as on her ascent to heavenly glory. The Catholic Church feast day dedicated to this event has received the name "The Taking of the Virgin Mary into Heaven" (*Assumptio*/Assumption). The opinions of Catholic theologians of what actually happened at the repose of the Theotokos differ. Some (the mortalists) assert that she, not subject to Original Sin, was not subject to death, but died voluntarily and therefore ascended to heaven. Others (the immortalists) consider that she genuinely could not die and was straightaway taken up into heavenly glory. In 1950, Pope Pius pronounced the dogma of the bodily assumption of the Virgin Mary into heaven, having referred to it in a special bull dedicated to this dogma, saying that Christ preserved her "from corruption and death."[45]

---

[44]The pronouncement of the Virgin Mary as "Co-redemptrix" is not a dogma of the Catholic Church, although this title was repeatedly used by popes of Rome (in particular, John Paul II), when speaking ex cathedra.

[45]The Apostolic Constitution of Pope Pius XII, "Munificentissimus Deus" (First of November, 1950).

The Dormition of the Most Holy Theotokos. Byzantine icon in relief. 10th c.

The Assumption of the Virgin Mary into heaven is not celebrated in the Orthodox East, but rather the Dormition of the Most Holy Theotokos is, reflected in iconography: in the West the Virgin Mary is depicted as ascending into the clouds surrounded by Cherubim, but in the East she is laid out on a funeral bier surrounded by the apostles. The Orthodox believe that the Lord preserved her body from corruption, although they profess that she died by virtue of being subject to the law common to human nature. In his homily on the Dormition, John of Damascus says that the Theotokos is the "one who overcame the defining nature in her childbearing now gives way to those same limits, and submits her unsullied body to death." At the same time the Damascene stresses that "still there is an infinite difference between God's servants and his Mother," and since, if the soul of the Mother of God is subject to the law of nature and was separated from her body, and that body was placed in a grave, this holy body "did not remain in death, nor was it dissolved by corruption."[46]

In contrast to the Catholic Church, the Orthodox Church never dogmatized a teaching on the assumption of the Most Holy Theotokos into heaven; nevertheless, belief in this event is an inseparable part of the Tradition of the Orthodox Church. John of Damascus says in his *Homily on the Dormition*:

> The angels and archangels carried you there. The unclean spirits of midair trembled at your departure. The air was blessed by your passing through it, the ether of the upper regions was sanctified. Heaven received your soul with joy. The powers [of heaven] met you with holy hymns and splendid ceremony. . . . The powers accompany you in procession, the principalities sing your blessings, the thrones praise you, the cherubim are struck dumb with joy, the seraphim praise you, for you are called, by nature and by God's own plan, the mother of their Lord. You have not simply gone up into the heavens like Elijah (2 Kg 2.11), nor have you simply been transported, like Paul, to the third heaven (2 Cor 12.2). You have gone on to the very royal throne of your Son, where you see him with

[46] *Homily on the Dormition* 1.10 (1998), 194–195.

your own eyes and rejoice; you stand beside him in great, indescribable freedom.[47]

The veneration of the Theotokos occupies an exclusive place in Orthodox liturgical services. The Marian feasts accompany the faithful throughout the whole church year, parallel to feasts of the Lord, dedicated to the remembrance of the foundational events in the life of the Savior. The first great feast of the church year is the Nativity of the Theotokos, and the last, her Dormition. Individually celebrated are the Entry of the Theotokos in the Temple, the Meeting of the Lord, and the Annunciation of the Most Holy Theotokos. In Russian Orthodox Church tradition, there is a widespread celebration in honor of icons of the Mother of God—the Vladimir icon, the Kazan icon, the Smolensk icon, the Tikhvin icon, and many others.

Every liturgical rite, whether in the liturgy, vespers, matins, compline, nocturns, or the hours, contains prayers dedicated to the Mother of God. Every ode of a canon contains a Troparion dedicated to the Theotokos; cycles of verses at vespers and matins contain a "Theotokion" verse as well. The innumerable quantity of prayers dedicated to the Theotokos bears witness to the fact that her image was the source of abundant inspiration for church poets and hymnographers. It remains so for all the generations of Orthodox Christians, who see in the Most Holy Theotokos a "Steadfast Protectress," a "Comfort in need and grief," a "Seeker of those who are perishing," and the "Joy of all who sorrow."

The veneration of the Theotokos grew out of the very depths of being of the Orthodox Church:

Union with Christ, which is the goal of the Church's existence—yes, and of every individual Christian—is above all participation in his sacrificial love toward mankind. In this, a huge role belongs to that which is the unique form connected with the Redeemer, the bonds of motherly love. The Mother of God becomes the Mother of all living things, of all Christianity, of every person who is born and raised in the Spirit and truth. . . . The mystery of Mary is the mystery of the Church. *The Mother-Church and the Mother of God* together give birth to new life. . . . The Church calls the faithful to itself and helps them grow into spirituality and these mysteries of the faith, mysteries of their own existence and spiritual destiny.

[47]Ibid. I.II, 196.

They learn to contemplate the living Christ in the Church together with the festive council, the Assembly "of the firstborn who are enrolled in heaven" (Heb 12.23), and bow down before them. And they discern in this radiant and glorious council the dazzling face of the Most Holy Mother of the Lord and Redeemer, a face full of grace and love, of compassion and mercy, a face "More Honorable than the Cherubim and more Glorious beyond compare than the Seraphim."[48]

---

[48]Georges Florovsky, *Dogma and History* (Moscow: 1995), 179–180.

PART SIX

Eschatology

E VERY RELIGION CONTAINS an eschatological dimension within itself, for each religion addresses not only the material world, but also the spiritual world, not only the present times, but the future times. However, it is in Christianity that eschatology plays so essential a role that Christianity loses its meaning outside the eschatological dimension, ceasing to be itself. Eschatology permeates the whole being of the Church, its liturgical services, its sacraments and rites, its theological and moral teachings, its asceticism and its mysticism. The entire history of the Church is filled with eschatological expectations, beginning with the resurrection and ascension of Christ into heaven and continuing up to the present day.

The Savior reigning in power. Theophanes the Greek. 15th c.

As Protopresbyter Georges Florovsky notes, the Western liberal theological tradition, beginning with the age of the Enlightenment, scorned eschatology: to many, it became a remnant of a long-forgotten past. However, the contemporary theological thought—in Catholicism as well as Protestantism—opens up the theme of eschatology anew, returning to the realization that the dogmata of the faith have a direct relation to it.[1]

As concerns Orthodox theology, it never lost the eschatological dimension. At the same time, the "pseudomorphosis" of Orthodox theology that occurred under the influence of Catholicism and Protestantism in the eighteenth and nineteenth centuries could not inform on eschatology. The aspect of the eschatological theme on dogmatic theology in Greek and Russian

[1]Georges Florovsky, *Dogma and History* (Moscow: 1995), 444–446.

489

The wise thief in paradise.
Central Rus'. 17th c.

textbooks in this period follows primarily Catholic schemes. In this sense, the twentieth century became for the Orthodox Church a time of rethinking eschatology, returning to that patristic foundation on which it was built up during the epochs of the early Church and the Byzantine period.

In the words of Protopresbyter Alexander Schmemann, eschatology is a distinguishing peculiarity of the Christian faith as a system of persuasion, that is as "faith in God, in the salvific power of specific historical events and, finally, in the conclusive victory of God in Christ and of the Kingdom of God." Eschatology is directed toward the future, to the mystical *eschaton* of the coming Kingdom. At the same time, "as Christians, we already possess that in which we believe. The Kingdom must come, but at the same time the approaching Kingdom is already amongst us. The Kingdom is not only some secret thing; we can know it here and now. And consequently, in each homily we bear the witness, *martyria*/μαρτυρία, not only to our faith, but to the possession of those things in which we believe." The authentic nature of the Christian faith, according to the theologian, is concluded with our "living within time, but living outside of time; we live in that which has not yet come, but we already know it and have it."[2]

These two aspects of Christian eschatology are already revealed in the New Testament teaching on the Kingdom of God. The expression "enter the kingdom of heaven" (Mt 5.20, 7.21, 19.23–24) is repeatedly used by the Savior, showing the perspective of the salvation of human souls in its future, posthumous existence. Jesus' words addressed to the Jews that "the kingdom of God will be taken away from [them] and given to a nation bringing forth the fruits [of the kingdom]" (Mt 21.43), again point out a kind of future perspective in which the Kingdom of God transfers to the New Israel, to those who believe in Christ. Christ bequeaths the Kingdom, which will begin in an eschatological

[2]Alexander Schmemann, *Liturgy and Tradition* (Kiev: 2005), 117.

perspective, to his disciples at his Second Coming: "I appoint to you a kingdom, as my Father has appointed [a kingdom] to me, that you may eat and drink at my table in my kingdom, and sit on thrones judging the twelve tribes of Israel" (Lk 22.29–30).

On the other hand, Christ's preaching, like the preaching of John the Baptist, began with the words that the Kingdom of Heaven "is at hand" (Mt 4.17, 3.2), that is, it has approached people in earnest. News of the Kingdom's proximity becomes a leitmotif in Christ's preaching: the Kingdom of God is not some far off eschatological viewpoint, not a reality "existing beyond the grave," but an experience that is accessible to man already in earthly life, provided he believes in Christ and fulfills his commandments. The eschatological "last times" began with the First Coming of Christ and his preaching on earth; they will end with his Second Coming, when Christ "delivers up the kingdom to the God and Father" (1 Cor 15.24).

Christ's moral teaching is built on the fundamental claim of the Kingdom of God as not only a future reality, an existence that is beyond the grave, but as a reality in the earthly life of man. In the Savior's words, "The kingdom of heaven suffers violence, and the violent take it by force" (Mt. 11.12), that is, they carry it away here, on earth. In Jesus' parables, the Kingdom of God is likened to a seed, thrown on the ground (Mt 13.24), to a mustard seed (Mt 13.31), to yeast in dough (Mt 13.33), to treasure hidden in a field (Mt 13.44), to a fine pearl (Mt 13.45), to a net thrown into the sea that caught fish of every kind (Mt 13.47), to a king who wished to settle accounts with his slaves (Mt 18.23), to a landowner who went out early in the morning to hire laborers for his vineyard (Mt 20.1), to a king who gave a wedding banquet for his son (Mt 22.2). All of these images are borrowed from everyday human life and relate to the experience of a person living in this world, and not of one who has already passed on to a different world.

Christ speaks of how the Kingdom of Heaven belongs to those who are poor in spirit (Mt 5.3), those who are persecuted for righteousness' sake (Mt 5.10), to children (Mt 19.14), of how the Kingdom "is not of this world" (Jn 18.36). Addressing his disciples, the Savior exhorts them: "Do not be afraid, little flock, for it is your Father's good pleasure to give you the kingdom" (Lk 12.32). Thus, the Kingdom of God is *already* given, *already* exists in the life of Christians. Through faith in Christ and following his commandments, people are joined to the Kingdom of God, which will be fully realized after the

Second Coming of the Savior, but which nevertheless already exists invisibly in the Church, comprising the core of its being.

This experience is revealed in the Orthodox liturgical services, particularly in the Divine Liturgy, which is not only an *anamnesis*, a recollection of past events (of the Last Supper, the passion, death, and resurrection of the Savior), but also a participation in the future reality.[3] The liturgy is the "fulfillment of the Church at the Lord's banquet in his Kingdom."[4] The Savior's promise is already realized at the completion of the liturgy: "You shall eat and drink at my table in my Kingdom." The words of the Eucharistic prayer pose events past, present, and future in one unbroken sequence: "Thou it was who brought us from non-existence into being, and when we had fallen away didst raise us up again, and didst not cease to do all things until thou hadst brought us up to heaven, and hadst endowed us with thy Kingdom which is to come." The Kingdom of God is in the "future," but it has simultaneously *already* been given, and the liturgy *already* calls people to heaven, it is *already* "heaven on earth."

Before moving on to the most important aspects of Orthodox eschatology, it is necessary to make two clarifications. First of all, it is necessary to say that eschatology is a subject of questions about, not answers to, the mysteries, and not of evidence of hopes and dreams, and not of categorical claims. Much of what concerns the future fate of the world and mankind is revealed to us in the Holy Scriptures and in the Tradition of the Church, but much remains hidden in the depths of the divine mysteries. Going down the line of eschatological issues, there are many divergences between the Eastern and Western (Orthodox and Catholic) theological traditions, but for some issues there is not even a unified view within Orthodox tradition. For this reason, V.N. Lossky warns of a twofold danger that lies in wait for the theologian who enters on the path of researching eschatological themes: "of being too explicit, or of giving too great a share to the 'inexpressible' mystery." Dealing with eschatological problems, we "enter a field where we constantly see our methods of theological research reduced to inadequacy by the multitude of aspects which must be grasped simultaneously—mobile intersecting planes which cannot be halted and held stationary in the mind without falsifying them."[5]

---

[3]Cf. John Zizioulas, *Being as Communion* (Moscow: 2006), 260.
[4]Alexander Schmemann, *Liturgy and Tradition* (Kiev: 2005), 119.
[5]"Dominion and Kingship: An Eschatological Study," *In the Image and Likeness of God* (Crestwood, NY: St Vladimir's Seminary Press, 1974), 211–212.

The second elucidation deals with the coexistence of two eschatologies at the root of the Christian theological tradition—a "personal" one and a "universal-historical" one.[6] The questions addressed to the realm of personal eschatology are connected with death and the posthumous fate of individual human identities. Universal eschatology, on the contrary, addresses future events that relate to the history of all of humanity—to the Second Coming of Christ, to the universal resurrection, to the Last Judgment, to the eternal blessedness of the righteous, and to the torment of sinners.

In accordance with these divisions that have but a methodological significance, inasmuch as the fate of an individual person is inseparable from the fate of humanity, the first section of this chapter will be dedicated to one of the fundamental aspects of "personal" eschatology—the theme of death as a way to eternity. In the later sections our attention will be concentrated on those eschatological themes that relate to the fate of humanity as a whole.

[6]N. A. Berdiaev, *Dukh i realjnost'* (Moscow: 2003), 550.

27

Death as a Way to Eternity

THE THEME OF DEATH DIVIDES HUMANITY into two camps—those who believe in an "afterlife" and those who do not believe in one. The religious person who does not belong to one particular confession of faith acknowledges the existence of life after death, even if the notions of what this is actually like differs one from the other in different religions. The non-religious person, on the contrary, rejects the existence of an afterlife, positing that a person's life is contained exclusively in the timeframe between birth and death. The divergence between the religious and non-religious worldview is not so radical and obvious in any other realm.

Above all, this divergence influences the concept of life, its meaning and purpose. The non-religious person strives to survive on earth as long as possible, "to get everything out of life," since after crossing the threshold of death, there is nothingness, emptiness. In Christian tradition, on the contrary, earthly life is not considered to be of absolute importance, since Christians continue on to the prospect of an eternal existence. Christians are preoccupied not so much with the number of years they can live as much as the quality of their own lives; moreover this quality is defined not by earthly gains as much as by spiritual richness, where "neither moth nor rust corrupt, and where thieves do not break through nor steal" (Mt 6.20).

The stated divergence absolutely influences how the believer and the non-believer relate to death and everything that accompanies it. The non-religious person fears death, fears thoughts of death, preparing for death, mortal disease: the widespread view that a sudden death is the best death comes from this fear. The faithful, on the contrary, prepare themselves for death and at the same time pray for deliverance from a sudden death. In Christian tradition, a mortal illness is looked at as a test possibly bearing spiritual benefit, and death, as a passage into another world.

For the non-believing person, death is a catastrophe and a tragedy, a rupture and a break. For the Christian, though, death is neither a catastrophe nor something evil. Death is a "falling asleep," a temporary condition of separation from the body until the final unification with it. As Isaac the Syrian emphasizes, the sleep of death is short in comparison with the expectant eternity of a person. For this reason, a person should not grieve over death, but should think of it with hope for a future eternal life:

Detail of the icon "The Ladder."
Nizhny Novgorod. 17th c.

There is no mourning for your going into the silent grave, O dead one. . . . How beautiful your members and how deplorable your decay! But do not be paralyzed by grief, for you will once again be wrapped in a body by the burning flame and by the Spirit, carrying in it the exact image of its Creator. . . . Do not be distressed that we will dwell in this corrupt death for many years under the earth, while the end of the world has not yet come. Death is not burdensome for us, for the continuation of our sleep in the grave is like a dream in the course of one night. For look, the most wise Creator made even death easy so that we would not not feel its load even a bit. Until we passed through it, it was heavy for us, but after death we do not feel any sort of corruption or decay of our members, but, like after a dream in the course of one night, we will awake on that day as if we had laid ourselves down to sleep the night before, and now have awakened. This is how easy our long sleep in the grave will be, and the passing of the years spent in it.[1]

The fear of death, characteristic of the non-believer, is cast out in Christianity by the hope of the resurrection:

Faith strengthens him in hope, so that with joy he endures all dangers that accompany him for the sake of these divine blessings, so that even in death he was not afraid and did not suffer as a bodily essence, but became like one who possesses super-physical hope, who has a steadfast heart and who believes in God. Every day he awaits the exodus from the body . . . so that he might safely attain the resurrection from the dead.[2]

[1]Isaac the Syrian *Chapters on Knowledge III* 74–75.
[2]*On the Divine Mysteries: Homily* 1.20.

In the treatise *On Death*, Cyprian of Carthage claims that "it is for him to fear death who is not willing to go to Christ. It is for him to be unwilling to go to Christ who does not believe that he is about to reign with Christ."[3] In Cyprian's words, "assuredly he may fear to die, who, not being regenerated of water and the Spirit, is delivered over to the fires of Gehenna; he may fear to die who is not enrolled in the cross and passion of Christ."[4]

Death is viewed in Christianity, on the one hand, as a consequence of the Fall: God created people as immortal, but as a result of turning away from fulfilling God's commandments, people became mortal and corruptible. On the other hand, the notion that death is a blessing from God is present in some fathers of the Church, for through death lies the way to resurrection and eternal life. As Gregory of Nyssa writes, "by the Divine Providence death has been introduced as a dispensation into the nature of man, so that, sin having flowed away at the dissolution of the union of soul and body, man, through the resurrection, might be refashioned, sound, passionless, stainless, and removed from any touch of evil."[5]

Interpreting the biblical narrative on God's cursing of Adam and Eve for their sin and on their expulsion from paradise, Isaac the Syrian discusses how the establishment of death and the expulsion were accomplished under the form of a curse, although a blessing was hidden in this very curse:

As he established death for Adam under the guise of a sentence for sin and as he revealed the presence of sin as means of a punishment, although the punishment itself was not his goal, as he showed, so death was established for Adam as a requital for his mistake. But he hid his true mystery, and under the form of something frightening he hid his pre-eternal intention relating to death and his wise plan regarding it: though death can be something quite frightening, shameful, and difficult in the beginning, nevertheless this is truly the means of our translation to that exalted and all-glorious world. . . . When he cast out Adam and Eve from paradise, he cast them out under the guise of wrath. . . . But the saving plan was already present in all of this, perfecting and leading all to that primordial intention of the Creator. It was not disobedience that brought death to Adam's house, and it was not the breaking of the commandment that cast Adam and Eve out

[3] *On Mortality* 2.
[4] Ibid. 14.
[5] *Great Catechetical Oration* 35.

of paradise, for it was clear that God did not create them for existence in paradise, which is only a small part of the earth; but they should have subjugated all the earth. . . . Even if they had not broken the commandment, they regardless would not have remained in paradise forever.[6]

Therefore death was a blessing, since it contained within itself from the beginning the potential for future resurrection, and the expulsion from paradise was for the good of humanity, since instead of "a piece of land," mankind received dominion over the whole earth. According to Isaac the Syrian, death was the consequence of divine "trickery": God hid his true purpose under the mask of punishment for sin, concluding with the salvation of humanity. Isaac maintains that it is necessary to see that God's actions can only be seen outwardly in the history of mankind as punishment and retribution, though in actuality God's goal is for us to attain blessing by any means possible. Knowing our propensity to all forms of evil beforehand, God cleverly prepares that which is fatal for us, but is actually a means for our improvement. Only in going through what is presented as a punishment for us from God do we come to know that it served us for the good. There is no retribution in God, but he always cares for the benefit that comes from all his activity in relation to people.[7]

In Christian tradition, death is considered from the perspective of "the death of God"—the death on the cross of the Lord and Savior. This death precisely bestowed significance and justification on the death of people. By his death, Christ "trampled" upon death, he conquered and annulled it, having opened to humanity the way to the resurrection. This does not signify that death ceased to exist: it exists, but for the one who believes in Christ, it lost its power: "We do indeed die, but we do not continue in it: which is not to die at all. For the tyranny of death, and death indeed, is when he who dies is never more allowed to return to life. But when after dying is living, and that a better life, this is not death, but sleep."[8]

What happens to a person's soul after death? In the words of Gregory the Theologian, "every fair and God-beloved soul, when, set free from the bonds of the body . . . departs hence, at once enjoys a sense and perception of the blessing which await it, inasmuch as that which darkened it has been purged

[6] On the Divine Mysteries: Homily 39.4.
[7] Ibid. 39.5.
[8] John Chrysostom Homily on Hebrews 17.4.

away, or laid aside." Having been set free from the body, the soul "feels a wondrous pleasure and exultation, and goes rejoicing to meet its Lord, having escaped as it were from the grievous poison of life here, and shaken off the fetters which bound it and held down the wings of the mind, and so enters on the enjoyment of the bliss laid up for it."[9]

The focus in Gregory the Theologian revolves only around the posthumous fate of the God-loving soul; Gregory does not deal with what happens to the soul of a sinner here. According to the patristic view widespread in the East, the soul of a righteous person encounters angels after its departure from the body (this opinion is partly based on Luke 16.22), but demons torture the soul of a sinner. One of the homilies of Macarius of Egypt speaks of this:

> When the soul of a man departs out of his body, a great mystery is there accomplished. If it is under the guilt of sins, there come bands of devils, and angels of the left hand, and powers of darkness take over that soul, and hold it fast on their side. No one ought to be surprised by this. If, while alive and in this world, the man was subject and compliant to them, and made himself their bondman, how much more, when he departs out of this world, is he kept down and held fast by them. That this is the case, you ought to understand from what happens on the good side. God's holy servants even now have angels continually beside them; and when they depart out of the body, the bands of angels take their souls over to their own side, into the pure world, and so they bring them to the Lord.[10]

We find a similar concept of the fate of a person after death in Blessed Diadochus, the bishop of Photike, who says that people who have not confessed their sins during life will be terror-stricken at the hour of death. And "he who then finds himself in fear will not pass freely by the princes of Hades, because they consider the timidity of this soul to be a sign of its co-participation in their evil deeds." But the soul of the God-loving person that bears repentance for sins, at the hour of separation from the body "is borne from the world by angels beyond all the dark hordes, because such a soul is inspired by spiritual love in some way."[11]

[9] *Oration* 7.21.
[10] *Spiritual Homilies* 22.
[11] *100 Chapters* 100.

It is said in both Macarius and Diadochus that demons meet the souls of sinners, while the souls of the righteous fall into the arms of angels. There exists, however, another idea, according to which the soul of every person, including the righteous, endures trials after death. Basil the Great, speaking on the "steadfast divine ascetics, who have sufficiently grappled with invisible enemies all their life," claims that when they find themselves at the end of life, "the prince of this age comes to know of it, in order to keep them for himself if there can be found any wounds on them received during the battle, or any kind of stain or imprint of sin."[12]

The Ladder of St John Climacus. Sinai. 12th c.

John Climacus describes the hours before death of a certain Stephen, who lived as a monastic for forty years and that "tears and fasting adorned his soul, as did many other fine achievements." A day before his passing he was afflicted with the illness by which he would die, and went into an ecstasy "and began to look to the right and left of his bed. He seemed to be rendering an account to someone, and in the hearing of the bystanders he said: 'Of course it is true. That was why I fasted for so many years.' Or again: 'Yes, that is correct, but I wept and served my brothers.' Or again: 'No. You are accusing me falsely.' Or sometimes: 'Quite right. No, I have no excuse. But God is merciful.'" As Climacus notes, "he died while it was happening leaving us unsure of the judgment passed on him, of his final end or sentence or of the verdict rendered him."[13]

The testimony of another type of patristic literature is the fundamental teaching on the "tribulations"–trials in the afterlife that the soul of each person endures. This teaching found reflection in various memorials of Byzantine ascetic and hagiographic literature, particularly in *The Torments of Blessed Theodora*. Described in this account is an experience of going through twenty torments ("toll-houses"), each of which correspond to one of the sins: a person must give answer to the demon-torturer for every sin committed, and if

---

[12] *Homily on Psalm Seven* 2.

[13] *The Ladder of Divine Ascent*, Colm Luibheid and Norman Russell, tr. (New York: Paulist Press, 1982), 142.

that person cannot prove their innocence, they will not be permitted to go on to the next torment. To a modern person, such descriptions can seem to be the stuff of fantasy or some kind of unhealthy "eschatological sadism," although the experience of people who have survived clinical death, researched by doctors, psychologists, and theologians, in some cases support the testimony contained in these ordeals.[14]

Regardless of how literally the testimonies of the toll-houses are perceived, whether in ancient or modern sources, the teaching that man awaits a trial after death is generally accepted in Orthodox tradition. This trial is called the "particular judgment" in dogmatic theology textbooks, as opposed to the general "Last Judgment," at which the final fate of every person is determined.

After the posthumous trial of a person's soul is completed, the soul either ends up at the gates of paradise, where it dwells in anticipation of eternal blessing, or at the gates of hell, where it can look forward to eternal torment. This is discussed especially in St Mark of Ephesus:

> We assert that neither the righteous have yet attained the fullness of their destiny and that blessed condition for which they have prepared themselves here through deeds; nor were sinners led away after death into eternal punishment in which they will be tortured for eternity; but both one and the other must needs occur after that last day of judgment and the resurrection of all. But for now both the one and the other find themselves in places appropriate for them: the former—in perfect repose and in freedom in heaven with the angels and before God himself as if they were already in paradise . . . and the latter, in their turn, locked away in Hades, dwelling in darkness and the shadow of death, laid in the depths of the Pit (Ps 88.6). . . . And the former abide in every joy and happiness, already expecting but not yet possessing in their hands the Kingdom promised them, and unspeakable blessing; the latter, on the contrary, dwell in every hardship and inconsolable suffering, as condemned, awaiting the sentence of the Judge and foreseeing such tortures. And neither have the former yet received the inheritance of the Kingdom and those blessings that no eye has seen, nor ear heard, nor the human heart

---

[14]A detailed account, in the light of Orthodox eschatology, of the experience of people who have survived clinical death, is contained in the book: Seraphim Rose, *The Soul After Death* (Platina, CA: St Herman Press, 1980).

conceived (1 Cor 2.9), nor have the latter yet been handed over to eternal torment and burning in the unquenchable fire.[15]

The interim condition in which the soul of a dead person lives before the Last Judgment is spoken of in the Synaxarion of Meatfare Saturday: "We should know that at present, that is, prior to the general resurrection, the souls of the righteous exist in certain specially designated places, and those of sinners in another region, the former rejoicing in their hope, but the latter grieving in expectation of the terrors that await them, since the saints have not yet received the promise of good things."[16] Proceeding from the fact that the final destiny of people after death is not determined before the Last Judgment and therefore it is possible to alter their fates, the Orthodox Church prays for every person who has fallen asleep, including those in Hades.[17]

How does the Orthodox Church view the destiny of people after death who do not bear moral responsibility for their actions and who by virtue of this are not allowed to associate either with the righteous or the sinners? This argument pertains especially to youths who have suffered a premature death, but also to those who are insane.

According to Gregory of Nyssa, the notion of retribution after death cannot be applied to youths, for the word "retribution" supposes the presence of acts committed either for evil or for good. If such acts were simply absent, then it is impossible to speak of a requital for them.[18] Sin is a disease of human nature, and in order to enjoy heavenly blessings, it is necessary to be cured of this disease. Since then an infant who has not yet been tempted by evil "has no such plague before its soul's eyes obscuring its measure of light . . . so it continues to exist in natural life; it does not need the soundness which comes from purgation, because it never admitted the plague into its soul at all."[19] At the same time, the life of a young child cannot be compared to the life of a virtuous person with feats of moral accomplishment, who has been crowned in the Kingdom of Heaven. Such a feat leads to incomparable great blessedness, rather than what a youth possesses who has been prematurely stolen by death.[20] It could turn out to be the contrary case, that "not

---

[15] *Second Oration on the Purifying Fire.*
[16] *Lenten Triodion.* Saturday before Meatfare. Matins. Synaxarion at the sixth ode of the canon.
[17] Discussion on prayers for the dead will continue in the ensuing volumes of our book.
[18] Gregory of Nyssa *On Infants' Early Deaths.*
[19] Ibid.
[20] Ibid.

participating in life is a greater blessing than living," that is, it could be better not to be born, or to be born and immediately die, than not to live a life in virtue and holiness.[21]

The argument in the above words of Gregory of Nyssa concerns those who have died in childhood, as well as those who have died in their mother's womb. Gregory does not see a principal difference in the fate of one or the other, excepting that those former ones were taken from life according to the unspeakable Providence of God, whereas the guilt of death of the latter ones lies with the parents.[22] Gregory says the following concerning those who died at an early age due to disease or some unfortunate accident: it is not characteristic of the Divine Providence only to make right the consequences of evil deeds, but also in some cases to prevent those that have not yet been committed. It is possible that, foreseeing some future sinful way of life for a person, the Lord steals the person away from life prematurely, "in order that the evil may not be developed."[23]

Gregory does not pose a question specifically on the fate of unbaptized children. There is no monolithic answer to this question in Orthodox tradition. The Synaxarion from the Saturday before Meatfare cited above says that "when baptized infants die, they enjoy the paradise of delight, whereas those not illumined by baptism and those born of pagans go neither to paradise nor to Gehenna."[24] The question, therefore, remains open, and the fate of unbaptized children is entrusted to the all-blessed Divine Providence. In any case, the view of Thomas of Aquinas, that unbaptized children are doomed to dwell in a special section of Hades (the *infernum puerorum*[25]) prepared for them, is foreign to Orthodox tradition.

---

[21]Ibid.
[22]Ibid.
[23]Ibid.
[24]*Lenten Triodion*. Saturday before Meatfare. Matins. Synaxarion at the sixth ode of the canon.
[25]Summa Theologica IIIa, 52.2. For more, see the section dedicated to the descent into Hades, Chapter 18.

28

The Second Coming of Christ

THE BASIC FOCUS OF CHRISTIAN ESCHATOLOGY is on the Second Coming of Christ. The whole history of Christianity unfolds during the period of time between the First and Second Coming of the Savior. The fate of all people, those both living and dead, is intertwined in this history. The anticipation of the Second Coming unites the Church of those who have wandered off and the triumphant Church. Those who lived before Christ, especially the Old Testament righteous, abide in the expectation of the Second Coming.

The Second Coming of Christ will differ in a radical way from his first manifestation. The first time, Christ came to earth in the kenotic "form of a servant, and was made in the likeness of men . . . and being found in fashion as a man" (Phil 2.7), but the second time he will come in the glory and majesty of his divinity. In the words of Hippolytus of Rome, "there are two manifestations of our Lord and Savior indicated in the Scriptures: one is the first, which was inglorious in the flesh by reason of his disparagement . . . but the other will be his appearance in glory, when he will come down from heaven with the hosts of angels and the glory of the Father."[1] Cyril of Jerusalem says: "We preach not one advent only of Christ, but a second also, far more glorious than the former. For the former gave a view of his patience; but the latter brings with it the crown of a divine kingdom. . . . In his first coming, he endured the Cross, despising shame (Heb 12.2); in his second, he comes attended by a host of angels, receiving glory. . . . The Savior comes, not to be judged again, but to judge them who judged him."[2]

Much attention is given to the theme of the Second Coming in the pages of the New Testament—in the Gospels, as in Acts, and the Apostolic Epistles, and Revelation. Each one of the Synoptic Gospels contains an eschatological

[1] *On Christ and the Antichrist* 44.
[2] *Catechetical Lecture* 15.1.

chapter in which Christ himself speaks of his Second Coming and of the signs of the end of the world (Mt 24; Mk 13; Lk 21). In the Savior's words, his coming will be preceded by a multitude of false messiahs and false prophets, who will call themselves Christ and "will lead many astray" by wonders and signs (Mt 24.5, 24.11, 24.23–25; Mk 13.5–7, 21–22; Lk 21.8). The time before the end of the world is described as a period of social and natural disasters, when wars will come, and "nation will rise against nation, and kingdom against kingdom, and there shall be famines, and pestilences, and earthquakes in divers places" (Mt 24.6–7; Mk 13.7–8; Lk 21.9–11). Christians will be hated because of Christ's name, and "be afflicted, and . . . killed" (Mt 24.9; Mk 13.9, 11–13; Lk 21.12–29). At the same time, the good news "shall be preached in all the world, for a witness to all nations; and then the end shall come" (Mt 24.14; Mk 13.10).

The Second Coming itself is described as an event of universal, cosmic significance:

An angel wrapping the heavenly firmament. Monastery of Chora. Constantinople. 14th c.

Immediately after the tribulation of those days the sun shall be darkened, and the moon shall not give her light, and the stars shall fall from heaven, and the powers of the heavens shall be shaken. And then the sign of the Son of man shall appear in heaven. And then all the tribes of the earth shall mourn, and thy shall see the Son of man coming in the clouds of heaven with power and great glory. And he shall send his angels with a great sound of a trumpet, and they shall gather together his elect from the four winds, from one end of heaven to the other. (Mt 24.29–31; cf. Mk 13.24–27; Lk 21.26–27)

Christian exegetical tradition understands the cross to be the "sign of the Son of Man." As John Chrysostom says, the cross of Christ, which is "brighter than the sun," will be a joy to Christians and a disgrace to the Jews. "Having heard of the cross, do not think of anything sad: Christ will come in power and great glory," writes Chrysostom. In Chrysostom's words, at the moment of the Second Coming, "angels will collect those who are resurrected, and clouds will bear them up, and all this will occur in but a moment."[3]

[3] *Homily on Matthew* 76.4–5.

The Savior's Second Coming will be sudden and unexpected; it will take unawares those who have not prepared themselves for it. Hence the call to constant vigilance:

> But of that day and hour no one knows, no, not the angels of heaven, nor the Son, but my Father alone. . . . Watch therefore, for you do not know at what hour your Lord comes. (Mt 24.36, 42; Mk 13.32, 35)

> And take heed to yourselves, lest at any time your hearts be overcharged with surfeiting, and drunkenness, and cares of this life, and that day come upon you unawares. For as a snare it shall come on all who dwell on the face of the whole earth. Watch, therefore, and pray always, that you may be accounted worthy to escape all these things that shall come to pass, and to stand before the Son of man. (Lk 21.34–36)

The book of the Acts of the Apostles begins with an account of how the disciples, filled with eschatological premonitions, asked Christ: "Lord, will you at this time restore again the kingdom to Israel?" Christ repeated in his reply that which he said to the disciples not long before his death on the cross: "It is not for you to know the times or the seasons that the Father has put in his own power." After this, the Lord was lifted up into the air before his disciples' eyes, before whom two angels appeared at that time and said: "This same Jesus, who is taken up from you into heaven, shall so come in like manner as you have seen him go into heaven" (Acts 1.6–11).

The expectation of the Second Coming of Christ began with the event described in Acts, and it has lasted almost two thousand years already. In the early Christian Church, it was thought that Christ's Coming would occur fairly soon—possibly even during the life of the apostles. Such a notion was based in part on a literal interpretation of Christ's words: "This generation will not pass until all these things be fulfilled" (Mt 24.34). It is said in the Catholic Epistles of the apostles: "The coming of the Lord draws nigh" (Jas 5.8); "the end of all things is at hand" (1 Pet 4.7). The Apostle Paul indeed suggested that Christ's Coming would occur during his life: "We shall not all sleep, but we shall all be changed" (1 Cor 15.51); "for yet a little while, and he that shall come will come, and will not tarry" (Heb 10.37). Paul writes in the First Epistle to the Thessalonians: "We who are alive and remain until the coming of the Lord, will by no means precede those who are asleep. . . . The dead in Christ will rise first. Then we who are alive and remain, shall be caught up together with them in the clouds to meet the Lord in the air" (1 Thess 4.15–17).

However, with the passing of time the Christian community came to the realization that the Lord's Second Coming might occur in some more distant future. In the Second Epistle to the Thessalonians, the Apostle Paul even dissociates himself from his first epistle in some places:

> Now we beseech you, brethren, concerning the coming of our Lord Jesus Christ, and our gathering together unto him, that you be not quickly shaken in mind, or be troubled, either by spirit, or by word, or by letter as if from us, that says that the day of Christ is at hand. Let no man deceive you by any means, for that day shall not come, unless there come first a falling away, and that man of sin be revealed, the son of perdition, who opposes and exalts himself above all that is called God, or that is worshipped; so that he as God sits in the temple of God, showing himself that he is God. Do you not remember that, when I was with you, I told you these things? . . . For the mystery of iniquity is already working; only he who now holds it back will continue to hold it back, until he is taken out of the way. And then that wicked one shall be revealed, whom the Lord shall consume with the spirit of his mouth, and shall destroy with the brightness of his coming, whose coming is after the working of Satan with all power and signs and lying wonders. (2 Thess 2.1–9)

The Apostle Peter, in his Second Catholic Epistle, directly answers the question: "Where is the promise of his coming?" (2 Pet 3.4). In the apostle's words:

> The Lord is not slack about his promise, as some men count slackness, but is longsuffering to us, not willing that any should perish, but that should come to repentance. . . . Wherefore, beloved, seeing that you look for these things, be diligent, thay you may be found by him at peace, without spot, and blameless. And count the longsuffering of our Lord as salvation, even as our beloved brother Paul also, according to the wisdom given to him, has written to you, as also in all his epistles, speaking in them of these things. In them there are some things hard to be understood, which those who are unlearned and unstable wrest to their own destruction, as they do also the other scriptures. (2 Pet 3.9, 14–16)

Peter's reference to the epistles of the Apostle Paul in connection to the theme of the Second Coming leaves no doubt as to the fact that he is dealing with the two epistles of the Apostle Paul to the Thessalonians, and referring precisely to those parts of the epistles that speak of the imminence of the Lord's Coming. It is clear that the issue of the timing of Christ's Coming became a rather delicate one, and challenged various interpretations and disputes amongst the first Christians. For this reason the apostles again and again reminded the addressees of their epistles that, instead of being dependent on the timing of the Lord's Coming, Christians are called to be ever vigilant, patient, and abstinent:

> Be patient, therefore, brethren, until the coming of the Lord. Behold, the husbandman waits for the precious fruit of the earth, and has long patience for it. . . . You also be patient; strengthen your hearts, for the coming of the Lord draws nigh. (Jas 5.7–8)

> But the day of the Lord will come as a thief in the night. On that day the heavens shall pass away with a great noise, and the elements shall melt with fervent heat, the earth also and the works that are in it shall be burned up. Seeing then that all these things shall be dissolved, what manner of persons ought you to be in all holy conversation and godliness, looking for and hastening to the coming of the day of God, on which the heavens shall be dissolved in fire, and the elements shall melt with fervent heat? (2 Pet 3.10–12)

> But of the times and the seasons, brethren, you have no need that I write to you. For you yourselves know perfectly that the day of the Lord comes as a thief in the night. For when they say, "Peace and safety," then sudden destruction comes upon them, as travail upon a woman with child; and they shall not escape. . . . Therefore let us not sleep, as others do; but let us watch and be sober. (1 Thess 5.1–3, 6)

The book of the Apocalypse, or the Revelation of John the Theologian, is a symbolic description of the Second Coming of Christ and of the events immediately preceding and following it. A leitmotif of Revelation is the fight between good and evil, resulting in the final victory of good. This victory, according to Revelation, is completed in two stages. First there appears on a white horse the "Faithful and True [one], and in righteousness he judges and

makes war. . . . His name is called The Word of God" (Rev 19.11–13). He wins
the battle with the serpent and the false prophets (Rev 19.19–21), after which
an angel binds "the dragon, that old serpent, who is the Devil, and Satan . . .
[for] a thousand years," and throws him into the pit (Rev 20.2–3). All the
righteous who have not bowed down to the beast are resurrected and rule
"with Christ a thousand years. . . . This is the first resurrection" (Rev 20.4–5).
At the conclusion of the thousand years, Satan is freed from his prison and
sets out to deceive the peoples, but fire from heaven burns those seduced by
him, and the devil himself is cast "into the lake of fire and brimstone, where
the beast and the false prophet are, and they shall be tormented day and night
for ever and ever" (Rev 20.7–10). Further on it describes the judgment of the
dead, at which "the sea gave up the dead that were in it; and Death and Hades
delivered up the dead that were in them, and they were judged, every one
according to his works. And Death and Hades were cast into the lake of fire.
This is the second death" (Rev 20.11–14). The book ends with a description of
the new Jerusalem, the heavenly city, in which the Lamb rules and where the
righteous enjoy eternal blessings.

There was never one understanding of the Apocalypse or one generally
accepted interpretation of it in Christian tradition. Perhaps it is due to the
difficulty of interpreting the prophecies in Revelation that this book, in contrast to all the other New Testament books, was never read in Orthodox liturgical services. A literal interpretation of some of the prophecies of Revelation
frequently resulted in the false understanding of the book's meaning. In the
second century, some church authors made a claim based on Revelation 20.4
that there would be a thousand-year reign on earth of the righteous after the
Second Coming of Christ and universal resurrection.[4] A similar opinion, a
result of the so-called chiliasm, divided Irenaeus of Lyons, Justin Martyr, and
Hippolytus of Rome, from the Latin writers—Tertullian. Towards the fourth
century, chiliasm was opposed in the East and in the West, although it reap-
peared in the Middle Ages in the preaching of Joachim of Fiore (1202), and
after that in the Anabaptists during the period of the Reformation.

The theme of the Second Coming of the Savior in Eastern Christian
patristic literature is covered, as a rule, by two different perspectives. On the
one hand, that spirit of joyful expectation of Christ's Coming was never fully
lost, so expressed in the Apostles Peter's words about Christians who are

[4]Cf. especially Justin Martyr *Dialogue with Trypho* 81.

anticipating and waiting for "the coming of the day of God" (2 Pet 3.12), in the outcry of "maranatha" (1 Cor 16.22), and "Amen. Come, Lord Jesus" (Rev 22.20), which reflect an early Christian liturgical practice.

On the other hand, church writers placed careful attention on those frightening and disturbing events that, according to the New Testament, ought to presage the Second Coming of Christ. The theme of the antichrist received development in the East especially. In the First Epistle of John, the term "antichrist" is used both in the singular and the plural, indicating by it both the "lawless one" spoken of by the Apostle Paul (2 Thess 2.8) as well as the enemies and false teachers of Christianity in general (1 Jn 2.18, 2.22, 4.3). In the patristic tradition, the term "antichrist" is connected only to that chief enemy of Christ and the Church, "who is bound to come at the end of the world,"[5] in order to deceive the whole universe and to turn people away from the true faith.

The main distinguishing feature of the antichrist, according to church Tradition, will be apostasy, antagonism toward God, a desire to pose as God. In the words of the Apostle Paul, the antichrist is he who "opposes and exalts himself above all that is called God, or that is worshipped; so that he sits as God in the temple of God, himself that he is God" (2 Thess 2.3–4). Interpreting these words of the apostle, Irenaeus of Lyons writes of the antichrist:

He, being an apostate and a robber, is anxious to be adored as God; and that, although a mere slave, he wishes himself to be proclaimed as a king. For he being endued with all the power of the devil, shall come, not as a righteous king, nor as a legitimate king, in subjection to God, but an impious, unjust, and lawless one; as an apostate, iniquitous and murderous; as a robber, concentrating in himself [all] satanic apostasy, and setting aside idols to persuade [men] that he himself is God, raising up himself as the only idol, having in himself the multifarious errors of the other idols. This he does, in order that they who do [now] worship the devil by means of many abominations, may serve himself by this one idol.[6]

The treatise that became the classic exposition on the theme of the antichrist is *On Christ and the Antichrist*, attributed to the name of Hippolytus of Rome and proving a huge influence on the development of Christian

[5]John of Damascus *An Exact Exposition . . .* 4.26.
[6]*Against Heresies* 5.25.1.

The holy martyr Hippolytus of Rome. Staro Nagoricane. Macedonia. 14th c.

eschatology in both East and West. In this treatise, the antichrist is presented as a political leader who gathers together the scattered Jewish tribes and rebuilds the razed temple in Jerusalem. By this all his life and actions will seem to replicate the life and actions of Christ, only from the opposite spectrum:

Now, as our Lord Jesus Christ, who is also God, was prophesied of under the figure of a lion, on account of his royalty and glory, in the same way have the Scriptures also aforetime spoken of Antichrist as a lion, on account of his tyranny and violence. For the deceiver seeks to liken himself in all things to the Son of God. Christ is a lion, so Antichrist is also a lion; Christ is a king, so Antichrist is also a king. The Savior was manifested as a lamb; so he too, in like manner, will appear as a lamb, though within he is a wolf. The Savior came into the world in the circumcision, and he will come in the same manner. The Lord sent apostles among all the nations, and he in like manner will send false apostles. The Savior gathered together the sheep that were scattered abroad, and he in like manner will bring together a people that is scattered abroad. The Lord gave a seal to those who believed on him, and he will give one in like manner. The Savior appeared in the form of a man, and he too will come in the form of a man. The Savior raised up and showed his holy flesh like a temple, and he will raise a temple of stone in Jerusalem.[7]

A significant portion of *On Christ and the Antichrist* is dedicated to the interpretation of the statue described in the book of Daniel with a head of gold, a chest and arms of silver, thighs of bronze, legs of iron, and feet partly of iron and partly of clay (Dan 2.32–32). According to Hippolytus of Rome, the different parts of the statue's body symbolize powerful ancient empires: the gold is the Babylonian empire, the silver represents the Persians and the Medes, the bronze is the Greeks, the iron is Rome, and that which is partly of iron and partly of clay represents those kingdoms that will arise in the future. The antichrist will appear amongst these kingdoms.[8]

[7]Hippolytus of Rome *On Christ and the Antichrist* 6.
[8]Ibid. 28.

The notion of the antichrist as a political leader is widely extended throughout patristics. Some authors tie in the coming of the antichrist with the fall of the "restraining one" about whom the Apostle spoke (2 Thess 2.7): the Roman empire is understood to be this "restraining one." In the words of John Chrysostom, "when the Roman rule ceases to be, then he [the antichrist] will come . . . because until that time, while people still fear this rule, no one would soon as submit themself [to the antichrist]; but after it is destroyed anarchy will be established and he will strive to steal all power, both human and divine."[9]

According to the Eastern fathers of the Church, the antichrist will combine spirituality with political power. In the words of John of Damascus, at the start of his rule the antichrist will put on a guise of holiness, although subsequently after gaining the victory, he will begin to persecute the Church and manifest all his evil. "He will come with signs and lying wonders, fictitious and not real, and he will deceive and lead away from the living God those whose mind rests on an unsound and unstable foundation, so that even the elect shall, if it be possible, be made to stumble."[10]

The Fathers of the Church understood the words of the Apostle Paul that the antichrist "sits as God in the temple of God, showing himself that he is God" (2 Thess 2.4) not to refer to a Christian temple, but to a Jewish one, that is the destroyed temple of Jerusalem. In the words of Cyril of Jerusalem, "for if he [the antichrist] comes to the Jews as Christ, and desires to be worshipped by the Jews, he will make great account of the Temple, that he may more completely beguile them; making it supposed that he is the man of the race of David, who shall build up the Temple which was erected by Solomon."[11]

The antichrist's identification with the Jewish religion and national leaders enters into early Christian anti-Semitic polemics, as already reflected in Hippolytus of Rome. The latter claims that the antichrist "will raise a Jewish kingdom."[12] Moreover, in Cyril of Jerusalem's opinion, the antichrist will be a Roman emperor: he "shall seize for himself the power of the Roman empire."[13] Andrew of Caesarea echoes Cyril, maintaining that the antichrist

---

[9] *Homily on the Second Epistle to the Thessalonians* 4.
[10] *An Exact Exposition . . .* 4.26.
[11] *Catechetical Lecture* 15.15.
[12] *On Christ and the Antichrist* 25.
[13] Cf. *Catechetical Lecture* 15.11.

will come "as the Roman emperor": under his unifying rule, the Roman empire, perishing from division, will become strong once again.[14]

Thus, if John Chrysostom saw the "restraining one" as Roman rule and considered that the fall of the Roman empire would mark the beginning of the antichrist's kingdom, then Cyril of Jerusalem and Andrew of Caesarea, on the contrary, conceived of the antichrist as the Roman emperor. This discord is certainly due to the subjective approach of the Fathers of the Church on the theme of the antichrist, as well as the different political and cultural contexts within which this or that author lived. To make absolute a proposed hypothesis of the Fathers of the Church, or to elevate one to the level of church dogma, is hardly possible. The dogmatic tradition of the Church contains within itself the concept of the antichrist as a political and religious leader who, in the time prior to the Second Coming of Christ, will deceive the whole world. However much one tries to define where and when the antichrist will appear, on which governments or ethnic structures he will lean, the data coming from this attempt has always been and always will be particular to that concrete historical period of the one making the attempt. Such attempts are made anew in every era.

There is also no universally-accepted interpretation of the "number of the beast" in Orthodox tradition, or the "number of the name" of the antichrist, which according to Revelation, is six hundred sixty-six (Rev 13.17–18, 15.2). Irenaeus of Lyons considers that the number is formed from the age of Noah at the start of the flood (600 years) and the size of the idol built by Nebuchadnezzar (sixty cubits tall, and six cubits wide),[15] although the arbitrary character of this interpretation is quite obvious. In the words of Hippolytus of Rome, with respect to the name of the antichrist, "it is not in our power to explain it exactly." Hipploytus offers some possible interpretations of this name, although it is stipulated that "we ought neither to give it out as if this were certainly his name, nor again ignore the fact that he may not be otherwise designated."[16] Andrew of Caesarea, with respect to the interpretations of the antichrist's name and the number of the name, notes: "If it were necessary to know his name, then, as some teachers say, a prophet would have revealed it, but the grace of God was not pleased that his pernicious name

[14]Cf. Andrew of Caesarea *Interpretation on Revelation* 36.
[15]Cf. *Against Heresies* 5.29.2.
[16]*On Christ and the Antichrist* 50.

should be written in a divine book. If one researches the words, then, according to Hippolytus and others, one can find a multitude of names, both proper and common nouns, which correspond to this number."[17]

In any case, any magical attitude toward numbers as such has always been foreign to Orthodox tradition, including the number six hundred sixty-six, which in and of itself has no more meaning than any other number. There is no notion in the patristic tradition that this number poses any kind of threat or spiritual danger. It appears clear that the number six hundred sixty-six in Revelation is some kind of secret symbol, the meaning of which is not revealed by the book's author; this symbol has not been convincingly interpreted in any patristic era.

Regarding the "mark" of the antichrist repeatedly referred to in Revelation (Rev 13.17–18, 14.9–11, 15.2, 16.2, 19.20), one can only say that, according to the book itself, as well as in the majority of patristic commentaries, it will be the symbol of those who voluntarily submit themselves to the antichrist. In other words, the mark, or seal, will not be placed automatically, and no one will be found to be with the antichrist in *involuntary* submission or service. Every person will have the possibility of making a conscious choice in favor of Christ or the antichrist, and true Christians will reject the temptation, even if it means the end of their lives:

> The forerunner and shield-bearer of the antichrist with the help of demons, having made an effigy of the beast, will present him falsely, saying he will order the forgiveness of all who did not submit themselves to him, and will try to place on everyone's right hand the disastrous mark of the apostate and seducer's name, in order to make those lured in to be bold in seduction and darkness. But those whose faces are marked by divine light will not accept him. And he will spread the mark of the beast everywhere, both in buying and in selling, so that those who do not accept it die an imposed death by want of those things necessary for life.[18]

The prophecies of the Apocalypse that, according to the teaching of the Church, will fully come to pass only at the end of time, began to come to pass already in the early Christian period and continued to occur over the course of the later centuries. The battle between Christ and antichrist,

[17] *Interpretation on Revelation* 38.
[18] Ibid. 37.

"O Only-Begotten Son."
Russian icon. 17th c.

between God and the beast, which was described in Revelation, has a character that is outside of time. The eschatological battle has already commenced, and it continues and will continue until the end of human history. Some Christians in this battle are on Christ's side, and others on the side of the antichrist, taking on his "mark," that is putting themselves on the path to compromise and apostasy. This deals with a moral choice that must be made by every person: in the end, the eternal fate of each person depends on this choice. Christians have made this choice during times of persecution, whether it be in the first or the twentieth century: some died for Christ and received the crown of martyrdom, while others accepted the mark of the beast and became apostates.

The apostle writes that "the mystery of iniquity is already at work" (2 Thess 2.7), meaning the exact same thing as the Apostle John the Theologian when he speaks of the appearance of many antichrists (1 Jn 2.18). The antichrist's war against Christ already began at the moment of Christ's First Coming, but the conclusive battle, as colorfully described in Revelation, will be at his Second Coming. Occurring then in the period between the two Comings is the division of humanity by a spiritual and moral principle, about which the author of Revelation speaks: "He that is unjust, let him be unjust still; and he that is filthy, let him be filthy still; and he that is righteous, let him be righteous still; and he that is holy, let him be holy still. And behold, I come quickly, and my reward is with me, to give every man according as his work shall be" (Rev 22.11–12).

In the perception of modern man, the word "apocalypse" (literally meaning "revelation") is falsely associated with the terrors and catastrophes that must precede the end of the world. Such a perception is not foreign to some Orthodox Christians, in whose minds the notion of "the end of the world" summons thoughts of terror, and the image of the antichrist almost displaces the image of Christ as the Conqueror of death and hell, the Savior and Redeemer of the human race. Resulting from this, attempts to guess the date of the coming of the antichrist, a multitude of predictions of the nearness of the end of the world, and panic with respect to the number six hundred and sixty-six, all create a supercharged atmosphere of fear and suspicion.

However, overlooked in all of this is the fact that the "protagonist" of the Second Coming is actually Christ, and not the antichrist, and that the Second Coming itself will not be a moment of defeat, but a great moment for the glory of God, the victory of good over evil, of life over death, and of Christ over the antichrist. It is no accident that the theme of victory is one of the leitmotifs of Revelation. All of those on the side of good in the global battle between good and evil will participate in this victory. According to Revelation, they will sit on the throne together with the Son of God and will themselves become sons of God; they will be clothed in white raiment, and their names will be written in the book of life:

To him that overcomes I will give to eat of the tree of life that is in the paradise of God. (Rev 2.7)

He that overcomes shall not be hurt by the second death (Rev 2.11).

To him that overcomes I will give to eat of the hidden manna, and I will give him a white stone, and on the stone a new name written that no one knows save him who receives it. (Rev 2.17)

He that overcomes shall be clothed in white raiment; and I will not blot his name out of the book of life, but I will confess his name before my Father, and before his angels. (Rev 3.5)

Him that overcomes I will make a pillar in the temple of my God, and he shall go out [of it] no more. And I will write upon him the name of my God, and the name of the city of my God, which is New Jerusalem, which comes down out of heaven from my God; and I will write upon him my new name. (Rev 3.12)

To him that overcomes I will grant to sit with me on my throne, even as I also overcame and have sat down with my Father on his throne. (Rev 3.21)

He who overcomes shall inherit all things; and I will be his God, and he shall be my son. (Rev 21.7).

Christ's Second Coming will be marked by the end of earthly history, but this marking is not a tragic and painful break in humanity's fate, but that glorious purpose toward which history, by Divine Providence, is steadfastly moving. Christian historical wisdom suggests precisely such a view of the "end of the world," a view that does not correspond to "apocalyptic" terrors and dangers, but a view permeated with joy and bright hope.

29

The Universal Resurrection

T HE DOGMA OF THE UNIVERSAL RESURRECTION is one of those Christian dogmata that is quite difficult for rational comprehension. All-powerful death, its implacability and finality, is presented as such an obvious fact that the teaching of the resurrection can seem to contradict reality itself. The decomposition and dissolving of the body after death does not seem to leave any kind of hope for its subsequent rising up. The teaching of the resurrection of the body contradicts the majority of philosophical theories that have existed since before Christianity, especially Greek philosophy, which considered freedom from the body, the transition to a purely spiritual, noetic existence, to be the greatest blessing.

The apostolic preaching had already exposed the radical divergence between ancient thought and the newborn Christian thought on exactly this point. The book of Acts contains a narrative of the Apostle Paul's preaching in the Areopagus—a sermon that began most successfully, accompanied by citations from ancient poets and which could have been quite intriguing for the Athenian senators, had Paul not started talking about the resurrection. As it is noted in Acts, having heard reference to the resurrection of the dead, some began to jeer, and others said: "We will hear you again about this." Paul then left the meeting (Acts 17.32–33). The Athenians called Paul a "babbler" for preaching about "Jesus and the resurrection" (Acts 17.18).

Nevertheless, the teaching of the universal resurrection is at the core of Christian eschatology. Without this teaching, Christianity loses its meaning, just as it does without faith in Christ's resurrection and, in the Apostle Paul's words, the Christian proclamation is in vain (1 Cor 15.12–14).

The Christian teaching of the resurrection of the dead is based above all on the fact of Christ's resurrection, on Christ's words on the resurrection, and on the apostolic preaching. However, there existed even in Old Testament times numerous prophecies on the resurrection of the dead. It is said in the

The descent into Hades.
School of Andrei Rublev. 15th c.

book of the Prophet Isaiah: "Your dead shall live, their dead bodies shall rise. Leap up and be jubilant, you who lie prostrate in the dust! For your dew is as the dew of herbs, and the earth will cast out the dead" (Isa 26.19). It is characteristic that the focus, just as in Christian tradition, is on the bodily resurrection specifically; moreover this resurrection is considered in a moral aspect, as a recompense for deeds done in life: "For behold, the Lord comes out from his dwelling place to punish the inhabitants of the earth for their iniquity; the earth also shall disclose its blood, and shall no more cover its slain" (Isa 26.21).

The theme of a recompense or retribution dominates the descriptions of the resurrection of the dead of the Prophet Daniel: "Many of those who sleep in the dust of the earth shall awake, some to everlasting life, and some to reproach and everlasting shame" (Dan 12.2). According to Daniel, the resurrection of the dead will occur "at the end of a time, two times, and half a time" (Dan 12.7). Preceding this event will "be a time of tribulation, such tribulation as has not been from the time that there was a nation" (Dan 12.1). At the universal resurrection, "the wise shall shine as the brightness of the firmament" (Dan 12.3), "Many must be tested, and whitened, and tried with fire . . . but the transgressors shall transgress: and none of the transgressors shall understand; but the wise shall understand" (Dan 12.10).

The most striking prophecy on the resurrection of the dead in the Old Testament is in the book of Ezekiel. This prophecy is read in the Orthodox Church at the service of Holy Saturday:

> The hand of the Lord came upon me, and the Lord brought me forth by the Spirit, and set me in the midst of the plain, and it was full of bones. And he led me round about them in a circle, and behold there were very many on the face of the plain, and they were very dry. And he said to me, "Son of man, will these bones live?" and I said, "O Lord God, you know this." And he said to me, "Prophesy upon these bones, and you shall say to them, 'You dry bones, hear the word of the Lord. Thus says the Lord to these bones: Behold, I will bring upon you the breath of life, and will

lay sinews upon you, and will bring up flesh upon you, and will spread skin upon you, and will put my Spirit into you, and you shall live; and you shall know that I am the Lord.'" So I prophesied as the Lord commanded me. And it came to pass while I was prophesying, that, behold, there was a shaking, and the bones approached each one to its joint. And I looked, and behold, sinews and flesh grew upon them, and skin covered them . . . and the breath entered into them, and they lived and stood on their feet, a very great congregation. And [the Lord] said to me, "Son of man, these bones are the whole house of Israel!" (Ezek 37.1–8, 10–11)

In this prophecy, as in the book of Daniel, the resurrection of the dead is presented as the resurrection of the people of Israel. This laid the ground for some interpreters to perceive the prophecy as an allegorical description of the rise to political power of the people of Israel. However, in Christian tradition the prophecy of Ezekiel was uniformly perceived as relating to the universal resurrection, which will come to pass after the Second Coming of Christ. If Ezekiel is speaking only of the resurrection of the house of Israel, then this can only be explained in the sense that the whole Bible is addressed to the people of Israel and tells the story and destiny of this people, somehow leaving out the fate of other peoples. However, the Bible is thought of in Christian tradition as addressing the fate of all humanity, and the prophecies concerning the people of Israel give way to a universal meaning.

The description contained in Second Maccabees of the martyrdom of the seven brothers and their mother, who refused to obey the decree of the gentile king and to break the laws of their fathers, bears witness to the fact that belief in the resurrection of the dead and in eternal life was widely extended throughout the tribes of Israel. One of the brothers, while dying, says to the king: "You, wretch, you dismiss us from this present life, but the King of the universe will raise us up to eternal life, because we have died for his laws." Another, at their demand, stretches out his hands, saying: "I got these from heaven, and because of his laws I do not begrudge them, and I hope to get them back again." Another one of the brothers says: "As I die by men it is fitting to put [my] hope in God, that he will raise [me] up again." The mother, strengthening her sons, says to them: "I do not know how you came into being in my womb. Neither did I give you breath and life, nor did I set in order the substance of each. So, the Creator of the world, who shaped the nature of man and arranged the beginning of all, in his mercy will give you again breath and life, just as you are not sparing yourselves now for the sake of his laws." All seven, after suffering terrible agony, were put to death. And after her sons, the mother also died. (2 Mac 7.1–41)

The resurrection of the dead is referred to several times in the Gospels. In one of the conversations with the Jews, recounted in the Gospel of John, Christ speaks of his Second Coming, of the universal resurrection, and of the Last Judgment:

> Amen, amen, I say to you: The hour is coming, and now is, when the dead shall hear the voice of the Son of God, and those who hear shall live. For as the Father has life in himself, so he has given to the Son to have life in himself, and has given him authority to execute judgment also, because he is Son of man. Do not marvel at this: for the hour is coming, in which all who are in the graves shall hear his voice, and shall come forth: Those who have done good, to the resurrection of life, and those who have done evil, to the resurrection of judgment. (Jn 5.25–29)

During the time of Jesus Christ, belief in the resurrection of the dead was widespread among the Hebrew people. The words of Martha, the sister of Lazarus who died, testify to this in particular: "I know that he shall rise again in the resurrection on the last day" (Jn 11.24). Concerning the people of Israel, then, two diametrically opposed views on the resurrection of the dead existed in their midst: the Pharisees acknowledged it, but the Sadducees did not—a small sect that arose during the time of the Hasmoneans (second century BCE), which included leading members of the aristocracy and the Levitical priesthood. The Gospel of Matthew contains a narrative in which the Sadducees, having come to Jesus, asked whose wife would the woman, who was married to seven brothers, be. Christ answered this: "You err, because you do not know the scriptures, nor the power of God. For in the resurrection they neither marry nor are given in marriage, but are as angels of God in heaven. But as touching the resurrection of the dead, have you not read what was spoken to you by God, 'I am the God of Abraham, and the God of Isaac, and the God of Jacob'? God is not the God of the dead, but of the living" (Mt 22.29–32).

The book of Acts recalls that the Sadducees were opposed to the apostolic preaching, "being grieved that they taught the people and preached through

Jesus the resurrection of the dead" (Acts 4.2). When the Apostle Paul was summoned to the Sanhedrin he, upon finding out that some were Pharisees and others Sadducees, said: "Men and brethren, I am a Pharisee, the son of a Pharisee. Of the hope of the resurrection of the dead I am called in question." These words of the apostle caused dissension "between the Pharisees and the Sadducees"; since the dissension became violent, the tribune ordered that Paul be removed from before the Sanhedrin. (Acts 23.6–10)

The Apostle Paul was the first Christian theologian who imparted a systematic aspect to the teaching of the resurrection of the dead: all ensuing development of the Christian teaching on the resurrection rests on those foundations that Paul laid. According to the apostle's teaching, the resurrection of the dead will occur at the Second Coming of Christ:

> For if we believe that Jesus died and rose again, even so those who sleep in Jesus God will bring with him. . . . For the Lord himself shall descend from heaven with a shout, with the voice of the archangel, and with the trumpet of God: and the dead in Christ shall rise first. Then we who are alive and remain shall be caught up together with them in the clouds, to meet the Lord in the air. And so we shall ever be with the Lord. (1 Thess 4.14–17)

The teaching on the resurrection of the dead is covered most fully by the apostle in the First Epistle to the Corinthians. Here, above all, he connects the resurrection of the dead to Christ's resurrection, placing one event in direct dependence on the other:

> Now if Christ is preached, that he rose from the dead, how do some among you say that there is no resurrection of the dead? But if there is no resurrection of the dead, then Christ has not been raised. And if Christ has not been raised, then our preaching is in vain, and your faith is also vain. Indeed, we are found false witnesses of God, because we have testified of God that he raised up Christ, whom he has not raised up, if the dead are not raised. For if the dead are not raised, then Christ has not been raised. And if Christ has not been raised, your faith is vain; you are still in your sins. Then those also who have fallen asleep in Christ have perished. If in this life only we have hope in Christ, we are of all men most miserable. (1 Cor 15.12–19)

The resurrection of all mankind then clearly follows the resurrection of Christ, as the death of all people follows the death of Adam. What was broken by Adam's Fall will be restored at the Second Coming:

The descent into Hades.
Portrait miniature. 12th c.

But now Christ has been raised from the dead, and has become the first fruits of those who have fallen asleep. For since by man came death, by man came also the resurrection of the dead. For as in Adam all die, even so in Christ shall all be made alive. But every man in his own order: Christ the first fruits, and afterward those who are Christ's, at his coming. . . . The first man is of the earth, earthy: the second man is the Lord from heaven. As is the earthy, such are those also that are earthy; and as is the heavenly, such are they also that are heavenly. And as we have borne the image of the earthy, we shall also be the image of the heavenly. (1 Cor 15.20–23, 47–49).

The Apostle Paul refers to Christian baptismal practice as well as to the personal experience of confession, which from his point of view would be senseless if there were no resurrection of the dead, as evidence for correct belief in the resurrection of the dead:

Else what shall they do which are baptized for the dead, if the dead are not raised at all? Why are they then baptized for the dead? And why do we stand in jeopardy every hour? I protest by your rejoicing which I have in Christ Jesus our Lord, I die daily. If after the manner of men I have fought with beasts at Ephesus, what advantage is it to me, if the dead are not raised? "Let us eat and drink, for tomorrow we die." (1 Cor 15.29–32)

The phrase "baptism on behalf of the dead" causes some commentators to suppose that a practice existed in the ancient Church of baptizing dead people, for whom some like person would stand in at the sacrament of baptism. Tertullian refers to a "vicarious baptism" in connection to this, which "would be beneficial to the flesh of another in anticipation of the resurrection,"[1] but he does not specify what this vicarious baptism consists of. John Chrysostom refers to the existence of a rite for the "baptism of the dead" in

---

[1] *On the Resurrection of the Flesh* 48.

the Gnostic sect of Marcion: when a catechumen dies in this sect, supposedly a living man lies beneath his or her bed so as to answer for the dead person at the baptism taking place over them.[2] Chrysostom considers that such a rite would "excite much laughter." In Chrysostom's view, the words of the Apostle Paul on the resurrection of the dead serve for understanding the baptismal creed in context: "I believe in the resurrection of the dead." Baptism for the dead is no more than the confession of faith in a bodily resurrection, for "if there be no resurrection, why art thou then baptized for the dead?" i.e., the dead bodies. For in fact with a view to this art thou baptized, the resurrection of thy dead body, believing that it no longer remains dead."[3]

A different interpretation is possible: the baptism of the dead is the baptism performed with the intent of being united with relatives who died in the bosom of the Church, or a baptism in memory of this or that revered Christian.

The Apostle Paul parses out in detail the question of the nature of the body into which the dead will be resurrected. This body, according to the apostle's teaching, will be spiritual, incorruptible, and immortal. Responding to the question, "How are the dead raised up? And with what kind of body do they come?" the apostle turns to the image of a seed, which "does not come to life, unless it dies." God gives this seed such a body as it pleases; he gives a body to every seed. "So also is the resurrection of the dead. It is sown in corruption; it is raised in incorruption. It is sown in dishonor; it is raised in glory. It is sown in weakness; it is raised in power. It is sown a natural body; it is raised a spiritual body." As the apostles emphasizes, "this corruptible [body] must put on incorruption, and this mortal [body] must put on immortality." (1 Cor 15.35–53)

In the Epistle to the Philippians, the Apostle Paul says that at the Second Coming Christ "will change our vile body, that it may be fashioned like unto his glorious body" (Phil 3.21). In other words, the bodies of resurrected people will be similar to the glorified body of Christ, that is, like his body after his resurrection from the dead. This body, according to the gospel testimonies, had only some approximation to the earthly body of Christ, since the Resurrected Christ was recognized not so much by his outward appearance as much as by his voice or gestures. Mary Magdalene, upon seeing the

---

[2]Cf. *Homily on First Corinthians* 40.1. In modern times, some Mormon communities revived the heretical practice of baptizing dead people.
[3]Ibid. 40.2.

resurrected Christ, took him to be the gardener and recognized him only after he addressed her by name (Jn 20.11–16). The disciples who met Christ on the road to Emmaus did not recognize either his outward appearance or his voice–they recognized him when he broke bread before their eyes (Lk 24.13–35). The resurrected Jesus passed through locked doors; at the same time the marks of the wounds left by the nails and the spear were preserved on his body (Jn 20.25–27). As John Chrysostom highlights, the appearances of Jesus to the disciples over the course of the forty days "had the purpose of informing and showing us how amazing our bodies will be after the resurrection. The resurrected body will need neither blood nor clothing. As the most pure body of the Lord ascended at the time of the divine ascension, so too we, who will be of one essence with him, will be taken up into the clouds."[4]

The theme of the resurrection of the dead continued to play a role in the preaching of Christian authors and apologists in the post-apostolic age. At the foundation of this preaching lies the teaching formulated by the Apostle Paul, although this teaching underwent substantial development and had many details to be worked out in the works of church writers of the second through fourth centuries.

Clement of Rome devotes great attention to the theme of the resurrection in his First Epistle to the Corinthians. Clement observes the evidence of the universal resurrection in the life of nature:

> Let us consider, beloved, how the Lord continually proves to us that there shall be a future resurrection, of which he has rendered the Lord Jesus Christ the first-fruits by raising him from the dead. Let us contemplate, beloved, the resurrection which is at all times taking place. Day and night declare to us a resurrection. The night sinks to sleep, and the day arises; the day [again] departs, and the night comes on. Let us behold the fruits [of the earth], how the sowing of grain takes place. The sower goes forth, and casts it into the ground; and the seed being thus scattered, though dry and naked when it fell upon the earth, is gradually dissolved. Then out of its dissolution the mighty power of the providence of the Lord raises it up again, and from one seed many arise and bring forth fruit. (1 Cor 15.35–38)[5]

---

[4] *On the Enjoyment of Future Blessings.*
[5] *First Epistle to the Corinthians* 24.

Clement borrows the tale of the phoenix bird from Herodotus as a witness of the universal resurrection.[6] Consequently, Tertullian[7] also uses this tale, as do many later Christian authors, for whom the phoenix becomes the symbol of the resurrection to newness of life.

The Christian apologist of the second century, Justin Martyr, speaking on the resurrection of the dead, insists that souls will be united with those very bodies that they possessed in life.[8] It is precisely in this teaching on the resurrection of the body that Justin sees a genuine newness of life and a distinction of the eschatological teaching of Christ from the teaching of the ancient philosophers:

> Considering, therefore, even such arguments as are suited to this world, and finding that, even according to them, it is not impossible that the flesh be regenerated; and seeing that, besides all these proofs, the Savior in the whole Gospel shows that there is salvation for the flesh, why do we any longer endure those unbelieving and dangerous arguments, and fail to see that we are retrograding when we listen to such an argument as this: that the soul is immortal, but the body mortal, and incapable of being revived? For this we used to hear from Pythagoras and Plato, even before we learned the truth. If then the Savior said this, and proclaimed salvation [only for the soul alone, what new thing] beyond [what we learned from] Pythagoras and Plato and all their band, did he bring us? But now he has come proclaiming the glad tidings of a new and strange hope to men. For indeed it was a strange and new thing for God to promise that he would not keep incorruption in incorruption, but would make corruption incorruption.[9]

Another Christian apologist of the same period, Athenagoras of Athens, while discussing the same theme, places the emphasis on the inseparable link between the soul and body in man. In his opinion, the bliss of the soul separated from the body cannot be the genuine state to which man is appointed, for man consists of both parts. The soul's existence without the body is incomplete and temporary, and it follows from this that "there must by all

---

[6]Ibid. 25.
[7]Cf. *On the Resurrection of the Flesh* 13.
[8]Cf. *First Apology* 9.
[9]*On the Resurrection* 10.

means be a resurrection of the bodies which are dead, or even entirely dissolved, and the same men must be formed anew, since the law of nature ordains the end not absolutely, nor as the end of any men whatsoever, but of the same men who passed through the previous life; but it is impossible for the same men to be reconstituted unless the same bodies are restored to the same souls."[10]

The decomposition of the body after a person's death is not, from Athenagoras' point of view, a hindrance to the restoration of the body. For "it is not possible for God to be ignorant, either of the nature of the bodies that are to be raised, as regards both the members entire and the particles of which they consist."[11] Even if a person's body had been torn by wild beasts, clarifies the apologist, it would not be too difficult for the Creator to extract the body from the beasts and "unite it again with the proper members and parts of members," regardless of whether it had passed through the body of one or many beasts, or even from one to another, or was even destroyed and then decomposed along with those animals that had eaten it.[12]

Naturalism is emphasized in the description of the universal resurrection found in Tertullian's treatise *On the Resurrection of the Flesh*, where the author parses out the Christian teaching on the resurrection in detail, arguing against the classical concepts of man's mortal fate. The treatise begins with the words: "The resurrection of the dead is the Christian's trust. By it we are believers."[13]

In his own clear, rhetorical manner, Tertullian proves the bodily character of the resurrection of the dead. In Tertullian's words, "flesh and blood, therefore, must in every case rise again, equally, in their proper quality,"[14] although this will be a transfigured and altered flesh and blood. The body that will rise "is that which was sown,"[15] that is, sown in the death of a person on earth. Like Clement of Rome, Tertullian sees proof of the resurrection of the dead in the rhythm of nature:

> In a word, I would say, all creation is instinct with renewal. Whatever you may chance upon, has already existed; whatever you have lost, returns

[10] *On the Resurrection of the Dead* 25.
[11] Ibid. 2.
[12] Ibid. 3.
[13] I.
[14] Ibid. 50.
[15] Ibid. 53.

again without fail. All things return to their former state, after having gone out of sight; all things begin after they have ended; they come to an end for the very purpose of coming into existence again. Nothing perishes but with a view to salvation. The whole, therefore, of this revolving order of things bears witness to the resurrection of the dead. . . . And surely, as all things rise again for man, for whose use they have been provided—but not for man except for his flesh also—how happens it that (the flesh) itself can perish utterly, because of which and for the service of which nothing comes to nought?[16]

Answering the question of whether people will be raised up in the form in which they died, that is, for example, blind, lame, or enfeebled, Tertullian proves that if the flesh is to be repaired after its dissolution, much more so will it be restored after some violent injury."[17] Tertullian clarifies that bodily harm is in essence a kind of extenuating circumstance, an accident, but wholeness is the natural characteristic of man. Even if the injury occurs in the maternal womb, the initial whole condition overcomes any injury. From here Tertullian comes to the following conclusion: "As life is bestowed by God, so it is restored by him. As we are when we receive it, so are we when we recover it. To nature, not to injury, are we restored; to our state of birth, not to our condition by accident, do we rise again. If God raises not men entire, he raises not the dead."[18]

Following after the Gospel (Mt 22.30), Tertullian says that resurrected people will be like angels. However, in his opinion, this does not at all mean that they will be devoid of bodies. Having taken on an angelic appearance, people will not be dependent on "the usual wants of the flesh"; their flesh will become spiritual, but the flesh will remain.[19] The flesh of man is the bride of Christ, which will be returned to Christ at the resurrection:

And so the flesh shall rise again, wholly in every man, in its own identity, in its absolute integrity. Wherever it may be, it is in safe keeping in God's presence, through that most faithful "Mediator between God and man, [the man] Jesus Christ" (1 Tim 2.5), who shall reconcile both God

---

[16]Ibid. 12.
[17]Ibid. 57.
[18]Ibid.
[19]Ibid. 62.

to man, and man to God; the spirit to the flesh, and the flesh to the spirit. Both natures has he already united in his own self; he has fitted them together as bride and bridegroom in the reciprocal bond of wedded life. Now, if any should insist on making the soul the bride, then the flesh will follow the soul as her dowry. The soul shall never be an outcast, to be had home by the bridegroom bare and naked. She has her dower, her outfit, her fortune in the flesh, which shall accompany her with the love and fidelity of a foster-sister. But suppose the flesh to be the bride, then in Christ Jesus she has in the contract of his blood received his Spirit as her spouse.[20]

St Methodius of Patara.
Monastery of St Bessarion,
near Meteora. 16 c.

In the third to the fourth centuries, the polemic-by-default on the issue of the nature of resurrected bodies was expanded between Origen and St Methodius of Patara. One finds in Origen's writings the view that the bodies of resurrected people will be non-material, spiritual, and ethereal, similar to the bodies of the angels.[21] According to Origen's teaching, the material bodies of people, in comparison to the new, spiritual bodies in which they will be resurrected, can be likened to a seed in comparison to the stalk that grows from the seed.[22]

St Methodius however, arguing with Origen, rejects the notion that material bodies will be eliminated and that the nature of the resurrected body will be like that of the angels, even if Christ does indeed say that the saints in the resurrection will be "like angels in heaven" (Mk 12.25; Mt 22.30). Christ's words, according to Methodius (in agreement with Tertullian's opinion), need to be remembered not in the sense that the saints will be devoid of bodies in the resurrection, but in the sense that the state of the saints' blessedness will be like that of the angels.[23]

[20]Ibid. 63.

[21]Origen *On First Principles* 3.6; *Against Celsus* 3.41; *Commentary on Matthew* 17.30.

[22]Ibid. 2.10. A more detailed development of Origen's teaching on the nature of the resurrected body can be found in: Makarii (Oksiuk), *The Eschatology of Gregory of Nyssa* (Moscow: 1999), 162–174.

[23]Cf. Methodius of Patara *On the Resurrection* 31.

[24]Ibid. 30.

In Methodius' words, God created man as one essence of soul and body and the final goal of man's existence is not the casting off of the body, but salvation together with the body:

> It is impermissible to assume that God, having made man bad or having made a mistake in his construction, thought to fashion him after an angel, repenting of his creation like the worst artist; or as if he wanted to make an angel from the start, but, not having power for this, created man. That is ridiculous. Why then did he create man, and not an angel, if he wanted man to be an angel and not man? Could it be because he could not? That is blasphemy. Or did he set aside the better things for the future and make something inferior? This too is ridiculous. He does not err in the creation of beauty, he does not postpone it, he does not feel powerless, but, as he wants and when he wants, he has the ability to create, just as he has the strength. For this reason, desiring man to be, he created man in the beginning. For if and when he so desires something, then he desires beauty, and man is beautiful, but man is also an existing thing composed of soul and body; thus, consequently, man will exist not without a body, but with a body. . . . "For God created us," says the Wisdom of Solomon, "for incorruption, and made us in the image of his own eternity" (Wis 2.23). Therefore, the body is not destroyed because man consists of soul and body.[24]

In the fourth century, St Gregory of Nyssa placed great attention on the theme of the resurrection of the dead. In the treatise *On the Making of Man* he dismantles those arguments against the resurrection of the body that Tertullian developed. In his words, "they point to the disappearance of the dead of old time, and to the remains of those who have been reduced to ashes by fire; and further, besides these, they bring forward in idea the carnivorous beasts, and the fish that receives in its own body the flesh of the shipwrecked sailor, while this again in turn becomes food for men, and passes by digestion into the bulk of him who eats it." Gregory says in response to this that even if the body of a man is devoured by a bird of prey or by wild beasts and is mixed with their flesh, even if it passes through the teeth of fish and is burned by fire and turned to vapor and dust, nonetheless the material substance of the body is preserved. Everything in the material world, broken down into its composite parts, returns to its own nature, "and not only does

[25]Gregory of Nyssa *On the Making of Man* 26.

earth, according to the divine word, return to earth, but air and moisture also revert to the kindred element, and there takes place a return of each of our components to that nature to which it is allied." It is not difficult then for God to gather precisely together those parts that are necessary for the renewal of the human body.[25]

What type of mechanism unites the soul with the body at the universal resurrection, and how will the souls recognize the bodies that belong to them? In answering this question, Gregory advances the view of the reciprocal natural attraction of the soul and body, an attraction that does not cease even after death:

> For as the soul is disposed to cling to and long for the body that has been wedded to it, there also attaches to it in secret a certain close relationship and power of recognition, in virtue of their commixture, as though some marks had been imprinted by nature, by the aid of which the community remains unconfused, separated by the distinctive signs. Now as the soul attracts again to itself that which is its own and properly belongs to it, what labor, I pray you, that is involved for the divine power, could be a hindrance to concourse of kindred things when they are urged to their own place by the unspeakable attraction of nature, whatever it may be? For that some signs of our compound nature remain in the soul even after dissolution is shown by the dialogue in Hades, where the bodies had been conveyed to the tomb, but some bodily token still remained in the souls by which both Lazarus was recognized and the rich man was not unknown.[26]

Each body has its own *eidos*/εἶδος, or form, which remains, like a stamp, on the soul even after its separation from the body. At the moment of the universal resurrection the soul identifies this *eidos* and is united with its body. At this point, the broken pieces that made up the material substance of the body are united one with the other, just like globules of spilled mercury. As St Gregory emphasizes, "if only the power were given it of God, the proper parts would spontaneously unite with those belonging to them, without any obstruction on their account arising to him who reforms their nature."[27]

[26]Ibid. 27.
[27]Ibid.
[28]*On the Soul and the Resurrection.*

In the dialogue *On the Soul and the Resurrection*, Gregory of Nyssa says that "we have a body that now consists of, and will again consist of, worldly elements," moreover "that one soul will once again be contained in that one body, composed of those same elements." Gregory places this teaching in opposition to the classical teaching on reincarnation, the transfer from one body to another.[28] At the same time he stresses that the material of the resurrected body will differ from the crude material of the earthly body: "For you will see what covered the bodily, destroyed for now by death, again woven from the same stuff, but not from crude and heavy ingredients, but a thread worked into something lighter and airier. Therefore the best parts of you will remain, but you will be raised again to a better and more perfect beauty."[29]

In Gregory's words, "the resurrection is the renewal of our nature to its original state." Man's original nature was susceptible neither to aging nor to sickness: all of this "was imposed on us together with the appearance of vice." Having been made impassioned, human nature encountered the necessary consequences of a passionate life, but, having been returned to a life without passion, it will not be subject to the consequences of vice. Fleshly copulation, conception, birth, feeding, growing older, old age, sickness, and death—all of this is a result of the Fall. But in the future, life "will follow some other state,"[30] devoid of all the myriad signs of an impassioned existence. St Gregory calls this state "spiritual and passionless."[31]

John Chrysostom has a similar concept of the nature of the resurrected body. In his words, at first people's bodies will disappear, but then they will be renewed and will be much better than those now, "they will transfer into a better state," and moreover "each one will receive its own, and not a foreign, body." The resurrected person will have "a body that will remain, and death and corruption disappear when it is robed in immortality and incorruption."[32] Chrysostom persistently shows that, as Christ rose not in another body, but in the same one, only altered a bit, so will people be raised in their own bodies, though renewed and transfigured.[33]

[29]Ibid.
[30]Ibid.
[31]Ibid.
[32]*Homilies on First Corinthians* 42.2.
[33]Ibid. 41.2.
[34]*On the Resurrection of the Dead* 6.

According to Chrysostom's teaching, a difference exists between the body and corruption: the former will remain, but the latter will be abolished. Truly freed from corruption, the body will be immortal:

> One is the body and the other is death; one is the body and the other is corruption; that which is the body is not corruption; that which is corruption is not the body; the body, true, is corruptible, although the body is not corruption; the body is mortal, but nevertheless it is not death; but the body was an act of divine creation, while corruption and death came from sin. . . . The body is in the middle of corruption and incorruption; it takes corruption from itself and wraps it in incorruption; it overthrows that which it received from sin, and acquires that which the grace of God bestowed upon it. . . . The coming life does not destroy the body, rather it destroys corruption and death. . . . In fact, the body is painful, burdensome, and crude, but not by its own nature, but by mortality, which was added to it later; the body itself is not corruptible, but incorruptible.[34]

There is no obstacle for the Almighty God, and for this reason it is not an impossible task for God to reconstitute the body that has been subject to decay:

> Do not say to me: how can the body rise again and be made incorruptible? When the power of God is acting, "how" has no place. . . . What is more difficult—to form from the earth flesh, sinews, skin, bones, nerves, veins, arteries, organic and simple bodies, eyes, ears, noses, legs, arms, and have each one of these members correspond to their specific and broader purposes, or to make something immortal that had been subject to corruption?[35]

In Chrysostom's words, the rejection of the resurrection of the body is a rejection of the resurrection in general: "If the body will not be resurrected, then man will not be resurrected, because man is not only soul, but soul and body." If only the soul will be resurrected, then it will not be resurrected fully, only partially. Then "it is impossible to speak of the resurrection in relation to the soul alone, since the resurrection is to those dead and decayed, for it is not the soul that decomposes, but the body." Chrysostom emphasizes that

[35]Ibid. 7.
[36]Ibid.

the resurrection will be universal: "both Greeks and Jews and heretics, and every person that has come into the world" will rise.[36]

If the resurrection will be universal for everyone–for the virtuous and the dishonorable, the evil and the good–then will not the pagans, vice-filled, and idol-worshippers not enjoy that same honor that will be afforded to Christians? Chrysostom answers that question thus: "The bodies of sinners will truly rise incorruptible and immortal, but this honor will be for them a means of punishment and torment: they will rise incorruptible so that they may gradually burn, because if that fire is unquenchable, then it requires bodies that will never be destroyed."[37] This will be that "resurrection of condemnation" of which Christ speaks in the Gospel (Jn 5.29).

St Ephraim the Syrian, discussing the universal resurrection, stresses that all those who died in childhood and even in their mother's womb will rise as "adults" at the resurrection of the dead:

> Whoever drowned at sea, whoever was torn apart by wild beasts, whoever was picked at by birds, whoever burned in fire, will, in the quickest blink of an eye, awake, rise, and be. Whoever died in their mother's womb, will be made as one who has completed their years in the same instant that life returns to the dead. The youth whose mother died with him or her during childbirth will become a complete person and will recognize his or her mother at the resurrection, and the mother will recognize her child. . . . The Creator resurrects the sons of Adam as equals since he created them as equals, and so they will wake from death as equals. There is no one who is greater or lesser in the resurrection. Those who were born premature will rise just as those who completed a long life. Only in deed and way of life will there be greater and more glorious ones, and some will be like the light, and others like the darkness.[38]

In the *Spiritual Homilies* of Macarius of Egypt, we find interesting discussions on the nature of resurrected bodies. Answering the question of whether all the members will be resurrected, Macarius says that all will be subjected to light and fire at the universal resurrection, although the body preserves its nature and the proper personal traits of each person are preserved:

[37]Ibid. 8.
[38]*On the Fear of God and on the Last Judgment.*
[39]*Spiritual Homilies* 15.10.

Nothing is difficult for God. Such is his promise. But to human weakness and human reasoning, this seems somehow impossible. As God, taking dust and earth, fashioned some other kind of essence, precisely a bodily essence unlike the earth, and created many kinds of essences, such as: hair, skin, bones, and sinews; and in the way that a needle, thrown into the fire, changes color and turns into flame, but nonetheless the essence of the iron is not destroyed but remains as it is, so all the members will be renewed at the resurrection and, as it is written, "not a hair . . . will perish" (Lk 21.18), and all will be made as clear as light, all will be gathered and subjected to light and fire, but will not be allowed to turn into fire, so that it will not become a previous essence, as some maintain. For Peter remains Peter, and Paul, Paul, and Philip, Philip; each, having been filled with the spirit, abides in one's own essence and nature.[39]

The testimonies taken from Holy Scripture and the compositions of the Christian authors of the second through fourth centuries, show that the Eastern Christian tradition is completely of one mind when it comes to understanding the universal resurrection. The tradition claims that the resurrection involves all people, beyond dependence on creed, nationality, or moral state, but only for some will this be a "resurrection to life," while for others it will be a "resurrection of condemnation." People's bodies will be resurrected, although these bodies will acquire new characteristics—incorruption and immortality. The body of the resurrected person will be free from the consequences of corruption, maiming, and imperfection. It will be illuminated, light, and spiritual, like Christ's body after his resurrection.

According to the teaching of the Orthodox Church, not only will all of humanity participate in the resurrection of the dead, but all of nature, the whole created cosmos. This teaching is based on the words of the Apostle Paul on the participation of all creation in the glory of the resurrected man:

> For I reckon that the sufferings of this present time are not worthy to be compared with the glory which shall be revealed in us. For the earnest expectation of the creature waits for the manifestation of the sons of God. For the creature was made subject to vanity, not willingly, but by reason of him who has subjected it in hope, because the creature itself also shall be delivered from the bondage of corruption into the glorious liberty of

[40]Cf. *Catechetical Lectures* 15.3.

the children of God. For we know that the whole creation groans and travails in pain together until now. And not only they, but we ourselves also, who have the first fruits of the Spirit, even we ourselves groan within ourselves, waiting for the adoption, that is, the redemption of our body. (Rom 8.18–23)

According to this teaching, nature suffers together with man, but it also arises and becomes transfigured at that very moment when people's bodies will be resurrected and transfigured. The fate of nature and the universe is inseparable from the fate of mankind: such is the idea behind New Testament eschatological teaching. The world and nature will not disappear after the Second Coming of Christ, but will pass away into a "new heaven and a new earth" (Rev 21.1). In the words of Cyril of Jerusalem, we do not await the resurrection of ourselves only, but that of heaven.[40] The Blessed Augustine teaches that "this world shall pass away," but "by transmutation, not by absolute destruction."[41] Like the resurrected bodies of people, nature and the cosmos will become spiritual and incorruptible.

The dogma on the resurrection of the dead has a deep spiritual-moral significance. From the point of view of many Fathers of the Church, this dogma reveals that eschatological perspective in the light of which Christian moral law acquires meaning. Gregory of Nyssa considers that outside of the dogma on the resurrection of the dead, not only does Christian morality lose power, but so does all morality and asceticism in general:

For what reason do people toil and philosophize, neglecting the pleasures of the womb, affectionate abstinence, allowing themselves only a little sleep, entering into battle with cold and heat? Let us speak to them using the Apostle Paul's words: "Let us eat and drink, for tomorrow we die" (1 Cor 15.32). If there is no resurrection, and death is the end to life, then leave off your accusations and reprimands, having been granted an unimpeded authority for homicide: let the adulterers destroy marriage; let the covetous live in luxury at the expense of their opponents; do not scold anyone; let the perjurers curse continuously, for death awaits him who sticks to cursing; let another lie as much as one may desire, because there is no reward for truth; let no one help the poor, for the merciful will

[41] *The City of God* 20.14.
[42] *Discourse on the Holy Pascha.*

remain without a prize. Such considerations occur in the soul of those more chaotic than the flood; they cast out every wise thought and encourage every foolish thought and thievery. For if there is no resurrection, there is no Judgment; if then the Judgment is denied, the fear of God is denied along with it. Where there is no one who is humbled by fear, there the devil exults.[42]

30

The Last Judgment

T HE NOTION THAT MAN WILL BE JUDGED for his deeds is already present in the Old Testament: "Rejoice, young man, in your youth, and let your heart cheer you in the days of your youth, and walk in the ways of your heart and in the sight of your eyes; yet know that for all these things God will bring you into judgment" (Eccl 11.9).

However, it is precisely in the New Testament that the teaching of the posthumous retribution and the Last Judgment is revealed most comprehensively. Christ himself repeatedly says to his disciples that he will come "in the glory of his Father with his angels, and then he will reward every man according to his works" (Mt 16.27; cf. 25.31). Conversing with his disciples on the Mount of Olives not long before his death on the cross, Christ paints a picture of the Last Judgment, when he "will sit on his throne of glory. And before him shall be gathered all nations, and he shall separate them one from

Detail of the icon "The Last Judgment." Northern Russia. 16th c.

another, as a shepherd divides his sheep from the goats. And he shall set the sheep on his right hand, but the goats on the left" (Mt 25.31–33). Acts of mercy bestowed on one's neighbor are the criteria by which the righteous will be separated from the sinners. At the Last Judgment, the people who committed such acts will hear from the Lord: "For I was hungry and you gave me food, I was thirsty and you gave me drink, I was a stranger and you took me in, I was naked and you clothed me; I was sick and you visited me; I was in prison and you came to me." But according to these criteria, the sinner, who did not perform acts of mercy, will be cast "into everlasting fire prepared for the devil and his angels." (Mt 25.35–41)

Jesus repeatedly emphasizes that he, and not God the Father, will judge mankind at the Last Judgment: "The Father judges no one but has committed all judgment to the Son" (Jn 5.22). The Father gave the Son authority to pronounce judgment "because he is the Son of Man" (Jn 5.27). It is precisely Christ, the Son of God and the Son of Man, who is "ordained by God to be the judge of the living and the dead" (Acts 10.42). At the same time, Christ says about himself: "And if any man hears my words, and does not believe, I do not judge him; for I came not to judge the world, but to save the world. He who rejects me and does not accept my words, has one who judges him: the word that I have spoken, that will judge him on the last day" (Jn 12.47–48).

What follows from these words of the Savior is, first of all, that mankind will be judged by Christ—not only as God, but as Man, who "was in all points tempted as we are, yet without sin" (Heb 4.15). Secondly, God's judgment will not somehow be thrust on humanity from without, not merely a consequence of a "just recompense" on God's part. The necessity of judgment flows from man's moral responsibility before God and before other people. The Last Judgment begins in a person's earthly life and occurs in every concrete moment, when a person decides whether or not to feed the hungry, to give drink to the thirsty, to visit the imprisoned, or to share with those who have none. Christ's words on the Last Judgment are no threat of retribution, but a call to virtuous acts. This saying is perceived exactly in this way in the Orthodox Church, which addresses the faithful during the Week of the Last Judgment with the following words:

> Knowing the commandments of the Lord, let this be our way of life: let us feed the hungry, let us give the thirsty drink, let us clothe the naked,

let us welcome strangers, let us visit those in prison and the sick. Then the Judge of all the earth will say even to us: "Come, ye blessed of my Father, inherit the Kingdom prepared for you."[1]

The Last Judgment, according to Christ's teaching, does not refer only to an eschatological reality. Christ's conversation with Nicodemus underscores this: "For God did not send his Son into the world to condemn the world, but that the world through him might be saved. He who believes in him is not condemned; but he who does not believe is condemned already, because he has not believed in the name of the only begotten Son of God. And this is the condemnation, that light has come into the world, and men loved darkness rather than light, because their deeds were evil" (Jn 3.17–19). But in the conversation with the Jews, Christ says: "He who hears my word and believes in him who sent me, has everlasting life, and shall not come into judgment, but has passed from death to life" (Jn 5.24).

Therefore, faith in Christ and the fulfillment of his words here already during earthly life become the key for a person's salvation, while those who do not believe in Christ and reject the Gospel are already condemned to perdition. The separation of the sheep and the goats occurs on earth, when some people choose the light, and others the darkness; some follow after Christ, others reject him; some do good deeds, and others stand on the side of evil. The separation of the sheep and the goats is not a result of divine arbitrariness: it is the consequence of that moral choice that each person makes for himself. The Last Judgment only confirms that choice made by the person him or herself. In the words of John Chrysostom, "on the day of Judgment our own thoughts will stand forth, both those that condemn and those that exonerate, and no person will need any other accuser at that trial."[2]

As Chrysostom emphasizes, Christ came to people "not to judge or to enquire, but to pardon and remit transgressions." If he had come seated on the judgment seat, people might have had grounds to flee from him, but he came with love and forgiveness so that people might run to him in repentance. Many have done so. But since some have stagnated in evil even up to this stage, who wish to remain in it, then Christ simply reveals such people. "'For since,' [Christ] saith, 'the profession of Christianity requires besides

[1]Lenten Triodion. Meatfare Week. Great Vespers. *Sticheron* at the Litya.
[2]*Homilies on Romans* 5.5.

right doctrine a sound conversation also, they fear to come over to us, because they like not to show forth a righteous life.'"[3]

According to the teaching of the Orthodox Church, all people without exception will stand at the Last Judgment—Christians and Gentiles, believers and non-believers: "If then the advent of the Son comes indeed alike to all, but is for the purpose of judging, and separating the believing from the unbelieving, since, as those who believe do his will agreeably to their own choice, and as, [also] agreeably to their own choice, the disobedient do not consent to his doctrine."[4]

The idea that believers in Christ will be judged with particular severity is already present in the Apostolic Epistles. In the Apostle Peter's words, "the time has come that judgment must begin at the house of God" (1 Pet 4.17), that is with the Christian Church. The fearful words of the Apostle Paul are addressed precisely to the members of the Church:

> For if we willfully sin after we have received the knowledge of the truth, there remains no more sacrifice for sins, but a certain fearful looking for of judgment and fiery indignation, which shall devour the adversaries. He who despised Moses' law died without mercy [at the testimony of] two or three witnesses. Of how much more severe punishment, do you suppose, shall the one be thought worthy, who has trodden under foot the Son of God, and has counted the blood of the covenant by which he was sanctified an unholy thing, and treated with contempt the Spirit of grace? For we know him who has said, "Vengeance belongs to me, I will repay, says the Lord." And again, "The Lord shall judge his people." It is a fearful thing to fall into the hands of the living God. (Heb 10.26–31).

According to the Apostle Paul, those who are outside the Church will be judged in correlation to the law of their conscience, written on their own hearts (Rom 2.14–15). This deals with that essential moral law that is placed in man by God and that is called conscience. According to John Chrysostom's teaching, "God created man with sufficient strength to choose virtue and flee evil": wisdom and conscience help a person make the right choice. Beyond wisdom and conscience, the Old Testament Jews had the law of Moses, but the Gentiles did not have this law. That is why the virtuous

---

[3] *Homilies on John* 28.2.
[4] Irenaeus of Lyons *Against Heresies* 5.27.1.

Gentiles were so amazing, "because they had no need for the law, but they discovered everything connected to the law, having not words inscribed in their minds, but deeds."[5]

Chrysostom comes to a radical conclusion: "Nothing more is needed for a Gentile's salvation than he be a fulfiller of the law."[6] These words do not serve to be perceived as a rejection of the principle already formulated by Cyprian of Carthage: "There is no salvation outside the Church." Chrysostom, it seems, does not put this in doubt. The term "salvation," if it is taken as a synonym for deification, entrance into the Kingdom of Heaven, and unification with Christ, is hardly altered by

The Three Hierarchs. Byzantium. 14th c.

addressing people outside Christianity and the Church. At the same time, the posthumous fate of the virtuous non-Christian will differ from the fate of the non-Christian living in sin and vice. The moral criterion at the appraisal of deeds committed during life will be applied to all people without exception, with the only difference being that Jews will be judged by the law of Moses, Christians by the Gospel, and Gentiles by the law of conscience written in their hearts. (We note that the criterion of confession of faith is absent in Christ's words on the Last Judgment: the separation of the sheep and the goats occurs exclusively according to moral criteria.)

According to Holy Scripture, Christ will judge mankind together with his apostles (cf. Mt 19.28; Lk 22.30) and the saints (cf. 1 Cor 6.2). Those judged will not just be people, but angels as well (cf. 1 Cor 6.3), but only those of them who turned away from God and became demons.[7] These "angels who did not keep their own position . . . [God] has kept in eternal chains in deepest darkness for the judgment of the great day" (Jude 1.6).

According to the teaching of Basil the Great, "we will be judged each in our own rank—whether simple folk, or elders, or princes."[8] Symeon the New Theologian develops this teaching, saying that a righteous person will be

---

[5]John Chrysostom *Homilies on Romans* 5.5.
[6]Ibid. 6.1.
[7]John Chrysostom *Homilies on First Corinthians* 16.3.
[8]*Interpretation on Isaiah* 3.14.

placed in opposition to each sinner of the same rank at the Last Judgment: sinful women will be opposed to holy women, dishonorable kings and rulers against virtuous governors, sinful patriarchs against holy patriarchs, "who were in the image and likeness of the true God not only in word, but in deed." Fathers will be judged by fathers, slaves and free by slaves and free, married and unmarried by married and unmarried. "Basically, every sinful person on the fearful day of Judgment will see the opposite of themselves in eternal life and the unspeakable light of someone who is like them, and will be judged by them."[9]

According to Holy Scripture, people will be judged by books in which their deeds are written, and each will be judged by his own acts (Rev 20.12–13; Dan 7.10). This way bears witness to the fact that everyone's actions remain in God's memory: in the words of Cyril of Jerusalem, God records every virtue of a person, including mercy, fasting, marital fidelity, and abstinence; but evil deeds are also recorded, including greed, calumny, blasphemy, occult arts, theft, and murder.[10]

On the other hand, in Basil the Great's opinion the reference to the books shows that God, at the moment of the Last Judgment, raises images in the memories of every person of all that they did, so that all might recall their acts and understand that the punishment is justified.[11] Basil warns against a literal understanding of the images used to describe the Last Judgment. In his words, Scripture presents the Last Judgment in a "personified way," that is anthropomorphically. But if, for instance, it says that the Judge will ask for an account from the judged, then this "is not because the Judge will ask questions of each of us or will give answers to the judged, but so as to instill thoughtfulness in us and so that we would not forget his statutes."[12]

In Basil's opinion the Last Judgment will not be so much an outside event as much as an inner process: it will occur above all in the conscience of a person, in his or her mind and memory. Moreover, the Last Judgment will be accomplished with lightning speed: "Clearly all the deeds of our life, by some kind of unspeakable force, will be imprinted in the memory of our soul like a painting in a moment's time";[13] "one should not think that much time will

[9]*Catechetical Oration* 5.559–672.
[10]Cf. Cyril of Jerusalem *Catechetical Lecture* 15.23.
[11]Cf. *Interpretation on Isaiah* 1.18.
[12]Ibid.
[13]Ibid.

pass while each one sees themselves and their deeds; all of this will be presented in a moment to the Judge and the results of God's judgment will be vividly imprinted by some unspeakable force before themselves, and the dominating soul,[14] as if in a mirror, will see the image made by itself."[15]

Basil the Great's elucidations bring in important correctives to that understanding of the Last Judgment that is reflected in many literary memorials and in Western medieval paintings, in particular the famed fresco by Michelangelo from the Sistine Chapel. Depicted on this fresco is Christ surrounded by the Old Testament righteous: Christ is sending all the sinners into the abyss of Hell with an arm upraised in a punitive gesture. The fundamental idea of the composition is that with right judgment accomplished, each shall inevitably receive requital from God for their actions.

Nevertheless, the Last Judgment in the Orthodox understanding is not so much a moment of requital, as much as a moment celebrating truth, not so much a manifestation of God's wrath, as much as a manifestation of divine mercy and love. "God is love" (1 Jn 4.8, 4.16), and he never ceases to be love, even at the moment of the Last Judgment. "God is light" (1 Jn 1.5), and he never ceases to be light, even when he comes to judge the living and the dead. But subjectively, the divine love and the divine light are perceived differently by the righteous and by sinners: for some it is a source of joy and blessing, while for others it is a source of torment and suffering.

Symeon the New Theologian says that the terrible day of the Lord is called the day of judgment not because of the literal sense of the word *day* as the time in which the judgment will take place. The day of the Lord is the Lord himself:

> While for some it is somehow about the day, to others it is about him who is to come on that day. But the Master and God of all, our Lord Jesus Christ, shines forth on that day in the divine radiance, and the effervescence of the Master overshadows the sensory sun, so that it will not be visible at all; the stars will darken, and everything visible winds down, like a scroll, that is, everything gets out of the way, making room for its Creator. And he will be alone—both the day and God at the same time. He who now is invisible for all and lives in the unapproachable light, then

---

[14]I.e. in the nous.
[15]Basil the Great *Interpretation on Isaiah* 3.13.

will appear for all as he is in his glory, and will fill all with his light, and will become for the saints the never-ending day on which night will never fall, replete with incessant joy; but for sinners and the unjoyful, like me, he will be totally inaccessible and invisible. While they, when they lived in life, did not try to purify themselves in order to see the glory of the Lord and to take him inside of them, then in that future age he will be inaccessible and invisible to them out of fairness.[16]

In the context of Christ's words that God is "kind" in relation "to the ungrateful and the wicked" (Lk 6.35), the Last Judgment is perceived as the manifestation of God's kindness, God's glory, divine love, and divine mercy, but not wrath or retribution on God's part. The Day of the Lord is the day of light, not the "day of darkness and gloom" as it is presented in the Old Testament prophets (Joel 2.2; Amos 5.18–20), and not the "day of wrath" (*dies irae*) as it is called in medieval Latin poetry. The reason for the torment of sinners is not God's anger and not the absence of God's love, but their own incapability to perceive God's love and the divine light as sources of joy and delight. This incapability flows from the spiritual-moral choice that a person made during earthly life.

Symeon the New Theologian emphasizes that the Last Judgment of the Lord begins during the earthly life of each person. It is precisely earthly life that is the time when a person communes with the divine light through the fulfillment of God's commandments and through repentance. Symeon considers that for such people, the day of the Lord will never come, because it has already come for them and they already abide in the divine light. The day of the Lord as Last Judgment comes only for those who knowingly turned away from repentance and the accomplishment of God's commandments:

> The grace of the Holy Spirit is inaccessible and invisible for those who possess disbelief and passions. But for those who manifest obligatory repentance and start to fulfill Christ's commandments with faith, and at the same time with fear and trembling, this grace is revealed and is visible and bears them itself to their judgment . . . or, it is better said, it is for them the day of divine judgment. Whoever always radiates and is illumined by this grace, this person truly sees oneself . . . this person sees all one's deeds in detail. . . . One is judged by this and is condemned by

[16] *Moral Oration* 10.1.

divine fire, and then, fed by the water of tears and washed all over the body, all is baptized in soul and in body by the divine fire and the spirit, becoming totally pure, totally spotless, a son of the light and of the day and no longer a son of mortal man. For this reason such a person will not be judged by a future trial, since one has already been judged before, not denounced by the light because one has been sanctified by it before, and will not enter that fire so as not to be burned eternally, because one entered it here before and was already judged. And one will not think that only then the day of the Lord will come, because it will already have become the day of light and radiance from communion and conversation with God, and one will have ceased to be in the world or with the world, but everything will be totally inside the person. . . . The day of the Lord is not for those who already radiate the divine light, but it will suddenly be revealed to those who are in the darkness of passions, living in the world in a worldly way and loving the blessing of this world; he will suddenly appear to these, and will seem to them to be fearful, like an unbearable and unquenchable fire.[17]

---

[17] *Moral Oration* 10.2.

31

Posthumous Retribution

T HE UNDERSTANDING OF THE LAST JUDGMENT expressed in the words of
Symeon the New Theologian (cited in the previous chapter) corresponds fully to the teaching of the Eastern fathers concerning the torments
of Hades. The torture of Hades is summed up above all by the impossibility
of partaking in God's love, in the impossibility of experiencing the divine
love as a source of joy and blessing. Isaac the Syrian says that sinners in
Gehenna are not at all deprived of God's love. On the contrary, this love is
given equally to all—both to the righteous in the Kingdom of Heaven and to
the sinner in the fires of Gehenna. But for the former it is a source of joy and
blessing, while for the latter it is a source of torment:

> Those suffering in Gehenna are struck with the lashes of love! How bitter
> and heavy is the torment of love! For having sensed that they have sinned
> against this love, they endure a suffering greater than any previous fear of
> torment; grief, afflicting the heart for sinning against love, more fearful
> than any other possible punishment. It is inappropriately thought some-
> times that sinners in Gehenna are deprived of God's love. Love . . . is
> given universally to all. But it enacts its power in two ways: it tortures the
> sinners . . . and cheers those who have fulfilled their debts.[1]

According to the opinion of the Eastern fathers of the Church, God is not
the creator of Hades, just as he is not the creator of evil. The existence of
Hades is in opposition to the will of the all-blessed God, "who will have all
men to be saved and to come to the knowledge of the truth" (1 Tim 2.4).
Hades does not exist because God wants it to, but because the will of those
created essences that are against the divine will inevitably create the existence
of Hades. God did not create Hades for the devil and his demons, but they
formed it for themselves. Irenaeus of Lyons writes:

[1] *Homily* 18 (*Ascetical Homilies*).

To as many as continue in their love towards God, does he grant communion with him. But communion with God is life and light, and the enjoyment of all the benefits which he has in store. But on as many as, according to their own choice, depart from God, he inflicts that separation from himself which they have chosen of their own accord. But separation from God is death, and separation from light is darkness; and separation from God consists in the loss of all the benefits which he has in store. Those, therefore, who cast away by apostasy these forementioned things, being in fact destitute of all good, do experience every kind of punishment. God, however, does not punish them immediately of himself, but that punishment falls upon them because they are destitute of all that is good. Now, good things are eternal and without end with God, and therefore the loss of these is also eternal and never-ending. It is in this matter just as occurs in the case of a flood of light: those who have blinded themselves, or have been blinded by others, are for ever deprived of the enjoyment of light.[2]

Thus, God does not send sinners to Hades, but people who oppose the will of God and stand against God make their choice in favor of Hades. This choice is not made from some kind of far off eschatological perspective, but in a person's earthly life. It is here on earth that the torture of Hell begins for some, but for others—"the kingdom of God . . . com[ing] with power" (Mk 9.1).

According to the thought of Protopresbyter Georges Florovsky, the original paradox of creation includes the possibility for Hell: "God did not create anything other than himself, some kind of "opposing" self, in the act of creation. Consequently, the created world has its own mode of existence." God granted freedom to the created world, and therefore, autonomy. This is expressed as the "kenotic self-restriction" of God, who "so to say, was pushed out and granted space for another being." As Florovsky writes, "the point of the kenotic paradox is not in the existence of the world, but in the potential for Hades. The world can obey God, and in its obedience serve God and manifest his glory. . . . Hades, on the contrary, means recalcitrance and estrangement."[3]

[2] Against Heresies 5.27.2.
[3] Georges Florovsky, Dogma and History (Moscow: 1995), 446–447.

Hades' existence is "not dependent on God's decision. God does not send anyone there. People create a hell for themselves."[4] Hades exists because sin exists. But "sin is not from the beginning: it is a tear, a turning away, an escape from the truth. Its essence is apostasy and revolt."[5] The reality of Hades is conditional on the reality of sin as a moral choice, made consciously and freely by a person:

> Hades is not a myth or a turn of phrase used to incite fear. . . . It is a reality in which many human beings participate by their own volition. . . . Hades lurks in sin itself, although to the one abiding in it, it is thought of as paradise. . . . The authority of sin is in direct rejection of the God-created reality, in its attempt to establish another level of being . . . to which the sinner intoxicated and blinded by pride can give preference forever. . . . God does not place barriers before the "universal conversion"—on the contrary, he "wishes that every person should be saved. . . ." Insurmountable hindrances only arise on the part of the creature.[6]

Detail of the icon "The Last Judgment." From the church of Saints Boris and Gleb. Novgorod. 16th c.

The reality of Hades, its existence for sinners, and even its potential for eternal existence, do not contradict the abolition and destruction of Hades by the resurrected Christ. We saw in considering the theme of Christ's descent into Hades that, according to many theological and liturgical texts of the Eastern Church, Christ freed everyone from Hell—in the sense that he opened the possibility of salvation and escape from Hades for everyone without exception. However, we also saw that the Tradition of the Church does not give a direct answer to the question whether all responded to Christ's preaching and whether all followed after him. If anyone remained in Hell after Christ's descent there, then it is not because Christ led some out but left others, but because these people did not want to follow Christ; they themselves wished to remain in hellish torment.

[4]Ibid., 465.
[5]Ibid., 448.
[6]Ibid., 461–462.

Hades was truly "abolished" by the resurrected Christ, that is, it is no longer inescapable for people, it no longer rules over them. But those who consciously stand on the path contrary to God's will, who knowingly commit evil and sins, reconstitute the destroyed and abolished Hades, for they do not want to be reconciled with God's love. The paradox of the mystery of Hades and eternal torment can be summed up in that God did not create Hades, but people created it for themselves; God destroyed and abolished it, but people reestablish it again and again. Hell is renewed every time a sin is consciously committed and when there is no repentance following this sin.

The reality of Hades is one of the axioms of the religious experience. The existence of Hades was known even in the Old Testament, where it was perceived as the kingdom of death, to which all people descended without exception–not only sinners, but the righteous too. The *Sheol* of the Old Testament is "a land of darkness and gloominess . . . a land of perpetual darkness, where there is no light, and no one can see the life of mortals" (Job 10.21–22). *Sheol*, according to the ancients, is located in the underworld, that is, beneath the earth (Gen 37.35; Deut 32.22). Those descending there cannot exit from it (Job 7.10). *Sheol* is the place of the God-forsaken: God does not remember those who have descended there, for they are cut from his hands (Ps 88.5). The Old Testament *Sheol* does not suggest any possibility for communion with God: those who dwell in it cannot stand and praise God (Ps 88.11).

Side by side with the Old Testament concept of *Sheol* as a house "appointed for all living" (Job 30.32) is the idea of Hades as a place of posthumous retribution for sins. There, those who did not repent at the words of God and despised the will of the Most High sit "in darkness and the shadow of death, fettered in poverty and iron" (Ps 107.10–11). It is said concerning those who have rebelled against God that "their worm shall not die, their fire shall not be quenched" (Isa 66.24). A notion of God's existence in the underworld is found in the Old Testament: "If I go up to heaven, you are there; if I make my bed in *Sheol*, you are there" (Ps 139.8). Finally, we find an idea of deliverance for the sons of Israel from Hades and death in the Old Testament: "I will deliver them out of the power of Hades, and will redeem them from death: where is your penalty, O death? O Hades, where is your sting?" (Hos 13.14).

Many Old Testament images and ideas are present in the New Testament teaching on Hades and eternal torture. Jesus Christ speaks of Gehenna as an "unquenchable fire": where "their worm does not die, and the fire is not quenched" (Mk 9.48), where "there shall be weeping and gnashing of teeth" (Mt 8.12, 22.13; Lk 13.28). The term "Gehenna" (*geenna*/γέεννα) is used in the New Testament as a synonym for the term "Hades" (*hadēs*/ᾅδης).[7] The terms "prison," "underworld," and "nether region" were also used synonymously.[8]

In the parable of the rich man and Lazarus, Christ speaks of the posthumous fate of two people, one of whom was taken into the bosom of Abraham, while the other was found in the flames of Hell, in torment. "A great chasm has been fixed" between the bosom of Abraham and Hades, so that it is impossible to cross over from one place to the other (Lk 16.19–26). According to the parable, there is no intermediate space or intermediate state between Hades and the bosom of Abraham; the condition of those found in Hades remains unalterable, and their entreaties for the abatement of their suffering go unanswered.

How much are biblical images of the underworld, fire, worm, darkness, and the gnashing of teeth literally understood in the patristic tradition? Many fathers of the Church characteristically see in these images a symbolic indication of the torment of Hell as more of a spiritual reality, as the condition of the soul after death, and less as a place of torture, where sinners are burned by fire or eaten by worms. Answering the question of where and in what kind of place the flame of Gehenna is located, John Chrysostom poses the supposition that it will be located "quite out of the pale of this world": "for as the prisons and mines are at a great distance from royal residencies, so will hell be somewhere out of this world."[9] In other words, Gehenna is beyond the bounds of the material cosmos; it is a reality of the spiritual world. The tortures of Gehenna bear not a material, but a spiritual character: they are essentially the state of the soul and nous of a person, separated from God because of one's sinful life.

What then is the nature of the torments of Gehenna? In the mind of the Church Fathers, the torture of Gehenna is the repentance for crimes committed.[10] This futile and belated repentance is effectively different from the

---

[7]The term "Gehenna" refers to a ditch in the environs of Jerusalem into which the filth and corpses of animals were thrown. During the time of Christ it was used as a common noun referring to a place of damnation.

[8]For Gehenna, see Mt 5.22, 5.29, 5.30, 10.28, 18.9, 23.15, 23.33; Mk 9.43, 9.45, 9.47; Lk 12.5; Jas 3.6. For Hades, see Mt 11.23, 16.18; Lk 10.15, 16.23; Acts 2.27, 2.31; 1 Cor 15.55; Rev 1.18, 6.8, 20.13, 20.14. For prison, cf. Lk 12.58; 1 Pet 3.19. For the underworld, see Phil 2.10. For nether region, see Eph 4.9.

[9]*Homilies on Romans* 31.3.

[10]Cf. Isaac the Syrian *Oration* 18.

repentance that a person can come to in life. Repentance is the regret of sins accompanied by a change of mind (such is the literal meaning of the Greek word *metanoia*/μετάνοια, translated as "repentance"), a change in one's way of life. The possibility to correct mistakes is available to a person only in earthly life. Symeon the New Theologian says that after death a state of inertia begins, when no one can do anything good or evil; for this reason, however someone may turn out, so will they remain.[11]

The feeling of repentance in Hades is accompanied by a sense of shame for the crimes committed:

> Those who did evil will be resurrected to chastisement and shame in order to see in themselves the loathsomeness and effect made on them by their sins. And perhaps a more terrible darkness and eternal fire is that shame that will linger with sinners for eternity, who have unceasingly before their eyes the consequences of the sin committed in the flesh, like some kind of unimaginable paint, ever remaining in the memory of their souls. . . . The harshest punishment of them all is this eternal shame and disgrace.[12]

But the most powerful torment that awaits sinners in Hades is excommunication from Christ, the inability to relate with God:

> No doubt hell, and that punishment, is a thing not to be borne. Yet though one suppose ten thousand hells, he will utter nothing like what it will be to fail of that blessed glory, to be hated of Christ, to hear "I know you not. . . ." Yea, better surely to endure a thousand thunderbolts, than to see that face of mildness turning away from us, and that eye of peace not enduring to look upon us.[13]

In the words of Symeon the New Theologian, the only source of torment for the sinners in Hades is separation from Christ:

> Master, of those who believe in you, no human being, no one of those who
> have been baptized in your name, will be able to endure this heavy and dreadful burden of being separated from you, oh, Merciful One:

[11]Cf. Symeon the New Theologian *Hymn 1.*
[12]Basil the Great *Homily on Psalm 33.*
[13]John Chrysostom *Homilies on Matthew 23.9.*

what a terrible trial, what a terrible, unbearable, eternal suffering!
Indeed what is worse than to be separated from you, Savior?
What is more painful than to be cut off from life,
to live down there like a corpse, deprived of life,
to be deprived at once of all blessings?[14]

Mark of Ephesus also speaks of this, asserting that "deprivation of the contemplation of God is a greater and heavier torture than all others, as it is the reason and basis of other sufferings." Sinners at the Last Judgment will see God for the last time "and will see him no more and will have no hope of seeing him, and the same thing by which they angered the Master will torment them the most of all."[15]

Symeon the New Theologian disproves the notion that there exists some kind of intermediate space between Gehenna and the Kingdom of Heaven, "which will not receive any light but will be also deprived of darkness, outside of the Kingdom, but outside of hell too, far from the banquet hall and far from the chastening fire all at once." Symeon considers that there is no such place and cannot be such a place:

This is not written down anywhere and neither will it be;
but those who will have lived according to your will
will be in the light of all that is good
while the doers of evil will suffer in the chastening
darkness and in the center there will be . . .
a frightful abyss separating one from the other. . . .
Yes, for the man who falls into the center, it will be worse
than the most horrid torments, than the worst punishments;
in an abyss of torments, in a pit of perdition
the unhappy man will roll, will be dragged
there where it is difficult to walk
for those who in torments would want to go to the land of the living
but who would prefer to be reduced to ashes in the dreadful fire
rather than throw themselves into this frightful pit.[16]

---

[14]*Hymn* 1.

[15]Mark of Ephesus *Answers to the Difficulties and Questions Posed to Him from the Cardinals and Other Latin Teachers, in Connection with the Proclaimed Speeches.*

[16]*Hymn* 1.

Isaac the Syrian also speaks of the absence of an intermediate state between Gehenna and the Kingdom of Heaven. According to his teaching, though there are many abodes in the Kingdom of Heaven, they are all contained within it; the fire of Gehenna is outside of the borders of the Kingdom:

> The subject for contemplation is one for all, and the place is one, and there is no other intermediate stage apart from these two states. I mean the one stage that is above, and the other that is below, but between them the difference is one of retribution. If then this is fair—and it is truly fair—then what could be more thoughtless and unwise than such words: "It is good enough for me to avoid Gehenna so as to enter the Kingdom, I do not care"? For to avoid Gehenna is the same as entering the Kingdom, just as being deprived of the Kingdom means to enter Gehenna. Scripture did not show us three countries, but what did it say? "When the Son of Man comes in his glory . . . he will put the sheep at his right hand and the goats at the left" (Mt 25.31–33). Have you not understood from this that there is a state set up in opposition to the higher stage, and that this is the torment of Gehenna?[17]

The teaching of the torments of Hades was a subject of theological discourse in the Christian East and West for many centuries. The following questions were especially posed in the course of these disputes: whether changing the posthumous fate of a sinner and one's liberation from Hades is possible; whether the torments of sinners in Hades are eternal or if they bear a temporary character; how do the eternal torments of sinners in Hades correspond to the notion of the limitless and unspeakable love of God toward mankind?

The Western and Eastern theological traditions did not always answer these questions identically. In particular, the teaching of purgatory—a kind of intermediate place between Paradise and Hell, or, rather, a special division of Hell where sinners are subjected to a purifying fire—was formulated in the West under the influence of the Blessed Augustine and a slew of other Latin fathers. This teaching is based on the understanding that all sins are subdivided into two categories: mortal and venial; a person who has committed a mortal sin and dies without repentance appears in Hell and suffers torture from which deliverance is impossible; the person who is culpable only of a venial sin will

[17] *Oration* 58.

end up in purgatory (*purgatorium*) after death, where one endures a purifying suffering over the course of a determined period of time, upon the completion of which one can be translated to paradise. A text long attributed to the Blessed Augustine says the following concerning the nature of the purifying fire: "He, who in a previous time [i.e. in earthly life] did not bear the fruit of conversion, must first be purified by the purifying fire; and although this fire will not be eternal, nonetheless I am surprised at the level of its severity, for it surpasses every torment that has ever taken place in this life."[18]

Above all concerning the biblical foundation of the teaching of purgatory are Christ's words on the length of the sentence: "Amen, I say to you, you will by no means come out from there, until you have paid the last penny" (Mt 5.26; Lk 12.59). In the opinion of the Western theologians, these words testify to the temporary and purifying character of the trials after death. They also point out the words of the Savior on the sin that "shall not be forgiven . . . neither in this world nor in the world to come" (Mt 12.32): they draw a conclusion from this that there are sins that are forgiven in the age to come, and consequently, deliverance from punishment for these sins is possible. Finally, they offer the words of the Apostle Paul: "If any man's work abide which he has built on [this foundation], he shall receive a reward. If any man's work be burned, he shall suffer loss, but he himself shall be saved, yet so as by fire" (1 Cor 3.14–15).

The legalism of the teaching on purgatory sparked antagonism and rejection in the Orthodox East, where it had always been considered that God's mercy cannot be limited to only one category of the dead. Orthodox eschatology proceeds from the fact that until the Last Judgment, changes for the good are possible in the fate of any sinner found in Hell. In this sense it can be said that Orthodox Christianity views the posthumous fate of a person with greater optimism than Roman Catholicism, and that the door of the salvific Kingdom of God is never closed to anyone. As long as the final resolution of judgment has not been pronounced, hope is maintained for all the departed–the hope of deliverance from eternal torment and entry into the Heavenly Kingdom.

At the same time, the Orthodox Church is far from the excessive optimism of those who maintain that at the end time God's mercy will extend to all of unrighteous humanity and all people, including great sinners, and together with

[18] *On True and False Repentance* PL 40:1128.

them the devil and his demons will be saved in a lofty form by will of the God who is Good. Origen expressed this idea in the third century, Origen whose teaching on *apokatastasis*/ἀποκατάστασις ("universal restoration") was condemned in its entirety by an ecumenical council as contrary to the teachings of the Fathers of the Church. Origen writes in the treatise *On First Principles*:

> All this bodily substance of ours will be brought, when all things shall be re-established in a state of unity, and when God shall be all in all. And this result must be understood as being brought about, not suddenly, but slowly and gradually, seeing that the process of amendment and correction will take place imperceptibly in the individual instances during the lapse of countless and unmeasured ages, some outstripping others, and tending by a swifter course towards perfection, while others again follow close at hand, and some again a long way behind; and thus, through the numerous and uncounted orders of progressive beings who are being reconciled to God from a state of enmity, the last enemy is finally reached, who is called death, so that he also may be destroyed, and no longer be an enemy.[19]

Origen writes in another place in the same treatise, answering the question of the possibility of those angelic ranks that "act under the rule of the devil and are guilty of evil" turning to good:

> You yourself, reader, may approve of, if neither in these present worlds which are seen and temporal, nor in those which are unseen and are eternal, that portion is to differ wholly from the final unity and fitness of things. But in the meantime, both in those temporal worlds which are seen, as well as in those eternal worlds which are invisible, all those beings are arranged, according to a regular plan, in the order and degree of their merits; so that some of them speak in the first, others in the second, some even in the last times, after having undergone heavier and severer punishments, endured for a lengthened period, and for many ages, so to speak, improved by this stern method of training, and restored at first by the instruction of the angels, and subsequently by the powers of a higher grade, and thus advancing through each stage to a better condition, reach even to that which is invisible and eternal, having traveled through, by a

[19]3.6.6.

kind of training, every single office of the heavenly powers. From which, I think, this will appear to follow as an inference, that every rational nature may, in passing from one order to another, go through each to all, and advance from all to each.[20]

Therefore all living beings, according to Origen, are joined to some kind of general hierarchy in which each one of them is found to have one or another degree of success. In the end, they will all be led into oneness with God: the only difference between them is the length of the process of crossing from one stage to the other and, so to say, the greater or lesser painfulness of this process. Origen repeatedly makes the supposition concerning the final salvation of the devil and his demons,[21] although in some places he speaks directly as to the impossibility of salvation for the devil and his demons:[22] clearly, this issue remained unresolved for him.

Origen borrowed the term *apokatastasis* from Acts of the Apostles (Acts 3.21), where it talks about the promised time of "universal restoration" (*apokatastasis tōn pantōn*/ἀποκατάστασις τῶν πάντων). Origen interpreted this term in the sense of a restoration to the original state,[23] following the principle: "the end is like the beginning."[24] Following the classical philosophers, Origen considered the history of the universe as a cyclical process—as a succession of "eons" in each of which what already took place in the previous eons may be repeated. In this distinctive system, *apokatastasis* is thought of as the completion of a full historical circle and the return to the initial condition, the condition before the Fall.[25]

However, such a theory, first of all, contradicts the Christian vision of the historical process as a path to the final transfiguration and transformation into a better state, and not at all as a return to the initial condition. Protopresbyter Georges Florovsky writes that "the whole pathos of Origen's system is concluded in the cancellation, the abolition of the enigma of time and being. It is precisely in this intimate thought that his famous teaching of the 'universal restoration' (*apokatastasis*) lies. . . . *Apokatastasis* is the rejection of history. The

---

[20]Ibid. 1.6.3.
[21]Cf., especially: Origen *Commentary on Romans* 5.10, 9.41; *Commentary on John* 16; *Commentary on Matthew* 13.17.
[22]*Homilies on Joshua* 8.5.
[23]Cf. Origen *Homilies on Jeremiah* 14.18.
[24]*On First Principles* 1.6.2.
[25]Ibid. 2.9.2–3.

whole content of historical time is dispersed without memory or consequence. And 'after' history remains only that which was already 'before' history."[26]

Second, Origen's teaching on *apokatastasis* practically excludes the teaching on free will—the understanding that only by virtue of free choice can one follow Christ into eternal life. In the words of Isidore of Pelusium, "the salvation of mankind is prepared not through coercion and imposition, but by persuasion and a kind disposition. Since every person is in full control of their salvation, whether they are crowned or are punished justly, they receive what they have chosen."[27] But in Origen it turns out that people's salvation is found to be exclusively in the merciful God's competence; he underestimates the possibility of the devil, demons, and evil people resisting the good will of God for eternity. As a modern theologian writes, "to accept with Origen that evil will exhaust itself at the end time and that God alone will abide forever means to forget the absolute nature of personal freedom: it is absolute precisely because this freedom is in the image of God."[28]

Third, in Origen's system, *apokatastasis* is closely linked to his theory, rejected by the Church, of the pre-existence of souls, according to which people's souls existed in a kind of initial ideal world, but after that, owing to a "cooling-off," they were sent into a body. The life of the soul in the body, as well as its posthumous existence, can be thought of as a punishment or test necessary for the spiritual-moral purification and renewal to the initial worthiness. Corresponding to these views, Origen perceived hellfire as purifying, and not as chastising, and suggested that the torments of Hell are one of the means for universal restoration. However, there is no such teaching in the Church, and the contradiction between Origen and the Church on this point is quite clear.

Fourth, the Origenist *apokatastasis* radically contradicts the basic fundamentals of Christian morality. Indeed, what moral sense is there throughout the whole drama of human history if good and evil end up being equal in the eyes of divine mercy and just judgment? What meaning does the separation of the sheep from the goats at the Last Judgment have, if the good is not the only and absolute criterion by which this division occurs, or if this division bears a temporary character? What meaning is there in suffering, prayer,

[26]*Dogmat i istoriya* (Moscow: 1995), 294–295.
[27]*Letter 629, to Paul.*
[28]Olivier Clement, *Sources: Theology of the Fathers of the Ancient Church* (Moscow: 1994), 296.

ascetical efforts, the fulfillment of the gospel commandments, if the right-eous will be sooner or later equal to the sinners? As Emperor Justinian asked, is it fair that "those who led a life full of perfection to the end should be united with the lawless and pederasts, and to acknowledge that both the for-mer and the latter should enjoy equal blessings?"[29] The Origenist under-standing of *apokatastasis* does not give an answer even to one of these questions.

Fifth, Origen's supposition on the potential salvation of the devil and his demons is in radical opposition to church tradition. As previously men-tioned,[30] the devil and demons' falling away from God is perceived in Chris-tian tradition as final and irrevocable. In the words of John of Damascus, repentance is impossible both for angels[31] and for the devil and his demons.[32] It is impossible for the former because they are incorporeal and do not sin, and for the latter because they cannot change and be saved, but the unquenchable fire and eternal torment await them.[33]

Finally, sixth, Origen's view on the non-eternal nature of the torment of Hades directly contradicts the Gospel, where this torture and perdition of sin-ners is repeatedly called eternal:

Depart from me, you cursed, into everlasting fire. (Mt 25.41)

And these shall go away into everlasting punishment, but the righteous into life eternal. (Mt 25.46)

. . . when the Lord Jesus is revealed from heaven with his mighty angels, in flaming fire taking vengeance on those who do not know God, and who do not obey the gospel of our Lord Jesus; and who shall be punished with everlasting destruction from the presence of the Lord and from the glory of his power. (2 Thess 1.7–9)

It is true that Origen placed much attention on the fact that the adjective "eternal" (*aiōnios*/αἰώνιος) comes from the word "age" (*aiōn*/αἰών) and there-fore can indicate a certain length, though not a never-ending stretch, of time:

[29]Justinian *Letter to the Holy Council on Origen and His Accomplices.* Cited in *Acts of the Ecumenical Councils in Four Volumes*, vol III (St Petersburg: 1996), 538.
[30]Cf. Chapter 3.3.
[31]Cf. *An Exact Exposition . . .* 2.3.
[32]Ibid. 2.4.
[33]Ibid.

in Origen's opinion, hellfire is exactly like this–eternal, but not never-ending.[34] The argument is on the two notions of the word "eternity"– on the
eternity of God in comparison to which nothing created is eternal, and on
eternity as an endless length of time. However, such a distinction is absent in
the very texts of Holy Scripture that speak of eternal torment and eternal
perdition, as well as any kind of allusions to the possibility of a spiritual progression and subsequent salvation of the devil and his demons.

Origen's teaching on *apokatastasis*, including other mistaken views of his,
was condemned at the Council of Constantinople in 543 and at the fifth ecumenical council. In his letter to the council in 543, Emperor Justinian relates
the teaching of the Origenists thus: "They claim . . . that there will be a complete destruction of the body and that all will return once more to unity and
will become noetic, as it was in former times; from here it is clear that the
devil himself and other demons will be restored to this very same unity, as
well as the dishonorable and godless people together with divine god-
bearering people and heavenly powers, that they will have the same unity
with God that Christ has and that they had before."[35] In a letter to Patriarch
Menas of Constantinople, the emperor suggested the following formulation
of anathema against this teaching: "If anyone says or thinks that the punishment of demons and of dishonorable people is temporary and will end after
a time, and that a restoration will take place of demons and of impious people, let him be anathema."[36] The fifth ecumenical council supported this
anathema.

Researchers repeatedly noted the fact that, having judged the Origenist
teaching on *apokatastasis*, the Fifth Ecumenical Council did not say one word
concerning a similar teaching contained in the works of St Gregory of Nyssa
(that, moreover, some fathers of the Council explain with much respect
toward him). Gregory of Nyssa specifically wrote:

> When evil shall have been some day annihilated in the long revolutions
> of the ages, nothing shall be left outside the world of goodness, but that
> even from those evil spirits shall rise in harmony the confession of Christ's
> Lordship. . . . He that becomes "all" things will be "in all" things too; and

---

[34]Cf. Origen *Commentary on Romans* 5.7.
[35]*Acts of the Ecumenical Councils in Four Volumes*, vol III, 537–538.
[36]Ibid., 537.

herein it appears to me that Scripture teaches the complete annihilation of evil. . . . The Cause of all things is one . . . and yet the existences produced by that Cause are not of the same nature. . . . When such, then, have been purged from it and utterly removed by the healing processes worked out by the fire, then every one of the things which make up our conception of the good will come to take their place; incorruption, that is, and life, and honor, and grace, and glory, and everything else that we conjecture is to be seen in God, and in his image, man as he was made.[37]

In some places Gregory of Nyssa also speaks of the possibility of a final salvation for the devil and his demons.[38] How can one explain the presence of this teaching in Gregory of Nyssa? Usually this is explained as the influence of Origen. In the sixth century, responding to the issue of how one ought to react to the teaching laid out by Gregory of Nyssa, St Barsanuphius the Great wrote:

Do not think that people, even if they are saints, can grasp the depths of the divinity. . . . Saints, having been made teachers, or making themselves such, or compelling other people to succeed greatly, succeed their own teachers and, having received support from above, exposited a new teaching, but simultaneously preserved what they took from their former teachers, i.e., the incorrect teaching. Having succeeded and afterwards been made spiritual teachers, they did not pray to God that he might reveal to them to be the first of their teachers: whether it was the Holy Spirit who suggested what their teachers taught them but, considering them to be wise and intellectual, did not examine their words; and therefore the opinions of their teachers got mixed up with their own teaching, and these saints sometimes said that which they learned from their teachers and sometimes the good which was suggested to them by their intellect; but subsequently these and other words were attributed to them.[39]

In the eighth century, St Germanus of Constantinople promoted the suspicion of heretical interpolations in the compositions of Gregory of Nyssa. Mark of Ephesus repeated this suspicion at the Council of Florence-Ferrara, having noted that those places in which Gregory of Nyssa speaks of

[37] *On the Soul and the Resurrection.*
[38] Cf. *On the Life of Moses* 2.82; *On the Soul and the Resurrection.*
[39] Barsanuphius and John *Direction on the Spiritual Life* 610.

universal salvation "are distortions and interpolations made by certain heretics and Origenists . . . proclaimed with the goal of showing that they have the protection of this saint and great enlightener." Moreover, in St Mark's words, if Gregory of Nyssa actually enforced the teaching of a universal salvation, then "this teaching was the subject of dispute and was not finally condemned and rejected by an opposing viewpoint brought forth at the Fifth Ecumenical Council; therefore there is nothing surprising that he himself, being a man, sinned in this particular instance."[40]

The works of St Maximus the Confessor examine most fully the question of the correlation between God's desire to save all of humanity and man's free will as a possible hindrance to this desire. His eschatological teaching repeatedly became the subject of academic analysis in the twentieth century. Maximus' theological thought is so complicated and dialectic that some scholars see in Maximus a hidden advocate of the teaching on *apokatastasis*;[41] others, on the contrary, suggested that he rejected this teaching and stood for traditional positions.[42]

Above all, St Maximus repeatedly speaks of God's desire to save all of creation and every person. In his words, God "equally loves all people and wants for all to be saved and obtain the knowledge of the truth."[43] Christ is "he who fulfilled in himself the divine salvation for all."[44] He "accepted human nature so as to save the whole race of man from the ancient sin"[45] and "fulfilled the salvation of the human race."[46] Maximus speaks in one of the texts of that final change that will occur "by the voluntary will and election" of people, when "thanks to him, our Savior and God, the universal and natural-in-grace restoration and change of the whole race of man from sin and corruption into eternal life and incorruption will occur at the

[40]Mark of Ephesus *Refutation of the Latin Chapters That Were Presented Concerning the Purifying Fire* II. Cited in Amvrosy (Pogodin), *St Mark of Ephesus and the Union of Florence* (Moscow: 1994), 68–69. The opinion on heretical interpolation in the compositions of Gregory of Nyssa however, is not supported by modern academic criticism. Cf. W. Lackner, "Ein hagiographisches Zeugnis für den Antapodotikos des Patriarchen Germanos I. von Konstantinopel," *Byzantion* 38 (1968), 42–104.

[41]Cf. especially: Hans Urs von Balthasar, *Cosmic Liturgy: The Universe According to Maximus the Confessor* (Einsiedeln: 1961), 355–359. B. Altaner and A. Stuiber, *Patrologie* (Freiburg: 1978), 523.

[42]Cf. P. Sherwood, "The Earlier Ambigua of St Maximus and his Refutation of Origenism," *Studia Anselmiana* 36 (Rome: 1955), 205–222.

[43]*Chapters on Love* 1.61.

[44]*Ambigua.*

[45]*Theological and Polemical Compositions* 8.

[46]*Ambigua.*

completion of the ages."[47] In another text, Maximus describes the hoped-for "completion of the ages" thus:

> Like the soul in the body, the intelligible world abides invisibly, though actually, in the sensory world. And this will be until that time that it does not please him who linked their union, and he will dissolve this link for the sake of the higher and more mysterious economy, at the time of the universal and expected completion of the ages, which we await. Then the world, like man, will die in its manifestation and in the blink of an eye will be restored again from its decrepitude at our resurrection. Then man, like a part with the whole and like the small with the great, will be co-resurrected with the world, having received back the virtue of intransient incorruption.[48]

There is no direct criticism of the Origenist concept of *apokatastasis* in the works of Maximus, although he addresses Gregory of Nyssa's teaching on *apokatastasis* and gives his own interpretation of this teaching. In Maximus' words, the Church knows three meanings of the word *apokatastasis*: first of all, this is a moral rebirth at which the identity "is reborn that realizes the plan of the virtuous life, which is like it"; second, this is a physical rebirth and transfiguration of "all nature at the resurrection, a rebirth into incorruption and immortality"; third, this is "the rebirth of the powers that the soul, fallen under the influence of sin, had before in its state upon the creation." At the universal resurrection, when the body of every person will be restored, "then the damaged powers of the soul . . . cast down through evil, yet still implanted in the soul and nearing the end of all the ages and not finding a place of repose, will come to God who has no end; and therefore, thanks to knowledge, not committed virtue, will the soul retake its powers back and will be restored to its original state, and then it will become clear that the Creator never participated in sin."[49] It is precisely the third meaning of the word *apokatastasis* that, in Maximus the Confessor's opinion, is most frequently found in Gregory of Nyssa.

Maximus decisively rejects this theory as being a sign along with the Origenist theory of the pre-existence of souls. At the same time he offers his own

---

[47] *Commentary on Psalm 60.*
[48] *Mystagogia 7.*
[49] *Questions to Thalassius 13.*

interpretation of the pre-existence of souls, leaning on the traditional teaching of Divine Providence. According to his teaching, all the souls of rational
creatures pre-existed in Divine Providence and at the fulfillment of God's
plan for every soul is its restoration, or *apokatastasis*:

> Each of the rational and thinking creatures—angels and people—by means
> of the plan for which it was created, abides in God and is directed to him,
> and is called and manifested to be "part of God," thanks to the plan
> which, as was already said, pre-existed in God. Thus, obviously, if each
> would be moved in correlation to this plan, then it would be proven in
> God, in whose plan its being pre-exists as an origin and principle, and if
> it does not strive by its own will to receive anything else more preferable
> to its own origin, then it will not move away from God and, moreover,
> thanks to its impulse to become a god and be called a part of God, its
> communion with god is perfected through its obligatory image. While it
> is wise and intellectual by nature, by moving closer to God it perceives its
> own origin and principle, not having any further possibility to move to
> any other place beyond the limits of its own origin and ascent and restora-
> tion in the plan, in conformity to which it was created.[50]

Here, "restoration" is linked to the traditional Eastern Christian teaching
of deification, while deification is perceived as the achievement of the purpose for which man was created. According to Maximus' teaching, this deification should seize all of humanity and the whole universe. In the
eschatological perspective, when Christ unites all that is sensory and rational
into himself, people "will finally find his image, carrying it on themselves
completely whole and unmarred; nor will the shadow of decay touch it, and
with us and through us he will fulfill all of creation in its center, as if it were
a member of his body, and indissolubly unite to himself paradise and the
world, heaven and earth, the sensory and the intelligible." Since Christ himself has a body, senses, soul, and nous, like us, then "taking each part as a
member of the body . . . he divinely joins everything to himself, showing in
this that all creation exists as one, as one identity."[51]

A whole series of other texts ascribed to Maximus' pen shows that he
places great significance on a person's free will in the issue of salvation. In

[50] *Ambigua.*
[51] *Ambigua.*

Maximus' words, Christ "became the path to salvation for all, leading to the Father by means of virtue and knowledge those who wish to follow him on the path of righteousness by observing the divine commandments."[52] In the eschatological Kingdom of God "every rational creature, whether angelic or human, will rejoice and break out in joy (those who did not, by negligence, at all distort the divine purpose, placed in their nature by the Creator)."[53] Interpreting the words of the Prophet Isaiah "and the glory of the Lord shall appear, and all flesh shall see the salvation of God" (Isa 40.5), Maximus clarifies: "All flesh means all faithful, believing flesh," "for not all flesh will see God's glory, since this will not happen with impious flesh."[54] Speaking on deification, Maximus questions: "What can be greater for those worthy . . . in whom God is united with those who became gods and makes all his by his grace?"[55]

Therefore, *apokatastasis* and the final deification of creation are the objectives of St Maximus' absolute eschatological hope, however only those who wish to follow Christ and observe his commandments will participate in this final deification—only the worthy, only the faithful; the impious will end up beyond its boundaries. Whoever then will turn out to be "worthy" and by what criteria will the worthy be separated from the unworthy? Maximus explains this in *Chapters on Love* in the following way: Christ "suffered for all of humanity and gave all equally the hope of the resurrection, although each makes himself worthy either of glory or of punishment."[56]

Thus each person makes himself worthy either of salvation and deification, or of punishment and eternal perdition. In the words of one researcher:

> For Maximus the universal salvific will of God and even the omnipotence in his love and grace are not guarantees for the success of his plan of salvation for all in the history of mankind. . . . Because of the fact that Maximus so paradoxically insists on the significance of a person's role, he is ready even to admit to the non-existence of a divine plan in the fates of separate individuals who depart from the intent, or *logoi* [λόγοι], previously with God at their creation, and preferable to the intent of destructive egocentricity or non-existence.[57]

[52] *To Thalassius* 63.
[53] *Ambigua.*
[54] *To Thalassius* 27.
[55] *Ambigua* 7.
[56] 1.71.
[57] B. Daley, "Apokatastasis and 'Honorable Silence' in the eschatology of St Maximus the

People who have not made their choice in favor of God will be subjected
to tortures, which Maximus labels eternal and without end:

> They will live in the depths of darkness and in oppressive silence, bitterly
> moaning and lamenting their existence and abiding in the deepest wrath.
> . . . They will take the eternal fire and darkness and insatiable worm, they
> will gnash their teeth and weep unceasingly and be in endless terror, from
> which every damned person will strive for endless torture all the more for
> eternity, rather than any other acceptable form of punishment.[58]

Maximus the Confessor is convinced that God will give to each everything necessary for salvation and that at the end he will be "all in all." However, for some of those awarded salvation, union with God will be a source
of joy, and for others, those "unlucky ones," a source of torment:

> Nature does not contain qualities that are supernatural, just as it does not
> contain laws that act against nature. By "supernatural," I mean that divine
> and incomprehensible joy with which God naturally operates when he is
> gracefully united with those who are worthy. By "against nature" I under-
> stand that inexpressible torment caused by the deprivation of that joy
> with which God acts in nature when he is united with the unworthy con-
> trary to grace. God is united with everyone in correlation with the given
> construction of each identity from nature; and to a certain image, known
> only to him, does he give to each a sensitive experience of himself, corre-
> sponding to that image by which each is created, so as to find him who
> is totally united with everything at the end of all the ages.[59]

The meaning of these words is the following: a person is given the freedom to accomplish or not accomplish that original intent for which he or she
existed in Divine Providence. Those who act "according to nature" accomplish it; those who live unnaturally, in sin and vice, destroy it. God equally
loves both one and the other, and does not deprive anyone of his presence
and love.[60] But love, as Isaac the Syrian said, "acts in two ways": it becomes

Confessor," *Maximus Confessor. Actes de Symposium sur Maxime le Confesseur, Fribourg, 2–5 septembre
1980*, Felix Heinzer and Christoph Scönborn, ed. (Éditions Universitaires: Fribourg, Switzerland,
1982), 333.
    [58]*Epistle* 4.
    [59]*To Thalassius* 59.
    [60]Cf. B. Daley, "Apokatastasis and 'Honorable Silence . . . ,'" 339.

a source of joy and blessing only for those who became worthy of salvation and deification, who united themselves with God and became like him.

The Kingdom of Heaven is constructed in such a way so as to be capable of containing all people within itself. The problem is that not every person wants to accept the Kingdom of God as his own home, to become an integral part of it. The possibility for universal salvation, as well as the possibility for eternal torment, directly flows from the free will of a person: as long as there remains even one person who is incapable or does not wish to be reconciled with God, the tortures of abandonment in Hades will be preserved for that person. From God's point of view, everything necessary for the salvation of every person has already been done, and the redemptive act of the God-Man is extended to all humanity. The adoption then of the fruits of Christ's Redemptive Sacrifice depends on the person him- or herself—above all the moral choice that he or she makes during life. Universal salvation is possible insofar as free acceptance of Christ's salvific Good News is possible by all people without exception, insofar as the free choice on behalf of God and the good, free, voluntary, and irrevocable denouncement of evil from all people and every person is possible.

God "will have all men to be saved," says the Apostle Paul (1 Tim 2.4). God will always, eternally desire the salvation of all people, and until the time universal salvation is accomplished, God's will remains unfulfilled. But God will always, eternally respect a person's will and will not save anyone in spite of his will. This is the greatest paradox of the mystery of salvation. If salvation depended only and exclusively on God, everyone would be saved. But since a person's salvation is the fruit of a joint creation, the fruit of the synergy of God and man, then a person's participation in the act of his own salvation is necessary.

The teaching on *apokatastasis* and universal salvation gained a whole group of supporters in the form of the theologians and philosophers of the Russian diaspora in the twentieth century. The consistent and decisive proponents of this teaching were Archpriest Sergius Bulgakov and N.A. Berdiaev. V.N. Lossky was more cautious, yet still spoke out in favor of this teaching. Metropolitan Anthony of Sourozh in particular also repeatedly defended it in his compositions, saying: "The surety of the salvation of all cannot be a surety of faith in the sense that there is no clear, definitive support of this in Holy Scripture, but this can be a surety of hope, since knowing God as we know him, we have the right to hope for everything." The phrase "eternal torment" is used in the Gospel; however, there is a difference between divine eternity and created eternity: the latter "is confined by the limits of time." If the devil succeeded "in creating a self-sufficient, eternal kingdom, independent from God," then this would be his victory over God: "he will have acquired that which he wanted, to be an indivisible king of eternity, of co-eternal Hades, parallel with God."[61]

However, the opinions of individual theologians and philosophers defending the teaching of universal salvation do not grant it legitimacy as a teaching of the Church. The Church condemned the concept of *apokatastasis*. Another matter in the spiritual life of the Christian is the issue of people's salvation that can be thought of from a different perspective—as a subject of hope and prayer.

St Silouan of Mount Athos

In this sense the response of St Silouan of Mount Athos to the monk who claimed, "God will punish all atheists. They will burn in everlasting fire" is characteristic. Silouan, upon hearing this, said with emotion: "Tell me, supposing you went to paradise and there looked down and saw somebody burning in hellfire—would you feel happy?" The monk answered: "It can't be helped. It would be their own fault." The elder then said sorrowfully: "Love could not bear that. . . . We must pray for all." His biographer writes, "And he did, indeed, pray for all men. . . . His soul was grieved by the realization that people lived in ignorance of God and his love, and with all his strength he prayed . . . for the living and the dead, for friend and foe, for all men."[62]

St Silouan considered the possibility of the torments of Hell only in relation to himself: "Soon I shall die, and my accursed soul will descend into hell."[63] Silouan said in reference to other people: "We should keep in mind only this thought—that all might be saved."[64] The genuine Christian attitude toward the theme of eternal torments should be to consider its possibility

[61]Anthony (Bloom), *God and Man* (Moscow: 1993), 59–65.
[62]Sophrony (Sakharov), *The Monk of Mount Athos* Rosemary Edmonds, tr. (Crestwood, NY: St Vladimir's Seminary Press, 1973), 32–33.
[63]Ibid., 117.
[64]Ibid., 119.

only as applicable to oneself, but not applicable to others. In the words of Olivier Clement, "it is impossible to speak of Hell for others in the spiritual sense. The theme of Hades can be discussed only in the terms You and I. The warnings in the Gospels are addressed to me, they reveal the seriousness and tragedy of my own spiritual fate."[65]

The ancient book of the sayings and the lives of the Egyptian desert fathers contains the story of Abba Anthony the Great, who once heard a voice during prayer in his cell: "Anthony! You have still not achieved the worth of the leather tanner who lives in Alexandria." The next morning the elder got himself to Alexandria and went to the leather tanner pointed out to him and said: "Tell me of your deeds, because I came here from the desert for this reason." The leather tanner was greatly surprised at the saint's request and answered him humbly: "I do not know about me, whether I did anything good. For this reason I get up early from bed, and rather than leaving for work, I say to myself: all the inhabitants of this city, from the greatest to the least, will enter the Kingdom of God for their virtuous deeds, but I alone will go unto eternal tortures for my sins. And these words I repeat in my heart before I go to sleep." Upon hearing this, Anthony answered: "Truly, my son, you, a skilled craftsman sitting quietly in his home, have gained the Kingdom of God; but I, although I have spent my whole life in the desert, yet I have not gained spiritual wisdom, I have not reached the level of consciousness that you express with your words."[66]

This patristic story presents the one perspective by which the Christian is allowed to think of universal salvation: "all will be saved, only I will perish." Such a mentality has nothing in common with Origenist *apokatastasis*. It flows from the inner spiritual experience of a man deeply conscious of his sinfulness and brought to repentance for his own sins and imperfection. Such repentance necessarily includes thoughts of eternal torments, not for others, but for oneself, as well as the hope for salvation, not for oneself, but for everyone else.

---

[65] *Sources*, 296.

[66] *Paterikon: A Selection of the Sayings of the Holy Monks and Stories from their Lives, compiled by Bishop Ignatius (Brianchaninov)* (Brussels: 1963), 41.

32

"New Heaven" and "New Earth"

Detail of the icon "The Apocalypse." Cathedral of the Dormition in the Moscow Kremlin. 15th c.

THE CHURCH'S CONDEMNATION OF THE TEACH-
ING on *apokatastasis* does not at all change the
belief that God will be "all in all" in the end, that
death will finally be defeated and annulled, that a
"new heaven" and a "new earth" will be inaugu-
rated. This belief is based on a whole series of testimonies in the New Testament Scriptures that speak
of the final change and transfiguration of the whole
creation. Among such testimonies, the words of the
Apostle Paul in the First Epistle to the Corinthians
address most of all the final abolition of death,
which will follow after the Second Coming of Christ:

> For as in Adam all die, even so in Christ shall all be made alive. But every
> man in his own order: Christ the first fruits; afterward those who are
> Christ's at his coming. Then comes the end, when he has delivered up the
> kingdom to God, even the Father; when he has put down all rule and all
> authority and power. For he must reign, until he has put all enemies under
> his feet. The last enemy to be destroyed is death. For he has put all things
> under his feet. . . . When all things are subdued to him, then shall the Son
> also himself be subject unto him that put all things under him, that God
> may be all in all. (1 Cor 15.22–28)

Further on, while developing the teaching on the resurrection of the dead,
the Apostle Paul returns to the idea of the abolition of death and Christ's
final victory over it:

> Behold, I show you a mystery: We shall not all sleep, but we shall all be
> changed, in a moment, in the twinkling of an eye, at the last trumpet. For

the trumpet shall sound, and the dead shall be raised incorruptible, and we shall be changed. . . . When this corruptible has put on incorruption, and this mortal has put on immortality, then shall be brought to pass the saying that is written, Death is swallowed up in victory. O death, where is your sting? . . . But thanks be to God, who gives us the victory through our Lord Jesus Christ. (1 Cor 15.51–57)

In the above text from the Apostle Paul, nothing is said about whether all people will participate in the final transfiguration and change of creation or only some of its parts. On the one hand, Paul presents this event as universal, as touching all of humanity and the whole universe. On the other hand, in saying "we," he means first of all Christians living in the hope of the resurrection of the dead and Christ's final victory. The eschatological Kingdom of God is the kingdom of the saved, but will all enter into this Kingdom?

Revelation provides the answer to this question, painting a picture of a new heaven and a new earth that will be ushered in, since "the first heaven and the first earth had passed away, and there was no more sea" (Rev 21.1). Here the eschatological state of transfigured creation is presented in the form of a new Jerusalem, descending from heaven: this heavenly city is "the tabernacle of God . . . among men. He will dwell with them; they shall be his people, and God himself will be with them, and be their God. And God shall wipe away all tears from their eyes; and there shall be no more death, neither sorrow, nor crying, neither shall there be any more pain; for the former things have passed away" (Rev 21.2–4). Entering into this heavenly city will be "the nations. . . . And there shall in no wise enter into it any thing that defiles, neither anything that works abomination, or makes a lie, but those who are written in the Lamb's book of life" (Rev 21.24, 27). Revelation says of those who will remain outside the heavenly city: "But the fearful, and unbelieving, and the abominable, and murderers, and whoremongers, and sorcerers, and idolaters, and all liars, shall have their part in the lake that burns with fire and brimstone, that is the second death" (Rev 21.8). Therefore the new Jerusalem is the Kingdom of the saved; however, not all people will enter into it: "Blessed are those who do his commandments, that they may have right to the tree of life, and may enter in through the gates into the city. For without are dogs, and sorcerers, and whoremongers, and murderers, and idolaters, and whoever loves and makes a lie" (Rev 22.14–15).

Thus, on the one hand, Holy Scripture teaches that some will remain "until the times of restitution of all things" (Acts 3.21), when God will "be all in all" (1 Cor 15.28). On the other hand, it is clear that along with the Kingdom of the saved, Scripture refers to those who will not enter into this Kingdom and will remain outside it. Such an understanding of Christ's eschatological victory over Hell and death is contained in the majority of the holy fathers of the Eastern Church, including, as we have already seen, in Maximus the Confessor.

What will the eschatological Kingdom of God be like for those who manage to enter it? And what will the source blessing be for those inhabitants of paradise? According to the teaching of the Fathers of the Church, the chief and only source of blessing in paradise will be God himself. Gregory of Nyssa writes:

> But, further, the Divine Being is the fountain of all virtue. Therefore, those who have parted with evil will be united with him; and so, as the Apostle says, God will be "all in all" (1 Cor 15.28). . . . For while our present life is active amongst a variety of multiform conditions, and the things we have relations with are numerous, for instance, time, air, locality, food and drink, clothing, sunlight, lamplight, and other necessities of life, none of which, many though they be, are God—that blessed state which we hope for is in need of none of these things, but the Divine Being will become all, and instead of all, to us, distributing himself proportionately to every need of that existence. . . . God becomes, to those who deserve it, locality, and home, and clothing, and food, and drink, and light, and riches, and dominion. . . . He that becomes "all" things will be "in all" things.[1]

Isaac the Syrian says that the heavenly blessing is a person's communion with God's love, which is "the tree of life" and "the heavenly bread," that is, God himself:

> Paradise is the love of God, in which is the enjoyment of all blessings. There the blessed Paul took his fill of the super-substantial food and, when he tasted of the tree of life that was there, he cried out saying: "No eye has seen, nor ear heard, nor the human heart conceived, what God

---

[1] *On the Soul and the Resurrection.*

has prepared for those who love him" (1 Cor 2.9). Adam was cast from this tree due to the devil's counsel. The tree of life is God's love from which Adam fell. . . . So long as we do not have love, our actions are thorns on the earth. . . . But when we acquire love, then we begin to eat of the heavenly bread. . . . This heavenly bread is Christ, who has come down from heaven and given life to the world (Jn 6.33). . . . Thus those who live in love reap life from God, and by this the world . . . breathes the air of the resurrection. The righteous partake of the resurrection by this air.[2]

The life of the future age is "constant and unspeakable repose in God."[3] This life "does not have an end or change."[4] Bodily activity there is occupied with intellectual action, which is "a delightful glance and an undiffused vision."[5] In the Kingdom of Heaven, a person's nous will be busy in contemplation of divine beauty in a condition of ceaseless amazement: "Human nature will not cease to be amazed by God there, having no thought at all of created things. . . . But as all the beauty of creation will be a restoration lower than God's beauty, then how can the nous consciously depart from God's beauty?"[6]

The hierarchical structure of the universe will disappear in the future age, according to which divine revelations are transmitted from God to the higher ranks of angels, and by their aid to the lower ranks and to mankind:

> Such order will be annulled in the future age because no one will accept from another the revelation of God's glory, to the right worship and rejoicing of one's soul, but each one by virtue of its powers will be given that which is due to him in terms of ascetical deeds and in worthiness from the Lord directly; and one will not receive this gift from another, as it is now. For there is neither a student nor a teacher nor one who has need for another to make up for one's deficiencies there. There is one Giver there, directly bestowing the ability to accept, and all accept from him the acquisition of heavenly happiness. There, all ranks of students and teachers are ceased, and the speedy wishes of everyone will go to him who is One.[7]

[2] Homily 83.
[3] Isaac the Syrian On the Divine Mysteries 18.3.
[4] Chapters on Knowledge I 19.
[5] On the Divine Mysteries 8.2.
[6] Homily 80.
[7] Isaac the Syrian Homily 18.

In the future, no one will enter the blessedness by force: each one has his or her own choice to make in favor of God. This choice is made by people during earthly life and is expressed in denying the passions and in repentance: "There is no coercion of any kind, but no one will inherit glory against their will, nor will they inherit it without repentance; but all are welcome to God's wisdom by choosing good by their free will and thus gaining access to him."[8] The future blessedness will become the destiny of those who already reached "the promised land" in their earthly life and united themselves to God. However, those who died in the hope of reaching the promised land, though they may never have seen it nearby, are not excluded from the Kingdom of Heaven. Not having achieved perfection, though striving for it, they will be like the Old Testament righteous who never saw Christ in life, but hoped in him.[9]

The entrance into the Kingdom of Heaven will be found in various degrees of proximity to God, in correlation with the capabilities of each person to contain the divine light. However, the various degrees will not signify a hierarchical inequality amongst the saved; there will be the highest degree of communion with God for each person in his or her own measure:

The Savior, with many who abide in the Father, names different levels of knowledge of those dwelling in that country, that is discrepancies and the difference in spiritual gifts that they enjoy by virtue of this knowledge. For it is not the difference of places, but the degrees of gifts that he called many of those who abide. As the material sun is enjoyed by each according to the purity and admissibility of the power of vision . . . so in the future age all the righteous will abide unseparated in one land, but each one will be seen in his or her own way as one with the intellectual sun and by their own worthiness will be drawn into joy and happiness. . . . No one sees the merits of one's friend as higher or lower so that if one would see the highest blessing of a friend and one's own

Detail of the icon "The Symbol of Faith." Moscow. 17th c.

[8]Isaac the Syrian *On the Divine Mysteries* 10.20.
[9]*Homily* 66.

deprivation, this would not be a reason for grief and sadness. Indeed this will not be there, where there is no grief or sighing! On the contrary, each one will rejoice according to their merit, within their merit.[10]

In the words of Gregory the Theologian, people in the future age will reach a state of complete deification and likeness to God:

> "God will be all in all" (1 Cor 15.28) at the time of restoration . . . when we are no longer what we are now, a multiplicity of impulses and emotions, with little or nothing of God in us, but are fully like God, with room for God and God alone. This is the "maturity" towards which we are speeding. Paul himself is a special witness here. . . . I quote: "Where there is neither Greek nor Jew, circumcision nor uncircumcision, Barbarian, Scythian, bond nor free; but Christ is all in all" (Col 3.11).[11]

Gregory the Theologian thinks of the Kingdom of Heaven, to which the righteous attain after the universal resurrection, as a kingdom of light where people, having been delivered from the perversion of earthly life, will shine "as lesser lights circling round the great Light."[12] This is the kingdom "where the sanctuary of all those rejoicing and singing the ceaseless hymn, where the voice of those rejoicing and voice of joy, where the most perfect and purest vision of God is, which we now understand only in riddles and shadows."[13] The final union of mankind with God, the communion with the divine light, and the restoration and deification of all human nature, all come to pass in this Kingdom.

[10] *Homily* 58.
[11] *Oration* 30.6 (Crestwood, NY: 2002), 98.
[12] *Oration* 18.42.
[13] *Oration* 24.19.

Abbreviations

ANF = Ante-Nicene Fathers. Philip Schaff, ed. Grand Rapids, MI. Eerdmans, 1984. Early Church Fathers, CCEL.

CCEL = Christian Classics Ethereal Library at Calvin College. CD-ROM. Version 4. Grand Rapids, MI: Calvin College, 2001.

CCSG = Corpus Christianorum, series graeca.

CSEL = Corpus Scriptorum Ecclesiasticorum Latinorum.

CSCO = Corpus Scriptorum Christianorum Orientalium. Edited by I.B. Chabot et al. Paris, 1903–

GPS = Γρηγορίου τοῦ Παλαμᾶ συγγράμματα. Thessaloniki: 1988.

NPNF-1 = Nicene and Post-Nicene Fathers, Series 1. Philip Schaff, ed. Grand Rapids, MI: Eerdmans, 1984. Early Church Fathers, CCEL.

NPNF-2 = Nicene and Post-Nicene Fathers, Series 2. Philip Schaff, ed. Grand Rapids, MI: Eerdmans, 1984. Early Church Fathers, CCEL.

PG = Patrologia graeca. Edited by J.-P. Migne. 162 vols. Paris, 1857–1886.

PL = Patrologia latina. Edited by J.-P. Migne. 217 vols. Paris, 1844–1864.

SC = Sources Chrétiennes.

Φιλοκαλία = Φιλοκαλία τῶν ἱερῶν νηπτικῶν. Thessaloniki: 1972–1976.

Bibliography

"Acts of the Ecumenical Councils" 4. Saint Petersburg: 1996.

Afanasiev, Nikolai. *The Church of the Holy Spirit*. Paris: 1971. [Russian].

Altaner, B. and A. Stuiber. *Patrologie*. Freiburg: 1978.

Ambrose of Milan. *On Repentance*. Translated by H. De Romestin, with the assistance of E. De Romestin and H. T. F. Duckworth. NPNF-2, vol. 10.

Amphilochius of Iconium. *On the True Faith*. *Eastern Fathers and Teachers of the Church of the Fourth Century* vol 2. Edited by Met. Hilarion (Alfeyev). Moscow: 2000. [Russian].

_____. *To Seleucus*. *Eastern Fathers and Teachers of the Church of the Fourth Century* vol 2. Edited by Met. Hilarion (Alfeyev). Moscow: 2000. [Russian].

Amvrosy (Pogodin). *St Mark of Ephesus and the Union of Florence*. Moscow: 1994. [Russian].

Anastasius of Sinai. *The Guidebook*. PG 89:36–310.

_____. *On the Creation of Man*. PG 44:1328–1345, PG 89:1151–1180.

_____. *Oration on the Holy Meeting*. *Venerable Anastasius of Sinai*. Edited by A.I. Sidorov. Moscow: 2003. [Russian].

Andrew of Caesarea. *Interpretation on Revelation*. PG 106:216–785.

Andrew of Crete. *Orations*. PG 97:805–1304.

Anthony (Bloom). *God and Man*. Moscow: 1993. [Russian].

Anthony the Great. *Exhortations to Monks*. PG 40:1079–1084.

_____. *Instruction on the Life in Christ*. *The* Philokalia *in a Russian Translation*, enlarged edition, vols. 1–5. Paris: 1988. [Russian].

_____. *Teachings on Good Morals*. *The* Philokalia *in a Russian Translation*, enlarged edition, vols. 1–5. Paris: 1988. [Russian].

Athanasius of Alexandria. *Against Apollinarius*. PG 26:1093–1165.

_____. *Against the Arians*. NPNF-2, vol. 4.

_____. *Commentary on Psalm 17* I. PG 27:109–124.

_____. *Definitions*. PG 28:533–553 (spuria).

_____. *Letter to Epictetus*. NPNF-2, vol. 4.

_____. *On the Exposition of Dionysius*. NPNF-2, vol. 4.

_____. *On the Holy Spirit*. NPNF-2, vol. 4.

_____. *On the Incarnation of the Word*. NPNF-2, vol. 4.

————. *Oration Against the Gentiles*. NPNF-2, vol. 4.

————. *To Adelphius*. NPNF-2, vol. 4.

————. *To the Bishop of Antioch*. PG 28:597–708 (spuria).

Athenagoras of Athens. *Apology*; *On the Resurrection of the Dead*. ANF, vol. 2.

Augustine. *The City of God*. NPNF-1, vol. 2.

————. *Concerning Man's Perfection in Righteousness*. NPNF-1, vol. 5.

————. *Contra epistolam Manichaei quam vocant fundamenti* liber 1. PL 42:173–206; CSEL 25/1:193–248.

————. *Epistles*. NPNF-1, vol. 1.

————. *Letters*. NPNF-1, vol. 1.

————. *On Baptism*. NPNF-1, vol. 4.

————. *On the Book of Genesis* 12. PL 34:245–486; CSEL 52:231–1873.

————. *On the Trinity*. Translated by Arthur West Haddan, with William G. T. Shedd. NPNF-1, vol. 3

————. *On True and False Repentance*. PL 40:1113–1130 (spuria).

————. *Psalm against the Donatist Party*. PL 43:23–32.

————. *Seventeen Questions Concerning Matthew*. PL 35:1321–1364; CCSL 44B.

————. *A Treatise on the Predestination of the Saints*. NPNF-1, vol. 5.

————. *Treatise on Rebuke and Grace*. NPNF-1, vol. 5.

Balthasar, Hans Urs von. *Liturgie Cosmique: Maxime le Confesseur*. Paris: 1947.

————. *A Theology of History*. Moscow: 2001. [Russian].

————, and A. Grillmeier. *Le Mystère Pascal*. Paris: 1972.

Barsanuphius and John. *Direction for the Spiritual Life*. Volos: 1960. [Greek].

"Basic Principles of the Russian Orthodox Church of Relation to Non-Orthodox." Moscow: 2000. [Russian].

Basil the Great. *Against Eunomius*. Edited by B. Sesboüé, G.-M. de Durand, and L. Doutreleau. Paris: 1982–1983.

————. *Conversation against the Sabellians*. PG 31:599–617.

————. *Epistles*. PG 32:219–1111.

————. *Homilies*. PG 31.163–618.

————. *Homily on the Hexaemeron*. NPNF-2, vol. 8.

————. *Homily on Psalm 7*. PG 29:227–249.

————. *Homily on Psalm 28*. PG 30:71–81.

————. *Homily on Psalm 33*. *The Works of Our Father Among the Saints Basil the Great, Archbishop of Caesarea in Cappadocia*. Moscow: 1993. [Russian].

————. *Homily on Psalm 48*. PG 29:432–460.

————. *Interpretation on Isaiah*. PG 30:117–665.

————. *The Letters*. R. Deferrari, trans. Volume III. Loeb Classical Library vol. 243. London: 1930. Reprinted by Harvard University Press.

_____. *On the Holy Spirit*. David Anderson, trans. Crestwood, NY: St Vladimir's Seminary Press, 1980.

Basil of Seleucia. *Oration 2: On Adam*. PG 85:37–49

Berdiaev, Nikolai. "Aleksei Stepanovich Khomiakov." *Sobraniye sochinenii* 5. Paris: 1997. [Russian].

_____. *Dukh i real'nost'* [Spirit and reality]. Moscow: 2003. [Russian].

_____. *Philosophy of the Free Spirit*. Paris: 1927–28. [Russian].

Bolotov, V.V. *Origen's Teaching of the Holy Trinity*. Saint Petersburg: 1879. [Russian].

Bouyer, Louis. *On the Bible and the Gospel*. Brussels: 1988. [Russian].

Bulgakov, S.N. *Orthodox Christianity, 3rd ed*. Paris: 1989. [Russian].

Calvin, John. *Instruction in the Christian Faith*. Moscow: 1998. [Russian].

Cheremukhin, Pavel. "The Council of Constantinople (1157) and St Nicholas, Bishop of Mephon." *Theological Works* 1 (Moscow, 1960), 85–110. [Russian].

Christian Dogmatics: Dogmatic Texts of the Teaching of the Catholic Church from the Third to the Twentieth Centuries. Saint Petersburg: 2002. [Russian].

Clement of Alexandria. *Exhortation to the Heathen*. ANF, vol. 2.

_____. *Pedagogue*. ANF, vol. 2.

_____. *Stromata*. ANF, vol. 2.

Clement, Olivier. *Sources: Theology of the Fathers of the Ancient Church*. Moscow: 1994. [Russian].

Clement of Rome. *First Epistle to the Corinthians*. ANF, vol. 1.

_____. *Second Epistle to the Corinthians. Early Church Fathers: Anthology*. Brussels: 1988. [Russian].

Cyprian of Carthage. *Epistle to Quintus Concerning the Baptism of* Heretics. ANF, vol. 5.

_____. *On Mortality*. ANF, vol. 5.

_____. *The Unity of the Catholic Church. On the Church: Select Treatises*. Allen Brent, trans. Crestwood, NY: St Vladimir's Seminary Press, 2006.

Cyril of Alexandria. *Commentary on John*. http://www.monachos.net/content/patristics/patristictexts/345-cyril-commentary-john-link.

_____. *Defense to the Emperor Theodosius*. PG 76:453–488.

_____. *Interpretation of Romans*. PG 74:773–856.

_____. *On the Holy Symbol*. PG 75:9–656

_____. *On the Incarnation*. PG 75:1413–1420.

_____. *On Worship in Spirit and Truth*. PG 68:133–1125.

_____. *The Twelve Chapters*. PG 76:293–312.

Cyril of Jerusalem. *Catechetical Lectures*. Translated by Edwin Hamilton Gifford. NPNF-2, vol. 7.

_____. *Mystagogical Catechesis. Lectures on the Christian Sacraments*. F. L. Cross, ed. Crestwood, NY: St Vladimir's Seminary Press, 1977.

Daley, B. "Apokatastasis and 'Honorable Silence' in the Eschatology of St Maximus the Confessor." *Maximus Confessor. Actes de Symposium sur Maxime le Confesseur, Fribourg, 2–5 septembre 1980*. Felix Heinzer and Christoph Scönborn, ed. Fribourg, Switzerland: Éditions Universitaires, 1982.

Diadochos of Photiki. *100 Chapters. The* Philokalia *in a Russian Translation*, enlarged edition, vols. 1–5. Paris: 1988. [Russian].

_____. *Ascetical Oration*. Edited by E. des Places. SC 5-bis: 1955

_____. *Oration on the Ascension*. Edited by E. des Places. SC 5-bis: 1955

Diogenes Laertius. *Lives and Opinions of Eminent Philosophers*. Moscow: 1979. [Russian].

Dionysius the Areopagite. *Celestial Hierarchy*. http://www.monachos.net/content/patristics/patristictexts/346.

_____. *Ecclesiastical Hierarchy*. http://www.monachos.net/content/patristics/patristictexts/347.

_____. *Mystical Theology*. http://www.monachos.net/content/patristics/patristictexts/348.

_____. *On the Divine Names*. Edited by B. R. Suchla. Berlin: 1990.

Divine Liturgy. South Canaan, PA: St Tikhon's Seminary Press, 2008.

Elias of Crete. *Anthology*. Φιλοκαλία 2:289–298.

Ephraim the Syrian. *Hymns on Faith*. Translated by J.B. Morris. NPNF-2, vol. 13.

_____. *Nisibene Hymn*. Translated by J.T. Sarsfield Stopford. NPNF-2, vol. 13.

_____. *On the Fear of God and on the Last Judgment*. Cited in: *Works*, vol. 4. Sergiev Posad: 1900. [Russian].

_____. *Words on Faith* (CSCO 212, Scr. syri 88). Edited by E. Beck. Louvain: 1961.

Epiphanius of Cyprus. *Panarion*. Edited by K. Holl. Leipzig: 1915.

Eusebius of Caesarea. *Commentary on the Gospel*. Moscow: 1993. [Russian].

_____. *Ecclesiastical History*. Translated by Arthur Cushman McGiffert. NPNF-2, vol. 1.

Evagrius of Pontus. *Gnostic Chapters*. A. Guillaumont. 1958.

_____. *The Knower*. Edited by A. Guillaumont and C. Guillaumont. 1989.

_____. *On Prayer*. Translation by Luke Dysinger, O.S.B. http://www.ldysinger.com/Evagrius/03_Prayer/00a_start.htm.

_____. *On Tempting Thoughts*. J. Muyldermans. *A travers la tradition manuscrite d'Evagre le Pontique*. Bibliothèque du Muséon, 3. Louvain: 1932.

_____. *Skemmata*. J. Muyldermans. *Evagriana et Nouveaux fragments inédits*. Paris: 1931.

Florensky, Pavel. "Theological Legacy." *Theological Works* 17, 91. [Russian].

Florovsky, Georges. *Dogma and History*. Moscow: 1995. [Russian].

_____. *Eastern Fathers of the Fifth to Eighth Centuries*. Paris: 1937. [Russian].

_____. *Selected Theological Writings*. Moscow: 2000. [Russian].

_____. "On the Limits of the Church." *Church Quarterly Review*. 1933. [Russian].

Formula of Concord. Translated by K. Komarov. Sterling Heights: 1996. [Russian].

The Gospel of Nicodemus. Cited in: *Pamyatniki drevnej christianskoj pis'mennosti v russkom perevode*, vol. 1. Moscow: 1860. [Russian].

Gregory of Cyprus. *On the Procession of the Holy Spirit*. PG 142:269–300.

Gregory Dialogus [Gregory I, the Great, Pope of Rome]. *Homilies on the Gospel*. Translated by James Barmby. NPNF-2, vol. 13.

_____. *Letters*. Translated by James Barmby. NPNF-2, vol. 13.

Gregory of Nyssa. *Against Eunomius*. Translated by William Moore and Henry Austin Wilson. NPNF-2, vol. 5.

_____. *Against the Teaching of Fate. Eastern Fathers and Teachers of the Church of the Fourth Century* vol 2. Edited by Hilarion (Alfeyev). Moscow: 1996. [Russian].

_____. *Great Catechetical Oration*. Translated by William Moore and Henry Austin Wilson. NPNF-2, vol. 5.

_____. *On Bliss (On the Beatitudes). Gregorii Nysseni Opera* VII. Edited by J.F. Callahan. Leiden-New York-Cologne: 1992.

_____. *On Holy Pascha*. PG 46:600–693.

_____. *On Infants' Early Deaths*. Translated by William Moore and Henry Austin Wilson. NPNF-2, vol. 5.

_____. *On Not Three Gods*. Translated by William Moore and Henry Austin Wilson. NPNF-2, vol. 5.

_____. *On the Life of Moses. Gregorii Nysseni Opera* VII, I: *De vita Moysis*. Edited by H. Musurillo. Leiden: 1964.

_____. *On the Making of Man*. Translated by William Moore and Henry Austin Wilson. NPNF-2, vol. 5.

_____. *On the Protomartyr Stephen*. PG 46:701–721.

_____. *On the Soul and the Resurrection*. Translated by William Moore and Henry Austin Wilson. NPNF-2, vol. 5.

_____. *Oration on the Meaning of "In the Image."* PG 44:1328–1345 (dubia).

_____. *Sermon on the Divinity of the Son and Spirit (De Deitate Filii et Spiritus Sancti)*. PG 46:553–576.

_____. *To Ablabius*. Translated by William Moore and Henry Austin Wilson. NPNF-2, vol. 5.

_____. *To the Greeks*. PG 45:176–186.

Gregory Palamas. *Against Akyndinos.* GPS 3:39–506.

————. *Apodictic Treatise.* GPS 1:23–153.

————. *Epistle to John Gavras.* GPS 2:325–362.

————. *Homilies.* PG 151–545.

————. *Natural Chapters.* Φιλοκαλία 4:134–187.

————. *On the Worship of Communion.* GPS 2:137–163.

————. *To the Most Reverend Nun Xenia.* Φιλοκαλία 4:91–115.

————. *Triads.* GPS 1:359–694.

Gregory of Sinai. *Chapters on the Commandments and Dogma.* Φιλοκαλία 4:31–62.

Gregory the Theologian. *Autobiographical Poems.* PG 37:969–1452.

————. *Christ the Sufferer.* "La passion de Christ. Tragèdie." Edited by A. Tuiller. 1969.

————. *Dogmatic Verses.* PG 37:397–522.

————. *Letter 101. On God and Christ.* Frederick Williams and Lionel Wickham, trans. Crestwood, NY: St Vladimir's Seminary Press, 2002.

————. *Moral Poems.* PG 37:521–968.

————. *On Oneself and on Bishops. Church and Time* vol 1 (22). Translated by Aleksei Yastrebov. 2003. [Russian].

————. *Oration 1, 38–40, 45. Festal Orations.* Nonna Verna Harrison, trans. Crestwood, NY: St Vladimir's Seminary Press, 2008.

————. *Oration 2, 4, 6, 7, 10, 11, 17, 18, 20, 21, 24, 25. 32, 34, 37, 42, 43, 44.* NPNF-2, vol. 7.

————. *Oration 27–31. On God and Christ.* Frederick Williams and Lionel Wickham, trans. Crestwood, NY: St Vladimir's Seminary Press, 2002.

————. *Poems on Others.* PG 37:1451–1600.

Grigorii (Yaroschevsky). *Explanation of difficult Passages in the First Epistle of the Holy Apostle Peter.* Simferopol': 1902. [Russian].

Hermas. *The Shepherd.* ANF, vol. 2.

Hilarion (Alfeyev). *Christ the Conqueror of Hell: The Descent into Hades from an Orthodox Perspective.* Crestwood, NY: St Vladimir's Seminary Press, 2009.

————. *Orthodox Christianity I.* Basil Bush, trans. Crestwood, NY: St Vladmir's Seminary Press, 2011.

Hilarion (Troitsky). "Holy Scripture and the Church." *Works: In Three Volumes.* Moscow: 2004. [Russian].

————. *Works.* 3 vols. Moscow: 2004. [Russian].

Hippolytus of Rome. *On Christ and the Antichrist.* ANF, vol. 5.

Honorius of Autun. *The Eighth Book of Questions on Angels and Man.* PL 172:1197.

Ignatius. *Epistle to the Ephesians.* ANF, vol. 1.

————. *Epistle to the Magnesians.* ANF, vol. 1.

_____. *Epistle to the Philadelphians.* ANF, vol. 1.

_____. *Epistle to the Smyrnaeans.* ANF, vol. 1.

_____. *Epistle to the Trallians.* ANF, vol. 1.

Ignatius (Brianchaninov). *Writings.* 5 vols., 3rd ed. St Petersburg: 1905. [Russian].

Irenaeus of Lyons. *Against Heresies.* ANF, vol. 1.

Isaac the Recluse. *Orations. The* Philokalia *in a Russian Translation,* enlarged edition, vols. 1–5. Paris: 1988. [Russian].

Isaac the Syrian. *Ascetical Homilies.* Translated from the Greek by S. Sobolevsky. Sergiev Posad: 1911. [Russian].

_____. *Chapters on Knowledge. Church and Time* vol. 4 (13). Translated by Hilarion (Alfeyev). 2000. [Russian].

_____. *On the Divine Mysteries* (CSCO 554, Scriptores syri 224). Edited by Sebastian Brock. Louvain: 1995.

_____. *Orations. De perfection religiosa.* Edited by Paulus Bedjan. Leipzig: 1909.

Isidore of Pelusium. *Letter 629, to Paul.* PG 78:177–1645.

Jacob Aphrahat. *Orations.* NPNF-2, vol. 13.

Jerome. *Against Helvidius.* PL 23:193A–216B.

John Chrysostom. *Against the Anomians.* PG 48:623–692.

_____. *Catechetical Oration on Holy Pascha.* PG 59:721–724 (spuria).

_____. *Homilies on Genesis.* http://www.scribd.com/doc/63012934/Homilies-on-Genesis-Saint-John-Chrysostom.

_____. *Homilies on the Gospel According to St John.* NPNF-1, vol. 14.

_____. *Homilies on Romans.* NPNF-1, vol. 11.

_____. *Homily in the Church of the Apostle Thomas.* PG 63:473–478.

_____, *Homily on Acts.* NPNF-1, vol. 11.

_____. *Homily on the Cemetery and the Cross.* PG 49:393–398.

_____. *Homily on the Cross and the Thief.* PG 49:399–408.

_____. *Homily on First Corinthians.* NPNF-1, vol. 12.

_____. *Homily on Hebrews.* NPNF-1, vol. 14.

_____. *Homily on John.* PG 59:23–482.

_____. *Homily on the Martyrs.* PG 50:645–654.

_____. *Homily on the Martyrs Juventinus and Maximinus.* PG 50:571–578.

_____. *Homily on Matthew.* NPNF-1, vol. 10.

_____. *Homily on Repentance.* PG 49:277–350.

_____. *Homily on the Second Epistle to the Thessalonians.* NPNF-1, vol. 13.

_____. *On the Enjoyment of Future Blessings.* PG 51:347–354.

_____. *On the Priesthood.* Graham Neville, trans. Crestwood NY: St Vladimir's Seminary Press, 1977.

_____. *Oration on the Martyr Romanus.* PG 50:605–612.

John of Damascus. *Apologetic Treatises Against Those Decrying the Holy Images. Orationes de imaginibus tres.* Edited by B. Kotter. PTS 17. 1975.

_____. *Dialogue against the Manicheans.* PG 94:1505–1584.

_____. *An Exact Exposition of the Orthodox Faith.* http://www.orthodox.net/ fathers/exactidx.html.

_____. *On the Dormition of Mary: Early Patristic Homilies: On the Dormition of the Holy Mother of God.* Brian E. Daley, trans. Crestwood, NY: St Vladimir's Seminary Press, 1998.

John Duns Scotus. *Opus Oxoniense.* Cited in: Florovsky, Georges. *Dogma and History.* Moscow: 1995. 155. [Russian].

_____. *Reportata Parisiensa.* Cited in: Florovsky, Georges. *Dogma and History.* Moscow: 1995. 155–156. [Russian].

John of Karpathos. *Exhortatory Chapters.* Φιλοκαλία 1:276–296.

John of the Ladder. *The Ladder of Divine Ascent.* Colm Luibheid and Norman Russell, trans. New York: Paulist Press, 1982.

John (Zizioulas). *Being as Communion.* Moscow: 2006. [Russian].

Justin Martyr. *Dialogue with Trypho.* ANF, vol. 1.

_____. *First Apology.* ANF, vol. 1.

_____. *Fragments.* ANF, vol. 1.

_____. *Second Apology.* ANF, vol. 1.

Kaiser, W.C. *The Messiah in the Old Testament.* Carlisle: 1995.

Kallistos Katafygiotis. *On Unity with God.* PG 147:835–942.

Karayannis, Basil. *Maximus the Confessor: the Essence and Energies of God.* Paris: 1993. [French].

Καρμίρις, I.N. ʿΗ εἰς ἅδου κάθοδος ᾿Ιησοῦ Χριστοῦ. Athens: 1939.

Kartashev, A.V. *Old Testament Biblical Criticism.* Paris: 1947. [Russian].

Khomiakov, A.S. *Izbranniye sochineniya.* NY: 1955.

_____. *The One Church.* Moscow: 2005. [Russian].

Kiprian (Kern). *Antropologia sv. Grigoriya Palamy.* Moscow: 1996.

Lackner, W. "Ein hagiographisches Zeugnis für den Antapodotikos des Patriarchen Germanos I. von Konstantinopel." *Byzantion* 38 (1968): 42–104.

Larchet, Jean-Claude. *Maximus the Confessor: Mediator between East and West.* Moscow: 2004. [Russian].

Leontius of Byzantium. *Against Nestorius and Eutychius.* PG 86/1:1273–1358.

Life of Avvakum. Moscow: 1960. [Russian].

Lossky, Vladimir. *Theology and the Vision of God: A Collection of Writings.* Moscow: 2000. [Russian].

_____. *Dogmatic Theology.* Moscow: 1991. [Russian].

————. *In the Image and Likeness of God*. Crestwood, NY: St Vladimir's Seminary
Press, 1974.

————. *Mystical Theology of the Eastern Church*. Moscow: 1991. [Russian].

Luther, Martin. *On the Slavery of the Will*. Moscow: 1986.

Macarius of Egypt. *New Spiritual Conversations. Works*. Moscow: 2001. [Russian].

————. *Spiritual Homilies*. *http://www.monachos.net/content/patristics/
patristictexts/179-macarius-homilies-1-5*, and *http://www.monachos.net/content/
patristics/patristictexts/180-macarius-homilies-6-11*, and *http://www.monachos.net/
content/patristics/patristictexts/181-macarius-homilies-12-22*.

MacGraham, A. *The Theological Meaning of the Reformation*. Odessa: 1994. [Russian].

Magdalino, P. "The Byzantine Holy Man in the Twelfth Century." *The Byzantine
Saint*. S. Hackel, ed. London: 1981.

Makarii (Oksiuk). *The Eschatology of Gregory of Nyssa*. Moscow: 1999. [Russian].

Malinovsky, N. *Study of Orthodox Dogmatic Theology. Sergiev Posad, 1911*. Moscow:
2003. [Russian].

Mansvetov, I. *The Book of Church Order (Typikon): Its Formation and Fate in the Greek
and Russian Churches*. Moscow: 1885.

Mark the Ascetic. *Epistle to the Monk Nicholas*. Φιλοκαλία 1:127–138.

————. *On Spiritual Law*. PG 65:905–929.

Mark of Ephesus. *Answers to the Difficulties and Questions Posed to Him from the Cardinals and Other Latin Teachers, in Connection with the Proclaimed Speeches*. Cited
in: Amvrosy (Pogodin). *St Mark of Ephesus and the Union of Florence*. Moscow:
1994. [Russian].

————. *Confession of the True Faith*. Cited in: Amvrosy (Pogodin). *St Mark of Ephesus and the Union of Florence*. Moscow: 1994. [Russian].

————. *The Dialogue Known as "to the Latins," or Additions to the Creed*. Cited in:
Amvrosy (Pogodin). *St Mark of Ephesus and the Union of Florence*. Moscow:
1994. [Russian].

————. *Second Oration on the Purifying Fire*. Cited in: Amvrosy (Pogodin). *St
Mark of Ephesus and the Union of Florence*. Moscow: 1994. [Russian].

————. *Syllogistic Chapters against the Latins*. Cited in: Amvrosy (Pogodin). *St
Mark of Ephesus and the Union of Florence*. Moscow: 1994. [Russian].

Maximus the Confessor. *Ambigua*. PG 91:1031–1418.

————. *Ascetical Oration*. PG 90:911–956.

————. *Chapters on Love*. PG 90:959–1073.

————. *Chapters on Theology and on Oikonomia*. PG 90:1083–1176.

————. *Commentary on Psalm 60*. PG 90:856–872.

————. *Dispute with Pyrrhus*. PG 91:288–353.

————. *Epistles.* PG 91:362–650.

————. *Letter to Marinus.* http://www.monachos.net/content/patristics/patristictexts/185-maximus-to-marinus.

————. *Mystagogia.* PG 91:658–718.

————. *On the Cosmic Mystery of Jesus Christ.* Paul M. Blowers and Robert Louis Wilken, trans. Crestwood, NY: St Vladimir's Seminary Press, 2003.

————. *Questions to Thalassius.* PG 90:243–786.

————. *Scholia on Dionysius.* PG 4:13–576.

————. *Theological and Polemical Compositions.* PG 91:9–285.

Melito of Sardis. *On Pascha.* Alistair Stewart-Sykes, trans. Crestwood, NY: St Vladimir's Seminary Press, 2001.

Methodius of Patara. *On the Resurrection.* Cited in *Works.* Edited by G. N. Bonwetsch. Leipzig: 1917.

Meyendorff, John. *Byzantine Theology.* Minsk: 2001. [Russian].

————. *The Life and Works of St Gregory Palamas.* St Petersburg: 1997. [Russian].

————. *Orthodoxy in the Modern World.* Klin: 2002. [Russian].

————. "The Time of Holy Saturday." *Moscow Patriarchate Journal* 4 (1992): 33–34. [Russian].

————. *Introduction to Patristic Theology.* Klin: 2001. [Russian].

Nemesius of Emesa. *On the Nature of Man.* PG 40:503–818.

Nicholas Cabasilas. *Homily on the Annunciation.* Cited in: Lossky, Vladimir. *In the Image and Likeness of God.* Crestwood, NY: St Vladimir's Seminary Press, 1974. 202–203.

Nikodim (Milash). *The Canons of the Orthodox Church, together with a Commentary by Nikodim, Bishop of Dalmatia and Istria* 1. Moscow: 2001.

"Octoechos." Unpublished English translation at St Vladimir's Orthodox Theological Seminary, Yonkers, NY.

Optatus of Milevis. *On the Donatist Schism* (CSEL 26). 1893.

Origen. *Against Celsus.* ANF, vol. 4.

————. *Commentary on the Gospel According to Matthew.* ANF, vol. 10.

————. *Commentary on John.* PG 14:21–830.

————. *Commentary on Romans.* PG 14:837–1292.

————. *Exhortation to Martyrdom.* Cited in *Works I: Exhortatio ad martyrium, Contra Celsum 1–4.* Edited by P. Koetschau. Leipzig: 1899.

————. *Homilies on Jeremiah.* SC 238. 1977.

————. *Homilies on Joshua.* SC 71. 1960.

————. *On First Principles.* ANF, vol. 4.

————. *Philocalie.* E. Junod and M. Harl, ed. Paris: 1976–1983.

Paterikon: A Selection of the Sayings of the Holy Monks and Stories from their Lives, compiled by Bishop Ignatius (Brianchaninov). Brussels: 1963.

Palladius. *The Lausiac History*. Klin: 2001.

Payne, J. Barton. *Encyclopedia of Biblical Prophecy*. New York: 1973.

"Pentecostarion." Unpublished English text at St Vladimir's Orthodox Theological Seminary, Yonkers, NY.

Philaret (Drozdov). *Selected Writings: Letters; Memoirs*. Moscow: 2003.

Philaret of Moscow. *Extensive Christian Catechesis*. [Russian].

_____. *On the Dogmatic Worthiness of the Septuagint*. Moscow: 1858. [Russian].

_____. *Colloquy between a True Believer and a Sceptic on the True Doctrine of the Greco-Russian Church*. Moscow: 1833. [Russian].

_____. *Words and Sayings*. Moscow: 1873–1885. [Russian].

Photius of Constantinople. *Mystagogy of the Holy Spirit*. PG 102:279–542.

_____. *To Amphilochius*. Leipzig: Bibliotheca Teubneriana, 1986–1987.

Pius IX, Pope. Apostolic Constitution *Ineffabilis Deus* of December 8, 1854.

Pius XII, Pope. Apostolic Constitution *Munificentissimus Deus* of November 1, 1950. Acta Apostolicae Sedis. Vatican City: 1950. Pp. 735ff.

Plato. *Phaedo*. Cited in *Writings* (3 vols.). Moscow: 1970. [Russian].

_____. *Republic*. Cited in *Writings* (3 vols.). Moscow. [Russian].

_____. *Timaeus*. Cited in *Writings* (3 vols.). Moscow: 1971. [Russian].

Plotinus. *Enneads*. Translated by Stephen Mackenna and B.S. Page. http://classics.mit.edu/Plotinus/enneads.1.first.html .

Prokhorov, G. M. *Memorials of Russian and Translated Literature of the Fourteenth and Fifteenth Centuries*. Leningrad, 1987. [Russian].

Quasten, J. *Patrology*, vols. 1–3, 5th ed. Westminster, MD: 1990.

Rose, Seraphim. *The Soul After Death*. Platina, CA: St Herman Press, 1980.

Sayings of the Desert Fathers. PG 65:71–440.

Schedrovitsky, D.V. *Introduction to the Old Testament: the Five Books of Moses*. Moscow: 2001. [Russian].

Schmemann, Alexander. *Liturgy and Tradition*. Kiev: 2005. [Russian].

Sherwood, P. "The Earlier Ambigua of St Maximus and his Refutation of Origenism." *Studia Anselmiana* 36. (Rome, 1955): 205–222.

Socrates Scholasticus. *Church History*. Moscow: 1996. [Russian].

Sophrony (Sakharov). *The Monk of Mount Athos*. Rosemary Edmonds, trans. Crestwood, NY: St Vladimir's Seminary Press, 2001.

_____. *Starets Siluan*. Paris: 1952. [Rusian].

Symeon the New Theologian. *Catechetical Lecture*. Cited in: *Catéchèses*. Edited by B. Krivochéine and J. Paramelle. SC 96: 1963; SC 104: 1964; SC 113: 1965.

_____. *Chapters*. Edited by J. Darrouzès. SC 51-bis: 1980.

————. *Hymns of Divine Love*. George A. Maloney, S.J., trans. New Jersey: Dimension Books.

————. *Letter on Confession*. Cited in: K. Holl. *Enthusiasmus und Bussgewalt beim griechischen Mönchtum: Eine Studie zu Symeon dem neuen Theologen*. Leipzig: 1898. [German].

————. *Moral Oration*. Edited by J. Darrouzès. SC 129: 1967.

————. *Theological Oration*. Edited by J. Darrouzès. SC 122: 1966.

Tatian. *Address to the Greeks*. Edited by E. Schwartz. Leipzig: 1888.

Tertullian. *On the Resurrection of the Flesh*. Edited by A. Kroymann. CSEL 47. 1906.

————. *Prescription Against the Heretics*. Edited by A. Kroymann. CSEL 70. 1942.

Theodoret of Cyrus. *Difficult Passages of Divine Scripture*. PG 80:75–858.

————. *An Exact Exposition of Divine Dogma*. PG 83:439–556.

Theophilus of Antioch. *To Autolycus*. PG 6:1023–1168.

Theophylact of Bulgaria. *Commentaries on the New Testament*. Saint Petersburg: 1911.

Thomas Aquinas. *Summa Theologiae*. London-New York: 1965.

S.V. Troitsky, S.V. "Athonite Troubles." *Additions to Church Statements* 20 (1913): 882–909. [Russian].

Vasily (Krivoshein). *Symbolic Texts in the Orthodox Church*. Nizhny Novgorod: 2004. [Russian].

Vassiliades, Nicholas. *The Mystery of Death*. Holy Trinity Sergius Lavra: 1998. [Russian].

Verkhovskoy, Serge. "On the Names of God." *Pravoslavnaya Mysl'* 6 (Paris, 1948): 37–55. [Russian].

Vysheslavtsev, B. *The Heart in Christian and Indian Mysticism*. Paris: 1929. [Russian].

Ware, Kallistos. *The Orthodox Church*. London: Penguin Books, 1991.

Ware, Kallistos and Mother Mary. *The Festal Menaion*. South Canaan, PA: St Tikhon's Seminary Press, 1998.

————. *The Lenten Triodion*. South Canaan, PA: St Tikhon's Seminary Press, 1994.

Winslow, D. *The Dynamics of Salvation: A Study in Gregory of Nazianzus*. Philadelphia: 1979.

Zenkovsky, Vasily. *The Basics of Christian Philosophy* 2. Paris: 1964. [Russian].

Index